Epidemiology and the Delivery of Health Care Services

Methods and Applications

Second Edition

Epidemiology and the Delivery of Health Care Services

Methods and Applications

Second Edition

Edited by

Denise M. Oleske

Rush University
Chicago, Illinois

Kluwer Academic / Plenum Publishers
New York, Boston, Dordrecht, London, Moscow

Library of Congress Cataloging-in-Publication Data

Epidemiology and the delivery of health care services: methods and applications/edited by
Denise M. Oleske.—2nd ed.
        p.   ; cm
      Rev. ed. of: Epidemiology and the delivery of health care services/edited by Denise
M. Oleske. c1995.
      Includes bibliographical references and index.
      ISBN 0-306-46525-6
        1. Health planning—Methodology. 2. Epidemiology. 3. Health services administration.
I. Oleske, Denise.   II. Epidemiology and the delivery of health care services.
      [DNLM: 1. Epidemiology.   2. Delivery of Health Care—organization & administration.
3. Epidemiologic Methods.   4. Health Planning—methods.   WA 105 E6433 2001]
RA394.9 .E64 2001
614.4—dc21

                                                                                          2001016490

ISBN: 0-306-46525-6

©2001 Kluwer Academic / Plenum Publishers, New York
233 Spring Street, New York, New York 10013

http://www.wkap.nl/

10 9 8 7 6 5 4 3 2 1

A C.I.P. record for this book is available from the Library of Congress

Contributors

Dolores G. Clement
Department of Health Administration
School of Allied Health Professions
Virginia Commonwealth University
Richmond, Virginia 23298-0233

Gerald L. Glandon
Department of Health Services Administration
University of Alabama at Birmingham
Birmingham, Alabama 35294

Jack Goldberg
Epidemiology/Biostatistics Division
School of Public Health
University of Illinois at Chicago
Chicago, Illinois 60612

Marcia B. Hargreaves
Quality Improvement and Volunteer Services
Rush-Presbyterian-St. Luke's Medical Center
and
Department of Health Systems Management
Rush University
Chicago, Illinois 60612

Ronald C. Hershow
Department of Epidemiology
School of Public Health
University of Illinois at Chicago
Chicago, Illinois 60612

Frances J. Jaeger
University of Illinois at Chicago Perinatal Center
Chicago, Illinois 60612

Sana Loue
Department of Epidemiology and Biostatistics
School of Medicine
Case Western Reserve University
Cleveland, Ohio 44106

Karl A. Matuszewski
Clinical Knowledge Service
University HealthSystem Consortium
Clinical Practice Advancement Center
Oak Brook, Illinois 60523
and
Department of Health Systems Management
Rush University
Chicago, Illinois 60612

Helen Jo Neikirk
Clinical Information Management
University HealthSystem Consortium
Oak Brook, Illinois 60523

Denise M. Oleske
Departments of Health Systems Management and Preventive Medicine
Rush University
Chicago, Illinois 60612

Marcia Phillips
Department of Health Systems Management
Rush University
Chicago, Illinois 60612

Iris R. Shannon
Department of Health Systems Management
Rush University
Chicago, Illinois 60612

Bailus Walker, Jr.
Environmental and Occupational Medicine Program
College of Medicine
Howard University
Washington, DC 20059

Thomas T. H. Wan
Department of Health Administration
School of Allied Health Professions
Virginia Commonwealth University
Richmond, Virginia 23298-0233

Diane R. Weber
Quality Services
University HealthSystem Consortium
Oak Brook, Illinois 60523

Preface

In the previous edition of this book, the predominant theme was applying epidemiology to assist managers in dealing with an environment in which the structure of health care financing was rapidly changing to managed care and in which there was increasing competition among health care providers. While these phenomena continue to exist, new challenges have emerged, and in particular the explosion of information technology has given way to a global society and decision making that is increasingly shared with consumers because of their access to the same sets of data. Thus, the questions with which health care managers are confronted on a daily basis are now exceedingly more complex: (1) How can a population be defined considering that both exposures and diseases originating in one corner of the globe can rapidly become a threat to any nation's security? (2) Where do influences on a population begin and end? (3) How can we protect and promote health in that population or any population if privacy is preeminent?

This edition brings in this editor's view of the increasing need for health care managers, be they in private or public settings, to use epidemiological concepts and methods. The challenges posed by health care delivery in the 21st century are immense, ranging from redefining life and health given the advances in genetic technology, global environmental changes, and multinational simultaneous increases in poverty and longevity, to economic decisions regarding technology and service levels that fewer and fewer can afford. Epidemiology, as the language of science, is the essential tool in health care management decision making, be it at the point of direct service or at the level of deciding national priorities in a limited health care budget.

This edition presents core epidemiological principles and their applications in the first six chapters. The next five chapters illustrate how epidemiology is used in management planning, decision making, and practice in specialty areas (health care quality management, transmissible disease control, genetic health services, technology assessment, and health care services for environmentally provoked health problems). The last set of chapters demonstrates how epidemiology at the macrolevel interfaces with other disciplines (economics, policy, and ethics) when health care management faces initiatives at the cusp of public and private sector interests. Prior or current enrollment in coursework in biostatistics and in health care organizations at the graduate level are highly recommended to better appreciate the material presented herein. Throughout the book, the need to use the scientific method in management decision making is emphasized. Specific content is presented (e.g., the scientific method, assessment of causality, study designs, survey form construction, etc.) such that this book can be used to teach principles of research methods to prepare students for their theses or other capstone projects in health care management.

As in the last edition, all chapters are written by individuals who apply epidemiological thinking and methods in their current positions. Additionally, since most chapter authors have had international health care experience, the topics presented in these chapters analyze the top priorities and concerns relative to health care globally. Following each chapter, the reader is challenged with case studies relevant to the theme of the chapter that require epidemiological concepts and techniques for their solution. Most of the cases are new and all are real-life or based on real-life situations that the reader is likely to encounter as a health care manager. Some of the cases have suggested answers provided in the end of the volume. It must be emphasized that these are suggested answers; different situations, depending on the context, resources, and time, may require different approaches. Some of the cases have questions without answers; this is intended so that users of the volume can develop their own creative solutions using epidemiological principles and methods. You are encouraged to use the "Websites for Health Care Managers Thinking Epidemiologically" in devising your own solutions.

Enjoy reading (and using) this new edition!

Denise M. Oleske, Ph.D., F.A.C.E.

Chicago, Illinois

Contents

Fundamentals

Chapter 1—An Epidemiological Framework for the Delivery of Health
Care Services 3

Denise M. Oleske

An Epidemiological Model for the Delivery of Health Care Services 3
The Population 4
    Population Trends 6
Need for Health Care 6
Utilization of Health Care Services 10
    Factors Affecting Health Care Utilization 12
    Accessibility of Health Care 13
    Availability of Health Care Resources 13
Health of Populations Served 14
Applying Epidemiology in Health Care Management Practice 15
    Monitoring Service Population Size 15
    Distribution of Health Needs in a Population 16
    Understanding the Genesis and Consequences of Health Problems 18
    Understanding the Relationship between Health System Characteristics and
        the Health Status of Populations Served 18
    Monitoring Health Care Systems, Organizations, and Program Performance ... 19
    Modifying the Structure and Processes to Respond to Environmental Change 20
    Formulation and Evaluation of Public Policy Affecting the Delivery of Health
        Care Services 20
Summary 21
Case Studies 22
References 27

Chapter 2—Measurement Issues in the Use of Epidemiological Data 29

Denise M. Oleske

Introduction 29
Methods of Measurement 29

Validity and Reliability of a Measure 31
  Validity 33
  Reliability 36
Logistics of Measurement 37
Classification of Health 38
  Disease 38
  Injuries 40
  Functioning and Disability 40
  Mental and Behavioral Disorders 41
  Quality of Life 41
  Other Health Measures 42
Classification of Health Services 42
  Classifying Organizational Units 42
  Classifying Procedures 43
Control of Measurement Error 43
Sources of Data 44
Summary 47
Case Studies 47
References 49

Chapter 3—Descriptive Epidemiological Measures 51

  Denise M. Oleske

Measuring the Frequency of Health Events in Populations 51
  Incidence Rate 51
  Prevalence Rate 53
Sources of Information for Incidence Rate Measures 54
Sources of Information on Prevalence 55
Format of Descriptive Epidemiological Measures 57
  Specific Rates 58
  Summary Rates 58
  Ratio Measures 64
Summary 68
Case Studies 68
References 73

Chapter 4—Assessing Causality: Foundations for Population-Based Health Care
  Managerial Decision Making 75

  Thomas T. H. Wan

Introduction 75
Scientific Inquiry 75
  Characteristics of Scientific Inquiry 76
  Logic of Scientific Inquiry 77

Stages in Scientific Inquiry 79
  Identification and Specification of the Study Problem 79
  Selection of an Informed Theoretical Framework 80
  Quantification of Study Variables 80
  Selection of a Study Design 82
  Specification of the Analytic Framework: Proposing the Hypothesis and
    Setting Error Tolerances 82
  Selecting a Statistical Test 84
Multilevel Analysis 87
  Evaluating Causality 90
  Meta-analysis 92
Conclusions 92
Case Studies 93
References 97

Chapter 5—Strategic Planning: An Essential Management Tool for Health Care
Organizations and Its Epidemiological Basis 99

Frances J. Jaeger

Epidemiological Basis of Strategic Planning 99
Theoretical Basis of Strategic Planning 104
The Strategic Planning Process 106
  Step 1. Plan the Planning and Ensure Favorable Conditions for Effective
    Strategic Planning 107
  Step 2. Review the Organization's Mission Statement and Revise It as
    Necessary to Ensure That It Remains Relevant to the Organization's Future.
    If No Written Statement of Mission Exists, Develop and Adopt One 107
  Step 3. Do a Situational Analysis that Encompasses Assessments of Elements
    of the Organization's External and Internal Environments as Well as an
    Evaluation of the Impact of the Organization's Efforts 108
  Step 4. Apply an Approach for Defining the Key Issues, Focusing the
    Attention of the Organization, and Establishing the Framework for the Next
    Step of Strategy Development 115
  Step 5. Generate, Evaluate, and Select Alternative Strategies for Achieving
    Organizational Goals and Objectives or the Best Alignment of the
    Organization with the Opportunities in Its Environment 116
  Step 6. Carry Out the Implementation Phase of Strategic Planning, Detailing
    Operational Action Plans and Budgets, Monitoring Impact, and Making
    Midcourse Adjustments as Necessary 116
Data Resources and Issues Related to Use in Strategic Planning 117
Tools to Facilitate Strategic Planning 117
Applicability of the Strategic Planning Process 119
The Format and Content of the Strategic Plan 122
Conclusions 123
Case Studies 124
References 130

Chapter 6—Evaluating Health Services, Programs, and Systems:
An Epidemiological Perspective 133

Dolores G. Clement and Thomas T. H. Wan

Dimensions of Health System Evaluation 134
   Determine the Population Targeted for Intervention 134
   Identify Aspects of Health Care To Be Evaluated 134
The Evaluation Process 137
   Planning 137
   Implementation 138
   Intervention 138
   Monitoring and Feedback 138
Conceptual Framework for Specifying Evaluation Criteria 138
Analytical Approaches to Evaluation: An Epidemiological Perspective 140
   Study Designs 140
   Analyzing Intervention Effects 145
   Other Analytic Methods 149
Prospects of Health Services Evaluation 150
Conclusion 150
Case Studies 151
References 153

Specialty Areas

Chapter 7—Epidemiology and Health Care Quality Management 157

Diane R. Weber, Helen Jo Neikirk, and Marcia B. Hargreaves

Introduction 157
Interrelationship between Health Care Quality Management and Epidemiology .. 157
Quality Management Defined 158
Organizational Approaches to Quality Management 159
Programmatic Options in Quality Management 159
Quality Planning 160
Performance According to Standards, Guidelines, and Other Management
   Strategies 161
   Performance According to Standards 161
   Clinical Practice Guidelines 162
   Utilization Management 162
   Case Management 163
   Risk Management 163
   Best Practices 163
Models for Systematic Improvement 164
   Plan–Do–Check–Act Model 164
   Clinical Value Compass 165
Quality Measurement 166
   Process Measures 167

Clinical Outcomes 167
Satisfaction 167
Health Status 168
Data Sources 168
Sampling 169
Levels of Quality Measurement 169
Quality Improvement Tools and Techniques 170
Brainstorming 171
Affinity Diagram 171
Cause-and-Effect Diagram 172
Flowchart 173
Statistical Quality Control Tools 173
Check Sheet 175
Histogram 175
Pareto Chart 175
Scatter Diagram 176
Run Chart and Control Chart 177
Comparison Charts 179
Application of Quality Control Tools 180
Risk Adjustment 181
Conclusion 182
Case Studies 183
References 186

Chapter 8—Control of Transmissible Diseases in Health Care Settings 191

Denise M. Oleske and Ronald C. Hershow

Introduction 191
Infectious Disease Concepts 192
Managing Disease Outbreaks 195
Managerial Responsibilities in Infection Control 196
Bloodborne Disease Transmission 197
Epidemiology of Hepatitis B 198
Epidemiology of Human Immunodeficiency Virus Infection 198
Bloodborne Disease Control Measures 199
Hazard Communication 201
Airborne Disease 203
Airborne Disease Control Measures 204
Special Considerations in Infectious Disease Control for Specific Health Care
    Service Settings 207
Inpatient Acute Care Facility 207
Ambulatory Care 208
Home Care 209
Long-Term Care/Skilled Nursing Facility 209
Hospice 210
Behavioral Health Care Settings 211
Conclusion 211

Case Studies 212
References 214

Chapter 9—Genetic Epidemiology: The Basis for a New Health Service
Delivery Model 217

Marcia Phillips and Jack Goldberg

Introduction 217
Basic Genetic Concepts 218
    Mendelian Genetics 218
    Exceptions to Mendel's Laws 218
The Human Genome Project 219
    Scope and Progress 219
    Genetic Mapping 220
    Epidemiology and the Human Genome Project 221
    International Implications 221
Genetics and Epidemiology 222
    Roles of Epidemiology 222
    Genetic Techniques and Epidemiology 223
    Genetic Epidemiology Studies 225
Health Services Management and Genetic Epidemiology 227
    Screening 227
    Population-Based Genetic Health Screening Service: Screening for
        Phenylketonuria, a Model 228
    Future of Genetic Screening Programs 229
    Economic and Health Impact of Genetic Testing 230
    Information Systems Support for Genetic Health Services ... 230
The Ethical Challenges of Genetics 230
Conclusion 231
Case Studies 232
References 234

Chapter 10—Technology Assessment 235

Karl A. Matuszewski

Defining Technology Assessment and Its Function 235
Categories of Technology 237
    Devices 237
    Procedures 238
    Pharmaceuticals 238
Technology Life Cycle 238
Targeting Technologies for Assessment 240
    High Utilization 240
    High Potential for Harm 241
    High Cost 241
How Is Technology Assessment Performed? 241

Literature Review and Synthesis 242
Consensus Panels 243
Decision Criteria 243
Meta-analyses 244
Outcomes Assessment 246
Randomized Clinical Trials 247
Other Methods 247
Who Does Technology Assessment? 248
US Food and Drug Administration 248
Agency for Healthcare Research and Quality 248
American College of Physicians 249
Blue Cross and Blue Shield Association 249
ECRI 249
Center for Practice and Technology Assessment (CPTA) 249
University Health System Consortium 250
Other Assessment Centers 251
International Efforts 251
Problems in Performing Technology Assessment 252
Lack of Evidence 252
Lack of Agreement on How to Perform the Assessment 252
Inconsistent Evidence 252
Legal Interference 252
Breadth of Topics 253
New Information 253
Imperfect Use of Technology 253
Future of Technology Assessment 253
Summary 255
Case Studies 255
References 257

Chapter 11—Health Risks from the Environment: Challenges to Health
Service Delivery 261

Bailus Walker, Jr.

Introduction 261
Problems in Environmental Health 262
Gene–Environment Interaction 262
Impact of the Environment on the Reproductive System 263
Impact of the Environment on the Immune System 264
Impact of the Environment on the Nervous System 265
Impact of the Environment on the Respiratory System 266
Environmental Terrorism 266
Climate Changes, Cataclysmic Events, and Other Disasters 267
Environmental Equity 269
Global Environmental Health 271
Recognition and Assessment of Environmentally Related Disease 271
Risk Assessment 273

Health Services for Environmentally Provoked Diseases 274
    Primary Prevention 274
    Secondary Prevention 274
    Tertiary Prevention 276
Summary and Conclusion 276
Case Studies 276
References 279

Spanning Topics

Chapter 12—Epidemiology and the Public Policy Process 285

Iris R. Shannon

A Contextual Framework for the Relationship between Public Policy and
    Epidemiology: Public Health 286
    Public Health 286
    National Health Objectives 287
Public Policy: An Interactive Process 287
The Interrelationship between Epidemiology and Public Policy 289
Application of Epidemiology in the Policy Process 290
    US Department of Health and Human Services Initiative to Eliminate
    Disparities in Health 290
    Infant Mortality 293
    Vaccine-Preventable Diseases 294
    Childhood Hepatitis B Infections and Hepatitis B Vaccine Use 296
Summary 301
Case Studies 301
References 307

Chapter 13—The Contribution of Epidemiological Information in Economic
Decision Making 309

Gerald L. Glandon

Introduction 309
Background: Public Goods 310
    Government Provision of Public Goods 310
    Health Care and Public Goods 311
Overview of the Definition and Core Elements of Cost–Benefit Analysis and
    Cost-Effectiveness Analysis 312
Cost-Effectiveness Analysis, Epidemiological Data, and Application to
    Managerial Decision Making 318
Conclusion 323
Case Studies 323
References 326

Chapter 14—Ethics, Epidemiology, and Health Service Delivery 329

Sana Loue

Introduction 329
Approaches to Resolving Ethical Dilemmas 330
   Principlism 330
   Casuistry 331
   Communitarianism 333
   Feminist Ethics 334
   Utilitarianism 335
Principles, Rules, and Guidelines 338
   The Nuremberg Code and Declaration of Helsinki 338
   The International Covenant on Civil and Political Rights 339
   CIOMS and WHO International Guidelines 340
   United States Guidelines and Regulations 340
Operationalizing Codes, Guidelines, and Regulations in the Context of Research
   and Patient Care 341
   Informed Consent 341
   Confidentiality and Privacy Concerns 344
Conclusions 346
Case Studies 346
References 349

Suggested Answers to Selected Case Study Questions 353

Appendix—Websites for Health Care Managers Thinking Epidemiologically 373

Glossary 385

Index 395

Fundamentals

1

An Epidemiological Framework for the Delivery of Health Care Services

Denise M. Oleske

An Epidemiological Model for the Delivery of Health Care Services

The organization and delivery of health care services is heavily influenced today by the dilemma of providing quality health care given limited resources. This challenge raises a number of questions: Should all health care services be equally distributed among or provided to the population? Are all health services equally effective among population subgroups? To what degree do health services improve health status? A population-based focus is required to answer these questions. Such a focus classically directs attention on the general population in a defined geopolitical area. Historically, private health care services typically have not undertaken responsibility for addressing the needs of geographically based populations. However, new community benefit legislation, challenges to not-for-profit status, increasing demands from consumers, increasing enrollment in capitated health plans, and an extremely competitive health care marketplace compel health care providers to be more responsive to population health care needs and status. Epidemiology can be the pivotal link in assisting providers to align services more effectively to enhance health status. This balance needs to occur both at the point of delivery as well as at the level of public policy.

To represent the application of epidemiology in the new era of the delivery of health care services, the following definitional orientation is offered:

> **Epidemiology is the study of the distribution of health needs, including disease, impairments, disability, injuries, and other health problems in human populations and factors contributing to their emergence, severity and consequences. The ultimate goal of epidemiology is to identify the causal factors that could be eliminated or modified to prevent or control adverse health outcomes and apply the knowledge of these to improve the health status of populations.**

Denise M. Oleske   Departments of Health Systems Management and Preventive Medicine, Rush University, Chicago, Illinois 60612.

Epidemiology and the Delivery of Health Care Services: Methods and Applications, Second Edition, edited by Denise M. Oleske. Kluwer Academic/Plenum Publishers, New York, 2001.

3

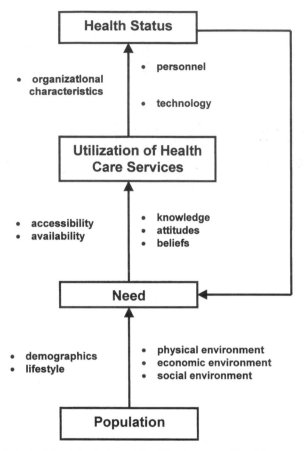

Figure 1.1. Epidemiological model of the delivery of health care services.

A population-based focus in the delivery of health care can influence health status. A model that represents how the orientation may be conceptualized is displayed in Fig. 1.1. This conceptual model is the focus of this chapter and provides the orientation for the remainder of the volume. First, each component of the model is discussed. An explanation of how the model provides a framework for management practice follows.

The Population

Defining the population and understanding its characteristics is fundamental to the epidemiological model of health services delivery. Populations targeted for health care services are defined in terms of geopolitical boundaries, users of a health provider (e.g., hospitals, physician group practice, public clinic), those in institutions (e.g., school children, prisons, orphanages, etc.), members of a health insurance plan (e.g., Medicaid, Medicare, members of a health maintenance organization, those receiving worker's compensation), because of special group membership (e.g., military personnel), or some combination thereof. Populations are characterized in terms of trends in size, demographic, economic characteristics, social charac-

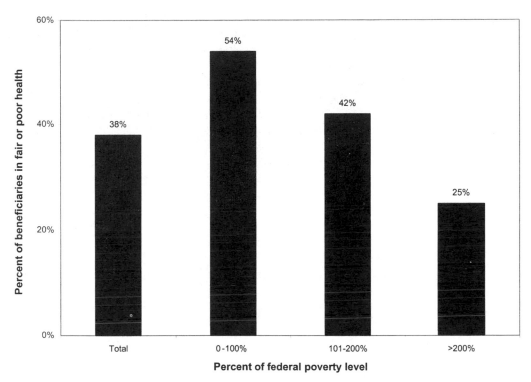

Figure 1.2.   Medicare beneficiaries in fair or poor health by federal poverty level. Data from Schoen *et al.* (1998).

teristics, and distribution of exposures that could influence health. Health and most diseases or health problems can be observed to vary with population characteristics. Figure 1.2 illustrates that even within the population of Medicare recipients, self-reported health status varies with income level, which is represented in this figure by federal poverty status.

The major factors affecting population size are birth rate or fertility rate, death rate, and migration. The greatest amount of change in the growth in a population over the short term is usually attributable to the difference between the birth rate and the death rate. However, over time, migration contributes a major influence to population change in terms of numbers and composition. Despite many technological advances in health care delivery, not all nations will experience population growth. Population declines of over 1% between 1990 and 1999 were observed for Bosnia and Herzegovina, Estonia, Kuwait, and Latvia largely attributable to declines in the fertility rates of these nations (World Health Organization, 2000).

With respect to demographic and social characteristics, attributes of a population known to be related to health events include age, gender, race, ethnicity, education, employment status, and income. Data from the decennial census provide the basic information on these and other characteristics of populations residing in the community. An act of Congress delineated the provision of the 1990 census and was codified in Title 13, United States Code. The census provides basic information for all inhabitants of the United States.

Health care claims data (pharmacy claims, hospital discharge abstracts), encounter data (numbers of visits made to a physician practice or clinic), health insurance membership or beneficiary files, and even birth certificates can also provide information on the characteristics of populations served by organizations, systems, types of insurers, or institutions. Populations also may be characterized in terms of the distribution of exposures or facts that may result in physical, emotional, or psychological harm. Epidemiological studies can determine which of these exposures are risk factors. A risk factor is a characteristic that is known to be associated with a health-related condition. Risk factors may be personal characteristics, lifestyle features, or the environment. Epidemiological measures can be used to characterize the distribution of the risk factors in the population, across geographic areas, and over time. Some characteristics are immutable (e.g., age, gender) and some are potentially modifiable (smoking, air pollution). The profound differences observed in the occurrence of health needs, use of health services, and resultant health status are driven by features of a population. Thus, knowledge of the characteristics of population targeted for health services is essential to plan and deliver health care services that optimize health.

Population Trends

The population of the world reached 6 billion persons in October 1999, doubling in size in under 40 years. There are 10 countries that have a population of 100 million or more: Bangladesh, Brazil, China, India, Indonesia, Japan, Nigeria, Pakistan, Russian Federation, and the United States of America. Overall, the population of the world is expected to increase at least at 1.3% per year, but the growth is concentrated in Asia and Oceania and in Africa (Fig. 1.3) where the income levels are among the lowest of all nations. By 2050, it is estimated that there will be at least an additional 1 billion persons added to the globe and eight additional countries with a population of 100 million or more: Ethiopia, Democratic Republic of the Congo, Mexico, Philippines, Viet Nam, Iran, Egypt, and Turkey (United Nations, 2001). The challenge to all health care managers worldwide will be how to promote and protect health and maintain quality of life given growing imbalances between social, economic, and environmental resources with continued dramatic population increases.

In the United States, one of the populations of particular concern is the growing Medicare population. One of three Medicare beneficiaries lives on an income below 200% of the federal poverty level and reports health problems. Forty-three percent of Medicare's disabled under age 65 lie at or below the poverty levels (Schoen et al., 1998). With expected increases in the number of Medicare recipients, significant challenges arise in ensuring and providing health care services to this population.

Another significant trend in the United States is the increasing percentage of the Hispanic population. In 1999, 12% of the US population was Hispanic, with people of Mexican origin comprising 65% of the US Hispanic population. In six states, the percentage Hispanic of the total population exceeds 17% (Fig. 1.4). High rates of immigration and fertility render this population the fastest growing segment in the United States. Continued low educational attainment and income, diverse ethnic and racial origins, and relative youth of the rapidly growing Hispanic population will present enormous challenges to the US health care system.

Need for Health Care

Any self-perceived deviation from societal norms of health or problem detected by a health profession may be considered a "need." An individual's perception of need is influenced by health information, health education, and changing financial situation. The pro-

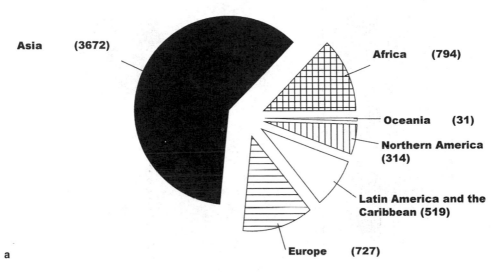

**World population of 2000
estimated 6057 million**

Asia   (3672)

Africa   (794)

Oceania   (31)

Northern America
(314)

Latin America and the
Caribbean (519)

a

Europe   (727)

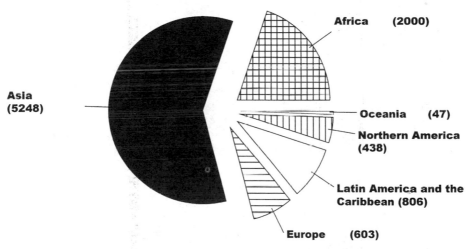

**World population of 2050
estimated 9322 million**

Asia
(5248)

Africa   (2000)

Oceania   (47)

Northern America
(438)

Latin America and the
Caribbean (806)

b

Europe   (603)

Figure 1.3. (a) Distribution of world population, 2000. (b) Distribution of estimated world population, 2050. Data from United Nations (2001).

vider's perception of the need is similarly influenced by health information (dissemination of practice guidelines) and diagnostic or treatment utilization restrictions imposed by health insurers or institutional policies (e.g., restriction to drugs dispensed only if on hospital formulary) (Andersen, 1995). Health needs may be expressed as a global measure of perceived health, disease, impairments, injuries, psychological/emotional distress, or behaviors that prompt seeking preventive care, health information, or therapeutic intervention. The use of

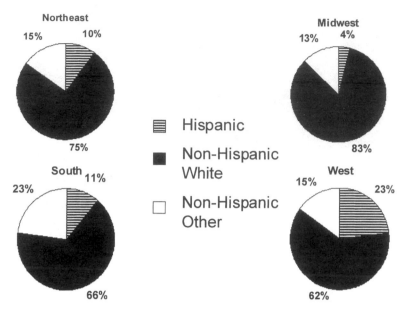

Figure 1.4. Distribution of the Hispanic population by region, United States, 1999. Data from US Census Bureau (2000).

health care services is influenced by the degree of deficits produced by a health need and/or the amount of services required for producing maximum attainable functioning (Steinwachs, 1989).

There are several approaches for quantifying health needs. Inferences can be made from census and vital data (records of births, deaths, marriages, and divorces). The birth certificate provides a wealth of information for this purpose. Lower levels of prenatal care, as measured through the birth certificate, among pregnant teens may suggest the need for special adolescent health services available in the community. A second approach is to measure self-report of perceived level of health, symptoms, diseases, injuries, and impairments. A third measurement of need is withdrawal behavior, such as absentee rates and work-loss days. For example, a high number of unscheduled days of employee absences is a proxy measure of a high level of stress among employees. A fourth approach is to assess the use of nonmedical services, such as nonprescription medications and treatments. A fifth measure is to evaluate levels of utilization of various types of formal health cares services, with the assumption that increasing utilization rates reflect increasing levels of need. Ambulatory sensitive hospitalization, or hospitalizations that are felt to be preventable if adequate primary care were available, is an important measure of need especially for vulnerable populations (Fig. 1.5). Last, a sixth approach for quantifying need is through clinical measurements of such variables as physical function, blood pressure, cognitive impairment, or cholesterol level. Variation of obesity (body mass index 30+) by age group, race/ethnicity, and gender are displayed in Fig. 1.6. This figure indicates the need for weight reduction interventions particularly for Mexican American and black females.

Where possible, physical measurements of need are desirable as persons with comparable symptoms and limitations exhibit high variability in how they perceive their health status and use medical care (Mechanic, 1995). The level of need in the population among population

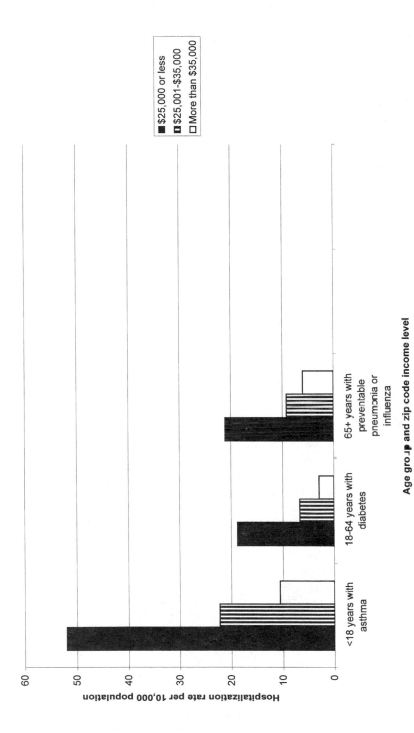

Figure 1.5. Ambulatory care sensitive conditions by age group and zip code income level. Source US Department of Health and Human Services (2000).

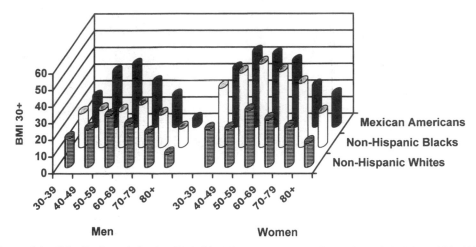

Figure 1.6. Distribution of obesity (BMI 30+) by age group, gender, and race/ethnicity, 1988–1994, United States. Data from National Center for Health Statistics (2000).

subgroups, across geographic areas, and over time may be represented through epidemiological measures (additional discussion on epidemiological measures may be found in Chapter 3). The selection of one measure of need over another for use in estimating the utilization of a health service depends on the type of level of health intervention anticipated. Screening for high blood pressure in a population is a means for providers to determine need by identifying persons with asymptomatic untreated hypertension.

Utilization of Health Care Services

Health care utilization refers to the category and purpose of health care services rendered or sought. Categories of health care services include physician or other individual health care professional services, facility use (hospitalizations, clinic visits), prescription use, or even the use of medical devises. Health care services for disease prevention may be rendered or sought through one of three levels: primary, secondary, or tertiary intervention. Primary prevention services are those activities or initiatives designed to reduce the likelihood or to prevent the onset of a health problem from ever occurring in healthy persons. Secondary prevention services are those activities or initiatives designed at reducing morbidity or morality from a health problem due to early identification of a disease before its signs and symptoms occur and which alters the course of a disease through early intervention. Tertiary prevention services are those activities or initiatives aimed at reducing morbidity and mortality and complications among individuals who have existing health problems (see Table 1.1).

In addition to measuring the capacity and productivity of a health care system, health care utilization also has been used as a proxy measure of health need, health status, or health outcome (e.g., hospital readmission rate for newborns). High utilization could mean there are unmet needs that cause the high utilization (e.g., high hospital admission rates in a community for asthma because of lack of physicians; high hospitalization rates among depressed persons because of lack of training in coping skills); low utilization rates could mean lack of adequate health care (e.g., low rates of breast conserving surgery). Hospitalization, the most costly form

Table 1.1. Level of Health Promotion and Examples of Health Care System Components

Level of prevention	Health care system components
Primary	• Aerobics classes
	• Immunization programs
	• Estrogen replacement therapy to prevent cognitive decline
Secondary	• Screening mammography
	• High blood pressure screening
	• Vision screening
	• Screening for BrCa1 gene
Tertiary	• Postoperative physical therapy for joint replacement surgery
	• Anticoagulant therapy to prevent secondary stroke
	• Cholesterol reduction by diet and/or medication in persons with coronary heart disease

of health care utilization, varies by geographic region even for similar age–gender groups (MacKay *et al.*, 2000). Procedure rates likewise vary. Figure 1.7 displays ambulatory and inpatient procedure rates in the United States according to gender and age group, with a 10.3% increase in the former procedure category and a 4.1% decline in the latter category. Both ambulatory and inpatient procedure rates increase with increasing age group and is parallel in that increase except for the slightly higher utilization rates in females aged 15–44 years primarily for childbearing reasons.

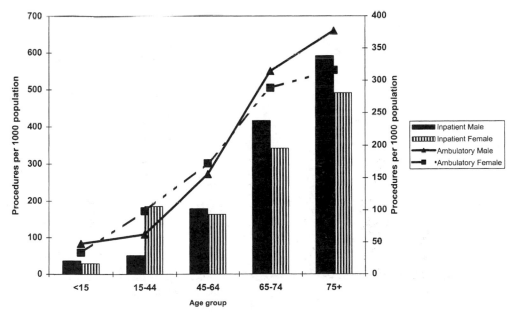

Figure 1.7.   Ambulatory and impatient procedure rates per 1000 population according to age group, and gender, United States. Note: Ambulatory rates are from 1996. Inpatient rates are from 1998. Source MacKay *et al.*. (2000).

Utilization of health services does not necessarily imply ultimately more favorable health status. This is exemplified with the high degree of variation in the use all common surgical procedures, particularly for cardiac procedures after acute myocardial infarction (AMI) (Wennberg, 1996). A high degree of procedure use for the management and prevention of AMI has only a mixed effect on mortality and other heart disease events (Selby *et al.*, 1996; Guadagnoli *et al.*, 1995).

Factors Affecting Health Care Utilization

Utilization is generally observed to vary with need, irrespective of the measure of need, with the highest levels of need typically associated with the highest levels of utilization. Figure 1.8 illustrates this concept showing that lower levels of perceived health are associated with a linear increase in numbers of contacts with the health care system related to poorer self-reported health. However, not all utilization is need driven. The high proportion of one to three visits in the last year by those with higher reported health status is attributable to seeking annual health exams. Wennberg (1996) demonstrated wide variability in the use of a variety of surgical procedures and acknowledged that the variation is not necessarily due to health care need. Health care utilization is influenced not only by a population's sociodemographic structure, but also its beliefs, knowledge, and attitudes regarding the efficacy of health services and curability of their condition and help-seeking behaviors. Characteristics of the health care system also influence utilization such as distribution of number and type of health care manpower and Medicare reimbursement factors.

Different theoretical models of health care utilization may be employed depending on whether the population under consideration is generally well or generally ill. Mechanic's

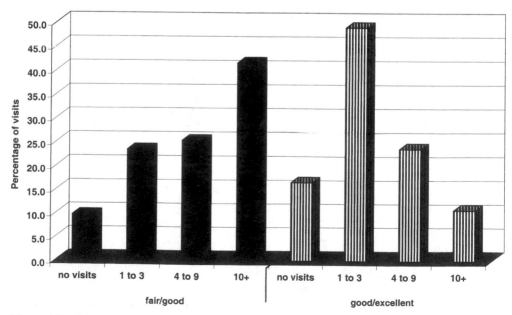

Figure 1.8. Distribution of health care visits to doctor's offices, emergency departments, and home visits within the past 12 months according to self-assessed health status, 1998, United States. Data from MacKay *et al.* (2000).

model focuses on the relationship of illness behavior and health care utilization. Self-appraisal of health, knowledge of symptoms, their seriousness, and knowledge of a procedure being available are highly associated with utilization of health care services (Mechanic, 1995). Beliefs about the curability of a condition may impede or promote the use of early detection. Attitudes are particularly important regarding influencing the action an individual takes regarding the utilization of health care if a symptom is not present. In addition, utilization is mitigated by accessibility and availability of services.

Accessibility of Health Care

Accessibility, as defined from an epidemiological point of view, is the proportion or number of a population that use a service or facility as a function of physical (e.g., distance, wheel chair access), economic (e.g., insurance type, income, copayment amount), or cultural factors (e.g., language barriers) or other aspects of the health care system (e.g., waiting time for an appointment, appointment mechanisms for hearing-impaired, insurance referral policies). Accessibility can be estimated from: (1) self-reports by the population on the difficulty of getting medical care when it is needed; (2) use of medical services for prevention and screening (e.g., percentage of the population having blood pressure checks, measles vaccine, etc); and (3) use of medical services for diagnosis, treatment, and rehabilitation. There are three specific indicators (known also as ambulatory-care-sensitive conditions) used to assess access to primary care in a population. These are hospitalization rates for children (asthma), working age adults (diabetes), and elderly persons (pneumonia and influenza). As with all health utilization measures, even these indicator rates vary by income (Fig. 1.5). The national goal is to reduce the hospitalization rates of the ambulatory-sensitive conditions by 25% in 2010 (US Department of Health and Human Services, 2000). One of the major access barriers to health care in the United States is lack of insurance, with 15.8% of the population of 42.3 million persons having neither private nor public health insurance (Rhoades et al., 2000). Persons with health insurance are much more likely to be in better health and have less disease and less disease risk factors; this applies to both physical health as well as mental health (Ford et al., 1998; Schoen et al., 1998; McAlpine and Mechanic, 2000) (Fig. 1.9). Access to primary health care is known to be inversely associated with hospital admission rates (Bindman et al., 1995).

Availability of Health Care Resources

Availability is the ratio between the population of an administrative or geographic unit and the health facilities, personnel, and technology to support the delivery of health care. Wennberg (1996) has demonstrated that use of health care in a community often is more related to the availability of physicians and hospital beds than to its population's health. Greater utilization occurs with greater availability of resources.

Utilization of services does not necessarily mean that health needs are addressed or that utilization is appropriate. Variations in physician practice styles and intensity in the use of medical resources and technology exist across systems of care and geographic areas independent of health care needs (Wennberg, 1996). Moreover, utilization of health care services per se does not always lead to improved health status. Adverse events such as surgical complications, nosocomial infections, and drug reactions can occur as a result of contact with health care services. An increasing literature is indicating that features of the organization such as the availability of specialized treatment centers can positively affect health status. Its culture, leadership, information services, and human resources activities can affect patient outcomes

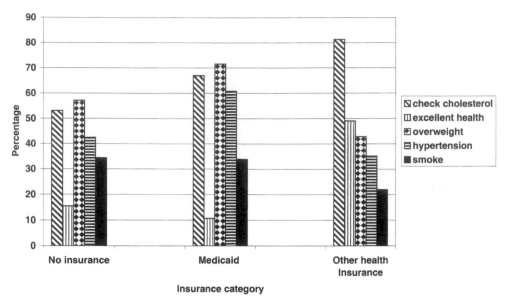

Figure 1.9. Distribution of health screening activities and selected risk factors for 50- to 64-year old women by health insurance status, National Health and Nutrition Examination Survey III, 1988–1994. Source Ford *et al.* (1998).

and ultimately population health status (Mitchell and Shortell, 1997; Herbert-Croteau *et al.*, 2000; Shortell *et al.*, 2000). The appropriateness of utilization also must be considered. The goal of the health care manager should be to identify the best or most appropriate match between health needs and resource utilization within a specific population. Thus, in the model presented health care services utilization becomes a primary "exposure" or potential risk factor that may have a causal relationship to population health status, favorably or unfavorably depending on the appropriateness of utilization. Inappropriate or unnecessary utilization can result in patient injury or even death.

Health of Populations Served

There are myriad different definitions and approaches for determining the health of populations. The World Health Organization (WHO, 1948) originally offered the definition of health as the optimal balance between physical, mental, and social functioning. The measure selected depends on the population (geographically defined, membership in health plan), the goal of the assessment (detailed or general), the validity and reliability of the measure, and the scope of the evaluation (international, national, local, or provider-specific).

Historically for geographically defined populations health status has been quantified with the proxy measure mortality because of the universality of recording of deaths and because of the widespread availability and general comparability of these records across international or other across-geographic areas (see Chapter 3 for computation). Thus, mortality rate indicators of health used for international comparisons have included the infant mortality rate (the number of deaths under 1 year of age per 1,000 live births), the maternal mortality ratio (number of deaths of mothers attributable to childbirth per 100,000 live births), and the life expectancy (the average number of years that an individual is expected to live assuming current mortality rates continue to apply). Infant mortality is felt to be the most sensitive indicator for evaluating the health status of populations for short-term interventions such as immunization or prenatal care programs. Life expectancy, another mortality measure, has been another common proxy measure of health status for long-term interventions, such as national health policy changes, the availability of medical intervention, or for changes in the economic conditions. The loss of over 15 years of life expectancy due to the AIDS epidemic in sub-Sahara Africa is in part due to the lack of availability of medical intervention. However, mortality rates alone may be insufficient as measures of provider impact on health status as smaller volume service units may have fewer deaths, rendering the mortality rates unreliable.

As computers and information systems become more widespread, the WHO has adopted a new summary measure of health for geographically defined populations: the disability adjusted life expectancy (DALE). This measure was developed in recognition of the fact that increasing life years as measured by life expectancy does not necessary measure all those years were "healthy." The DALE subtracts from the expected number of years of life for a person born in the current year and is weighted by disability severity (Murray and Lopez, 1997). This new measure rates Japanese people has having the highest healthy life expectancy at 74.5 years, Sierra Leone the lowest with less than 26 years, and the United States as 24th with 70 years (World Health Organization, 2000). The DALE is a promising new measure for comparing geographically defined populations with the caveat that since the disability component of the measure is obtained through surveys of the population to develop composite measures, differences in the perceptions of disability are highly culturally dependent.

Health status assessed in reference to a specific intervention is referred to as a health outcome. In addition to the proxy measures of health mentioned above, health status can be determined by a health care provider or can be self-reported (see also Chapter 2). Surveys may be used to evaluate health status in populations, but the logistics of administering these may be problematic and may not be appropriate or feasible for certain populations.

Regardless of the measure of health status used, better health should be the overall goal of any health care service, organization, or system. A corollary of this is that with the appropriate and timely use of health services broadly defined, health status should be improved.

Applying Epidemiology in Health Care Management Practice

From this conceptual orientation, it should be clear that a basic knowledge of epidemiological methods and their applications is essential for all health care managers. Specifically, the health care manager must consider (1) monitoring population size served by health care providers, (2) distribution of health needs in a population, (3) the genesis and consequences of health care problems, (4) how the health care system and organizational characteristics impact the health status of persons served, (5) the necessity of monitoring the health system, organizational, and program performance with epidemiological techniques, (6) the continuous need to restructure the health care system, organization, and its processes to fit the changing environment, and (7) the development and evaluation of public policy affecting health care delivery. An explanation of the significance of each of these challenges faced by health care managers in the context of epidemiology follows.

Monitoring Service Population Size

The primary role of the health care administrator is to manage resources with the goal of enhancing the health status of populations served. This function requires managers to have a population-based perspective and to be cognizant of trends affecting population size. The manager must understand the factors that influence the size of the service population in order to project resource needs of populations targeted for services. These factors include those resulting from sociodemographic changes (birth rate, death rate, and migration) and those due to changes in the structure of the health care system (Table 1.2). An examination of trends in the United States reveals a substantial increase in the overall size of the population, which is attributable to continued declines in mortality rates in all age groups, continued immigration into the United States, and recent increases in the birth rate in certain age groups of women (Fig. 1.10). Although as described earlier most of the world population's is increasing, in some areas the population is decreasing. Declining annual growth is observed in Albania, Bosnia, and Herzegovina, Bulgaria, Croatia, Georgia, Hungary, and the Ukraine, to name a few (World Health Organization, 2000). Although population growth typically follows declines in mortality (from disease), fertility decline accompanies or soon follows the decline in mortality. However, for some of the aforementioned countries, recent wars and civil conflict and future such anticipated events elsewhere in the world will have a major impact on both population size as well as mass migrations of populations.

Other factors affect the size of a population to be served, such as the closure of inner-city and rural hospitals and the shifts of the population served by these facilities to facilities elsewhere. Another factor is implementation of strategic initiatives by health care providers. Vertical integration of organizations (e.g., an academic medical center aligns itself with community hospitals associated with an HMO), the formation of multihospital systems (e.g., Columbia/HCA), collaboration among providers and insurers (e.g., Uni-Health American and California Blue Shield), joint ventures between providers and vendors (e.g., Caremark, Inc.), and growth in specialty for-profit health service corporations (e.g., Vencor) are examples of these initiatives. Larger populations also result from such trends as the emergence of health care purchasing coalitions of small businesses. The trend in increasing service population size will continue as it is viewed as consistent with achievement of cost-efficient care as a result of economies of scale. The substantial gains in enrollment in managed care health plans, even for the Medicaid population, illustrates this trend (Table 1.3). Thus, today the term "population based" may be viewed as also extending from a population defined by geographic boundaries to any large population served by a health care system or health-insuring arrangement.

Distribution of Health Needs in a Population

Knowledge of the distribution of health needs in a population is particularly essential for planning the types of health care services that should be provided. Epidemiological measures enable the distribution of health needs in a population to be characterized in terms of, "Who is

**Table 1.2. Factors Affecting the Size of the Population
Served by Health Care Systems**

Birth rate or fertility rate
Mortality rate
Migration
Facility closures
Horizontal integration of organizations (e.g., affiliations, joint ventures)
Vertical integration of organizations (primary, secondary, and tertiary care)
New service configurations (provider–vendor; provider–insurer)

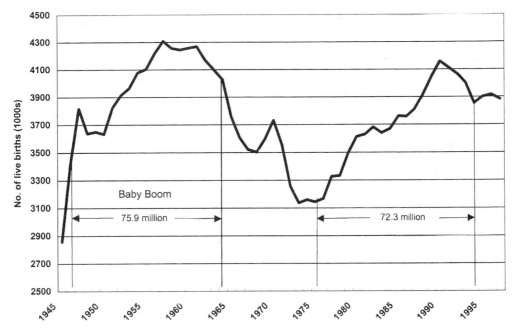

Figure 1.10.   Trends in the number of US births. Sources US Census Bureau (1975); MacKay *et al.* (2000).

affected? When? Where?" For example, infectious disease is a priority concern in populations with a large percentage of individuals 5 years of age and under. Therefore, the provision of immunization services would be an appropriate priority response. Mortality from heart disease is highest in those aged 65 years and over. Organizations within a community with a large proportion of elderly persons should provide services to address this health problem, such as instruction and skills on basic life support techniques. An estimate of the distribution and frequency of health needs in a population enables the projection of the amount of resources that would have to be expended. For example, diabetics have high rates of hospital utilization and experience a high incidence of various comorbidities such as myocardial infarction and diabetic retinopathy. Health maintenance organizations or other capitated programs that have a

Table 1.3. **Trends in Medicaid Managed Care Enrollment**

Year	Total medicaid population	Fee-for-service population	Managed care population	Percent managed care enrollment
1993	33,430,051	28,621,100	4,808,951	14.39
1994	33,634,000	25,839,750	7,794,250	23.17
1995	33,373,000	23,573,000	9,800,000	29.37
1996	33,231,147	19,911,028	13,330,119	40.10
1997	32,082,380	16,746,878	15,345,502	47.82
1998	30,896,635	14,322,639	16,573,996	53.64

[a]Data from http://www.hcfa.gov/Medicaid/

high proportion of diabetics may find it cost-effective to initiate screening programs to identify diabetics. Once identified, diabetics could be targeted for intense education and follow up to optimize management of the diabetes and to avoid complications such as diabetic retinopathy and prevent unnecessary hospitalization. Another potential predictor of the consumption of health care resource is the proportion of the population who are cigarette smokers. Smokers have a higher utilization of health care services than nonsmokers (Vogt and Schweitzer, 1985). Thus, knowledge of the prevalence of risk factors for disease in a population may be applied as a provider negotiating the nature of services provided relative to a fixed cost per person. Epidemiological information allows the manager to anticipate the resources to meet population needs and to anticipate the risks that may be incurred if the needs are not met also may be estimated. This information also allows managers to distribute resources and to assess the impact of developing affiliation and joint venture agreements.

The profile of the disease burden will be changing dramatically in the next 20 years. Worldwide, ischemic heart disease, unipolar major depression, road traffic accidents, cerebrovascular disease, and chronic obstructive pulmonary disease will be the five leading causes of disease burden (Institute of Medicine, 1997). The future distribution of diseases will challenge health systems that traditionally have been very independent to become more mutually connected with local governmental agencies and with foreign governments where borders are affected. This applies not only to the United States but to all countries of the world.

Understanding the Genesis and Consequences of Health Problems

Risk factors are attributes or exposures that increase the chance of the occurrence of an outcome or disease. Preventive health services are aimed at eliminating or otherwise mitigating risk factors. So, for an HMO with a large proportion of elderly members who are at risk for fracture injuries mass education aimed at improving physical activity (even mall walking) could lessen the likelihood of certain hospitalization for fracture injuries. For some diseases such as breast cancer there are no risk factors known to date that are modifiable. But even when risk factors are known, individuals may or may not be able to take measures to avoid these factors (e.g., because of lack of knowledge, heritable factors, etc.), thereby reducing the likelihood of health problems arising. Thus, health care services must be available to address the resultant health problems and manage the consequences. Epidemiological methods help identify prognostic factors, which are aspects of the disease or the individual from which the probability of recovery (or death) can be determined. For example, hip fracture patients who receive immediate rehabilitation therapy are more likely to live longer and have less morbidity than those who do not receive such services. The implications of this are that early intervention, be it through primary, secondary, or tertiary prevention services, may measurably improve health status.

Understanding the Relationship between Health System Characteristics and the Health Status of Populations Served

There is a growing body of literature indicating that features of a health system, its organization, its personnel, its available technology and programmatic efforts often have been linked to changes in the health status of populations served, even when considering medical conditions and therapeutic regimens of the patients. In drawing an analogy to classic epidemiology, these organizational features may be characterized as "exposure factors." An *organization* is characterized by its volume, ownership (e.g., governmental, for-profit, not-for profit, etc.), configuration (e.g., affiliation, system member, etc.), other features such as duration of encounter (e.g., 23-hour, overnight, long-term care), and other factors such as type of accreditation or type of service (e.g., wellness program, home care, etc.). Examples of the impact of organizational features upon health status are plentiful. The outcomes for mother having hospital newborn deliveries differs according to organizational characteristics. Lower cesarean section rates are observed in hospitals that are members of the Council of Teaching Hospitals even when considering the characteristics of women delivering (Oleske *et al.*, 1991).

Personnel considerations of an organization pertain to the number of staff, their qualifications and experience, and other factors of manpower (e.g., physical ability, interpersonal skills, etc.). The personnel associated with an organization can have a substantial effect on the health status of patients served. For example, hospitals with a higher percentage of physicians who are board-certified specialists and hospitals with a higher percentage of registered nurses on their nursing staff have a lower patient mortality (Hartz *et al.*, 1989). A low nurse–patient ratio in nursing homes has been linked to an increased likelihood of falls, medication errors, and other adverse outcomes (Spector and Takada, 1991). With increasing manpower shortages, it becomes increasingly important to understand whether some degree of cross-training or use of lower levels of trained manpower can be incorporated into health care delivery without compromising the health of populations. Mundinger *et al.* (2000) demonstrated that it was possible to achieve similar patient outcomes at least when comparing nurse practitioners and physicians in an ambulatory setting.

The *technology* of an organization includes devices, procedures, and pharmaceuticals available to diagnose and treat populations served (see also Chapter 10). The availability of technology generally improves the outcome of the care provided. For example, the technology of neonatal intensive care is long known to directly benefit select high-risk pregnancies and neonates, including those who are preterm or low birth weight or born to mothers with diabetes mellitus (Svennignsen, 1992). Mammography can be used for the early detection of breast cancer. If the cancer is identified in an early stage, the likelihood of death and high medical expenditures associated with the treatment of more advanced disease is reduced. For this reason, the prevalence of mammography screening in women served by health plans is a marker of organizational quality. Managers also can use epidemiology to assess whether the use of a particular technology is associated with any risks, such as a new transplant procedure. Epidemiological data also are useful in cost-benefit/cost-effectiveness evaluations of technology by providing both the benefit and effect information (see also Chapter 13).

Programmatic efforts represent what services are provided, how these are organized, or the means by which they are delivered. Programmatic efforts include quality assurance programs, total quality management programs, and clinical practice guidelines (see also Chapter 7). An example of a programmatic effort is a genetic screening service to identify women at high risk for breast and ovarian cancer (see also Chapter 9). While organizational factors are critical for successful guidelines implementation, in particular the need for clinical leaders and subject experts need to champion the guidelines, the size of the target population to which the guideline is relevant, and its burden of disease should be of sufficient magnitude before an institution undertakes the massive amount of planning, implementation, and monitoring of compliance of the guideline.

Monitoring Health Care Systems, Organizations, and Program Performance

The increased necessity for the continuous monitoring the health care system, organization, and program line performance is another reason for the use of epidemiology in management practice. The impetus for monitoring performance has been stimulated by the total quality management/continuous quality improvement movement and is formalized as part of various accreditation standards. The quality principles are espoused under the assumption that performance monitoring is one type of quality initiative and as such may be a means of improving organizational effectiveness and efficiency in the use of resources (e.g. personnel, supplies, equipment, etc.). For health care managers, the impact of these initiatives on patients is the ultimate concern. Performance can be assessed through the use of epidemiological measures or by means of analytic studies. (Subsequent chapters provide further discussion of these topics.)

Modifying the Structure and Processes to Respond to Environmental Change

In addition to considering the internal environment of an organization, epidemiology enables managers to understand how forces external to the organization can affect the organization and delivery of care. A classic example of how hospitals were compelled to change their processes occurred with the introduction of the prospective payment system (PPS) in 1983 (Svahn and Ross, 1983). PPS introduced reimbursement for treating Medicare patients on the basis of a single fixed amount per patient. The amount of reimbursement per hospital admission was determined by the diagnostic-related group (DRG) in which the patient fell. The DRG is based on the patient's clinical diagnosis, surgical procedures performed, age, and comorbidities present, which except for age rely on coding from the *International Classification of Diseases*. The new method of payment stimulated the restructuring of hospital processes. Some of the changes included the introduction of utilization review programs and more prehospitalization (outpatient) testing. The major response by hospitals to the introduction of PPS was to reduce the length of stay as a means of providing services within a fixed price per case. Cases with lengths of stay longer than what could be accommodated by a fixed price created losses for the institution. Epidemiology provides a framework for examining excess variability and causes of variability that could create losses to a health care system receiving capitated payment for the provision of services to a population. For example, an epidemiological investigation of delays in a teaching hospital found that the most frequent cause of an extended length of stay was difficulty in scheduling tests (Selker *et al.*, 1989). At the organizational level, epidemiology also can be used to assess the effects of restructuring. The increasing shortages in allied health professions also influence health care organizations. The impact of this on patient health status can be assessed with epidemiological methods.

Formulation and Evaluation of Public Policy Affecting the Delivery of Health Care Services

Epidemiological data and methods also are critical for the development and assessment of public policy affecting the delivery of health care services that health care executives may have the occasion to influence. Epidemiological data consisting of cancer incidence, mortality, and survival rates are collected by the Surveillance, Epidemiology, and End Results (SEER) Program of the National Cancer Institute to assess the impact of cancer in the general population. Specifically, these data provide information on changes over time on the extent of disease at diagnosis and survival associated with various forms of therapy. Health care providers can benchmark their experience relative to such national data. Extensive use of epidemiological data has been incorporated into defining priorities and strategic directions for the health of the nation and state governments (US Department of Health and Human Services, 2000; see also Chapter 12).

Epidemiological data also have been used to evaluate the impact of policies such as minimum drinking age laws (Zador *et al.*, 1989; see also Chapter 6). The End Stage Renal Disease (ESRD) Program is a classic example of a public policy that did not utilize epidemiological data in planning. Prior to the implementation of ESRD, estimates of future utilization of dialysis and transplant services were based on current recipients of those services. Those individuals were predominantly white, male, educated, and employed. When the ESRD Program extended Medicare coverage to all persons under age 65 with end-stage renal disease, the demographic characteristics of the recipients paralleled that of the general population. The incidence of those on treatment doubled within a few years. The result was an extraordinary expenditure of resources, with ESRD patients representing 0.25% of the Medicare patients and approximately 10% of the Medicare Part B budget (Rubin, 1984). This could have been anticipated and perhaps the extent and nature of coverage modified if population-based data were used in planning prior to the implementation of the program. As new national efforts are introduced, epidemiological methods also can be used to assess some of the other impending changes in health care delivery that would influence organizational restructuring. Epidemiology will be used to determine whether the health status of populations served will improve in a new configuration of health care delivery. As local and national health care systems change in response to external pressures, epidemiological methods will be used to assess the responsiveness of organizations to those changes in terms of meeting the needs of populations served.

Summary

The use of epidemiology in management decision making associated the delivery of health care services is now essential. Through an epidemiological framework, we can assess

Table 1.4. Questions for Health Care Executives
When Managing Health Systems from an Epidemiological Framework

1. Who is the population served?
   a. How is this population defined?
   b. What are the major size and demographic trends in this population?
   c. From what distances do individuals travel to receive health care?
2. What are the population's health care needs?
   a. How can these needs be measured?
   b. What is the prevalence of risk factors?
   c. What is the burden of disease and other problems?
3. What health services are feasible for addressing the population's health care needs?
   a. What are barriers the population can experience when attempting to access health care services?
   b. What are the capabilities of the organization/system relative to the size and needs of the population? (personnel, equipment, facilities)?
   c. How do the services of the local health system link to national or regional policy goals or initiatives?
   d. What environmental influences affect health services delivery? (payment conditions/provisions, market competition, trends affecting preferred delivery mode/setting)
4. What is the population's health status?
   a. How will the health status be measured at the present and over time?

how and why health care needs are distributed throughout a population and evaluate the use and efficacy of interventions. Thus, to improve the health status of a population, one needs to understand the population characteristics, the distribution and level of need, factors affecting the use of health care services, and the implications on the system if the desired level of health status is not achieved. The author leaves this chapter advising the reader to have in hand both the epidemiological model of the delivery of health care services from Fig. 1.1 and the list of questions in Table 1.4 as a framework for preparing to meet the challenges of managing health systems delivering population-based health care.

In Chapters 2 and 3, the issues and methods for measuring need and health that managers commonly encounter are discussed. Chapters 4, 5, and 6 illustrate analytic approaches to decision making when evaluating the impacts of health care programs and policies. The remaining chapters focus on the application of epidemiology of health care in specialty and spanning areas.

Case Studies

Case Study No. 1
Racial Differences in the Incidence of Cardiac Arrest and Subsequent Survival

There are known differences between blacks and whites for the prevalence of many cardiovascular diseases. There is less information on the differential rates of occurrence of cardiac arrests. Becker *et al.* (1993) examined racial differences in cardiac arrest and survival using data from the emergency medical system (EMS) in Chicago. The City of Chicago covers 228 square miles and its EMS system responds to more than 300,000 calls per year through the 911 telephone system. There are 55 two-person units providing advanced life support 24 hours a day. Patients with cardiac arrest are transported to 1 of 46 hospitals and treatment protocols used by the EMS follow the recommendations of the American Heart Association. In every age group, both black men and black women had more cardiac arrest than whites. Factors related to differences in survival are displayed in Table 1.5.

Q.1. Why would there be a difference in the occurrence of cardiac arrest between blacks and whites?

Q.2. Why would there be a difference in survival from cardiac arrest between blacks and whites?

Q.3. What services could the Chicago Department of Public Health provide in response to a community concern about the high number of fatal cardiac arrests?

Table 1.5. Percentage Surviving According to Race and Risk Factors[a]

Risk factor	Whites	Blacks	P value
Witnessed arrest	49%	42%	<0.001
CPR attempted by bystander	25%	18%	<0.001
Response interval < 6 min	3.3%	0.8%	<0.001
VF/VT[b] as initial cardiac rhythm	4.6%	1.6%	<0.001

[a]Data from Becker *et al.* (1993).
[b]VF/VT denotes ventricular fibrillation or ventricular tachycardia.

Case Study No. 2
Variability in the Use of Coronary Artery Bypass Grafting (CABG)

Wennberg (1996) observed wide variation in the use of a number of health care procedures. Table 1.6 displays the variation in the use of CABG procedures in the Medicare population admitted to selected US hospital service areas. A hospital service area was defined by the percentage of Medicare discharges by zip codes assigned to a town or city by the plurality method where the zip code was contiguous with the service area. The CABG utilization rate per 100,000 Medicare enrollees varied more than a factor of 4, with the lowest being in the Grand Junction, Colorado, hospital referral region and the highest in the Joliet, Illinois, region.

Q.1. What level of health service intervention is a CABG procedure: primary, secondary, or tertiary prevention and why?

Q.2. Considering the epidemiological framework for the delivery of health care services (Fig. 1.1), what factors of the population influence the CABG utilization rates?

Q.3. Considering the epidemiological framework for the delivery of health care services (Fig. 1.1), what factors of the health care system influence the CABG utilization rates?

Case Study No. 3
Rural Populations and Public Health Services

Jackson and Union Counties are adjacent rural counties located in southern Illinois. During the period 1920 to 1950, the coal mining industry prospered in the region. Since that time, the mines have closed and a few small farms are the mainstay of agricultural activity, the only remaining industry of any size, except for a large state-supported university in Jackson County. Local taxes are insufficient to support a large county health department. No new industry growth is expected. Thus, the State Health Department must subsidize public health activities in that area. Due to budget cuts in the State Health Department, the nature and amount of public health activities is being reexamined. Strategies for regionalized public health services are being examined. Data from the State's Office of Vital Statistics and the US Census are as follows:

	Total population by year		Number of births by year	
	1985	1991	1990	1999
Jackson County	61,100	60,900	690	705
Union County	18,000	17,600	241	198

Q.1. What other data should be compiled?

Q.2. Based on this preliminary assessment, what initial course of action should the state consider?

Case Study No. 4
Black–White Disparities in Breast Cancer Mortality

Considerable progress has been made in controlling morbidity and mortality from breast cancer. Advances in mammography technology have allowed smaller breast tumors to be detected. Widespread

Table 1.6. Coronary Artery Bypass Graft Surgery Rates by Selected Hospital Referral Region

Hospital referral region name	Hospital referral region state	Total population n (1990)	Medicare population n	CABG procedure rate per 100,000	Hospital referral region name	Hospital referral region state	Total population n (1990)	Medicare population n	CABG procedure rate per 100,000
Grand Junction	CO	57417	29020	2.07	Manchester	NH	164646	82822	5.22
Albuquerque	NM	264319	117763	2.66	Columbia	SC	215258	108229	5.28
Denver	CO	380137	163270	3.12	Raleigh	NC	253253	128251	5.31
Honolulu	HI	249501	91283	3.35	Sioux Falls	SD	235367	117471	5.34
Dubuque	IA	42821	21508	3.60	Chicago	IL	555335	252551	5.36
Charlottesville	VA	112762	56899	3.63	Billings	MT	120822	60821	5.36
Tucson	AZ	227366	86986	3.69	Houston	TX	701110	354234	5.38
Duluth	MN	110860	55265	3.77	Las Vegas	NV	207303	86110	5.41
Springfield	MA	206398	102782	3.82	Philadelphia	PA	1088052	522192	5.43
Arlington	VA	202392	102581	3.92	Ann Arbor	MI	255856	128729	5.49
Anchorage	AK	48768	24821	3.99	Tampa	FL	229592	94672	5.53
Sun City	AZ	119569	48484	4.04	Baltimore	MD	548831	274625	5.55
San Francisco	CA	303017	137196	4.07	Pittsburgh	PA	1046066	523354	5.55
Missoula	MT	82422	41374	4.12	Oklahoma City	OK	413680	204818	5.56
Portland	OR	492638	168475	4.16	Grand Forks	ND	49928	24851	5.59
Rockford	IL	169883	85221	4.19	Nashville	TN	473628	238276	5.64
Boise	ID	136451	68514	4.20	Evanston	IL	231368	108566	5.68
Hattiesburg	MS	63460	31739	4.23	Hartford	CT	375616	188277	5.72
Providence	RI	323129	152455	4.28	Durham	NC	280019	141273	5.73
Phoenix	AZ	458829	191774	4.29	Greenville	SC	170890	86153	5.73

City	State			Rate	City	State			Rate
San Diego	CA	580299	185903	4.32	Detroit	MI	471035	233448	5.85
Worcester	MA	191634	78247	4.33	Wichita	KS	352720	173960	5.87
New York	NY	1012093	475687	4.36	Cleveland	OH	601249	287654	5.88
San Bernardino	CA	410855	104442	4.41	Richmond	VA	301182	151733	5.89
Minneapolis	MN	630496	278212	4.44	Iowa City	IA	84837	42355	5.95
Topeka	KS	110532	55327	4.45	Bismarck	ND	61250	30726	6.00
Bangor	ME	108853	54720	4.51	Louisville	KY	371995	184422	6.08
Boston	MA	1177153	578227	4.56	St Louis	MO	837617	418988	6.09
Newark	NJ	360757	179074	4.57	Charleston	WV	252516	126593	6.09
Los Angeles	CA	1525138	523261	4.65	Greenville	NC	159535	80765	6.17
Washington	DC	424100	212972	4.67	Lubbock	TX	150437	75365	6.20
Seattle	WA	490706	207503	4.68	Chattanooga	TN	145807	73291	6.26
Salt Lake City	UT	262005	132143	4.71	Fort Lauderdale	FL	842301	333215	6.32
Colorado Springs	CO	117417	56562	4.76	New Orleans	LA	183269	91028	6.37
San Antonio	TX	396618	173173	4.78	Jacksonville	FL	255066	128785	6.55
Miami	FL	651143	236134	4.85	Huntsville	AL	102842	51975	6.87
Lincoln	NE	158565	79126	4.88	Little Rock	AR	386377	193215	7.05
Marshfield	WI	106541	53474	4.93	Saginaw	MI	185287	93134	7.16
Dallas	TX	570414	284100	4.97	Texarkana	AR	70646	35094	7.33
Omaha	NE	308292	151270	5.01	Hinsdale	IL	61934	30199	7.52
Buffalo	NY	430720	210491	5.03	Memphis	TN	370246	184400	7.70
Kansas City	MO	507563	241129	5.04	Birmingham	AL	533325	267273	7.73
Burlington	VT	136818	68714	5.10	Joliet	IL	95883	47952	8.50

aData from Wennberg (1996).

efforts have been undertaken by many cancer organizations aimed at educating women in the importance of breast self-exam and early detection. New treatment protocols that include multimodality therapy (surgery, chemotherapy, and radiation therapy) have been introduced. New drugs, such as tamoxifen, have been discovered to reduce the recurrence of breast cancer and are routinely used in practice. Despite all these advances, mortality rate (the number of deaths from breast cancer in a population) for breast cancer has increased in black women since 1973 but has decreased in white women during this same time period. The incidence rate (the number of new cases in a population) among white women is higher than among black women (Fig. 1.11).

Q.1. What population characteristics could account for these differences?

Q.2. How could differences in health care utilization account for a higher mortality rate in black women?

Case Study No. 5
Why Aren't 100% of Children Immunized Against Common Childhood Illnesses?

Despite a philosophy and financial structure that supports preventive health care, vaccination coverage levels for recommended childhood vaccinations are highly variable in health maintenance organiza-

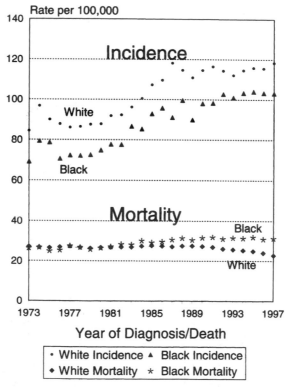

Figure 1.11. Breast cancer incidence and mortality, white women and black women, SEER areas, 1973–1997. SEER, Surveillance, Epidemiology, and End Results Program of the National Cancer Institute.

tions and have been reported to be as low as 39%. Immunization data were reviewed by McPhillips-Tangum *et al.* (1996) in a non-Medicaid, independent practice association (IPA) model health plan with approximately 150,000 members and 4300 affiliated primary care physicians in southern California. Medical charts of 1396 children aged 2 years who were continuously enrolled in the plan as of 1993 were reviewed. A survey was sent to the 97 physicians of the children in this sample to assess physician knowledge, attitudes, and practices regarding pediatric vaccination.

Q.1. What characteristics of the IPA could present barriers to immunization?

Q.2. What physician practices could be barriers to immunization?

References

Andersen, R. M., 1995, Revisiting the behavioral model and access to medical care: Does it matter? *J. Health Soc. Behav.* **36**:1–10.

Becker, L. B., Hahn, B. H., Meyer, P. M., Wright, F. A., Rhodes, K. V., Smith, D. W., Barrett, J., and the CPR Chicago Project, 1993, Racial differences in the incidence of cardiac arrest and subsequent survival, *N. Engl. J. Med.* **329**:600–606.

Bindman, A. B., Grumbach, K., Osmond, D., Komaromy, M., Vranizan, K., Lurie, N., Billings, J., and Stewart, A., 1995, Preventable hospitalizations and access to health care, *J.A.M.A.* **274**:305–311.

Ford, E. S., Will, J. C., De Proost Ford, M. A., and Mokdad, A. H., 1998, Health insurance status and cardiovascular disease risk factors among 50- to 64-year-old US women: Findings from the Third National Health and Nutrition Examination Survey, *J. Women's Health* **7**:997–1006.

Goodman, E., 1999, The role of socioeconomic status gradients in explaining differences in US adolescents' health, *Am. J. Pub. Health* **89**:1522–1528.

Guadagnoli, E., Hauptman, P. J., Ayanian, J. Z., Pashos, C. L., McNeil, B. J., and Cleary, P. D., 1995, Variation in the use of cardiac procedures after acute myocardial infarction, *N. Engl. J. Med.* **333**:573–578.

Hartz, A. J. Krakauer, H., Kuhn, E. M., Young, M., Jacobsen, S. J., Gay, G., Muenz, L., Katzoff, M., Bailey, R. C., and Rimm, A. A., 1989, Hospital characteristics and mortality rates, *N. Engl. J. Med.* **321**:1720–1725.

Herbert-Croteau, N., Brisson, J., and Pineault, R., 2000, Review of organizational factors related to care offered to women with breast cancer, *Epid. Review* **22**:228–238.

Institute of Medicine, 1997, *America's Vital Interest in Global Health: Protecting Our People, Enhancing Our Economy, and Advancing Our International Interests*, National Academy Press, Washington, DC.

McAlpine, D. D., and Mechanic, D., 2000, Utilization of specialty mental health care among persons with severe mental illness: The roles of demographics, need, insurance, and risk, *HSR: Health Services Res.* **35**:277–292.

McPhillips-Tangum, C. A., Lewis, N. A., Ward-Coleman, C., Koplan, J. P., Lee, P., Batchlor, E., Kamil, I. J., and Small, A., 1996, Use of a data-based approach to identify and address physician barriers to pediatric vaccination-California, 1995, *Morbid. Mortal. Week. Rev.* **45**:188–190.

Mechanic, D., 1995, Sociological dimensions of illness behavior, *Soc. Sci. Med.* **41**:1207–1216.

Mitchell, P. H., and Shortell, S. M., 1997, Adverse outcomes and variations in organization of care delivery, *Med. Care* **35**:NS19–NS32.

Mundinger, M., Kane, R. L., Lenz, E. R., Totten, A. M., Tsai, W., Cleary, P. D., Friedewald, W. T., Siu, A. L., and Shelanski, M. L., 2000, Primary care outcomes in patients treated by nurse practitioners or physicians: A randomized trial, *J.A.M.A.* **283**:59–68.

MacKay, A. P., Fingerhut, L. A., and Duran, G. R., 2000, *Health United States, 2000, with Adolescent Health Chartbook*, National Center for Health Statistics, Hyattsville, MD.

Murray, C. J. L., and Lopez, A. D., 1997, Regional patterns of disability-free life expectancy and disability-adjusted life expectancy: Global Burden of Disease Study, *Lancet* **39**:1347–1352.

National Center for Health Statistics, 2000, *Prevalence of BMI, overweight and obesity: United States, 1960–1994* (http://www.cdc.gov/nchs/about/major/nhanes/overweight.pdf).

Oleske, D. M., Glandon, G. L., Giacomelli, G., and Hohmann, S., 1991, The cesarean birth rate: Influence of hospital teaching status, *HSR: Health Services Res.* **23**:325–337.

Rhoades, J., Brown, E., and Vistnes, J., 2000, *Health Insurance Status of the Civilian Noninstitutionalized Population: 1998*, AHRQ Pub. No. 00-0023, Agency for Healthcare Research and Quality, Rockville, MD.

Rubin, R. J., 1984, Epidemiology of end stage renal disease and implications for public policy, *Pub. Health Rep.* **99:**492–498.

Schoen, C., Neuman, P., Kitchman, M., Davis, K., and Rowland, D., 1998, *Medicare Beneficiaries: A Population at Risk*, The Henry J. Kaiser Family Foundation and the Commonwealth Fund, Menlo Park, CA; New York.

Selby, J. V., Fireman, B. H., Lundstrom, R. J., Swain, B. E., Truman, A. F., Wong, C. C., Froelicher, E. S., Barron, H. V., and Hlatky, M. A., 1996, Variation among hospitals in coronary angiography practices and outcomes after myocardial infarction in a large health maintenance organization, *N. Engl. J. Med.* **335:**188–196.

Selker, H. P., Beshansky, J. R., Pauker, S. G., and Kassirer, J. P., 1989, The epidemiology of delays in a teaching hospital, *Med. Care* **27:**112–129.

Shortell, S. M., Jones, R. H., Rademaker, A. W., Gillies, R. R., Dranove, D. S., Hughes, E. F. X., Budetti, P. O., Reynolds, K., and Huang, C., 2000, Assessing the impact of total quality management of organizational culture on multiple outcomes of care for coronary artery bypass graft surgery patients, *Med. Care* **38:**207–217.

Spector, W. D., and Takada, H., 1991, Characteristics of nursing homes that affect resident outcomes, *J. Aging Health* **30:**427–454.

Steinwachs, D. M., 1989, Application of health status assessment measures in policy research, *Med. Care* **27:** S12–S26.

Svahn, J. A., and Ross, M., 1983, Social Security amendments of 1983: Legislative history and summary of provisions, *Soc. Sec. Bull.* **5:**3–48.

Svennignsen, N. W., 1992, Neonatal intensive care, *Int. J. Technol. Assess. Health Care* **8:**457–468.

United Nations, 2001, *World Population Prospects: The 1998 Revision*, United Nations Press, New York (http://www.popin.org/pop1998/4.htm).

US Census Bureau, 1975, *Historical Statistics of the United States: Colonial Times to 1970*, Series B-14, 93rd Congress, 1st Session, House Document, No. 93–78 (Part 1).

US Census Bureau, 2000, *Characteristics of the Hispanic Population* (http://www.census.gov/population/socdemo/hispanic/cps99/99gifshow/sld002.htm).

US Department of Health and Human Services, 2000, *Healthy people 2010-Conference ed.* US Government Printing Office, Washington DC.

Vogt, T., and Schweitzer, S., 1985, Medical costs of cigarette smoking in a health maintenance organization, *Am. J. Epidemiol.* **122:**1060–1066.

Wennberg, J. E., 1996, *The Dartmouth Atlas of Health Care*, American Hospital Publishing, Chicago, IL.

World Health Organization, 1948, *Test of the Constitution of World Health Organization* Official Records, WHO, Geneva, Switzerland.

World Health Organization, 2000, *The World Health Report 2000*, WHO, Geneva, Switzerland.

Zador, P. L., Lund, A. K., Fields, M., and Weinberg, K., 1989, Fatal crash involvement and laws against alcohol-impaired driving, *J. Public Health Policy* **10:**467–485.

2

Measurement Issues in the Use of Epidemiological Data

Denise M. Oleske

Introduction

Health services, regardless of their purpose (e.g., health promotion, disease prevention, screening and diagnosis, treatment, or rehabilitation) are designed to support the health of populations. It is the health care manager's responsibility to continuously monitor these services, to assess their efficacy, and to determine the most appropriate allocation of resources for achieving desired health status goals. These tasks require managers to accurately measure the exposure factors that influence utilization of health services as well as health itself. Exposure factors may be harmful or beneficial and may be the health services themselves, lifestyle, or the environment. Accurate measurement of exposure to health services and resultant health status is essential and necessarily precedes any attempt to analyze the impact of health services delivery.

Health care managers must decide what data should be collected on a routine or periodic basis and select an appropriate measurement of the desired data elements. The trade-offs in terms of costs and time must be considered as decisions are made about the amount of information that should be collected. This chapter discusses the major issues pertinent to the measurement of exposure to and the outcomes of health service delivery, including the methods and logistics of measurement, reliability, and validity, the classification of results, and reduction of measurement error.

Methods of Measurement

Numerous methods exist for measuring exposure factors and health status including surveys, clinical assessments, imaging techniques, laboratory tests, and physical measure-

Denise M. Oleske   Departments of Health Systems Management and Preventive Medicine, Rush University, Chicago, Illinois 60612.

Epidemiology and the Delivery of Health Care Services: Methods and Applications, Second Edition, edited by Denise M. Oleske. Kluwer Academic/Plenum Publishers, New York, 2001.

ments. The data obtained from these measures are called primary data. Regardless of measurement method(s), the key question is: "Does it obtain the information needed?"

The most widely used method for obtaining information about both exposure factors and health status is a survey or the use of forms to collect information. Survey forms may be designed to collect information from personal and telephone interviews, self-administered questionnaires, or medical or administrative records. The advantages and disadvantages of each approach are contrasted in Table 2.1. Survey information may be recorded onto hard copy or onto a computer screen linked to a database software package. In practice, a combination of these approaches may be most effective in reducing nonresponse bias and to promote data quality (Brambilla and McKinlay, 1987).

A survey form, regardless of the medium on which it resides, consists of three elements: (1) any special instructions to the participant (or to the data collector), (2) the questions (or items) themselves, and (3) the scaling of each item. The survey form should begin with the title of the study and a brief statement of its purpose, followed by brief instructions for completing the form. Instructions direct the data abstractor, interviewer, or respondent to provide or select one or more answers for each item, indicate how the choice(s) or answers should be provided (circled, checked), and specify how to proceed through the form when an item does not apply.

The content of the items depends on whether or not they concern exposure or outcomes. If measuring exposure, information should be sought on the exposure itself: periods of exposure, sources, intensity, frequency, and duration. If measuring outcomes, evidence is sought to enable classification based on specified criteria (additional discussion on this follows). Whether measuring exposure or outcomes, the survey form should contain cues to facilitate the retrieval of information. Cues may be provided relevant to the timing of the occurrence of

Table 2.1. Advantages and Disadvantages of Various Types of Surveys

	Advantages	Disadvantages
Record surveys	Rules for coding/abstraction in place	Source documents not uniform in order or content
	Nonreactive	Missing data may not be retrievable
	Source data may be more accurate	Time consuming even for health care professionals
		More complex cases likely to be missing
Telephone surveys	Quick to obtain	Physical measures not obtainable
	Less costly than personal interviews	Some persons do not have phones
	Can administer a lengthy form, with branching questions	Confused with sales calls
	Wide geographic coverage possible	Behavioral cues missed
	Can maintain tight quality control	Choices not able to be presented visually
		Hearing impairments affect responses
Self-administered	Anonymous	May overrepresent women and higher socioeconomic status
	Inexpensive	
	No interviewer effects	Recording errors, missing data may not be corrected
Personal interviews	Can obtain physical measurements	Responses may be modified by interviewer's characteristics
	Can administer a lengthy form	
	Allows impressions to be recorded	Expensive and time-consuming

the event or the degree of exposure. For example, in a study investigating the impact of the level of patient participation in treatment decisions (exposure) on health outcomes, the first item or question (intended as a cue) could be: "When was your most recent hospitalization?" Paffenbarger *et al.* (1993) utilized cartoons of different sized body figures to stimulate the recall of past weight changes (exposure) which could affect current health status.

The level of measurement desired and the past use of a measure determine the type of scaling techniques used. Levels of measurement may be **nominal** (a variable categorized into two or more levels representing mutually exclusive categories: HMO, Medicare, or self-pay insurer categories; diseased or not diseased; male or female), **ordinal** (a variable categorized into levels that representing ordered values: e.g., <$10,000, $10,000–11,999, >$11,999), or **interval** (a variable with units each of which have meaning: e.g., charges for hospitalization). For nominal and ordinal scales, the categories should be mutually exclusive. Responses for ordinal scales should reflect the most conventional options. A common ordinal scale is called Likert-type, whereby a response with varying degree of intensity is represented between two extremes. It also is very important to always have a time referent for the respondent when querying health events or exposures (e.g., in the last week, in the past 30 days, ever, etc.). The recording of pain frequency may be as follows:

In the past week, how bothersome has the following symptom been?

	None	Very little	Some	Quite a bit	Very much
Q.1. Low back pain	0	1	2	3	4

When recording values for an interval level item, the units desired and the maximum number of integers should be indicated. For example:

Q.2. On the average, about how many cigarettes a day do you now smoke?
(1 pack = 20 cigarettes)   a. Number of cigarettes   ____ ____
                             b. Don't smoke regularly   8   8
                             c. Refused   9   9

Coding conventions designate the use of "8" for responses not applicable and "9" for unknown, refused, or missing responses.

In deciding the particular response scale to be used or cut points for the scale, it may be helpful to review previous studies on the same topic. For example, survey forms used in national health surveys are public domain. The Behavioral Risk Factor Surveillance Survey form can be downloaded from the Centers for Disease Control (CDC) website and a module of that form as it pertains to access to health care is displayed in Fig. 2.1. Cut points may be determined by: (1) historical convention (e.g., age group); (2) clinical significance; (3) data-based rules such as quartiles of a distribution; (4) plots of exposure versus outcome (e.g., Q–Q plots; receiver operating characteristic [ROC] curves) (Wartenberg and Northridge, 1992; Simmons *et al.*, 1995); or (5) statistical models such as recursive partitioning analysis (tree-based models) (Zhang and Bracken, 1995).

Validity and Reliability of a Measure

A measure should be both reliable and valid. Therefore, in selecting or interpreting a measure, validity and reliability should be assessed. Many studies now report the level of reliability and validity for the measures used.

To the correct respondent   HELLO, I'm _____ calling for the _____
and the Centers for Disease Control and Prevention. We're
gathering information on the health practices of _____
residents to guide state health policies. You have been chosen
randomly to be interviewed, and we'd like to ask some questions
about day-to-day living habits that may affect health.

We do not ask for your name, address, or other personal information that identifies you. The phone
number is erased once we finish all interviews at the end of the year. There are no risks or benefits to
you being in this survey. Taking part is up to you. You don't have to answer any question you don't
want to, and you are free to end the interview at any time. The interview takes _____ minutes. All
information you give us will be confidential. If you have any questions about this survey, I will
provide a toll free telephone number for you to call to get more information.

Section 1: Health Status

1.1. Would you say that in general your health is:

> **Please read**
>
> | | | |
> |---|---|---|
> | a. | Excellent | 1 |
> | b. | Very good | 2 |
> | c. | Good | 3 |
> | d. | Fair | 4 |
> | | or | |
> | e. | Poor | 5 |

Do not   Don't know/Not sure   7
read these Refused   9
responses

1.2. Now thinking about your physical health, which includes physical illness and injury, for how
many days during the past 30 days was your physical health not good?

> | | | | |
> |---|---|---|---|
> | a. | Number of days | ____ | ____ |
> | b. | None | 8 | 8 |
> | | Don't know/Not Sure | 7 | 7 |
> | | Refused | 9 | 9 |

1.3. Now thinking about your mental health, which includes stress, depression, and problems with
emotions, for how many days during the past 30 days was your mental health not good?

> | | | | |
> |---|---|---|---|
> | a. | Number of days | ____ | ____ |
> | b. | None | 8 | 8 |
> | | Don't know/Not Sure | 7 | 7 |
> | | Refused | 9 | 9 |

1.4. During the past 30 days, for about how many days did poor physical or mental health keep you
from doing your usual activities, such as self-care, work, or recreation?

> | | | | |
> |---|---|---|---|
> | a. | Number of days | ____ | ____ |
> | b. | None | 8 | 8 |
> | | Don't know/Not Sure | 7 | 7 |
> | | Refused | 9 | 9 |

Figure 2.1.   Selected text from the 2000 Behavioral Risk Factor Surveillance Survey Questionnaire.

Validity

Validity represents the precision to which the measure truly characterizes the phenomenon being studied. A measure must be reliable in order for it to be valid. Validity can be assessed through qualitative and quantitative means.

Qualitatively, the validity of a measure is influenced by its inherent structure and the method by which it is administered. If the measurement method uses a survey form, Aday (1996) proposes that the following guidelines be followed to promote the validity of a survey form:

1. Formatting
   a. should be consistent with the manner in which it is administered (e.g., telephone, personal interview, self-administered, data abstraction)
   b. the form should have a clear title of the project name, purpose of project, and instructions on completing the form
   c. local Institutional Review Board (IRB) requirements may have to be considered in the format including: explaining procedures for maintaining confidentiality of response and voluntary nature of participation
   d. questions should be numbered, with letters for subcategories and numbers assigned to response choices and presented in a logical sequence
   e. responses should be listed vertically
   f. use consistent numeric codes for responses (e.g., 1 always equals "yes")
   g. always phrase full and complete questions, not single words or incomplete sentences
   h. obtain opinions from convenience sample of target audience on appearance of survey form (e.g., color, font, layout)
   i. take into consideration the special needs of the target population (e.g., need for large font)
2. Clarity
   a. provide instructions as necessary to complete
   b. never leave a space with no instructions
3. Balance
   a. avoid providing a series of questions with the same response categories (e.g., strongly agree, agree, disagree)
   b. all parts of a question and associated responses should be on the same page
4. Length
   a. determine the length of each item and the form itself as increased length may promote fatigue and inaccurate responses and coding
5. Order and context (a logical order facilitates data abstraction and participant recall)
   a. provide clear skip instructions
   b. demographic questions should be last, even for screening purposes, except for data abstraction forms where they should be first
   c. leave space for comments last
   d. end the questionnaire with a thank you and return information (if relevant)
   e. clarify the referent (events in last six days versus ever; satisfaction with communication in a department versus a division)

Figure 2.1 displays a segment of the CDC's Behavioral Risk Factor Surveillance Survey telephone interview form. This interview form illustrates many of the principles recommended by Aday for formatting survey forms.

To ensure the validity of information obtained, a protocol for collecting the information should be formulated. The elements of the protocol should include the development of an operations manual; provisions for training the data collectors; specification of rules for handling conflicting or missing data; pilot testing of the process and form, a definition of a standard environment in which the data are collected; routine checks of the completeness, corrigibility, and accuracy of the data collected; periodic retraining of the data collectors; and means of transmitting the data for computer entry.

The most commonly used methods for evaluating validity are **content validity** (or face validity), **criterion validity**, and **construct validity**. The determination of content validity is based on the degree to which experts, usually at least three, make a subjective determination that the measure represents the full domain of the concept or condition. Content validation is typically the first step in the validation process. Comparing the test measure to known measure of the phenomenon assesses criterion validity. When a measurement contains interval-level values, comparing the mean and standard deviation of the difference between the test measure and the valid reference can assess validity mean. When measures are at the normal level (e.g., tests to identify diseased from disease-free persons), validity is assessed through the construction of a 2×2 table that determines the sensitivity (the proportion of those who test positive for the outcome and have the outcome), the specificity (the proportion of those who test negative for the outcome and do not have the outcome), and the positive predictive value (the proportion of those testing positive who have the outcome) (Table 2.2). The values from criterion validity can help predict traits at a later time. From information on the sensitivity and

Table 2.2. Evaluation of the Criterion Validity of a Measure

Measure results	Disease		Total
	Present	Absent	
Positive	True positive (TP)	False positive (FP)	
	A	B	A + B
Negative	False negative (FN)	True negative (TN)	
	C	D	C + D
Totals	A + C	B + D	A + C + B + D

Sensitivity[a] (those who have the disease, and are so classified by the test)
$$= A/(A + C) \times 100\% = TP/(TP + FN) = TP/\text{All those with disease}$$
Specificity[a] (those who do not have the disease and are so classified by the test)
$$= D/(B + D) \times 100\% = TN/(TN + FP) = TN/\text{All those without the disease}$$
False negative rate[a] (those with the disease not identified by the test)
$$= C/(A + C) \times 100\%$$
False positive rate[a] (those without the disease identified by the test)
$$= B/(B + D) \times 100\%$$
Proportion of the population with the disease (disease prevalence rate)
$$= (A + C)/(A + B + C + D) \times 100\%$$
Positive predictive rate (those with the disease who test positive)
$$= A/(A + B) \times 100\%$$
Diagnostic accuracy = No. of true positives + No. of true negatives/total evaluated
$\times 100\%$
$$= (A + D)/(A + B + C + D) \times 100\%$$

[a]Can also be expressed as a probability.

specificity of a diagnostic test applied to a population to detect diseases before its signs and symptoms occur (a process called screening or secondary prevention), estimates can be made of the number of diseased persons who will require referral for treatment. Ideally, a measure should be 100% sensitive and 100% specific and have a 100% positive predictive value.

When the test measure values are ordinal and the outcome is nominal level of measurement, likelihood ratios (LR) and receiver operating characteristic (ROC) curves can be constructed to assess criterion validity. A ROC curve is a plot of the true positive rate versus the false positive rate for various levels of the test (Fig. 2.2). The challenge is determining the optimal cut points for the levels of the test. The LR for a positive test is defined as the ratio of the true positive rate to the false positive rate for various levels of the measure. The test level where a LR of 1.0 is exceeded is defined as the threshold for positivity or the cut point at which the value for the level of the test measurement will significantly predict the outcome. Statistical software is available to easily construct LRs and ROC curves (SPSS, 1999). Table 2.3 provides information on the cut points of quintiles of peak serum estradiol (PES). Increasing PES is known to be associated with high-order multiple births. A high rate of high-order multiple births is an undesirable outcome for fertility centers. The ROC curve for these data is presented in Fig. 2.2. The more area under the curve (AUC), the greater is the accuracy of the test measure in predicting the outcome (an AUC = 1.00 is a perfect prediction). ROC curves aid management decision making. Chapter 10 (this volume) illustrates how ROC curves are used in choosing from available technologies. Garnick *et al.* (1995) used ROC curves to determine what would be the optimal postadmission time cut point for using a risk-adjusted mortality rate after hospitalization as a measure of hospital quality for cardiac care. Further detail on the uses of ROC curve construction and interpretation can be obtained elsewhere (Metz, 1986; Peirce and Cornell, 1993; Choi, 1998).

Construct validity is the use of two or more measures yielding similar results to account

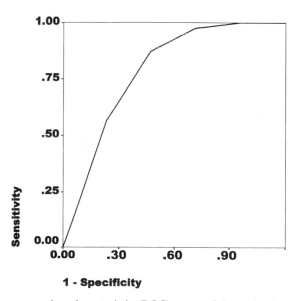

Figure 2.2. Receiver operating characteristic (ROC) curve of the optimal cut-points of peak serum estradiol that predict higher order multiple births. From Gleicher *et al.*, (2000).

Table 2.3. Data for Constructing a Receiver Operating Characteristic (ROC) Curve

Gold standard	Cutpoints[a] for positivity								Total
	4		≥3		≥2		≥1		
	Pos	Neg	Pos	Neg	Pos	Neg	Pos	Neg	
Positive	21	18	32	7	39	0	39	0	39
Negative	92	230	174	148	261	61	307	15	322
True positive rate	21/39 = .54		32/39 = .82		39/39 = 1.0		39/39 = 1.0		
False positive rate	92/322 = .29		174/322 = .54		261/322 = .81		307/322 = .95		
Likelihood ratio (LR)	21/39 ÷ 92/322 = 1.88		32/39 ÷ 174/178 = 1.52		39/39 ÷ 261/322 = 1.23		↑[b] 39/39 ÷ 307/322 = 0.95		

[a]Cut points are based upon peak serum estradiol concentrations where $4 \geq 1385$ pg/ml; ≥ 3 is 1384–935 pg/ml; ≥ 2 is 934–661 pg/ml; and $\geq 1 \leq 660$ pg/ml. Positivity means that a higher-order birth (3 or more) occurred at the cut point.
[b]↑ Threshold for positivity, i.e., the cut point where the LR statistically significantly predicts the outcome.
From Gleicher *et al.* (2000).

for a phenomenon. Construct validity is used when multiple criteria are thought to measure a concept such as quality of life. Thus, if one wanted to evaluate the validity of a new severity of illness measure, the numerical values of the measure could be compared against mortality rates or the relative risk of mortality. The Charlson comorbidity index was validated in this manner (Charlson *et al.*, 1994). Stratification of a population subgroup by comorbidity level allows for greater precision in estimating resource consumption by stratum and enables controlling for morbidity when comparing organizational health care units with respect to effectiveness. A correlation coefficient or *R*-squared from a linear regression model can be used to statistically assess construct validity.

Reliability

Reliability represents the extent to which a measurement instrument has consistency over time (stability or reproducibility), among various versions or applications (equivalence), and within the instrument itself (homogeneity). Various means can be employed to assess reliability, depending upon the level of measurement and the aspect of reliability being assessed. Three common statistical techniques used for assessing reliability are **correlation coefficients**, the **kappa statistic**, and the **coefficient of variation**.

Reliability may be determined from the product moment (Pearson) correlation coefficient when the independent and dependent variables are continuous and each have a normal distribution. When the independent or dependent variables are at least ordinal or when the sample is less than 30, a rank-difference correlation coefficient (Spearman's rho) may be utilized. The valid values for both correlation coefficients range from −1, a perfectly inverse correlation, to +1, a perfectly positive correlation. The value "0" represents no correlation. The larger the value of the correlation coefficient, the greater the reliability, with values of at least 0.70 in either direction representing a strong correlation. Spread sheet packages and all statistical software packages are capable of generating both parametric and nonparametric correlation coefficients.

The kappa statistic (k) is used to assess reproducibility when the ratings from two measures or one measure at two-time periods are being compared and both are categorical levels of measurement. The kappa represents the extent to which agreement exists beyond that expected on the basis of chance (Maclure and Willett, 1987). It is represented as follows:

$$k = (P_o - P_e)/(1 - P_e)$$
where: P_o = proportion of observations for which there is agreement
P_e = proportion of observations for which agreement is expected by chance alone

A scheme for assessing the strength of agreement beyond chance of the kappa statistic proposed by Fleiss (1981) is 0 to < 0.40, poor; 0.40 to 0.75, fair to good; > 0.75 excellent. The kappa statistic can conveniently be computed using Epi Info (version 6.04b) software (Dean et al., 1997). If the measures compared are ordinal (i.e., level of agreement), a weighted kappa should be used. The reader is advised to consult Soeken and Prescot (1986) for a discussion and advice on the use of weights.

The coefficient of variation is used to compare the dispersion or variability of two measures whose order of magnitude of numeric values are very disparate. The coefficient of variation (CV) is represented as:

$$CV = \text{s.d.} / \bar{x}$$
where: s.d. = standard deviation of x_i observations
$\bar{x}$ = mean of x observations

For example, the results of high-density lipoprotein (HDL) ("good lipoproteins") and low-density lipoproteins (LDL) ("bad lipoproteins") are often used to determine an individual's risk of cardiovascular disease. But since the average values for LDL are higher (mean = 120 mg/dl, SD = 27.5 mg/dl) than the values of HDL (mean = 20 mg/dl, SD = 2.5 mg/dl), does this mean that one test result is more reliable than the other? Substituting the values for LDL and HDL and computing the coefficient of variation for each reveals not only comparable measures of dispersion (CV_{HDL} = 22.9%; CV_{LDL} = 12.5%), but also that the two tests are reliable measures. A coefficient of variation over 50% indicates poor reliability and the use or purchase of the diagnostic material is not advised.

Factors affecting the reliability of a measure are:

- Accuracy or specificity of the measurement (inconsistency, coding differences across diagnoses and procedures, ambiguity of diagnoses)
- Stability of the variables (consistent definition or criteria for diagnoses, consistent or standardized method of data collection)
- Timing and method of data collection (collected at same time of data under same circumstances)

Measures should be both reliable and valid in order to accurately classify exposure to a causative factor or to determine the presence or absence of an outcome. Reliability and validity assessments should not be considered absolute, as what is reliable and valid in one setting or among a certain type of population may not be so for another.

Logistics of Measurement

Regardless of the measurement method selected, the logistics for the collection of information should be determined. Logistics encompass administration of the measure, super-

Table 2.4. Questions for Evaluating the Logistics of Measurement

1. How is the measure administered?
2. Has it been used in other similar situations and to what degree of success?
3. Is the measure understandable by the study sample? by those who administer it?
4. Will the sample (patients, records, specimens) be accessible?
5. Are there any risks associated with its administration?
6. What are the potential restrictions of its use (e.g., cost, copyright, patent)?
7. Are special training and equipment required?
8. What is the length of time involved in measurement?
9. How is it scored?
10. Will the results of the measurement be available in a timely manner?
11. Are normative data and interpretation guidelines available? If so, what is the cost?

vision of the data collection, and data processing. The questions in Table 2.4 must be addressed to determine whether the measurement process is feasible. Simultaneously, the quality of data collected must be continuously monitored included checks of the staff collecting the data, corrigibility and completeness of information, and timeliness of submission of information.

Classification of Health

Decisions about initiating efforts to improve the health of populations and to more effectively target resources may be aided with the use of an appropriate system for classification of health. Health (or absence of) may be measured as observed such as diseases, injuries, death, or by self-report. Health may be represented as an index that is a single score derived from a series of observations such as functional ability or cognitive function. Health may be represented as a profile that is a measurement of multiple concepts, such as a quality of life instrument. A **classification system** is a method for assigning individuals evaluated into one of k mutually exclusive categories or units representing a degree of health, pathology, or manifestation of a condition. Classification aids in the precision of measurement as it provides for a way of structuring information. Classification is essential for health planning: for characterizing health problems in the potential service population, for conducting studies of risk factors, for devising and evaluating patient intervention strategies, for monitoring organizational effectiveness, and for projecting resource utilization. Common methods for classifying aspects of health are discussed below.

Disease

Disease refers to a state of dysfunction of the normal physiological processes manifested as signs, symptoms, and abnormal physical or social function. The most commonly used schema for classifying disease is the *International Classification of Diseases* (ICD), which is currently in its 10th revision (World Health Organization, 1999a), replacing the ICD 9th revision as of January 1, 1999 for coding and classifying mortality data. The tabular list of disease is now alphanumeric (A00.00–Z99.9) instead of numeric, but still retains three-digit categorization of the disease entity. Its application in other areas of health service delivery (e.g., for coding hospital discharge abstracts) is scheduled for introduction in 2001. The ICD with clinical modifications (ICD-10-CM) provides a method for classifying diseases and injuries as well as procedures and reasons for utilizing health care. The implementation of ICD-10-CM will be based on the standards set through the Health Insurance Portability and Accountability Act of 1996 (http://aspe.os.dhhs.gov/adminsimp). Although the ICD was originally designed to serve as a template for the uniform coding of death, it also may be used to classify symptoms, physical findings, severity, pathological processes, procedures, and etiologic factors. ICD-10 enables information relevant to ambulatory and managed care encounters to be coded and expands injury codes. Laterality of organs (right breast, left breast) will be able to be coded. Codes are assigned to states on a nominal scale. Although there are many more codes available through ICD-10, the new revision attempts to reduce clinical vagueness, that is, reducing the number of codes could be used to represent the same trait.

Table 2.5 compares the coding of low back disorders between the two versions and is an example of how ICD-10 has created combination diagnosis/symptom codes to reduce the number of codes needed to fully describe a condition. With advancement in classifying disease, one always must be aware of the potential for heterogeneity that may exist within individual diseases. Another caution regarding the use of ICD coding is that codes have changed over time for a number of conditions (e.g., AIDS, pneumonia, dementia). For example, although human immunodeficiency virus (HIV) infection was recognized in 1981, the ICD-9-CM code until 1986 was 279.19, "other deficiency of cell-mediated immunity." Effective 1987, the codes for AIDS were changed to 042.0, 042.1, 042.2, and 042.9. The classification system was later expanded to include more diagnostic entities for AIDS (ICD-9-CM codes 042-044). In ICD-10, HIV disease with disease sequelae will be the axis for expanded codes that range from B20.0 "HIV disease resulting in infection" to B24 "unspecified HIV disease." AIDS is no longer a separate code. Immunodeficiencies are coded separately depending on the type, e.g., from D80.8 "Other immunodeficiencies with predominantly antibody defects," to D81.2 "Severe combined immunodeficiency [SCID] with low or normal B-cell numbers."

When properly mapped, the move to ICD-10 from and ICD-9 coding system should not affect a patient's diagnosis-related group (DRG) classification that is based on ICD coding. Accurate disease coding of encounters with health care providers is essential to ensure appropriate monitoring of resource use in the management of a particular disease as well for

Table 2.5. International Classification of Diseases (ICD) Codes
Used to Classify Low Back Pain, 9th and 10th Revisions

Revision/ICD Code	Label
9th/Code	
724.2	Lumbago, low back pain, low back syndrome, lumbalgia
724.5	Backache, unspecified
846.0–.9	Sprains and strains of sacroiliac region
847.2	Sprains and strains, lumbar
847.3	Sprains and strains, sacrum
847.4	Sprains and strains, coccyx
10th/Code	
M54.3	Sciatica
M54.4	Lumbago with sciatica
M54.5	Low back pain

budgeting and reimbursement purposes. A draft version of ICD-10 is available through the electronic library of the National Center for Health Statistics: ftp://ftp.cdc.gov/pub/Health_ Statistics/NCHS/Publications/.

Injuries

Injuries are physical manifestations of bodily harm resulting from contact with temperature extremes, objects, or substances or from bodily motion. In the United States in 1997, there were 34.4 million medically attended episodes of injury and poisoning among the civilian noninstitutionalized population (Warner et al., 2000). In ICD-9, injury, poisoning, and certain other consequences of external causes and related procedures were coded from E800-999, but in ICD-10 they will be coded with greater specificity as to the mechanism in the disease tabular list as S00-T98. External causes of morbidity and mortality are now coded V01-Y98. There are four axes of coding external causes: (1) injured person's mode of transport, (2) collision versus noncollision, (3) information on the injured person activity (traffic or nontraffic), and (4) specific activity (e.g., V27.0 "Driver of motorcycle injured in nontraffic accident with fixed or stationary object"). Attention has been given to detailed coding for "Intentional self-harm," X60-X84 (e.g., "Intentional self-poisoning [suicide] by and exposure to alcohol," X65) and for "Assault," X85-Y09 (e.g., "Assault [homicide] by drugs, medicaments, and biological substances," X85).

Coding of the external cause of injury is required whenever an injury is the principal diagnosis or directly related to the principal diagnosis. When coding multiple trauma cases, codes are advised to sequence first the condition that presents the most serious threat to life. While the level of coding detail will aid providing more detail for developing prevention initiatives, the increased coding demands upon acute and emergency health care providers will provide a challenge.

Functioning and Disability

The intent of classifying functional ability is to represent how independently an individual can perform or fulfill expected social roles. Function may be either directly assessed by a physician or other trained practitioner or be self-reported. Independence is the highest achievable outcome level of functioning in these scales. Measures of physical performance are widely used in assessment and longitudinal follow-up of the health status of elderly, disabled, and chronically ill persons. They also are utilized to measure the response to intervention (e.g., rehabilitation services).

An aberration in functioning is termed disability; it can be physical or social. Physical disability is manifest by aberrations in an individual's sensory and motor performance. The disability classification system utilized depends on the population that needs to be assessed. Institutionalized elderly may be expected to have low levels of physical performance, and therefore any changes in the ability to bathe, dress, eat, and toilet are important to monitor. Social disability is characterized by an inability to interact with persons or to handle problems in the course of performance of expected social roles and responsibilities. The measures of function selected to measure disability depend on the degree of specificity required to assess the problem (e.g., assessment of return to work based upon an ability to lift 25 pounds without pain after an acute episode of low back pain), the expected degree of impairment, the population being assessed (inpatient, community dwelling), and if functioning needs to be assessed over time. The Roland–Morris (1983) scale is an example of a condition-specific scale (back pain) that considers both physical and social functioning and is appropriate for measuring the effectiveness over time of product line services, such as rehabilitation services. With the increasing aging of the population and the need to determine how health care services provide healthy life outcomes and prevent disability, measures of disability increasingly will be used to routinely distinguish among treatments and providers and justify reimbursement and to predict populations at particular risk for services. Functional limitations, both physical and social, are predictors of disability, morbidity, and high health care resource use (Mendes de Leon *et al.*, 1999).

To better describe the human functioning and disability associated with health conditions and permit comparisons of data across health services in different cultures, the International Classification of Functioning and Disability (ICIDH-2) (World Health Organization, 1999b) was developed and is intended to be complementary to ICD-10. ICIDH-2 is based on the philosophy that impairments are not necessarily manifestations of pathology. Classification addresses four components: (1) body functions and structure, (2) activities at the individual level, (3) participation in society, and (4) contextual factors (e.g., environmental factors influencing functioning). The goals of this new classification system include improving the ability to assess clinical outcomes relative to vocational or rehabilitation interventions and to aid in social security and compensation system planning and design.

Mental and Behavioral Disorders

The two main classification systems for mental and behavioral disorders are the *Diagnostic and Statistical Manual of Mental Disorders*, 4th edition (DSM-IV) (American Psychiatric Association, 1994) and the ICD-10. There are differences in the coding systems with respect to criteria, most commonly with respect to duration criteria. Among the most striking is with respect to schizophrenia (DSM-IV, 6 months; ICD-10, 1 month). In the ICD-10, psychiatric conditions are organized as follows:

- F00–F09 Organic including symptomatic mental disorders
- F10–F19 Mental and behavioral disorders due to psychoactive substance use
- F20–F29 Schizophrenia, schizotypal and delusional disorders
- F30–F39 Mood [affective] disorders
- F40–F48 Neurotic, stress-related and somatoform disorders
- F50–F59 Behavioral syndromes associated with physiological disturbances and physical factors
- F60–F69 Disorders of adult personality and behavior
- F70–F79 Mental retardation
- F80–F89 Disorders of psychological development
- F90–F98 Behavioral and emotional disorders with onset usually occurring in childhood and adolescence
- F99 Unspecified mental disorders

A feature of ICD-10 is an annex that contains information on culture-specific disorders (e.g., *skinkeishitsu*, Japan; *Pa-leng*, Taiwan, province of China).

Quality of Life

Quality of life (QOL) is a multidimensional classification consisting of measures covering symptoms/problem complexes, mobility, physical activity, emotional well-being, and social functioning. Quality of life represents the perceived relationship of preferred states.

There are both general and disease-specific measures. Examples of a general quality of life survey form are the Short Form 36 Health Survey (SF-36 form) (Stewart *et al.*, 1989) and the quality of life questions on the Behavioral Risk Factor Surveillance Survey form (Campbell *et al.*, 1999). Condition-specific measures of QOL include the Functional Assessment of Human Immuno-deficiency Virus Infection quality of life (Cella *et al.*, 1996) and the Arthritis Impact Measurement Scales (Meenan *et al.*, 1992). QOL measures also can be used to measure the impact of health policy changes on the status of potential populations. QOL measures do not require any assumptions about the intensity or duration of symptoms or about the existence of any underlying pathology. A limitation of most QOL instruments is that they only measure perceptions at the present moment in time.

Other Health Measures

In addition to the above, there also are measures of social health, psychological well-being, mental health, and other general health measures. A large compilation of health measures can be found in McDowell and Newell (1996).

Classification of Health Services

Classifying Organizational Units

Classification also is important in identifying components of a health care system or organization. An example classification of service units is the case of intensive care units (ICUs). ICUs can be classified according to service area (e.g., medical, surgical, etc.), specialty function (e.g., cardiac, burn unit, etc.), intensity of services (e.g., high dependency, subacute, stepdown, etc.), or age group of patient (e.g., neonatal, pediatric, adult, etc.). In classifying health services, insurers and funders hope to distinguish which health services are essential and effective from those that may be only supportive and may not be essential for all categories of patients or the general population. It also is important to classify health services in order to appropriately place patients relative to intensity of care. Harvey *et al.* (1992) sought to develop a model to determine which patients would benefit from hospital environment for rehabilitation versus other continuum of care levels such as a day rehabilitation program.

The issue of classification of health service systems will become more important as a greater understanding is gained of how organizations could be reconfigured to more efficiently and effectively serve larger populations. For example, as an increasing number of the population is served by "managed care" systems concern emerges over the impact on vulnerable patient subgroups. Studies exist that compare outcomes between managed care and fee-for-service care for different patient populations, but the results are not consistent (Sullivan, 1999). Differences in the classification of capitated care entities, namely coverage and copayment, render this body of research difficult to interpret. Oleske *et al.* (2000) identified 12 different forms of managed care operating in two states. Managed care can be an organization such as a health maintenance organization, a group of providers providing discounted services as necessary to persons from a group (a PPO, or preferred provider organization), or individual providers responsible for all the nonspecialty care of a defined population for a capitated annual amount.

Health care services may be even classified according to Milner (1997) based on their effectiveness based on quality research evidence such as available through the Cochrane

Evidence Site. Classification under this scheme would be: completely ineffective, ineffective for certain people, or appropriate for all persons.

Lack of uniformity in classifying health services units gives rise to difficulty in the precise evaluation of the outcome of patients served. For example, the admission of less acutely ill patients to an ICU could result in more favorable patient outcomes, implying that treatment at a particular health care provider is more advantageous when in fact the outcomes may be largely due to differing patient characteristics. Even the content and the value of the process of care known as prenatal care has been challenged because many have questioned the manner in which the adequacy of prenatal care is classified (Fiscella, 1995). Currently, the adequacy of prenatal care is measured by proxy measures that use the number of visits and the timing of the visits relative to gestational age with information available from the birth certificate (Kotelchuck, 1994). A better way of classifying prenatal care adequacy would be to allow the process of care to be directly measured and recorded (e.g., weights taken, woman screened for sexually transmitted diseases, etc.), but the cost in accurately obtaining this information may be prohibitive. Better classification of what classifies adequate from inadequate prenatal care services may aid in reducing the high infant mortality, a major outcome measure of the efficacy of prenatal care, among certain ethnicities, races, and countries.

With a more precise definition of health service units, a more precise estimate of the impact organizational "risk factors" (services or structure) can be made. Without more precise classification of service units, it is difficult for a manager to interpret the effectiveness of the units of an organization and to understand the biases associated with selection into one health service unit versus another.

Classifying Procedures

Procedures, a special form of health care services, will be classified according to the ICD-10 procedure coding system (ICD-10-PCS). ICD-10-PCS coding will be required by the US Health Care Financing Administration of hospitals reporting inpatient procedures (Medicare Part A) for reimbursement. It also is a very different coding structure from ICD-9 procedure coding. In contrast to the current procedural terminology (CPT) coding system of the American Medical Association, which has 7000 procedures codified, ICD-10-PCS will have hundreds of thousands of codes when its final version is implemented. ICD-10-PCS will have seven-character procedure codes. The first character is the specialty (e.g., 6 = nuclear medicine); the second characteristic is the body system on which the procedure is performed. The third character represents the type of procedure (e.g., systemic therapy). The body part is specified by the fourth character. The fifth through seventh characters in combination specify details concerning the procedure (e.g., type of radiopharmaceutical used). Concerns over the ICD-10-PCS include that it prohibits usage of commonly accepted terms in clinical practice and instead requires the procedure to be described in detail (e.g., "hysterectomy," not accepted, versus "resection of the uterus," accepted) and that lack of provisions for not otherwise specified codes (NOS/NEC) will force inaccurate coding. A comprehensive review of ICD-10-PCS is described in Averill *et al.* (1998).

Control of Measurement Error

Measurement error is not perfectly capturing what is intended. Inherent in every measure, be it medical records, responses to surveys, or a laboratory test, is the possibility for error. One strategy for the control of error, assuming the validity of the measure is acceptable, should be aimed at reducing variation in measurement. Variability of response can emanate from transitory personal factors (e.g., technician or participant illness), measurement format (e.g., letters too small), coder/technician/interviewer effects (e.g., required elements for data entry not clear, differences in response due to gender; technician unable to calibrate an auto-analyzer), and variations in the measurement environment (e.g., noise, temperature). Warnecke *et al.* (1997) provide additional insight into how to improve questionnaire design taking into account obtaining accurate responses from a racially and culturally diverse population. Prior to initiation of the measurement process, a plan should be in place for the control of error. The aspects that should be considered in this plan are displayed in Table 2.6. Once the measurement is developed and is available for routine use, a manual should be prepared that contains the following information: the development of the instrument, procedures used for the administration, methods for routinely assessing the quality of information measure, and the results of the reliability and validity testing of the measure.

Sources of Data

Before embarking on the collection of primary data, the health care manager should determine whether there are data sources (secondary data) that could be used to assess the health care access, utilization, or health status of the population under concern. Table 2.7 lists national data sources commonly used in health care planning or evaluation. Some of the data sources listed are of limited value for a particular hospital service delivery area and are only generalizable to large regions. Governmental agencies should be consulted for the availability local information and for specially developed data sets (e.g., state tumor registry, perinatal network data, trauma system registry). Also, private organizations may collect information on health status of a community [e.g., Metropolitan Chicago Information Center; Community Tracking Study (Ginsburg *et al.*, 1996)], hospital market area [Center for the Evaluative Clinical Sciences, *Dartmouth Atlas of Health Care*, (Wennberg, 1996)], or population sub-groups such as reproductive health in women of childbearing age (Alan Guttmacher Institute, http://www.agi-usa.org). The reader is referred to other data sources can be found in the Appendix, Websites for Health Care Managers Thinking Epidemiologically.

Regardless of the data set used, the health care manager must be cautious in interpreting

---

Table 2.6. Strategies for the Control of Measurement Error

- Have a written protocol for measurement.
- Develop a standard procedure for training study staff.
- Conduct a pilot study to determine the feasibility of administering the measure, its acceptability, and the time require for its administration.
- Institute procedures to ensure the completeness and accuracy of recording measurements.
- Monitor data collection staff's adherence to data collection protocol.
- Use an outside referent (person or lab standard) to compare data abstractor, interviewer (or technician) staff findings.
- Ensure that data are collected (or are available) from all eligible records or persons.
- Perform reliability checks among those performing measurements.
- Review data collected (in raw form and summary statistics) on a regular basis.

Table 2.7. Select Useful National Data Sources for Assessing the Population, Health Care Access, Health Care Utilization, and Health Status

Data set	Population/sample	Variables of interest
Census of the US population	Complete enumeration of population every 10 years since 1790	Gender, age, race and marital status from 100% of population, more detailed information (income, education, housing, occupation, and industry from a representative sample
US natality data	All US resident births	Infant birth characteristics, prenatal care use
Behavioral Risk Factor Surveillance Survey (BRFSS)	Random monthly telephone surveys of persons in all states, the District of Columbia, and three territories	Health care access, use of screening tests, tobacco, alcohol, nutrition, physical activity, quality of life, health care insurance
National Hospital Discharge Survey	Stratified national sample from hospitals	Medical diagnoses using ICD codes, procedures, gender, age, payer
National Health Interview Survey	40,000 households	Demographic, socioeconomic, health status, health care utilization, incidence of acute illnesses, prevalence of chronic conditions and impairments, extent of disability
National Household Survey on Drug Abuse	Sample of households	Incidence, prevalence, and patterns of substance abuse
Area Resource File	Mortality files, natality files, members of the American Hospital Association and the American Medical Association	County level data on health professions, population characteristics and economic data, health facility number and types, hospital utilization, physician data, HMO enrollment, environmental features, health professions training resources

(continued)

Table 2.7. (*Continued*)

Data set	Population/sample	Variables of interest
National Ambulatory Medical Care Survey	3000 physicians, 34,000 patient records	Visits to office-based physicians by type of visit, age and gender
HIV/AIDS Cost and Services Utilization Study	National probability sample of 2,864 HIV-infected adults receiving medical care, including those in HMOs in 28 urban areas and 24 counties in the US	Access, use, quality of care. Quality of life, clinical outcomes, mental health, unmet needs for care, provider characteristics
Medical Expenditure Panel Survey	Updates the 1987 National Medical Expenditure Survey to adequately sample poor, elderly, families, veterans, uninsured, and racial and ethnic minorities. Data from a nationally representative sample for the (1) household component: 10,000 families, 24,000 individuals; (2) nursing home component: 5,000 residents; (3) medical provider component: 17,000 physicians, 500 home health, 3,000 hospitals; (4) insurance component: 40,000 businesses	Demographics, employment, health status, health services spending, in those with (including in managed care plans) and without health insurance
Medicare National Claims History Files	Claims histories of 38 million Medicare beneficiaries, 48,826 institutional providers, including 6,246 hospitals, 14,610 skilled nursing facilities, 10,487 home health agencies, 2,239 hospices, 2,689 outpatient physical therapy, 472 comprehensive outpatient rehabilitation facilities, 3,274 end stage renal dialysis facilities, 3,447 rural health clinics, 1,175 community mental health centers, 2,406 ambulatory surgical centers, and 1,772 federally qualified health centers	Patient demographics; diagnoses; procedures; drug utilization; membership in a managed care plan; provider type
Medicaid Information Files	Counts of eligibles and recipients categorized on the basis of eligibility as of the first appearance during the Federal fiscal year covered. Duplicates may occur as some states report the person in as many categories as the individual is eligible for	Patient demographics; health plan enrollment; category of Medicaid eligibility; provider characteristics

the data. Duplicate reports, differences in reporting periods, reporting delays, and misclassification all affect the validity of conclusions that may be drawn.

Summary

Because of the complexity associated with the emergence of health problems, precision in measuring exposure to both risk factors and types of health services used as well as health status is essential for precision in the decision-making process. The more accurately the health care manager can quantify exposure and outcome, the less likely he or she is to make a false claim about a causal relationship between the two. The soundness of the measurements used always should be a consideration when interpreting the magnitude of the health problems confronted, the factors that contribute to their emergence, and the strategies employed. The next chapters illustrate the importance of valid and reliable information.

Case Studies

Case Study No. 1
Measuring Recovery from a Work-Related Low Back Disorder

Low back disorders (LBD) are a major source of disability and pain. The cause of these disorders in the workplace may be due to frequent bending, twisting, or lifting, forceful movements, or vibrations. Treatment may include pain medication, muscle relaxants, physiotherapy, use of back supports, counseling on lifestyle management, or surgery. After an acute episode of LBD, the course of recovery may be long, as much as 45 days. Dimensions of recovery measured may be pain, physical functioning, or physical disability, or some combination thereof. Stress, cigarette smoking, perceptions of health status, and depression may influence recovery from a work-related LBD. The measurement of effectiveness of tertiary prevention requires careful consideration of the recovery measure because recovery outcomes are multidimensional with multiple potential prognostic factors (Oleske *et al.*, 2000). Individuals with uncomplicated LBD (e.g., not due to cancer, fracture, etc.) can be managed in an ambulatory setting. The Center for Comprehensive Back Care is a freestanding midwestern facility, which contrasts with a large automotive manufacturing company to provide rehabilitation services to its 30,000 employees. The center utilizes exercise equipment, biofeedback, occupational therapy, and classroom education in the rehabilitation process. In order to receive reimbursement from insurance agencies, the Center needs to provide data documenting patient progress during treatment for a LBD.

Q.1. Choose one measure that could be used to evaluate the efficacy of rehabilitation interventions by the center for low back disorders. Describe the measure, including how the data are collected.

Q.2. Discuss the reliability and validity of the measure.

Case Study No. 2
Inappropriate Emergency Department Visits by Members
of a Health Maintenance Organization (HMO)

Studies indicate that 15–53% of all emergency department (ED) utilization is inappropriate. Since ED charges are expensive, HMOs should analyze inappropriate utilization of EDs by its members. A study by Freeway Medical Center's Health Plan (FMCHP) was conducted to determine how many inappropriate visits to a specific ED its members made. FMCHP is a large urban HMO with 18 offices located throughout the metropolitan area, each of which is open daily from 8 AM to 10 PM. The ED studied was located within two blocks of FMCHP's central office. Despite this, there were 6,819 visits to the ED from the 39,000 enrollees of FMCHP served by its central office location. The first phase of the study was to obtain agreement on what constituted an "inappropriate" visit. Criteria were developed regarding what constituted "inappropriate" ED use (i.e., service or care that could have been rendered in a primary care setting). One set of criteria represented a list of services that were considered routine primary care and inappropriate for receiving treatment in the ED (e.g., urine culture, immunization, redressing of a wound, etc.). The other was a list of medical conditions that could be treated in a primary care setting and were inappropriate for an ED (e.g., upper respiratory infection, pharyngitis, sprained ankle, etc.). The next step was to determine whether physicians agreed on what was considered to be "inappropriate." One physician from the ED and one physician from FMCHP conducted a retrospective chart review of 1,745 cases from FMCHP who visited the ED in a 3-month time period. The results of their reviews are displayed in Table 2.8.

Q.1. How should the level of agreement between the two physicians be determined?

Q.2. What is your interpretation of the analysis from Q.1?

Case Study No. 3
A Breast Cancer Screening Program

Westchester is a city of approximately 500,000 persons over 21 years of age, about half of whom are female. The number of deaths among women from breast cancer is high. To address the problem, the local health department decided to initiate a program to screen for breast cancer. In this program, mammography would be used to screen for the presence of breast cancer. Mammography has a 99% sensitivity and 99% specificity. About 0.3% of women in the community are estimated to have breast cancer.

Q.1. Approximately how many cases of breast cancer would you expect to find from screening?

Q.2. How many women testing false positive would be found?

Q.3. Is mammography a good test to use for screening? Why?

Table 2.8. Evaluation of Agreement Between Two Physicians Regarding the Appropriateness of Emergency Department (ED) Visits

	ED physician		
	Appropriate	Inappropriate	Total ED visits
Health plan physician			
Appropriate	257	57	314
Inappropriate	20	1411	1431
Total ED visits	277	1468	1745

Case Study No. 4
Health Services Data

Health care managers need data to plan, establish baselines, and assess the impacts of any health system change. To perform these functions, access to data is vital. Often multiple data sources must be accessed in order to make these determinations. Primary and secondary data sources should be used as necessary.

Select as many data sources as necessary to answer the question, "Would dissemination of information to elderly persons in a managed care plan about the importance of receiving pneumococcal vaccine reduce their incidence of hospitalizations during the winter quarter of the year?" Choose your data set(s) based on the epidemiological model of the delivery of health care services (Fig. 1.1).

Q.1. Describe the sample or population from which the data came.

Q.2. Discuss the reliability and validity of the information from this data set.

Q.3. Discuss how the sample or population characteristics influence the types of conclusions that can be drawn from these data.

Q.4. Compare and contrast a comparable data source from another country with respect to Q.1–Q.3.

References

Aday, L., 1996, *Designing and Conducting Health Surveys: A Comprehensive Guide*, 2nd ed., Jossey-Bass, San Francisco, CA.

American Psychiatric Association, 1994, *Diagnostic and Statistical Manual of Mental Disorders*, 4th ed., Author, Washington, DC.

Averill, R. F., Mullin, R. L., Steinbeck, B. A., Goldfield, N. I., and Grant, T. M., 1998, Development of the ICD-10 procedure coding system (ICD-10-PCS), *J. Am. Health Info. Manage Assoc*.

Brambilla, D. J., and McKinlay, S. M., 1987, A comparison of responses to mailed questionnaires and telephone interviews in a mixed mode health survey, *Am. J. Epidemiol.* **126:**962–971.

Campbell, V. A., Crews, J. E., Moriarty, D. G., Zack, M. M., and Blackman, D. K., 1999, Surveillance for sensory impairment, activity limitation, and health-related quality of life, *Morbid. Mortal. Week. Rev.* **48:**131–156.

Cella, D. F., McCain, N. L., Peterman, A. H., Mo, F., and Wolen, D., 1996, Development and validation of the Functional Assessment of Human Immunodeficiency Virus Infection (FAHI) quality of life instrument, *Qual. Life Res.* **5:**450–463.

Charlson, M., Szatrowski, T. P., Peterson, J., and Gold, J., 1994, Validation of a combined comorbidity index, *J. Clin. Epidemiol.* **47:**1245–1251.

Choi, B. C. K., 1998, Slopes of a receiver operating characteristic curve and likelihood ratios for a diagnostic test, *Am. J. Epidemiol.* **148:**1127–1132.

Dean, A. G., Dean, J. A., Coulombier, D., Burton, A. H., Brendel, K. A., Smith, D. C., Dicker, R. C., Sullivan, K. M., and Fagan, R. F., 1997, *Epi Info Ver 6, a Word Processing, Database, and Statistics Program for Public Health on IBM-Compatible Microcomputers*, Centers for Disease Control and Prevention, Atlanta, GA.

Fiscella, K., 1995, Does prenatal care improve birth outcomes? A critical review, *Obstet. Gynecol.* **85:**468–479.

Fleiss, J. L., Jr., 1981, *Statistical Methods for Rates and Proportions*, 2nd ed., John Wiley & Sons, New York.

Garnick, D. W., DeLong, E. R., and Luft, H. S., 1995, Measuring hospital mortality rates: Are 30-day data enough? *HSR: Health Serv. Res.* **29:**679–695.

Ginsburg, P. B., Kemper, P., Baxter, R., and Kohn, L. T., 2000, The Community Tracking Study analyses of market changes: Introduction, *HSR: Health Serv. Res.* **35**(1:1): 7–16.

Gleicher, N., Oleske, D. M., Tur-Kaspa, I., Vidali, A., and Karande, V., 2000, Reducing the risk of high-order multiple pregnancy after ovarian stimulation with gonadotropins, *N. Engl. J. Med.* **343:**2–7.

Harvey, R. F., Silverstein, B., Venzon, M. A., Kilgore, K. M., Fisher, W. P., Steiner, M., and Harley, J. P., 1992, Applying psychometric criteria to functional assessment in medical rehabilitation: III. Construct validity and predicting level of care, *Arch. Phys. Med. Rehabil.* **73:**887–892.

Kotelchuk, M., 1994, An evaluation of the Kessner adequacy of prenatal care index and a proposed adequacy of prenatal care index, *Am. J. Pub. Health* **84:**1414–1420.

Maclure, M., and Willett, W. C., 1987, Misinterpretation and misuse of the kappa statistic, *Am. J. Epidemiol.* **126:** 261–269.

McDowell, I., and Newell, C., 1996, *Measuring Health*, 2nd ed., Oxford University Press, New York.

Meenan, R. F., Mason, J. M., Anderson, J. J., Guccione, A. A., and Kazis, L. E., 1992, AIMS2, The content and properties of a revised and expanded Arthritis Impact Measurement Scales health status questionnaire, *Arthritis Rheum.* **35:**1–10.

Mendes de Leon, C. F., Glass, T. A., Beckett, L. A., Seeman, T. E., Evans, D. A., and Berkman, L. F., 1999, Social networks and disability transitions across eight intervals of yearly data in the New Haven EPESE, *J. Gerontol.* **54B:**S162–S172.

Metz, C. E., 1986, ROC methodology in radiologic imaging, *Invest. Radiol.* **21:**720–733.

Milner, P., 1997, A new national classification of health services based on clinical effectiveness, *J. Pub. Health Med.* **19:**127–128.

Oleske, D. M., Andersson, G. B. J., Lavender, S. A., and Hahn, J. J., 2000, Association between recovery outcomes for work-related low back disorders and personal, family, and work factors, *Spine* **25:**1259–1265.

Paffenbarger, R. S., Jr., Blair, S. N., Lee, I., and Hyde, R. T., 1993, Measurement of physical activity to assess health effects in free-living populations, *Med. Sci. Sports Exercise* **25:**60–70.

Peirce, J. C., and Cornell, R. G., 1993, Integrating stratum-specific likelihood ratios with the Analysis of ROC curves, *Med. Decision Making* **13:**141–151.

Roland, M., and Morris, R., 1983, A study of the natural history of back pain. Part I: Development of a reliable and sensitive measure of disability in low-back pain, *Spine* **8:**141–144.

Simmons, E., Hedges, J. K., Irwin, L., Maassberg, W., and Kirkwood, H. A., Jr., 1995, Paramedic injury severity perception can aid trauma triage, *Ann. Emerg. Med.* **26:**461–468.

Soeken, K. L., and Prescott, P. A., 1986, Issues in the use of kappa to estimate reliability, *Med. Care* **24:**733–741.

SPSS, 1999, *SPSS Ver. 10.0 Computer Software*, Chicago, IL.

Stewart, A. L., Hays, R. D., and Ware, J. E., 1989, The MOS short-form general health survey: Reliability and validity in a patient population, *Med. Care* **26:**724–735.

Sullivan, K., 1999, Managed care plan performance since 1980: another look at 2 literature reviews, *Am. J. Pub. Health* **89:**1003–1008.

Warnecke, R. B., Johnson, T. P., Chavez, N., Sudman, S., O'Rourke, D. P., Lacey, L., and Horm, J., 1997, Improving question wording in surveys of culturally diverse populations, *Ann. Epidemiol.* **7:**334–342.

Warner, M., Barnes, P. M., and Fingerhut, L. A., 2000, Injury and poisoning episodes and conditions: National Health Interview Survey, 1997, *Vital Health Stat.* **10**(202).

Wartenberg, D., and Northridge, M., 1992, Defining exposure in case-control studies: A new approach, *Am. J. Epidemiol.* **133:**1058–1071.

Wennberg, J. E., 1996, *Dartmouth Atlas of Health Care*, American Hospital Publishing, Chicago, IL.

World Health Organization, 1999a, *International Classification of Diseases*, 10th rev., Clinical Modification (ICD-10-CM), Geneva, Switzerland.

World Health Organization, 1999b, *International Classification of Functioning and Disability*, Beta-2 Draft, Full Version, Geneva, Switzerland.

Zhang, H., and Bracken, M. B., 1995, Tree-based risk factor analysis of preterm delivery and small-for-gestational-age birth, *Am. J. Epidemiol.* **141:**70–78.

3

Descriptive Epidemiological Measures

Denise M. Oleske

Suppose you were responsible for drafting legislation for a new citywide public health initiative aimed at reducing the rate of HIV infection in African Americans. How would you present evidence to show this is a problem that differentially affects persons of color? Suppose you were charged with evaluating the impact of a new quality of care initiative on reducing adverse patient events in your health system, how would you represent the magnitude of the adverse patient events now and over the time in which your initiative is in place? In either scenario, your first step would be to measure the frequency of health events in the population for which services, programs, or policies are planned. In addition, the relationship of the health event to factors that may account for its occurrence and distribution should be described. This chapter presents common descriptive epidemiological measures and sources of information concerning these. It also discusses how the measures are constructed and interpreted as well as how they are applied in the delivery of health care services.

Measuring the Frequency of Health Events in Populations

In order to quantify the magnitude of a health problem, it must be measured. In epidemiology, the measurement of events is expressed in terms of a referent population instead of raw numbers. Epidemiological measures of the frequency of health events in populations may be quantified as rates.

Incidence Rate

An incidence rate is a descriptive measure in which the numerator consists of new or incident cases of a health event occurring in a population at risk for the event. A rate is computed as follows:

Denise M. Oleske   Departments of Health Systems Management and Preventive Medicine, Rush University, Chicago, Illinois 60612.

Epidemiology and the Delivery of Health Care Services: Methods and Applications, Second Edition, edited by Denise M. Oleske. Kluwer Academic / Plenum Publishers, New York, 2001.

Rate per $10^k = E_{(t)}/P_{(t)} \times 10^k$

where E = number of events occurring in the population during a specified period of time t

P = population in the same area at the same time t in which the events where expected to occur

10^k = a unit of population to which the rate apples expressed as a power of 10

Thus, the incidence rate of breast cancer per 100,000 women given 500 new cases of breast cancer in a population of 500,000 women would be computed as follows:

$$500 \text{ cases}/500,000 \text{ women} \times 100,000 = 100 \text{ per } 100,000$$

This is the same as:

$$500 \text{ cases} = 500,000 \text{ women} \times 100/100,000$$

The events in the numerator must be derived from a defined referent population, and both the event and the population should be related to the same time period and the same geographic area. In most circumstances, an individual hospital or provider cannot be a singular source of information for the construction of rates for a community unless all cases of the event occurring within a population in a well-defined geographic area come to the attention of the hospital or provider. In reality, most populations are served by multiple health care facilities and providers, and hence data from only one source would yield an underestimate of the true rate of the event within a population.

The denominator should not include those who already have the condition or who are not susceptible to it by virtue of immunity, immunization, surgery, or other factor that excludes the potential for being exposed. For example, a study of the incidence rate of uterine cancer among menopausal women using estrogen supplements should exclude women from the denominator who have had a hysterectomy. The choice of a denominator for a rate measure depends on the manner in which time is represented. The denominator used to construct rate measures for community populations is derived from the decennial census or interim population projections based on census data. In this circumstance, the identification of persons who are truly at risk for the health event is not feasible. Thus, the average population at risk, the population at mid-year (July 1), is used in computing the rate. The denominator for the rate may consist of the total population who develops the health event over a specified period of time. This is called the **cumulative incidence rate**. The denominator may consist of the number of persons who could develop the event in consideration of how long each person was observed. This measure is called the **incidence density**. The denominator for this measure expressed in terms of person-time units, is illustrated below:

> *Given a group of four persons:*
> Person A is observed for 5 days
> Person B is observed for 1 day
> Person C is observed for 1 week
> Person D is observed for 1 month*
> Total = 43.5 person-days of observation

If *Salmonella* infection developed in one of the four persons on a skilled care unit, the incidence density rate (IDR) would be:

$$\text{IDR} = [\text{No. of new events} / \text{Person-time uits of observation}] \times 10^k$$
$$= 1/43.5 \times 100 = 2.3 \text{ infections per 100 person-days}$$

---

*Assumes the average month is 30.5 days.

The incidence density rate measure is used when persons at risk for an event are observed for different lengths of time as in a longitudinal study, a randomized clinical trial where the outcome is not immediately ascertainable, and in survival analysis. Incidence density rates that are averaged over a period of time to represent the instantaneous occurrence of an event are called **hazard rates**.

The factor of 10 is used in the computation of a rate to make the relationship between events and the population more meaningful by removing the decimal fraction created by dividing a small number of events relative to a large population. The particular power of 10 used depends on convention (e.g., per 100,000 population for disease-specific rates in a community, per 1,000 population when representing the total death rate in a community) or on convenience. Generally, a power of 10 is used such that the lowest level of the variable for which the rate is calculated is one digit to the right of the decimal. The same factor of 10 must apply to all levels within a variable.

Incidence rates may refer to the onset of an illness or condition (morbidity) or death (mortality). In order to identify a new case of an illness or condition, knowledge of the time of onset of the event is essential. This can only be achieved if the population is already under surveillance for changes in health status or will be involved in such monitoring. For acute onset conditions such as gastroenteritis, myocardial infarction, and nonfatal trauma, the identification of a "new" case can be pinpointed. When the onset is not readily apparent, as is the case with chronic conditions, mental disorders, and behavioral problems (e.g., substance abuse), surrogate measures are used. For defining an incident cancer case, the date of pathology confirmation of the malignancy is used as the date of onset. The date of first use of an intravenous, nonprescription drug may be considered in defining the onset of drug addiction. In defining incident events, the numerator should specify whether events or persons are being counted. In some circumstances, multiple new events may occur within the same population. This is exemplified in the calculation of nonfatal injury rates. The numerator in the computation of the injured persons rate consists of the number of persons who experienced an injury, whereas the numerator of the injury rate represents the number of episodes of injury in persons at risk during a specific time period.

The period of time identified for the observation of incident cases must be clearly defined. Incidence rates can be computed for short time periods—hours, days, and weeks as for epidemics—or over longer periods of time. Examples of incidence rates referring to short time intervals are attack rates and case-fatality rates. An attack rate is the number of persons experiencing illness during a specified time period, usually the same time interval for all persons, in relationship to a defined set of conditions. The case-fatality rate is the number of persons dying from a specific condition that was diagnosed within a short period of time, usually a year or less. The case-fatality rate is a proxy measure of disease severity. The case-fatality rate also is used as measures of effectiveness of health service units where the mortality is expected to be high, for example, in ICUs. Rare or infrequent events in a population may yield unstable rate estimates even if calculated on an annual basis. In such circumstances, incident cases may be pooled over a few years (3–5) with the denominator consisting of the population from the previous census year or at a mid-point of the interval being averaged. Because the incidence rate describes the likelihood of an event occurring in a population susceptible to its occurrence, the incidence rate is synonymous with the term "risk."

Prevalence Rate

A prevalence rate is a measure of event frequency that represents the total number of persons with a health event (or other characteristic) divided by the total number of persons at a specific point in time (t) multiplied by a power of 10, as with incidence rates. The individuals with the health event examined who constitute the numerator also must be included in the denominator, that is, they both come from the same geographic area and in the same time period. The prevalence rate is represented as follows:

$$\text{Prevalence rate}_{(t)} = \frac{\text{Total number of persons with characteristic}_{(t)}}{\text{Total population}_{(t)}} \times 10^k$$

The prevalence rate is influenced by how many individuals develop the condition in a particular time frame (incidence rate) and how long it lasts (duration). Thus, factors that influence the development of an incident case (e.g., changes in exposures that result in a disease, changes in the way the delivery system accesses new cases, or changes in diagnostic methods) also affect the prevalence. Intervention programs for the prevention or treatment of cases, changes in the physical manifestation of the incident case (e.g., increased virulence of organism), selective in- or out-migration of susceptible or immune persons for treatment also may affect the prevalence rate. Thus, if a community has an unexpected low prevalence of a health problem, this may be explained by a low disease incidence, a disease that is selectively more serious or fatal in that community (e.g., due to lack of access to health care), or a disease that is very curable (e.g., high access to effective care). The selection of the time period for the computation of the prevalence rate is discretionary and may reflect cases existing over an interval of time such as one year (annual prevalence) or a specific moment in time such as one day (point prevalence).

The prevalence rate reflects the total burden of a condition within a population. As such, it is useful for estimating the level and intensity of health care services required within a population. For example, the prevalence rates of hypertension in a community would be useful in determining if the initiation of a screening program would be worthwhile.

In addition to quantifying the proportion of persons in which an outcome has occurred (e.g., disease prevalence), the proportion of persons who have a characteristic that may be a determinant of a health outcome (exposure prevalence) also may be useful. For example, knowing that an HMO has a high prevalence of smokers, an administrator may consider initiating educational and smoking cessation clinics for its service population in order to prevent premature births, chronic obstructive pulmonary disease, heart disease, and various forms of cancer such as cancer of the lung, larynx, and bladder, which are all associated with smoking.

Sources of Information for Incidence Rate Measures

The source of incidence information about the onset of illnesses or conditions varies according to the event studied. Physicians are responsible for defining most incident health events through clinical signs and symptoms, laboratory, radiological, or pathological means. However, all health professionals have responsibility for reporting certain events to the local health authority as required by state law (e.g., selected communicable diseases) or to the designated supervisor as required by the policies of a health care facility (e.g., patient falls). The list of health-related events to be reported by law varies somewhat from state to state, but selected infectious diseases must be reported in all jurisdictions of the United States (see Chapter 8, this volume). In addition to communicable diseases, malignant neoplasms, selected occupational diseases, and other health problems such as lead poisoning may be required by law to be reported. Reportable morbidity data are available through local health departments, and the Centers for Disease Control and Prevention (CDC) provides regular national summaries for transmissible diseases in its periodical, *Morbidity and Mortality Weekly Review*. The incidence of some conditions requiring hospitalization, such as hip fracture, may be available from data files of hospital claims (Lauderdale *et al.*, 1993).

The primary source of information about deaths is the death certificate, one of the items of vital data required by law in each state in the United States and in all industrialized and many developing nations throughout the world. The death on the certificate is described in terms of an immediate cause (the mode of dying) and underlying causes (the injury or disease that initiated the chain of events that led directly to the death). In addition, the death certificate contains demographic information about the decedent including sex, race, birth date, social security number, residence, usual occupation, manner of death, and other significant conditions (that contributed to death and are not listed in the chain of events), and information about next of kin (Fig. 3.1). All states also require filing of a fetal death certificate if the fetus is determined to be a product of 20 or more completed weeks of gestation and not born alive. On the death certificate, a physician, medical examiner, or coroner provides information on the cause of death. The funeral director records the demographic information and files the certificate with the state vital registration office. The deaths listed on the certificate are classified by a nosologist at the state vital statistics office according to the most recent edition of the *International Classification of Diseases* (ICD). All states and the District of Columbia periodically submit death certificate information on computer tape to the National Center for Health Statistics (NCHS), where data are coded and quality-control checked. The NCHS then disseminates the mortality data as annual volumes of *Vital Statistics of the United States*. The World Health Organization (WHO) collects, classifies, and tabulates mortality statistics from the United States and other countries. When using death certificates, caution must be used. First, the assignment of the primary cause of death may not be accurate because the physician may be unfamiliar with the decedent or may lack autopsy information. One must be wary in using mortality data to describe trends for several reasons including the codes used to identify diseases change with each revision of the ICD, the diagnostic technology used to detect diseases changes over time, and new conditions may emerge (see also Chapter 2, this volume). Because many hospitals maintain registries such as tumor registries, issues of cost and manpower are paramount. However, many accrediting bodies require at least a 90% annual rate of ascertainment of the follow-up status of individuals in registries. Individuals difficult to locate may be deceased. There are two major sources of information about individual death records: (1) the National Death Index, for a fee, provides death records in response to user submission of 12 potential matching variables, and (2) the Internet site http://www.ancestry.com, which provides free access to the death master file from Social Security Administration payment records (Sesso *et al.*, 2000).

Incidence data are used for studies of the etiology of diseases, the evaluation of program or treatment outcomes (e.g., effectiveness of a vaccine program for reducing measles in a community), disease surveillance (e.g., cases of repetitive motion disorder due to workplace exposures), and monitoring the quality of health care provided (e.g., nosocomial infection rate). Because recording of deaths is widely practiced, mortality rates represent the most universal method for prioritizing health problems within a population and for comparing the health status of populations across geographic areas.

Sources of Information on Prevalence

Population surveys provide information on prevalence, exposure or disease. Two agencies are primary sources of health-related prevalence data for the United States population.

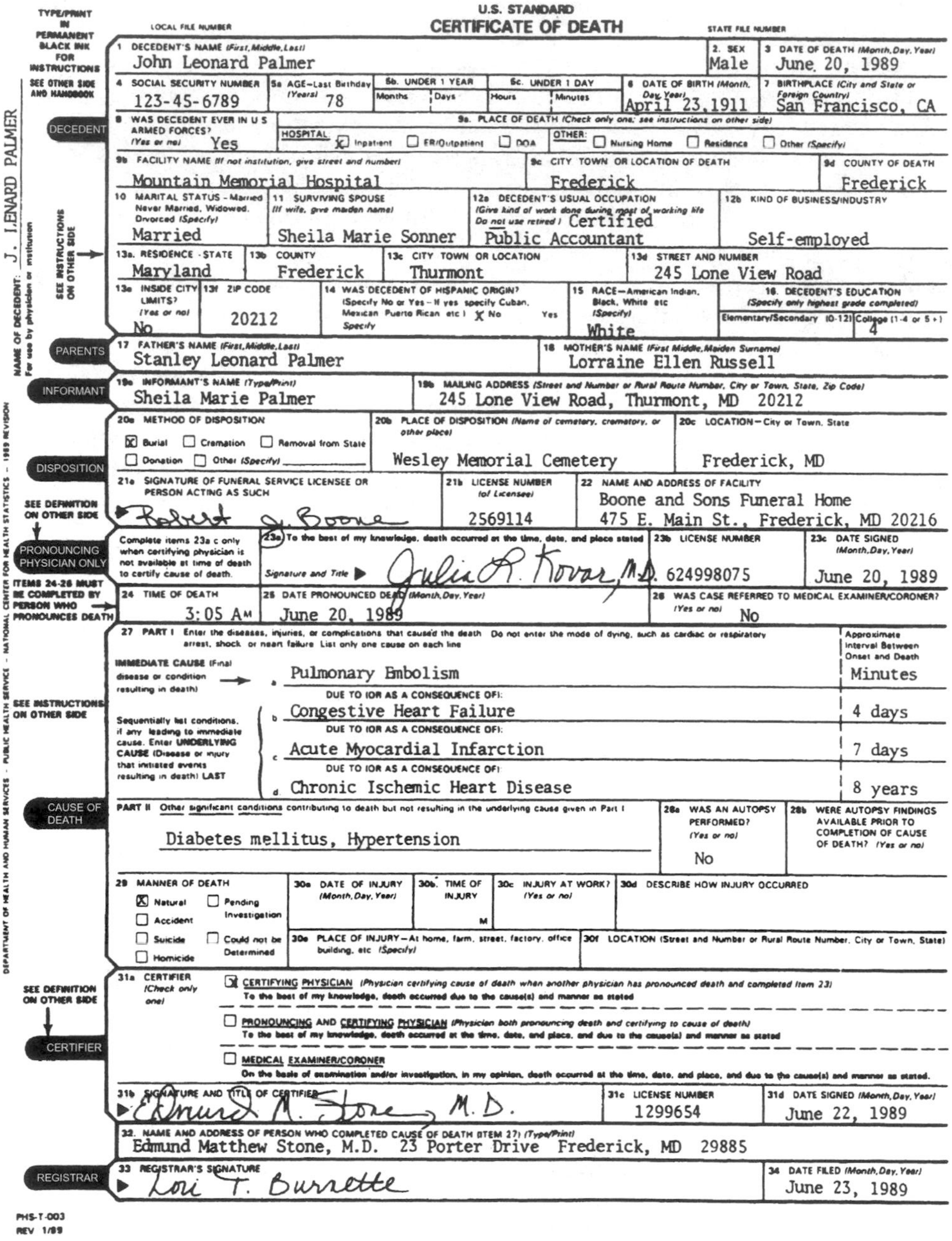

U.S. STANDARD
CERTIFICATE OF DEATH

TYPE/PRINT IN PERMANENT BLACK INK FOR INSTRUCTIONS SEE OTHER SIDE AND HANDBOOK

LOCAL FILE NUMBER — STATE FILE NUMBER

DECEDENT
1. DECEDENT'S NAME (First, Middle, Last): John Leonard Palmer
2. SEX: Male
3. DATE OF DEATH (Month, Day, Year): June 20, 1989
4. SOCIAL SECURITY NUMBER: 123-45-6789
5a. AGE—Last Birthday (Years): 78
5b. UNDER 1 YEAR: Months / Days
5c. UNDER 1 DAY: Hours / Minutes
6. DATE OF BIRTH (Month, Day, Year): April 23, 1911
7. BIRTHPLACE (City and State or Foreign Country): San Francisco, CA
8. WAS DECEDENT EVER IN U.S. ARMED FORCES? (Yes or no): Yes
9a. PLACE OF DEATH (Check only one; see instructions on other side): HOSPITAL: [X] Inpatient [ ] ER/Outpatient [ ] DOA; OTHER: [ ] Nursing Home [ ] Residence [ ] Other (Specify)
9b. FACILITY NAME (If not institution, give street and number): Mountain Memorial Hospital
9c. CITY, TOWN, OR LOCATION OF DEATH: Frederick
9d. COUNTY OF DEATH: Frederick
10. MARITAL STATUS—Married, Never Married, Widowed, Divorced (Specify): Married
11. SURVIVING SPOUSE (If wife, give maiden name): Sheila Marie Sonner
12a. DECEDENT'S USUAL OCCUPATION (Give kind of work done during most of working life. Do not use retired): Certified Public Accountant
12b. KIND OF BUSINESS/INDUSTRY: Self-employed
13a. RESIDENCE—STATE: Maryland
13b. COUNTY: Frederick
13c. CITY, TOWN, OR LOCATION: Thurmont
13d. STREET AND NUMBER: 245 Lone View Road
13e. INSIDE CITY LIMITS? (Yes or no): No
13f. ZIP CODE: 20212
14. WAS DECEDENT OF HISPANIC ORIGIN? (Specify No or Yes—If yes, specify Cuban, Mexican, Puerto Rican, etc.) X No / Yes
15. RACE—American Indian, Black, White, etc. (Specify): White
16. DECEDENT'S EDUCATION (Specify only highest grade completed): Elementary/Secondary (0-12) / College (1-4 or 5+): 4

NAME OF DECEDENT: J. LENARD PALMER — For use by physician or institution — SEE INSTRUCTIONS ON OTHER SIDE

PARENTS
17. FATHER'S NAME (First, Middle, Last): Stanley Leonard Palmer
18. MOTHER'S NAME (First, Middle, Maiden Surname): Lorraine Ellen Russell

INFORMANT
19a. INFORMANT'S NAME (Type/Print): Sheila Marie Palmer
19b. MAILING ADDRESS (Street and Number or Rural Route Number, City or Town, State, Zip Code): 245 Lone View Road, Thurmont, MD 20212

DISPOSITION
20a. METHOD OF DISPOSITION: [X] Burial [ ] Cremation [ ] Removal from State [ ] Donation [ ] Other (Specify)
20b. PLACE OF DISPOSITION (Name of cemetery, crematory, or other place): Wesley Memorial Cemetery
20c. LOCATION—City or Town, State: Frederick, MD
21a. SIGNATURE OF FUNERAL SERVICE LICENSEE OR PERSON ACTING AS SUCH: Robert J. Boone
21b. LICENSE NUMBER (of Licensee): 2569114
22. NAME AND ADDRESS OF FACILITY: Boone and Sons Funeral Home, 475 E. Main St., Frederick, MD 20216

SEE DEFINITION ON OTHER SIDE

PRONOUNCING PHYSICIAN ONLY
Complete items 23a-c only when certifying physician is not available at time of death to certify cause of death.
23a. To the best of my knowledge, death occurred at the time, date, and place stated. Signature and Title: Julia R. Kovar, M.D.
23b. LICENSE NUMBER: 624998075
23c. DATE SIGNED (Month, Day, Year): June 20, 1989

ITEMS 24-26 MUST BE COMPLETED BY PERSON WHO PRONOUNCES DEATH
24. TIME OF DEATH: 3:05 AM
25. DATE PRONOUNCED DEAD (Month, Day, Year): June 20, 1989
26. WAS CASE REFERRED TO MEDICAL EXAMINER/CORONER? (Yes or no): No

CAUSE OF DEATH
27. PART I. Enter the diseases, injuries, or complications that caused the death. Do not enter the mode of dying, such as cardiac or respiratory arrest, shock, or heart failure. List only one cause on each line.

	Cause	Approximate Interval Between Onset and Death
IMMEDIATE CAUSE (Final disease or condition resulting in death) a.	Pulmonary Embolism	Minutes
DUE TO (OR AS A CONSEQUENCE OF): b.	Congestive Heart Failure	4 days
DUE TO (OR AS A CONSEQUENCE OF): c.	Acute Myocardial Infarction	7 days
DUE TO (OR AS A CONSEQUENCE OF): d.	Chronic Ischemic Heart Disease	8 years

Sequentially list conditions, if any, leading to immediate cause. Enter UNDERLYING CAUSE (Disease or injury that initiated events resulting in death) LAST

PART II. Other significant conditions contributing to death but not resulting in the underlying cause given in Part I: Diabetes mellitus, Hypertension
28a. WAS AN AUTOPSY PERFORMED? (Yes or no): No
28b. WERE AUTOPSY FINDINGS AVAILABLE PRIOR TO COMPLETION OF CAUSE OF DEATH? (Yes or no)
29. MANNER OF DEATH: [X] Natural [ ] Accident [ ] Suicide [ ] Homicide [ ] Pending Investigation [ ] Could not be Determined
30a. DATE OF INJURY (Month, Day, Year)
30b. TIME OF INJURY: M
30c. INJURY AT WORK? (Yes or no)
30d. DESCRIBE HOW INJURY OCCURRED
30e. PLACE OF INJURY—At home, farm, street, factory, office building, etc. (Specify)
30f. LOCATION (Street and Number or Rural Route Number, City or Town, State)

CERTIFIER
31a. CERTIFIER (Check only one):
[X] CERTIFYING PHYSICIAN (Physician certifying cause of death when another physician has pronounced death and completed item 23) To the best of my knowledge, death occurred due to the cause(s) and manner as stated.
[ ] PRONOUNCING AND CERTIFYING PHYSICIAN (Physician both pronouncing death and certifying to cause of death) To the best of my knowledge, death occurred at the time, date, and place, and due to the cause(s) and manner as stated.
[ ] MEDICAL EXAMINER/CORONER On the basis of examination and/or investigation, in my opinion, death occurred at the time, date, and place, and due to the cause(s) and manner as stated.
31b. SIGNATURE AND TITLE OF CERTIFIER: Edmund M. Stone, M.D.
31c. LICENSE NUMBER: 1299654
31d. DATE SIGNED (Month, Day, Year): June 22, 1989
32. NAME AND ADDRESS OF PERSON WHO COMPLETED CAUSE OF DEATH (ITEM 27) (Type/Print): Edmund Matthew Stone, M.D. 23 Porter Drive Frederick, MD 29885

REGISTRAR
33. REGISTRAR'S SIGNATURE: Lori T. Burrette
34. DATE FILED (Month, Day, Year): June 23, 1989

PHS-T-003 REV 1/89

DEPARTMENT OF HEALTH AND HUMAN SERVICES - PUBLIC HEALTH SERVICE - NATIONAL CENTER FOR HEALTH STATISTICS - 1989 REVISION

Figure 3.1. Sample death certificate.

One is the NCHS, which collects health-related data from self-reports of conditions, physical examination, and laboratory evaluation of individuals surveyed. Individuals are selected based on probability selection of the population. Other surveys conducted by the NCHS useful for prevalence information are the National Health Interview Survey (NIHS) and the National Health Examination Survey. The prevalence rate of hypertension of 233.2 per 1000 men aged

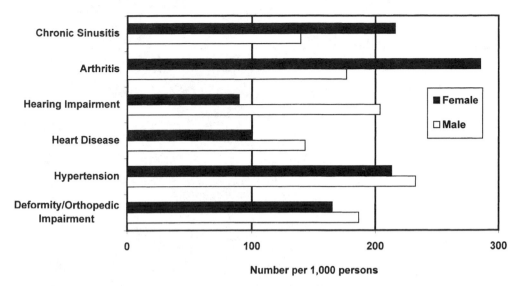

Figure 3.2. Prevalence rate of selected chronic conditions, United States, 1997. From National Center for Health Statistics (1999).

45 to 64 years is displayed in Fig. 3.2. This rate means that among every thousand men aged 45 to 64 years of age in the general population, 233 have reported a doctor told them they had hypertension. Another way of representing the prevalence rate is through a percentage. Thus, the rate also can be interpreted as 23% of the men aged 45 to 64 years have hypertension. The disadvantage of the NCHS prevalence surveys is that the precision of the survey provides estimates only reliable for large geographic regions of the United States. The estimates are not generalizable to smaller population subgroups.

The CDC is another major source of prevalence data, providing information on exposure to factors known to be associated with the major causes of death through the Behavioral Risk Factor Surveillance System (BRFSS). The BRFSS is a state-based random-digit-dialing telephone survey of noninstitutionalized adults developed by the CDC. Examples of the information collected in the BRFSS include the prevalence of certain high-risk behaviors (smoking, chronic or binge alcohol consumption, overweight, physical inactivity, and safety belt nonuse) and the use of selected medical screening tests (blood cholesterol screening, mammography, clinical breast examination, and Papanicolaou or pap smear). Because the survey is operational in 47 states and the District of Columbia, trends at the national as well as the state level can be monitored.

Format of Descriptive Epidemiological Measures

Descriptive epidemiological measures can be represented as specific rates, summary rates, or ratio measures. These measures are used in descriptive epidemiological studies the purpose of which is to characterize a disease, health problem or exposure in terms of person (who gets the disease or is exposed), place (where does it occur), and time (how has it changed over time).

Table 3.1. Common Specific Rates

$$\text{Gender-specific death rate} = \frac{\text{No. of deaths for gender during specified period}}{\text{Population (for the gender) at the midpoint of the period}} \times 100,000$$

$$\text{Race-specific death rate} = \frac{\text{No. of deaths for the race during a specified period}}{\text{Population (for the race) at the midpoint of the period}} \times 100,000$$

$$\text{Age-specific death rate} = \frac{\text{No. of deaths for the age group during a specified period}}{\text{Population at the midpoint of the period}} \times 100,000$$

$$\text{Infant mortality rate} = \frac{\text{No. of deaths} < 1 \text{ year of age}}{\text{No. of live births}} \times 1,000$$

$$\text{Neonatal mortality rate} = \frac{\text{No. of deaths} < \text{age 28 days}}{\text{No. of live births}} \times 1,000$$

$$\text{Perinatal mortality rate} = \frac{\text{No. late fetal deaths plus deaths} < \text{age 7 days}}{\text{No. of live births plus late fetal deaths}} \times 1,000$$

$$\text{Fertility rate} = \frac{\text{No. of live births}}{\text{No. of women 15–44 years of age}} \times 1,000$$

$$\text{Case fatality rate} = \frac{\text{No. of deaths from a disease (in a specified time)}}{\text{No. diagnosed with that disease (in same time)}} \times 100$$

Specific Rates

Specific rates pertain to a subgroup of the population and the number of events that occur in that subgroup. Specific rates assist in identifying population subgroups (i.e., by age group, gender, race, etc.) at risk for an event. Common specific rates are listed in Table 3.1. Through an examination of specific rates, unique patterns, especially for age, are observed for all health problems, regardless of whether the event is infectious, chronic, or resulting from injury (Fig. 3.3a c).

Summary Rates

Summary rates represent the total events occurring in a population. Summary measures included crude rates, standardized rates, years of potential life years lost, and disability-adjusted life year. The disadvantage of summary measures is that unique patterns in specific population subgroups that may be particularly vulnerable cannot be discerned.

Crude (or **total**) **rates** relate the total number of events in a population multiplied by a factor of ten. The crude mortality rate represents the average risk of mortality in a population. Crude death rates are also used to rank deaths in a population in a specific time period. Overall, heart disease is the major cause of death in the United States, comprising 33.2% of all deaths (Table 3.2).

Figure 3.3. (a) Age-specific mortality rates for human immunodeficiency virus (HIV) infection, all races, both genders, United States, 1997. (b) Age-specific mortality rates for motor vehicle accidents, all races, both genders, United States, 1997. (c) Age-specific mortality rates for malignant neoplasms, all races, both genders, United States, 1997. From National Center for Health Statistics (1999).

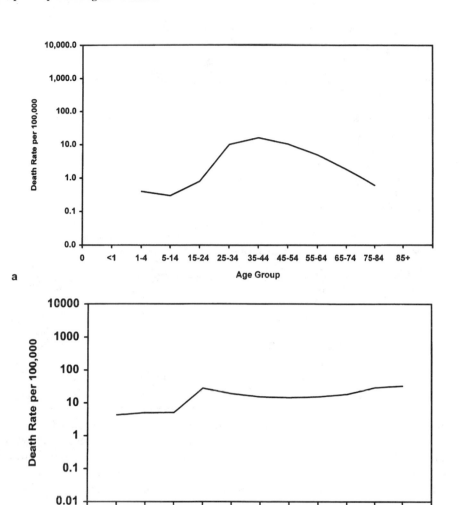

a

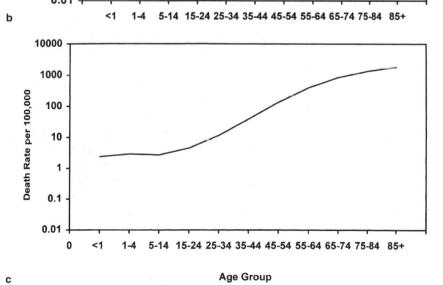

b

c

**Table 3.2. Crude Death Rates and Percent of Total Deaths
for the 10 Leading Causes of Death, United States, 1997**

Rank order	Cause of death	Rate per 100,000 population	Percent of total deaths
	All causes	864.7	100.0
1	Diseases of heart	271.6	31.4
2	Malignant neoplasms	201.6	23.3
3	Cerebrovascular diseases	59.7	6.9
4	Chronic obstructive pulmonary diseases and allied conditions	40.7	4.7
5	Unintentional injuries	35.7	4.1
6	Pneumonia and influenza	32.3	3.7
7	Diabetes mellitus	23.4	2.7
8	Suicide	11.4	1.3
9	Nephritis, nephrotic syndrome, and nephrosis	9.5	1.1
10	Chronic liver disease and cirrhosis	9.4	1.1

SOURCE: Kramarow et al. (1999)

A **standardized** (or **adjusted**) **rate** is a summary rate for a total population in which the frequency of events is weighted by the number of persons in the stratum of the variable whose effect we wish to control (or remove). Since it was demonstrated earlier that each health event has a unique demographic "signature," the influence of population characteristics has to be "neutralized" in order to determine whether the disease events have increased or decreased independent of key population characteristics. A standardized rate is used when it is necessary to compare rates of an event across geographic areas or time periods or because the populations compared have markedly different demographic characteristics. Summary measures also are useful when cause-specific information is not comparable and comparisons are likely to be unreliable. Such is often the case in making comparisons of specific conditions (e.g., perinatal mortality rate) across nations. The most profound variations in the disease patterns are attributable to age; as a result, standardization is most often concerned with removing the effects of age as a confounding variable in order to more accurately characterize the magnitude of disease frequency in a population. This type of standardization is referred to as "age-adjustment." The principle behind standardization is to compute rates for the populations being compared that take into account possible differences in demographic characteristics that could influence the disease frequency. In order to do this, standardization takes into account the disease frequency in the study populations in the context of some "normative" or standard population. There are two approaches for standardization of rates, direct and indirect.

Direct adjustment is performed to enable comparison of the frequency of health events in a population over time periods or geographic areas. In this method, the stratum-specific rates in a comparison population are weighted according to the number of persons in the same subgroups or stratum of the standard or reference population and summed over all strata. The directly standardized adjusted rate is algebraically represented as:

$$\sum_{i=1}^{n} r_i \times (p_i/P)$$

where: n = the total number of subgroups over the range of the adjusted rate

r_i = the specific rate for the subgroup in the population of interest

p_i = the number in standard population in subgroup i

$P = \sum_{i=1}^{n} p_i$ is the total population fo the subgroups that comprise the range of the rate being adjusted

Alternatively, the steps that come to the same end as the above algebraic process are:

1. Determine if there are a sufficient number of events (usually at least 10) in the comparison population for each level of the variable whose influence you wish to control.
2. Determine a standard population. The standard population can be the combined populations of the groups being compared, the larger population, or some predefined standard population.
3. Compute the rate of the event of interest for each level of the variable whose influence you wish to neutralize (e.g., age) in the comparison population using the events and population information from the comparison population.
4. Multiply the rate in the study population by the number of persons in the standard population for each level of the variable.
5. Sum the product obtained across all levels.
6. Divide the sum from step 5 by the total number in the standard population and multiply by an appropriate factor of 10 (usually 100,000). This results in the adjusted rate for the comparison population.
7. Repeat steps 1–6 for each comparison population.

Table 3.3 illustrates the application of direct age-adjustment to enable the comparison of the breast cancer incidence between white and black females. The conclusion suggested by directly standardized rates is that the age-adjusted incidence of breast cancer is higher among white females (113.0 per 100,000 women) than among black females (101.5 per 100,000 women). Another way of saying this is that white females have a higher overall incidence rate of breast cancer when the age distribution of the two groups is the same. The major disadvantage of direct rate adjustment is that since it is a summary measure, disparities in the variation of specific rates among the population subgroups compared may be missed. In the example presented, if one were to only examine the adjusted rate, one would not be aware of the higher incidence of breast cancer among every age group under 50 years of black females compared to white females, but after age 50 years this is reversed.

Indirect adjustment is performed when the number of events for each level of the variable whose effect is to be removed is either unknown or too small. This limitation is often present when attempting to make between-institution comparisons or comparisons over time for uncommon events or between small geographic areas. For example, an administrator may wish to determine whether the mortality rate from acute myocardial infarction (AMI) is higher at one hospital than at other hospitals in the system. The distribution of deaths from AMI according to age group may not be known, or even if known the number of deaths according to age group may be small. Thus, indirect standardization should be performed in order to make the desired comparisons. The process of indirect rate standardization is as follows:

1. Compute the crude rate (C) of the event in the standard population.
2. Using data from the standard population, compute the rate of the event (r) for each level of the event whose effect is to be removed.
3. Obtain the number (n) in the comparison population according to each level for which rates were computed.

**Table 3.3. Calculation of Directly Standardized Incidence Rates[a]
per 100,000 Population for Breast Cancer, Females, SEER Areas, 1992–1996**

Age group (i) at diagnosis	White females incidence rate (r_i) per 100,000 pop.	$r_i \times P_i$	Black females incidence rate (r_i) per 100,000 pop.	$r_i \times P_i$	US standard million population, 1970[b] (P_i)
0–4	0.0	0.0	0.0	0.0	84,416
5–9	0.0	0.0	0.0	0.0	98,204
10–14	0.0	0.0	0.0	0.0	102,304
15–19	0.0	0.0	0.2	0.1877	93,845
20–24	0.9	0.7251	2.7	2.1752	80,561
25–29	7.4	4.9077	10.3	6.8310	66,320
30–34	23.4	13.1623	31.5	17.7184	56,249
35–39	58.2	31.8098	62.3	34.0507	54,656
40–44	117.6	69.3346	120.3	70.9265	58,958
45–49	198.2	118.1708	199.1	118.7074	59,622
50–54	264.6	144.5854	241.4	131.9082	54,643
55–59	304.0	149.1941	280.2	137.5138	49,077
60–64	364.2	154.4317	294.2	124.7496	42,403
65–69	423.2	145.6061	341.9	117.6341	34,406
70–74	473.9	126.9531	390.7	104.6646	26,789
75–79	500.7	94.4871	424.1	80.0319	18,871
80–84	487.1	54.7549	372.8	41.9064	11,241
85+	416.5	30.9668	353.0	26.2456	7,435
Total population		1139.0894		1015.2510	1,000,000

Age-adjusted rate per 100,000 population:
Sum of ($r_i \times P_i$)/total population $\times$ 100,000 =

| | White females | 113.9 | Black females | 101.5 |

SEER, Surveillance, Epidemiology, and End Results Program of the National Cancer Institute.
[a]SOURCE: Ries *et al.* (1999).
[b]SOURCE: U.S. Bureau of the Census, Census of Population, 1970.

4. Obtain the total number of events (O) that occurred in the comparison population.
5. Multiply the number in each level in the comparison population by the rate from the respective level in the standard population.
6. Divide the number of observed events by the sum of the expected number of events. This will yield a standardized mortality (or morbidity) ratio (SMR).
7. Multiply the SMR by the crude rate of the event in the standard population. This yields an indirectly adjusted rate.

Table 3.4 illustrates the application of indirect rate adjustment. It may be concluded that the observed number of deaths is lower for AMI cases at hospital A than the rate in the system hospitals even when adjusting for the differences in age.

The variance, standard error, and confidence interval of the rate adjusted by the direct and indirect methods may be obtained and the significance of adjusted rate variation among geographic areas may be tested. The reader is advised to consult Anderson and Rosenberg

Table 3.4. Calculation of Indirectly Standardized Rate Utilizing Hypothetical Data on Acute Myocardial Infarction (AMI) Fatality Rates, 30 Days Post-Hospitalization

	All Hospitals	Hospital A		
	AMI death rate per 100 AMI cases (r)	No. AMI cases	AMI deaths (O)	Expected AMI Deaths (E)
65–69	22.7	17	*	3.9
70–74	24.5	15	*	3.7
75–79	22.3	10	*	2.2
80+	30.5	29	*	8.8
Overall	24.2	71	11	18.6

Crude mortality rate (C) all hospitals = 24.2 per 100 AMI cases
Standardized mortality ratio (SMR) for Hospital A = O/E = 11/18.6 = 0.59
Indirectly age-adjusted rate = C × SMR = 24.2 deaths per 100 AMI cases × 0.59
= 14.3 deaths per 100 AMI cases

Conclusion: AMI patients in hospital A have a lower risk of death from AMI at 30 days posthospitalization.

(1998), Carriere and Roos (1994), or Kahn and Sempos (1989) for details about these computations.

In reviewing data representing adjusted rates, it is critical to understand on what year the standard population used to calculate adjusted rates was based. The numerical value of the standardized rate depends on what standard population was used. The standard population can be the combined population of all the comparison populations (e.g., world population for the standard population in comparing mortality rates across nations). The standard population could be the larger population of two or more comparison populations. However, in reality there is no established criteria for selecting a standard population, only that the standard population selected should be considered "normal" relative to the comparison populations being studied and reflect a reasonable age distribution (Anderson and Rosenberg, 1998). Rates standardized to the year 2000 population distribution will yield considerably higher rates for chronic conditions, even doubling some rates, but will narrow race differentials in the age-adjusted rates (Sorlie et al., 1999). Thus, age-adjusted death rates calculated prior to the implementation of the year 2000 standard will not be comparable to rates using the new standard population.

The rate standardization method described above utilize arithmetic weighting procedures to adjust for confounding variable. The direct and indirect methods described above are one-factor adjustments. Higher-order adjustments using arithmetic weighting procedures can be found in Fleiss (1981). Other methods exist for performing adjustment of rates, depending on how many variables need to be controlled, the size of the comparison population, and the number of events in each of the various levels of the confounding variable(s) whose effect is to be removed. **Regression-based adjustment** is a technique used when the sample size of the comparison population is small and large numbers of confounding variables need to be considered (Kahn and Sempos, 1989).

The **years of potential life lost** (YPLL) is a summary measure of premature mortality. To compute the YPLL for a specific cause, the numbers of deaths for that cause in each age group are tallied and multiplied by the years of life lost calculated as the difference between the midpoint of the age group and 75 years of age (in the United States the average life expectancy is over 75 years). The midpoint values for the most common age groups used are 0.5, 7.5, 19.5, 29.5, 39.5, 49.5, 59.5, and 69.5. Thus, 100 persons dying from HIV in the 25–34 years age group multiplied by 29.5 (midpoint of interval) represents 2950 years of life lost. When summed up over all age groups examined, the value is termed the YPLL. The number of years of life lost may be formatted as a rate using the number of persons less than 75 years of age in the denominator expressed per 100,000.

The YPLL is useful for summarizing the frequency of events that disproportionately affect younger persons or for assessing the impact of community-based interventions in geographic areas with a large minority or immigrant population which are typically younger than the population of the larger community. This is in contrast to mortality data represented as crude or adjusted rates whose values are weighted by the disease processes common to the elderly. Table 3.5 shows substantial declines in the YPLL due to external causes but a large increase in a chronic condition, diabetes mellitus.

Disability-adjusted life year (DALY) is a composite measure representing the sum of years of life lost because of premature death and years of life lived with disability. One DALY is one lost year of healthy life. The disability component of the summary measure (YLD) is weighted according to the severity of the disability and is multiplied by the expected duration of the disability and the incidence of the disability. Murray and Lopez (1996) developed the specific algorithms for this calculation as well as the disability weights.

Ratio Measures

It may be necessary to describe the presence or absence of a health event relative to some characteristic. When this characteristic is thought to be associated with an increased probability of a specific outcome, the characteristic is referred to as a "risk factor." A risk factor

Table 3.5. Years of Potential Life Lost (YPLL) Before Age 65
by Cause of Death, United States, 1990 and 1997

Cause of death (ICD-9 code)	YPLL per 100,000 persons under 65		Percentage change, 1990–1997
	1990	1997	
All causes (total)	8518.3	7398.4	−13.1
Unintentional injuries (E800–E949)	1263.0	1115.2	−11.7
Malignant neoplasms (140–208)	1713.9	1523.5	−11.1
Suicide (E950–E959)	405.9	378.0	−6.9
Homicide (E960–E978)	466.4	368.9	−20.9
Diseases of the heart (390–398, 402, 404–429)	1363.0	1190.2	−12.7
Human immunodeficiency virus infection (042–044)	366.2	208.7	−43.0
Cerebrovascular disease (430–438)	221.1	207.1	−6.3
Chronic liver disease and cirrhosis (571)	168.8	141.7	−16.1
Pneumonia/influenza (480–487)	128.5	112.6	−12.4
Diabetes mellitus (250)	133.0	149.9	12.7
Chronic obstructive pulmonary disease (490–496)	156.9	158.9	1.3

SOURCE: National Center for Health Statistics (1999).

may be potentially modifiable (e.g., high cholesterol) or it may be immutable (e.g., age). The calculation of the risk ratio, the relative risk, the odds ratio, or the population attributable risk is used to determine how strong the relationship is between a risk factor and an outcome of interest.

The **risk ratio** compares two rates representing risk (e.g., incidence or mortality rates). Generally, the group with the higher risk or the group in whom exposure to the risk factor is the greatest is placed in the numerator. The rate of the lower-risk group or the group with little or no exposure is in the denominator. The rate in the numerator and the rate in the denominator typically will be an adjusted rate so that the effect of age is removed when comparing the two groups. For example, the male–female risk ratio for mortality due to HIV infection from Table 3.6 is computed as:

Risk ratio = adjusted rate in the higher risk group or exposed group ÷ adjusted rate in the
     lower risk or nonexposed group
   = 9.1 age-adjusted HIV mortality rate per 100,000 among men ÷ 2.6 age-adjusted
    HIV mortality rate per 100,000 among whites
   = 3.5

The risk ratio in this example means that men are 2.43 times more likely to die from HIV than women. Since this ratio compares two adjusted rates, the conclusion can be extended to state that the elevated risk of death from HIV in men is higher than women even after consideration of the differences in age distribution between the genders. Risk ratios can be utilized to identify health problems that differentially occur in certain population subgroups. An examination of the male to female risk ratios for leading causes of death reveal that in addition to

Table 3.6. Ratio of Age-Adjusted Rates per 100,000 Population
for Selected Causes of Death by Gender and Race, United States, 1997[a]

Cause of death	Ratio of	
	Male to female	Black to white
All causes	1.60	1.54
Natural causes	1.51	1.54
Diseases of heart	1.81	1.47
Malignant neoplasms, including neoplasms of lymphatic and hematopoietic tissue	1.40	1.34
Cerebrovascular diseases	1.15	1.77
Chronic obstructive pulmonary diseases and allied conditions	1.47	0.80
Pneumonia and influenza	1.54	1.39
Chronic liver disease and cirrhosis	2.33	1.19
Diabetes mellitus	1.19	2.43
Human immunodeficiency virus infection	3.50	7.54
External causes	1.93	1.55
Motor vehicle accidents	2.13	1.06
Suicide	4.24	0.56
Homicide and legal intervention	3.79	5.98

[a]SOURCE: National Center for Health Statistics (1999).

HIV/AIDS, over a twofold greater risk of death among males is observed for accidents, suicide, and homicide and legal intervention, with the largest male–female difference observed from suicide. The risk ratio of black to white age-adjusted mortality rates indicates over a twofold greater risk of death among blacks for diabetes mellitus, homicide and legal intervention, and HIV (Table 3.6).

The **relative risk** (RR) is determined in a cross-tabulated format and represents the strength of the association between a risk factor classified at a nominal level (exposed to a risk factor versus not exposed) and an event also classified at a nominal level (present or absent) (Table 3.7). Table 3.8 presents hypothetical data which compares the proportion of elderly patients in fee-for-service (FSS) and health maintenance organization (HMO) systems of care with joint pain or with chest pain who were referred for specialist care. "Exposure" in this case is the system of care; "referral to physician specialist" is the event of interest. The RR of referral to a physician specialist is the incidence rate of referral to physician specialist in the FSS group divided by the incidence rate of referral to physician specialist in the HMO group. From the data in this example, referral to a specialist is more likely for chest pain patients in FFS than HMOs (OR = 1.88 and RR = 1.39). However, for patients with joint pain, elderly in FFS are less likely to be referred to a physician specialist than elderly persons in HMOs (OR = 0.61; RR = 0.75).

Because true measures of risk cannot always be readily derived, some method for estimating chances of events occurring relative to exposure is required. For this reason, the odds ratio, which is an approximation of the relative risk, is used. The odds of an event is the ratio of the occurrence of some exposure that exists relative to it not existing. Thus, in 100 persons with lung cancer, if 80% of them were smokers, the odds in favor of being a smoker would be 80:20 or 4:1. The odds ratio (OR) is the ratio of the odds of an event in the exposed group to the odds of the event in the unexposed group. The representation and interpretation of the OR depends on whether or not the odds of exposure or the odds of an event is being compared between two groups (Table 3.7). The OR in Table 3.8 is computed as an event odds ratio, since the data are derived from a quasi-experimental design. Thus, the odds of referral to a specialist (event) is 1.49 times more likely for patients with repetitive chest pain in the FFS group than those who were in a managed care group (exposure).

It must be kept in mind that both the RR and the OR are descriptive measures used to appraise the strength of an association between exposure and event. The valid values of the RR and the OR range from 0 to $+ \infty$. When data are presented in the format as in the 2×2 table arrangement found in Table 3.7, a RR or OR greater than 1 means that the exposure increases

Table 3.7. Computation of Relative Risks and Odds Ratios

	Event		
	Yes	No	Total
Exposure			
Yes	a	b	a + b
No	c	d	c + d

Relative risk of event = Incidence rate in high risk group ÷ Incidence rate in low risk group
= a/(a + b) ÷ c/(c + d)
Odds ratio of exposure = (a/c) ÷ (b/d)
Odds ratio of event = (a/b) ÷ (c/d)

Table 3.8. Calculation of the Relative Risk (RR) and Odds Ratio (OR) Using Hypothetical Data of the Relationship between Insurance Plan Type and Referral to a Specialist, Those with Joint Pain and Those with Chest Pain, Persons Aged 65 Years and Over

Plan type	Referral to a specialist for those with chest pain		
	Yes	No	Total
Fee-for-service	292 (a)	232 (b)	524
Health maintenance organization	223 (c)	333 (d)	556

RR = [a/(a + b)]/[c/(c + d)] = 1.39
OR = (a/b)/(c/d) = 1.88

Plan type	Referral to a specialist for those with joint pain		
	Yes	No	Total
Fee-for-service	199 (a)	325 (b)	524
Health maintenance organization	278 (c)	278 (d)	556

RR = [a/(a + b)]/[c/(c + d)] = 0.75
OR = (a/b)/(c/d) = 0.61

the likelihood of the event. A RR or OR less than 1 means that exposure decreases the likelihood of the event. A RR or OR equal to 1 means that the chances of the event occurring in the exposed and unexposed are equal. A statistical test, such as a chi-square or Fisher's exact test, must be applied to the data to determine whether the association represented by the RR or OR is statistically significant. Since the RR or OR are point estimates based on a sample of what the true values of the RR or the OR should be in the general population, a confidence interval usually 95%, can aid in determining significance. A 95% confidence interval that contains a RR or OR of 1.0 means the association is not significant. If either the upper or lower limit of the interval does not contain 1, then the association is either significantly lower (in the case of the former) or significantly higher (in the case of the latter circumstance). Additionally, the confidence interval is a measure of the precision of the RR and the OR. The wider the interval, the less precise the RR or the OR, usually because of few events in the exposed group. Computations of the statistical significance and the confidence interval are facilitated through the use of the interactive public domain statistics program for microcomputers, Epi Info 2000, which can be downloaded through www.cdc.gov/epiinfo (Dean *et al.*, 2000).

To assess the proportion of the risk of exposure due to a particular factor, the **population attributable risk** (PAR) percent, may be computed (Walter, 1978). This measure has importance as it assesses the theoretically achievable reduction in risk if the risk factor were entirely removed from a population. It is for this reason that the PAR can be used as a measure of the efficacy of a population-based intervention. The PAR percent is calculated as follows:

$$PAR \% = [P_e(RR - 1)]/[1 + P_e(RR - 1)] \times 100\%$$

Where PAR % = population attributable risk percent
P_e = proportion of the population exposed
RR = ratio of the incidence rate among the exposed to the incidence rate among the nonexposed.

The PAR percent also can be estimated from the OR (Cole and MacMahon, 1971).

Table 3.9. Prevalence of Risk Factors for Stroke and Population Attributable Risk Percent[a]

Risk factor	Percentage of population exposed	Relative risk	Population attributable risk %
Hypertension	56.2	2.73	49.3
Cigarette smoking	27.0	1.52	12.3
Atrial fibrillation	4.0	3.60	9.4
Heavy alcohol consumption	7.2	1.68	4.7

[a]From Gorelick (1994).

When confronted with a variety of risk factors for a disease and limited resources, the PAR percent can help determine which interventions may have the greatest impact for a population. Table 3.9 displays modifiable risk factors for stroke. The PAR percent for hypertension was derived as follows:

$$PAR \% = [0.562 \ (2.73 - 1)]/[1 + 0.562 \ (2.73 - 1)] \times 100\% = 49.3\%$$

Thus, of the risk factors displayed, interventions aimed at preventing stroke through hypertension control would have the greatest impact on the health status of the population, potentially eliminating 49.3% of strokes.

Summary

This chapter has presented common descriptive measures, namely rates and ratios, useful in planning and evaluating health care services, policies, and programs. Rates are used to identify and prioritize health problems within a population, assess variability of the utilization of health care resources, evaluate progress toward achieving health goals, and propose hypotheses regarding the etiology and control of health problems. Rates also are used to assess health, disease, and exposure patterns and their variability in populations. Ratios aid in evaluating the degree of the relationship between exposure and outcome. Descriptive measures, in general, are useful in identifying the components of the health care system that could be modified to improve the health status of populations. The specific type of epidemiological measure used depends on the objective of the assessment, the nature of the health problem being evaluated, and the type of data available.

Case Studies

Case Study No. 1
In-Hospital Mortality from Hip Fractures in the Elderly

Hip fractures are an important cause of mortality and morbidity in the elderly population. The incidence rate of hip fractures rises with increasing age, with the highest rates being among white females followed by white males, black females, and black males. Following hip fracture, persons are at greater risk of death than the general population. In addition, marked differences in survival following a hip fracture are noted according to gender and race, with black males and females being at highest risk of death. Differences in survival have been hypothesized to be due to differences in medical care utilization and the delivery of services provided during hospitalization or subsequent to discharge. Since virtually all

Table 3.10. In-Hospital Deaths among Admissions for Hip Fractures
by Age, Race, and Gender, Maryland, 1979–1988[a]

Characteristic	No. of admissions for hip fractures	No. of deaths
Age group		
65–69	2,542	68
70–74	3,842	140
75–79	5,374	216
80–84	6,541	297
≥85	9,071	618
Race and gender		
White males	4,980	392
White female	20,675	847
Black males	506	38
Black females	1,209	62
Total	27,370	1,339

[a]From Myers *et al.* (1991).

hip fractures are likely to be hospitalized, the examination of factors contributing to mortality during hospitalization may suggest areas where measures could be implemented to improve survival for these persons. Myers *et al.* (1991) examined factors contributing to inpatient mortality. Data from this study are displayed in Table 3.10. Hospital discharge abstracts provided information on patient demographic, clinical characteristics, and vital status at discharge.

Q.1. Compute the age-, race-, and gender-specific mortality rates for hip fracture per 100 persons admitted using data from Table 3.10. Which population subgroups are at highest risk of death?

Q.2. Although women have a higher incidence of hip fractures than men, why would the mortality rate for men be higher?

Q.3. Why were data pooled over 10 years?

Q.4. What other source of mortality data could have been used in this study instead of the hospital discharge abstracts?

Q.5. What measurement errors could enter into the computation of the inpatient mortality rates using hospital discharge abstract data? How would these affect the estimates of the mortality rates?

Case Study No. 2
Medicaid Prenatal Care: Fee-for-Service Versus Managed Care

There has been a rapid nationwide increase in the enrollment of the Medicaid population into managed care arrangements to cover their health care services. One way of assessing the quality of care between these two payer systems would be to compare outcomes of care for pregnant Medicaid recipients who were enrolled in either fee-for-service (MFFS) or managed care (MMC) plans. To accomplish this evaluation, Oleske *et al.* (1998) examined birth certificate data for one calendar year from two California counties where a particular form of managed care was in operation. These counties operated not-for-profit mixed-model managed care plans whose regulatory framework is characterized as a county-organized health system/health insuring organization. Both plans involved providers, beneficiaries, local government officials, and other interested parties in their operations. Control counties were selected based on geographic proximity, size, and social and economic factors and did not have any form of managed care available for their Medicaid populations. A computerized file of birth certificates was used to obtain information on characteristics of the women, payer group assignment, and pregnancy outcomes. There were 13,453 women who gave birth through the MFFS group and 6,122 women who gave birth in the MMC group. The incidence of low birth weight among women in the MFFS plan was 6.1% and 4.5% in the MMC plan.

Q.1. What is the odds ratio (OR) of low birth weight in managed care versus fee-for-service? What do you conclude from the OR?

Q.2. What would the OR be if the incidence rate of low birth weight in the MFFS group was twice that of the MMC group?

Q.3. How could the sources of data used affect the OR calculated in Q.1?

Case Study No. 3
Gender Differential Trends in Prevention, Diagnosis, Classification, and Treatment of Coronary Heart Disease

Early efforts aimed at reducing coronary heart disease (CHD) mortality saw rates declining earlier and steeper in women than among men. The relative contribution of prevention versus improvements in

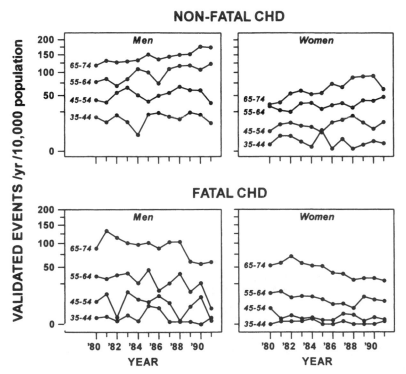

Figure 3.4. Nonfatal and fatal coronary heart disease (CHD) rates per 10,000 population, by gender, and aged 35–74 years, southeastern New England, 1980–1991. Reprinted from Derby, *et al.* (2000), with permission of the Society of Epidemiologic Research and Oxford University Press.

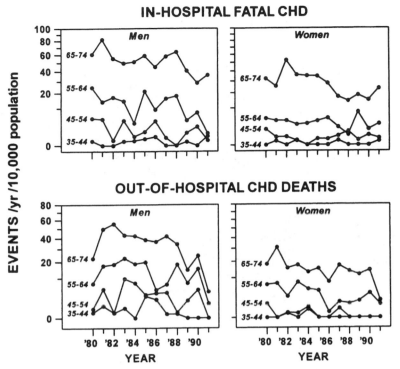

Figure 3.5. In-hospital fatal and out-of-hospital coronary heart disease (CHD) rates by gender, 35–74 years, southeastern New England, 1980–1991. From Derby *et al.* (2000), with permission of the Society of Epidemiologic Research and Oxford University Press.

diagnosis and treatment in the decline are controversial. Differences in classification of coronary heart disease over time, differences in health care utilization patterns, and differences in the use of diagnostic and therapeutic technology over time also make it difficult to study this problem. Derby *et al.* (2000) examined 6282 in-hospital and out-of-hospital coronary disease events ascertained through the surveillance system of the Pawtucket Heart Health Program. Nonfatal and fatal CHD rates and in-hospital fatal and out-of-hospital CHD death rates were compared by gender, calendar year, and age group (Figs. 3.4 and 3.5).

Q.1. What type of rates are displayed in these figures?

Q.2. What groups are at highest risk of fatal CHD? What groups are at high risk of in-hospital fatal CHD?

Q.3. What can be concluded about these rate patterns over time?

Q.4. What reasons could explain the gender differential over time?

Q.5. What biases affect the rate measures in this study that could account for the gender difference?

Q.6. What implications do these data have for a capitated health care plan?

Case Study No. 4
The Burden of Disease in Los Angeles County

The Los Angeles County Department of Health Services (LACDHS) in its recent community-based planning efforts acknowledged that too often the health of populations is evaluated in terms of a proxy measure of health, namely mortality (Los Angeles County Department of Health Services and UCLA Center for Health Policy Research, 2000). With the aging of society and improved control of many transmissible diseases, some of the greatest health problems will be chronic disabling conditions. One of the core functions of public health agencies is measuring the health status of populations. The Los Angeles County Department of Health Services with the assistance of a local university assessed the health status of Los Angeles County residents using the summary measure known as disability adjusted life years (DALYs). The DALY was felt to be a more appropriate method for characterizing the burden of ill health in the community for both private and public organizations to better prioritize efforts to improve the public's health. Table 3.11 compares the results of the assessment using DALYs, crude mortality rate, and years of life lost (YLL) rank.

Q.1. Define the terms DALY, YLL, and crude mortality.

Q.2. Why are the rankings from the crude mortality rate and the YLL rank different? Would there be a difference in these rankings if either measure were age adjusted?

Q.3. What biases enter into the calculation of the DALY, YLL, and crude mortality?

Case Study No. 5
Risk Factors for Coronary Artery Disease

One of the leading causes of death in the United States is coronary artery disease (CAD). The Framingham Heart Study has provided a wealth of death on risk factors for CAD for which to guide the development of health promotion programs. From longitudinal studies, such as the Framingham Study, various epidemiological measures are possible to compute including incidence, relative risk, and population attributable risk. Each measure of risk has its own meaning and utility in planning health services and

Table 3.11. Leading 10 Causes of Premature Death and Disability in Los Angeles County Based for Disability-Adjusted Life Years (DALY), with Crude Mortality Rank and YLL in 1997

Rank	Cause	DALYs (years)	Crude mortality rank	YLL rank
1	Coronary heart disease	72,886	1	1
2	Alcohol dependence	60,872	39	29
3	Homicide/violence	45,548	8	2
4	Depression	43,449	91	91
5	Diabetes mellitus	42,456	6	10
6	Osteoarthritis	39,811	70	80
7	Stroke	33,351	2	4
8	Lung cancer	29,785	3	3
9	Emphysema	29,333	5	11
10	Motor vehicle crashes	29,040	14	5

health policy. Wilson and Evans (1993) report the following data from the Framingham Study: Prevalence of smokers, 42%; nonsmokers, 58%; rate of CAD in smokers, 12.6 per 100 population, and in nonsmokers, 7.7 per 100 population.

Q.1. What is the relative risk (RR) of CAD for smoking?

Q.2. What does a RR of 1.6 mean?

Q.3. What is the risk of CAD attributable to smoking?

Q.4. If you were planning to introduce health promotion services on a individual level, which epidemiological measure would be most useful?

Case Study No. 6
Violence As an Occupational Risk Factor for Health Care Workers

Health professionals, heretofore, have accepted that assault by a patient was part of the "hazards" associated with the job. In May 1993, the Occupational Health and Safety Administration (OSHA) laid out its policy on workplace violence. One of the implications of this policy was that suffering attacks by patients was no longer acceptable. Subsequent to the introduction of the policy, an employee of a Midwestern psychiatric hospital reported to OSHA excessive exposure to patients' violent behaviors. The hospital was cited for failing to protect hospital employees from patients' violent behavior. This was the first OSHA citation for an employer failing to deal with workplace violence. Violent behavior is common among patients in a psychiatric hospital. Patients who exhibit violent behavior are the elderly who may be cognitively impaired, individuals undergoing detoxification from a chemical dependency, those with severe psychiatric problems, and adolescents with behavioral disorders. The hospital did not contest the citation and provided a detailed description of how it analyzed its problem and would modify policies and procedures based on the data. Epidemiological measures were used in the analysis to develop strategies for prevention.

Q.1. The first thing the hospital did was established a system to monitor the incidence rate of violence. Propose what events should be included in the numerator and how the denominator should be constructed.

Q.2. Describe how epidemiological rate measures could be used to identify which patients pose the highest risk of violence to hospital personnel and when and where this occurs.

References

Anderson, R. N., and Rosenberg, H. M., 1998, Age standardization of death rates: Implementation of the year 2000 standard, *National Vital Statistics Reports*, Vol. 47, No. 3, National Center for Health Statistics, Hyattsville, MD.

Carriere, K. C., and Roos, L. L., 1994, Comparing standardized rates of events, *Am. J. Epidemiol.* 140:472–482.

Cole, P., and MacMahon, B., 1971, Attributable risk percent in case-control studies, *Br. J. Prevention and Soc. Med.* 25:242–244.

Dean, A. G., Arner, T. G., Sangam, S., Sunki, G. G., Friedman, R., Lantiga, M., Zubieta, J. C., Sullivan, K. M., and Smith, D. C., 2000, Epi Info™ 2000, a database and statistics program for public health professionals for use on Window 95, 98, NT, and 2000 computers, Centers for Disease Control and Prevention, Atlanta, GA.

Derby, C. A., Lapane, K. L., Feldman, H. A., and Carleton, R. A., 2000, Sex-specific trends in validated coronary heart disease rates in southeastern New England, 1980–1991, *Am. J. Epidemiol.* 151:417–429.

Fleiss, J. L., 1981, *Statistical Methods for Rates and Proportions*, 2nd ed., John Wiley & Sons, New York.

Gorelick, P. B., 1994, Stroke prevention: An opportunity for efficient utilization of health care resources during the coming decade, *Stroke* **25:**220–224.

Kahn, H. A., and Sempos, C. T., 1989, *Statistical Methods in Epidemiology*, Oxford University Press, New York.

Kramarow, E., Lentzner, H., Rooks, R., Weeks, J., and Saydah, S., 1999, *Health and Aging Chartbook: Health United States, 1999*, National Center for Health Statistics, Hyattsville, MD.

Lauderdale, D. S., Furner, S. E., Miles, T. P., and Goldberg, J., 1993, Epidemiologic uses of Medicare data. *Epidemiol. Rev.* **15:**319–327.

Los Angeles County Department of Health Services and the UCLA Center for Health Policy Research, 2000, *The Burden of Disease in Los Angeles County*, County of Los Angeles, CA.

Murray, C. J. L., and Lopez, A. D. (eds.), 1996, *The Global Burden of Disease: A Comprehensive Assessment of Mortality and Disability from Diseases, Injuries, and Risk Factors in 1990 and Projected to 2020*, Harvard University Press, Cambridge, MA.

Myers, A. H., Robinson, E. G., Van Natta, M. L., Michelson, D., Collins, K., and Baker, S. P., 1991, Hip fractures among the elderly: Factors associated with in-hospital mortality, *Am. J. Epidemiol.* **134:**1128–1137.

National Center for Health Statistics, 1999, *Health United States, 1999 with Health and Aging Chartbook*, Hyattsville, MD.

Oleske, D. M., Branca, M. L., Schmidt, J. B., Ferguson, R., and Linn, E. S., 1998, A comparison of capitated and fee-for-service Medicaid reimbursement methods on pregnancy outcomes, *HSR: Health Services Res.* **33:**55–73.

Ries, L. A. G., Kosary, C. L., Hankey, B. F., Miller, B. A., Cleff, L., and Edwards, B. K. (eds.), 1999, *SEER Cancer Statistics Review 1973–1996*, National Cancer Institute. Bethesda, MD.

Sesso, H. D., Paffenbarger, R. S., and Lee, I., 2000, Comparison of national death index and world wide web death searches, *Am. J. Epidemiol.* **152:**107–111

Sorlie, P. D., Thom, T. J., Manolio, T., Rosenberg, H. M., Anderson, R. N., and Burke, G. L., 1999, Age-adjusted death rates: Consequences of the year 2000 standard, *Ann. Epidemiol.* **9:**93–100.

Walter, S. D., 1978, Calculation of attributable risks from epidemiological data, *Int. J. Epidemiol.* **7:**75–182.

Wilson, P. W. F., and Evans, J. C., 1993, Coronary artery disease prediction, *Am. J. Hypertens.* **6:**309S–312S.

4

Assessing Causality
Foundations for Population-Based Health Care Managerial Decision Making

Thomas T. H. Wan

Introduction

The scientific bases for making managerial decisions is the use of evidence generated from explicit, experiential, and confirmed knowledge. This knowledge management approach is a systematic thought process, beginning with the collection of observable facts and the analysis of these facts to provide adequate explanations of the phenomenon or problem under study. Ideally, scientific data should be gathered under a theoretically informed framework, so that evidence can be derived from the application of data warehousing and data-mining techniques. Such evidence-based knowledge can be integrated with practical and experiential knowledge to shed light on the cause–effect relationships between the problems and solution sets in the field of health care management.

This chapter will provide readers with the principles of causal analysis, including qualitative causal criteria and selected multivariate analytic methods. This chapter also will prepare readers to select appropriate techniques for problem solving and decision-making as they relate to health services administration.

Scientific Inquiry

This section will introduce the fundamentals of scientific inquiry, discuss a variety of research designs, introduce the principles and methods employed in causal analysis, and explain the variety of analytical designs and statistical approaches to identifying the determinants of health service problems. Scientific thinking aids the health care manager in organizing vast amounts of information including those responses from competing or dissenting interests

Thomas T. H. Wan Department of Health Administration, School of Allied Health Professions, Virginia Commonwealth University, Richmond, Virginia 23298-0233.

Epidemiology and the Delivery of Health Care Services: Methods and Applications, Second Edition, edited by Denise M. Oleske. Kluwer Academic/Plenum Publishers, New York, 2001.

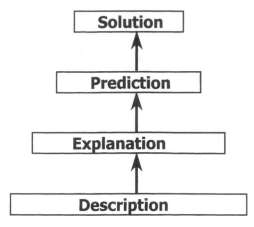

Figure 4.1. Foundation of scientific inquiry.

so as to derive the most appropriate decision for the circumstances in consideration of the time limits imposed on making that decision. Scientific inquiry is used in all forms of problem solving, specifically to support and verify, or to reject preconceived concepts and propositions about situations (Wan, 1995). At the lowest level, scientific inquiry helps to describe an observed phenomenon and the facts that surround it. At the next level, by identifying causal relationships, scientific inquiry helps to explain the phenomenon. Predicting future events, from the historical patterns of a phenomenon is another use of scientific inquiry. At the highest level, scientific inquiry can provide the necessary information to control, modify, and design solutions to the problems presented by a phenomenon (Fig. 4.1).

Characteristics of Scientific Inquiry

The process of scientific inquiry has four characteristics: observability, verifiability, tractability, and manipulability. Each characteristic has a precise meaning for the process of scientific inquiry. Although all four elements are typically found in scientific investigation, they need not all be present in every case.

Observability is central to the empirical approach to the natural world: observations of sensory data that can be confirmed. Facts or data must be observable through either an objective or a subjective procedure. For example, health status may be identified through clinical assessment and by laboratory results, which are objective measures of health. However, subjective measures such as surveys also provide observable, i.e., empirical data about health status.

Verifiability is the second characteristic of scientific inquiry and is closely related to the first characteristic. A phenomenon is considered verifiable when its existence or pattern is detected by repeated observations and is corroborated by diverse observers. An example is the historical trend of the continued disparity of mortality and morbidity rates between whites and nonwhites and by socioeconomic class (Howard *et al.*, 2000). This is observed for most major disease categories and has been observed worldwide as well as among all health plans.

A third characteristic of scientific inquiry is the *tractability* of the data, which means that observed facts and data must be both accessible and amenable for statistical and causal analysis. From an epidemiological perspective, for example, a tractable disease is one that has traceable etiology and therefore is preventable or controllable. Epidemiological data must be subject to causal analysis in order to tease out the cause and effect relationship.

The final characteristic of scientific inquiry is *manipulability*, or can an intervention or manipulation be performed on the observed subjects. For example, a genetic disease is considered manipulable if early detection and gene therapy are possible. The manipulability is precisely determined by explicit knowledge, so that predictable results can be achieved as well as the known risks and benefits.

The above characteristics are necessary conditions for conducting a scientific inquiry. Thus, these essential features of scientific inquiry can solidify the deductive and/or inductive logical reasoning of epidemiological studies.

Logic of Scientific Inquiry

The ultimate goal of scientific inquiry is to generate a set of hypotheses, which repeated observations then test and either confirm or reject. To derive, test, and confirm a theory, an explication of concepts in a theoretical framework is essential in addition to following the process of scientific inquiry while attempting to establish the theory. In health services management research, although some existing theoretical frameworks may be useful in many instances, other unique aspects of health care delivery and organizations relative to the populations they serve have not yet been given theoretical formulations. New theories are formulated by using two basic approaches: induction and deduction. The respective roles of these two logical methods in causal inference in epidemiology have been hotly debated. Readers who are interested in further reading about causation and causal inference should consult Rothman and Greenland (1998).

Inductive inquiry starts by observing specific facts and then formulates general principles based on them to develop a theory. For example, the Joint Commission on Accreditation of Healthcare Organizations has set forth a series of activities for quality monitoring and improvement to enhance the overall performance of health care organizations. Quality indicators are collected routinely by assessing the presence of sentinel events (baby abduction, injuries due to treatment, unanticipated deaths, etc.) or rates of adverse patient outcomes (unscheduled hospital readmission rate, medication error rate, surgical complication rate, etc.). Then conclusions are drawn as to which aspects of the health care process are associated with greater risks of adverse events. The specific observations, when analyzed in terms of organizational theory, have suggested that both poor clinical support system designs and human errors may be adversely affecting the quality of patient care. Such generalization based on specific facts is called logical induction.

Deductive inquiry starts with general principles and derives specific expectations from them to develop a theory. In this case, the theory or framework provides the starting point from which specific hypotheses are proposed. They then are tested empirically. Using the previous topic of rates of adverse outcomes, the investigator would first formulate a hypothesis, such as "Presence of an automated pharmacy prescription system reduces hospital nurses' medication error rates." If the theoretical framework was chosen that concerned the effects of care process design in a health care delivery system, the deductive principles supporting the hypothesis sets the expectation that case management with an automatic system for tracking patient outcome would reduce undesirable mishaps, because care planning and coordination can be organized effectively to reduce errors or mishaps. Data on medication errors then would be compiled for units with and without automated pharmacy prescription systems.

Often the deductive and inductive approaches are used together; in fact, in scientific inquiry they may be inseparable. For in actuality observations of specific events may lead inductively to a conclusion and generalization about a phenomenon. Then, from this generalization, concepts and propositions may be formed and organized into an abstract theoretical structure. Using that theoretical structure, specific hypotheses can be proposed and tested by empirical data. Let us now illustrate the construction of a theory by the use of both inductive and deductive processes.

Prevention of sentinel health events is a pressing quality-of-care issue for which existing organizational theory or epidemiological theory offers little guidance. The first step in constructing a theory to aid in solving this problem is to specify two observed phenomena: (1) the rates of medication errors vary greatly by hospital units, and (2) hospital units with a clinical decision support system such as automated prescription records have lower annual medication error rates than do those hospitals with no such system. In order to postulate the relationship between these observations, they must be accurately defined and measured. So the next step in the theory development cycle is to measure the two variable: quality of prescribing behavior and medication errors.

After the two variables—prescribing behavior (care process) and medication errors—have been defined and measured, the necessary data about them are collected. Then data analysis is done to identify any association or correlation, as well as to measure the magnitude of any relationship between the two variables; furthermore, the effect that a change in one variable may have on the other variable can be examined using predictive analytical techniques. In this step, any relationship between the two variables is defined and described.

Our example began with a focus on specific data about an observed phenomenon. Now, after the data analysis step, generalizations can be made. These generalizations, or tentative explanations about the relationship between the two variables, might include:

1. Effective use of an automated prescription record system leads to a lower rate of medication errors.
2. Use of an integrated clinical care process varies directly with the size of hospitals.
3. Integration of clinical care is more likely if an automated system for patient care has positively affected the efficiency and effectiveness of patient care.
4. Hospital financial performance varies directly with the degree of clinical and informational integration.

These generalizations describe relationships between care technology use and hospital performance, as defined within a health system framework (Wan, 1995).

From such generalizations, founded in observation and empirical data analysis, it is then possible to move into a deductive model. In this phase of the theory construction, propositions can be formed. Propositions, or statements about the relationships between concepts, are an important part of the theoretical framework, because they can be tested as hypotheses.

Two propositions that could be deductively derived here are:

1. More clinical and informational integration leads to higher efficiency in care processing, and in turn, reduces annual rates of adverse patient outcomes.
2. Clinical and informational integration has enhanced hospital performance because the design and use of care technology offer better decision support and reduces the rate of adverse patient outcomes.

These theoretical propositions, describing possible relationships between the two concepts, constitute hypotheses that can be tested. They return us to the point of making observations about relationships in the real world, thus completing the circle of observation–deduction–concept formulation–hypothesis testing–observation.

Stages in Scientific Inquiry

When designing solutions for a health care management problem, the initial and most crucial decision is to define the condition or problem to be addressed. Epidemiological surveys for needs assessment are particularly useful in defining the problem, after which an intervention can be designed. Then evaluation research methods appropriate to that intervention design and measures for quantifying the criteria can be selected. This process, which follows the stages of scientific inquiry, consists of seven steps (Table 4.1): (1) identification and specification of the study problem; (2) selection of a theoretically informed framework to guide the inquiry (the research process); (3) quantification of the study variables; (4) selection of a study intervention design; (5) specification of the analytic framework; (6) confirmatory statistical analysis; and (7) evaluation of causality. These seven steps are described below.

Once research questions have been developed, it is necessary to state the study problem in clear, precise terms and to specify its salient aspects. A useful problem statement will guide the investigator in the design and execution of quantitative root-cause analysis.

Identification and Specification of the Study Problem

The starting point for this process is to identify the key issues and variables contained in the problem. Every problem affects three dimensions: person (the sample or population involved), place (the location, setting, or circumstance), and time (the time element or sequencing of exposures and events must be clearly identified). Specification of the study problem thus means elucidating its precise attributes. Attributes of particular importance are the problem's magnitude and its significance, its location and boundaries, and its determinants and consequences. Magnitude and significance refer to two important statistics: the incidence of the problem and the prevalence of the problem. The incidence of a problem is the number of new episodes of the problem that occur within a certain time interval. Prevalence is the number of old and new episodes of a problem existing at a given point in time, and hence represents the burden of the condition on the population. Incidence refers to the timing of the problem; prevalence refers to the sheer numbers of the events. Considered together, these two aspects of the problem provide a good picture of its seriousness.

The specification process must provide operational definitions for these attributes, so they can be clearly understood and interpreted. An operational definition describes a variable or

---

Table 4.1. The Seven Steps of Scientific Causal Inquiry

1. Identification and specification of the study problem
2. Selection of an informed theoretical framework
3. Quantification of the study variables
4. Specification in analytical modeling
5. Selection of the intervention study design
6. Confirmatory statistical analysis
7. Establishment of causality

concept in terms of the procedures by which it can be measured. For example, if the study problem is an examination of whether patients are being discharged too soon, the variable of early discharge could be defined as "discharged on the first or second postoperative day."

Selection of an Informed Theoretical Framework

Theories can be defined as abstract generalizations that present systematic explanations about the relationships among phenomena; theories also knit together observations and facts into an orderly system. A theoretical framework is a statement by the researcher of the assumptions and beliefs that guide a particular research process. Theory also provides an analytical framework through which to form logical interpretations of the facts collected in the study, and it guides the search for new information. Selecting a theoretically informed framework consists of five stages: (1) conceptualization, (2) model selection, (3) critique of previous work in the field, (4) review of evidence, and (5) refinement or reformation of the model.

Conceptualization is a means of formulating the study problem as a flow diagram, specifying all the relationships among the variables, both those under study as well as those affecting the relationship(s) but which are not under study. This formulation will ultimately help to explain the data. It is important to remember, however, that conceptual thought is a deductive process and so requires testing in the real world.

Model selection assigns real-world attributes and manifestations of the study problem in an abstract way. This abstract representation of variables and relationships is the basis for proposing hypotheses and facilitating analysis of variable later in the research process. The selection of a theoretical model enables the investigator to identify causal links among the study constructs and to make logical interpretations of the study results.

Review of the literature involves obtaining information on research findings, theory, methodological approaches, reviews of the current literature, opinions, and viewpoints, as well as anecdotes and experiential descriptions. Often there is a wealth of available literature, and the investigator has to decide how relevant particular material is to the study problem. Questions to ask when reviewing an epidemiological study or other article to formulate a model are displayed in Table 4.2.

Examining the evidence involves reviewing the information that led to the selection of the study problem. For example, if the quarterly audit of patient incident reports at a general hospital indicates that there has been an increase in patient falls, it would be useful to compare data from the hospital's risk management or quality improvement office from that audit with information in the literature. The literature suggests that elderly patients are at high risk for falls while in the hospital, but the audit data revealed that the majority of patients who fell were middle-aged, postoperative patients who were receiving narcotics for pain relief. Thus, age, hospital unit, and practices of narcotic administration should be included as variables in a theoretical framework for a health care management study about the causes of patient falls. In addition, any confounding factors that might distort or suppress the relationship between an intervention variable and a response variable should be considered in the formulation of the model.

Quantification of Study Variables

If the results of the study are to be meaningful to the health care manager and to allow clear communication to those who use them, the variables examined must be quantified with a

Table 4.2. Questions to Ask When Reviewing An Epidemiological Study or Other Article

- What is the study hypothesis?
- What is the population to which the study intends to refer the results?
- What is the background and nature of the problem that stimulated this study?
- What contributions will this study make?
- What is the study design?
- What are the independent, dependent, and confounding variables? How are they classified?
- What is the reliability and validity of the measures? The data sources if secondary data?
- What statistical methods are used to test the hypothesis? Were these used appropriately?
- What is the major conclusion drawn from the study?
- How could the measures used and the sample affect the conclusion?
- Health care management practice: What action should be taken based on results to improve the health status of the population served?
- Technology assessment: Should this technology be discarded or accepted?
- Health Policy: Are the results consistent with national health goals? What programmatic action is suggested by the results?
- Organization/program performance: Did the organization/program meets its stated goals and target population? Was it effective?

reliable and valid measure (review Chapter 2, this volume). The study variables can be measured at the individual (patient) or aggregate (patient care unit, organization, or community) level. An operational definition is how the variable is defined and how it will be measured. Operationalizing links an abstract concept from the problem statement (e.g., medication errors occur at a high rate in patient care units with low nurse–patient ratios) and the theoretical framework to a variable that can be measured and quantified. For very broad concepts, proxy measures are used. For example, patient satisfaction is often used as a proxy measure for quality of care, which is a much more ambiguous concept. Once the variables have been operationalized, propositions stating the relationships between the variables are presented as theoretical hypotheses. Variables differ considerably in the ease with which they can be described, observed, and measured. Even something as seemingly simple as body weight can be measured in pounds or kilograms, as well as in fractions of either. In addition, body weight may show diurnal variation, which suggests that the time of day when the weight is measured should be specified in the operational definition. Furthermore, body weight also may be examined using anthropomorphic or electrical impedance measurements to determine the percentages of lean muscle mass or body fat.

To explore the example further: an operational definition of body weight will depend on the problem under study and where it fits in a theoretical framework. If the problem concerns overall population health, then a random weight to the nearest pound is adequate. In a weight reduction clinic, on the other hand, detecting small weight losses might be of concern, and so the operational definition might specify weights taken first thing in the morning. Another example would be research by an exercise physiologist studying long-distance runners, which would require more precise anthropomorphic measurements.

This example of body weight research has described a number of options for linking that concept with measurements. The most precise observations and measurements must be chosen to describe the attributes, magnitude, and significance of variables, as well as to identify causal relationships between them. Beyond that, however, the validity and reliability of the measurement techniques used to arrive at an operational definition must be established. Only if a measurement of a variable is both valid and reliable can it be depended on as an accurate representation of a concept or attribute (see Chapter 2).

The study questions and the theoretical framework guide specification of a statistical or causal model. Statistical modeling simplifies, summarizes, organizes, interprets, and communicates numerical data. The model is based on a priori information about the data structure (e.g., significant associations detected) and those from theory, hypothesis, and/or knowledge from previous research, management, or clinical experience. On the basis of the available data, one wants to test the validity of the model and to test hypotheses about the parameters of the model. In evaluating treatment outcomes, researchers often need to analyze multiple outcomes (e.g., the complication rate, repeated hospitalization rate, hospital mortality rate, etc.). Sometimes these outcome variables are correlated with each other. In that case, it is imperative to use a multivariate statistical technique to examine the effects of an intervention on multiple outcome variables, with or without correlated errors or residuals. The outcome or response variables are treated as endogenous variables (that are determined within the model), and the intervention variable is treated as an exogenous variable (that is determined outside of the model).

The specification of causal links among multiple study variables is not a simple matter. There is no single definition of causality that has emerged that is the standard across all health care fields. However, the explication of causal links in terms of either a reciprocal (both directional) or a recursive (unidirectional) relationship can serve well in the search for causality. There is no best way to fit the model in reality as suggested by Bollen (2000). In comparing alternative models with constraints, one might generate results to shed some light on the plausible causal relationships between the study variables. With an informed theoretical framework, investigators can map out their ideas, the theory, and hypothesized relationships, and can portray the structural or causal relationships among the study variables.

Selection of a Study Design

A study design is the template for specifying the sampling strategy to obtain information about the exposure or intervention (independent variable) and the health outcome or problem (dependent variable). The choice for selection of a study design depends on how much is known about a relationship between exposure and outcome. The more that is known, the more complex the design. There are three major categories of study design using in health care management epidemiology: descriptive, correlational, and experimental. Further details concerning factors influencing the choice of a study design when evaluating program and health system performance are illustrated in Chapter 6 (this volume).

Specification of the Analytic Framework: Proposing the Hypothesis and Setting Error Tolerances

The application of inferential statistical methods provides an objective, systematic framework so that health care managers working with identical data will be likely to come to the same conclusions. Examples of inferential statistical methods include estimation of population parameters, hypothesis testing of population parameters (e.g., comparing means), and identification and estimation of variance or error and hypothesis testing of variances (e.g., comparing variability in the use of coronary angiography in two health service market areas). Health care managers scientifically evaluate a problem by proposing a hypothesis, and, testing the hypothesis with an appropriate statistical method.

An important part of the analytic process is comparing the study results to the proposed hypotheses. Hypothesis testing helps the health care manager make objective decisions about the results of an intervention or organizational change. Using statistical methods, the health care manager can decide whether the study results reflect change differences between groups or true differences.

Hypothesis testing follows the rules of negative inference, in which a contradictory, or null, hypothesis is proposed. The null hypothesis states that there is no relationship between the variables and that any observed relationship is due to chance. In formulating a hypothesis, use the following template: (1) independent variable, (2) relation or parameter tested, (3) dependent variable, and (4) population to which the results are intended to be generalized to. For example, a manager believes that a certain staffing ratio of RNs to patients can lower the risk of falls in elderly hospitalized patients. The process of determining whether the staffing ratio is indeed critical would begin with formulating a null hypothesis (H_0): "Nurse staffing ratios are not associated with the rate of patient falls." The independent variable is the "nurse staffing ratio." The relationship proposed for examination is one of "association" and would cue the use of a statistical test evaluated with a chi square distribution. The dependent variable is rate of "patient falls." The population to which the results will be generalized is "elderly hospitalized patients." Sometimes the factors that will be controlled for are included in the hypothesis, setting a template for a more complex statistical analysis. To illustrate the use of control, the above hypothesis may then be stated, "Nurse staffing ratios are not associated with the rate of patient falls, controlling for characteristics of patients and hospitals." Statistical testing would then determine if the null hypothesis were correct (accept H_0) or if it is incorrect and the staffing ratio does have an effect in the rate of patient falls (reject H_0); this rejection or acceptance of the null hypothesis is decided by statistical analysis of the study data.

The two types of errors in testing a hypothesis are: rejecting a null hypothesis as false when it is actually true (type I error) and accepting a null hypothesis as true when it is actually false (type II error). The term *level of significance* is used to describe the probability of committing a type I error, and this level can be preset. The level of significance also is referred to as the alpha (α) level. The alpha level is the cut-point for determining whether the value of a test statistic (e.g., $t = 2.95$) computed through a statistical test (e.g., one-sample t-test) represents a sample parameter (e.g., mean) that is more extreme relative to the population distribution of means than would be expected by chance alone. An alpha level of 0.05 by convention is the maximum acceptable probability beyond which the differences or the associations are significant. So in this example, if an alpha level of significance of 0.05 for a one-sample t- test, one-tailed with 20 degrees of freedom is represented by a value of 1.725, the t statistic of 2.95 represents a mean that is much more extreme than would be expected by chance alone. The probability of committing a type II error is beta (β), and its complement ($1-\beta$) is referred to as the power of a statistical test. The power of a statistical test is its ability to detect differences when differences really exist. Another way of saying this is that power is the ability to reject a null hypothesis when it is false. The major source of bias in most studies of evaluating health care initiatives is having too low a power resulting from too small a sample to detect a difference between the interventions studied. A power of at least 80% is desired in observational studies. A power of 90% is optimal in intervention studies to lessen the likelihood of adopting interventions with a low probability of efficacy in other settings.

Hypothesis testing verifies the model that was specified in the theoretical framework, through procedures that analyze the attributes and relationships of the variables described in the study problem. For example, if a study on the utilization of emergency services examined whether certain age groups were more likely to use certain types of services, one hypothesis might be that young adults, middle-aged adults, and the elderly utilized emergency services at the same rate. However, analysis of the data on young adults, middle-aged adults, and the elderly shows that young adults and the elderly have similar utilization patterns for treatment of skeletal trauma and head injuries, but the main cause for young adults is motor vehicle accidents and for the elderly it is falls, while middle-aged adults' emergency service use is more for medical problems such as myocardial infarction and hypertension. Using inferential statistics, the investigator would decide what were the sources of variation and whether these differences were statistically significant. Furthermore, a statistical test evaluating the predictability of the relationship specified by the hypothesis (e.g., the goodness of fit statistic, R-squared, etc.) would indicate the usefulness of the relationship for an overarching theoretical model (Mulaik *et al.*, 1989). The better the statistical model predicts the relationship, the more convinced one is that a causal relationship exists. This confirmatory approach does not necessarily reveal the truthfulness of the causal model in reality, but only the extent to which a hypothesized model can be nullified. In any case, an alternative model with more carefully specified causal paths or study variables can help reduce the residual error and search for additional sources of error (Bullock *et al.*, 1994; Szeinbach *et al.*, 1995).

An experiment or new program initiative can involve a single intervention or multiple interventions. The outcome of the experiment or the assessment of the program performance can likewise be measured by either a single (or aggregate) outcome indicator or a set of correlated outcome indicators. Following the specification of intervention and outcome measures, the nature of their relation in the population of interest, appropriate statistical methods are selected to analyze program performance.

Selecting a Statistical Test

The hypothesis guides in the selection of a statistical test. Assuming that a sample or samples have been drawn randomly or have been assigned to a group by a random process, the factors that should be taken into consideration when selecting a statistical test are: (1) number of independent and dependent variables; (2) level of measurement of the independent variable; (3) level of measurement of the dependent variable; (4) number of samples studied; (5) the distribution of the units of measurement in the independent and dependent variables (normal or nonnormal); (6) time frame of measurement (once or repeated over time); and (7) number and type of variables used to control for confounding.

Since the reader is assumed to have a basic understanding of biostatistics, this author only refers herein to the more advanced statistical approaches (Table 4.3). With the ready availability of high-process capability personal computers, computerized databases of health care information, and statistical software packages, the use of these tests becomes the norm in evaluating any health care service, program, or system. Selected tests are described below and their applications are illustrated in Chapter 6 (binary logistic regression model, time series, and proportional hazards model) and Chapter 10 (meta-analysis) where they are commonly applied in management decision making. Structural equation modeling and multilevel analysis are considered in this chapter.

A **logistic regression model** is used when the dependent variable is a nominal or binary level of measurement and the independent variables (risk factors of interventions) are continuous and nominal level or ordered variables. Since the dependent variable is a discrete variable (e.g., the probability of being hospitalized in a specified period), the predicted probability should lie in between 0 and 1. Logistic regression is preferable to ordinary least squares (OLS), because OLS estimates are biased and yield predicted values that are not between 0 and 1. The

Table 4.3. Statistical Methods for Analyzing Program, Organization, or System Performance by Study Design and Outcome

Number of independent variables (design)	Number of dependent variables measuring performance outcome	
	Single outcome (level of measurement)	Multiple outcomes
Single intervention or exposure group (true experiment or quasi-experimental design)	• Ordinary least squares linear regression analysis (continuous) • Logistic regression model (dichotomous or ordinal) • Proportional hazards model (dichotomous)	• Linear structural relations (LISREL) model • Meta-analysis
Multiple interventions or exposure groups (factorial design or quasi-experimental design)	• Repeated measures multiple analysis of variance (continuous) • Single or multiple time-series analysis (continuous) • Proportional hazards model (dichotomous) • Meta-analysis (dichotomous or continuous)	• LISREL model

logistic model can be expressed in two ways. The logistic model can be expressed in terms of the log odds ratio (the ratio of two individual odds) for a given outcome (e.g., improved population health) relative to some number (n) of independent variables (x) with a coefficient of βi and a model intercept of α:

Log odds ratio (OR) = log [prob(event)/prob(no event)] = log $(P/1-P)$ = lx = α + $\beta_i x_n$ where P is the probability of an event under study.

The logistic model also can be expressed in terms of the probability of an event (e.g., the probability of an adverse outcome). If $P(x)$ is the probability of an event occurring, then:

$$P(x) = e^{\alpha + \beta i}/1 + e^{\alpha + \beta i}$$

which also is the same as

$$P(x) = 1/[1 + e^{-(\alpha + \beta x)}]$$

When the probability is relatively small, $P(x)$ is roughly equivalent to eβx. When there is more than one independent variable in the model, the method is referred to as *multiple logistic regression analysis*. If there are multiple independent ($\beta_i X_i$) variables in a model, their values are modified, that is controlled for, by the presence of the other. Ordinal logistic regression is utilized when the outcome variable represents an ordering, such as degree of patient satisfaction or pain level (Bender and Grouven, 1997). Statistical software packages are available for binary, polytomous, and ordinal logistic regression (PROC LOGISTIC in SAS, 1995; MULTINOMIAL LOGISTIC in SPSS Version 10). Refer to Chapter 6 for an application of this statistical technique and to the recommended text on this technique by Hosmer and Lemeshow (1989).

Structural equation modeling (SEM) is used in evaluating the performance of health care organizations when multiple outcomes (e.g., the surgical complication rate, medication error rate, treatment problem rate, and so on of a particular hospital) in relationship to an exposure are expected. The basic idea behind SEM is that linear relationships among variables are represented as path diagrams and path coefficients. Associated and causal paths on the diagram are traced according to predefined rules. This method aids in sorting out relationships when there is a moderate number of variables to study but is not recommended when the number of variables is large. Sometimes these outcome variables are correlated with each other. In that case, use of a multivariate statistical technique is required to examine the effect of an intervention on multiple outcome variables, with or without correlated measurement errors or residuals (unexplained variances for the study equations). The outcome variables are treated as endogenous variables, and the intervention variable is treated as an exogenous variable. In addition, confounding or control variables can be included in the model specification so that the net effect of an exogenous variable on the endogenous variable(s) can be ascertained when the effects of extraneous factors are simultaneously controlled.

The analysis of linear structural (causal) relationships (LISREL) among quantitative outcome variables is useful in data analysis and theory construction. The LISREL model has two parts (Jöreskog and Sörbom, 1979; Long, 1983a,b; Bollen, 1989). One is the measurement model, which specifies how the latent variables or theoretical constructs (e.g., adverse patient outcomes) are measured by observable indicators (e.g., medication error rate, complication rate, patient fall rate, etc.). The other is the structural equation model, which represents the causal relationships among the exogenous and endogenous variables. Path analysis, a form of structural equation model, presents a graphic picture of the functional relationships between the exogenous variables (Xs) and the endogenous variables (Ys). All variables are measured at the interval level without measurement errors. The exogenous variables are assumed to be independent with no association. The effects of Xs on Y are additive and linear. For example, health services use (measured by the number of physician visits) is treated as an endogenous variable when health status (X_1), age (X_2), and family income (X_3) are the predictor or exogenous variables. Y_1 regresses on X_1, X_2, and X_3 and generates standardized regression coefficients (path coefficients). These coefficients are interpreted as the net effects of one predictor variable on Y_1 when the effects of other predictor variables are simultaneously considered. The relative importance of the predictor variables explaining the variation in Y_1 can be determined by the magnitude of the coefficients; 1 minus R_2, the residual term, in Y_1 computes the unexplained variance, the total variance unexplained by the predictor variables in the equation.

LISREL's structural equation model is like the path-analytic model in three aspects: (1) model construction, (2) parameter estimation of the model, and (3) testing the fit of the model to the data by comparing observed correlations with predicted correlations among the study variables (Jöreskog, 1977). However, the LISREL model differs from the path analytical model in three useful ways. First, it is less restrictive than the path-analytic model (Mulaik, 1987; Al-Haider and Wan, 1991). For instance, it allows the investigator to ask direct questions about the data, in the form of different restrictions on the coefficients. Second, LISREL can easily handle errors in measurement, correlated errors and residuals, and reciprocal causation (Y_1 affects Y_2 and Y_2 also affects Y_1). Last, LISREL's advanced procedures can specify, compare, and evaluate the impact of an intervention on a set of correlated outcome variables (Bollen, 1989; Jöreskog, 1977, 1993).

It is growing increasingly important to consider the relationship among different outcomes (Wan, 1992; Wan et al., 1998). For example, the beneficial effects of home care services on improved physical, mental, and social functioning outcomes of geriatric patients. Failure to recognize the concomitant effects of the intervention can lead to inappropriate conclusions about program effects. The use of structural equation modeling techniques (such as LISREL) not only allows assessment of the effects of the intervention on multiple outcome (endogenous) variables, but also of the net effect of the intervention variable when the effects of other extraneous factors are simultaneously controlled.

A variety of epidemiological statistical techniques are appropriate in longitudinal program evaluations. Structural equation modeling techniques can be applied to longitudinal (cohort) data. Because this technique analyzes the relationships between endogenous (outcome) variables, one can examine the relationships between those variable across time as well. For example, structural equation modeling can control for other factors when assessing how interventions affect behavioral changes (Short and Hennessy, 1994). Campbell *et al.* (1986) compares multivariate analysis of variance and structural equation modeling in greater detail. Statistical software packages facilitate analysis when using the structural equation approach (PROC CALIS in SAS, LISREL in SPSS, AMOS through SmallWaters Corp., LISREL through SSI Products, Mplus, and STREAMS).

An example of the determinants of health care outcomes of patients for coronary artery bypass procedures evaluated using the LISREL method is presented in Fig. 4.2. Sahin *et al.* (1999) examined the self-report health status (e.g., SF- 36) that was measured by indicators of physical functioning, role limitations due to physical health problems, bodily pain, general health, vitality, social functioning, role limitation due to emotional problems, and mental health functioning at preoperative and postoperative periods.

Multilevel Analysis

With the wealth of computerized epidemiological information available to health care managers now, one must be careful to define what the unit of measurement is. Is the patient the unit of observation? Is the organization the unit of observation? Is the community the unit of observation? When statistical analysis includes both individual-level and macro-level data, this is referred to as multilevel analysis. Multilevel analysis has the advantage of explaining health outcomes that are more consistent with social theory than are conventional analyses. For example, we know that individual risk factors are influenced by contextual factors (e.g., social, physical, economic environments) and heretofore have typically eliminated these from the analyses. Thus, a greater understanding of the macro-level factors should allow us to develop more effective interventions, particularly when those contextual factors significantly influence health outcomes.

The challenge in performing multilevel analysis is organizing the data. Data sets may be organized through various levels of aggregation in epidemiological or organizational research. For example, in a study of nursing unit performance, patients' perceptions of care quality can be aggregated to reflect the mean level of patient satisfaction across all patients of a hospital regardless of unit or the patient responses can be aggregated to the unit level and then the means of the units can be compared across all hospital units. The data set that comprises individual patient characteristics, organizational unit, and hospital-contextual variables constitutes multilevel data. When multilevel data are used in a study, researchers tend either to disintegrate the aggregated data to the lower level (e.g., nursing unit), i.e., assign the value of aggregated data to the lower level, or to aggregate the lower level data to the upper (e.g., hospital) level, i.e., use the mean or median of the lower level to compromise the need of the upper level. From the methodological viewpoint, the former cannot satisfy the assumption of the independence of observations that underlies the traditional statistical approach (Bryk and Raudenbush, 1992; Duncan *et al.*, 1998). Another problem posed by disaggregating is that statistical tests involving the variable at the upper-level unit are based on the total number of

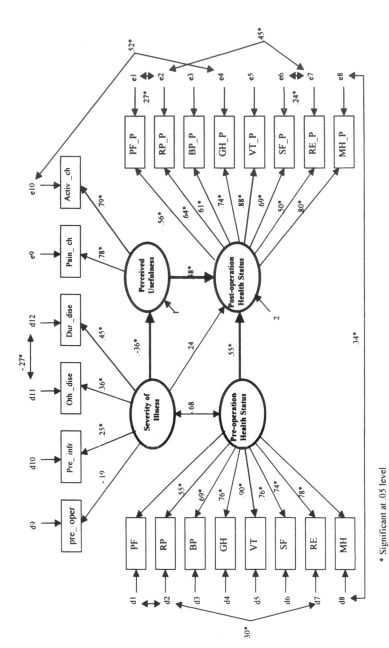

Figure 4.2. Structural equation model of the determinants of coronary artery bypass (CAB) outcomes.

* Significant at .05 level

lower-level units, which can influence estimates of the standard errors and the associated statistical inference (Bryk and Raudenbush, 1992; Hoffman, 1997). The aggregation may lose valuable information, in that the meaningful lower level variance in the outcome measure is ignored due to the process of aggregation (Hoffman, 1997). Aggregation also may cause the "ecological fallacy," i.e., analyzing upper-level data but interpreting the result at the lower level. In fact, most data are hierarchical; for example, individuals are nested in families, families are part of communities, and communities are nested in counties and/or states. The hierarchical nature of data should not be neglected in either theory building or data analysis (Muthén, 1991, 1994; Phillips *et al.*, 1998).

Multilevel analysis is frequently used when contextual and/or ecological variables are involved in the investigation of individual differences. It can be used to identify contextual effects and to derive accurate estimates of individual-level effects on an outcome variable (Morgenstern, 1998; Heck and Thomas, 2000). The multilevel model is an important step to tease out the net effect of each individual-level predictor variable on an outcome variable when the effects of ecological predictors, other individual-level predictors, and their interaction terms are simultaneously being considered. A special feature of multilevel modeling is using intercept and slope as outcomes (Bryk and Raudenbush, 1992), as illustrated in the following example: Home care$_{ig}$ = B_{0g} + B_{1g} (comorbidity) + r_{ig}. Home care of ith patient in the gth county is influenced by the comorbidity, where comorbidity is expressed as the difference between the number of comorbidities for an individual in the gth and the average number of comorbidities of that county ($x_{ig} - \bar{x}_{.g}$). B_{0g} is the expected utilization for a patient with value of zero on the predictor, i.e., no comorbidity; B_{1g} is the comorbidity slope for county g, and r_{ig} is the error term. It is believed that county-level variables of home care resources (W_g) have impacts on the utilization of home care through the intercept and slope, which are illustrated as follows:

$$B_{0g} = r_{00} + r_{01} (W_g) + U_{0g}, \text{ and}$$
$$B_{1g} = r_{10} + r_{11} (W_g) + U_{1g}$$

where r_{00} is the mean of home care use for a community that lacks adequate home care resources, i.e., a patient lives in a poor county; r_{01} is the difference in communities with varying levels of home care resources; r_{10} is the average comorbidity slope for communities with different levels of home care resources; r_{11} is the average difference in comorbidity slope between different communities; U_{0g} is the unique effect of county g on average home care use given the level of home care resources available; U_{1g} is the unique effect of county g on the comorbidity slope conditioned on home care resources.

After substituting intercept and slope by corresponding elements in the latter two equations, we obtain the following for the original equation:

$$\text{Home care}_{ig} = r_{00} + r_{01} (W_g) + r_{10} (x_{ig} - x_{.g}) +$$
$$r_{11} (W_g(x_{ig} - \bar{x}_{.g})) + U_{1g} (x_{ig} - \bar{x}_{.g}) + U_{0g} + r_{ig}$$

When analyzing two or more levels of information, consideration must be given to the selection of a statistical test that accommodates the different levels of data. Two-stage linear or logistic regression methods (illustrated above) as well as SEM are common statistical methods for multilevel analysis of population-based data (Bryk and Raudenbush, 1992; Kaplan and Elliot, 1997; Wong and Mason, 1985).

Evaluating Causality

Causality is said to be established whenever the occurrence of one event is reason enough to expect the production of another. The first step in the determination of causality is to consider only those relationships that are statistically significant. Next, the removal of the confounding influences of variables extraneous to the causal pathway is a critical requirement for causal inference. A confounding variable is a factor that is associated with both the exposure and the outcome. Removal of confounding involves holding the variables constant or varying them systematically so their effects can be phased out from a study or compared to other conditions. Specifically, confounding may be removed by active manipulation of subjects or conditions, restricting the study eligibility criteria (control of confounding by design), or performing stratified or multivariate statistical analyses.

In experimental study designs, control of confounding usually refers to applying the intervention across levels of a variable such as hospital teaching status or age group of patients. Control also may be achieved through study design by deliberately setting criteria to exclude certain observations. An example of initiating control by design would be a health care manager interested in studying the effect of quality improvement initiatives on neonatal mortality in urban hospitals should remove all rural hospitals the population from which the study data are being compiled. However, studies limited to certain values of a confounding variable may not be generalized to other values, e.g., studies conducted on hospitals may not be generalized to nursing homes.

Once statistical association has been established and confounding has been addressed, the context of the relationship must be examined. This can be done through either qualitative or quantitative means (e.g., meta-analysis). Approaches to assessing causality through qualitative criteria have been proposed by several individuals (Hill, 1965; Susser, 1991; Rothman and Greenland, 1998). Causal assessment using a qualitative approach is summarized:

1. *Causal Ordering*: The presumption that one exposure or event causes another requires that the first event or exposure (X_4) produce an expectation for the occurrence of the final event or outcome (X_5). The variables should refer to time points that span intervals known to be consistent with the latency or incubation period and direction for the outcome to occur (see Fig. 4.3).

2. *Statistical Probability*: A precursor factor $(X_1, X_2,$ or $X_3)$ may or may not show any statistical significance in its relevance to the occurrence of X_4 in reality. A priori hypotheses are subject to empirical tests so the presence of statistical significance is the basis for nullifying the hypotheses in question.

3. *Strength of the Association*: The stronger the statistically significant correlation or association between the two variables, the more it supports a causal link between them. The association of itself, no matter how strong, does not necessarily imply causality. Strength can be assessed using an odds ratio, relative risk, rate ratio, correlation coefficient, beta value, or r-squared value.

4. *Specificity*: The specificity of an association entails a description of the precision with which the occurrence of one specific causal factor to the exclusion of other factors will predict the occurrence of an effect (Rothman and Greenland, 1998). The linear model assumes a unidirectional cause–effect relationship. However, in reality, in health care the problems do not always match the conventional wisdom and variables are often related in reciprocal causation (see Fig. 4.4). For example, inpatient care services use (Y_1) and outpatient care services use (Y_2) are two factors that are influenced by a selected group of predictor variables that include perceived health status (X_1), age (X_2), and social class (X_3). Reciprocal causal links

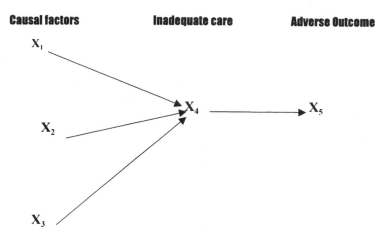

Figure 4.3. Conceptualization of causal ordering for an adverse outcome.

or paths can be determined between the two endogenous variables such that the increase in inpatient care is affected by the increase in outpatient care used by patients, or vice versa.

5. *Consistency of the Relationship*: Repeated results under the same constraints using different study designs and in different populations can aid in assessing the existence of the relationship between the exposure factors and the outcomes.

6. *Coherence*: The substantive meaningfulness of the cause–effect relationship must be theoretically based and corroborated with existing knowledge (Bullock *et al.*, 1994). Statistically determining the fit of the model (that the distribution of the observed variables is that is what is predicted by a multivariate model) may be biased for different reasons, such as a biased

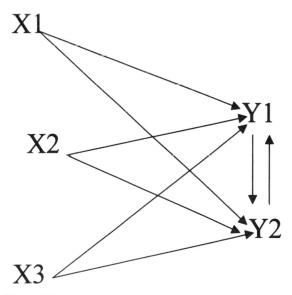

Figure 4.4. Mutual causation or reciprocal causal paths.

sample, small sample size, homogeneity of the study population, and so forth. Thus, the meaningfulness of the postulated causal relationships must be supported by a coherent logic and interpretation. For instance, in explaining the coronary artery bypass (CAB) patients' outcomes in the study by Sahin *et al.* (1999), they found that the procedure helped patients gain better functioning abilities in all eight dimensions of the SF-36 measure of health status. This result shows that the intervention effect is positive and also coherent.

7. *Prediction*: If the occurrence of a specific outcome or effect can be predicted with great certainty when a direct causal factor is present, that implies that the causal model has a predictive power in reality. Predictability is an important ingredient of causal inference (Rothman and Greenland, 1998). For example, the CAB procedure has contributed to the improved health and functional status of patients. This conclusion was drawn for the analysis of the net effect of CAB patients' postoperative health status when the effect of preoperative health status and other personal factors were simultaneously considered. The statistical control of confounding or biased factors is essential in the development of predictable, causal model.

8. *Simulation*: Modeling strategies vary by the types of data and designs. One can utilize data mining techniques to simulate the model so that optimal solutions can be obtained. Most of regression techniques are parametric; they require the users to specify the functional form of the statistical solution. If the underlying form of the statistical function is not known, as is very often observed in health care research, neural networks or other simulation techniques can be employed to capture functional, fussy, structural, and probabilistic relationships among the study variables.

Meta-analysis

Meta-analysis is an analytical strategy for combining the results of many studies as a means of attempting to assess causality between a particular intervention or technology and selected outcomes of interest. Meta-analysis is used to summarize the effect size (intervention effect) in terms of a summary measure (e.g., mean, proportion) of specific health outcomes and the strength of the summary measure and to determine whether that effect size is consistent across all studies examined (heterogeneity) (Takkouche *et al.*, 1999). If it is properly used, meta-analysis can strengthen causal interpretations of nonexperimental data (Chalmers, 1988; Greenland, 1994). The current knowledge management approach stresses the use of data warehousing and data-mining strategies to organize a database for meta-analysis by simulating analytical results (Liebowitz, 1999). Results from meta-analysis can help to confirm or refute a theoretical model that implies a causal linkage between exogenous and endogenous latent variables. However, the results from meta-analysis are retrospective and viewed with the same caution as cross-sectional and case-control studies. Also, nonsignificant findings may be excluded from publication or inclusion in the meta-analysis. The application of meta-analysis is discussed in Chapter 10 (this volume).

Conclusions

This chapter is written to identify and explain the fundamental principles in conducting causal analysis in health services management. Epidemiological study designs and methods are reviewed and illustrated as the orientation of health care managers is increasingly focused on population-based concerns. The application of the scientific thinking, and hence a knowledge management approach to health service problems, can guide the development and implementation of solution sets (i.e., interventions). The principal criteria of causality and their application in the conduct of causal analysis are central to developing scientific, evidence-based knowledge for navigating organizational changes (Keats and Hitt, 1988) and innovations (Scott and Bruce, 1994).

The causal approach advocated here does not imply that employing explicit and practical knowledge in organizational sciences can solve every managerial problem. However, causal analysis and its application can make it possible to search more efficiently for errors that may be amenable to organizational and behavioral interventions. The health care manager thinking causally will recognize that multiple pathways, intermediate factors, the measures used and the multiple levels of effect that risk factors have along the pathway affect the differences in outcomes observed.

Case Studies

Case Study No. 1
Applying the Scientific Method to Develop a Strategy
for Assessing HMO Performance in Preventive Practice

While more and more of the population required or encouraged to enroll in capitated health care plans, consumers are faced with making choices among HMO's with little or no data to guide them in plan selection. Now, data collected from the National Committee for Quality Assurance (NCQA) have been used to rank HMOs' preventive performance in immunization, prenatal care, mammography, Pap smear testing, and cholesterol testing.

A preventive score for each HMO was calculated by summing the deviation points from the national goal for all five areas, and if the deviation was higher than the national goal, the HMO received a positive point and vice versa. Information about the HMO's physicians, enrollment size, accreditation status, the type of practice model, and service market area characteristics was obtained from the survey conducted by the Inter-Study and the Area Resources File in the United States A model of practice performance of HMOs was formulated using the practice score and the market share as endogenous variables, and six organizational, market, and community health characteristics as exogenous variables. The definitions of the variables are presented as follows:

PREV-S	Total prevention score
IMMUNI	Percent elderly immunized
MAMMO	Percent women 21+ years receiving mammography
PAP	Percent women 21+ years receiving Pap smear test
CHOLES	Percent adults receiving cholesterol test
ACCRED	NCQA accreditation status (yes = 1; no, unknown = 0)
%BD-PCP	Percent primary care physicians
%BD-SPEC	Percent specialists
%TURN	Percent physician turnover each year
ENROLL	Total number of enrollees in specific geographic area
NHMO	Number of HMOs in the market area
GROW	Percent growth of the HMO in numbers
MORT	Adjusted mortality rate in the market area
SHARE	Percent HMO enrollees served by a given HMO in the market area
OPEN	Type of HMO (open physician panel = 1; else = 0)

Health care managers of capitated health plans are responsible for monitoring the practice performance of their plans and for identifying factors that influence the variation in preventive services among by different market and organizational characteristics of HMOs. This case study is designed to identify organizational and community factors that affect the variation in HMOs' preventive practice.

Q.1. Construct a conceptual model of a hypothesized causal relationship among the study variables, specifically those factors that influence performance of a plan with respect to preventive services.

Q.2. Propose a null hypothesis for this conceptual relationship.

Q.3. What statistical test would you select to determine if a causal relationship exists between the variables you specified in Q.1 and HMO performance for preventive services? Give the reasons why you selected this statistical test.

Q.4. How would you determine what factors from your statistical test influence an HMO's performance for preventive services?

Case Study No. 2
Optimizing the Assessment of Health Outcomes

The 36-item, Short-Form Health Survey (SF-36) was developed by Dr. John Ware and his medical outcomes study (MOS) colleagues to provide generic measures of health status and outcomes from the patient's point of view. Such generic measures are not specific to age, disease, or treatment and are useful

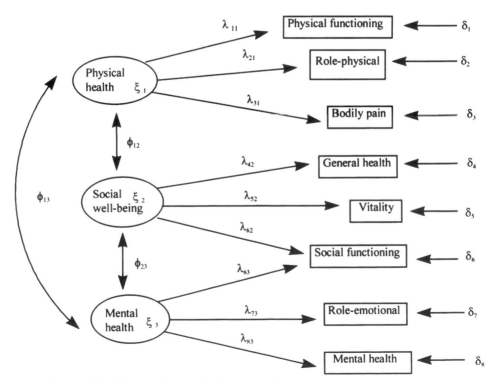

Figure 4.5.   The generic model of the three-factor measurement model of SF-36.

for assessing general health system or organizational performance. The SF-36 is practical because it is shorter than many other such surveys and can be self-administered. By constructing scales from more efficient items, the SF-36 attempts to reduce the burden on the respondent without bringing measurement precision below the critical level. The SF-36 has been used in various health care settings with different patient groups, including among those who have diabetes, undergo rehabilitative care, or require outpatient dialysis. The SF-36 measures nine health concepts: (1) general health perceptions (general health); (2) health transition; (3) limitations on physical activities because of health problems (physical functioning); (4) limitations on usual role activities because of physical health problems (role–physical); (5) limitations on usual role activities because of emotional problems (role–emotional); (6) limitations on social activities because of physical or emotional problems (social functioning); (7) bodily pain; (8) psychological distress or well-being (mental health); and (9) energy and fatigue (vitality) (Fig. 4.5). Scales are scored using Likert's method of summated ratings, which assumes that the distributions of responses to items within the same scale and item variances are roughly equal. Each item is also assumed to have a substantial linear relationship with the score for its scale, that is, item internal consistency. The use of each item to score only one scale assumes substantial item discriminant validity, that is, each item clearly measures one health concept more than other health concepts. When these assumptions are well satisfied, items in the same scale can be scored without standardization and can be simply summed. Results from SF-36 tests of scaling assumptions strongly support the use of summated ratings to compute SF-36 subscales. The SF-36 subscales are scored so that a higher score indicates a better health state. Transforming each raw scale score to a 0 to 100 scale is strongly recommended. Estimates of score reliability for eight SF-36 subscales (internal consistency reliability, test–retest reliability, or alternate-form reliability) have been reported in 15 studies. All the estimates show high reliability, ranging from 0.6 to 0.96. Physical functioning tends to have the highest internal consistency reliability, probably due to the fact that more items are used to measure physical functioning. It is not known how well aggregated indices measured by SF-36 represent certain major health concepts in terms of the construct validity of the sub-indices (Hays *et al.*, 1994).

Q.1. Discuss how you would choose to test the validity of an aggregate index of SF-36, that is, the validity of a three factor measurement model of the health indicators that constitute the generic core of the health status measurement as presented in Figure 4.5. Search the literature and identify studies that attempt to accomplish this. Critique these studies using the questions from Table 4.2 as your guide.

Q.2. Do an online search of the literature and find studies that compare the SF-36 to its even shorter version, the SF-12.

Case Study No. 3
Organizational Determinants of Patient Satisfaction

Patient satisfaction can be measured at both patient and organizational-unit levels. This case study is designed to identify organizational factors or nursing unit characteristics that affect the variation in patient satisfaction, using structural equation modeling. Patient satisfaction is an endogenous latent construct that can be reflected by numerous individual indicators of patient satisfaction considering interpersonal and technical aspects of quality of care on the nursing units as well as the physical environment (Boles and Wan, 1992). Information about the nursing unit characteristics and patient satisfaction typically is determined from the survey of patients after their hospital experience.

Q.1. Propose a hypothesis to solve the management problem of "How can the patient satisfaction level be improved in the hospital system?"

Q.2. What is the unit of your analysis and why?

Q.3. Gather and critique other studies of patient satisfaction with hospital care. What are the pros and cons from the literature on the use of a composite or aggregate index to reflect the construct—patient satisfaction—versus using individual indicators of satisfaction?

Q.4. What does the literature indicate are the key organizational characteristics that may influence the variation in patient satisfaction? Critique this literature.

Case Study No. 4
Identification of Motor Vehicle-Related Risk Factors for Accidents in Almaty, Kazakhstan

Motor vehicle accidents rank the second highest of all causes of deaths in Kazakhstan. Much higher mortality rates due to motor vehicle accidents was observed in urban than rural areas. No systematic information is available to identify the causes and effects of motor vehicle related deaths. In formulating a national strategy for prevention of motor vehicle accidents, it is imperative to gather epidemiological information about the accidents and deaths. You are asked by the US Agency for International Development to develop a project to tackle the causes and effects of motor vehicle deaths in Almaty, with a total population of 1.2 million.

Q.1. How would you identify the agent, host, and environmental etiological factors in motor vehicle accidents? [HINT: See also Chapter 11.]

Q.2. How would you determine what are the causal (etiologic or risk factors) involved in motor vehicle accidents in this city?

Q.3. After you identify the risk factors, how do you go about designing and implementing an evaluation of preventive intervention? [HINT: Use the process of scientific inquiry.]

Case Study No. 5
Developing a Conceptual Framework for Community-Based Violence Prevention

Research on intimate partner violence is extensive and has identified numerous individual, household, and societal factors. Most of the research has focused on individual level characteristics such as marital status, substance abuse, marital discord, education, and income. There is increasing evidence that community variables, such as crime rate and unemployment rate, also may be strong predictors. Cunradi et al. (2000) sought to investigate the relationship of neighborhood poverty and intimate partner violence among heterosexual white, black, and Hispanic couples in the United States. The strategy in evaluating the relationship was to use existing (secondary) data.

Q.1. Draw a conceptual model of the relationships studied.

Q.2. Propose a hypothesis to test.

Q.3. What secondary sources of data could be used to test this hypothesis?

Q.4. What statistical approach would be appropriate for testing this hypothesis?

References

Al-Haider, A. S., and Wan, T. T. H., 1991, Modeling organizational determinants of hospital mortality, *Health Services Res.* **26:**303–323.

Bender, R., and Grouven, U., 1997, Ordinal logistic regression in medical research, *J. R. College Physicians Lond.* **31:**546–551.

Boles, R., and Wan, T. T. H., 1992, Longitudinal analysis of patient satisfaction among Medicare beneficiaries in different HMOs and fee-for-service care, *Health Serv. Manage. Res.* **5:**198–206.

Bollen, K. A., 1989, *Structural Equations With Latent Variables*, John Wiley & Sons, New York.

Bollen, K. A., 2000, Modeling strategies: In search of the holy grail, *Structural Equation Modeling* **7:**74–81.

Bryk, A. S., and Raudenbush, S. W., 1992, *Hierarchical Linear Models*, Sage Publications, Newbury Park, CA.

Bullock, H. E., Harlow, L. L., and Mulaik, S. A., 1994, Causation issues in SEM research, *Structural Equation Modeling* **1:**253–267.

Campbell, R. T., Mutran, E., and Parker, R. N., 1986, Longitudinal design and longitudinal analysis, *Res. Aging* **8:**480–502.

Chalmers, T. C., 1988, *Data Analysis for Clinical Medicine*, International University Press, New York.

Cunradi, C. B., Caetano, R., Clark, C., and Schafer, J., 2000, Neighborhood poverty as a predictor of intimate partner violence among white, black, and Hispanic couples in the United States: A multilevel analysis, *Ann. Epidemiol.* **19:**297–308.

Duncan, T. E., Alpert, A., and Duncan, S. C., 1998, Multilevel covariance structure analysis of sibling antisocial behavior, *Structure Equation Modeling* **5:**211–228.

Greenland, S., 1994, Invited commentary: A critical look at some popular meta-analytic methods, *Am. J. Epidemiol.* **140:**290–296.

Hays, R. D., Marchall, G. N., Yu, E., Wang, I., and Sherbourne, C. D., 1994, Four year crosslagged associations between physical and mental health in the medical outcomes study, *J. Consult. Clin. Psychol.* **62:**441–449.

Heck, R. H., and Thomas, S. L., 2000, *An Introduction to Multilevel Modeling Techniques*, Lawrence Erlbaum Associates Publishers, Mahwah, NJ.

Hill, A. B., 1965, The environment and disease: Association or causation? *Proc. R. Soc. Med.* **58:**295–300.

Hoffman, D. A., 1997, An overview of the logic and rationale of hierarchical linear models, *J. Management* **23:**723–744.

Hosmer, D. W., Jr., and Lemeshow, S., 1989, *Applied Logistic Regression*, John Wiley & Sons, New York.

Howard, G., Anderson, R. T., Russell, G., Howard, V. J., and Burke, G., 2000, Race, socioeconomic status, and cause-specific mortality, *Ann. Epidemiol.* **10:**214–223.

Jöreskog, K. G., 1977, Structural equation models in the social sciences: Specification, estimation and testing, in *Applications of Statistics* (P. R. Krishnaiah, ed.), pp. 265–287, North-Holland Publishing, Amsterdam.

Jöreskog, K. G., 1993, Testing structural equation models, in *Testing Structural Equation Models* (K. A. Bollen and J. S. Long, eds.), pp. 294–316, Sage Publications, Newbury Park, CA.

Jöreskog, K. G., and Sörbom, D., 1979, *Advances in Factor Analysis and Structural Equation Models*, ABT Books, Cambridge, MA.

Kaplan, D., and Elliott, P. R., 1997, A didactic example of multilevel structural equation modeling applicable to the study of organizations, *Structural Equation Modeling* **4:**1–24.

Keats, B. W., and Hitt, M., 1988, A causal model of linkages among environmental dimensions, macro-organizational characteristics, and performance, *Acad. Manage. J.* **31:**570–598.

Liebowitz, J. (ed.), 1999, *Knowledge Management: Handbook*, CRC Press, New York.

Long, J. S., 1983a, *Confirmatory Factor Analysis*, Sage Publications, Beverly Hills, CA.

Long, J. S., 1983b, *Covariance Structure Models: An Introduction to LISREL*, Sage Publications, Beverly Hills, CA.

Morgenstern, H., 1988, Ecologic studies, in *Modern Epidemiology* K. J. Rothman and S. Greenland, eds., pp. 459–480, Lippincott Williams and Wilkins, Chestnut Hill, MA.

Mulaik, S. A., 1987, Toward a conception of causality applicable to experimentation and causal modeling, *Child Dev.* **58:**18–32.

Mulaik, S. A., James, L. R., Van Alstine, J., Bennett, N., Lind, S., and Stilwell, C. D., 1989, Evaluation of goodness-of-fit indices for structural equation models, *Psychol. Bull.* **105:**430–445.

Muthén, B. O., 1991, Multilevel factor analysis of class and student achievement components, *J. Educ. Measure.* **28:**338–354.

Muthén, B. O., 1994, Multilevel covariance structure analysis, *Sociol. Res. Meth. Res.* **22:**376–399.

Phillips, K. A., Morrison, K. R., Anderson, R., and Aday, L. A., 1998, Understanding the context of healthcare utilization: Assessing environmental and provider-related variables in the behavioral model of utilization, *Health Ser. Res.* **33:**571–596.

Rothman, K. J., and Greenland, S., 1998, Causation and causal inference, in *Modern Epidemiology* (K. J. Rothman and S. Greenland, eds.), pp. 7–28, Lippincott Raven, Philadelphia.

Sahin, I., Wan, T. T. H., and Sahin, B., 1999, The determinants of CABG patients' outcomes, *Health Care Manage. Sci.* **2:**215–222.

SAS Institute Inc., 1995 Logistic regression examples using the SAS® system, version 6, first edition, SAS Institute, Cary, NC.

Scott, S. G. and Bruce, R. A., 1994, Determinants of innovative behavior, *Acad. Manage. J.* **37:**580–607.

Short, L. M., and Hennessy, M., 1994, Using structural equations to estimate effects of behavioral interventions, *Structural Equation Modeling* **1:**68–81.

SPSS, Inc., 1999, *SPSS Advanced Models™ 10.0*, Chicago, Illinois.

Susser, M., 1991, What is a cause and how do we know one? A grammar for pragmatic epidemiology, *Am. J. Epidemiol.* **133:**635–648.

Szeinbach, S. L., Barnes, J. H., and Summers, K. H., 1995, Comparison of a behavioral model of physicians' drug product choice decision with pharmacists'; product choice recommendations: A study of the choice for the treatment of panic disorder, *Structural Equation Modeling* **2:**232–245.

Takkouche, B., Cadarso-Sqarez, C., and Spiegelman, D., 1999, Evaluation of old and new tests of heterogeneity in epidemiologic meta analysis, *Am. J. Epidemiol.* **150:**206– 215.

Wan, T. T. H., 1992, Hospital variations in adverse patient outcomes, *Qual. Assurance Utilization Rev.* **7:**50– 53.

Wan, T. T. H., 1995, *Analysis and Evaluation of Health Systems: An Integrated Approach to Managerial Decision Making*, Health Professions Press, Baltimore, MD.

Wan, T. T. H., Pai, C. W., and Wan, G. J., 1998, Organizational and market determinants of HMOs' performance in preventive practice, *J. Healthcare Qual.* **20:**14–129.

Wong, G. Y., and Mason, W. M., 1985, The hierarchical logistic regression model for multilevel analysis, *J. Am. Stat. Assoc.* **80:**513–524.

5

Strategic Planning

An Essential Management Tool for Health Care Organizations and Its Epidemiological Basis

Frances J. Jaeger

Organizations charged with the delivery of health services exist in an environment in which no single organization can isolate itself from the change that surrounds it. Strategic planning offers organizations a tool for analyzing the impact of changing trends and environmental conditions. It equips health care managers with a systematic process for setting future direction, developing effective strategies, and ensuring that the organization's structure and systems are compatible with long-term survival and success. Through the use of strategic planning, organizations learn to think and to act strategically, thereby making better judgments about the future and becoming more proactive in shaping it.

Epidemiological Basis of Strategic Planning

To influence health positively by anticipating and responding to changes in needs and health status among populations targeted for service is the epidemiological basis of strategic planning for health care organizations. Typically, such organizations exist to deliver a service or set of related services in response to the health needs of defined populations. Thus, an appropriate measure of the effectiveness of health care organizations is the extent that they attain through service delivery specific outcomes that improve the health status of those served.

Over time, the characteristics and the health needs of populations change. Consequently, health care organizations (as well as larger health systems) must employ a process, such as strategic planning, to maintain awareness of demographic changes and altered disease patterns. Otherwise, they risk obsolescence by responding to old and irrelevant sets of health needs and service demands.

Frances J. Jaeger   University of Illinois at Chicago Perinatal Center, Chicago, Illinois 60612.

Epidemiology and the Delivery of Health Care Services: Methods and Applications, Second Edition, edited by Denise M. Oleske. Kluwer Academic/Plenum Publishers, New York, 2001.

The size of a population is considered the most useful predictor of future needs and the utilization of health services (MacStravic, 1984). As a population increases or decreases in size, the demand for health services generally varies in the same direction. Thus, a country experiencing significant population growth will require expansion of its health system and mobilization of additional resources to satisfy health needs.

Other demographic variables, including age, race, ethnicity, gender, family structure, education, and income, affect population transformations that also alter needs and demand for health care (see "Epidemiological Model of Health Care Delivery" in Chapter 1, this volume). Figure 5.1 illustrates the decrease in total fertility rates (or rates based on the expected number of children a woman would bear at the prevailing age-specific fertility rates) that all regions of the world have experienced during recent decades. In many countries, declining birth rates have decreased family size and led to stabilization in the size of younger age cohorts. In addition, populations are being characterized as "graying" due to longer life expectancies and substantial growth in the number of elderly persons compared to other age segments. The global phenomenon of aging will cause the world's median age to increase from 26 years in 1998 to a projected 32 years in 2025 (McDevitt, 1999).

Figure 5.2 represents the growth in the elderly population of the United States. As the post-World War II "baby boomers" reach 65 (around 2011), the country will experience a comparable "senior boom." If current life expectancy and fertility trends continue, those 65 and over will constitute one fifth of the population in 2030 and their absolute number will be more than double the number in 1990 (Day, 1996).

Other countries of the world are experiencing similar growth in their aged populations. In an article prepared for the Spring 1998 issue of *CommonHealth* (which was devoted to the new era of aging), Kinsella and Velkoff (1998) made the following comment:

> The graying of the population has been well-publicized in the industrialized nations of Western Europe and North America.... Not as well appreciated is the fact that most countries of Central and Eastern Europe and the former Soviet Union are also well into the process of demographic aging. This region is home to 7 percent of the world's population, but accounts for 12 percent of the world's elderly (defined here as persons age 65 and over). (p. 7)

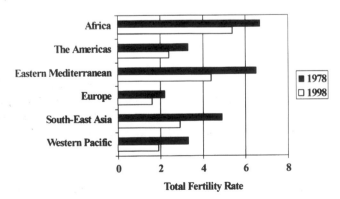

Figure 5.1. Declines in fertility by WHO region, 1978–1998. SOURCE: United Nations Population Division (1999).

Number in millions

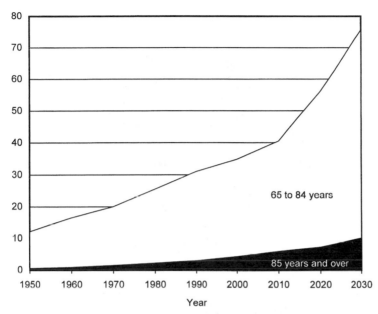

Figure 5.2. Population 65 years of age and over, United States, 1950–2030. SOURCES: National Center for Health Statistics (1999) and Day (1996).

Age trends associated with defined populations can be summarized visually by population pyramids, which utilize stacked bars to represent age and gender distribution. Pyramids can be constructed to reflect either actual counts of persons in each age-gender subgroup or the percentages that result when the number of persons in each group is divided by the total number of persons in the population at a specific time. When bars of a pyramid represent percentages, the total pyramid must equal 100%. The population pyramids found in Fig. 5.3 were presented in *The World Health Report 1999* (World Health Organization, 1999) to provide an example of population transformation over time. The US Bureau of the Census maintains an international data base and a visit to its web site can result in generation of similar pyramids (with a recent year contrasted with future years) for almost any country in the world.

As the absolute numbers and the relative size of age categories change, the characterization of disease within a population and the impact of illness are altered as well. In countries with substantially more people growing older and experiencing lives into the 70s and beyond, heart disease, cancer, and stroke are now the most common causes of illness and the leading causes of death. Even in developing regions, the high rates of disability and death from malnutrition and infectious diseases are being surpassed by chronic diseases (World Health Organization, 1999). The prevalence as well as severity of these diseases influence the types and quantity of services required to meet health needs. For example, the prevalence of hypertension in women 70 and over is nearly 40 per 100 (Kramarow *et al.*, 1999). Since hypertension is likely to be managed in an ambulatory care setting, this means that among 100 elderly patients who present themselves for outpatient care, 40 will require treatment for hypertension. However, the entire group could benefit from periodic screening to ensure that

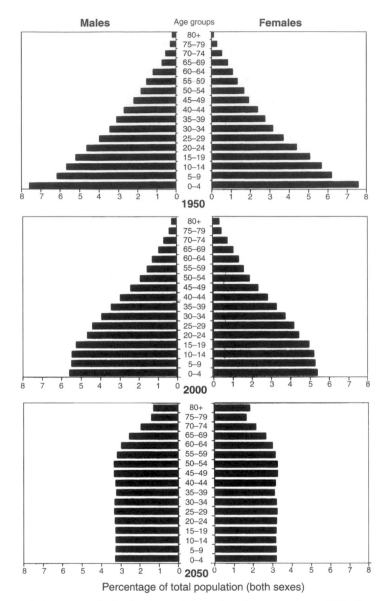

Figure 5.3. Population pyramids for Southeast Asia region, by age and sex, 1950, 2000, and 2050. SOURCE: United Nations Population Division (1999). Reprinted from *The World Health Report 1999: Making a Difference* (World Health Organization, 1999), with permission.

the disease is diagnosed and effectively controlled once found. Figure 5.4 provides data on the magnitude of limitations in physical activity in the elderly. Over 20% of women age 70 years and older are unable to perform at least one physical activity such as climbing stairs; by age 85 years, this increases to 52.5%. These epidemiological data illustrate that as populations age, an increasing number of its members will require assistance. The demand for physical rehabilitation, restorative, and community support services is likely to increase, even in developing

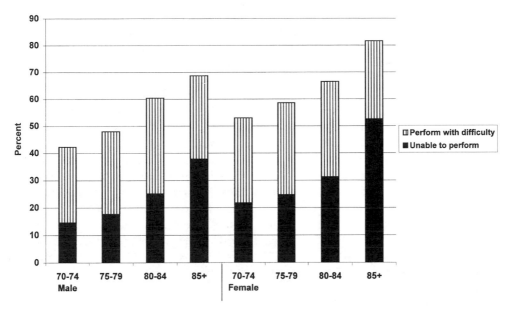

Figure 5.4. Percent of persons 70 years of age and over who have difficulty performing one or more physical activities, by gender, United States, 1995. SOURCE: National Center for Health Statistics (1999).

nations. Further, chronic diseases and conditions will predictably consume a growing portion of health care resources unless more population-based health promotion and prevention initiatives (e.g., encouraging calcium and vitamin D supplementation) are undertaken by health plans and government agencies.

As the diseases affecting the world's populations have changed as well as the populations themselves and their environment, the "disability-adjusted life year" (DALY) increasingly is being used as a measure to prioritize health needs in strategic planning (World Bank, 1993; Murray and Lopez, eds., 1996; World Health Organization, 1999; see also Chapter 3, this volume). Use of DALYs has served to highlight not only the growing significance of noncommunicable diseases but also the increasing contribution of injuries (both intentional and nonintentional) and neuropsychiatric conditions to the disease burden of both high and lower income groups (World Health Organization, 1999). Whereas the World Health Organization (1999) estimated that noncommunicable diseases accounted for 43% of the global disease burden in 1998, it projects that noncommunicable diseases will represent 73% of the disease burden by 2020. This prediction is based on the following assumptions: continued aging of the world's population, extension of the recent downward trend in overall mortality, and augmentation of the number of people exposed to risk factors such as tobacco use, obesity, physical inactivity, and heavy alcohol consumption. In the world-to-be, disorders such as depression, alcoholism, drug dependence, and psychoses will afflict growing numbers and increase the need for mental health services. Reversing the trend related to rising injuries will require identification of underlying causes and initiation of preventive measures.

In the 1980s and continuing into the 1990s, countries in Western Europe and North America focused attention on the new killer diseases and achieved notable declines in death rates for several leading causes of death, including heart disease and stroke. However, just as progress was being made in the control of major chronic illness, the world was confronted with

a new communicable disease—acquired immune deficiency syndrome (AIDS). First identified in the early 1980s, AIDS, which results from infection with the human immunodeficiency
virus (HIV), spread so rapidly that it soon reached epidemic proportions. Initially, AIDS was
considered a uniformly fatal disease despite the long interval frequently occurring between
initial infection and serious disease state. Although AIDS still deserves the characterization of
a deadly disease, individuals testing positive for HIV may benefit from new drug regimens that
discourage or postpone the onset of full-blown AIDS. Thus, this relatively new disease is
taking on characteristics of a chronic disease, at least in parts of the world where affected
individuals have access to effective treatments. In countries like England and the United
States, planning for the delivery of care to AIDS patients has shifted away from acute care
settings. Emphasis now is being placed on long-term maintenance in the community, outpatient medical services, and alternative and supportive therapies to improve the quality of life
for people living with the disease. Unfortunately, more than 95% of all HIV-infected people
live in the developing world, and AIDS is canceling otherwise expected increases in life
expectancy, especially in sub-Saharan African countries that have 10% and more of their populations infected (UNAIDS/WHO, 1998a). Thus, the consensus among world governments is
that increased attention must be given to prevention to impede the terrible consequences of this
disease.

Epidemiological methods identify the variables that are associated with patterns of health
problems, the need for care, and the utilization of services. What people do at work and during
leisure hours, the level of attention given to good nutrition and exercise, and personal lifestyle
behaviors can result in lesser or greater risks to health. Socioeconomic factors influence both
disease patterns and the ability to access services to ameliorate health problems. Biological,
hereditary, and genetic factors account for some differences in health status, and at least some
countries of the world are beginning to gain competence in controlling and altering the effects
of these factors. Changing beliefs, values, perceptions of health status, and consumer expectations influence service utilization and judgments about the adequacy of available services.

An organization once effective in addressing traditional health problems may be un-
prepared to tackle the challenges that arise when a population is transformed or when new
disease patterns emerge. Strategic planning is not the sole ingredient for success among health
care organizations, but failure is almost guaranteed without an appropriate response to the
demographic and epidemiological changes that affect health care needs and demands.

Theoretical Basis of Strategic Planning

Barry (1986) defines strategic planning as a process directed at finding the "fit" between
the mission, purpose, and goals of an organization, the forces external to the organization
(including the needs of the target population, competitors and allies, and social, political,
economic, and technological forces), and the internal resources and capabilities under the
organization's control. In the present age of "health care reform," an organization defining its
mission as delivery of health care must be cognizant of altered health needs as well as
changing organizational requirements that may be imposed from outside the organization.
Payers, for example, may elect to do business only with providers organized into a health care
alliance or community care network.

In the past, closed-system models were common among the theories proposed to explain
organizational behavior. The classical works of Taylor (1947) and Weber (1964) presented
closed-system views that were based on the assumption that the internal structures and
processes of an organization are its most important features. More recently, the analysis of

organizations has moved toward an open-systems approach that recognizes the importance of the interface or optimum fit between an organization and its environment (Starkweather and Cook, 1983). According to open systems theory, organizations are not self-contained units. They must relate to elements in their environments to acquire resources for organizational maintenance and for production of outputs associated with goals. They must also interact with their environments for disbursement of goods and services once these are produced. Shortell and Kaluzny (1983, 1994) provide a discussion of open- and closed-system concepts and argue that both organizational constructs are needed to understand and manage health service organizations.

Once it was realized that an organization's ability to thrive could be affected by other organizations in its environment, studies were initiated to test numerous hypotheses related to organizational success and interorganizational relationships. These studies led to the development of the tenets of exchange theory, which is the foundation of marketing. According to Day (1984), marketing is the primary means by which an organization looks outward and aligns itself with its environment. It is a tool for selecting customers to be served and competitors to be challenged and it is a means for managing the exchange of valued resources among organizations.

Marketing is associated with the *voluntary* exchange of resources, and this implies that organizations exercise choice in marketing relationships. Organizations can generally select the parties and sometimes the values to be involved in transactions, but they must interact with other organizations if they are truly open systems. They cannot afford to direct all their energies to issues of internal control. An external orientation is critical to survival because the interconnections or resource dependencies that exist among organizations require them to replenish their resources by relinquishing the products or services they generate with the resources controlled by others (Pfeffer and Salancik, 1978). Health care organizations, which are designed primarily for the delivery of services rather than goods, nevertheless can benefit from the practice of good marketing, which is simply the effective management of the exchange process associated with providing services to selected beneficiaries and obtaining the resources for continued operations.

Strategic planning is generally considered essential for effective marketing because it facilitates an organization's understanding of its present and probable future environments and empowers the decisions associated with exchange interactions. An organization that successfully integrates strategic planning and marketing into its managerial functions will take advantage of environmental situations that improve relationships with other organizations, thereby satisfying its resource needs and strengthening its capabilities for achieving goals and objectives associated with its mission.

The strategic planning process requires the application of epidemiology to ensure that planning is market based—that is, responsive to the needs, demands, and wants of targeted populations or the markets to be served. The use of epidemiology within the context of strategic planning has been limited in the past for two reasons. First, the market areas of health care organizations have been difficult to define because of problems in identifying the populations at risk who require specific health services and competing interests among providers. For example, a physician may staff more than one hospital or multiple hospitals may provide the same service to the same geographic area or to areas that partially overlap. Second, disease and health status data have typically been reported only for large geographic areas or for civil units. With advances in small-area analysis (see Chapter 7) and automated management information systems that offer improved efficiency and expanded storage capabilities, it is possible to gain an increased level of confidence when constructing the probable future market of a health care organization based on epidemiological analysis.

Organizational theory and the principles related to the behavior of organizations in their environments provide the conceptual framework for strategic planning. Ideally, when an organization finds itself in a hostile environment or poorly aligned with opportunities as a result of changes in technology, unfavorable political circumstances, changing consumer needs and expectations, or any number of reasons, the organization will adjust its objectives and strategies accordingly. Unfortunately, this ideal scenario is not the reality for many health care organizations. Adjustments may be difficult because of inflexible organizational structures (which fail to alter personnel resources and relationships consistent with changing requirements), outdated management systems (or systems for information, planning, and control that are no longer workable under new conditions), or a general paralysis or inability to respond quickly enough when confronted with an accelerating rate of change. However, deliberative and conscientious application of the strategic planning process can minimize time lags between the recognition of changed environmental forces and the initiation of action to alter the organization's objectives, strategies, structure, and management systems (Kotler and Clarke, 1987). Additionally, when an organization realizes a need to identify new markets or otherwise redefine the population to be served, epidemiology can provide a framework for compiling and analyzing data for consideration during the strategic planning process.

The Strategic Planning Process

Strategic planning is a systematic process that involves a series designed to define a situation or problem, develop strategies, and implement solutions. The process may be represented as six major steps formatted around a circle to suggest that strategic planning is a cyclical and continuous process (Fig. 5.5). The steps and related tasks of this process are discussed below.

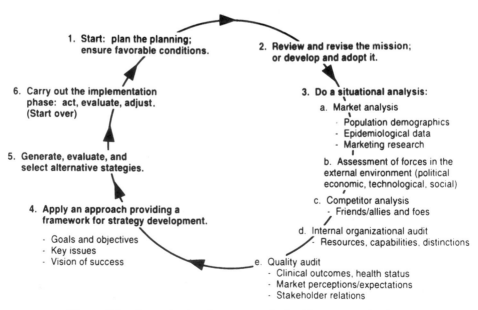

Figure 5.5. Strategic planning process for health care organizations.

Step 1. Plan the Planning and Ensure Favorable Conditions for Effective Strategic Planning

There are certain conditions that are necessary for an organization to think and act strategically: a strategic orientation or ability to recognize the influence of the external environment and to sense significant changes in that environment; a commitment from top-level management to participate in the process and to implement the resulting recommendations; allocation of sufficient resources to carry out the process, including time and technical expertise (such as that required for market research and interpretation of data); consensus on the plan for planning with agreement on how planning participants will be selected, the timetable for initiation and completion of various phases of the process, the approaches and techniques to be employed, and the anticipated benefits or outcomes associated with the effort; and absence of barriers that could prevent completion of the process or interfere with strategic action. When the prerequisites for effective strategic planning are missing, the energy of the organization should be directed at establishing the necessary conditions before initiating the process.

Step 2. Review the Organization's Mission Statement and Revise It as Necessary to Ensure That It Remains Relevant to the Organization's Future. If No Written Statement of Mission Exists, Develop and Adopt One

Consideration of the organization's mission should occur early in the planning process because it is the mission that captures an organization's reason for being and defines its domain (or the territory in which the organization conducts its business). Later in the planning process (when an organization develops a better appreciation of its situation and unique capabilities), it may be necessary to refine the original mission statement or even replace it with one that is judged to be more appropriate for the present as well as the future.

The elements that Bryson (1988) recommends for inclusion in a well-defined mission statement, adapted for a health care organization, are presented in Table 5.1. Organizations that deliver health care should delineate the markets or populations that are targeted for service as well as the specific needs that will be addressed. Markets may be determined by geography or legal mandate, or other considerations (such as severity of need or purchasing power) may affect the selection and definition of the organization's customers.

Table 5.1. Key Elements of a Mission Statement[a]

- Identification of the organization
- Specification of the population targeted for service (and the basis for selecting this "market," e.g., geography, disease category, other)
- The health-related needs or problems the organization intends to address
- In general terminology, what the organization will do to respond to specified needs or problems of the population targeted for service
- How the organization will relate to key stakeholders and the values to be promoted in stakeholder relationships
- An indication of the organization's philosophy and values
- Features that distinguish the organization

---

[a]Adapted from Bryson (1988).

Step 3. Do a Situational Analysis that Encompasses Assessments of Elements of the Organization's External and Internal Environments as Well as an Evaluation of the Impact of the Organization's Efforts

This step encompasses the core set of analytic activities that distinguish strategic planning from other types of planning. The five tasks associated with a situational analysis are a market analysis, an assessment of forces in the external environment, a competitive analysis, an internal organizational audit, and a quality audit. Demographic and epidemiologic data are crucial to this step.

Task A: Market Analysis

A market analysis is a planning task initiated for the purpose of defining and characterizing the market and its health care needs and preferences. The term *market* usually refers to the constituency (of individuals, groups, or other organizations) that the focal organization actually serves or desires to serve through involvement in exchange transactions. A market analysis is essential for ensuring that health care organizations employ an approach for planning and delivering services that is market-based, that is, truly responsive to the needs and wants of current and prospective patients or customers. This market is what may be referred to in classical epidemiological terms as the population at risk that a provider organization targets for the delivery of health care services.

To characterize both the current and future market, the analysis should include assessment of the number of individuals constituting the actual or potential market; the numbers by sex and age associated with its subgroups (or market segments); fertility patterns and the life-cycle stage of the market; income, employment, and educational levels; racial, ethnic, and cultural characteristics; and the anticipated changes in the population over time. Data from a census can be used for determining the numbers of persons in each of these market segments.

Relative to a defined market and within the context of strategic planning, epidemiology presents a conceptual framework and tools for describing the frequency of health problems in targeted populations. For organizations designed to serve market segments (such as specific diagnostic groups), epidemiological methods can be used to provide estimates of the number of individuals currently affected by certain diseases and to project patterns of disease over time to facilitate a match between future needs and service availability. Table 5.2 illustrates an example of how epidemiology can be used to estimate the level of use of a diagnostic procedure.

In planning services to address health problems using an epidemiological framework, Baker and Reinke (1988) state the following questions should be answered: What is the magnitude of the problem? What trends are evident? What populations and population subgroups are affected by the problem? In order to address these questions, health status data may be presented for the market population of interest to the service provider. Data may consist of population data related to health status and its determinants (e.g., the number and percentage of the population living below the poverty level or depending on public assistance, the proportion of pregnant women without a source of prenatal care, the percentage of unmarried mothers, vaccination levels of children); data that help to describe the intensity of a problem, such as incidence, mortality, and prevalence rates (of disease and of exposure); data for other rates, such as those related to fertility; and the results of epidemiological studies pertinent to risk factors (person-related, lifestyle, or environmental). These data may be cross-tabulated based on selected demographic variables and contrasted with one or more sets of

Table 5.2. Estimating Inpatient Cardiac Catheterization Volume for Columbia, SC
(Metropolitan Statistical Area)

Age group (a)	Number of persons[a] (b)	Rate of cardiac catheterization procedures in short-stay hospitals[b] (c)	Number expected to be hospitalized annually (d = b × c)
< 15	97,641	2.2 per 10,000	21
15–44	244,592	6.9 per 10,000	169
45–64	97,641	81.8 per 10,000	799
65+	48,333	166.7 per 10,000	806
Total	488,207	36.8 per 10,000	1,795

[a]Source for total population (1996): US Bureau of the Census (Internet release date: December 1997); source for population distribution by age: Table B-2, US Bureau of the Census (1998).
[b]Lawrence and Hall (1999).

national, state, or local data. Such comparisons enable an understanding of differences in the distribution of diseases and determinants and they provide guidance for development of actions. For a health care organization to address health needs, it is essential to perform a market analysis utilizing epidemiological data.

The determination of appropriate measures of health status and the selection of formats for the presentation of data are among the most difficult tasks of a health planner charged with facilitating strategic planning. Crude death rates are easy to calculate and may suffice for purposes of a market analysis. However, when differences in needs among population segments are of concern, then specific rates may be preferred. When the rates of two or more populations are compared, it is usual to age-adjust rates in order to distinguish differences that result from better or poorer health from those that can be attributed to differences in the age composition of the groups (see Chapter 3 on how adjusted rates are computed).

Data on morbidity and disability may be obtained from a variety of sources. In the United States, the National Center for Health Statistics is the principal governmental agency that generates vital and health statistics. On an annual basis, the center publishes *Health, United States*, a report summarizing the nation's health status. The National Center also conducts special surveys (such as the *National Health Interview Survey*, the *National Nursing Home Survey*, and the *National Ambulatory Care Survey*) that yield data on acute and chronic conditions and utilization of health services. Almost all reports of the National Center for Health Statistics are now placed on the worldwide web, thus allowing widespread access.

For more than a decade, the United States has established national objectives for disease prevention and health promotion under what is now known as the Healthy People Initiative. Consequently, several reports that track progress in meeting objectives have been issued in recent years. Additional examples of references and data sources useful for strategic health planning can be found in Table 5.7 as well as in the appendix, "Websites for Health Care Managers Thinking Epidemiologically."

Sources of international health data are becoming more and more numerous, although reliability of data varies and data elements may not be comparable from country to country. Population census reports, birth and death registration systems, disease reporting and surveillance programs, and epidemiological studies represent the primary sources for population and health-related data. The World Health Organization Statistical Information System (WHOSIS) has a web site with links to health ministries and statistical offices as well as other sources of health information. On a yearly basis, the World Health Organization releases (and enables access on its web site) *The World Health Report*, which generally discusses important health topics in chapter format and includes a statistical annex with a comprehensive set of demographic and health-related data for regions and countries of the world. The United Nations is another source of relevant data and it has a web site with links to the statistical offices of many countries. The US Bureau of the Census maintains the *International Data Base*, a computerized data bank containing demographic and socioeconomic data for 227 countries and areas of the world. The *International Health Data Reference Guide, 1997* (National Center for Health Statistics, 1998) provides information on the availability of selected national vital, hospital, health manpower resources, and population-based health survey statistics for 44 nations. The worldwide web can be a valuable resource for those engaging in strategic planning as can health ministries and private and public agencies having a mission related to improving health status.

Market analysis facilitates assessment of psychographic variables of the targeted population such as values, attitudes, and belief systems that affect need, the perception of need, and the actual utilization of health services. Marketing also can identify the most favorable conditions for ensuring that exchanges occur and that mutually beneficial results are realized by the parties participating in exchange transactions—that the right clients or patients receive the right services, in a timely manner and in the right places, and that the organizations delivering the services are offered appropriate values in return.

Although many health care organizations define the market to be served on the basis of history and tradition (that is, the market remains the same population that was selected for service from the organization's very beginning), it is important to realize that an organization may find its chances of survival improved by a redefinition of its market: by expanding the traditional delineation, by selecting only specified segments or subsets of the market as originally defined, by turning to an entirely new market, or by applying these strategies in any of a number of combinations. A market audit thus may include the assessment of the various scenarios and consequences of altering the organization's current market. Will a change increase or decrease the types and level of resources available to an organization? What new needs must be addressed if the organization attempts to serve a new market? Which of several potential markets has the greatest needs, would generate the highest level of demand for a given service, or return the greatest benefit if selected for a new venture? These and other questions may require consideration to ensure that an organization and the market it elects to serve receive mutual benefit from the relationship so that it can be sustained over time.

Task B: Assessment of Forces in the External Environment

An assessment of external trends and forces is necessary to achieve a clear understanding of the opportunities and threats inherent in the present as well as the future environment of the organization. The assessment should consider factors that affect patterns of disease and disability, the health needs of the population or markets to be served, the actual expression of needs into service demand, and the capabilities of the organization to respond.

Bryson (1988) has used the acronym PEST to refer to the political, economic, social and technical forces in the external environment. Use of this device may serve as a memory aid, but the external trends and forces should not simply be considered nuisances (or pests). The challenge of strategic planning is to think strategically, and thus to design strategies that interface with these forces and trends so that they represent opportunities, not annoyances or threats.

Task C: Competitive Analysis

A competitive analysis assesses an organization's position in the marketplace relative to other organizations, some of which may compete for the same customers or valued resources or otherwise interfere with an organization's ability to serve its selected markets. Porter (1980, 1985) argues that an organization should analyze key forces that shape its industry and identify strategic options for gaining competitive advantage through modification of variables under its control. If an organization performs a competitive analysis and judges itself weak in comparison to its competition, then it should seek strategies to improve its position. If the organization is already positioned well, a situational analysis can strengthen awareness of the elements of the organization's advantage and increase the probability of sustaining it.

Health systems worldwide are becoming more complex in their structures and more pluralistic every day. For example, hospitals in the United States began experiencing a decline in admissions in the early 1980s, but the US health system continued to expand due to an "explosion" of demand for outpatient care and the growth of long-term care (American Hospital Association, 1991). Table 5.3 indicates that between 1977 and 1997, the number of nonfederal short-term hospitals declined by 12.2%. Admissions decreased by 8.0% and average stay by nearly 20.0%, resulting in a 26.2% decline in patient-days (hospital admissions multiplied by the stay in days). However, outpatient visits more than doubled during the same period (Health Forum, 1999). Many different types of providers now function in a variety of settings under numerous organizational arrangements. In response to increasing competition, many health delivery organizations have become engaged in aggressive pursuit of competitive strategies to improve market share. In today's climate, competitive analysis must do more than identify competitors; it also must find those who could be allies or potential collaborators. Thus, joint ventures, mergers, and partnerships are among the cooperative relationships that could represent suitable strategies for ensuring the adequacy of resources for organizational maintenance and effectiveness. Coddington and Moore (1987) include a discussion of several noncompetitive strategies (e.g., physician bonding, networking, and development of multihospital systems) that should be evaluated as options for attaining competitive advantage.

Complexity and diversity are not characteristics unique to the US system of health care. *The World Health Report 1999* states: "Most countries have no single health system, but several distinct health financing and provision sub-systems, embracing different types of traditional or alternative practice, as well as public, private and not-for-profit hospitals and clinics" (World Health Organization, 1999, p. 31). The same report identifies the primary goals

Table 5.3. Changing Patterns of Health Utilization, United States, 1977–1997[a]

Year	Hospitals (nonfederal/short-term)	Beds (in thousands)	Admissions (in thousands)	Average stay (days)	Outpatient visits (in thousands)
1977	5,973	974	34,353	7.6	204,238
1980	5,904	992	36,198	7.6	206,752
1985	5,784	1,003	33,501	7.1	222,773
1990	5,420	929	31,203	7.3	302,691
1995	5,220	874	30,966	6.5	415,710
1997	5,082	855	31,595	6.1	450,907

[a]From Health Forum (1999).

of most health systems as: "improving health status; reducing health inequalities; enhancing responsiveness to legitimate expectations; increasing efficiency; protecting individuals, families and communities from financial loss; enhancing fairness in the financing and delivery of health care" (World Health Organization, 1999, p. 31). Thus, an important question relevant for comparing health systems competing within the same market area or the dominant system of one country compared to another is: "How well does each health system under study perform against these goals?"

Task D: Internal Organizational Audit

An internal organizational audit is an assessment of the resources under an organization's control (or in the case of a health system, available for application to the system's mission). It encompasses current and projected staff resources and capabilities, financial assets and sources of reimbursement, facilities and equipment, planning and decision-making systems, and market assets (such as a favorable reputation in the community and good public relations). The purpose of this type of audit is to develop an understanding of the strengths and weaknesses of the organization so that it will balance what is needed and wanted by its markets against what it can feasibly do to respond to such needs and wants (Kotler and Clarke, 1987).

Since health care is a personnel-intensive field, it can be affected significantly by changes in the quantity and quality of the human resource pool that is prepared and available to deliver services. Ratios of major categories of health personnel to a specified population are useful indicators for assessing availability. Table 5.4 provides an example of such ratios for US registered nurses to the country's population. Although the table indicates increasing ratios over past years, ratios are expected to decline in future years. This is because enrollments in nursing educational programs have been declining in the past few years; consequently, the production system will not be able to fully replace members of the current pool as they reach retirement age. A 1999 publication of the Bureau of Health Professions, *United States Health Workforce Personnel Factbook*, presents a compilation of data on students and practitioners in the health professions, and the web site of this Bureau is a source of other data useful for planning purposes.

Few countries in the world have as many categories of health personnel as the United States, but the challenge for all countries is the same: to ensure an adequate supply of appropriately prepared personnel to assign to the tasks essential for improving and maintaining health. An assessment of ratios alone is inadequate for determining the adequacy of human

Table 5.4. Ratio of Registered Nurses to the US Population, 1970–1996[a]

Year	Ratio per 100,000 population
1970	366
1975	449
1980	555
1985	640
1990	710
1995	798
1996	808

[a]From Bureau of Health Professions (1999).

resources. Personnel requirements change over time and are influenced by such factors as changing needs and demands, structural changes in the health system, and changing productivity levels due to use of supportive personnel and technological advances (Baker, 1988). Therefore, the current and projected supply of any personnel category must be compared to the requirements for that category based on a model that incorporates multiple factors for determination of need. This comparison is called "gap analysis," and it results in the quantification of deficits or surpluses based on a comparison of the actual or projected supply against numbers representing current or anticipated requirements.

Table 5.5 represents a macrolevel resource analysis which projects the primary care practitioner requirements for the United States in year 2005 based on 1995 provider levels. In 1994, the Bureau of Health Professions (BHP) succeeded in organizing a joint workgroup of representatives from the Council on Graduate Medical Education (COGME) and the National Advisory Council on Nurse Education and Practice (NACNEP). The workgroup provided input into development of a computerized model, known as the integrated requirements model (IRM). The model was used to estimate requirements for physicians, physician assistants, nurse practitioners, and certified nurse midwives under six scenarios associated with assumptions about insurance coverage, managed care penetration, and use of nonphysician providers. Findings from the six illustrative analyses for 1995 through 2020 were published in the *Report on Primary Care Workforce Projections, Council on Graduate Medical Education and National Advisory Council on Nurse Education and Practice, December 1995* (Council on Graduate Medical Education and National Advisory Council on Nurse Education and Practice, 1996). The simulation model has been made available to promote integrated planning. It allows a user to forecast requirements under an unlimited number of scenarios by varying model input and parameters. The web site of the BHP's National Center for Health Workforce Information and Analysis (as updated December 1, 1999) states that the site will have an interactive demonstration of the IRM in 2000 and that an expanded IRM model is being developed to predict future need for both physician and nonphysician providers in 18 specialties.

Restructuring and changing roles among personnel are not unique features of the US health care system, and many countries are currently examining the assumptions related to educating and training personnel to meet health care needs. For example, many new independent states (NIS) of the former Soviet Union are engaged in partnership programs sponsored by the American International Health Alliance and the US Agency for International Develop-

Table 5.5. Changes in Practitioner Requirements Compared to 1995 Levels According to the Six Illustrative Projection Scenarios[a]

Provider	Status quo	Baseline insurance	High managed care	Universal coverage	Equal access under universal coverage	High NP/PA/ CNM use
Physicians	10.4%	11.5%	12.1%	20.3%	22.7%	−2.2%
Physician assistants	11.4%	15.1%	20.6%	30.7%	33.3%	130.0%
Nurse practitioners	12.3%	15.4%	19.2%	21.2%	23.6%	130.4%
Certified nurse midwives	1.8%	−0.3%	−1.4%	9.5%	11.7%	99.3%

[a]From Council on Graduate Medical Education and National Advisory Council on Nurse Education and Practice (1996).

ment. Partnerships between health care institutions in the United States and their NIS counterparts are designed to improve health care by creating more efficient and accountable delivery
systems and changing the focus of care to better meet primary health needs. Many NIS
countries have physician to population ratios considerably higher than many developed
countries. However, physicians were less adequately educated and trained (based on standards
of Western medicine) and most have been disbursed to specialty areas resulting in limited
resources for basic health care. Nurses were educated at barely a high school level and
generally did nothing more than carry out orders of physicians and perform tasks typically
assigned to dietary, housekeeping, and other supportive staff. Now, as medical schools
lengthen educational programs and institute policy reforms to strengthen primary care, nursing
is responding by preparing case managers and advanced practice nurses to be able to provide a
broader array of primary services. A recent publication of the American International Health
Alliance (1997a) discusses some of these changes and provides examples of nurses assuming
more responsibility in direct patient care, educational leadership, and management. Changes
in the NIS are being shaped for the most part through collaborative planning processes
sponsored by health ministries and involving educational leaders to ensure commitment to
implementation.

    Although national and regional manpower trends may have an impact on the capabilities
of a health care organization, the focus of an internal audit should be on resource variables that
are subject to change through alteration of organizational strategies. If an organization is
affected by constrained resources (personnel, financial, or otherwise) or resources that vary in
availability, it may be difficult to provide health services consistent with the needs of its
service population. The "resourceful" organization will recognize and evaluate several alternatives for adjusting to a troubling set of circumstances. Alternatives may include identifying
and employing new resources to accomplish essentially the same mission, defining a new
mission that can be accomplished with diminished resources, or determining how resources
can be used more efficiently to achieve an equal effect with fewer resources. Planning for
resource needs within an organization or on a larger scale requires similar attention to finding
solutions that are feasible within current resource limitations or practical through the manipulation of controllable variables.

Task E: Quality Audit

    A quality audit is an assessment of how well an organization (or a state or nation) is
meeting expectations. A quality audit should consider the objectives the organization has set
for itself (as reflected in its mission, goals, and objectives) as well as the expectations that
affect consumer judgment about quality. In addition, the audit should assess the ability of the
organization to satisfy the expectations of stakeholders or constituencies that have an interest
in or an influence on the organization (Table 5.6). The various reports issued by the US federal
government as well as some states to assess performance against Healthy People objectives
often have components of a quality audit performed at a macrolevel.

    Within the context of strategic planning, quality audits should address the traditional
elements of clinical outcomes (or effects that result from the application of medical science
and technology) and the processes of delivering care. However, it is not enough for a health
care organization to decrease mortality, morbidity, disability, pain, and discomfort in the
population served. It also must determine whether consumers are satisfied with the behavior of
caregivers and the attributes and conditions of service delivery (i.e., timeliness, price, convenience, and the attractiveness of surroundings). Based on findings of a quality audit, the

Table 5.6. Questions to Address in the Quality Audit Component of the Situational Analysis
(of the Strategic Planning Process)[a]

- What does quality mean to staff of the organization (at various levels) and to members of its governing or policymaking board? What does quality mean to those the organization seeks to serve?
- What gaps in service quality do consumers experience in the use of our services?
- Does the organization meet performance standards commonly utilized for measuring services like ours?
- Is there evidence that the organization is achieving objectives pertinent to improving the health status of the population (by decreasing morbidity, mortality, disability, pain or discomfort)?
- What does the organization need to achieve desirable clinical outcomes and meet the expectations of consumers as well as the expectations set by organizations which monitor quality in health care (such as the Joint Commission on Accreditation of Healthcare Organizations)?
- Does the organization have the capability to provide quality, and if not, what does it lack?
- What specific mechanisms (such as committee structures and approaches for monitoring satisfaction) should be implemented to ensure that the organization meets quality expectations?

[a]Adapted from: Baynham (1991).

organization should position itself to promote its positive image or implement modifications to improve patient–customer satisfaction. In addition, the organization should strive to maintain productive and beneficial relationships with organizations with the potential for greatest impact (positive or negative) due to control of certain values, either concrete resources or the ability to grant or withhold approval or recognition. Third-party payers and licensing and accrediting organizations are examples of such stakeholders. Since it generally is impossible to satisfy all stakeholders at once, it is important to concentrate on effective management of relationships with key stakeholders.

Step 4. Apply an Approach for Defining the Key Issues, Focusing the Attention of the Organization, and Establishing the Framework for the Next Step of Strategy Development

Generally, this step involves proposing and achieving consensus on goals and measurable objectives relating to an organization's desired future. A goal can be defined as a broad statement indicating general direction toward a desired future state. Objectives are more specific statements that indicate in measurable terms what is to be accomplished and when. Each objective should make a contribution toward achievement of a goal, but a single objective need not lead to full attainment of the goal. The situational analysis that precedes the formulation of goals should result in the generation of objectives that are meaningful and significant to the organization, realistic, sufficiently ambitious and yet attainable, consistent with the organization's responsibilities and authority, and compatible with its goals and values. When appropriate objectives are developed, they provide both a framework for designing strategies as well as one for measuring performance. Epidemiological data are used in the formulation of the goals and objectives as well as in the formulation of strategies. For example, the epidemiological catchment area study (discussed in Johnson et al., 1992) concluded that 23% of the population had depressive symptoms. Depressive symptoms are associated with high population-attributable risk percentages of emergency department use, medical consultations for emotional problems, and suicide attempts (Johnson et al., 1992). These data may prompt an organization to insure the inclusion of mental health services in its future plans.

Step 5. Generate, Evaluate, and Select Alternative Strategies for Achieving Organizational Goals and Objectives or the Best Alignment of the Organization with the Opportunities in Its Environment

Characteristic of any true planning process is the systematic generation of potential strategies, or the means to achieve a defined end. Depending on the planning approach utilized, the strategies also must be evaluated to assess their potential for achieving objectives, addressing strategic issues, or moving the organization toward its vision of success.

Bandrowski (1985, 1990) recommends that strategies be developed through the use of a sequential thought process and "creative planning" techniques. The first step in the thought process (which is comparable to the situational analysis discussed in step 3) is to gain an understanding of issues to be addressed, problems to be solved, or the future to be created. Next, an unconstrained thought process is employed for combining ideas and generating a sufficiently large number of potential strategies; this is to be done in a nonjudgmental manner to facilitate creative leaps in the design of new visions and innovations. Nutt (1984) provides a detailed description of useful creative thinking techniques, including brainstorming and synectics (or the combining of seemingly unrelated things), nominal groups, and Delphi surveys. Day (1984) elaborates five other approaches for generating creative strategy options: challenging present strategies, looking for strategic windows, playing on competitor's vulnerabilities, changing the rules of the competitive game, and enhancing customer value. Following the development of options, judgmental thinking should be utilized to narrow the field of potential strategies to those that can achieve the desired results and meet selection criteria such as technical and financial feasibility, acceptability to key decision makers, consistency with objectives, adaptability, and cost-effectiveness. The number of strategies to be selected generally depends on the level of resources available for application during the implementation phase. When resources are plentiful, multiple strategies may be selected. In the more usual scenario of scarce resources, a limited number of alternatives can be selected and some order of priority may be assigned.

Step 6. Carry Out the Implementation Phase of Strategic Planning, Detailing Operational Action Plans and Budgets, Monitoring Impact, and Making Midcourse Adjustments as Necessary

This step encompasses translating decisions about strategic directions into plans that specify the organization's programs, tactics for attracting customers and promoting the organization's products and services, and the application of resources to support implementation efforts. Generally, action plans contain a purpose or objective for each program (or set of related services), the steps or series of actions required to implement the program, a timetable, and identification of the individuals responsible for carrying out the actions. For complex organizations, strategic action plans may be developed for major programs or groupings of related services on a departmental basis or by functional areas. Budgets serve as a control and coordinating mechanism for integrating all aspects of strategy within available resources. Therefore, if implementation of the strategic plan requires organizational restructuring, modification of staff assignments, or redistribution of resources from one program or service to another, then these changes should be reflected in approved budgets.

Effective implementation requires a control system for monitoring organizational performance, assessing the impact of overall strategies and specific tactics, and providing feedback about adjustments that may be necessary to achieve desired outcomes. If specific and quantifiable objectives were delineated previously, then evaluation of effectiveness will focus on two questions:

1. Were the recommended tactics or actions carried out?
2. If yes, did they accomplish the stated objectives?

If an organization identified strategic issues or created a vision of success, then performance would be measured against key indicators of success. Epidemiological data can provide measures of that success and answer such questions as: "Did the health status of the population improve as a result of the strategic initiative?" Performance of a quality audit (discussed previously as a component of the situational analysis) is another means of determining if the organization improved its ability to deliver health services in a manner consistent with quality expectations.

Data Resources and Issues Related to Use in Strategic Planning

Each step of the planning process requires data. However, the analytical phase of the situational analysis (step 3) is especially dependent on the compilation of relevant and accurate data and the transmittal of information that will directly aid decision-makers (see Table 5.7 for examples of useful data resources). For many countries of the world, lack of data is not the primary challenge for the health planner. Rather, the planner may have to review a considerable amount of data and then select that most appropriate for the purpose of a specific planning task. A common problem for a planner or data user is determining whether data collected for a larger geographic area (such as a nation) is generalizable to a smaller area. The data user also must be cautious when attempting to apply findings from a study to a larger population beyond the study group. With the increasing ease of use of geographic information systems (GIS), health care managers thinking epidemiologically will be able to understand more fully the spatial properties of health care delivery systems and their accessibility (Moore and Carpenter, 1999). This technique will aid in bringing precision to the definition of population. In addition to these issues, a committee operating under the Institute of Medicine noted the following data issues in its final report: quality of data, limitations of self-reported data, validity and reliability, periodicity of data, and timeliness of data availability (Committee on Leading Health Indicators for Healthy People 2010, 1999). If such issues are ignored, there is the possibility that a planning process will result in erroneous conclusions and inappropriate strategies.

Tools to Facilitate Strategic Planning

Decisions stemming from strategic planning are appropriately influenced by facts, the subjective interpretation of factual data as well as the attitudes, preferences, values, and beliefs that are held by planning participants. Various tools and group techniques have been utilized to summarize important facts and to build consensus around key issues and preferred strategies. One tool that has been recommended for strategic planning is a SWOT analysis (or an assessment of *s*trengths, *w*eaknesses, *o*pportunities, and *t*hreats). A SWOT analysis combines the systematic analysis of an organization's internal strengths and weaknesses with the

Table 5.7. Examples of Useful References for Strategic Planning in Health Care

Source	Description
United States	
AHA Guide to the Health Care Field	Annual comprehensive directory that provides data on hospitals and other health-related providers (published by the American Hospital Association)
Area Resource File	Information system provided by the Health Resources and Services Administration (includes a county-specific database and contains data on health facilities and professions)
Census reports and current population estimates/ projections	Bureau of the Census (of the US Department of Commerce) reports on the decennial population and housing survey; sample surveys (Current Population Surveys) are conducted between decennial censuses; population estimates and projections are generated for counties
Health, United States	Annual report of the National Center for Health Statistics on the health status of the nation
Morbidity and Mortality Weekly Report	Data obtained by state disease surveillance systems and forwarded to the Center for Disease Control for weekly publication and compilation into an annual report
Sample surveys	National Health and Nutrition Examination Survey, National Health Interview Survey, National Home and Hospice Care Survey, National Hospital Discharge Survey, National Household Survey of Drug Abuse, National Nursing Home Survey, National Ambulatory Medical Care Survey, Youth Risk Behavior Survey, National Survey of Family Growth, Behavioral Risk Surveillance System (some of these surveys are periodic/some are ongoing)
Statistical Abstract of the United States	Annual publication of the Census Bureau with data for the nation, states, and metropolitan areas plus selected international data
TrendWatch	Health care marketing experts rate the importance and significance of trends affecting the health care industry in quarterly newsletters published by the Alliance for Healthcare Strategy and Marketing
Vital statistics	Data on births, deaths, marriages, divorces, and abortions collected by states and forwarded to the National Center for Health Statistics, which publishes yearly summary reports as well as monthly reports; states also may provide data
International Data	
Country studies	Library of Congress resource files for about 60 nations that can be accessed from the worldwide web
International Data Base	A computerized source of demographic and socioeconomic statistics for countries and areas of the world developed by the US Census Bureau's International Programs Center
WHOSIS	A world wide web site of the World Health Organization Statistical Information System provides direct or indirect access to various statistical databases compiled by WHO and has links to other health-related web sites
World Health Report	Annual report of the World Health Organization that provides demographic and health data for most countries of the world; this report also contains chapters that discuss and analyze important health topics

Table 5.7. (*Continued*)

Source	Description
World Population Profile: 1998	Report prepared by the International Programs Center within the Bureau of the Census that provides demographic data and projections for countries and regions of the world (also includes discussion of HIV/AIDS in developing countries)
World wide web site of the United Nations/Economic Commission for Europe, Statistical Division	World wide web site that has links to international statistical agencies of member countries as well as links to other sites providing demographic and health-related data

externally oriented assessment of the opportunities and threats in the environment (Bryson, 1988). The same type of systematic analysis has been recommended (and named by various acronyms) by others who propose that such an analysis is a prerequisite for an organization to undertake conscientious action to improve its alignment with new opportunities in the environment.

Figures 5.6 and 5.7 provide examples of worksheets that can be utilized for purposes of obtaining input for a SWOT analysis. They are designed as tools to stimulate discussion among members of a planning group. Additional examples of tools that can be used during the strategic planning process can be found in the growing body of literature on this subject (Barry, 1986; Kotler and Clarke, 1987; Spiegel and Hyman, 1991).

Applicability of the Strategic Planning Process

In the past, the strategic planning process was most often applied within a single organization. However, the techniques and steps of the process can be utilized across organizational boundaries to identify and address the health care needs of health systems, communities, regions, states, or nations. To help promote an accurate picture of the AIDS problem as well as an appropriate response, the Joint United Nations Programme on HIV/AIDS (UNAIDS) and the World Health Organization (WHO) issued a publication, *AIDS Epidemic Update: December 1998* (UNAIDS/WHO, 1998a). The same organizations published *Strategic Planning: Guide to a Strategic Planning Process for a National Response to HIV/AIDS* (UNAIDS/ WHO, 1998b), which promotes use of strategic planning for assessing a country's manifestation of AIDS, mobilizing resources, and tailoring strategies for addressing the current reality of the disease and ultimately preventing it.

The *Healthy People 2010 Toolkit: A Field Guide to Health Planning* (Public Health Foundation, 1999) was developed under contract with the Office of Disease Prevention and Health Promotion [US Department of Health and Human Services (USDHHS)] in order to provide guidance, technical tools, and resources for developing and promoting state-specific plans in response to the goals set forth by the USDHHS. The *Toolkit*, which can be accessed in its entirety from a web site, also is designed to provide a strategic planning resource for communities and other entities committed to improving health.

The WHO initiated sponsorship of a Healthy Cities project in 1988 and it has served as a

Sample Opportunities and Threats Worksheet for a Health Care Organization

Instructions:

1. Utilize this worksheet to identify and describe: (a) the current and future market(s) targeted for service, (b) key stakeholders and their expectations, (c) current and potential competitors and allies, and (d) important environmental forces and trends.
2. After completing sections a–d, label each entity or force/trend as an opportunity (**O**) or a threat (**T**) or a combination of opportunity/threat (**O/T**).

A. **Current/Future Market(s):**   Clearly describe the current population (of patients/customers) that the organization is serving as well as the population it intends to serve in the future. Specify size, geographic base (if relevant), as well as *demographic and epidemiological factors* that are relevant to the health needs of the market(s).

B. **Key Stakeholders:**   List the key stakeholders that influence your organization (such as accrediting bodies and funding sources); briefly summarize the expectations of these stakeholders relative to your organization.

C. **Competitors and Allies:**   Identify both current or potential competitors as well as current or potential allies; briefly indicate the factors that affect the nature of the relationship with these and rate the probability of a change (positive or negative).

D. **Environmental Forces and Trends:**   List the PESTs—political, economic, social, and technological—that will affect the market(s) and its health needs as well as the abilitiy of the organization to respond to needs. Examples: changing fertility patterns and family/household structures, attitudes toward self versus governmental responsibility for health care, probability of technological improvements and anticipated treatment breakthroughs, passage of new health insurance provisions to cover indigent care.

Figure 5.6.

Sample Internal Organization Audit Worksheet to Identify Strengths and Weaknesses of a Health Care Organization

Instructions:
1. In column A, summarize the status or current level of each resource.
2. In column B, indicate the ideal current level and the level that will be required 3–5 years in the future.
3. In column C, summarize strengths related to each resource category as well as weaknesses. Be specific and identify what health outcome cannot be achieved or what quality expectation cannot be achieved at current or projected future resource levels.

	A. Current status/ level of resource	B. Desirable current and future status or level	C. Strengths and weaknesses (and associated problems related to poor health outcomes and quality expectations)
Staff:			
Financial resources:			
Reimbursement sources:			
Facilities:			
Systems for planning, information, and control:			
Market assets:			

Figure 5.7.

means of promoting the WHO Health for All Agenda, which includes not only improving access to health care but also promoting healthy lifestyles and reducing inequalities in health status. The American International Health Alliance has created Healthy Community Partnerships between US academic medical centers and communities in Eastern Europe, promoting application of a six-phase community change process that can be considered a strategic planning process. This process is described in an American International Health Alliance (1997b) publication.

An example of a broad-based, public-private partnership engaged in a strategic development effort to redefine the public health system in Illinois is the Turning Point Initiative that is funded by a grant from the Robert Wood Johnson Foundation. The steering committee for the effort, known as Public Health Futures Illinois, represents more than 30 organizations with representatives from traditional public health agencies (state and local), business, labor, insurance, managed care, the faith community, community-based organizations, universities, and philanthropic organizations. The committee produced *Illinois Plan for Public Health Systems Change* (Public Health Futures Illinois, 1999) following an extensive strategic planning process. The plan defines a vision, presents a mission statement for the Illinois public health system, establishes strategic priorities and goals, and details an action plan to guide infrastructure improvements and implementation of integrated prevention systems.

Those designing a process for strategic planning now can find many examples of its application. Nevertheless, tailoring a process for a specific purpose and ensuring consistency with available resources (of time, people, and expertise) remains an important first step.

The Format and Content of the Strategic Plan

By definition, a strategic plan captures the organization's plans for the future and discusses how the organization intends to achieve its vision or desired future state. Strategic plans usually include a mission, broad goals, and specific objectives that are to be accomplished over a period of time, such as 5 years; for some organizations, these elements constitute the entirety of the document labeled "strategic plan." A written plan, as opposed to one expressed verbally, provides a more effective tool for influencing budgeting and resource allocation decisions. It also can be a useful tool for gaining consensus during the strategic planning process and communicating the logic and the assumptions underlying strategy recommendations to those who will be responsible for implementation over time.

There is considerable variation in the format and content of strategic plans. They may be very short or detailed and complex. They may include the situational analysis with all data collected and analyzed to generate alternatives and recommendations, or this data may be compiled as an appendix or published as a separate document.

Organizations may publish their strategic plans together with their shorter-term, operational plans and budgets that are generally prepared on a yearly basis. It is not essential that the long-range, strategic plan and the operational plan be printed under one cover. However, it is important that an organization use its strategic plan as the framework for the design of its tactical or operational plan. The two plans must "hang together" or achieve consistency with each other. To ensure this, it is sound practice for an organization to review its strategic plan, assessing the need for changes, prior to preparation of the next operational plan. A sample outline of a strategic plan may be found in Table 5.8.

Table 5.8. Sample Outline, Strategic Plan for a Health Care Organization

- Executive summary (brief statement of overall strategy)[a]
- Mission and long-range perspective on where the organization or system should be 3, 5 or more years in the future[a]
- Market(s) or population(s) targeted for service (includes demographic and epidemiological descriptors)[a]
- Products or program of services to be offered with volume projections[a]
- Goals: what the organization or system hopes to accomplish as a result of the products and services to be offered[b]
- Description of the organization's or system's structure with details pertinent to products, services, and resources (staff, facilities, etc.)[b]
- Description of governance structure, including function, composition, and membership[b]
- Staffing plans and identification of developmental needs; the quantity and quality of personnel required to implement selected strategies[a]
- Description of facilities and plans for facility expansion, renovation, or closing[b]
- Financial plans with revenue and expenses projected; capital budgets if relevant; for an organization, cash flow or balance sheet projections; for a larger system, resource needs and sources of support for the system[a]
- Implementation steps: what major tasks should be carried out over the next year and beyond[a]
- Identification of obstacles and organizational or system constraints and contingency plans indicating what the organization or system will do under varying circumstances (recognizing that the future cannot be predicted precisely)[b]
- Broad operating policies for the future and an overview of anticipated changes to maintain the organization's or system's viability[b]

[a]Sections generally included in strategic plans.
[b]Additional sections recommended for inclusion in strategic plans, but not essential.

Conclusions

If an organization engages in effective strategic planning—performing an accurate situational assessment, developing a clear sense of direction, and achieving consensus on appropriate overall strategies—then it should produce a plan suitable for motivating and guiding its actions for at least a few years into the future. Because many variables in the health care field are surrounded by uncertainty and defy precise prediction, strategic plans typically focus on a planning horizon of 3 to 5 years. It is appropriate for an organization to apply a mechanism for at least a cursory review, and revision as necessary, of its strategic plan on an annual or biannual basis.

Because planning is an adapting and ongoing activity, it can accurately be presented as a circular process—one that is never really finished because the end of one planning process signals the beginning of the next cycle (Day, 1984). During intervals when planning is not occurring on a formal or intensive basis, organizations must nevertheless maintain systems for monitoring compliance with plans, assessing impact, and determining whether the assumptions underlying strategies remain valid. Given that change is constant and that change will affect the delivery of health care around the world, organizations must be prepared to change as well. Strategic planning must be used to determine what changes are required to promote organizational survival and to provide the organization (system, state, or nation) with the benefits of functioning proactively, not simply reactively.

Case Studies

Case Study No. 1
Strategic Planning for a County Health Department

A County Health Department that serves a population of 358,000 in a collar county of a major metropolitan area was recently faced with the resignation of the director of the Mental Health and Alcoholism Division. This division is the Health Department's largest; five other divisions support traditional public health functions. Since the Board of Health gained recognition as a community mental health provider, the division is operated with public funding from the state's Department of Mental Health and Developmental Disabilities (DMH-DD), the Department of Alcohol and Substance Abuse, and a local tax levy.

During the 20-year tenure of the mental health director, change had been incremental and gradual. But at the time he retired, the Health Department was confronted with numerous changes both from within the department and external to it. Within a 6-month time frame, both state agencies funding the Mental Health and Alcoholism Division announced that new conditions on the receipt of funds (such as the implementation of new quality assurance measures) would become effective at the beginning of the next fiscal year. These agencies also offered financial incentives for increasing addiction services to the youth of the county. Medicaid reimbursement for mental health services also was expanded, and DMH-DD allocated new monies to provide mental health services to the homeless and to develop community residential programs for the mentally ill. Other providers in the county also expressed interest in applying for funds, since grant awards for these new initiatives were to be provided on a competitive basis.

The staff of the division varied in their reactions to the prospects of new leadership. Some of the "old timers" were saddened by the division director's departure. Others, especially members of the staff who had been hired in recent years, felt that it was time for a change; they welcomed the beginning of a new era. They felt that the division had been reactive rather than proactive in the face of changing needs and growing demands for services.

The executive director, who felt he had the responsibility of attending a range of community meetings and business affairs, sensed increasing discontent in the county with certain areas of health care, especially the availability of primary health care. He frequently heard suggestions that the Health Department should do more. Although the county had been gradually aging, there had been recent support of economic development. Many light manufacturing and service-oriented businesses were relocating to the area and young adults were moving to the county to take advantage of new job opportunities. The number of births occurring in the county was increasing, as well as the demand for prenatal care and maternity services. One of the hospitals located in the county had almost discontinued its maternity service a few years ago due to poor occupancy of beds; now it was actively recruiting obstetricians and helping them establish their practices. So far this effort had limited success. Families with young children were having difficulty finding pediatricians who would accept new patients. Just before the opening of school in the fall, the Health Department was inundated with calls from parents who were seeking the location of clinics that would provide school physicals and immunizations.

The executive director of the Health Department was relatively new to the health department, having arrived only 6 months prior to the resignation of the Mental Health Director. Members of the Health Department's board expressed various opinions to him about the hiring of a new director. Some suggested that a young, ambitious, entrepreneurial individual with credentials in health care as well as business administration was needed to direct the Mental Health Division; such an individual could provide the leadership required for the division to take advantage of the new opportunities in the field. Other board members expressed concern that the Mental Health and Alcoholism Division had grown too big; they did not want the community to think only of mental health services when they thought of the Health Department. Some board members felt more attention should be given to expanding the resources for primary care and to monitoring and improving the quality of the environment, especially since the county was experiencing so much industrial growth all at once.

Q.1. Is this a good time for the Board of Health to initiate strategic planning? Why or why not?

Q.2. Does the scenario, as described, suggest that those involved with the county Health Department share a sense of a common mission?

Q.3. Assuming that a decision is made to proceed with strategic planning, what types of data should be reviewed for the purpose of identifying the key issues?

Q.4. How could these data be used to make an epidemiological assessment of the needs of the county's service population?

Q.5. Who should be involved in the strategic planning process? Why?

Q.6. Does the scenario suggest any pitfalls or problems that could be encountered during the strategic planning process? Can anything be done to avoid these?

Case Study No. 2
Strategic Planning for In-Patient Rehabilitation Services

In 1998, University Center (UC) Hospital realized that providing patients with comprehensive, inpatient rehabilitation services had become a money-losing endeavor, although other area hospitals had found these services to be among those most profitable. UC is part of a major state-supported university and academic medical center. Its problem seemed to be that it had failed to obtain exemption from the Medicare prospective payment system (PPS) for its inpatient rehabilitation program. The hospital therefore received reimbursement for older patients (who tended to utilize more rehabilitation services than other groups) on the basis of each patient's diagnosis-related group (DRG) classification. Since DRGs were designed as a payment mechanism for acute care episodes, these payments were inadequate to fully reimburse the care of patients who stayed in the hospital beyond the acute phase to undergo rehabilitative therapy designed to improve physical and psychosocial functioning.

Under certain conditions, a hospital could obtain exemption from the PPS and this would result in more favorable cost-based reimbursement for Medicare patients served in the rehabilitation unit. One of the conditions associated with exemption was recognition from the appropriate state agency that the hospital operated a unit meeting state qualifications for a comprehensive rehabilitation service. The hospital was located in Illinois, which operated a certificate-of-need (CON) program. The hospital had never sought recognition of beds for a distinct unit; the service utilized beds licensed as acute care beds. Thus, the first conditions for exemption did not exist.

The hospital director and other members of the management team, including several associate directors, the chief of the medical staff, the director of nursing, the chief financial officer, and the dean of the medical school met to address the question of whether a rehabilitation unit was really needed since average daily census was only eight patients over the past year. The state mandated that a rehabilitation unit have at least 12 beds for approval. The first decision made by the hospital director and the management team was to hire a consulting firm specializing in development of rehabilitation services. No one on the management team had experience in preparing a CON or addressing the host of legal and political issues surrounding the process of attaining exemption from PPS. In addition, the management team was concerned with so many other issues that it felt it was impossible to adequately solve the rehabilitation problem without additional personnel.

The consulting firm hired by the hospital was directed to undertake a preliminary feasibility study to assess the probability of gaining state approval through award of a CON for a rehabilitation unit. The firm's consultants also were requested to determine whether the hospital could demonstrate compliance with other exemption conditions. When the consultants completed this initial study and indicated that the hospital's chances of gaining both a CON and exemption were relatively good, the management team endorsed a more comprehensive feasibility study to assess other factors.

Q.1. Using an epidemiological framework, what elements should be included in a more comprehensive feasibility study?

Q.2. Did hospital administration abdicate its role in providing leadership to a strategic planning process?

Q.3. Does the scenario describe the best approach for engaging in strategic planning around the issue of the hospital's future direction relative to the delivery of rehabilitation services consistent with epidemiological trends?

Case Study No. 3
Health Care Reform in Uzbekistan

Uzbekistan, one of the New Independent States (NIS) located in Central Asia, has committed itself to reform of its health care system. The country has a relatively high physician to population ratio; the WHO estimated the ratio of Uzbek physicians per 100,000 population to be 335 in 1994. Canada's ratio was 221 when estimated in 1992 (by WHO) and the United States had a ratio of about 260 per 100,000 population when estimated by the Bureau of Health Professions. However, Uzbek physicians had shorter periods of medical education and less practical experience prior to entering practice than counterparts in countries where the practice of medicine is considered more advanced. Further, nurses in Uzbekistan received barely more than education at a high school level. Thus, hospital nurses did tasks like making beds, fetching pharmaceuticals for physicians, and performing other supportive tasks requiring minimum skills. Likewise, nurses were not well used in polyclinics (outpatient care centers) and there was little appreciation of a "nursing role" with distinctive patient care responsibilities.

Reform measures in Uzbekistan have been enhanced by participation in a partnership program made available to many NIS countries by the American International Health Alliance (AIHA). AIHA is an organization formed by a consortium of major US hospital associations to provide humanitarian aid, consultation, and assistance in health care reform after the disintegration of the Soviet Union. The activities of partnership programs have been supported financially with funds provided to AIHA by the US Agency for International Development.

The largest institute for medical education in Uzbekistan, together with Ministry of Health officials, have spearheaded nursing reform and a set of objectives have been developed and are currently in various stages of implementation. Objectives include upgrading formal nursing education (for example, by developing core nursing curricula), creating clinical nurse educator positions (to promote expansion of nursing education within clinical settings), and initiating a national nursing association to facilitate development of the nursing profession, delineate nursing roles, establish standards and promote leadership development (including educating nurses to replace physicians as faculty for nursing programs).

As a result of its partnership with an academic medical center in Chicago (that has a College of Nursing in addition to five other health professional schools), Uzbek physicians, nurses, educational leaders, and clinical administrators have been able to visit the United States and participate in intensive training/education programs hosted by the Chicago partner. AIHA also has sponsored many conferences that provided Uzbekistan and other NIS countries opportunities to share experiences and learn from each other. Nursing reform has been a focus of most partnerships sponsored by AIHA, and the interactions among NIS countries have been determined to be at least of equal value to the opportunity to interact with

American partners. Uzbekistan's government still has centralized control over most of its oblasts, with the federal government maintaining a primary role in development of policy in the areas of health, education, and economic development. The country is being challenged with a slowly developing economy and high inflation. The health system is underfinanced and lacks resources for capital improvement and repair. Too many hospital beds exist (even after several years of bed reduction efforts), and the country is experimenting with a number of approaches for improving the financing and effectiveness of its health services. Despite the many challenges faced by Uzbekistan, the president of the country and its minister of health have expressed commitment to nursing reforms as a component of larger health system and medical education reform. Recently, a chief nursing position was created within Uzbekistan's Ministry of Health to ensure that nursing reforms would be sustained and realize optimal results.

Q.1. Could strategic planning have any utility in this scenario?

Q.2. If a strategic planning task force was to be organized under sponsorship of the Ministry of Health, who should be involved in this task force and why should their involvement be sought?

Q.3. What might be the nature of the PESTs in Uzbekistan that would impact on the task of reforming nursing?

Case Study No. 4
Strategic Planning for a Perinatal Center

For several decades, Illinois has maintained a state-funded system of perinatal care based on a model of a regional "network" of maternity and neonatal service providers. The leadership within each of the state's ten networks is provided by an officially designated perinatal center consisting of a medical school and its associated tertiary care hospital. By law and regulation, every hospital licensed to provide maternity care must be affiliated with a perinatal center, and a letter of agreement must be written between a center and each hospital in its network. Although the service areas of downstate networks are geographically distinct, the six centers serving metropolitan Chicago attempt to coordinate care among hospitals and other service providers that tend to be scattered throughout the metropolitan area.

When networks were initially organized in the late 1970s, public health officials provided guidelines for the structure of networks and supervised negotiations among representatives of Chicago area hospitals as they determined the membership of the various networks. At that time, it was determined that six centers were needed for the area and that the hospitals in a single network should account for approximately 20,000 deliveries. Primary consideration was given to maintenance of relationships that existed between medical schools and the community hospitals they utilized as clinical resources for medical education programs. Attention was also given to ensuring that each network had a fair distribution of facilities with high-risk, specialized resources.

Over the years, many changes have occurred and the configuration of some of the Chicago area networks presents problems. For example, there is a wide range (from 3 to 20) in the number of hospitals affiliated with each center, and two networks have responsibility for deliveries far in excess of the recommended 20,000. More importantly, the distribution of specialized services and high-risk beds appears poorly matched to the needs of the populations served by the hospitals in each network. When an affiliated community-based hospital refers a high-risk maternal patient for delivery or tries to send a sick neonate to a neonatal care unit, some Chicago-area perinatal centers are unable to identify an available bed within its own hospital. However, other perinatal centers in the area have very low occupancies, and the administrations of a few of these hospitals are beginning to question why they continue to offer such expensive services without an adequate return on investment. Some hospital administrators feel that the state is unnecessarily restraining the operation of free market principles by applying rules for linking hospitals and operating networks that are no longer relevant to changing times and environments. In addition to poorly distributed resources between networks, there are other reasons why membership in metropolitan networks no longer reflects the rationality that existed in the past. Some networks have a much higher percentage of low-income patients (and therefore a relatively sicker population) than other networks, but the state's formula for providing perinatal centers with funds to administer their networks does not adequately take this into account.

Medical school alignments have changed and more and more hospitals are bonding together and forming multi-institutional systems. Some hospitals have formally changed their perinatal network affiliations to achieve consistency with the pattern of new relationships, but others have not (and this sometimes results in weak linkage with a perinatal center and less than ideal relationships). Another factor confounding the situation is the growing importance of health maintenance organizations (HMOs) and other forms of managed care. Sometimes the gatekeepers associated with these programs will not approve the transfer of a high-risk patient to the specified perinatal center, in accordance with established referral provisions, because the center is not a recognized HMO or managed care provider.

Recently, the administrators of all six metropolitan networks forwarded a request to the Department of Public Health to provide staff assistance as they study the problems and explore a more rationalized approach for network configuration. The department agrees that some restructuring of networks may be necessary, but it refuses to dictate the membership of each network, preferring that local providers assume responsibility for correcting deficiencies.

Q.1. Discuss how epidemiological data could be used in strategic planning to resolve some of the problems suggested in this case.

Q.2. What might be recommended in this scenario as a means to explore the advantages and disadvantages of maintaining the status quo versus designing alternative models for the delivery of perinatal services?

Case Study No. 5
Building a Healthier Community in Slovakia

Banska Bystrica, a town of about 85,000, is located in central Slovakia. Although the town experienced rapid growth in the 1970s and 1980s, growth slowed during the early 1990s. Then around 1996, the town began to lose inhabitants as a result of emigration from the region. Both birth rates and death rates have shown declines in recent years. The town expects to have a drop in population after 2000, and by 2010 the population decrease will be even more significant if residents continue to leave the area. Current average age of the population is nearly 35, whereas the WHO estimated that the average age of the world was only 26 in 1998.

In 1997, the mayor's office of this town prepared a publication entitled *The Profile of Health, Banska Bystrica*. This publication stated: "The amount of illnesses and number of deaths caused by modern environmental influences has grown, while in contrast, the number of deaths caused by other illnesses, has declined because of the development of health care." The publication compiled a comprehensive range of data for the town and compared it with data for a larger region and the Slovak Republic. Health status data addressed life expectancy and causes of death; for cancer, respiratory disease, and cardiovascular disease, deaths as well as morbidity were discussed. Since Banska Bystrica inhabitants had participated in a study of risk factors, the profile reported on findings and noted that "smoking is one of the most important and most frequently observed risk factors." For the entirety of the population 15 and over, it was found that 22.3% of females and 30.5% of males smoked. However, certain subsets of the population smoked more frequently. For females, 31.7% of those 25 to 34 years old smoked (compared to 26.2% for the males in this age group). For males 35–44 years of age, 40.3% smoked (while only 20.7% of females in this age group smoked). The other lifestyle indicators found to be significant in the town's population were high blood pressure, high total cholesterol levels, and obesity. Indeed, 75% of the population was found to have one or more of these risk factors (Mayor's Office, Banska Bystrica, 1997).

The *Profile* also addressed levels of air pollution, water pollution in the city canals, drinking water, waste management, noise, sources of electric and gas power, and town parks. A very short section on health facilities and personnel was presented. The town's characteristics related to education, housing, employment, economic dependency, social and family structure, and municipal social services also were discussed.

In 1998, Banska Bystrica published the *City Health Plan*, which was subsequently used when applying for grants from sponsors such as the European Union and the WHO Healthy Cities program (in which this town participated). Banska Bystrica maintains a community coalition consisting of representatives of schools and academic institutions, the urban planning office, health providers, the state health institute, nongovernmental organizations, businesses, city legislative representatives, and the city hall administration. This coalition has committees that help the town establish objectives for social, health, and educational programs and monitor impact of efforts.

Q.1. The town is getting ready to update its profile. Are there other areas relevant to the life of the town that should be addressed?

Q.2. Are there any special health needs suggested by this case?

Case Study No. 6
Strategic Planning for a University-Based Wellness Center

A comprehensive wellness center (CWC) associated with a major state university and academic medical center experienced great success and rapid growth during its initial years of operation. The CWC achieved designation as one of only seven health promotion and disease prevention centers recognized nationally by the Centers for Disease Control. It went from a program with three faculty and two staff working on four projects funded at less than $200,000 during the first year, to a unit with over 60 people (approximately 35 full-time equivalents) involved with projects worth over $4.4 million during its seventh year. The CWC, which was started in less than 700 square feet of office space, now is located on an entire floor of a large office building. In the next year, CWC will begin utilizing another floor, thus occupying nearly 23,000 square feet of office, computer, and general research space.

Since its inception, CWC has received nearly $20.0 million to support three training programs and 50 research projects on a wide range of diseases, behaviors, and populations. The CWC has attempted to maintain a good sense of its mission, described by its leadership as the following: "To provide a multidisciplinary research focus for the study, analysis and dissemination of information on health promotion and the prevention of the major causes of morbidity and mortality among the diverse population groups of the city (in which CWC is located) and the state."

CWC has determined that its overall direction for the next 5 years will be to consolidate and build on strengths in ways that support the urban mission of the major university with which it is associated. It also has determined that its focus should be diverted from continuing expansion (since there is some sense that CWC will soon be big enough) to assurance of high-quality research and effectiveness of impact. The CWC has been able to involve faculty from 35 departments in eight colleges across the university campus. The benefits offered to participating faculty include collegial advice and review during grant proposal preparation, ongoing interaction with other prevention researchers, the services of its business office, computer facilities, research offices, and support of graduate students. The CWC's success and favorable reputation are responsible for attracting an ever-growing number of faculty who desire assistance with their research activities. Can the CWC continue to respond to anyone and everyone? Should it lend support to research on any topic related to the broad category of health promotion and disease prevention? How will the new era of "health care reform" affect the CWC's future? The CWC's leadership has begun asking these questions as they direct their attention to positioning CWC for success in the years to come.

Q.1. Discuss how strategic planning could be utilized by the CWC to address the questions raised in this case.

Q.2. Considering the mission of the CWC, how might epidemiological and demographic data be utilized to assist it in becoming more focused?

Case Study No. 7
Strategic Planning for Professional Health Care Associations

Members of one of the largest state medical societies in the United States have expressed concern that the various models proposed for health care reform will have a detrimental impact on physicians, especially those engaged in subspecialties. Even as the debate rages over which reform plan will be implemented, the increasing popularity of managed care already has eroded the position of subspecialists. Concern over escalating costs has resulted in greater scrutiny of the need for referral to specialists and increased emphasis is being placed on the role of the primary care provider, who frequently is charged as gatekeeper to the larger system.

Several years ago, the Council on Graduate Medical Education, an advisory group to Congress, estimated that the United States would have 115,000 too many medical specialists and 35,000 too few general practitioners in the year 2000. This prediction resulted in implementation of physician retraining programs in a few areas of the country. Specialists were being retrained to ensure their competency in the delivery of primary care. However, the projection of too few physicians is not held by all (Hart *et al.*, 1997), assuming increasing health care delivery through managed care plans and lean physician staffing of HMOs.

An ad hoc committee of the state medical society has been charged with assessing existing retraining programs and determining whether sponsorship of such a program would be an appropriate activity for the society. If the committee recommends initiation of the retraining program, it also is charged with developing objectives and implementation procedures.

As the committee begins its work, it is aware that the society's membership could be split on the need for and the benefits of a retraining program. A southern California hospital that offered a retraining program experienced the resignation of many physicians from its medical group because of issues associated with retraining.

Q.1. What type of epidemiological and demographic data could be used by the committee to assist in assessing the need and feasibility of a training program?

Q.2. If the committee approaches its charge as undertaking strategic planning for the medical society, describe a process that may be employed in this situation. Since the medical society is a professional association, should the strategic planning process it utilizes differ from the process for an organization responsible for direct delivery of care?

References

American Hospital Association, 1991 (December), A decade of change: AHA's annual survey traces national trends, 1980–1990, *Hospitals* **20:**32–33.

American International Health Alliance, 1997a, *Nurse Leaders Creating Change: A Revolution in Progress*, American International Health Alliance, Washington, DC.

American International Health Alliance, 1997b, *Safer Streets, Longer Lives: Creating a Healthy Community*, American International Health Alliance, Washington, DC.

Baker, T. D., 1988, Health personnel planning, in *Health Planning for Effective Management* (W. A. Reinke, ed.), pp. 131–146, Oxford University Press, New York.

Baker, T. D., and Reinke, W. A., 1988, Epidemiologic base for health planning, in *Health Planning for Effective Management* (W. A. Reinke, ed.), pp. 117–130, Oxford University Press, New York.

Bandrowski, J. F., 1985, *Creative Planning Throughout the Organization*, AMA Membership Publications Division, American Management Association, New York.

Bandrowksi, J. F., 1990, *Corporate Imagination Plus: Five Steps to Translating Innovative Strategies into Action*, Free Press, New York.

Barry, B. W., 1986, *Strategic Planning Workbook for Nonprofit Organizations*, Amherst H. Wilder Foundation, St. Paul, MN.

Baynham, B., 1991 (February), Strategic planning and evaluation for QA, *Dimensions* 21–24.

Bryson, J. M., 1988, *Strategic Planning for Public and Nonprofit Organizations*, Jossey-Bass, San Francisco.

Bureau of Health Professions, Health Resources and Services Administration, US Department of Health and Human Services, 1999, *United States Health Workforce Personnel Factbook*, US Department of Health and Human Services, Rockville, MD.

Coddington, D. C., and Moore, K. D., 1987, *Market-Driven Strategies in Health Care*, Jossey-Bass Publishers, San Francisco, CA.

Committee on Leading Health Indicators for Healthy People 2010, 1999, *Leading Health Indicators for Healthy People 2010: Final Report* (C. Chrvala, and R. Bulger, eds.), Division of Health Promotion and Disease Prevention, Institute of Medicine, Washington, DC.

Council on Graduate Medical Education and National Advisory Council on Nurse Education and Practice, 1996, *Report on Primary Care Workforce Projections, December 1995*, Bureau of Health Professions, Health Resources and Services Administration, US Department of Health and Human Services, Rockville, MD.

Day, G. S., 1984, *Strategic Marketing Planning*, West Publishing Company, St. Paul, MN.

Day, J. C., 1996, *Population Projections of the United States by Age, Sex, Race, and Hispanic Origin: 1995 to 2050*, Current Population Reports, P25–1130, US Bureau of the Census, US Government Printing Office, Washington DC.

Hart, L. G., Wagner, E., Pirzada, S., Nelson, A. F., and Rosenblatt, R. A., 1997, Physician staffing ratios in staff-model HMOs: A cautionary tale, *Health Affairs* **16**:55–70.

Health Forum, 1999, *Hospital Statistics, 1999 Edition*, American Hospital Association, Chicago.

Johnson, J., Weissman, M. M., and Klerman, G. L., 1992, Service utilization and social morbidity associated with depressive symptoms in the community, *JAMA* **267**:1478–1483.

Kinsella, K., and Velkoff, V., 1988 (Spring), Aging populations signal demographic sea change, *CommonHealth* 7–9.

Kotler, P., and Clarke, R., 1987, *Marketing for Healthcare Organizations*, Prentice-Hall, Englewood Cliffs, NJ.

Kramarow, E., Lentzner, H., Rooks, R., Weeks, J., and Saydah, S., 1999, *Health and Aging Chartbook. Health, United States, 1999*, National Center for Health Statistics, Hyattsville, MD.

Lawrence, L., and Hall, M., 1999, *1997 Summary: National Hospital Discharge Survey. Advance Data from Vital and Health Statistics*, No. 308, National Center for Health Statistics, Hyattsville, MD.

MacStravic, R. S., 1984 *Forecasting Use of Health Services*, Aspen Systems Corporation, Rockville, MD.

Mayor's Office, Banska Bystrica, 1997, *The Profile of Health, Banska Bystrica*, Mayor's Office, Banksa Bystrica, Slovakia.

McDevitt, T., 1999, *World Population Profile: 1998*, US Department of Commerce, Bureau of the Census, Washington, DC.

Moore, D. A., and Carpenter, T. E., 1999, Spatial analytic methods and geographic information systems: Use in health research and epidemiology, *Am. J. Epidemiol.* **21**:143–160.

Murray, C. J. L., and Lopez, A. D. (eds.), 1996, *A Comprehensive Assessment of Mortality and Disability from Diseases, Injuries, and Risk Factors in 1990 and Projected to 2020*, Global Burden of Disease and Injury Series, Vol. I, Harvard School of Public Health (on behalf of the World Health Organization and the World Bank), Cambridge, MA.

National Center for Health Statistics, 1998, *International Health Data Reference Guide, 1997*, US Department of Health and Human Services, Hyattsville, MD.

National Center for Health Statistics, 1999, *Health, United States, 1999 with Health and Aging Chartbook*. US Department of Health and Human Services, Hyattsville, MD.

Nutt, P. C., 1984, *Planning Methods for Health and Related Organizations*, John Wiley & Sons, New York.

Pfeffer, J., and Salancik, G. R., 1978, *The External Control of Organizations, A Resource Dependence Perspective*, Harper & Row, New York.

Porter, M., 1980, *Competitive Strategy*, Free Press, New York.

Porter, M., 1985, *Competitive Advantage: Creating and Sustaining Superior Performance*, Free Press, New York.

Public Health Foundation, 1999, *Healthy People 2010 ToolKit: A Field Guide to Health Planning*, Public Health Foundation, Washington, DC.

Public Health Futures Illinois, 1999, *Illinois Plan for Public Health Systems Change*, Illinois Department of Public Health, Springfield.

Shortell, S. M., and Kaluzny, A. D., 1983, Organization theory and health care management, in *Health Care Management: A Text in Organization Theory and Behavior* (S. M. Shortell and A. D. Kaluzny, eds.), pp. 5–37, John Wiley & Sons, New York.

Shortell, S. M., and Kaluzny, A. D., 1994, Organization theory and health services management, in *Health Care Management: Organization Design and Behavior*, 3rd ed. (S. M. Shortell and A. D. Kaluzny, eds.), pp. 3–29, Delmar Publishers, Albany, NY.

Spiegel, A. D., and Hyman, H. H., 1991, *Strategic Health Planning*, Ablex Publishing Corporation, Norwood, NJ.

Starkweather, D., and Cook, K. S., 1983, Organization–environment relations, in *Health Care Management: A Text in Organization Theory and Behavior* (S. M. Shortell and A. D. Kaluzny, eds.), pp. 333–377, John Wiley & Sons, New York.

Taylor, F., 1947, *Scientific Management*, Harper & Row, New York.

UNAIDS (Joint United Nations Programme on HIV/AIDS) and the World Health Organization, 1998a, *AIDS Epidemic Update: December 1998*, UNAIDS, Geneva, Switzerland.

UNAIDS (Joint United Nations Programme on HIV/AIDS) and the World Health Organization, 1998b, *Strategic Planning: Guide to a Strategic Planning Process for a National Response to HIV/AIDS*, UNAIDS, Geneva, Switzerland.

United Nations Population Division, 1999, *World Population Prospects: The 1998 Revision*, United Nations, New York.

US Bureau of the Census, Population Estimates Program, Population (Internet release date: December 1997). *MA-96-5 Estimates of the Population of Metropolitan Areas: Annual Time Series, July 1, 1991–July 1, 1996*, US Bureau of the Census, Washington, DC.

US Bureau of the Census, 1998, *State and Metropolitan Area Data Book 1997–98*, US Government Printing Office, Washington, DC.

US Bureau of the Census, 1999, *World Population Profile: 1998*, Report WP/98, US Government Printing Office, Washington, DC.

Weber, M., 1964, *The Theory of Social and Economic Organization*, Free Press, Glencoe, IL.

World Bank, 1993, *World Development Report 1993—Investing in Health*, Oxford University Press (For the World Bank), Cambridge, MA.

World Health Organization, 1999, *The World Health Report 1999: Making a Difference*, World Health Organization, Geneva, Switzerland.

6

Evaluating Health Services, Programs, and Systems
An Epidemiological Perspective

Dolores G. Clement and Thomas T. H. Wan

Health care service and program evaluation is vitally important to the efforts directed at reforming and improving the performance of a health system. Evaluation is a means by which a program, service, or a process is examined and an informed judgment is made concerning the extent of success in reaching predetermined goals. Evaluation plays major roles in health care: (1) assuring the delivery of a high quality of health care; (2) serving as a tool for monitoring care and controlling costs; and (3) promoting accountability for public and private program expenditures. Evaluation is not merely the application of methods, but involves managerial and political decision making pertinent to the resource allocation to other functions such as program planning, design, implementation, and ongoing monitoring. Evaluations are done for a variety of purposes: to improve the delivery of care, to test an innovation, to determine the effectiveness of regulatory policy, to assess the appropriateness of continuing or altering an intervention, or to compare health system effectiveness across nations.

The use of epidemiological principles and methods in evaluation can clarify information required for health service or program development or to guide decisions relevant to continued operations. Epidemiology provides a framework for planning, monitoring the health of a population, identifying changes in risk factors over time, and prioritizing health problems requiring correction. In addition, epidemiology provides measures, analytic study designs, and methods for investigating the effectiveness of programs in controlling disease, disability and other health problems, and for measuring their consequences in populations receiving health care services.

The purpose of this chapter is to present the conceptual dimensions of program evaluation, promote an understanding of study design, explain issues related to the introduction of interventions in populations, and describe specific statistical approaches for analyzing the

Dolores G. Clement and Thomas T. H. Wan   Department of Health Administration, School of Allied Health Professions, Virginia Commonwealth University, Richmond, Virginia 23298-0233.

Epidemiology and the Delivery of Health Care Services: Methods and Applications, Second Edition, edited by Denise M. Oleske. Kluwer Academic / Plenum Publishers, New York, 2001.

impacts of services, programs, and systems. The use of epidemiological techniques is especially appropriate at this time for population-based planning as larger and more diverse populations are using health care services. As health care becomes increasingly customized to meet the needs of specific populations, particularly those vulnerable or at high risk for certain problems, program evaluation based on epidemiological principles becomes necessary in order to determine the most effective delivery strategies.

Dimensions of Health System Evaluation

Program evaluation must address several conceptual issues in the design and conduct of analysis. These are summarized in Table 6.1 and described in this section.

Determine the Population Targeted for Intervention

The most important design consideration is determining the people, organizations, or communities to whom the intervention should be directed. Over sampling, undersampling, or exclusion of those who could benefit should be addressed during the design of the intervention and reexamined during the evaluation phase. Ethical considerations arise if a social program overlooks portions of the population at risk or benefits those with no need of the services encompassed by a program. Epidemiological methods can determine a population's need, identify those who could benefit most from an intervention, and determine whether care is being provided at an acceptable level. For example, ongoing evaluation can be performed to monitor the quality of care provided by individual hospitals to a population covered by a national health care system. Examples of epidemiological measures that might be used in such an evaluation should include hospital mortality rates categorized by case mix, iatrogenic morbidity rates for specific infections, and perinatal infant mortality rates.

Identify Aspects of Health Care To Be Evaluated

In evaluating health care, the major aspects to be considered include the:

- Quality of care
- Accessibility and availability of resources
- Continuity of care
- Effectiveness of health care
- Efficiency involved in care delivery
- Acceptability of care provided

Table 6.1. Summary of Conceptual Issues Addressed in Evaluation of Health Services, Programs, and Systems

1. Determine the population to whom the program applies.
2. Identify aspect(s) of the health care system to be evaluated.
3. Identify and develop evaluation criteria: standards and measures.
4. Specify the design and analytic approaches appropriate to the evaluation.
5. Identify who will conduct the evaluation and how it is to be financed.
6. Assess the impact of the evaluation on cost, quality and access to medical care.
7. Identify limitations of findings and implications.

Epidemiological methods are appropriate for evaluation of each of these aspects, since the focus of evaluation is the impact of interventions within populations. Descriptive measures alone or in combination with analytic studies (which are discussed later in this chapter) can be used to assess each system aspect. Several examples follow.

Quality

In order to evaluate quality, the concept must first be defined. Donabedian (1980) states:

> ... quality is a property of, and a judgement upon, some definable unit of care, and that care is divisible into at least two parts: technical and interpersonal ... At the very least, the quality of technical care consists of the application of medical science and technology in a manner that maximizes its benefits to health without correspondingly increasing its risk. (p. 5)

Quality assessment, in epidemiological terms, examines variation in rates and likelihood of both beneficial and adverse outcomes. An epidemiological approach in assessing the health of a population, monitoring morbidity and mortality trends, and comparing variation in the prevalence and incidence of health problems indicate the quality of health services and programs.

Retchin and Brown (1990) provide an example of the use of analytic epidemiological methods to evaluate quality in a quasi-experimental study of the delivery of routine and preventive care. The likelihood of receiving various forms of preventive care are presented as an odds ratio with a specified confidence interval. This study suggests that routine and preventive advice are more likely to be offered to Medicare enrollees in staff–group model health maintenance organizations (HMOs) than in the traditional fee-for-service setting. Wan *et al.* (1980) used a variety of patient outcome measures, including mortality rates, to assess the impact of daycare and homemaker services. Significantly higher mortality was found in the control group relative to the intervention group who received both categories of service. Further discussion on the interrelationship between quality, epidemiology, and health care management can be found in Chapter 7 (this volume).

Accessibility

Donabedian (1980) defines accessibility of care as the ease with which care is initiated and maintained. Public and private programs often are initiated to alleviate problems of access. Thus, the evaluation of these programs frequently focuses on changes in accessibility. Universal access through national programs for provision of services or insurance do not guarantee universal coverage for all services, which leaves access as an issue when benefits are restrictive as in when international programs are being evaluated. Young and Cohen (1991) examined patient insurance status, a variable that affects access to care, in relation to outcomes of care. Significantly greater mortality rates were observed among uninsured patients compared to rates for HMO and traditionally insured fee-for-service patients. Okada and Wan (1980), in their study of the impact of community health centers and Medicaid on the utilization of health services, found that health centers in low-income areas contributed to increased access to care among the disadvantaged. They also documented the extensive Medicaid coverage of study populations was an indicator of increased access to care.

Accessibility in situations of restrictive benefits packages is an issue that requires further evaluation. For example, Clement *et al.* (1994) found that access to specialists for those enrolled in HMOs was more restrictive than a fee-for-service comparison group. Variation between plans can be compared, using epidemiological techniques for monitoring prevention screening and treatment rates among different segments of the population. Onetime or time-limited access to the system also must be considered, which leads to assessment of whether care, once accessed, is continuous.

Continuity

Continuity can be defined as maintaining a relationship between successive episodes of health care. Evaluation of continuity generally focuses on interruptions in needed care.

Donabedian (1980) suggests that an important feature of continuity is the retention of past findings and the recording of decisions so that they may be used in the management of current problems in a manner reflecting constancy in the objectives and the methods of care. Continuous monitoring may be required in an evaluation, because reports at a single point in time only portray a segment of an ongoing intervention. Assessment of results that can improve or deteriorate should continue, unless a study is designed to be time-limited. When feasible, a longitudinal study should be conducted to monitor changes in care and outcomes over time and to evaluate the continuous effects of an intervention. For example, recidivism is an indicator of program outcome that is utilized to evaluate behavioral change associated with substance abuse and smoking cessation programs. The effectiveness of such programs is most appropriately quantified several months after the intervention has taken place (Bibeau et al., 1988).

Effectiveness

Effectiveness is the degree to which a health care system succeeds in meeting stated or accepted goals in the ordinary setting in which the intervention is conducted (Greenlick, 1981). In assessing effectiveness, two distinct variables should be evaluated: effectiveness of care and the psychosocial impact of the delivery of care on outcome. The evaluation of technical effectiveness is concerned with the degree to which a system can influence a favorable patient physiological or physical outcome (e.g., patient survival rates). The consideration of psychosocial dimensions is concerned with how the provider–patient relationship affects the outcomes of care (e.g., patient satisfaction rates). An example of evaluating technical effectiveness using epidemiological methods was demonstrated in a study done by Lane et al. (1992). Breast cancer screening rates among the socioeconomically disadvantaged women attending publicly funded health centers were found to be comparable to (or even higher than) screening rates for the general population.

Efficiency

Efficiency is the ability to produce a desired result using minimal resources. Cost is often the resource measure used to evaluate program efficiency, and efficiency evaluations are often concerned with whether the same end result can be achieved at lower cost. An example would be comparing the in-hospital mortality rates (outcomes) and length of intensive care unit stay (efficiency measure) between a group of physicians who are hospitalists (physicians who only see hospitalized patients) and a group of attendings in single specialty group practices. If the patients in the hospitalist group have the same in-hospital mortality rate as that of the attending group, but the former patients have a significantly shorter length of intensive care unit stay, then using hospitalists would improve efficiency.

Acceptability

Acceptability evaluations consider whether expectations of various persons within the health system are met. The expectations of planners, participants, providers, and patients should be reflected in the goals and outcomes to be achieved by a program. The manner in which a service is delivered and received determines the level of cooperation, compliance, and achievement of expected results. Health care might be deemed to be effective or efficient in its delivery, but if it is provided in an inappropriate setting or without respect and dignity, it may be unacceptable to intended beneficiaries. Acceptability is particularly critical when new technology is introduced into a population subgroup that has special challenges (e.g., culturally, physically).

Acceptability can be determined by using preestablished criteria or by surveying those involved with the program. A study assessing the acceptability of freestanding birth centers compared to hospital confinement for labor and delivery utilized the following epidemiological data to assess program outcomes: maternal and newborn complication rates and intrapartum and neonatal mortality rates (Rooks *et al.*, 1989). It was concluded that freestanding centers represent an acceptable alternative to a hospital for selected women, particularly those who had a prior delivery. Acceptability can also be measured through process criteria, such as dropout rates and lost-to-follow-up rates as was used in the European Natural Family Planning Study Group determination of symptothermal methods of contraception (Anonymous, 1999).

The Evaluation Process

Evaluation is a dynamic process that is bounded by a formal application to specific problems. There are four interrelated aspects of the evaluation process: planning, implementation, intervention, and monitoring/feedback. The evaluation process is iterative, continuous, and repetitive in nature (Fig. 6.1).

Planning

What is to be evaluated and accomplished by a health care system or an organization or program is determined in a planning stage as described in the previous chapter. Since a program or intervention is designed as a response to a recognized or perceived problem, the initial stage of program development should include assessment of the magnitude of the health problem and establishment of criteria for use during evaluation. Epidemiological data may provide essential information supportive of need and some of the same data may be applicable in the evaluation process. For example, Kotchen *et al.* (1986) cite the high cardiovascular

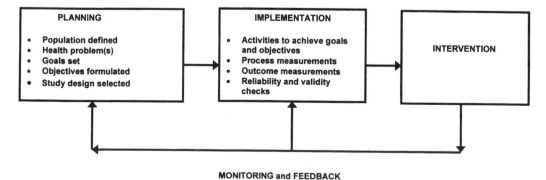

Figure 6.1. The evaluation process: A reiterative model.

disease death rate in the rural Southeast as one reason for initiating a high blood pressure control program in two counties in southeastern Kentucky. The same rate became one of the epidemiological measures used to monitor the impact of the program.

The goals of the intervention, specific and measurable objectives, the processes by which the objectives can be accomplished, budgetary considerations, and the means of monitoring progress are all established through planning. Sufficient documentation of plans is required for inclusion of planning phase considerations into the overall evaluation of a program. The study design to be utilized to assess an intervention should be determined during the planning stage and included in the plans.

Implementation

Implementation is the process of carrying out the activities planned to achieve goals and monitor an intervention. It involves not only doing what is needed but also measuring and documenting all the tasks of an evaluation or process. An ongoing evaluation process is needed from the beginning to ensure reliability, to safeguard the integrity of the program or intervention, and to ensure fiscal accountability.

Intervention

A well-planned service or program is established to effect change and interventions are designed to modify expectations and actions. Evaluations of interventions measure change and enable modification in direction or the design of alternative, innovative services or programs. It is important to note that the design of an evaluation should be customized for the specific intervention used.

Monitoring and Feedback

Effective administration and coordination of tasks associated with evaluation are necessary for monitoring an intervention. Periodic reports may indicate interim trends, and concurrent monitoring can ensure accountability and the appropriate allocation of resources. An evaluation should include a system to relay information or feedback about a program or process so that planned change is achieved. Rosen and Feigin (1983) have suggested that feedback can lead to improved performance, and they stress three principles of feedback. First, the group that is most likely to be influenced by the feedback must participate in selecting what is to be measured. Second, the feedback must be relevant to that group's goals. Third, the feedback should be used in a positive and supportive manner, rather than in a negative or punitive way. Corrective mechanisms to address deficiencies in a program or process must also be incorporated into the evaluation process. The changes instituted as a result of feedback and implementation of corrective measures should then be monitored in this reiterative process.

Conceptual Framework for Specifying Evaluation Criteria

A component of the process of evaluation includes the determination of goals and objectives to be accomplished through a program's intervention. Ideally, a variety of measures pertinent to the goals and objectives are used in an evaluation. The delineation of clear objectives and evaluation criteria during a program's planning phase facilitates evaluation. Objectives for what will be accomplished, who will be affected, and the expected time frame should be explicitly stated and quantified. Evaluation criteria must be developed to assess a program's performance against the standards. Utilizing the classic conceptual framework of Donabedian (1980), evaluation criteria may be categorized into structural, process, and outcome measures (SPO) that can be used to determine achievement of program, health service, or system objectives.

Structural measures represent characteristics of the people performing or receiving an intervention, the location where service is given, and the resources needed and used, including the resources required to plan, perform, and monitor the intervention. Structural criteria are derived from the design and objectives of the intervention. Human, material, and capital resources expended on a program are all structural variables.

Process measures represent what you do to accomplish the objectives of an intervention. These measures have several advantages including the relative ease of specifying process criteria to characterize what occurs in the program and the availability of administrative documentation and other records containing information about the intervention. Specific responsibility for tasks associated with the process of care can be determined in evaluations using process measures; this, in turn allows for specific corrective action to be taken. Process criteria identify standards for assessing the means employed to achieve the purpose of the intervention. The disadvantages of process criteria are that they tend to overemphasize technical care at the expense of the interpersonal process.

An **outcome** is the change achieved through the intervention. Outcome criteria must relate to results specifically attributable to the intervention being evaluated. For example, an outcome criterion for a smoking cessation program could be that 80% of those in the program will stop smoking for at least 2 years after program completion. The major difficulty in assessing an outcome is determining how much of an outcome can be considered a direct result of the intervention. Therefore, it is necessary to monitor other factors that could contribute to the outcome. In the case of smoking cessation programs, these factors could include illness or a large increase in cigarette taxes. Caution also must be used when assessing a program based on a singular outcome. The duration of the intended behavior change is an important outcome consideration for smoking cessation programs; it would be inadequate to evaluate these programs only on the outcome achieved at a point in time (such as immediately after the conclusion of a program intervention).

An alternative framework to SPO has been proposed by Glasgow *et al.* (1999) and used to evaluate the public health impact of health promotion. The RE-AIM model assesses five dimensions of program impact: reach, efficacy, adoption, implementation, and maintenance of a program. This model reflects who is affected by a program, policy, or service (**reach**), the consequences or outcomes (**efficacy**), how influential the program is (**adoption**), how effective a program is (**implementation**), and whether or not long-term change is sustained (**maintenance**). Each of these dimensions can be measured at different levels (e.g., individual, organizational or community). The relationships across dimensions and levels would need to be evaluated to determine the population-based impact of a service, program, or health system.

At the international level, the World Health Organization (WHO) (2000) has proposed an evaluation framework that is more oriented to the systems level. Five dimensions are utilized for assessing a health system: (1) overall level of health; (2) the distribution of health in the population; (3) the overall level of responsiveness; (4) the distribution of responsiveness; and (5) the distribution of financial contribution. The disability-adjusted life expectancy (DALE) is the measure of health used by the WHO (refer back to Chapter 3, this volume, for computation). The distribution of DALEs according to gender, global geographic subregions, and member nations has been examined. Responsiveness is the manner in which a system promotes utilization, namely respect for persons and client orientation as obtained through surveys of the country's population. Financing considers the balance between out-of-pocket health care expenses relative to prepaid insurance coverage. According to the WHO evaluation methodology, Japan outranks the United States in terms of the overall efficacy of the health system; Chile, Colombia, and Cuba rate higher than other Latin American countries; and that most of the worst-off countries are all in Africa.

Regardless of the conceptual framework, the evaluation determines whether or not the goals and objectives are met by assessing the level of conformance to evaluation criteria. But ultimately, the results of the evaluation must address the adequacy of the intervention be it a change in a national health insuring mechanism or the addition of new services to a hospital relative to the health status of the intended target population.

Analytical Approaches to Evaluation: An Epidemiological Perspective

Evaluation studies are an essential part of the assessment of health program performance. Since the success of a program in achieving its goals is influenced by the characteristics of the population served, an epidemiological perspective is crucial in the evaluation process. Programs are instituted in defined populations; thus epidemiological methods can be used to quantify the problem and measure and analyze program outcomes. Since epidemiological research also focuses on defined populations, the study designs and statistical methods applicable for conducting program evaluations are often those used in epidemiological research. A description of these designs and statistical methods follows.

Study Designs

Once it has been determined what aspect of the health care delivery system will be evaluated, the design of the evaluation can be developed. The initial and most crucial consideration in design selection is the timing for introduction of a program (or intervention) relative to the evaluation process. If the program has been ongoing when the evaluation is initiated, an observational study may be selected. If the program is introduced simultaneous with the evaluation process, an experimental design is more appropriate. The distinction among the observations designs is determined by how sample was drawn relative to when exposure and outcome was determined and when (Fig. 6.2).

Observational Studies

The three common observational designs used in evaluation studies are: case series, descriptive, cross-sectional, case–control, and longitudinal (or prospective). These designs are termed observational as no manipulation occurs of the independent variable.

The **case series** compiles information from a set of organizations or persons who have some predetermined characteristics. The sample is based on convenience, but some referent is maintained by either time or place. The purpose of the case series is to aid in the initial estimate of the magnitude of a problem or in framing a question about a relationship. A case series based on a set of organizations, such as teaching hospitals, would allow the question of, "Is the readmission rate to teaching hospitals high?" A case series based on patients using this theme

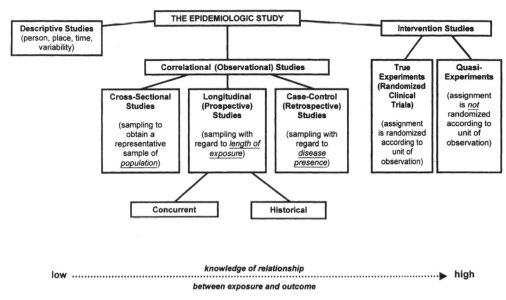

Figure 6.2. Categories of common epidemiological study designs.

would be to describe all the reasons patients were readmitted to a set of urban teaching hospitals in one year.

The **descriptive study** seeks to obtain information about the variability of an outcome, usually through rate measures relative to selected characteristics in particular by person, place, and time. Small-area analysis is one example of a descriptive study as its purpose is to assess the main dimensions of health system performance, namely cost control, access, and quality (Rohrer, 1993).

A **cross-sectional study** can be done to estimate population parameters (e.g., means, proportions, odds ratios, totals) that represent the magnitude of a risk factor, to determine the extent of a health problem in a population, and/or to test a hypothesis related to the degree of association between a causative factor and a health outcome in a defined population. The estimates provided by a cross-sectional study are static, representing the amount of the exposure, condition, or association at one point in time or period. Seldom is an entire population studied; rather, a sample or a collection of individual or group members is selected in order to estimate the desired population parameters. The sample for a cross-sectional study is selected in a random manner to represent the population from which it came. The reader is advised to consult Levy and Lemeshow (1999) for a discussion of the various methods for selecting a random sample. The source of data used in cross-sectional studies most often is obtained from some form of survey, namely telephone or personal interviews, self-administered questionnaires, or record reviews. Some studies also may obtain information derived from clinical examinations and biological measurements.

The cross-sectional study design provides a quick assessment of the strength of the relationship between a factor (experience in treatment in the above example) and a health outcome (e.g., mortality) associated with it. However, because the sample is cross-classified with respect to the attributes present at the time of sample selection, a cross-sectional study has limited use for determining causality because its design does not enable delineation of the timing of the onset of the putative cause relative to its hypothetical outcome. An example of a cross-sectional analysis is a study by Shea *et al.* (1999) that examines the relationship between patient sociodemographic and likelihood of referral to a specialist. A random sample of Medicare beneficiaries was drawn. Physician specialist referrals (classified as referral: yes or no) were 1.49 times more likely among those Medicare beneficiaries who also had Medicaid (classified as Medicaid: yes or no).

The purpose of a **case–control study** is to compare the prevalence of exposure factors between two or more groups. One group possesses the outcome under investigation; the other group or groups, known as control or comparison groups, do not. Information pertaining to exposure is obtained after the outcome has occurred. When rapid assessment of the relationship between exposure and outcome is required, for example when an initial assessment of a new medical technology is required, a case–control study may be conducted. Ideally, such evaluations should be done with a randomized clinical trial. However, this may not be feasible or economical during initial assessment.

Controls might be identified from a variety of sources. A sample from the general population might be drawn from birth registries, tax lists, driver's license lists, commercially prepared lists (Olson *et al.*, 2000), or through random digit dialing for telephone interviews (Olson *et al.*, 1992; Funkhouser *et al.*, 2000), depending on the subject of the evaluation. Bohlke *et al.* (1999) evaluated resident lists or published population rosters for three case–control studies of ovarian cancer and found greater than 90% of the cases on the lists. It is important to test that the source of controls is not biased. Bohlke *et al.* (1999) noted that age was a factor to be considered: cases under 40 years old were less likely than older cases to be on the lists of residents.

An example of an evaluation using different control groups to assess differences in result inferences is illustrated in a study by Moritz *et al.* (1997) utilizing a case–control design. Hip fracture cases and two different control groups, one from the general population of the community served by a hospital and another from persons admitted to the same hospital, were compared in a case–control study of risk factors for hip fracture in women 45 years of age or older. The study found that community controls were more representative of community-dwelling older women than the hospital control sample that was somewhat sicker and more likely to smoke. The study concludes that community controls are more appropriate for hip fracture studies of the elderly.

How are controls selected for a case–control study? Controls may consist of the total population or a sample that is alike in every way to the cases, including being selected from the same population and independently of their exposure status, except that they do not have the outcome under investigation. If a control sample is selected, it may be a random or a matched sample. Matching may be pairwise or nonpairwise. In pairwise matching, comparison members of a sample are selected when they have exactly the same value or nearly the same within a given tolerance of a confounding variable. Thus, if a case is a white male, 30 years of age, the control must be a white male, 30 plus or minus 1–5 years, depending on the desired matching tolerance for age. One of the most common approaches for nonpairwise matching is frequency matching. In frequency matching, cases are randomly selected and controls are selected in proportion equal to that of the cases. Thus, if the cases are 20% white, 40% male, and 10% over 65 years of age, controls must be selected to achieve a comparable distribution. Matching is recommended when the number of cases is small (<50) and when the available comparison or control pool is large. Matching must not be done on exposure. If numerous variables are required in order to control for the confounding variable, multivariable matching should be considered. The reader is advised to consult Anderson *et al.* (1980).

Case–control studies can be done relatively quickly and inexpensively and they can be performed with a comparatively small sample size. The limitations of case–control studies arise from the manner in which the study sample was acquired (because of the possibility of missing incident cases due to high mortality or other types of losses) and from the retrospective measurement of exposure to the suspect causative factors. The limitations include participant definition bias, self-selection bias, and lead-time bias.

Relevant questions to ask to assess participant definition bias include (1) Do criteria accurately distinguish between cases and controls? (2) Were the criteria uniformly applied? Questions relevant to self-selection bias are (1) Did the cases and controls arise from different service populations? (2) Are the controls a "healthier" population? A question related to lead-time bias is (1) Did the cases come to diagnostic attention sooner?

A major disadvantage of a case–control study is the reliance on the recall of past events or the abstraction of records that may have incomplete information on exposure to causative factors. Case–control studies cannot be used to establish cause and effect per se. However, historical sequencing of suspect causative events relative to the outcome under investigation can be preliminarily gleaned with careful structuring of interview questions and data abstraction forms. Sackett (1979) discusses in-depth other potential biases of case–control studies.

The major purposes of a **longitudinal study** (or **prospective study**) are to observe and document the time between exposure to a factor and outcome, as well as the amount of change in outcome relative to variation in exposure to a factor; or to measure change over time resulting from cohort, aging, or period effects. The sample for a longitudinal study consists of individuals who are free of the outcome variable(s) of interest at the time the study begins but are heterogeneous with respect to exposure (e.g., some have been exposed to a case manager and some have not). The distinguishing feature of this study design is that information on exposure is collected before the outcome occurs.

The two types of longitudinal studies are concurrent prospective and historical prospective. A **concurrent prospective study** is usually conducted in two stages. The first stage consists of the recruitment of participants. The sample selected must be stable (i.e., unlikely to move away or drop out of the study) and representative of the demographic and health status characteristics of the population from which it was drawn. In the second stage, participants are carefully evaluated to determine that they do not have the health outcome being examined. The individuals who are determined to be "outcome-free" are then followed and observed for a preestablished period of time to determine the occurrence of an outcome relative to exposure levels. A **historical prospective study** uses existing records from a cohort of persons thoroughly and uniformly characterized from a past time, such as persons receiving a comprehensive medical examination and history upon enrollment in a health insurance plan. Although exposure data are assumed to be complete, information on outcome events of interest may have to be compiled.

When the sample of outcome-free individuals is selected for a longitudinal study on the basis of some common event, such as birth year or period of employment at a company, this type of longitudinal study is referred to as a **cohort study**. A sample may be selected to study **period effects** or the impact of some event on all groups over time. Changes in health service utilization rates during economic recessions or in the incidence of back injuries after introduction of a new process in the workplace are topics that could be examined for period effects using a longitudinal study design. A sample may also be selected to study **aging effects**, whereby the context of the study is concerned with the changes occurring with the passage of time, regardless of cohort or period of measurement, that are physiological, cognitive, and functional in nature. This type of study could be important to a large employer attempting to project the demand for health care benefits among retirees. It also is important for any country that is experiencing an aging population and wanting to ensure better quality of life. Leveille *et al.* (1999) followed male and female participants who were aged 65 and older prospectively between 1981 and 1991 to evaluate being disability-free in the year prior to death. They found that moderate physical activity helps prevent disability in later life.

Longitudinal studies offer both advantages and disadvantages. By following individuals over time, measurement of the causative factors as well as the outcome can be more precise. In addition, more than one outcome can be studied if the parameters for defining the outcomes are established at the onset of the study. The duration of observation of participants depends on the estimated average time between exposure to the causative factor(s) and the occurrence of the outcome(s) of interest. Significant potential for selection bias may exist in a longitudinal study as a result of differential participation by age, gender, education, and health status. Other disadvantages include the necessity of a long observation period to accurately ascertain the outcome in the sample, the potential for excessive attrition (>20%) if sample members refuse continued participation, and loss in follow-up or death before the outcome is observed. As the trend toward contracted health care continues, longitudinal studies will become increasingly important due to the need to characterize the experience of population subgroups known to have high utilization rates such as older adults and cigarette smokers (Wolinsky and Johnson, 1991; Vogt and Schweitzer, 1985).

Observational studies often serve as precursors to experimental studies. When associations are detected that suggest that a program has impact upon health status and the intervention(s) can be well defined, the next stop is to evaluate a program using an experimental study design.

Experimental Studies

In experimental studies, an outcome is measured after a program is introduced or an intervention has been applied. The measurement of the outcome can either be immediately after the intervention or at some designated time in the future. Interventional studies may be experimental or quasi-experimental. The elements of **experimental studies** in human populations are: (1) volunteerism, (2) randomization, (3) intervention, and (4) control. An experimental design is the preferred method for evaluating a program.

Volunteerism means that for individuals whose outcomes are observed, informed consent (usually in writing) must be given regarding the nature of the intervention and the benefits and risks of participation in the study (see also Chapter 14). Volunteers may be different in terms of demographic characteristics and health status than nonparticipants.

Control means to have a comparison group as similar as possible to the intervention group with the exception that no intervention is received. The control group may be a group only observed, receiving some placebo, or receiving whatever is felt to be standard care. In the case of evaluating a new health education program, the control group would receive either the standard education given in the clinic or a brochure by one of the staff persons that contains an abbreviated set of information on the health education topic being studied. This is done for ethical reasons.

Randomization means the random assignment of the units of observation to which the conclusions will be drawn into one of the treatment groups. This can be done by a coin toss, use of a table of random numbers, or computer generated. Even with random assignment into study groups, there still is the possibility that there will be an uneven distribution of characteristics in the study groups that could influence the outcome (Murray, 1998). So, for example, consider the evaluation of the impact of a case manager on hospitalization. If more individuals who by chance are disabled and also h   tilizers of health care services are randomized to the no-case-manager group, one might   ne to a false conclusion about the efficacy of a case manager.

If an intervention is to be underta en but randomization or adequate control requirements cannot be achieved, evaluation of planned interventions in the field of health care can be carried out by a **quasi-experimental design**. For example, if assignment to a group is not random, depending instead on current referral patterns, current enrollment in a health plan type, or if health service units not the population within them are randomly assigned, then the study design would be quasi-experimental and less convincing in its conclusions. An example of a quasi-experimental design is the WHO evaluation of a structured antenatal care program (Villar *et al.*, 1998). In this program evaluation, antenatal clinics across the countries in the study were the unit of randomization, not the pregnant women attending the clinics. The study compares the program activities in four countries: Argentina, Cuba, Saudi Arabia, and Thailand. The new antenatal program will be compared with traditional prenatal care activities. Evaluation measures of this program are comprehensive and include outcomes pertaining to mother (e.g., rate of eclampsia) and to the newborn (e.g., rate of very low birth weight), process (e.g., rate of cesarean section), economics (cost-effectiveness), and patient satisfaction.

A **time series design**, which utilizes multiple measurements before the intervention and multiple measurements after the intervention also is considered a type of quasi-experimental design because there is manipulation and control (before versus after). This design is schematically represented as:

$$O_1, O_2, O_3, O_4, \ldots O_i \ X \ O_{i+1}, O_{i+2}, O_{i+3} \ldots O_{i+n}$$

Where O_i are the measurements taken before and after the introduction of the intervention at time interval i, n is the observation number at time i, and X represents at what time the intervention is introduced. This design is most useful when no cyclical or seasonal shifts are expected in the occurrence of the dependent variables. An evaluation of the introduction of Washington State Labor and Industries lumbar fusion guidelines for elective lumbar spinal fusion in injured workers, created in an attempt to curb escalating medical costs for injured workers, was performed using this method (Fig. 6.3). The time series technique can easily be performed using available statistical software (PROC FORECAST) (SAS Institute, 2000).

Although a randomized, controlled experiment is an ideal design for program evaluation, it often is difficult to meet the requirements of such an experiment in social research. Political and economic circumstances may occur during the course of an evaluation and render it difficult to determine whether an intervention had the desired effects. For example, legislation may be passed that substantially changes eligibility to include higher income groups; characteristics of program participants may change and this may affect the outcome, confounding the impact of the intervention. An ethical concern may be raised if randomization is seen as presenting some deprivation or harm to a set of participants. This could occur if study participants are randomized into groups provided different health insurance coverage. If one group has a high copayment, this could be perceived as adversely affecting health by restricting access to care. Since randomized trials rely on volunteers, the individuals comprising a study group may be different from the general population.

Analyzing Intervention Effects

The statistical methods selected to assess program impact depend on both the design and the level of measurement applied for evaluating outcome. A program intervention or indepen-

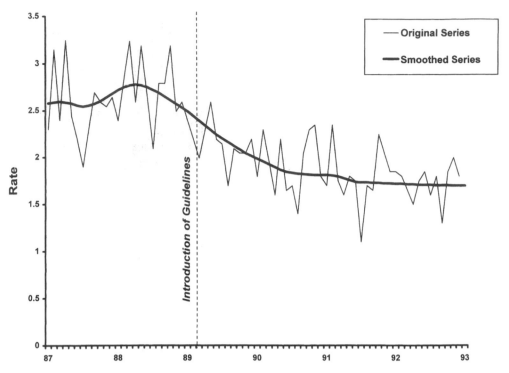

Figure 6.3. Monthly rates of low back operations involving fusion per 100,000 Washington State population. SOURCE: Elam *et al.* (1997).

dent variable is commonly represented as a discrete variable (presence or absence of an intervention). Outcome or dependent variables are commonly concerned with the presence or absence of a condition in the population served by the program being evaluated. Because the dependent variables are typically binary, logistic regression, survival analysis, or Cox regression are commonly used in program evaluation. A description of these methods follows.

Logistic regression is the statistical method used to evaluate an intervention when the outcome variable is categorical (binary or ordinal) and the independent variables (intervention) are continuous or discrete variables, or both. It is also required that all the units of measurement have been observed for the same amount of time, otherwise the Cox regression is used.

Data from Table 6.2 contain the results of a multiple logistic regression of a number of factors that could influence the likelihood of an HMO failing. The odds ratio (OR) for the variable pertaining to HMO size (OR = $e^{2.974}$ = 19.57) indicates that an HMO with less than 10,000 members is nearly 20 times more likely to fail than one with more than 100,000 members (the referent group). The significance of the OR also can be assessed using the Wald chi-square statistic:

$$\text{Wald chi-quare} = [b_i/\text{SE}(b_i)]^2 = (2.97/1.07)^2 = 7.69$$

The Wald chi-square indicates that a statistically significant relationship exists between HMO size and likelihood of failure. However, since the Wald statistic can be very unstable when the error is high in circumstances where the incidence of the outcomes are low, the Wald statistic may not reject the null hypothesis of an exposure factor represented as $\beta X_i = 0$. The likelihood

Table 6.2. Odds Ratio (OR) of HMO Failure
by Various Characteristics Obtained from Multiple Logistic Regression

Characteristic	Beta coefficient	SE[a]	Wald statistic	OR	95% CI[a]
<10,000 members	2.97[b]	1.07	7.69	19.57	2.39, 158.72
10–24,000 members	1.75	1.08	2.61	5.76	0.69, 48.10
25–99,999	1.34	1.12	1.43	3.82	0.42, 34.44
Profit status	−0.08	0.46	0.03	0.92	0.37, 2.25
Federal qualification	0.04	0.38	0.01	1.04	0.49, 2.18
IPA model	0.60	0.38	2.56	1.81	0.86, 2.81
Staff model	−0.66	0.51	1.76	0.52	0.19, 1.41
Network model	0.79	0.62	1.63	2.19	0.65, 7.47
Region 1	−1.43[b]	0.49	8.52	0.24	0.09, 0.62
Region 2	−1.15[b]	0.41	7.79	0.32	0.14, 0.71
Region 3	−0.86	0.53	2.56	0.43	0.15, 1.21

[a]SE, Standard error of the beta coefficient; CI, confidence interval for the odds ratio.
[b]Chi-square significant at the .05 level.
NOTE: The odds ratios are those derived from the simultaneous inclusion of all the characteristics in the model.

ratio test is recommended in these circumstances to assess the significance of a coefficient or OR.

Because the OR, a descriptive parameter, is only an estimate, a 95% confidence interval (CI) containing the true OR can be estimated from computing the upper confidence limit (UCL) and lower confidence limit (LCL). Using the data from Table 6.2, the confidence limits for the OR = 19.57 as follows:

$$\text{UCL for } \ln OR = b_1 + 1.96[\text{SE}(b_1)] = 2.97 + 1.96(1.07) = 5.07$$
$$\text{LCL for } \ln OR = b_i - 1.96[\text{SE}]b_1)] = 2.97 - 1.96(1.07) = 0.88$$

These values can be transformed from the natural log scale:

$$\text{UCL for } OR = e^{b+1.96[\text{SE}(b)]} = e^{2.97 + 1.96(1.07)} = 158.72$$
$$\text{LCL for } OR = e^{b-1.96[\text{SE}(b)]} = e^{2.97-1.96(1.07)} = 2.39$$

This means that the true value for the odds of an HMO failing lies somewhere between 2.39 and 158.72. Since the 95% CI does not contain unity, the OR of an HMO failing is increasing when the membership panel is less than 10,000 persons, which is a statistically significant association. The conclusions reached from a two-sided test statistic will be identical to those from an assessment of the CI. The wider the confidence interval, the less precise is the estimate of the OR. A small sample size and a limited number of events contribute to the imprecision.

Survival analysis examines the probability of an event (e.g., death, recidivism) in relationship to the amount of time each member in the sample was observed. For program evaluation, the period of concern is the time from a group's exposure to an intervention to the occurrence of the outcome of interest. This requires that the members of the sample be routinely monitored to document when an outcome occurs. The most common method for computing survival estimates is the product-limit method (Kaplan and Meier, 1958). Table 6.3 displays survival estimates (expressed as percentages or probabilities) of patients in a rehabilitation program. These estimates were obtained by applying the Kaplan–Meier approach. The steps necessary to obtain survival estimates are: (1) compute the interval from the

**Table 6.3. Computation of Product-Limit Survival Estimates
of a Hypothetical Cohort of Liver Transplant Patients**

Ordered survival time in months (t_x)	Number at risk[a]	Number censored	Number of deaths	Conditional probability of survival	Survival function $s(t)$
2	15	0	1	$1 - 1/15 = 1 - .067$	$14/15 = 0.933$
3	14	0	1	$1 - 1/14 = 1 - .071$	$0.933 \times 13/14 = 0.866$
6	13	1	1	$1 - 1/13 = 1 - .077$	$0.866 \times 12/13 = 0.799$
12	11	2	1	$1 - 1/11 = 1 - .091$	$0.799 \times 10/11 = 0.726$
18	8	2	0	$1 - 0/8 = 1.000$	$0.726 \times 8/8 = 0.726$
20	6	0	2	$1 - 2/6 = 1 - .333$	$0.726 \times 4/6 = 0.484$
22	4	0	0	$1 - 0/4 = 1.00$	$0.484 \times 4/4 = 0.484$

[a]Number at risk at time t_x is the number alive and under observation just before t_x who have the potential for experiencing the outcome.

beginning of the observation to the date the subject was last seen or the date of occurrence of the outcome of interest for each member of the cohort (the survival time); (2) order the survival times; (3) compute the probability of surviving from the beginning to the end of an interval by dividing the number experiencing the outcome during the interval by those alive at the beginning of the interval (the conditional probability); and (4) compute the probability of surviving beyond this point, $\hat{s}(t)$, by multiplying together the conditional probabilities from each successive time interval. Individuals not experiencing the event by the end of the study are termed "censored" in their contribution of time to the estimation of the survival experience. Individuals experiencing the event are "uncensored" observations. The validity of the survival estimate is enhanced by following the cohort long enough to enable documentation of all the events of interest (i.e., there is a large proportion of "uncensored observations"). A graph of these estimates (Fig. 6.4) illustrates that the 1-year survival of the group is 72.6% and the median survival is 19 months.

   If all events could not be observed by the end of a study period, it is desirable to have at least half the events occur and to have the censored events distributed evenly throughout the study period. If the survival estimates of two or more groups are to be statistically compared, the log-rank test or the Mantel–Haenszel chi-square test should be used. The reader should consult Kahn and Sempos (1989).

   Unlike the log-rank or the Mantel–Haenszel test, which divide variables into groups to test the equality of survival curves, the **Cox regression** can handle both continuous and discrete variables (e.g., gender, educational attainment) and time-varying independent variables, such as those related to duration of a program (Cox, 1972). The formula below states that a hazard at time t, or $h(t)$, is the probability of an outcome m at time t, or $m(t)$, given that the population at risk in a given time, $p(t)$, has survived to time t_{x+n}:

$$h(t) = m(t)/p(t)$$

In Cox regression, the comparison of two groups with respect to an outcome is expressed as an exponential set of independent variables (X_i), as in a regression equation with coefficients (β_i):

$$h_i(t)/h_o(t) = e^{\beta_i X_i}$$

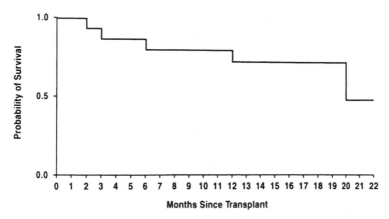

Figure 6.4. Plot of product-limit survival estimates of hypothetical liver transplant patients. NOTE: The plot of survival probabilities starts at 1.0 (100% of the sample is alive at the start of observation).

The ratio of the hazards in the above equation represents a relative risk. A major assumption in Cox regression is that the effect of the relative risk associated with a variable does not change over time, that is, the hazard functions are proportional over time. This method should be considered for use only if a small proportion of the observations are censored. Cox regression analysis and Kaplan–Meier survival analysis can be performed in both SAS and SPSS.

Other Analytic Methods

In reality, many programs are simultaneously operating within a health care system. Administrators may wish to isolate the significance of the occurrence of multiple outcomes (e.g., those associated with complications, repeated hospitalization, and mortality) given multiple, ongoing programs. At times, these outcome variables may be correlated with each other and considered indicators of a single underlying latent construct (e.g., adverse patient outcomes). An administrator also may be interested in assessing the effect of an intervention on more than one outcome variable at a time for the purpose of assessing the relationships between the outcome variables as well as the relationship between the intervention and the outcomes. An analytic method called **structural equation models** (SEM) can be used in evaluating these relationships, and is described more fully in Chapter 4 (this volume).

When the design calls for the measurement of multiple observations over a duration of time, such as in the case of a time series design, an analytical model called **autoregressive integrated moving average** (ARIMA) may be used (Box and Jenkins, 1976). This method uses a regression structure to predict future values from past values.

Because studies may not always support the same finding, even when the same design and analytic methods are used, **meta-analysis** may be appropriate in terms of attempting to evaluate an overall effect (DerSimonian and Laird, 1986). In the context of program evaluation, meta-analysis may be used to summarize the estimate of the size of the program's effect (commonly measured by an odds ratio or relative risk) on specific program outcomes across several studies. Chapter 10 presents an application of meta-analysis.

There are two major approaches to analyzing the costs and benefits of health care that are not within the scope of epidemiological applications but are often used to supplement evaluations. These two approaches are **cost-benefit** and **cost-effectiveness** analysis (Drummond *et al.*, 1997). Cost-benefit analysis plots the dollars expended for each program against the monetary value of benefits represented as society's value of the outcome (e.g., how much is a life worth?). In cost-effectiveness analysis, costs are calculated and programs are compared based on their achievement of a specific outcome expressed in terms of years of life saved or days of illness avoided. For both methods, the direct program costs (personnel, equipment, etc.) and indirect costs (e.g., caregiver time and time lost from work) are computed, with indirect costs being the most difficult to quantify. Benefits and costs also should be discounted as they are factored into the computations because their present values may not be the same as the future values. See Chapter 13 for further discussion of the interrelationship between economic analysis, epidemiology, and health care management in the evaluation of health services and policies.

Prospects of Health Services Evaluation

Who should evaluate health care and how these evaluations should be financed are issues of increasing importance for those administering a health care system. The answer to the first question is contingent on what aspects of the health care system are being evaluated. If the technical quality of care is being assessed, then the medical profession has the knowledge required to capably evaluate this aspect (Greenlick, 1981). If the broader interrelationships of access, availability, effectiveness, efficiency, and acceptability are being evaluated, the competencies of a range of medical and nonmedical professions and the public may be necessary to accomplish the assessment.

The answer to the question of financial responsibility for evaluations depends on who mandates the implementation of a program. If it is initiated because of a governmental mandate, then the responsibility for financing the evaluation lies with the government. For example, programs implemented at a national level for hospitals or nursing homes should be evaluated using federal funds. Similarly, mandated state and local interventions should be financed through state/local initiatives. Alternately, if the focus of an evaluation is a program implemented by a single hospital or nursing home, a chain of one of these, or an individual group practice, then the responsibility for funding lies with the entity responsible for implementation of the program, whether the funding comes from internal resources or an external source such as a private foundation.

Conclusion

Evaluation will continue to play an important role for health care managers in all countries, particularly in light of population-based planning, for several reasons. First, the organization of formal and informal alliances in the health care industry and the competition among them will prompt managers to continuously evaluate morbidity, mortality, and disability trends associated with service delivery and treatment of health problems in order to modify or discard services and treatments that are not efficient, effective, and of high quality. Second, the number and size of social programs have grown over time with the broadening scope of government involvement in health and social service issues. The application of epidemiological methods is useful for monitoring the health of the population and identifying changes over time. Epidemiology is based on the premise that health problems that can be identified often can be corrected. Last, programs addressing the needs of aging populations will proliferate and necessitate evaluation to assess changing needs, assure that expectations are met, and promote achievement of the desired health outcomes. Epidemiological methods can be used effectively to target identified needs and to assess the implications of programs or interventions for health care policy.

Case Studies

Case Study No. 1
Evaluation of an Influenza Vaccination Program

Each year the government recommends that vulnerable populations should be protected against new strains of influenza. There is a voluntary program that encourages the elderly population of the country to seek prevention by getting an injection to protect against potentially life-threatening influenza. Despite getting their "flu shot" in the past, some people still got the "flu." The government mandates that an evaluation be done to assess the effectiveness of this protective measure. The mandate requires a comparison of those who obtained the vaccination and those who did not, for those who got the flu and those who did not.

Q.1. Propose an evaluation study design to assess the elderly eligible for the program.

Q.2. What would be important factors to control for to determine why some elderly persons got the flu despite getting the vaccination?

Q.3. What epidemiological methods can be employed to examine the differences between elderly who received the vaccination and those who did not?

Q.4. How can the evaluation results be used to improve participation in the program in future years?

Case Study No. 2
Impact of a Smoking Prevention Program

The youth of the nation continue to begin smoking despite known risks for cancer and other potentially life-threatening illnesses. You are asked to design a program that will assess the magnitude of the problem in your community or nation and to develop a smoking prevention campaign that includes an evaluation of the campaign. Since it is important to prevent children from starting to use tobacco, it is suggested that schools be used as the organizations through which the intervention could be delivered.

Q.1. What is the initial step in beginning to design this intervention? What epidemiological methods can be used at this stage?

Q.2. How could the level of awareness of tobacco risk factors among teachers, students, and people in the community be determined?

Q.3. Design a school-based program for smoking prevention. How would you evaluate the effectiveness of the school-based program in preventing the new use of tobacco?

Case Study No. 3
Evaluation of Exposure to Tuberculosis

Approximately 8 million new cases of tuberculosis (TB) occur each year in the world. TB associated with HIV infection is at least in part responsible for the increasing incidence. The hospital staff is at higher risk of exposure to airborne pathogens than other occupations. It is recommended that hospital personnel be screened annually for exposure to TB. You work in an office monitoring the reporting of communicable diseases and note that a higher incidence of new cases is coming from one hospital in a region where there are only two hospitals to serve the community. On contacting the hospital with the higher incidence you discover that the staff had not yet been tested this year. You have been directed to assess exposure to TB and implement standard guidelines.

Q.1. How would you begin to identify and monitor cases where there may be increased risk of exposure to TB?

Q.2. What organizational and epidemiological data are needed to begin an assessment of exposure?

Q.3. Design an evaluative study to compare the TB control programs of the two hospitals in the area.

Case Study No. 4
Comparison of Leading Causes of Death by Age Group

Planning is the first step in devising a program evaluation. In this phase, data are carefully selected that also could be used to prioritize need for selecting a programmatic strategy as well as used for evaluating program impacts. The data in Table 6.4 rank order the 10 leading causes of death by age group.

Q.1. What type of data are used in the table?

Q.2. Interpret the data from table focusing on comparisons across age groups.

Q.3. Assuming that a large managed care plan represents a microcosm of America, choose one cause of death and outline a program that a managed care plan could implement that would address lowering the rate among its members, including how the program would be evaluated.

Case Study No. 5
Organized versus Spontaneous Pap Smear Screening for Cervical Cancer

Nieminen et al. (1999) compared two different strategies for reducing the incidence of invasive cervical cancer. The organized approach consists of a centralized organization inviting women between 30 and 60 years of age for screening every 5 years by letter. The invitation describes the place, date, and time for taking the screening test. The spontaneous screening approach consists of women seeking a Pap smear from a gynecologist. Cases were 179 incident cases of invasive cervical cancer treated at the Helsinki University Central Hospital (HUCH). Controls were 1507 women sampled from the Finnish Population Registry who also were residents of the HUCH catchment area. Questionnaires were sent to cases and controls concerning Pap smear history (before diagnosis date of cancer for cases; before corresponding date for controls), sociodemographic characteristics, and other health habits. The odds ratio of the likelihood of cases ever participating in an organized mass screening for cervical cancer was

Table 6.4. Top 10 Leading Causes of Death in 1998 for Different Age Groups of Americans[a]

Cause	Rank in leading cause of death in			
	Toddlers (1–4 years)	Children (5–14 years)	Adults (25–44 years)	Elderly (65+ years)
Congenital anomalies	2	4		
Unintentional injuries	1	1	1	7
Heart disease	5	5	3	1
Pneumonia and influenza	6	7	10	5
Homicide and legal intervention	3	3	6	
Cerebrovascular disease	9	10	8	3
Benign neoplasms	10			
Chronic liver disease and cirrhosis		7		
Malignant neoplasms	4	2	2	2
Human immunodeficiency virus infection		8	5	
Chronic obstructive pulmonary disease		9	10	4
Suicide		6	4	
Diabetes			9	6
Nephritis				8
Septicemia	7			10
Alzheimer's disease				9

[a]From National Center for Health Statistics (2000).

0.36 (95% CI of 0.26–0.56). The odds ratio of the likelihood of cases ever involved in spontaneous Pap smear activities was 0.82 (95% CI of 0.53–1.26).

Q.1. What can you conclude regarding the effectiveness of organized Pap smear screening?

Q.2. What are some potential confounding variables in this study?

Q.3. Propose an analytic strategy which could be used to evaluate the effectiveness of screening strategy and provide a rationale for its use.

References

Anderson, S., Auquier, A., Hauck, W. W., Oakes, D., Vandaele, W., and Wersberg, H. I., 1980, *Statistical Methods for Comparative Studies*, John Wiley & Sons, New York.

Anonymous, 1999, European multicenter study of natural family planning (1989–1995): Efficacy and drop-out. The European Natural Family Planning Study Groups. *Adv. Contracep.* **15**:69–83.

Bibeau, D., Mullen, K., McLeroy, K., Green, L., and Foshee, V., 1988, Evaluations of workplace smoking cessation programs: A critique. *Am. J. Prev. Med.* **4**:87–95.

Bohlke, K., Harlow, B. L., Cramer, D. W., Spiegelman, D., and Mueller, N. E., 1999, Evaluation of a population roster as a source of population controls: The Massachusetts resident lists, *Am. J. Epidemiol.* **150**:354–358.

Box, G. E. P., and Jenkins, G. M., 1976, *Time Series Analysis: Forecasting and Control*, Holden-Day, San Francisco.

Clement, D. G., Retchin, S. M., Brown, R. S., and Stegall, M. H., 1994, Access and outcomes of elderly patients enrolled in managed care, *JAMA* **271**:1487–1492.

Cox, D. R., 1972, Regression models and life-tables, *J. R. Statist. Soc.* **B34**:187–220.

DerSimonian, R., and Laird, N., 1986, Meta-analysis in clinical trials, *Controlled Clin. Trials* **7:**177–188.

Donabedian, A., 1980, *Explorations in Quality Assessment and Monitoring—Volume I: The Definition of Quality and Approaches to Its Assessment*, Health Administration Press, Ann Arbor, MI.

Drummond, M. F., O'Brien, B. J., Stoddart, G. L., and Torrance, G. W., 1997, *Methods for the Economic Evaluation of Health Programmes*, 2nd ed., Oxford University Press, Cary, NC.

Elam, K., Taylor, V., Ciol, M. A., Franklin, G. M., and Deyo, R. A., 1997, Impact of a worker's compensation practice guideline on lumbar spine fusion in Washington State, *Med. Care* **35:**417–424.

Funkhouser, E., Macaluso, M., and Wang, X., 2000, Alternative strategies for selecting population controls: Comparison of random digit dialing and targeted telephone calls, *Ann. Epidemiol.* **10:**59–67.

Glasgow, R. E., Vogt, T. M., and Boles, S. M., 1999, Evaluating the public health impact of health promotion interventions: The RE-AIM framework, *Am. J. Pub. Health* **89:**1322–1327.

Greenlick, M. R., 1981, Assessing clinical competence: A society view, *Eval. Health Profess.* **4:**3–12.

Kahn, H. A., and Sempos, C. T., 1989, *Statistical Methods in Epidemiology*, Oxford University Press, New York.

Kaplan, E. L., and Meier, P., 1958, Nonparametric estimation from incomplete observations, *J. Am. Statist. Assoc.* **53:**457–481.

Kotchen, J. M., McKean, H. E., Jackson-Thayer, S., Moore, R. W., Straus, R., and Kotchen, T., 1986, Impact of a rural high blood pressure control program on hypertension control and cardiovascular disease mortality, *JAMA* **255:**2177–2182.

Lane, D. S., Polednak, A. P., and Burg, M. A., 1992, Breast cancer screening practices among users of county-funded health centers vs. women in the entire community, *Am. J. Pub. Health* **82:**199–203.

Leveille, S. G., Guralnik, J. M., Ferrucci, L., and Langlois, J. A., 1999, Aging successfully until death in old age: Opportunities for increasing active life expectancy, *Am. J. Epidemiol.* **149:**654–664.

Levy, P. S., and Lemeshow, S., 1999, *Sampling of Populations*, 3rd ed., John Wiley & Sons, New York.

Moritz, D. J., Kelsey, J. L., and Grisso, J. A., 1997, Hospital controls versus community controls: Differences in inferences regarding risk factors for hip fracture, *Am. J. Epidemiol.* **145:**653–660.

Murray, D. M., 1998, *Design and Analysis of Group-Randomized Trials*, Oxford University Press, New York.

National Center for Health Statistics, 2000, *Health United States, 2000, with Adolescent Chartbook*, Author, Hyattsville, MD.

Nieminen, P., Kallio, M., Anttila, A., and Hakama, M., 1999, Organised vs. spontaneous Pap smear screening for cervical cancer: A case–control study, *Int. J. Cancer* **83:**55–58.

Okada, L. M., and Wan, T. T. H., 1980, Impact of community health centers and Medicaid on the use of health services, *Pub. Health Rep.* **95:**520–534.

Olson, S. H., Kelsey, J. L., Pearson, T. A., and Levin, B., 1992, Evaluation of random digit dialing as a method of control selection in case–control studies, *Am. J. Epidemiol.* **135:**210–222.

Olson, S. H., Mignone, L., and Harlap, S., 2000, Selection of control groups by using a commercial database and random digit dialing, *Am. J. Epidemiol.* **152:**585–592.

Retchin, S. M., and Brown, B., 1990, The quality of ambulatory care in Medicare health maintenance organizations, *Am. J. Pub. Health* **80:**411–415.

Rohrer, J. E., 1993, Small area analysis: Descriptive epidemiology in health services research, *Clin. Perf. Qual. Health Care* **1:**35–42.

Rooks, J. P., Weatherby, N. L., Ernst, E., Stapleton, S., Rosen, D., and Rosenfield, A., 1989, Outcomes of care in birth centers, *New Engl. J. Med.* **321:**1804–1811.

Rosen, H. M., and Feigin, W., Sr., 1983, Quality assurance and data feedback, *Health Care Manage. Rev.* **8:**67–74.

Sackett, D. L., 1979, Bias in analytic research, *J. Chronic Dis.* **32:**51–63.

SAS Institute, Inc., 2000, *SAS/ETS Software: Time series forecasting system*, version 6, 1st ed., SAS Institute, Cary, NC.

Shea, D., Stuart, B., Vasey, J., and Nag, S., 1999, Medicare physician referral patterns, *HSR: Health Serv. Res.* **34:**331–348.

Villar, J., Bakketeig, L., Donner, A., Al-Mazrou, Y., Ba'aqeel, H., Belizan, J. M., Carroli, G., Farnot, U., Lumbiganon, P., Piaggio, G., and Berendes, H., 1998, The WHO Antenatal Care Randomised Controlled Trial: Rationale and study design, *Paediatr. Perinat. Epidemiol.* **12**(Suppl.2):7–58.

Vogt, T. M., and Schweitzer, S. O., 1985, Medical costs of cigarette smoking in a health maintenance organization, *Am. J. Epidemiol.* **122:**1060–1066.

Wan, T. T. H., Weissert, W. G., and Livieratos, B. B., 1980, Geriatric day care and homemaker services: An experimental study, *J. Gerontol.* **35:**256–274.

Wolinsky, F. D., and Johnson, R. J., 1991, The use of health services by older adults, *J. Gerontol.* **46:**S345–357.

World Health Organization, 2000, *The World Health Report 2000*, WHO, Geneva, Switzerland.

Young, G. J., and Cohen, B. B., 1991, Inequities in hospital care, the Massachusetts experience, *Inquiry* **28:**255–262.

Specialty Areas

7

Epidemiology and Health Care Quality Management

Diane R. Weber, Helen Jo Neikirk, and Marcia B. Hargreaves

Introduction

Quality management parallels the goal of epidemiology in that it also seeks to improve health of populations. Quality management involves analysis of variation and identifying factors affecting health outcomes in populations. Epidemiological principles provide a foundation for the measurement of quality and ensure that quality management efforts are reflective of and relevant to the populations of interest. We examine the methodologies used to measure, analyze, and improve quality in health care and explore the epidemiological concepts that facilitate quality management procedures. Health care organizations' use of various tools and techniques to assess quality, identify improvement opportunities, and implement change are presented. Readers are encouraged to review the case studies at the end of the chapter to further explore the relationship between health care quality management and epidemiology.

Interrelationship between Health Care Quality Management and Epidemiology

Epidemiological methods are essential components of quality management providing a conceptual framework and tools for the assessment of adverse (sentinel) events and variation in processes and outcomes, elimination of unwanted variation, surveillance (monitoring) strategies, and improvement of average performance levels. Epidemiological techniques help the quality manager to: (1) describe variation in quality; (2) identify the causes of that variation; (3) select methods to reduce unwanted variation and improve quality; and (4) assist

Diane R. Weber   Quality Services, University HealthSystem Consortium, Oak Brook, Illinois 60523.   Helen Jo Neikirk   Clinical Information Management, University HealthSystem Consortium, Oak Brook, Illinois 60523.   Marcia B. Hargreaves   Quality Improvement and Volunteer Services, Rush-Presbyterian-St. Luke's Medical Center, and Department of Health Systems Management, Rush University, Chicago, Illinois 60612.

Epidemiology and the Delivery of Health Care Services: Methods and Applications, Second Edition, edited by Denise M. Oleske. Kluwer Academic/Plenum Publishers, New York, 2001.

health care organizations and systems in applying these methods to improve performance and ultimately outcomes of care. The quality concepts and tools originated in industrial settings. Collectively known as total quality management or continuous quality improvement, these methods have been applied to the health care setting since the mid to late 1980s (Berwick *et al.*, 1990; Laffel and Blumenthal, 1989; James, 1990; Neuhauser *et al.*, 1995).

The emergence of the application of epidemiology to health care quality was the identification of wide variation in the processes and outcomes of care among patients receiving routine treatment for the same conditions in different geographic areas and care settings (Wennberg and Gittelsohn, 1973; Vayda, 1973). Although some of this variation could be attributed to patient characteristics and disease severity, differences in provider preferences and practice patterns that could not be supported by research or corresponding improvements in outcome were found. This led to an impression that much of medical practice was not based strictly on science. Because health care delivery is an extremely complex activity involving patients, providers, and different care settings, some variation in the processes and outcomes is inevitable. The challenge for providers and all those interested in improving the quality of health care is to identify those practices that produce the best outcomes. Epidemiology provides methods and tools to help meet this challenge.

Quality Management Defined

The Institute of Medicine (IOM) defines quality of care as "the degree to which health services for individuals and populations increase the likelihood of desired health outcomes and are consistent with current professional knowledge" (Institute of Medicine, 1990, p. 180). The definition supports the inherent goal of health care to produce beneficial outcomes for patients, providers, and society. It also emphasizes the need to continuously provide evidenced-based, contemporary care. Finally, the IOM recommends that the outcomes of individuals as well as groups of patients be examinied as part of any quality assessment (Institute of Medicine, 1999b).

Quality management involves continuous planning, control, and improvement (Palmer *et al.*, 1991). Quality planning requires health care organizations to strategically design and provide services using effective processes. Quality control refers to the assurance that processes are functioning within standards and that levels of performance are achieved. To monitor levels of performance, quality control requires quality assessment and quality measurement. Quality improvement pertains to the actions taken to improve performance. Donabedian and colleagues (Palmer *et al.*, 1991) assert that manage health care quality covers three dimensions: the structures supporting care, the processes used to deliver care, and the outcomes or results of the care rendered. All play a critical role in quality. Structures might include medical equipment, buildings, and staff, which if inadequate or inaccessible might lead to adverse consequences. Process concerns the procedures involved in delivering care. By measuring the steps taken to provide patient care, providers can examine variation in practices and uncover processes that work well. Outcomes describe how care changes the health status of a patient (Palmer *et al.*, 1991). Sample outcome measures might include customer satisfaction, health-related quality of life, or clinical endpoints of care (complications, mortality, test results) (Nelson *et al.*, 1996). Most outcomes are influenced by patient factors outside of provider control (such as severity of illness), suggesting the need to adjust for these factors when comparing providers (see "Risk Adjustment," later in this chapter).

With this structure–process–outcomes framework, various quality theorists introduced the concept of "systems-thinking" in the 1980s and revolutionized health care quality management. Earlier efforts often relied on the "bad apple" theory to correct deficiencies or error and focused on punishing individuals after an adverse outcome occurred. This later approach did little to change the process of care. Systems thinking, on the other hand, encourages health care leaders to understand all the processes and structures comprising the system of care and to improve these in a proactive, mutually supportive manner (Batalden and Stoltz, 1993). In 1999, the IOM issued a report that urged health care organizations to fix faulty systems leading to medical mishaps like medication errors, unexpected deaths, or surgeries performed on the wrong side of the patient. The incidence of serious adverse drug reactions (ADR) alone is estimated to be 6.7% annually and fatal ADRs 0.32% of hospitalized patients (Lazarou *et al.*, 1998).

Organizational Approaches to Quality Management

Many health care quality programs were formally established to meet standards set forth by accreditation, government, and licensing agencies (Roberts *et al.*, 1987). Basic minimal functions included quality measurement, medical staff quality monitoring, peer review, blood usage review, medical records review, drug usage evaluation, surgical appropriateness review, and infection control. Often, attention was focused on compliance to these externally imposed mandates without any real measurement to determine whether compliance actually enhanced the quality of care within a given organization.

Quality management programs have evolved in response to strong external pressures challenging health care organizations' ability to provide appropriate care at a reasonable cost. For example, in England there is an increasing emphasis on organizations measuring performance (Naylor, 1999). In the United States, there is an increasing demand for accountability and shared data on health care performance from purchasers, consumer groups, managed care agencies, accreditation agencies, and legislators.

Ever-escalating health care costs have led to financial downsizing and other cost-cutting measures. Worldwide, health care quality in the public sector presents unique challenges. The motivating factors to drive improvement may stem from a need to better conserve resources. Projects may focus on providing better continuity, reducing length of stay and reducing unnecessary hospital admissions (Ensor and Thompson, 1999).

Although quality management does not directly produce revenue, it can be a protective maneuver for organizations in that clinical risks are minimized and cost-control opportunities become apparent. In addition, customer satisfaction may result, leading to improved competitive positioning, where applicable.

Programmatic Options in Quality Management

Health care organizations across the globe are challenged to improve the quality of care provided while reducing costs. A much wider variety of quality management programs, functions, and improvement processes are being utilized in health care now than ever before, the common denominator being the desired end result: seeking to improve one or more of the dimensions of quality (accessibility, efficiency, safety, timeliness, appropriateness, or effectiveness of care). Examples of health care improvement programs and initiatives appear below. It is important to understand that an organization may have more than one program in place.

The focus of a quality management program can be reflected in its title. In response to government and regulatory requirements for quality management, early programs were known as "quality assurance," later "quality assessment," "quality improvement," "quality management," and "performance improvement." Continuous quality improvement and total quality management programs became popular in the 1980s, and introduced the new systems thinking to health care organizations. Health care quality programs added new functions, such as quality improvement training, use of teams, team facilitation, storyboard creation, and the routine use of decision management tools and statistical process control techniques.

Over time, some health care organizations dropped the stale "quality" reference and attempted to more clearly define the area of focus. For example, a clinical process improvement program has a different focus than an operations improvement program. A clinical resource management program focuses on the costs of providing care in an effort to provide efficient yet appropriate care. A variety of programmatic quality initiatives pertinent to hospital obstetrical services are displayed in Table 7.1. Although these programs can promote favorable improvement of health care outcomes, success is predicated on the existence of other necessary components of quality improvement such as upper management commitment, quality as a central priority, and a focus on processes (Joint Commission on Accreditation of Health Care Organizations, 1992).

Quality Planning

Consistent with health care quality guru, Joseph Juran, quality improvement in some organizations is perceived as a way of managing business (Oberle, 1990). When truly capitalized upon, quality improvement approaches can guide and support all business operations. Like any business initiative, planning is the key to success. Yet, it often is an overlooked step in quality management.

Table 7.1. Examples of Programmatic Quality Initiatives for Hospital Obstetrical Care[a]

✓ Reports to physicians on
  • Their own individual cesarean section rates
  • The obstetrical department's overall C-section rates
  • Their own individual VBAC[b] rates
  • The obstetrical department's VBAC rates
✓ Multidisciplinary conferences held on individual obstetrical cases
✓ Other review of obstetrical cases within the department
✓ External review of obstetrical cases
✓ Practice guidelines for
  • Nursing monitoring of labor
  • VBAC
  • Electronic fetal monitoring
  • Breech deliveries
  • Induction and augmentation of labor
  • Fetal distress

[a]From Oleske (1997).
[b]VBAC, vaginal birth after cesarean.

Quality projects are often undertaken indiscriminately, with little thought to the resources required or the potential benefit (Clark *et al.*, 1994). Adding fuel to the problem is the failure to implement a review process by which projects are discontinued. As a result, health care organizations often find themselves with countless initiatives and measurement activities, finding themselves "data rich and information poor."

To effectively manage quality initiatives, organizations must determine strategic priorities for improvement based on the products and services needed by customers (Berwick *et al.*, 1990). Ultimately, projects should be linked to an organization's mission, vision and survival (Clark *et al.*, 1994). Often, such efforts focus on managing performance according to standards of care, the reduction of risk, and/or the improvement of performance according to a new level of excellence.

Performance According to Standards, Guidelines, and Other Management Strategies

To ensure that processes are working as planned and that appropriate levels of performance are achieved, various quality control functions are undertaken in health care. This involves compliance with laws, standards, implementation of guidelines or other determined thresholds, and other management strategies (utilization management, case management, risk management, and best practices).

Performance According to Standards

Although laws and regulations do not drive improvement projects, regulatory compliance is an absolute requirement for operations, and hence are a means of setting standards for health care organizations. A standard is a statement that defines the performance level, processes, and structures that must be in place to assure quality of care. Any issue associated with licensure, accreditation, or other external inspection must be given due attention or a hospital, health plan, or other health care facility will risk losing significant resources in the effort to reverse a larger problem. It is advantageous to address regulations in a proactive manner to avoid costly, time-consuming repercussions that could be related to minor oversights of specific standards or requirements. Of particular concern are regulations related to medical and other staff (e.g., nurse anesthetists) credentialing, licensure, staff competency, safety (staff and patients), the environment of care, and the environment surrounding the health care facility (e.g., for biomedical waste disposal). Standards data reporting requirements for each of these are now an essential part of accreditation criteria or licensure of a hospital or its various program components and have been developed in response for the need to monitor quality. Reporting can also be legislated. For example, delayed reporting of cancer incidence data as required by state law to a state health department may result in severe fines. Other aspects of health care delivery may be legislated as well. On October 10, 1999, Governor Davis of California signed AB394 into law the first legislation that will set nurse-patient ratios in all aspects of acute care hospitals.

There is ample evidence that standards, licensure, and accreditation affect the quality of care offered through health service units. For example, the National Committee for Quality Assurance (NCQA) (1999) reported that those health plans with NCQA Accreditation outperform those that have not earned NCQA Accreditation.

Clinical Practice Guidelines

Clinical practice guidelines have been utilized to reduce variation that is undesirable and unnecessary in clinical practice (Roberts, 1998). The key features of a clinical practice guideline according to the National Guideline Clearinghouse (NCG) (2000) are that it should: (1) have a structured abstract about the guideline and its development; (2) be focused on a specific clinical circumstances; (3) be based on a verifiable, systematic literature search and review of existing evidence published in peer-reviewed journals; and (4) be current (developed or revised within 5 years). Clinical practice guidelines (CPG) may be general recommendations, detailed clinical pathways (care maps), algorithms (decision-trees), or protocols. CPGs have been developed by agencies such as the Agency for Health Care Policy and Research (AHCPR) and professional societies (e.g., American College for Obstetricians and Gynecologists; North American Spine Society, American Geriatrics Society to name a few). They can also be developed by expert consensus within an organization (Gleicher *et al.*, 2000). The best CPGs are those that are developed through a multidisciplinary team and integrate the latest pathophysiological rationale, caregiver experience, and patient preferences with valid and current clinical research evidence (Ellrodt *et al.*, 1997). To set the pathway in motion at the right moment, applicable patient groups qualifying for pathway assignment must first be identified in a timely (often by nursing personnel) and accurate manner.

Each pathway should have clear criteria regarding milestones in the patient's progress. Nurses and/or case managers can intervene in a timely manner when processes are not occurring as outlined in the pathway. They also can help collect data on variances from the pathway and use this information in case management.

Variance tracking and outcome measurement can help demonstrate the success of the CPG. Variance tracking refers to the monitoring of how frequently aspects of the CPG were carried out as described. Not all variations from the CPG are undesirable, however. Each patient requires a plan of care that is unique to his or her physical and psychosocial needs (Joint Commission, 1999). Clinical practice guidelines, pathways, and care maps are not meant to replace clinical experience or judgment; they act only as a guide in the treatment of a particular disease or procedure. Some variation from the guidelines to meet individual patients' needs is expected and even desirable.

Patient outcomes also can be measured as part of the CPG effort. However, since data collection is a costly endeavor, it is suggested that only significant outcomes be measured. Measures to be considered might include adverse drug reaction rates, infection rates, mortality, patient satisfaction, mobility, return to previous activity level, and readmission rate (Roberts, 1998).

Critical success factors for CPG implementation include physician commitment; a multidisciplinary team of caregivers leading the effort, dissemination, and use of data; and computerized information systems support. To reinforce the intent of the CPG or pathway, organizations should consider developing supplemental tools, such as standing order sets on key areas of consensus, pathway reminders, and computerized informational system prompts.

Utilization Management

Utilization management is "the review of services delivered by a health care provider to determine whether, according to pre-established standards, the services were medically necessary" (University Hospital Consortium, 1994, p. 6). Utilization management staffs become familiar with criteria and thresholds set by multiple payer representatives in order to validate the need for initial or continued care. Utilization management is performed concurrent with a patient's stay, during which the appropriateness and quality of care are monitored. Since long lengths of hospital stay have been associated with increased nosocomial infection rates, utilization management aimed at reducing length of stay can benefit the patients as well as a hospital reimbursed under some form of capitated arrangement.

Case Management

Similar to utilization management, case management involves more in-depth mobilization, monitoring, and rationalization of the resources patients use over the course of an illness (Henderson and Wallack, 1987). Case management programs are either centralized across an institution or decentralized according to major categories of patients, such as service lines or clinical conditions. Working with members of the health care team, the patient, family members, and payers, case managers facilitate the efficient use of time and resources to coordinate effective care. Some case managers are employed by inpatient facilities and others by health care insurers. Satinsky (1995) explains that case management "can cross provider lines and coordinate care rendered in multiple locations…(and)…can monitor quality and cost across a continuum of care, helping providers deal with the shifting of financial risk" (p. 2). Organizations employing both case management and utilization management must avoid duplication of effort, as there is considerable similarity in functions.

Risk Management

Risk management functions are closely tied to quality performance management in that they seek to reduce the chance of injury or other adverse event resulting from clinical error. Clinical errors, such as medication errors, wrong side surgeries, and falls or injuries resulting from an unsafe situation, deserve constant attention to eradicate such problems. Many of these errors are measured continuously, and some of the more serious errors are intensively reviewed to identify root causes. The most serious errors are known as "sentinel events."

A sentinel event is "an unexpected occurrence involving death or serious physical or psychological injury, or the risk thereof. Serious injury specifically includes loss of limb or function" (Joint Commission, 1999, p. PI-6). Lucian L. Leape (1994), authority on medical mistakes, believes that such errors are evidence of system flaws, not character flaws. Consistent with Leape's philosophy, the focus of a root cause analysis is not on individuals but rather on systems and processes. For example, the incident of an amputation of the wrong leg reflects a deeper message than "it was the surgeon's fault." In fact, there are many ways to prevent wrong side surgeries, many of which involve various processes and systems of care. For example, it may be the process of patient identification, or the communication among staff members, or the physical assessment procedures that necessitate a closer look. Because the health care industry thus far has not been able to successfully reduce errors, new regulatory demands may emerge. The IOM has suggested increased regulatory oversight in an effort to reduce medical errors by 50% by the year 2004 (Institute of Medicine, 1999a; also view this online at http://www.iom.edu).

Best Practices

Health care organizations are finding that some of the best improvement ideas stem from the best practices of other institutions. The practice of best practices involves the

Table 7.2. Example of Benchmarking Quality Performance Indicators and Outcomes
for Acute Myocardial Infarction (MI) in Top 100 and Peer Hospitals, by Hospital Type, 1994–1996

Indicator or outcome	Small rural		Small urban		Nonteaching		Teaching	
	Top 100	Peer	Top 100	Peer	Top 100	Peer	Top 100	Peer
Thrombolytics adminstered	39.3%	64.6%	63.5%	63.6%	60.3%	61.5%	53.7%	55.4%
Ideal candidates receiving beta-blockers	51.7%	51.5%	56.3%	60.5%	67.6%	59.8%	67.4%	65.5%
30-day mortality risk adjusted	18.1%	19.8%	20.3%	18.8%	18.4%	18.4%	17.2%	17.3%
Readmission 180 days after discharge among survivors for MI	6.6%	7.2%	7.0%	6.8%	6.6%	6.4%	5.4%	6.4%

[a]From Chen *et al.* (1999).

adoption or adaptation of the good features of the best-demonstrated practices of other organizations. Benchmarking seeks to identify the performance possible rather than performance that is within acceptable parameters. Magazine "report cards" of "Top Hospitals," "Top Doctors," and "Top Health Plans" are a form of benchmarking. Table 7.2 displays an example of the format for these results when benchmarking quality of care given to patients admitted for treatment of acute myocardial infarction for hospitals of various bed sizes and geographic area. Besides benchmarking hospitals and health plans, benchmarking home care practices also is growing (Woomer *et al.*, 1999). Benchmarking is not unique to the US health care. The National Health Service (NHS) of England benchmarks various performance indicators by NHS Health Authority and by Hospital Trust according to geographic area, type, and size of hospital. This information is available in its website: http://www.doh.gov.uk/nhsperformanceindicators/hlpi2000/arealist_t.html.

Models for Systematic Improvement

To be most effective, quality management and improvement efforts must employ a systematic process based on the scientific method (Joint Commission, 1998a) (see also Chapter 4). Such processes or improvement models provide an organized framework for improving quality. Two examples of systematic processes for quality measurement are the plan–do–check–act model and the clinical value compass. These are described below.

Plan–Do–Check–Act Model

The statistical methods suggested by Shewhart (1939) were transformed into a diagram depicting how a process or product can be improved. The plan–do–check–act (PDCA) cycle, also known as the Shewhart cycle or the Deming cycle, was popularized in Japan in the 1950s by W. Edwards Deming (1986) and is increasingly used by health care organizations. The improvement steps in the PDCA cycle include:

- Plan. To plan a change or fix a problem, a process must be studied. Once data are evaluated, team members must decide upon a plan for improvement.
- Do. In the "do" step, the improvement plan is implemented on a small scale, perhaps a pilot test.
- Check. In this step, team members must observe or otherwise evaluate the results of the change.
- Act. If the change was successful, it is implemented to a larger degree so that it may be maintained. If the change was not successful in improving processes, the change is abandoned and the cycle repeated.

Once a model for improvement is identified, health care organizations often make modifications so that it is reflective of the organization's culture. One organization's adaptation of the PDCA cycle is depicted in Fig. 7.1.

Clinical Value Compass

The clinical value compass is a quality measurement model designed to help manage and improve the value of health care services (Nelson *et al.*, 1996). The clinical value compass aims its directional points at four main measurement areas that will aid health care organizations in managing and improving care. The compass point measures include:

- North: functional health status, risk status, and well-being
- South: costs (physicians, hospitals, drugs, and social costs

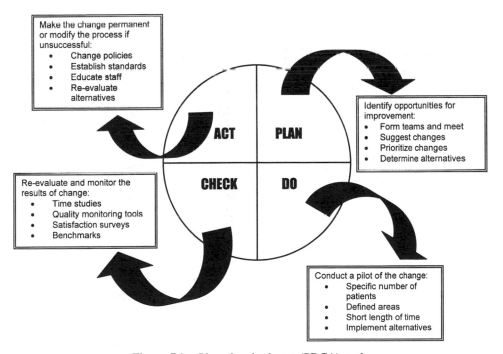

Figure 7.1. Plan–do–check–act (PDCA) cycle.

- East: satisfaction and perceived benefit of services
- West: clinical outcomes (e.g., mortality, morbidity)

To use the compass, health care organizations first must measure the value of care provided and then analyze the delivery processes contributing to outcomes and costs. Any changes made to the delivery process then are tested and examined to see whether the changes led to improved outcomes and lower costs.

Some organizations have found that the completion of a cycle of improvement could take from 6 months to more than 1 year (Carboneau, 1999). Delays might be related to time management, team leadership, the need for better education on quality principles, and the need for an effective improvement methodology. When a quality issue is in need of attention, it is unreasonable to allow months to pass before improvement is realized. To combat project lag time, some organizations have adopted rapid improvement cycles. In rapid-cycle improvement models, team activity is closely monitored and kept on track. Implementation of new ideas occurs more quickly, sometimes under a pilot test (Carboneau, 1999).

Quality Measurement

Quality measurement serves a variety of objectives: providing data to support improvement efforts, monitoring compliance with standards, making comparisons between providers of care, finding best and substandard performers, monitoring changes over time, and addressing the health needs of populations (Donaldson, 1999). Given both these varying goals and the complex nature of health care processes and outcomes, comprehensive quality assessment requires the application of graphical approaches (e.g., flow charts), descriptive measures (e.g., rates of nosocomial infection), and a variety of study designs and statistical techniques.

To evaluate themselves against their peers, many health care organizations participate in performance measurement systems or databases that offer comparative quality statistics on a regional or national level. Some systems are privately owned (available only through subscription), whereas others are publicly available. Databases of health care facility characteristics, process measures, and selected patient outcomes are maintained by companies, professional organizations, health care associations, peer review organizations, governmental agencies, and accrediting agencies. Because the type of data and procedures for data collection often vary, it is often difficult to make comparative analyses across the systems.

To establish consistency for nationwide analyses, the Joint Commission has been working to arrive at sets of standardized, core measures that will be uniformly applied across health care organizations (Joint Commission, 1999). Known as the ORYX initiative, it relies on measurement systems to embed the core measures and supply the data to the Joint Commission. Although nonstandardized measures are currently being collected by thousands of hospitals for ORYX, collection of standardized core measures will begin in 2002 (Joint Commission, 2000).

In a similar effort, the National Committee for Quality Assurance has established a set of commonly defined measures for use by practice plans and health maintenance organizations. Known as the Health Plan Employer Data and Information Set (HEDIS), these measures focus on clinical issues in the outpatient setting, such as diabetes management, cancer screening, and immunizations (Bodenheimer, 1999). Common quality measures used in health care management include process measures, clinical outcomes, satisfaction, and health status. A brief description of each appears below.

Process Measures

Process measures are typically utilization rate measures and are used to assess whether standards are met, the degree of compliance with practice guidelines, or a level of health system quality. Examples of process measures include:

- Surgical prophylaxis usage rates
- Cesarean section rates
- Immunization rates in health plans
- Tumor registry follow-up rates
- Mammography rates in health plans
- Completeness of tumor staging
- Rates of appropriate utilization of specific pharmaceuticals

Clinical Outcomes

A clinical outcome is the health status in relationship to a treatment or other intervention. Clinical outcomes can be expressed in terms of an individual practitioner, health care organizational unit (e.g., hospital trust in England), or system level (e.g., health authority in England). Clinical outcome measures include rates of death (inpatient, 30 day), complications, errors, infections, and other results of treatment (e.g., duration of graft). Clinical outcomes also aid in determining whether care was rendered according to established standards or practice guidelines. Clinical outcomes are also used to gauge efficacy. Specific examples of outcome indicators are rates of:

- Postoperative bleeding
- Mortality 2 days postprocedure involving anesthesia
- Medication error
- Readmission for same diagnosis within 30 days
- Surgical site infection
- Nosocomial infection
- Patient falls

As with any rate measure, the validity of the numerator and the denominator affect the accuracy of the estimate. For the numerator, validity is enhanced with the use of classification systems (see Chapter 2). Rate measures of quality are difficult to interpret where classification is not uniform, and such is the case with readmission rates. Readmission rates have not been consistently linked to quality. Weissman et al. (1999) propose a classification methodology to determine if a readmission indicates less than adequate quality of care.

Satisfaction

Patient, physician, and payer satisfaction is becoming increasingly important in competitive health care markets. Patient satisfaction survey instruments are widely used in the United States to generate data on patients' perceptions of the care received. Patient surveys of satisfaction with health care are common for inpatient services and outpatient services (Nelson and Niederberger, 1990; Holland *et al.*, 1995; Ware *et al.*, 1997), and health plans (Nelson and Niederberger, 1990; Hynes *et al.*, 1998; http:/www.hcfa.gov/about/acsipage.htm). The content of the satisfaction survey depends on the customer segment of interest. For example, the Customer Satisfaction Initiative of the US Health Care Financing Administration includes an assessment of ease of enrollment, ease of obtaining information, and staff courtesy and professionalism. Results from satisfaction surveys provide data to guide the development of ways to continuously improve service.

There are several ways to collect satisfaction data such as phone surveys, mailed surveys, presenting surveys to patients at the time of discharge, and interviewing patients during hospitalization (Ross *et al.*, 1995). Research shows that a mailed survey that protects patient anonymity is the best ongoing method for quantifying the quality of care and identifying processes that require attention. Many patients fear retribution if they provide negative comments via phone surveys or face-to-face interviews. Mailing the survey reduces the possibilities that patients will be influenced by the person administering the survey, will provide only positive comments, or will be excluded from the survey process because they are perceived as being difficult (Hall, 1995).

In a typical survey patients are asked to rate their experiences based on a Likert scale of 1 to 5 (5 being the most satisfied). A patient who rates his or her experience as "5" will usually return to the institution. A rating of "4" means the patient might return, "3" means they might not return, a "2" the patient will not return, and if the patient rates his or her experience a "1," he or she is gone. The notion that only patients with complaints respond to patient satisfaction surveys is untrue. Generally, only a small percentage of patients will respond with a rating of poor or very poor. The opportunity lies in focusing on those patients who rank the organization good.

Response rates to patient surveys vary depending on characteristics of the patient population served (with lower rates in lower income, less educated groups, non-English speaking) and organizational types (lower urban and larger hospitals). Improving rates can be accomplished by sending a follow-up postcard, mentioning the survey at discharge from care, and conducting a second or third mailing (very costly).

Health Status

Patient-based health status measurement tools (such as the Short Form 36 [SF-36] and the Health Status Questionnaire) address a variety of concepts including physical functioning, bodily pain, mental health, vitality, role functioning, and general health (Smith *et al.*, 1998). These instruments have been used to compare the quality of life of patients in different stages of disease progress (Vu and Escalanta, 1999), to examine the impact of personal behaviors (such as smoking) on health (Woolf *et al.*, 1999), and even to examine the general health of practitioners (Berardi *et al.*, 1999).

Similar to the collection process used in satisfaction measurement, health status tools require patient feedback and are often quite detailed. Though these measures are valuable, they can be expensive to collect and pose barriers to receipt of responses.

Data Sources

Data used to assess quality can be obtained from a variety of sources. The most common sources of data for quality assessment in health care are patient medical records, electronic hospital discharge abstract, physician billing systems, and patient surveys. Medical records are the source of very detailed clinical data including patient and family medical histories, physical examination findings, radiology and laboratory test results, operative reports, nursing observations, and physician orders for drugs and other therapies. Electronic discharge abstract and billing systems provide data elements needed by government and commercial insurers to pay the providers of care. These data elements include patient characteristics such as age, gender, length of stay (LOS); the principal diagnosis or reason for admission or treatment and secondary diagnoses or comorbidities; the procedures performed; and charges for services.

There is considerable debate among quality assessment professionals concerning which of these data sources is most appropriate for quality measures. Although the medical record may be the best source for detailed data on the processes and outcomes of care (e.g., the medications of beta blockers and thrombolytics for acute myocardial infarction) (Brown *et al.*, 1997; Widdershoven *et al.*, 1997), extraction of data from medical records can be very resource intensive. This often limits sample sizes and may compromise the validity of statistical analyses. In addition, the reliability of medical record data is dependent on the accuracy of the individual who does the data abstraction. Electronic discharge abstract and billing data have been extensively used to assess quality of hospital care. For example, through the Healthcare Cost and Utilization Project quality indicators software was developed to allow quality indicators, with and without standardization, to be compared within population subgroups and relative to US rates (Johantgen *et al.*, 1998). While hospital discharge abstract data are easy to obtain, the elements collected may only emphasize those patient characteristics, diagnoses, and procedures that are felt to be important for determining equitable payment for services. The accuracy and completeness of diagnosis and procedure coding also are of concern for measures that rely on discharge abstract data. An effective quality assessment and improvement program probably will use a combination of data sources and a variety of measures appropriate to each source.

Sampling

Ideally, a census of all patients should be monitored for quality performance. A census has the advantage of eliminating any doubts about sampling error. However, it is often cost-prohibitive to evaluate all patients receiving services or resource-prohibitive through a physical audit all medical records; computerized records of patient information typically do not contain a level of detail to perform outcomes assessments (e.g., only 8 diagnosis fields where 13 would be optimal). It is for these reasons that sampling may be an alternative. The sample must be representative of the people served, and thus selected using some random selection process (e.g., a computer software package, SAS, Microsoft Excel, EpiInfo Ver. 6.04b). The size of the sample that should be drawn to check error rates or to estimate patient outcomes or process measures can be easily calculated using a statistical software package (EpiInfo Ver. 6.04b: Dean *et al.*, 1997; nQuery Advisor: Elashoff, 1995–1999; PASS: Hintze, 2000) or sample size formulae from one of several recommended statistical texts (Fleiss, 1981; Rosner, 1995; Levy and Lemeshow, 1999). For example, the Joint Commission (1997) recommends a random sample of 5% or 30 cases during a specific time frame for examining error rates. For patient-based data collection, response rate also is an important factor in determining sample size.

Levels of Quality Measurement

The level of measurement used in quality assessment will determine which analytic and statistical methods are selected for analyses. Rate, ratio, and continuous measures are described.

Rate measures are the most common methods for assessing the quality of care in terms of process and outcome. Rates are used to show the proportion or percentage of a particular

Table 7.3. Common Rate Measures of Quality of Care for Processes and Outcomes

Process measures
- Percentage of pregnant women with prenatal care in the first trimester
- Childhood immunization completion rate, by individual vaccine type and all of recommended
- Mammography rate within 2 years for women aged 50+
- Percent of diabetics receiving insulin or oral hypoglycemic and who had an eye exam in past year
- β-Blocker prescription filled for those after myocardial infarction with no evidence of contraindication

Outcome measures
- Mortality rates:
  1. In-hospital death rates by procedure, clinical service (e.g., neonatal ICU), or diagnosis
- Incidence rates:
  1. Nosocomial infection rates
  2. Adverse incidence rate (fall rates, medication error rates, etc.)
- Survival rates:
  1. Cancer patient survival rate, by anatomic site and stage
  2. Patient and graft survival rate, by transplant procedure and type
- Other rates:
  1. Percentage of postoperative patients with pain control
  2. Patient satisfaction rates with the services provided and the patient care environment

patient group in which a particular event, either adverse or favorable, occurred. When calculating a rate, the individuals included in the numerator of the expression are a subset of the patient group represented by the denominator (see Chapter 3). Examples of rate measures commonly used to assess the quality of care are in Table 7.3. Small area analysis is a method for comparing utilization rates in populations from different small geographic areas. The highest rates in these areas are compared to the lowest rates, the degree of difference is evaluated and an attempt is made to explain the variation. In the early 1980s, rate measures were used to illustrate the high degree of variability in medical care, particularly at the local level (Connell *et al.*, 1981; Wennberg and Gittelsohn, 1982; McPherson *et al.*, 1982). Small-area analysis has identified differences in hospitalization rates and procedure use that have been attributed to differences in physician practice styles; access to community, ambulatory, and preventive care; and lack of professional consensus regarding optimal treatment strategies (Wennberg, 1996).

Ratio measures are similar to rates but the individuals or cases included in the numerator are not a subset of the denominator, i.e., the numerator and denominator measure different phenomena. An example of a ratio measure is the number of adverse drug reactions per 1000 inpatient days.

Continuous measures are those values in which each unit of the measurement has meaning. Continuous measures include days of hospital stay, deciliters of blood glucose, and number of in-hospital deaths.

Quality Improvement Tools and Techniques

As opportunities to improve are identified, various decision management tools can be used in combination with statistical tools to lead to improvement and process change. Much can be gained from measurement activities and a thorough analysis of the process. However, it is not until action is taken that future patients will actually benefit from what was learned. Improvement ideas must be generated, prioritized, clarified, and implemented.

There are various quality improvement tools and techniques designed to help organizations measure and analyze variation in any process. Use of these tools and techniques is key to successful planning and helps ensure that performance improvement efforts:

- Unlock creativity
- Encourage participation
- Capture objective data
- Document processes
- Measure performance
- Analyze causes and effects (Joint Commission, 1992)

Most tools have been developed for use by teams rather than individuals. Many improvement theorists assert that staff with firsthand knowledge of the processes and systems must be involved in improvement efforts. This expanded base of experience and knowledge allows the team to get directly to the root of a problem and to pinpoint improvement opportunities. Project teams can be time limited and focused on particular issues or on going and empowered to deal with new issues as they arise.

Brainstorming

Brainstorming is used to "stimulate group creativity and problem solving when faced with the need to change" (Strongwater and Pelote, 1996, p. 31). Free-flowing brainstorming sessions require that everyone takes a sequential turn in responding (passing is allowed), during which time no team member is allowed to criticize or discuss the idea. Team members are allowed to build on others' ideas or to offer new ideas during their turn (Scholtes, 1988). Goldman *et al.* (1996) utilized brainstorming in a multidisciplinary group to develop a process for a hospital to implement a strategic plan to combat antimicrobial resistance.

Affinity Diagram

Often, the output of a brainstorming session is a very long list of ideas representing a wide variety of areas. A useful follow-up exercise is an affinity diagram, which helps to categorize responses into a logical framework. The ideas from the brainstorming session are individually listed on small pieces of paper. Then, using a large surface, such as a wall, window, or table, the team members simultaneously arrange them into logical groups. Team members can disagree with one another and continue to rearrange the notes silently until consensus is reached. Once the categorization has ceased, team members are allowed to speak and to label the categories they have created.

As opportunities for improvement are uncovered, the team decides where to focus its energy. If numerous opportunities are identified, the team must engage in a prioritization exercise. This can be accomplished in a variety of ways. One approach is to use a voting technique, where each team member assigns a set number of points to the idea(s) of highest priority (Scholtes, 1988). Another approach is to have each team member complete a prioritization matrix that includes specific criteria and rating scales.

Cause-and-Effect Diagram

A cause-and-effect diagram represents pictorially the relationship between an effect and all of its potential causes. A cause-and-effect diagram is used to identify influencing factors that may contribute to problems. It originated from Kaoru Ishikawa, head of the Japanese Union of Scientists and Engineers, who in the 1960s expanded the use of this and other quality control tools in Japanese manufacturing. For this reason, the cause-and-effect diagram is sometimes referred to as the Ishikawa diagram, or the fishbone diagram, because of its shape.

Cause-and-effect diagrams clarify the potential causes of a problem and/or the sources of variation. To construct the diagram, the problem to be examined (e.g., long emergency room waiting times) is placed in a box on the right side of the page. A long line is then drawn horizontally from the box to the left side of the page. From this center horizontal line, lines are drawn diagonally above and below and titled with major categories thought to be contributing to the development of the problem. Typical health care categories are procedures, environment, equipment, and people.

For each category, the question "Why?" is asked. For each response, a diagonal line is added to the main branch of the category to represent a hypothetical explanation. "Why" continues to be asked in a category until the possibilities become unknown or exhausted. For example, if an organization is analyzing why there are problems with inaccurate or absent identification of patients on the admission record, the team may suggest that causes are primarily related to policies, procedures, people, and equipment/materials (Fig. 7.2). These major issues would serve as the large "fishbone" labels.

For each major issue, the team then asks, "Why?" For example, a series of "why" questions on the issue of patient identification might include:

- "Why is there inaccurate patient identification?"
- "Because there is wrong demographic information on the patient plate." *Wrong demographic information* is added as branch of the fishbone.

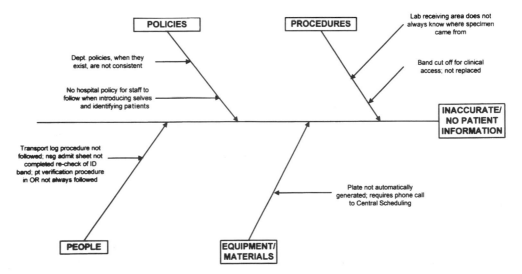

Figure 7.2. Cause-and-effect diagram.

- "Why is there *wrong demographic information*?"
- "Because the incorrect information is given by the physician's office to the operating room," or "Because the handwritten or verbal information is not clear or complete," or "Because the patient must be a John Doe or may give an alias." All these causes are added to the fishbone.

The cause-and-effect diagram keeps the team focused on the issue and generates a lot of active discussion. The participants in this process can gain new knowledge about improving a process from examining different aspects of a process. Last, the construction of this diagram presents an opportunity for staff to develop teamwork in problem solving thereby facilitating for future team problem-solving activities.

Flowchart

Based on performance data analysis and an examination of the root causes of a problem, it may be helpful to reevaluate how a process works. Many processes involve redundant or inefficient steps, too many handoffs (leading to failures), and/or may be ordered inappropriately. A flowchart is a useful tool for process analysis in that it provides a picture of the steps involved in a process.

Flowcharts allow teams to examine each step of the process, leading them to identify the potential sources of variation. The team must decide how detailed the flow diagram should be. A diagram depicting only the major steps of a process would take less time to complete and offer opportunity for further review. A helpful step in defining the process for review is setting start and end points for review. For example, if the team discovered that among the vital few causes of inpatient readmissions for congestive heart failure patients was "inadequate discharge planning," a flowchart should be created depicting the current process of discharge planning. Perhaps discharge planning begins at admission to the facility or even before admission. Perhaps it ends at discharge from the facility or during the first postdischarge visit to a clinic. Once the time points are agreed on, the team draws the sequential and simultaneous steps involved, working backward or forward in time.

There are standardized symbols for flowcharts, but these are not always followed. A special shape (such as a cloud) should be used for any process steps that are unknown or unclear. A sample flowchart appears in Fig. 7.3. During the discussion, a facilitator should keep the team focused, because discussions about detailed process steps often stimulate other conversations. As the chart is documented, suggestions for improvement will arise, including reduction of handoffs or unresolved problems, better interdepartmental workflow, and potential intervention points. The team then has the option of recreating the "ideal process" in a new flow diagram. The team returns to the improvement model (e.g., PDCA cycle) to evaluate ideas, check data, and pilot test a solution. Later, follow-up monitoring will ensure that the new performance level has been achieved.

Statistical Quality Control Tools

Originally developed in industrial settings, quality control tools consist of a set of graphic and statistical methods for analyzing variation in processes and promoting the achievement of statistical process control.

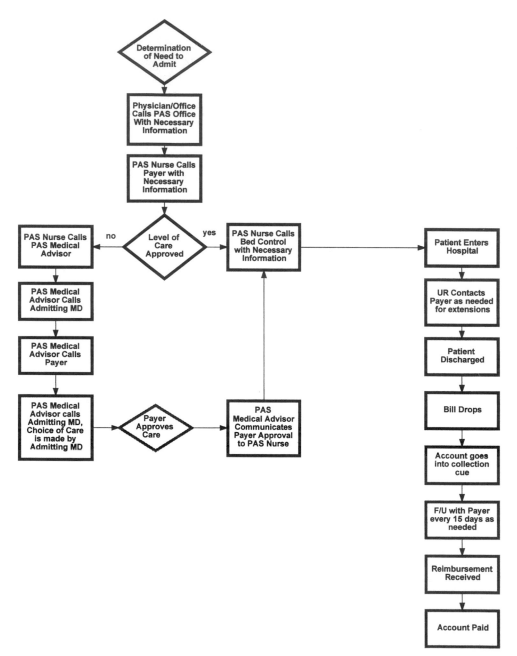

Figure 7.3. Flowchart of the process of admission and reimbursement for cardiology patients. Used with permission from Cynthia Barginere and Kathleen Papagni.

Check Sheet

The simplest of these techniques is the check sheet, which is a simple form for making sample observations. A check sheet can be used to count discrete events (or observations) such as postoperative complications or to record observations of continuous variables such as length of stay for patients with community-acquired pneumonia. These counts or observations then can be graphically displayed using a more advanced statistical quality control tool as appropriate.

Histogram

A histogram is a two-dimensional graph with bars representing the frequency of values on the y axis as a function of values on the x axis. Note that as a compared to a bar chart (or Pareto chart), the values along the x axis represent interval level measurement. Figure 7.4 represents a histogram of the hospital length of stay in days. The bar representing the peak in a histogram is the median of the distribution. In this figure, 5 days is the median length of stay.

Pareto Chart

A Pareto chart (bar chart) displays a frequency distribution of categorical data in descending rank order. Figure 7.5 represents the rate of surgical wound infection by number of patient risk factors. This chart illustrates that surgical wound infection increases with increasing number of patient risk factors. Pareto charts are a natural follow up to a cause-and-effect diagram. The Pareto diagram is based on Joseph Juran's 80–20 rule, meaning that 20% of the causes contribute to 80% of the problem (Juran, 1988). The diagram, similar to a bar graph, helps separate the "vital few" causes that account for the majority of the problem. Once sufficient data exist on the frequency of a number of causes, the relative frequencies are displayed on a bar chart. The measure of frequency is plotted on the vertical axis and the causes on the horizontal axis (in descending order). A third right vertical axis can be drawn to indicate the cumulative percentage of the total number of occurrences (Joint Commission, 1992). The 80–20 rule then can be visualized.

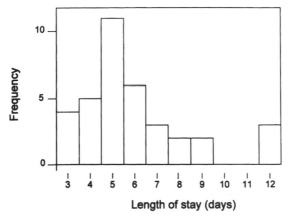

Figure 7.4. Histogram.

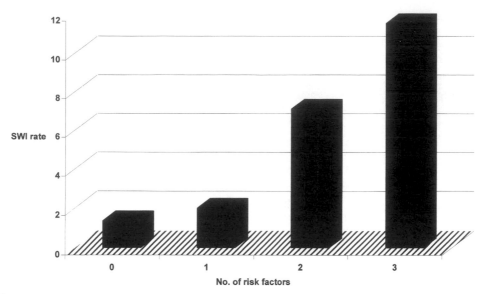

Figure 7.5. Pareto chart of surgical wound infection (SWI) rates by number of risk factors. Risk factors are any of the following: an operation that involved the abdomen, an operation lasting longer than 2 hours, an operation classified as either contaminated or dirty-infected, and a patient having three or more diagnoses at discharge. From Culver *et al.* (1991).

Scatter Diagram

A scatter diagram is a two-dimensional plot of the relationship between two variables. The values of the observations are plotted as x, y coordinates on a graph with x representing the independent variable and y the dependent (or response) variable. This diagram illustrates what happens to one variable when the other variable changes value. Figure 7.6 is a scatter diagram of the relationship between the ratio of primary care physicians per 100,000 population and mammography rates among non-HMO Medicare enrollees in selected hospital referral regions

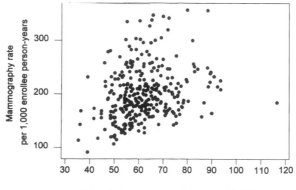

Figure 7.6. Scatter diagram.

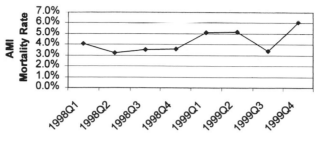

Figure 7.7. Run chart.

of the United States. This scatter diagram illustrates that with an increasing ratio of primary care physicians per 100,000 population, there is an increasing mammography rate.

Run Chart and Control Chart

A **run chart** (Fig. 7.7) is a line graph showing the result of an outcome measure, such as in-hospital mortality rate for acute myocardial infarction over time. The outcome measure is displayed on the y axis and the time is shown on the x axis. A **control chart** (Fig. 7.8) is a run chart to which horizontal lines are added to represent a measure of central tendency, such as the mean of the sample means or rates and upper and lower control limits on either side of this mean, which represent a measure of dispersion such as the standard deviation or standard error. Upper and lower control limits can be set at one, two or three times the standard deviation or standard error. The center line of a control chart can represent the historical center point for that health care unit or some normative value. The control limits are typically calculated based on an average sample size for the period examined; otherwise, the limits will vary with each sample across the time periods examined. Computation of limits based on individual time unit samples is desirable when the process is reexamined before and after some change has been introduced.

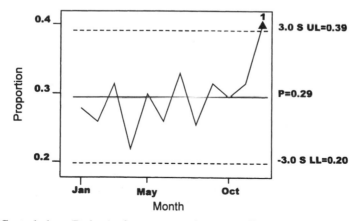

Figure 7.8. Control chart (P-chart) of cesarean section rate at Freeway Medical Center. UL, Upper limit; LL, lower limit; S, standard deviation; 1, special cause identified, point exceeds 3S at the upper limit.

The formulas for constructing the lines of the control chart depend on the level of measurement (e.g., interval, rate, etc.), the variability of the sample size over time, and the existence of an objective standard that would replace the mean as the center line. For most measures of quality in health care, objective or preset numerical standards do not exist. Formulas for calculating the lines for three common types of control charts follow:

Rate (or Proportion) Measures (P Chart)

Step 1: $x_i = n_i \cdot P_i \qquad \overline{P} = \dfrac{\Sigma\, n_i}{\Sigma\, n_i} \qquad \overline{n} = \dfrac{\Sigma\, n_i}{k}$

Step 2: $\sigma_{\overline{P}} = \sqrt{\dfrac{(\overline{P} \cdot (1 - \overline{P}))}{\overline{n}}}$

Step 3: $\overline{P} \pm z \cdot \sigma_{\overline{P}}$

Where:

k = number of time periods

n_i = total number in the denominator ("population at risk")

P = rate = events/population at risk × factor of 10 (or calculate as a proportion)

σ_P = standard deviation of the rate

z = standard deviate of the normal distribution to set the level of confidence, usually 99%

Continuous Measures [X Bar S Chart ($n \geqslant 10$) or X Bar R Chart ($n < 10$)]

Step 1: $\overline{\overline{X}} = \dfrac{\Sigma\, \overline{X}_i}{k} \qquad \overline{S} = \dfrac{\Sigma\, s_i}{k} \qquad \overline{n} = \dfrac{\Sigma\, n_i}{k}$

Step 2: $\overline{X} \pm z \cdot \dfrac{\overline{S}}{\sqrt{\overline{n}}}$

Where:

k = number of time periods

n_i = number of events

s_i = standard deviation

$\overline{X}_i$ = standard deviate of the normal distribution to set a level of confidence, usually 99%

Rate Measures (U Chart)

$$\overline{U} = \dfrac{\Sigma\, x_i}{\Sigma\, n_i} \qquad \sigma_u = \dfrac{\sqrt{\overline{U}}}{\sqrt{n}} \qquad \begin{array}{l} \text{UCL} = \overline{U} + 3\sigma_u \\[4pt] \text{LCL} = \overline{U} - 3\sigma_u \end{array}$$

Where:

$\overline{U}$ = mean ratio value

X_i = number of events, e.g., number of adverse drug reations

n_i = number of units of measurement, e.g., 1000 patient day increments

σ_u = standard deviation

UCL = upper 99% confidence limit

LCL = lower 99% confidence limit

Table 7.4. Data for a Control Chart of Cesarean Section Rates at Freeway Medical Center

Month (i)	Number of births in month (n_i)	Number of births by cesarean in month (e_i)	Proportion of cesarean birth per month (r_i): $r_i = e_i/n_i$
January	190	56	.29
February	180	52	.29
March	210	63	.31
April	188	44	.23
May	213	60	.28
June	216	52	.24
July	224	66	.29
August	202	51	.25
September	205	63	.31
October	195	59	.30
November	216	63	.29
December	180	80	.44
Total	2419	709	.29

Using the data from Table 7.4, a P control chart (Fig. 7.8) is drawn to examine variability cesarean section rates across a calendar year using Minitab (1999) software and to identify whether at any point the "process is out of control." The graph identifies that the process is under control relative to the average for the year in December where the cesarean rate exceeds the 99% confidence limit.

Comparison Charts

Comparison charts provide a method for determining whether performance (or outcomes achieved) differs significantly from a known standard at any given point in time, and hence allow performance to be benchmarked. An example might be the readmission rate accepted by experts as ideal and the overall mean readmission rate of an appropriate comparison group such as a state rate or rate for similar type of hospitals. Figure 7.9 compares the infant mortality rate (IMR) for selected states with the highest rates in all regions of the United States. The "standards" graphed are the current overall US IMR and the 2010 goal for the nation. Comparison charts also can be made for smaller time periods, for example, quarter of the year.

The comparison chart will display the sample rate or mean, the comparison standard rate or mean, and upper and lower statistical confidence intervals for the comparison rate or mean. The confidence intervals are at the 99% confidence level, which is comparable to an alpha level of .01, two-tailed. The formulae of the 99% confidence interval for continuous and rate measures are:

Continuous measures

$$\mu \pm 2.576 \cdot \frac{\sigma}{\sqrt{n}}$$

Where μ = mean of the comparison standard
σ = standard deviation of the comparison standard mean
n = total number of cases in the sample

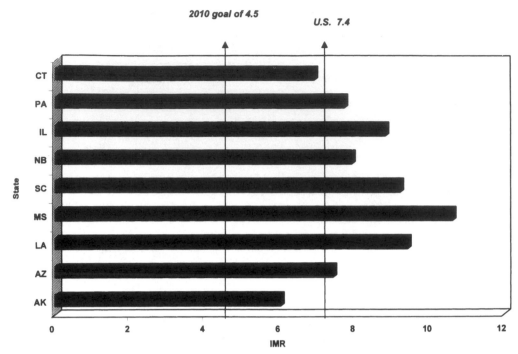

Figure 7.9. Comparison chart of infant mortality rate (IMR) by state. From US Department of Health and Human Services (2000a,b).

Rate measures

$$\rho \pm 2.576 \cdot \frac{\sigma}{\sqrt{n}}$$

Where ρ = mean rate for the comparison standard
σ = standard deviation of the comparison standard mean rate
n = total denominator cases in the sample

Application of Quality Control Tools

Control of unwanted variation, especially during the processes of health care delivery, may significantly reduce the likelihood of adverse clinical outcomes. This is because the unwanted variation may represent individual, organizational, or system performance problems. For example, high nosocomial infection rates in a pediatric unit only on weekends during the quarter may signal staffing problems in that patient car area. The most effective means of controlling unwanted variation is to identify the specific type that exists. Quality control tools, particularly control charts, help identify and distinguish both special and common causes of variation in health care delivery.

Common causes of variation are random fluctuations inherent to a process such as compliance with organizational policies. They are identified by random distributions of points occurring within the control limits of a control chart. Changes in the process must occur in order to reduce common causes of variation.

Special causes of variation are nonrandom events that are not inherent to a process (Deming, 1986), but rather are related to persons, places, or time. They produce deviations from the expected beyond the random variation related to common causes and often may be corrected without redesign of the process. Examples of special causes of variation include contamination of the sterile field during a surgical procedure, not properly calibrated laboratory equipment, and providing the wrong medication dose to a patient. Control charts are used to detect nonrandom variation in length of stay, mortality, readmissions, and complications for Medicare patients with pneumonia (Hand *et al.*, 1994). The U chart (Minitab, 1999) aids in evaluating whether or not a special cause is the source of the unwanted variation. The U chart plots the "defects" for a given sample across all samples, and hence is a ratio measure. Samples can be the same size or different sizes, but are assumed to come from a Poisson distribution with parameter μ that is both the mean and the variance. The average number of "defects" from the data set becomes the centerline, or μ can be specified by the user to represent the process mean. Special cause variation is said to exist if any one of the following are identified on a flowchart: (1) any single point more than 3 standard deviations from the center line; (2) 9 points in a row on the same side of the center line; (3) six points in a row all increasing or decreasing; or (4) 14 points in a row alternating up and down. Special cause is flagged automatically when using Minitab (1999) software, as occurs in Fig. 7.8 in the month of December when the cesarean section rate during that month exceeds 3 standard deviations from the centerline of the average annual rate for that hospital.

Risk Adjustment

The acceptance of quality assessment methods by health care providers and their usefulness in promoting quality improvement will be determined largely by confidence in the power of these methods to reliably measure "real" variations in processes and their relationship to outcomes. An essential factor in fostering this confidence is the ability to determine acceptable or expected norms through the process known as "risk adjustment" or "case mix." Quality improvement efforts based on comparisons of the performance or outcomes of care, in the absence of an attempt to account for differences in the severity of illness and other patient characteristics, are likely to end in failure.

The first large-scale attempts to measure severity of illness were a consequence of changes in hospital reimbursement (Iezzoni, 1989). The prospective payment system adopted by Medicare in 1983 created clinically interpretable patient classes based on variables commonly available in hospital abstract and billing systems (Fetter *et al.*, 1980). The patient classes, known as diagnosis-related groups (DRGs) were based primarily on the *International Classification of Diseases*, Ninth revision, *Clinical Modification* (ICD-9-CM) diagnostic and surgical codes, patient age, and discharge status. The DRG classification was widely criticized. It was believed to account only for major variations in severity of illness, while being insensitive to more subtle variations that might be delineated only through the use of detailed clinical data. An alternative to the DRG system is the all patient refined-diagnosis-related groups (APR-DRG), a population commercial system (3M) for adjusting hospital severity of illness that has been found to be a strong predictor of death (Romano and Chan, 2000).

Another use for severity of illness assessment is to adjust for the risk of undesirable outcomes when the underlying state of health of the population subgroups compared is highly variable. Poor outcomes in a given population or those not predicted after statistical adjustment for severity could indicate poor quality of care (Blumberg, 1986). Risk adjustment has been applied to many different types of adverse outcome including death, surgical complications, unexpected admissions after outpatient surgery, nosocomial infections, readmissions shortly after discharge, cesarean section rates, and excessive length of stay (Culver *et al.*, 1991; Tsuyuki *et al.*, 1994; Iezzoni *et al.*, 1994, 1996a; Salemi *et al.*, 1995; Fujita and Sakurai, 1995; Reiley and Howard, 1995; Normand *et al.*, 1996; Cariou *et al.*, 1997; Leung *et al.*, 1998; Aron *et al.*, 1998). These uses of severity of illness assessment for risk adjustment generally rely on patient condition and characteristics on admission to the hospital or at initial contact with a provider. This establishes risk before therapeutic intervention so that risk is not confounded with poor quality of care leading to adverse outcomes.

Other risk adjustment methods exist and these are reviewed in Iezzoni *et al.*, (1996b). The primary distinction among these is related to the source of the data used to define severity levels. Two major types of systems are identified: those that rely exclusively on discharge abstract or billing data and those that require primary data collection from medical records. Examples of severity of illness systems include the Acute Physiology and Chronic Health Evaluation (APACHE) system (Knaus *et al.*, 1981), the Computerized Severity Index (Horn and Horn, 1986), disease staging (Gonnella *et al.*, 1984), MedisGroups (Brewster *et al.*, 1985), and patient management categories (Young, 1984).

There are two final caveats here. One is that the adjustment is only as good as the quality of the data that are collected. So if large numbers of patient records are missing or incomplete or improperly coded, even the most sophisticated case mix/risk adjustment system will not be able to compensate for validity. Also, one must keep in mind that most case mix/risk adjustment methods focus on clinical factors and do not account for all possible factors that could affect patient outcomes. Differences in gender and age structure of the population that seeks care at a particular facility as well as other demographic and economic influences may explain some of the observed variations. Even the population may have different diagnostic composition that could affect outcome. For example, Cleves and Golden (1996) point out that even comparisons of hospital-specific mortality rates for hip arthroplasty adjusted for age and gender can be flawed if the proportion of arthroplasty's done for patients with and without hip fracture at the time of the procedure. For this reason, facilities or health plans should be aggregated into groups that facilitate "like" with "like" comparisons.

Conclusion

Quality management and quality improvement tools applied with an epidemiological framework can bring health care service units to a new level of performance. This performance, in some markets, plays a large role in establishing viability as a business. Consumer advocacy groups, business coalitions, accreditors, and regulators frequently evaluate health care organizations and integrated delivery networks. Because the accountability of health care providers now stems beyond the immediate health care setting and knowledge of epidemiological principles and their use are now essential to all health care managers. "Report cards" are commonly available to rank hospitals and doctors, many based on publicly available patient (e.g., Medicare data). Some use five-star rating systems, which greatly simplifies presentation for consumers of health care, but unfortunately they can lack risk adjustment or the descriptions required to understand performance data. It behooves health care organizations to investigate how they are being evaluated and by whom. To ensure organizationwide application of quality principles, some organizations have joined industrial companies in competing for awards for their quality efforts. One such award is the Malcolm Baldrige

National Health Care Quality Award. The award criteria include visionary leadership, organizational and personal learning, being customer-driven, valuing employees and partners, focus on the future, management by fact, managing by innovation, public responsibility and citizenship, focus on results and creating value, and a systems perspective (National Institute of Standards and Technology, 2000). Regardless of the type of health care organization—be it an office setting, an ambulatory surgery center, mental health center, hospital or long-term care facility—to be effective, the management of quality must be done in a coordinated, efficient, systematic approach that is closely aligned with the organization's strategic priorities. To do any less would limit the value of quality initiatives.

Case Studies

Case Study No. 1
Managing a Hospital Specific Cesarean Section Rate

A perennial problem faced by hospitals is confronting management of the cesarean rate. At Freeway Medical Center (FMC), the current total cesarean section rate is 33% over the last 6 months. During the same time period, the state average is 20.4%. Also, at nearby Gold Coast Medical Center, a private academic health center, the total cesarean section rate was 15.5% and at a local state university hospital the cesarean section rate was 15.4%. FMC wishes to reduce its cesarean section rate because it is being reported to the Joint Commission as a performance measure of quality to be assessed in its next accreditation review. The Cesarean Section Reduction Team from FMC is charged with tackling this problem and proposing solutions. The Cesarean Section Reduction Team decided to tackle this problem using an epidemiological framework.

Q.1. What would be your first steps in solving the problem?

Q.2. How is the cesarean section rate computed?

Q.3. What quality improvement tools could be used?

Q.4. What types of biases in the data affect the interpretation?

Q.5. What intervention can be used to affect the hospital cesarean section rate?

Case Study No. 2
Measuring and Improving Patient Satisfaction

Research shows that the mail-back survey is the best ongoing method for quantifying a patient's satisfaction with care, in a nonthreatening, confidential manner (Hall, 1995). In a typical survey patients are asked to rate their experiences based on a Likert scale of 1 to 5 (5 = most satisfied). A patient who rates his or her experience a "5" will usually return to the institution. A rating of "4" means the patient might return, a "3" means they might not return, a "2" the patient probably will not return, and if the patient rates his/her experience a "1," he or she definitely will not return. You present a quarterly data report to your hospital system's quality council. You represent hospital B. The report reflects other hospitals in the region including your competitors (Table 7.5). The quality council has set as a strategic priority the improvement of customer service.

Table 7.5. Hypothetical Patient Satisfaction Data
for Hospitals in a Health System

	Very poor 1 (9)	Poor 2 (25)	Fair 3 (50)	Very good 4 (75)	Good 5 (100)
Hospital A 60th percentile score of 85.1	1%	2%	8%	32%	57%
Hospital B 95th percentile score of 88.1	1%	2%	5%	25%	67%
Hospital C 5th percentile score of 83.0	2%	4%	12%	41%	41%

Q.1. How would you summarize the findings from Table 7.5?

Q.2. What are some additional ways in which the council could derive additional information form these data?

Q.3. What quality improvement tools might be helpful in determining how hospital B compares to its competitor hospitals?

Q.4. If the data revealed that patients were unhappy with hospital surroundings (noisy, dark, sterile décor), what might you do to generate ideas on how to improve the situation?

Q.5. To increase the likelihood of a favorable change in the patient satisfaction scores relative to the hospital environment, what management strategy should be undertaken?

Case Study No. 3
Investigation of a Medical Error

You have been called in to help investigate a medical error, one that has been highly publicized in the local news. A patient was scheduled to undergo a left below the knee amputation and the amputation was done to the right leg in error. The patient is a long-standing insulin-dependent diabetic with severe peripheral vascular disease. An accreditation agency has requested a copy of the analysis you and your team have conducted. Wrong-site surgery cases are difficult to defend and they often end in legal settlement. While the frequency of these types of cases remains low, they do generate a great deal of publicity and they are thought to be preventable. Although the surgeon is ultimately responsible for the verification of laterality (or correct side) of the patient for the surgery, settlements are often shared on an equal basis between both the physician and the hospital (Bosh, 1999).

Q.1. List various representatives you would like to have included on the team who will investigate the issue.

Q.2. The risk manager indicated that in the Joint Commission's (1998b) investigation of wrong-site surgery cases, most root causes related to "communication, preoperative assessment of the patient, and the procedures used to verify the operative site." What would you suggest the team do to uncover root causes?

Q.3. The team found several factors they believe contributed to the error. For example, the surgical technicians involved in preparing the site for surgery were not kept involved in the site verification process, and the surgeon was solely relied on to determine the correct operative site. How should new procedures be implemented?

Case Study No. 4
Chronic Pain in Older Persons

The medical director and the manager of the geriatric inpatient unit ask for your help in implementing a clinical practice guideline focused on chronic pain in older persons. This is a priority concern in this unit, since the prevalence of patients who complain of chronic pain caused by arthritis, joint, or back problems is high. These patients take a wide variety of therapies for their pain. The use of clinical pathways is encouraged at your facility and is supported by standards set forth by regulators and accrediting bodies. The Joint Commission on the Accreditation of Health Care Organizations announced in 1999 a comprehensive set of standards pertaining to pain assessment and management, compliance with which will be required by 2001. You agree to help and meet with a small team composed of hospital staff and one patient representative to develop and implement such a practice guideline. Through an Internet search, you find the National Guideline Clearinghouse (2000: http://www.guideline.gov) website where you discover there are dozens of existing evidence-based guidelines pertaining to pain management. You locate a guideline titled, "The Management of Chronic Pain in Older Persons" developed in 1998 by the American Geriatric Society. The guideline addresses pain assessment, pharmacological treatments, nonpharmacological strategies, and recommendations for health systems that care for older persons (American Geriatrics Society, 1999). The geriatric unit team adopts this guideline and creates a clinical care pathway for all staff to utilize in caring for these patients.

Q.1. What considerations should be given prior to implementing a new idea such as a pathway?

Q.2. What outcomes might be tracked to see whether the pathway is working? How should the data be collected? What tools should be used to analyze the data?

Q.3. What action(s) should be taken if the clinic staff does not follow the pathway?

Q.4. What are some of the critical success factors to implementation of the pathway?

Q.5. Describe how pathways can assist in case management.

Case Study No. 5
Outcome Measures and Control Charts

The governing board of a rehabilitation facility has asked you to help them develop a report card to monitor the overall clinical value provided by their organization. One of the board members has heard of the clinical value compass and asks you to give a description of it. After you do, the board agrees that the clinical value compass is an ideal format for the report on facility performance. You are asked to bring the first of such reports to the next meeting. Based on the four points of the compass, you find that the facility has been collecting data on costs, satisfaction, and a few clinical outcomes. These data are arranged using histograms, bar charts, and run charts.

Nothing appears out of the ordinary until you examine the clinical outcomes. While examining a comparison chart of nine rehabilitation hospitals in the region, the rate of readmissions was significantly higher this quarter in your rehabilitation facility. Before you bring the report to the board, you decide to research the observation further using the scientific method described in Chapter 4 (this volume). Fortunately, the database is rich in detail and contains diagnoses, procedures, and complications for each patient (patient identification is absent from the database).

Q.1. Would the determination of the risk of readmitted to the facility is considered as a count of the number of readmissions or a rate-based measure?

Q.2. What quality improvement statistical technique will allow you to examine the data over time and identify whether the process has been stable?

Q.3. If a control chart showed isolated points outside of the control limits or persistent upward or downward trends within control limits, what type of variation is being detected? What are some causes of this type of variation?

Q.4. Why would it be important to risk-adjust a measure of readmission? What variables do you use in risk adjustment of the readmission rate?

References

American Geriatrics Society, 1998, *AGS Clinical Practice Guidelines: The Management of Chronic Pain in Older Persons*, American Geriatrics Society, New York.

Aron, D. C., Harper, D. L., Shepardson, L. B., and Rosenthal, G. E., 1998, Impact of risk-adjusting cesarean delivery rates when reporting hospital performance, *JAMA* **279:**1968–1972.

Berardi, D., Berti, Ceroni, G., Leggieri, G., Rucci, P., Uston, B., and Ferrari, G., 1999, Mental, physical and functional status in primary care attenders, *Int. J. Psychiatr. Med.* **29:**133–148.

Berwick, D., Godfrey, B., and Roessner, J., 1990, *Curing Health Care*, Jossey-Bass, San Francisco.

Batalden, P. B., and Stoltz, P. K., 1993, A framework for the continual improvement of health care, *J. Qual. Improve.* **19:**424–447.

Blumberg, M. S., 1986, Risk adjusting health care outcomes: A methodologic review, *Med. Care Rev.* **43:**351–393.

Bodenheiimer, T., 1999, The American health care system—the movement for improved quality in health care, *N. Engl. J. Med.* **340:**488–492.

Bosh, D. F., 1999, Prevention of wrong-site surgery, *QRC Advisor* **1:**6–8.

Brewster, A. C., Karlin, B. G., Hyde, L. A., Jacobs, C. M., Bradbury, R. C., and Chae, Y. M., 1985, MEDISGRPS: A clinically based approach to classifying hospital patients at admission, *Inquiry* **22:**377–387.

Brown, N., Young, T., Gray, D., Skene, A. M., and Hampton, J. R., 1997, Inpatient deaths from acute myocardial infarction, 1982–92: Analysis of data in the Nottingham heart attack register, *Br. Med. J.* **315:**159–164.

Carboneau, C., 1999, Achieving faster quality improvement through the 24-hour team, *JHO* **21**(4); http://www.allenpress.com/jhq/080/080.htm.

Cariou, A., Himbert, D., Golmard, J. L., Juliard, J. M., Benamer, H., Boccara, A., Aubry, P., and Steg, P. G., 1997, Sex-related differences in eligibility for reperfusion therapy and in-hospital outcome after acute myocardial infarction, *Eur. Heart J.* **18:**1583–1589.

Chen, J., Radford, M. J., Wang, Y., Marciniak, T. A., and Krumholz, H. M., 1999, Performance of the "100 top hospitals": What does the report card report? *Health Affairs* **18:**53–68.

Clark, G. B., Schyve, P. M., Lepoff, R. B., and Reuss, D. T., 1994, Will quality management paradigms of the 1990s survive into the next century? *Clin. Lab. Manage. Rev.* **8:**426–428, 430–434.

Cleves, M. A., and Golden, W. E., 1996, Assessment of HCFA's 1992 Medicare hospital information report of mortality following admission for hip arthroplasty, *HSR: Health Service Res.* **31:**39–48.

Connell, F. A., Day, R. W., and LoGerfo, J. P., 1981, Hospitalization of Medicaid children: Analysis of small area variations in admission rates, *Am. J. Pub. Health* **71:**606–613.

Culver, D. H., Horan, T. C., Gaynes, R. P., Martone, W. J., Jarvis, W. R., Emori, T. G., Banerjee, S. N., Edwards, J. R., Tolson, J. S., and Henderson, T. S., 1991, Surgical wound infection rates by wound class, operative procedure, and patient risk index. National Nosocomial Infections Surveillance System, *Am. J. Med.* **91**(3B): 152S–157S.

Dean, A. G., Dean, J. A., Coulombier, D., Burton, A. H., Brendel, K. A., Smith, D. C., Dicker, R. C., Sullivan, K. M., and Fagan, R. F., 1997, *EpiInfo Ver 6, a Word Processing, Database, and Statistics Program for Public Health on IBM-Compatible Microcomputers*, Centers for Disease Control and Prevention, Atlanta, GA.

Deming, W. E., 1986, *Out of the Crisis*, MIT Center for Advanced Engineering Study, Cambridge, MA.

Donaldson, M. S. (Institute of Medicine) (Ed.), 1999, *Measuring the Quality of Health Care*, National Academy Press, Washington, DC.

Elashoff, J. D., 1995–1999, *nQuery Advisor® Statistical Software*, version 3.01, Cork, Ireland.

Ellrodt, G., Cook, D. J., Lee, J., Chao, M., Hunt, D., and Weingarten, S., 1997, Evidence-based disease management, *JAMA* **278**:1687–1692.

Ensor, T., and Thompson, R., 1999, Rationalizing rural hospital services in Kazakstan, *Int. J. Health Plan. Manage.* **14**:155–167.

Fetter, R. B., Shin, Y., Freeman, J. L., Averill, R., and Thompson, J. D., 1980, Case mix definition by diagnosis-related groups, *Med. Care* **18**(2 suppl): 1–53.

Fleiss, J. L., Jr., 1981, *Statistical Methods for Rates and Proportions*, 2nd ed., John Wiley & Sons, New York.

Fujita, T., and Sakurai, K., 1995, Multivariate analysis of risk factors for postoperative pneumonia, *Am. J. Surg.* **169**:304–307.

Gleicher, N., Oleske, D. M., Tur-Kaspa, I., Vidali, A., and Karande, V., 2000, Reducing the risk of high-order multiple pregnancy after ovarian stimulation with gonadotropin, *New Engl. J. Med.* **343**:2–7.

Goldman, D. A., Weinstein, R. A., Wenzel, R. P., Tabian, O. C., Duman, R. J., Gaynes, R. P., Schlosser, J., and Martone, W. J., 1996, Strategies to prevent and control the emergence and spread of antimicrobial-resistant microorganisms in hospitals, *JAMA* **275**:234–240.

Gonnella, J. S., Hornbrook, M. C., and Louis, D. Z., 1984, Staging of disease: A case-mix measurement, *JAMA* **251**:637–644.

Hall, M. F., 1995, Patient satisfaction or acquiescence? Comparing mail and telephone survey results, *J. Health Care Market.* **15**:54.

Hand, R., Piontek, F., Klemka-Walden, L., and Inczauskis, D., 1994, Use of statistical control charts to assess outcomes of medical care: pneumonia in Medicare patients, *Am. J. Med. Sci.* **307**:329–334.

Henderson, M., and Wallack, S., 1987, Evaluating case management for catastrophic illness, *Business Health* **4**:11.

Hintze, J. L., 2000, *PASS 2000 User's Guide*, Kaysville, UT.

Holland, M. S., Counte, M. A., and Hinrichs, B. G., 1995, Determinants of patient satisfaction with outpatient surgery, *Qual. Manage. Health Care* **4**:82–90.

Horn, S. D., and Horn, R. A., 1986, The Computerized Severity Index: A tool for case-mix management, *J. Med. Syst.* **10**:73–78.

Hynes, M. M., Reisinger, A. L., Sisk, J. E., and Gorman, S. A., 1998, Women in New York City's Medicaid program: A report on satisfaction, access, and use, *J. Am. Med. Women's Assoc.* **53**:83–88.

Iezzoni, L. I., 1989, Measuring the severity of illness and case mix, in *Providing Quality Care: The Challenge to Clinicians*, N. Goldfield and D. B. Nash, eds., pp. 70–105, American College of Physicians, Philadelphia, PA.

Iezzoni, L. I., Daley, J., Heeren, T., Foley, S. M., Fisher, E. S., Duncan, C., Hughes, J. S., and Coffman, G. A., 1994, Identifying complications of care using administrative data, *Med. Care* **32**:700–715.

Iezzoni, L. I., Schwartz, M., Ash, A. S., and Mackiernan, Y. D., 1996a, Does severity explain differences in hospital length of stay for pneumonia patients? *J. Health Serv. Res. Policy* **1**:65–76.

Iezzoni, L. I., Schwartz, M., Ash, A. S., Hughes, J. S., Daley, J., and Mackiernan, Y. D., 1996b, Severity measurement methods and judging hospital death rates for pneumonia, *Med. Care* **34**:11–28.

Institute of Medicine, 1990, *Medicare: A Strategy for Quality Assurance* (K. N. Lohr, ed.), National Academy Press, Washington, DC.

Institute of Medicine, 1999a, *To Err Is Human: Building a Safer Health System*, National Academy Press, Washington, DC.

Institute of Medicine, 1999b, *Measuring the Quality of Health Care*, National Academy Press, Washington, DC.

James, B. C., 1990, TQM and clinical medicine, *Front. Health Serv. Manage.* **7**:42–46.

Johantgen, M., Elixhauser, A., Ball, J. K., Goldfarb, M., and Harris, D. R., 1998, Quality indicators using hospital discharge data: State and national applications, *J. Qual. Improve.* **24**:88–105.

Joint Commission on Accreditation of Health Care Organizations, 1992, *Using Quality Improvement Tools in a Health Care Setting*, JCAHO, Oakbrook Terrace, IL.

Joint Commission on Accreditation of Health Care Organizations, 1997, *Comprehensive Accreditation Manual for Hospitals* JCAHO, Oakbrook Terrace, IL.

Joint Commission on Accreditation of Health Care Organizations, 1998a, *Comprehensive Accreditation Manual for Hospitals*, JCAHO, Oakbrook Terrace, IL.

Joint Commission on Accreditation of Health Care Organizations, 1998b, *Lessons Learned: Wrong Site Surgery*, Sentinel Event Alert (6) August 8, 1998, http://www.jcaho.org/edu_pub/sealert/sealert_frm.html.

Joint Commission on Accreditation of Health Care Organizations, 1999, *Comprehensive Accreditation Manual for Hospitals*, JCAHO, Oakbrook Terrace, Il.

Joint Commission on Accreditation of Health Care Organizations, 2000, Plan to implement core measures approved, *Joint Commission Perspect* **20:**9–11.

Juran, J. M., 1988, *Juran on Planning for Quality*, Free Press, New York.

Knaus, W. A., Zimmerman, J. E., Wagner, D. P., Draper, E. A., and Lawrence, D. E., 1981, APACHE-acute physiology and chronic health evaluation: A physiologically based classification system, *Crit. Care Med.* **9:**591–597.

Laffel, G., and Blumenthal, D., 1989, The case for using industrial quality management science in healthcare organizations, *JAMA* **262:**2869–2873.

Lazarou, J., Pomeranz, B. H., and Corey, P. N., 1998, Incidence of adverse drug reaction in hospitalized patients: A meta-analysis of prospective studies, *JAMA* **279:**1200–1205.

Leape, L. L., 1994, Error in medicine, *JAMA* **272:**1851–1857.

Leung, K. M., Elashoff, R. M., Rees, K. S., Hasan, M. M., and Legorreta, A. P., 1998, Hospital- and patient-related characteristics determining maternity length of stay: A hierarchical linear model approach. *Am. J. Public Health* **88:**377–381.

Levy, P. S., and Lemeshow, S., 1999, *Sampling of Populations: Methods and Applications*, John Wiley & Sons, New York.

McPherson, K., Wennberg, J. E., Hovind, O. B., and Clifford, P., 1982, Small-area variations in the use of common surgical procedures: An international comparison of New England, England, and Norway, *N. Engl. J. Med.* **307:**1310–1314.

Minitab, 1999, *Minitab Reference Manual*, Release 12.23, State College, PA.

Naylor, G., 1999, Using the business excellence model to develop a strategy for a health care organization, *Int. J. Health Care Qual. Assur.* **12:**37–44.

National Committee for Quality Assurance, 1999, *The State of Managed Care Quality*, 3rd ed., Washington, DC.

National Guideline Clearinghouse, 2000, *Fact sheet*, AHRQ Pub. No. 00-0047, Agency for Healthcare Research and Quality, Rockville, MD.

National Institute of Standards and Technology, Baldrige National Quality Program, 2000, *Criteria for Performance Excellence*, Baldrige National Quality Program, National Institute of Standards and Technology, Gaithersburg, MD.

Nelson, C. W., and Niederberger, J., 1990, Patient satisfaction surveys: An opportunity for total quality improvement, *Hospital Health Serv. Admin.* **35:**409–427.

Nelson, E., Mohr, J., Batalden, P., and Pume, S., 1996, Improving health care, part 1: The clinical value compass, *J. Qual. Improve.* **22:**243–258.

Neuhauser, D., Headrick, L., Katcher, W., and Lucas, P., 1995, Applying the statistical methods of continuous quality improvement to primary care: Hypertension, in *Improving Clinical Practice: Total Quality Management and the Physician* (D. Blumenthal and A. C. Scheck, eds.), pp. 111–136, Jossey-Bass, San Francisco, CA.

Normand, S. L. T., Glickman, M. E., Sharman, R. G. V. R. K., and McNeil, B. J., 1996, Using admission characteristics to predict short-term mortality from myocardial infarction in elderly patients, *JAMA* **275:**1322–1328.

Oberle, J., 1990 (January), Quality gurus, the men and their message, *Training* 47–52.

Oleske, D. M., 1997, *Hospital Obstetrical Care: A Comparison of Quality Indicators in Medicaid Fee-for-Service and Medicaid Managed Care Groups*, Final Report, Health Care Financing Administration Grant No. 18-P-90429/5, Baltimore, MD.

Palmer, R., Donabedian, A., and Povar, G., 1991, *Striving for Quality in Health Care: An Inquiry into Policy and Practice*, Health Administration Press, Ann Arbor, MI.

Reiley, P., and Howard, E., 1995, Predicting hospital length of stay in elderly patients with congestive heart failure, *Nurs. Econ.* **13:**210–220.

Roberts, J. S., Coal, J., and Redman, R., 1987, A history of the Joint Commission on Accreditation of Hospitals, *JAMA* **258**(7): 936–940.

Roberts, K., 1998, Best practices in the development of clinical practice guidelines, *J. Healthcare Qual.* **20:**16–20.

Romano, P. S., and Chan, B. K., 2000, Risk-adjusting acute myocardial infarction mortality: Are APR-DRGs the right tool? *HSR: Health Services Res.* **34:**1469–1489.

Rosner, B., 1995, *Fundamentals of Biostatistics*, Wadsworth Publishing, Belmont, CA.

Ross, C. K., Steward, C. A., and Sinacore, J. M., 1995, A comparative study of seven measures of patient satisfaction, *Med. Care* **33:**392.

Salemi, C., Morgan, J., Padilla, S., and Morrissey, R., 1995, Association between severity of illness and mortality from nosocomial infection, *Am. J. Infect. Control* **23:**188–193.

Satinsky, M. A., 1995, *An Executive's Guide to Case Management Strategies*, American Hospital Publishing, Chicago, IL.

Scholtes, P. R., 1988, *The Team Handbook: How to Use Teams to Improve Quality*, Joiner Associates, Madison, WI.

Shewhart, W. A., 1939, Statistical method from the viewpoint of quality control. Graduate School, Department of Agriculture, Washington, DC.

Smith, S., Stevic, M., and Livingston-Cooper, J., 1998, *Patient-Reported Health Status Outcomes*, University HealthSystem Consortium, Oak Brook, IL.

Strongwater, S. L., and Pelote, V., 1996, *Clinical Process Redesign: A Facilitator's Guide*, Aspen Publishers, Gaithersburg, MD.

Tsuyuki, R. T., Teo, K. K., Ikuta, R. M., Bay, K. S., Greenwood, P. V., and Montague, T. J., 1994, Mortality risk and patterns of practice in 2,070 patients with acute myocardial infarction, 1987–92: Relative importance of age, sex, and medical therapy, *Chest* **105:**1687–1692.

University Hospital Consortium, 1994, *Critical Issues Shaping Medical Practice*, UHC, Oak Brook, IL.

US Department of Health and Human Services, 2000a, *Health, United States, 2000*, National Center for Health Statistics, Hyattsville, MD.

US Department of Health and Human Services, 2000b, *Healthy People 2010--Conference Edition*, US Government Printing Office, Washington, DC.

Vayda, E., 1973, A comparison of surgical rates in Canada and in England and Wales, *N. Engl. J. Med.* **289:**1224–1229.

Vu, T. V., and Escalante, A., 1999, A comparison of the quality of life of patients with systemic lupus erythematosus with and without endstage renal disease, *J. Rheumatol.* **25:**2595–2601.

Ware, J. E., Jr., Kosinski, M., and Davies, A. R., 1997, *The Consumer Satisfaction Survey* (CSS): *Putting Health Care Performance into Context*, Health Assessment Lab, National Research Corporation, Boston, MA.

Weissman, J. S., Ayanian, J. Z., Chasan-Taber, S., Sherwood, M. J., Roth, C., and Epstein, A. M., 1999, Hospital readmissions and quality of care, *Med. Care* **37:**490–501.

Wennberg, J., and Gittelsohn, A., 1973, Small area variations in health care delivery, *Science* **182:**1102–1108.

Wennberg, J. E., and Gittelsohn, A., 1982, Variations in medical care among small areas, *Sci. Am.* **246:**120–134.

Wennberg, J. E. (ed.), 1996, *The Dartmouth Atlas of Health Care*, American Hospital Publishing, Chicago, IL.

Widdershoven, J. W. M. G., Gorgels, A. P. M., Vermeer, F., Dijkman, L. W. N., Verstraaten, G. M. P., Dassen, W. R. M., and Wellens, H. J. J., 1997, Changing characteristics and in-hospital outcome in patients admitted with acute myocardial infarction: Observations from 1982–1994, *Eur. Heart J.* **18:**1073–1080.

Woolf, S. H., Rothemich, S. F., Johnson, R. E., and Marsland, D. W., 1999, Is cigarette smoking associated with impaired physical and mental functioning status? *Am. J. Prevent. Med.* **17:**134–137.

Woomer, N., Long, C. O., Anderson, C., and Greenberg, E. A., 1999, Benchmarking in home health care: A collaborative approach, *Caring Magazine* November 22, 22–28.

Young, W. W., 1984, Incorporating severity of illness and comorbidity in case-mix measurement, *Health Care Financ. Rev.*(Suppl):23–31.

8

Control of Transmissible Diseases in Health Care Settings

Denise M. Oleske and Ronald C. Hershow

Introduction

Infectious diseases are a major cause of mortality and disability worldwide as well as in the United States. Leading global infectious killers are acute respiratory infections (including pneumonia and influenza), acquired immunodeficiency syndrome (AIDS), diarrheal diseases, tuberculosis, malaria, and measles (Fig. 8.1).

In addition to the increasing incidence and mortality, the resurgence of concern about transmissible diseases has been fueled by myriad factors. The ability of microbes to mutate, adapt, and survive was underestimated. Viruses evolve through replication errors, rearrangement of gene fragments, and invading new species. Resistant genes are transmitted from one bacterium to another on plasmids. These mechanisms promote new strains of influenza that traverse the globe along with tourists and immigrants. Resistance of many infectious diseases to current antimicrobial drugs is common. Antimicrobial resistant diseases include gonorrhea, malaria, pneumococcal disease, salmonellosis, shigellosis, tuberculosis, and staphylococcal infections. Medical practice and social and behavioral factors also have promoted a milieu for increasing the incidence of infectious diseases. Aggressive medical treatments (chemotherapy, bone marrow and organ transplantation, renal dialysis, indwelling medical devices) have increased the number of individuals living in an immunocompromised status. Increased use of illicit intravenous drugs has contributed to the spread of AIDS and hepatitis because of the use of contaminated needles. The behavior of exchanging sex for drugs also has been associated with an increase in the incidence of transmissible diseases, particularly for many sexually transmitted diseases, notably syphilis. A myriad of new infectious diseases including *Escherichia coli* O157:H7, hantaviruses, hepatitis C virus, human immunodeficiency virus (HIV), Legionnaire's disease, Ebola virus, toxic shock syndrome, and Lyme disease have

Denise M. Oleske   Departments of Health Systems Management and Preventive Medicine, Rush University, Chicago, Illinois 60612.   **Ronald C. Hershow**   Department of Epidemiology, School of Public Health, University of Illinois at Chicago, Chicago, Illinois 60612.

Epidemiology and the Delivery of Health Care Services: Methods and Applications, Second Edition, edited by Denise M. Oleske. Kluwer Academic/Plenum Publishers, New York, 2001.

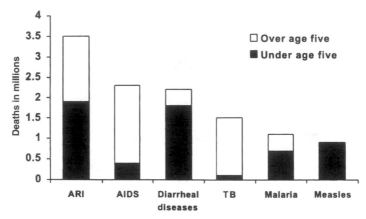

Figure 8.1. Leading infectious disease mortality, worldwide. ARI = acute respiratory infection; AIDS = acquired immunodeficiency syndrome; TB = tuberculosis. From World Health Organization (1999).

emerged in recent years. The incidence of many infectious diseases previously under control such as tuberculosis, rabies, dengue, and malaria recently has undergone a resurgence. In addition, the rise coupled with the potential of large foodborne outbreaks and bioterrorism threats create new challenges to managers of health care services.

The purpose of this chapter is to provide an introduction to the principles and knowledge of infectious disease epidemiology required for managers of health care services in light of the new challenges and threats posed by transmissible diseases in the 21st century. Avenues for action in the prevention and control of these diseases in health care settings are also suggested.

Infectious Disease Concepts

In order to understand the manager's role in the control of transmissible diseases in health care settings, a basic knowledge of terms and concepts is essential. To understand how to control transmissible disease, a health care manager must understand how infectious diseases arise and are transmitted.

There are five elements involved in the emergence of an infectious disease. It is essential for managers to know these as they guide the decision-making process. The elements are: (1) characteristics of the infectious agent, (2) reservoir of the agent, (3) mode of transmission, (4) portal of entry/exit, and (5) a susceptible host.

An infectious agent is characterized in terms of its biological classification, manifestation, and incubation period. The major categories of microbiological agents relevant to human diseases are bacteria, fungi, parasites, and viruses. Most human diseases caused by microbial factors are due to bacteria or viruses. Biological agents are classified according to the presence or absence of specific traits. For example, bacteria are classified based on the mechanism of movement and character of the cell wall. Viruses are classified based on the type of nucleic acid and the size, shape, substructure, and mode of replication of the viral particle. Table 8.1 illustrates the medically important microorganisms and their commonly associated diseases. In order to determine whether a biological factor is causative in a disease, it must be isolated and identified in the host. According to Brook *et al.* (1998), determination of the presence of microbial agents includes the following:

Table 8.1. Selected Medically Important Microorganisms
by Major Category and Associated Disease[a]

Category	Microorganism	Disease
Aerobic and facultative bacteria	*Staphylococcus aureus*	Toxic shock syndrome
Anaerobic bacteria	*Clostridium botilinum*	Food poisoning (botulism)
Viruses	*Rhinovirus*	Common cold
Fungi	*Trichophyton*	Ringworm
Parasites	*Plasmodium falciparum*	Malaria

[a]From Brooks *et al.* (1998).

1. The identification of agent in sections of tissues or stains of specimens morphologically
2. Culture isolation
3. Detection of antigen from the agent by fluorescein-labeled antibody stains or by immunologic assay
4. DNA–DNA or DNA–RNA hybridization to detect pathogen-specific genes in specimens
5. Antibody or cell-mediated immune responses at clinically important levels

The most important components of accurately identifying an infectious agent are the specimen, the adequacy of the quantity of material tested, the selection of the appropriate body area for testing, the method of collection (preferably from a site normal devoid of microorganisms), and the timeliness in the transport of the specimen to the laboratory. These steps are within the purview of the health manager and are essential processes to monitor in providing quality care to patients. In addition, the health care manager should have a knowledge of which diseases need to be reported to local health departments. A list of these is displayed in Table 8.2.

An agent also can be described in terms of its pathogenicity and virulence. Pathogenicity is the ability of an organism to alter normal cellular and physiological processes. Virulence is the ability of an organism to produce overt disease. The incubation period is the time from the introduction of the agent into the host to the onset of the signs and symptoms of disease. Each infectious agent has a unique incubation period that may be hours, days, weeks, months, or even years. For example, microbial agents that cause food poisoning typically have an incubation period of 24–72 hr; microbial agents that cause respiratory infections typically have an incubation period of 7–10 days, while hepatitis B and HIV infections have incubation periods that may be several months to years long (Chin, 2000).

A reservoir is where the agent lives, grows, and multiplies. Reservoirs can be living (human, animal, plant) or inanimate (soil, water). Human reservoirs can be clinical cases or carriers. Clinical cases are those persons who manifest signs and symptoms of the disease (acute cases) or who are infected but who do not manifest signs and symptoms of the disease (subclinical or inapparent cases). Carriers are those persons who serve as a potential source of infections and harbor a specific infectious agent, but they themselves are not manifesting any signs or symptoms of the disease.

The process of producing disease from biological agents begins with the introduction (or the portal of entry) and multiplication of the biological agent in the host. The mode of transmission is the next critical link in the chain of infection. Transmission is the mechanism

Table 8.2. Infectious Diseases Designated as Notifiable at the National Level, United States, 1997

Acquired immunodeficiency syndrome (AIDS)	Measles
Anthrax	Meningococcal disease
Botulism	Mumps
Brucellosis	Pertussis
Chancroid	Plague
Chlamydia trachomatis, genital infections	Poliomyelitis, paralytic
Cholera	Psittacosis
Coccidiomycosis	Rabies, animal
Cryptosporidiosis	Rabies, human
Diphtheria	Rocky Mountain spotted fever
Encephalitis, California serogroup	Rubella
Encephalitis, Eastern equine	Rubella, congenital syndrome
Encephalitis, St. Louis	Salmonellosis
Encephalitis, Western equine	Shigellosis
Escherichia coli O157:H7	Streptococcal disease, invasive Group A
Gonorrhea	*Streptococcus pneumoniae*, drug-resistant invasive
Hemophilus influenzae, invasive disease	disease
Hansen disease (leprosy)	Streptococcal toxic-shock syndrome
Hantavirus pulmonary syndrome	Syphilis
Hemolytic uremic syndrome, post-diarrheal	Syphilis, congenital
Hepatitis A	Tetanus
Hepatitis B	Toxic-shock syndrome
Hepatitis C/non-A, non-B	Trichinosis
HIV infection, pediatric	Tuberculosis
Legionellosis	Thyroid fever
Lyme disease	Yellow fever
Malaria	

by which an infectious agent is spread from a source to a host. There are four modes of transmission: (1) contact, (2) common vehicle, (2) airborne, and (4) vector borne.

Contact can be direct, indirect, or droplet spread. In direct contact transmission, there is physical contact, usually person-to-person, between the source and the host (e.g., transmission of *Staphylococcus* from hand of infected health care worker to a patient or a needlestick injury). Indirect refers to the passive transmission of a microorganism from the source to the host, usually on an inanimate object (e.g., *E. coli*-contaminated patient serving trays). Droplet spread transmission refers to those particles usually larger than 5 μm whose route of transmission is through the air, but only for very short distances as occurs with talking or sneezing. The common vehicle mode of transmission is a single inanimate vehicle that transmits the infectious agent to multiple hosts. Food and water are the most frequent common vehicles, although blood products and intravenous fluids also can be common vehicle sources. Airborne transmission involves infected particles in either droplet nuclei (less than 5 μm in diameter that contain the residua of evaporated larger particles) or dust that travel over 1 m in the air from the source to the host. Coughing and forceful sneezing are ways of transmitting tuberculosis from a human source into the air. Vector borne transmission can involve external or internal transmission of disease with insects. Flies can transmit *Salmonella* on their appendages from contaminated feces to food, representing external transmission. The passing of Lyme disease from ticks that have fed on infected deer to a human host represents internal vector-borne transmission. Knowing the manner in which microorganisms are transmitted aids in developing control measures for interrupting transmission. Some infectious organisms can

Table 8.3. Common Infectious Diseases, Reservoirs, and Routes of Transmission

Infectious disease	Reservoir	Route of transmission
Measles	Man	Respiratory
Hepatitis A	Man	Fecal–oral
Claymdia	Man	Sexual intercourse
Hepatitis B	Man	Percutaneous, permucosal, sexual intercourse, perinatal
Lyme disaese	Wild rodents, deer	Vector, ticks
Encephalitis	Wild birds, rodents, bats, reptiles, amphibians	Vector, mosquitos
AIDS	Man	Sexual contact, percutaneous, permucosal, perinatal

be transmitted by multiple routes, such as salmonellae, which can be transmitted by direct contact, airborne transmission, a common vehicle, and even by insects. Common infectious diseases, the reservoir, and route of transmission are displayed in Table 8.3.

The portal of exit is where the organism leaves the host. The portal of entry is where the organism invades the host. The portals of entry may be the respiratory (mouth and nose), gastrointestinal, or genitourinary tracts, or through the mucous membranes or skin. Usually, the portal of entry and the portal of exit are the same. For example, *Salmonella*-contaminated feces could produce an infection via ingestion of food contaminated with the feces.

Host susceptibility is not having sufficient resistance to protect against acquiring a pathogenic agent if exposed to it. Susceptibility depends on genetic factors, general health, and immunity. General health is influenced by nutrition and the presence of comorbidities. Disease caused by the biological agents occurs when the normal immune response of the host is overcome and destruction of cells and tissues occurs, producing physiological alterations in the host. Immunity is a resistance provided by the production of antibodies from lymphocytes or from monocytes having a specific action on the microorganism or on its toxin. Immunity can be characterized as passive (natural or artificial) or active (natural or artificial). Passive natural immunity is the transplacental transfer of antibodies from mother to fetus. Passive artificial immunity is the inoculation of specific protective antibodies in globulin preparations. Passive immunity has a short-term duration of efficacy (less than 6 months). Active immunity can be natural, as in the case of acquiring an infection (with or without clinical manifestation of disease), or artificial in which the agent itself in a killed or modified form (via a vaccine) is injected to stimulate protective antibodies. In fact, a relatively small subset of organisms causes disease.

Thus, to develop an infectious disease, an individual must be both susceptible and exposed. An exposure is a factor that, in the case of infectious disease transmission, is harmful and allows for entry or interaction with the organism to produce harmful effects or clinical disease. However, just because an individual is both susceptible and exposed does not mean that clinical (or overt) disease will develop. Circumstances and attributes of the exposure (frequency, dose, intimacy) and the degree of susceptibility of the host determine whether or not an infectious disease will emerge.

Managing Disease Outbreaks

In the health care setting, general infectious disease concepts guide the formulation of policies and procedures regarding the prevention of the emergence of infection in patients and health care workers. However, circumstances may arise in which an epidemic may occur. An epidemic is the occurrence of cases of a condition in excess of what would be expected. An epidemic may occur for several reasons, including: (1) an increase in the number of susceptible persons; (2) the emergence of a new organism; (3) changes in the environment; (4) changes in behavior; (5) new media for the growth of organisms; (6) the migration of infected persons, animals, birds, or insects into an area; (7) change in the virulence of an organism; and (8) inadequate immunization levels. Some epidemics develop slowly in nature, such as the recent epidemics of syphilis and tuberculosis, whose increased incidence had underlying causes in societal changes, i.e., the increased use of illicit intravenous drugs and noncompliance with treatment plans leading to multidrug resistant strains of tuberculosis. Other epidemics occur more suddenly and unexpectedly, such as an outbreak of salmonella, whose root cause may be the improper handling of food.

Health care settings that treat patients are susceptible to epidemics and must take precautions to not only prevent their occurrence, but to also respond to an epidemic in a quick fashion to decrease added risk to patients. Both the patient population and health care providers may be at risk in a hospital epidemic. An example of a slowly evolving epidemic that could occur in health care workers would be that of an increase in the incidence of needle-stick injuries. Although each incident is documented, trends in incidence typically are noted over a longer time period. An epidemic that is faster would be an outbreak of nosocomial infection in an intensive care unit, although only certain types (e.g., chicken pox, tuberculosis) would place health care providers at risk.

The health care organization's approach to epidemics must be both proactive and reactive. It is important to have the resources available to identify an epidemic and to respond accordingly. This requires specialized personnel such as an epidemiologist and safety experts. Additionally, the health care manager should have a firm understanding of how the occurrence of an epidemic could have an impact on other departments of the organization. It is important to remember that employees who do not have direct patient contact, such as housekeeping, laundry, and laboratory staff, are also at risk in an epidemic. An epidemic in a health care setting also potentially affects (1) liability (possible lawsuits and litigation); and (2) health care costs (increased total treatment costs for a patient because of additional medical resources required to treat the patient, and increased length of stay).

Due to the broad impact that an epidemic can have, the fundamental role of the health care manager is to ensure that an organized strategy for this activity is in place. Elements of that strategy would include (1) define the case; (2) screen all persons potentially exposed with laboratory studies to define the magnitude of the outbreak; (3) characterize the epidemic by persons, place, and time; (4) isolate the source or cohort of infected persons; (5) disinfect portals of exit; (6) break identified chains of transmission; (7) defend portals of entry; (8) immunize host; (9) investigate risk factors for developing the infection using an observational study design (most commonly a case-control study); and (10) establish and maintain surveillance systems that serve to identify outbreaks and gauge the efficacy of control measures.

Managerial Responsibilities in Infection Control

In addition to the prevention and control of epidemics, the health care manager also has general responsibilities in the control of transmissible diseases in health care service delivery settings. The tasks associated with this role are found in Table 8.4. Managers also have

Table 8.4. Management Responsibilities Regarding Infection Control

Prevention
   1. Classification of work activity and exposure level for all job classes
   2. Development of policies and procedures for workplace exposure control
   3. Provision of training and education
   4. Development of procedures to ensure and monitor compliance
Management of workplace environment
   1. Needle and sharps disposal
   2. Handwashing facilities
   3. Cleaning, disinfecting and sterilizing (equipment, room, laundry, body fluids)
   4. Provision of protective equipment
   5. Safe disposal of biohazardous waste
   6. Maintenance of isolation rooms
Medical response to individual exposure
   1. Baseline assessment and appropriate labortory testing at time of exposure
   2. Documentation in medical record circumstances of exposure (activities, work practices, protective equipment, source of exposure)
   3. Appropriate follow-up assessments and laboratory testing (e.g., HIV antibody tests at 6 weeks, 12 weeks, and 6 months following sharps exposure to HIV+ source patient)
   4. Provide treatment and evaluation for symptomatic diseases or source-related infection that develops during follow-up (e.g., PPD skin test conversion)
Management
   1. Report to OSHA[a] and state health department
   2. Decision to have patient duties depend on worker's personal physician and employer's medical advisors (NOTE: Persons with impaired immune system are highly susceptible to contagious disease to which they may be exposed in patient care contact)

[a]Occupational Safety and Health Administration.

responsibilities for coordinating the general effort of the prevention and control of transmissible diseases in health care organizations. The establishment of an infection control program is essential for any health care service delivery setting. The elements of an infection control program are outlined in Table 8.5. Two particular concerns to health care managers are bloodborne disease transmission and the other is airborne disease transmission.

Bloodborne Disease Transmission

Bloodborne pathogens are defined as pathogenic microorganisms that are present in human blood and can cause disease in humans. These pathogens include but are not limited to the hepatitis B virus (HBV), hepatitis C virus, and the human immunodeficiency virus (HIV). Potentially infectious materials are semen, vaginal secretions, amniotic fluid, cerebrospinal fluid, pericardial fluid, peritoneal fluid, pleural fluid, synovial fluid, saliva in dental procedures, any body fluid that is visibly contaminated with blood, all body fluids in situations where it is difficult or impossible to differentiate between body fluids, any unfixed tissue or organ, HIV- or HBV-containing culture medium or other solutions or tissue, cell, or organ cultures, and blood, organ, or other tissues from experimental animals infected with HIV or HBV.

Table 8.5. Elements in an Infection Control Program

1. Establish staffing, organizational position, and authority of infection control
2. Construct an exposure matrix for all employee job classifications
3. Develop, implement, and operate mechanisms for infection surveillance
   • Targeted (e.g., high-risk patients, ICUs)
   • Active (e.g., encourage reporting of needlestick injuries, culturing for a specific organism, Legionella)
   • Passive (e.g., monitor microbiolgical reports of Transplant Unit)
   • Periodic (rotating wards)
4. Develop policies and procedures in accordance with regulatory and credentialing bodies for the management of on-the-job exposures (e.g., isolation policies) and infections requiring work restrictions (e.g., chicken pox)
5. Conduct education for all new employees and annually thereafter on latest CDC[a] recommendations for infection control
6. Provide support for personnel health (e.g., employee wellness programs)
7. Conduct preemployment testing and mandatory imunization (rubella)
8. Conduct periodic screenings (e.g., for tuberculosis)
9. Provide recommended immunization (hepatitis B, influenza)
10. Provide treatment for on-the-job exposures if indicated
11. Establish mechanisms for communicable disease reporting
12. Feedback to staff on organizational progress in infection control

[a]Centers for Disease Control and Prevention.

Epidemiology of Hepatitis B

With respect to HBV infections, 10,258 new cases (incidence rate of 3.8 per 100,000) were reported in the United States in 1998 (National Center for Health Statistics, 2000). Due to underreporting, it is estimated that the actual occurrence of HBV is close to 200,000 cases per year. Worldwide, HBV infection is hyperendemic in sub-Saharan Africa, southern and eastern Asia, and the Amazon Delta. In these areas, hepatitis B carriage rates are generally greater than 10% (as compared to less than 1% in the US population). Approximately 25% of infected adults will develop an acute hepatitis syndrome and 6–10% will become HBV carriers. Carriers are at risk of developing chronic liver disease and of infecting others. Due to the availability and successful deployment of the hepatitis B vaccine, health care workers account for less than 2% of recent HBV infections in the United States.

Epidemiology of Human Immunodeficiency Virus Infection

In addition to HBV, HIV represents another virulent agent of concern to health care providers and managers. HIV is a retrovirus that in the late stages of infection gives rise to a condition known as AIDS. AIDS is clinically manifest as a progressive destruction of the immune system and other organ systems, particularly the central nervous system. Since the reporting of the disease, 687,863 cases have been recorded in the United States representing an incidence rate in 1999 of 16.9 per 100,000 persons (National Center for Health Statistics, 2000). In the United States, the highest HIV infection prevalence rate is among men who have sex with men (19.3%), and this group represents the largest proportion (60%) of men diagnosed with AIDS. However, the incidence rate is highest among black non-Hispanic males

(145.3 per 100,000) and black non-Hispanic females (54.1 per 100,000). Of men with AIDS, 57% were men who have sex with men and 22% were injection drug users (IDU). In women, 43% of AIDS cases were attributed to IDU and 39% were attributed to heterosexual contact with either an IDU, a bisexual male, a person with hemophilia, a transfusion recipient with HIV, or an HIV-infected person. The HIV prevalence parallels the prevalence rate of sexually transmitted disease in a geographic area (Centers for Disease Control, 1998b). Worldwide, there are 34 countries in which 91% of all AIDS death have occurred; 29 of these are in sub-Saharan Africa, 3 are in Asia (Cambodia, India, Thailand), and 2 in the Western Hemisphere (Brazil and Haiti). Particularly hard hit are Botswana, Zimbabwe, and South Africa, where more than 12% of the adult population is infected (United Nations, 1999).

Globally, the HIV pandemic has evolved in a variety of ways in different countries. In sub-Saharan Africa, for example, HIV infection is mainly spread heterosexually leading to a fairly equal incidence of AIDS by gender. Mother-to-child transmission is a common mode of transmission in this area and HIV prevalence rates exceed 20% in the general populations of many African countries. A number of opportunistic infections such as *Pneumocystitis carinii* and several cancers such as Kaposi's sarcoma are indicators of underlying AIDS (Chin, 2000). The mode of transmission for HIV is through the exchange of body fluids such as blood, semen, and vaginal fluids. These fluids can be exchanged through sexual contact, sharing of intravenous drug equipment, or other means where the integrity of the portals of entry—the mucous membrane and circulatory system—are violated. Once infected, the host enters into a period of several weeks before having an immune conversion to test positive as a carrier of the virus. The carrier may or may not exhibit signs and symptoms of AIDS because of its long incubation period.

Bloodborne Disease Control Measures

Because of the increased incidence of bloodborne diseases and the serious consequences of these diseases, the Centers for Disease Control and Prevention (CDC) established "standard precautions" in 1996. Standard precautions stress two points. First, excluding sweat, all body fluids, secretions, excretions, mucous membranes, and nonintact skin are presumed to be potentially infectious so that contact with these portals of exit and body fluids can be avoided. Second, these precautions mandate engineering controls, specific personal protective equipment (e.g., gloves, gowns, masks, eye protection), and specific work practices. These procedures are aimed at minimizing the exposure of health care workers to blood and body fluids that may be potentially infectious when performing duties or tasks. The responsibilities of health care managers regarding precautions specifically for bloodborne disease are outlined in Table 8.6. The elements of a bloodborne disease control program are outlined below.

Establishment of Policies, Procedures, and Employee Risk Assessment

Management should be aware of the latest CDC and OSHA regulations regarding the control of bloodborne disease transmission and implement an organizationwide plan that is reviewed annually. The first step is to classify all employees according to risk of exposure to bloodborne pathogens. Level I are employees who have the highest risk because they work with blood or related products, are exposed to sharps, perform invasive tasks, or frequently come in contact with equipment contaminated with blood or body fluids (e.g., nurse, lab technician). Level II are employees who are at medium exposure due to limited contact with patients, blood, or body fluids (e.g., laundry personnel or counseling staff). Level III em-

Table 8.6. Elements of an Exposure Control Plan for Bloodborne Pathogens

- List types of employees exposed to bloodborne pathogens by job classification
- Describe engineering controls implemented to handle sharp, infected objects
- Provide directions outlining safe work practices
- Offer in-service programs to educated and train employees on following the safe work practices on an annual basis
- Describe type of risk exposure (sharp objects, splash or spray of infectious agents, etc.)
- Describe and demonstrate the use of personal protective equipment
- Illustrate proper labeling and signage of high-risk areas and objects
- Assign responsibility for ensuring compliance with the safety plan and monitoring this compliance
- Promote hepatitis B vaccination

ployees have no patient contact and no contact with contaminated items such as sharps (e.g., clerks, computer operators). Volunteers also should be assessed and their risk determined by their departmental manager. Health facilities should use their own data to further refine job risk categories. Indeed, the identification of risk in different employee subgroups is a compelling reason to establish systematic monitoring of blood and body fluid exposures.

Employees who are levels I and II should be offered hepatitis B vaccine unless the employee is immune, has previously received the complete hepatitis vaccination series, has medical contraindications for receipt of vaccine, or is immune as determined by antibody testing.

In the event of exposure to potentially infectious materials, the health care organization should have in place policies that describe in detail the response to be taken. The exposed area should be thoroughly washed, appropriate treatment obtained, the incident should be reported to the appropriate manager, and appropriate follow-up of the incident by the safety or other designated department. Exposure should be evaluated according to the type of exposure (e.g., blood, saliva, etc.), nonpenetrating versus penetrating, and the source patient's HIV or hepatitis status, if known. Small cutaneous exposure on intact skin may not require postexposure prophylaxis (PEP); however, exposure to a large volume of blood, prolonged exposure time, or large areas of the body surface involved may. Significant exposure requires urgent intervention, preferably within 1 hour postexposure and not more than 24 hours postinjury. For suspect exposure to HIV or AIDS, current PEP involves the prompt administration of antiretroviral therapy using two to three drug combinations. The choice of the specific drugs depends on the level of risk of the exposed employee and the prior antiretroviral exposure of the source patient. It behooves health care managers to make an assessment of the stock of their postexposure drugs and the current PEP protocols by the CDC (see website: www.cdc.gov).

The organization should follow local laws regarding consent for testing individuals and should include legally valid steps for testing individuals when consent cannot be obtained (e.g., an unconscious patient). Due to the nature of a possible immune conversion following exposure, policies should be extremely sensitive to issues of confidentiality and both pretest and posttest counseling should be available to the exposed individual. This counseling should be actively offered at any point during the incident. Policies also should ensure that the safety office or appropriate recording department not only should be notified of the incident, but the circumstances leading to the incident also should be reported. A review of this information can be helpful in changing practice, policies, and approaches to education in an attempt to decrease exposure of bloodborne pathogens to health care workers.

Engineering Controls

Engineering controls are those devices that isolate or remove the bloodborne hazard from the workplace. Controls include sharps containers that are leak-proof and puncture resistant, needless intravenous connections, syringes with safety sheaths (to avoid recapping of needles), emergency mouth-to-mouth resuscitation mouthpieces, leak-proof and puncture-resistant medical waster containers, certified biological safety cabinets, and materials for biohazard spill clean up.

Personal Protective Equipment

Health care workers are primarily protected through the use of barriers (personal protective equipment) that reduce the risk of exposure of a health care worker's skin or mucous membrane (ports of entry) to potentially infective materials. Personal protective equipment (PPE) includes gloves, gowns, masks, masks with visors, face shields, shoe covers, and goggles. Additional consideration in the use of PPE are fluid resistance, appropriate size, and proper disposal of contaminated PPE in biohazard waste container or appropriate laundry bin. It is the responsibility of health care managers to provide these for any health care workers who may come in contact with body fluids. Although these barriers provide frontline protection, the health care provider and manager must realize that they may not protect against penetrating injuries from needles, sharp instruments, or broken glass. Protective equipment/barriers should never be used more than once and always should be changed between patients.

Work Practice Controls

Safe work practices consider both the employee personal practices as well as their care of the environment to control the risk of exposure to bloodborne pathogens. Handwashing is the single-most important work practice control measure. Hands also should be washed before and after wearing gloves, prior to and at the completion of any procedure, and between patient contacts. The next-most important work practice concerns the proper handling of used needles or other sharp instruments. Used needles must not be recapped or manipulated, but placed only in a puncture resistance container. All procedures should be performed in a manner as to minimize splashing, spraying, or aerosolization.

A clean and sanitary environment is essential. Thus, immediately after the completion of a procedure or the spill of any body fluid or potentially infectious materials, or as soon as feasible after visible contamination, all contaminated equipment and work surfaces should be cleaned and decontaminated with an appropriate disinfectant. When cleaning, employees should wear appropriate PPE. Soiled laundry should be handled as little as possible with a minimum of agitation and bagged in impervious bags or containers.

Hazard Communication

Communication of hazards to employees is an essential management responsibility. Approved warning labels must be affixed to all biohazardous waste containers, refrigerators, and freezers. Biohazardous waste bags are identified by their red color. For hospital inpatients who present unusually high risk of bloodborne-transmissible disease (e.g., AIDS, hepatitis), a sign regarding precautionary measures may be posted on the door to the patient's room (Fig. 8.2). Levels I and II employees must be given initial training on where the occupational exposure may take place with annual refresher training and retraining if tasks have changed.

STOP STANDARD PRECAUTIONS (*Las Precauciones Uniformes*) ALTO

Used for the Care of ALL PATIENTS (Usado para el cuidado de todos pacientes)

WASH HANDS:
- if contact blood, body fluids, secretions, excretions, and contaminated equipment.
- after gloves removed.
- between patient contacts.

WEAR GLOVES:
- when touching blood, body fluids, secretions, excretions, and contaminated equipment.

CHANGE GLOVES:
- just before touching mucous membranes or broken skin.
- after contact with any contaminated material.

REMOVE GLOVES:
- promptly after use.
- before touching non-contaminated items and environmental surfaces.

WEAR MASK, EYE PROTECTION, FACE SHIELD:
- to protect mucous membranes of the eyes, nose, and mouth during procedures likely to splash or spray blood, body fluids, secretions or excretions.

WEAR GOWN:
- during procedures likely to splash or spray blood, body fluids, secretions or excretions.

REMOVE GOWN:
- promptly after use to avoid transfer of contaminants to other patients or environments.

AVOID / PREVENT INJURY FROM SHARPS:
- Never recap used needles.
- Do not bend or break used needles by hand.
- Do not remove used needles from disposable syringes by hand.
- Place used needles/sharps in appropriate containers.
- Never attempt to remove sharps from containers.

LE LAVADO ENTREGA:
- *si avisa sangre, los liquidos del cuerpo, secretions, las excreciones, y el equipo contaminado.*
- *después guantes quitados.*
- *entre contactos pacientes.*

LLEVE GUANTES:
- *cuando tocar sangre, los liquidos del cuerpo, secretions, las excreciones, y contaminó el equipo.*

CAMBIE GUANTES:
- *apenas antes de tocar membranas de mucous o piel rota.*
- *después del contacto con alguna materia contaminada..*

QUITE GUANTES:
- *inmediatament después de uso.*
- *antes de tocar artículos no contaminados y superficies de entorno.*

LA MASCARA DEL USO, LA PROTECCIÓN DE OJO, Y/O LA CARA:
- *protegen a protege mucous membranas de los ojos, de la nariz, y de la boca durante procedimientos probables a salpica o rocia sangre, los liquidos del cuerpo, secretions o excreciones.*

LA BATA DEL USO:
- *durante procedimientos probables a salpica or rocia sangre, los liquidos, del cuerpo, secretions o excreciones.*

QUITE BATA:
- *inmediatamente después que está acostumbrado a evita la transferencia de contaminants a otros pacientes o ambientes.*

EVITE Y PREVENGA LA HERIDA DE AGUDO:
- *Nunca recap usó las agujas.*
- *Nodoble ni rompa las agujas usadas a mano.*
- *No quite las agujas usadas del syringes para tirar a mano.*
- *El lugar usó las agujas y agudo en contenedores apropiados.*
- *Nunca tentative a quita agudo de contenedores.*

Figure 8.2. Signage for isolation room for standard precautions, English and Spanish.

Although the mode of transmission for both HBV and HIV are similar, the potential for HBV acquisition in the health care workplace is greater than that of HIV due to greater concentrations of HBV found in blood and other plasma-derived body fluids to which health care workers are exposed in patient therapies or procedures. However, due to the availability of a vaccine with 90–95% efficacy, health care workers may now be rendered at extremely low risk of serious hepatitis B infection. Health care managers should institute measures to ensure that this vaccination is available to all at-risk HCWs at the beginning of their employment. This process should include postvaccination testing for antibodies to hepatitis B surface antigen (anti-HBs) 2–3 months after series completion to assess response to vaccine. Non-responders should receive a second series followed by retesting for anti-HBs.

Airborne Disease

One of the major serious and common threats to both patient and staff in the health care setting from airborne disease is from the etiologic agent for tuberculosis (TB), *Mycobacterium tuberculosis*. In the United States in 1997, there were 19,851 TB cases, representing an incidence rate of 7.4 per 100,000 population. Six states (California, Florida, Illinois, New Jersey, New York, and Texas) reported 57% of all TB cases (Centers for Disease Control, 1998a). Worldwide, TB remains one of the most important causes of mortality with the prevalence of infection exceeding 50% in most developing nations. Since the mid-1980s, the proportion of foreign-born persons with TB has continued to increase, while the overall number of cases in the United States continues to decrease (after a period of increased incidence in the late 1980s and early 1990s) (Centers for Disease Control, 1998a).

Individuals who are immunosuppressed (e.g., those with HIV) are at increased risk of developing active TB. The immune response to TB enhances HIV replication. Because of this, individuals infected with HIV should be medically evaluated for TB. The CDC has published recommended management strategies for patients with HIV infection and TB that emphasizes the need for a continuum of health care services to support the success of the treatment (Centers for Disease Control, 1998b). In addition to increased morbidity due to coinfection, strains of bacteria are able to mutate and become resistant to drug therapy. Over time, TB has become resistant to many of the antibiotics that had previously been used mainly as a result of noncompliance with treatment programs. New strains of multidrug-resistant TB (MDR-TB) are spreading creating a new challenge for the medical community. The risk of drug-resistant TB is greater among persons with known HIV infection as compared to others and may be as high as 11% (Centers for Disease Control, 1998b).

The transmission of TB within the environment must be of priority concern to health care managers. The most common method of TB transmission is exposure to bacilli in airborne droplet nuclei produced by infected persons who cough, sing, or sneeze. Infection occurs when an individual inhales droplet nuclei contaminated with *M. tuberculosis*. The bacteria then traverse the portal of entry (mouth or nasal passages) and deposit within the lungs. Usually the human immune system limits the multiplication and spread of the bacteria within 2–10 weeks. High-risk occupational situations are being in close contact with persons who have TB or medical procedures that are cough-inducing (bronchoscopy) or generate aerosols (nebulizers). In 90% of infected persons, these bacteria remain dormant throughout life and this is known as latent TB infection. Individuals with latent TB usually have a positive response to the protein purified derivative (PPD) skin test but are not symptomatic or infectious.

Factors affecting infection with TB are highly variable and depend on the virulence of the strain of TB, environmental conditions, and the health of the exposed individual. Outside the patient's rooms, infectious droplets may remain airborne and move within a building's air currents until inhaled by another worker or patient, settled out of the air, or exhausted from the building. As a control measure, managers should ensure that the ventilation system is in compliance with the CDC standards. The use of ultraviolet radiation, disinfection, and high-efficiency air filtration and electrostatic precipitation are other control measures that augment but do not obviate the need for maintenance of appropriate ventilation standards.

Airborne Disease Control Measures

Health care managers must always consult current guidelines on the latest measures for the control of TB. Elements of a TB control program are based on a hierarchy of control measures that are administrative, engineering, and personal protection. These are summarized in Table 8.7 and are more fully described below.

Administrative Procedures

Administrative controls are the development and implementation of written policies, procedures, and protocols to ensure the rapid detection, isolation, and treatment of patients with infectious TB, as well as implement effective work practices by health care workers in the facility. It also is the manager's responsibility to ensure compliance with these measures.

Risk Assessment. The first step toward implementing a TB exposure control plan is an initial risk assessment of each hospital area and employee type. The risk assessment should

Table 8.7. Optimum Tubercuosis Control Program for All Health Care Facilities[a,b]

Initial and periodic risk assessment
Evaluate HCW PPD skin test conversion data
Determinate TB prevalence among patients
Reassess risk in each PPD testing period
Written TB infection control program
Document all aspects of TB control
Identify individual(s) responsible for TB control program
Explain and emphasize hierarchy of control
Implementation
Assignment of responsibility
Risk assessment and periodic assessment of the program
Early detection of patients with TB
Management of outpatients with possible infectious TB
Isolation for infectious TB patients
Implement effective engineering controls
Provide respiratory protection
Contain/limit cough-inducing procedures
HCW TB education, HCW counseling and screening
Evaluate HCW PPD test conversion and possible nosocomial TB transmission
Coordinate effort with public health education

[a]TB, tuberculosis; HCV, health care worker; PPD, protein purified derivative.
[b]From *Federal Register*, Volume 58, No. 195, Tuesday, October 12, 1993.

receive input from qualified personnel such as an epidemiologist, infectious disease and pulmonary medicine specialists, engineers, and management. The assessment should include a review of the number of TB patients seen in the organization as a whole and for specialized areas such as TB, pulmonary, and HIV units. A review of the drug-susceptibility pattern of TB patients should be conducted along with an analysis of PPD skin test results of health care workers across the organization.

Rapid Detection, Isolation, and Management.   Rapid detection is probably the most important step in the control of TB within a health care organization. All medical and nursing staff should assess each patient admitted to any area of the organization for the signs and symptoms of TB. TB is suspect when any of the following are present: persistent cough greater than 2 weeks in duration, bloody sputum, night sweats, weight loss, anorexia, fever, or undiagnosed pulmonary infection. Suspicion of TB is higher in certain groups where the prevalence of TB is high (HIV, homeless, contacts of TB cases, injecting drug users, foreign born, elderly) or in patients at risk for progression from latent infection to active disease (undergoing immunosuppressive therapy, malignancy, renal failure, >10% below ideal weight).

In an individual suspected of having active TB, or who is in a high-risk group, or who is symptomatic for active TB, diagnostic measures should be initiated and airborne precautions should be instituted immediately (see Fig. 8.3). Implementation of these measures begins with

---

STOP AIRBORNE PRECAUTIONS ALTO
(*Las Precauciones en el Aire*)

Visitors: Report to Nurse Before Entering
(*Visitantes: Informarse conla enfermera antes de entrar*)

PRIVATE ROOM:
- Keep **DOOR CLOSED.**
- negative airflow room.

LA HABITACIÓN PRIVADA:
- *Mantenga PUERTA CERRÓ.*
- *La habitación con corriente de aire negativo.*

RESPIRATORY PROTECTION:
- AFB+ or rule out AFB use **N95 Respirator Mask**
- Chickenpox or Measles do not enter room if you have no history of disease or immunity - if unavoidable use **N95 Respirator Mask**

LA PROTECCIÓN RESPIRATORIA:
- *AFB+ o excluye AFB use la máscara de respiradora de N º95.*
- *No entre la habitación si el paciente tiene china o sarampion y usted no tiene ninguna historia de la enfermedad o no hacido inmunisado. Si es necesario use la máscara de respiradora de N º95.*

TRANSPORT:
- Place surgical mask on patient.
- Transport only if essential.

EL TRANSPORTE:
- *Coloque máscara quirúrgica en el paciente.*
- *Transporte sólo si esencial.*

DISCHARGE CLEANING:
- Routine cleaning sufficient.
- Keep room vacant for at least one hour.

• LA DESCARGA LIMPIANDO:
- *Limpiar de rutina suficiente.*
- *Mantenga la habitación vacía por lo menos una hora.*

Figure 8.3.   Signage for isolation room for airborne disease precautions, English and Spanish.

instructing the patient on the reasons for the precautions and the importance of complying with them. The patient is placed in a private room with negative airflow. The door is to remain closed at all times, an "airborne precaution" sign is placed on the door by nursing and the patient's chart, and all visitors should wear standard surgical masks. Health care workers entering the room must wear a particulate filter respirator. A mask should be provided to patients when they are being transported within the health care facility for tests that cannot be performed inside the TB isolation unit. Outpatient facilities should schedule these patients as the first or last appointment of the day. Upon arrival in a clinic, persons known or suspected to have TB should be asked to wear a surgical mask and placed immediately into an examination room apart from other patients. Ideally, ambulatory-care settings in which patients with TB are frequently examined or treated should have TB isolation rooms available. After the patient is discharged or leaves the exam room, airborne precautions remain in effect (including closed door) until 1 hour after the affected patient is discharged.

Confirmed active TB patients should be started on therapy in accordance with current CDC guidelines. If available, directly observed therapy (DOT) may be appropriate, particularly if nonadherence to therapy is likely.

Engineering Controls

Engineering controls are aimed at preventing the spread of disease and reducing the concentration of infected droplet nuclei through measures directed at local exhaust ventilation, air flow direction, and air cleaning. Specifically, rooms used for isolation should be under negative pressure, have air exchange at least six times per hour, have room air exhausted directly to the outside of the building away from any air intakes, and room air that is recirculated should be filtered through a high-efficiency particular air (HEPA) filter system. The design and installation of all ventilation systems in the facility should be supervised by a professional with expertise in ventilation who also has had experience and knowledge of health care settings. Areas where cough-inducing procedures such as bronchoscopy or suctioning are performed may have a higher concentration of airborne infected nuclei and may need more air exchanges on an hourly basis to decrease the concentration of airborne nuclei. Additionally, health care facilities that serve populations with a higher prevalence of TB also may need to supplement air-handling systems in general use areas.

Use of Personal Protection

According to the Occupational Safety and Health Administration (OSHA), all employees who are exposed to a patient classified with suspected or known TB must wear appropriate respiratory protection. Both disposable and motorized respirators are available. Prior to the issuance of a N95 particulate filter respirator (PFR95), a medical questionnaire is completed by the employee to determine whether he or she can be fit-tested for the respirator. A surgical face mask is not approved by OSHA for employee respiratory protection against exposure to TB droplet nuclei. Managers must make available safety glasses when procedures or treatments involving TB-infected patients give rise to the potential for splashing.

Monitoring and Surveillance

Monitoring and surveillance for TB using Mantoux skin testing (using PPD) is required of all employees in a medical setting regardless of their role in the organization. The test must be part of a preemployment screening, in a two-step procedure, and performed on an annual basis thereafter. High-risk employees, such as those employed in intensive care units, respiratory therapy, emergency room, and the pulmonary service are tested every 6 months. The exception to this is employees with a history of a positive PPD test, disease treatment, or who are currently on preventive TB therapy. These employees must be screened annually for the presence of signs or symptoms of TB. Policies also should be in place outlining steps to follow should a PPD "convert" (initial negative PPD reaction, followed by a positive reaction on follow-up testing) or if an active TB case in a health care worker is identified particularly if such conversions are clustered in employees from a specific geographic unit of the health care facility or within a specific employee category. A plan also should be in place to perform postexposure investigations when patients and staff are exposed to a TB case who is not isolated appropriately on initial presentation.

Education and Training

As with testing, education also should be on a continuous schedule. At a minimum, all employees should be required to attend an annual in-service program that describes the risk of exposure to TB and the individual's responsibility to reduce their own probability of exposure. Educational programs may be required sooner than planned if an increase in active TB cases is noticed or if a lapse in clinical practice has caused the spread of disease. At all times, educational material such as brochures, pamphlets, and federal, state, and local guidelines should be available to all employees upon request. Managers have the responsibility of ensuring that all their employees are current in their training.

Special Considerations in Infectious Disease Control for Specific Health Care Service Settings

It is the responsibility and a special challenge to the health care manager to provide a safe work area for the settings of employees as well as a treatment environment that reduces the likelihood or transmissible disease risk to patients. This priority also must be addressed during stages of program development, renovation, and reconstructions. Although concerns regarding communicable diseases exist in every health care setting, the types of disease that are of priority concern vary somewhat according to the setting because of the types of patients seen and the nature of the care provided. The specific settings addressed in this chapter are: inpatient, ambulatory care, long-term care, home care, and hospice facilities.

Inpatient Acute Care Facility

In the hospital, nosocomial infections and infectious diseases as comorbidities are of special concern. A nosocomial infection is an infection that is acquired while in an inpatient setting that was not incubating or present on admission. The incidence of nosocomial infection various according to organization characteristics, service area within a hospital, and anatomic site. The highest nosocomial infection rate is among patients in intensive care units (ICU) (Centers for Disease Control, 2000). The use of invasive devices (e.g., urinary catheters, central lines, ventilators) is a major contributor to this risk. Ventilator-associated pneumonias were the highest device-associated nosocomial infection in all types of ICUs.

Recommendations for the specific infrastructure and activities of infection control for hospitals have been proposed by the Society for Healthcare Epidemiology of America

(Scheckler *et al.*, 1998). Essential components of a hospital infection control program include an organized hospitalwide surveillance of nosocomial infections and other adverse events (e.g., monitoring antibiotic-resistance patterns), a system of reporting infection rates to practitioners, policies and procedures based on scientifically valid information found to positively impact infection control, ensuring the hospital's compliance with legal and accreditation standards, a trained hospital epidemiologist, and an infection control practitioner (e.g., nurse, medical technologist) assisted by surveillance technicians. The hospital control and surveillance program should collect and monitor data to evaluate conformance with the guidelines of accrediting bodies such as those of the local and state health departments, Health Care Financing Administration (if the hospital receives payment for Medicare patients), and the Joint Commission for the Accreditation of Health Care Settings (JCAHO), and others.

To promote the standardization of hospital surveillance data collection (e.g., uniform case definitions) and analysis methods, the National Nosocomial Infections Surveillance (NNIS) system was begun. It is a voluntary, hospital-based reporting system to monitor hospital-acquired infections. The NNIS is intended to provide national risk-adjusted benchmarks for hospital-acquired infection rates and device-associated rates. The NNIS has found that patients in intensive care units (ICU) are at highest risk for nosocomial infection and that rates vary by device and type of patient care unit. Infection rates for urinary catheters are highest in medical ICUs. Central line-associated bloodstream infections are highest in pediatric ICUs. Surgical ICUs have the highest ventilator-associated rates (Centers for Disease Control, 2000).

Infectious diseases as coexisting conditions among hospitalized patients render the patient at high risk for mortality. Staphylococcal infection is among the most common in elderly Medicare patients and has increased by 28% between 1991 and 1996 (Baine *et al.*, 1999). The case-fatality rate, or number of patients diagnosed with the condition dying from it within the year, varied by discharge setting. Among those who were discharged alive from the hospital to a skilled nursing facility, 31.5% died (Fig. 8.4).

Ambulatory Care

Ambulatory care clinics should follow infection control measures for the disposal of infectious waste that are the same as those for an inpatient treatment setting. For airborne pathogen transmission, health care workers should be aware of the risk of TB among their

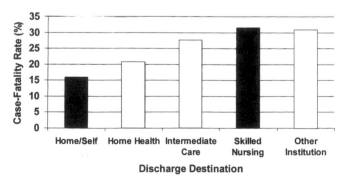

Figure 8.4. Case-fatality rates 90 days after hospitalization for staphylococcal septicemia in patients discharged alive to common discharge destinations (elderly Medicare, 5% sample, 1991–1996). SOURCE: Baine *et al.*, 1999.

patient population and especially aware of coinfection of patients with HIV and TB. Patients who are infected with HIV should receive a PPD skin test during the first visit to an outpatient clinic. If the signs and symptoms of active TB occur, steps to diagnose infection should be undertaken. At the onset of symptoms, measures should be implemented to ensure that the patient's mouth and nose are covered while ambulating through the clinic (i.e., the patient should be asked to wear a surgical mask).

All ambulatory care clinics should be equipped with either an isolation area or an area ventilated with the appropriate amount of air exchange to reduce the concentration of infected airborne nuclei for the examination and treatment of patients. Individuals who are known to have active TB infection should be provided, if possible, with a separate waiting and examination area or should be kept a minimum distance from other patients who may be immunocompromised.

Home Care

There are two special concerns in preventing the spread of both bloodborne and airborne pathogen in the home care setting. The first is to adequately provide both the visiting health care provider and the patient with the supplies necessary to handle infectious waste. Containers for contaminated sharps should be inside the home, and the home care provider should educate the patient on what constitutes contaminated waste and how to adequately dispose of it.

In the event of the possible spread of pathogens via airborne transmission, the home care provider should provide education to the patient. Methods to prevent the spread of disease to other individuals with whom the patient comes in contact should be described. This should include instructing the patient to cover the mouth and nose with tissue while coughing.

Long-Term Care/Skilled Nursing Facility

Similar to hospitals, nosocomial infections are a significant source of morbidity and mortality in long-term care and skilled nursing facilities (LTC/SNF). The characteristics of long-term care residents, old age, multiple chronic conditions, poor oral intake, and limited physical functioning make them highly vulnerable to nosocomial infections. Unique features of long-term care, namely resident and staff mingling in homelike environments promotes the spread of many transmissible diseases, particularly those with airborne routes of transmission, the most difficult to control.

Because of these reasons, outbreaks of gastrointestinal and respiratory infections are common. Outbreaks of respiratory infections often include influenza (primarily type A), TB, respiratory syncytial virus, and group A streptococcus (Li *et al.*, 1996). Thus, the major goal of infection control in LTC/SNF is surveillance to aid in early detection of outbreaks and to identify preventable endemic infections. Since many long-term care facilities have relatively limited resources, comprehensive methods of surveillance may not be feasible. Because of crowded living conditions and many of residents who are often in a compromised health status, a highly transmissible agent, such as influenza, can rapidly affect many residents. An important control measure then becomes the provision of vaccinations where feasible, such as against influenza A, for residents and staff, as well. A high vaccination rate can provide herd immunity. Herd immunity is the protection of an entire population from infection brought about by the presence of a critical number immune individuals (Fine, 1993). Other control measures include (1) restricting visitors, (2) delaying new admissions, (3) quartering residents with signs and symptoms of influenza, and (4) implementing respiratory isolation measures for acutely ill patients. The health care manager must keep in mind that these efforts still may not prevent cases of influenza from occurring because of poor antibody response in the elderly, improper handling of vaccines during administration, and incompatibility between virus strain and vaccine.

Since the number of TB cases in the United States is rising in some population subgroups, the likelihood of having long-term care patients becoming infected with TB is greater now and will only increase in the future, given the demographics of the population now infected with TB. Additionally, there are many persons who are over the age of 65 who carry tubercle bacilli in dormant lesions acquired earlier. These individuals may reactivate their tuberculosis infections and develop active, infectious tuberculosis as natural resistance wanes and adequate nutrition and physical activity decline. It is important for managers and providers in long-term care facilities to be aware of this possibility, since active TB is often incorrectly diagnosed as being either bronchitis or bronchopneumonia. Such an eventuality could expose a number of health workers to TB (Stead and Dutt, 1991).

Infection control in long-term care facilities is becoming increasingly complex as the population ages and the trend away from inpatient hospital care increases the number of persons treated in this type of facility. Additional challenges that increase the risk of nosocomial infection in the LTC/SNF environment are group activities, crowding, nursing staff working on more than one unit in a shift, multiple nursing units in a facility, and shared staff across nursing units (Li et al., 1996). Infection control strategies commonly and effectively used in acute care hospitals may not be applicable in the homelike ambience of the nursing home. For example, patient isolation is an impractical strategy to protect against spread of infection from residents found to be chronically colonized or infected with antibiotic-resistant microorganisms. Furthermore, isolation may be unnecessary because patients in long-term care are less likely to have the medical devices in place that provide a portal of entry for antibiotic resistant microorganisms.

To assist in addressing the infection control challenges in LTC/SNF, the Joint Commission on Accreditation of Healthcare Organizations published functional standards for infection control in long-term care facilities (Pritchard, 1999). Among the recommendations are that health care managers should outline procedures for: (1) administrative support for infection control, (2) outbreak detection and control system, (3) preventive health program for residents, (4) preventive health and exposure control program for employees, (5) antibiotic review and use protocols, (6) disease reporting support, and (7) well-designed policies and procedures related to reducing the risk of foodborne and environmental infection. Once implemented, these policies and procedures should be reviewed on a scheduled basis.

Hospice

Hospice programs provide specialized care to persons who are in the final stages of the disease. Owing to advances in drug therapy contributing to their longevity, AIDS patients are increasingly prevalent among hospice patients. Due to a compromised immune system, patients who are HIV positive or who have AIDS are more susceptible to coinfection with TB. Given that some hospices have inpatient services, precautions for the detection and prevention of the spread of TB should follow the same steps as those in place at an inpatient hospital setting. Thus, a comprehensive infection control program also is essential for hospice providers. If the hospice is not associated with a larger hospital or does not have direct access to the infection control staff of a larger organization, steps should be taken to ensure well-defined policies that detail steps to be taken for infection control which include contractual arrangements with outside infection control expertise.

Behavioral Health Care Settings

Freestanding behavioral health care facilities are becoming increasingly prevalent. A variety of services are offered through these agencies such as shelters for homeless or battered women and daycare centers for the elderly. Most of these facilities have policies and procedures in place that relate to the infection control standards required by their respective accrediting bodies. However, regardless of the mission of the behavioral center, the development of policies and procedures according to a level of prevention model is a useful adjunct in infection control that combined the management of infection control with epidemiological principles. The steps in developing an infection control program for behavioral health require an assessment of the services provided by the agency, review of the mission statements, and staff interviews to determine the activities that put staff or clients at risk for infection (Salloway and Downie, 1999). For example, in daycare for geriatric patients, primary prevention would emphasize flu immunization of patients and staff, secondary prevention would include screening for TB, and tertiary prevention focusing on the early identification of active infectious illnesses among staff and clients.

Conclusion

In addition to the administrative structure necessary to support infection control in a health care organization, the implementation of a comprehensive infection control plan that prioritizes the safety of both the workforce and their patients.

One of the primary means to prevent the spread of disease is education. Instruction about universal precautions and isolation measures should be a dynamic experience. Records documenting proper training should be maintained for reporting to accrediting agencies and a system for monitoring compliance with infection control protocols should be in place as a proactive aid in reducing the probability of unexpected disease exposure in the health care setting.

With health care shifting away from the inpatient setting and now being delivered in a variety of areas such as hospice, home care, and increasingly in the outpatient setting, infection control practices need to be adapted to the unique characteristics of each of these settings. Since these settings often rely on the compliance of patients for successful treatment, education of the patient also is a factor. Specifically, patients with TB need to be properly instructed about their role in preventing the spread of disease, namely, shielding others from exposure through the use of barriers when coughing, sneezing, and so on, and a firm understanding of compliance with drug treatment. Long-term care and skilled nursing facilities face obstacles when working with the sick and elderly who already may have a compromised system. Hospice patients are at risk of infectious comorbidities, especially those patients affected with HIV.

Today, health care managers are faced with the immense challenge of meeting regulatory agency requirements for infection control and planning strategies for keeping the workforce and patient population safe while at the same time of decreasing costs of patient care. The financial and legal impact of an unsafe workforce and patient population cannot be underestimated. Given the rapidly changing environment of not only health care but of the financial, political, and legal framework in which it must function, the health care manager needs to be acutely aware of the importance of a properly designed infection control program to prevent the spread of transmissible diseases in a health care organization. Regardless of the particular health care setting, the proactive health care manager will seek to ensure an infrastructure that is committed to improved surveillance as a means of "early warning" and initiate effective prevention programs before outbreaks occur.

Case Studies

Case Study No. 1
Decreasing HBV Infection in Health Care Workers

Health care workers are at occupational risk for HBV infection. At highest risk are those with frequent exposure to body fluids (nursing staff, phlebotomists, laboratory personnel). Despite the availability of free vaccinations available through employee health services, not all hospital employees are immunized to HBV. In a survey reported by Mahoney et al. (1997), the HBV vaccination coverage rates were observed in the following occupations: phlebotomist or technician, 81%; nurse, 72%; and nurse aid, 63%. Vaccination coverage was higher for smaller hospitals (<100 beds) than larger ones and lowest among black employees (65%). In order to improve vaccination coverage, hospitals have tried a variety of strategies. Displayed in Table 8.8 are various hospital policies associated with increase HBV coverage.

Table 8.8. Hospital Policies Associated with Increased Hepatitis B Vaccination Coverage: National Survey of Hospital Employees, 1994 and 1995

Policy	Total	No (%) vaccinated	Prevalence ratio	95% confidence interval
Incentive encouragement				
Yes	136	114 (81)	1.6	1.4–2.0
No	2033	1441 (69)		
Notify supervisor				
Yes	966	727 (76)	1.6	1.2–2.1
No	1346	909 (63)		
Sanctions imposed for refusing vaccine				
Yes	354	259 (78)	1.5	1.0–2.3
No	1887	1329 (66)		
Prerequisite vaccination for employment				
Yes	273	204 (76)	1.4	1.0–2.1
No	2101	1492 (67)		
Send out reminder notices				
Yes	2044	1465 (69)	1.2	1.0–1.5
No	304	197 (62)		
Tracking system to monitor coverage				
Yes	1977	1431 (69)	1.2	0.9–1.6
No	415	272 (63)		

[a]From Mahoney et al. (1997).

Q.1. Which policy is the most effective and why?

Q.2. Which policy is the least effective and why?

Q.3. What are some biases in the data used to evaluate hospital policy?

Q.4. Why could vaccination coverage be lower in larger hospitals?

Case Study No. 2
Outbreak of HBV Infection among Hemodialysis Patients

During a period of three months, 7 cases of acute HBV infection were identified in 131 susceptible patients at a dialysis center. None of the patients had been vaccinated against hepatitis prior to admission to the center (Hendricks *et al.*, 1996). Staff in the center was frequently assigned to provide care to all patients regardless of their HBV status. Common medication and supply carts were moved among dialysis stations within the center and medications and supplies were shared among susceptible and infected patients. Heparin, a medication commonly administered to these patients, was administered using a multiple-dose vial. Partially used vials were routinely returned to a common medication cart. A cohort study found that the HBV infection was associated with one particular shift (relative risk = 7.0, confidence interval of 1.5–42.8). During that shift, all the infected patients had been clustered in one area of the unit and all staff had been shared among all patients. One multidose heparin vial had been shared among these patients.

Q.1. What is the most likely source of the HBV transmission?

Q.2. What are other ways the HBV virus can be transmitted?

Q.3. How could future outbreaks be avoided at this dialysis center?

Case Study No. 3
Methicillin-Resistant *Staphylococcus aureus*: A Prevalent Nosocomial Pathogen in US Hospitals

Methicillin-resistant *Staphylococcus aureus* (MRSA) has become a prevalent nosocomial pathogen in US hospitals. Both patients and hospital personnel can be a reservoir for this organism. Recently hospital personnel have become the more common reservoir and may harbor the organism for many months. The primary mode of transmission of MRSA is by the hands. Thus, hands serve as a mode of transmission if contaminated by contact with infected patients, body sites of personnel themselves, devices, or items of environmental surfaces contaminated with body fluids contains MRSA.

Q.1. What is a nosocomial infection?

Q.2. What is a "reservoir" in the context of this case?

Q.3. "Standard precautions" for infection control are recommended for the prevention of MRSA. What constitutes "standard precautions" in the hospital setting?

Q.4. Outline a policy for preventing MRSA in a Women's and Children's Hospital.

Table 8.9. Incidence of Nosocomial Infections
by Type and Patient Care Unit[a]

Patient care unit	All	LRTI[b]	UTI	GI	No. of patients at risk
PICU	168	89	26	7	710
Neonatal	80	12	4	1	1,146
Hematology	46	8	22	4	561
General	54	7	1	41	5,051
Overall	373	123	43	53	14,675

[a]From Raymond et al. (2000).
[b]LRTI, Lower respiratory tract infection; UTI, urinary tract infection; GI, gastro-intestinal tract infection.

Case Study No. 4
Nosocomial Infections in Pediatric Patients

A major source of morbidity and mortality in the ICU is nosocomial infections. They prolong hospital stay and increase costs of care. Nosocomial infections are a particular problem because patients in an ICU (1) are immunocompromised due to the disease process, (2) have altered flora from treatment with high-dose and multidrug antibiotics, and (3) may have disrupted skin and mucosal membranes because of invasive procedures and devices. There are five common types of nosocomial infections in pediatric units: bacteremias, lower respiratory tract infections, urinary tract infections, postsurgical wound infections, and gastrointestinal infections. A 6-month prospective study of 20 pediatric units in eight European counties was conducted to determine the epidemiology of nosocomial infections in hospitalized pediatric patients (Raymond et al., 2000). Use the data from Table 8.9 to answer the questions below.

Q.1. What is the overall incidence of nosocomial infection in this population?

Q.2. What is the relative risk of nosocomial infection in pediatric ICU patients compared to those in general units?

Q.3. Which type of nosocomial infection has the highest incidence rate?

Q.4. What are some of the biases entering in to these data?

References

Baine, W. B., Yu, W., and Summe, J. P., 1999, Hospitalization of elderly Americans for staphylococcal septicemia, 1991–1996, Ann. Epidemiol. 9:456.

Brooks, G. F., Butel, J. S., and Morse, S. A., 1998, Jawetz, Melnick and Adelberg's Medical Microbiology, 21th ed., Appleton & Lange, Stamford, CT.

Centers for Disease Control, 1991, Nosocomial transmission of multidrug-resistant tuberculosis among HIV-infected persons—Florida anu New York, 1988–1991, Morbid. Mortal. Week. Rev. 40:585–591.

Centers for Disease Control, 1998a, Tuberculosis morbidity—United States, 1997, Morbid. Mortal. Week. Rev. 47:253–256.

Centers for Disease Control, 1998b, Prevention and treatment of tuberculosis among patients infected with human immunodeficiency virus: Principles of therapy and revised recommendations, Morbid. Mortal. Week. Rev. 47(No. RR-20):4–26.

Centers for Disease Control, 2000, Monitoring hospital-acquired infections to promote patient safety—United States, 1990–1999, *Morbid. Mortal. Week. Rev.* **49:**149–153.

Chin, J., 2000, *The Control of Communicable Diseases in Man*, The American Public Health Association, Washington, DC.

Fine, P. E. M., 1993, Herd immunity: History, theory, practice, *Epidemiol. Rev.* **15:**265–302.

Hendricks, K., Sehulster, L., Bell, R. L., Cousins, J., MacNeeley, W., Payne, A., des Vignes Kendrick, M., Simpson, D., Tormey, M., Itano, A., Mascola, L., Vugia, D., Rosenberg, J., Waterman, S., and Safranek, T. J., 1996, Outbreaks of hepatitis B virus infection among hemodialysis patients—California, Nebraska, and Texas, 1994, *Morbid. Mortal. Week. Rev.* **45:**285–289.

Li, J., Birkhead, G. S., Strogatz, D. S., and Coles, F. B., 1996, Impact of institution size, staffing patterns, and infection control practices on communicable disease outbreaks in New York state nursing homes, *Am. J. Epidemiol.* **143:**1042–1049.

Mahoney, F. J., Stewart, K., Hu, H., Coleman, P., and Alter, M. J., 1997, Progress toward the elimination of hepatitis virus transmission among health care workers in the United States, *Arch. Intern. Med.* **157:**2601–2605.

Pritchard, V., 1999, Joint Commission standards for long-term care infection control: Putting together the process elements, *Am. J. Infect. Control* **27:**27–34.

Raymond, J., Aujard, H., and the European Study Group, 2000, Nosocomial infections in pediatric patients: A European, multicenter prospective study, *Infect. Control Hosp. Epidemiol.* **21:**260–263.

Salloway, S., and Downie, J., 1999, Infection control programs for behavioral health care settings, *QRC Advisor* **15:** 6–12.

Scheckler, W. E., Brimhall, D., and Buck, A. S., 1998, Requirements for infrastructure and essential activities of infection control and epidemiology in hospitals: A Consensus Panel report, *Am. J. Infect. Control* **26:**47–60.

Stead, W. W., and Dutt, A. K., 1991, Tuberculosis in elderly persons, *Ann. Rev. Med.* **42:**267–276.

United Nations, 1999, *The Demographic Impact of HIV/AIDS*, United Nations, New York.

World Health Organization, 1999, *Removing Obstacles to Healthy Development*, WHO, Geneva, Switzerland.

9

Genetic Epidemiology
The Basis for a New Health Service Delivery Model

Marcia Phillips and Jack Goldberg

Introduction

Genetics will have an increasingly important role in all aspects of public health, epidemiology, and health care service delivery. In 2000, more than 2 years ahead of schedule, the international collaborative effort known as the Human Genome Project (HGP) completed the map of the entire genetic makeup of the human species. The most carefully coordinated international scientific research project in history, the HGP is designed to accelerate the progress of genetics by determining the structure of the human genome. The mapping of the human genome will provide an unprecedented opportunity to identify the genetic and nongenetic etiology for a far greater number of diseases than was possible just a few years ago. There are estimated to be 5000 clearly hereditary diseases such as sickle-cell anemia, cystic fibrosis, and Huntington's disease. Information on the sequencing of the human genome will be of particular interest to health care service planners, who will have a base of information that can be used to assess community health needs and to implement effective delivery of genetic health care services. Among the growing components of health services will be improved diagnostic precision, treatments at the molecular level, improved reliability in predicting the course of a disease, and the challenge of communicating to patients their risk of genetic diseases while at the same time maintaining their privacy and preventing genetic discrimination.

This chapter introduces the health care manager to the concepts that are essential in understanding genetic health. It will illustrate how epidemiological information provides crucial data on which management decision making is based when formulating and implementing genetic health care services to address legal, social, and ethical issues.

Marcia Phillips   Department of Health Systems Management, Rush University, Chicago, Illinois 60612.
Jack Goldberg   Epidemiology/Biostatistics Division, School of Public Health, University of Illinois at Chicago, Chicago, Illinois 60612.

Epidemiology and the Delivery of Health Care Services: Methods and Applications, Second Edition, edited by Denise M. Oleske. Kluwer Academic / Plenum Publishers, New York, 2001.

Basic Genetic Concepts

Mendelian Genetics

The fundamental principles of genetics were first described by an Austrian monk, Gregor Mendel, in 1865. However, his paper was ignored and did not receive attention from the scientific community until about 1900. Mendel's description of his experiments in breeding peas (and some other flowering plants) provided the foundation for our understanding of genetic inheritance.

Mendel formulated two laws, which explain how most genetic information is transmitted from an organism to its offspring. The **law of independent assortment of alleles** relates how an observable characteristic, or **phenotype**, is determined. An **allele** is a particular form of a gene. For example, the gene for human blood type has three possible alleles: A, B, and O. However, an organism will have only two alleles of each gene, one from each parent. This combination of genes is called the **genotype**. An allele for a characteristic (such as blood type) can be **dominant** or **recessive**. Recessive alleles are masked (not expressed as a phenotype) in the presence of its dominant allele. When two alleles form a pair, there are four possible combinations:

dominant (A) + dominant (A)
dominant (A) + recessive (a)
recessive (a) + dominant (A)
recessive (a) + recessive (a)

Mathematically, the probability of the possible combinations can be represented as follows:

$$AA + 2Aa + aa = 1 \text{ or } .25 + .50 + .25 = 1$$

Unless both alleles are recessive, the phenotype will have the dominant characteristic. Thus, assuming that each parent has a dominant and recessive allele, there is a 75% chance that the offspring will have the dominant characteristic.

Mendel's second law, the **independent segregation of genes**, tells us that any expression of a phenotype for a characteristic is independent of other phenotypic characteristics of the organism. In other words, the combination of alleles to produce blood type is independent of the combination of alleles to produce another characteristic, such as color blindness.

It became clear early in the last century that not all genetic transmission is as simple as postulated by Mendel. While Mendel's laws held true as an explanation of phenotypes for common characteristics, and for easily identified rare conditions, the transmission ratios of many characteristics varied greatly.

Exceptions to Mendel's Laws

The first major exception to Mendel's laws was the discovery of sex-linked inheritance. It was found as early as 1911 that the inheritance of certain traits studied in fruit flies could not be explained by Mendel's ratios. Wilson (1911) demonstrated that color blindness was linked to the sex of the organism, with only males being subject to the condition, except in rare cases. It was found that some characteristics are associated with the X and Y sex chromosomes and are only transmitted to one sex. (Much of the knowledge we have about Mendelian genetics resulted from research about *Drosophila melanogaster*, a species of fruit flies that has a short reproductive cycle and a relatively small genome. These conditions allow for easy study of mutations and transmission of genetic characteristics.)

The second major exception was the finding that some genetic characteristics were not independent of each other but seemed to be inherited together. In 1937, Bell and Hadane showed that color blindness and hemophilia were inherited together too often to be independent of each other. They formulated a theory that some genes are "linked" on the same chromosome and that these genes would be transmitted together in offspring. The study of **genetic linkage**—how and which genes are associated with each other—is one of the most important activities in genetic research.

Most of the diseases initially identified as having a genetic basis were caused by single genes. As our knowledge of the human genome has increased, it is clear that many more conditions are genetically related, but are caused by the interaction of numerous genes, often in conjunction with environmental factors. These multifactorial disorders are referred to as **complex diseases** by geneticists. Identifying and determining the genetic basis of complex disorders is one of the principal challenges of molecular and genetic epidemiology. The ability to undertake such studies has been made possible by the HGP.

The Human Genome Project

Scope and Progress

The HGP is the largest international scientific collaboration in history. The daunting goal of the project is to determine the entire DNA sequence of the human genome. The human genome includes approximately 35,000 protein-coding genes (as compared to the 13,600 genes of *Drosophila melanogaster*), which comprises about 5–10% of the genetic material in an individual. These coding materials are called **exons**. The remaining 90–95% of the DNA material, most notably **introns** (noncoding sequences), do not encode proteins and their functions and importance are not yet understood. The entire genome consists of more than 3 billion nucleotide sequences of DNA. Before the HGP, only a small fraction of genes had been identified, mostly those causing single-gene disorders, such as Huntington's disease.

The HGP is coordinated in the United States by the National Human Genome Research Institute (NHGRI) of the National Institutes of Health, and by the US Department of Energy. In several other countries, including Britain, France, Italy, Sweden, and Japan, the efforts are coordinated by similar agencies. Begun in 1990, the project was originally scheduled to take over 15 years. However, on June 26, 2000, President Clinton and British Prime Minister Tony Blair announced that the HGP and Celera Genomics Corporation have both completed an initial sequencing of the human genome.

The HGP has three specific goals: mapping the genome, establishing database systems to disseminate the information, and developing cooperative efforts to take advantage of the information to lead to new ways to diagnose, treat, and prevent diseases. The first of these goals is the heart of the project and has been pursued in a complex, closely coordinated effort. The first stage, accomplished from 1990 to 1995, consisted of completing a rough draft of a genetic maps for humans, and sequencing the genome of bacteria, yeast, nematode, and fruit fly. These organisms were selected because of their relatively simple genomes, which would help in understanding the more complex human genome.

Other goals during the first stage included improving the technology to identify and map genes, creating databases to capture and organize the incredible amounts of data generated from the project, and exploring the ethical and social issues involved in the resulting information. The final stage ending in 2003 will be "proofreading" to correct any errors in the maps.

Genetic Mapping

Two important concepts for understanding the mapping of the genome are the use of genetic maps and physical maps. Physical maps show the actual location of the genes and/or markers on each chromosome (Fig. 9.1, right). Physical maps allow researchers to determine

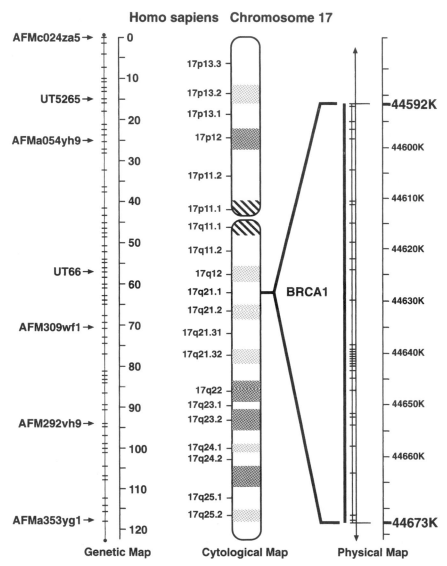

Figure 9.1. Correlation of the genetic, cytological, and physical maps of chromosome 17 (illustration by Janna Lundak).

the location of specific genes that are associated with particular diseases, such as BRCA1 for breast cancer, located at 17q21.1 on chromosome 17. BRCA1 consists of 81 K base pairs. Genetic maps (Fig. 9.1, left), on the other hand, show the position of its known genes and/or markers relative to each other based on recombination frequencies (the rates at which they are inherited together). Measured in centiMorgans, markers specific to chromosome 17 are shown in the genetic map in Figure 9.1. The cytological map (Fig. 9.1, center) is observed after microscopically viewed with various stains to show the specific banding patterns of chromosomes. The ultimate goal of the HGP is to produce accurate physical and genetic maps to assist researchers in identifying the genetic basis of human disease.

Epidemiology and the Human Genome Project

Epidemiology will play a major role in using the information produced by the HGP to refine etiologic models for disease development. Recognition of this important role resulted in the initiative known as the Human Genome Epidemiology Network (HuGE Net). This project has the potential for becoming one of the most important collaborative resources for translating the findings of the HGP into practical medical and public health advances. Coordinated by the US government's Centers for Disease Control (CDC), the purposes of the program are to: (1) establish information exchanges to promote global collaboration in the development and dissemination of epidemiologic data on human genetics; (2) establish and maintain Internet-based knowledge bases about the human genome that will be useful to epidemiologic researchers; and (3) promote the use of these knowledge bases among health care providers, researchers, governments, industry, and the public for making decisions about the use of genetic tests and services for disease prevention and health promotion (Khoury and Dorman, 1998). A website has been created as the home for the network at http://www.cdc.gov/genetics/hugenet/. The Internet has been a tremendous resource for making genetic information available to the research community and to the public. Table 9.1 lists a few of the hundreds of sites dedicated to cataloging and communicating newly discovered information about human genetics.

International Implications

HuGE Net's emphasis on international collaboration is indicative of the global implications of the HGP. The World Health Organization (WHO) has established its own human genetics program to develop genetic approaches for the prevention and control of common hereditary diseases and genetic predisposition to more complex disease. A central goal is promoting international collaboration and information exchange about genetic links to disease. Just as with HuGE Net, the primary vehicle for information exchange and dissemination will be the Internet, in this case at http://www.who.org/.

The importance of an international perspective can be illustrated by the genetic epidemiology of hemoglobin disorders. One of the most common genetically related hemoglobin disorders—sickle cell disorder—is a major health problem in sub-Saharan Africa, where approximately 70% of sickle cell anemia occurs. However, it is also a major health problem among African Americans in the United States, as well as large segments of the French-Canadian population. Thalassemia, another hemoglobin disorder, is a serious public health concern among different ethnic groups in areas including the Mediterranean, Africa, the Middle East, India, China, and Southeast Asia. The director of the WHO genetics program has stated, "it is highly probable that genetic approaches to the prevention of common diseases

Table 9.1. Representative Genetic Internet Resources

Supporting host	Website	Features
National Human Genome Research Institute	http://www.nhgri.nih.gov/	The U.S. home of the Human Genome Project; has an on-line, audio, video glossaries of genetic terms
GenBank	http://www.ncbi.nlm.nih. gov/Genbank/index.html	National Institutes of Health genetic sequence database, collection of publicly available DNA sequences
United States Department of Energy	http://www.er.doe.gov/ production/ober/hug top.html	Human Genome Project information, a primer on molecular genetics
Rockefeller University	http://linkage.rockefeller.edu	Provide software tools for genetic analysis
Centers for Disease Control	http://www.cdc.gov/genetics/	Links to medical genetic literature, news, reports, and results of national committee work including strategic planning on subject of genetics in public health
GeneClinics	http://www.geneclinics.org	Contains disease profiles including diagnosis, management, and counseling
Human Genome Project Ethical, Legal, and Social Issues	http://www.ornl.gov/hgmis/ elsi.html	Information on ethics, social issues, public policy, and education

will emerge as one of the dominant strategies for the improvement of health" (Boulyjenkov, 1998, p. 58).

Epidemiology will play a central role in realizing the medical and public health potential of the HGP. For instance, descriptive studies of the prevalence of genetic mutations in diverse populations are needed to characterize populations. The adaptation of the tools of traditional epidemiology to genetic concerns, as well as the adaptation of the basic methods of genetic research to epidemiological studies, has important implications for health systems planners throughout the world.

Genetics and Epidemiology

Roles of Epidemiology

Although the tools of epidemiology have been used in the study of genetics for most of the past 100 years, an important milestone in the development of genetic epidemiology occurred in the aftermath of the atomic bombing of the Japanese cities of Nagasaki and Hiroshima during World War II. After the end of the war, the US National Academy of Sciences commissioned a long-term study of the effects of radiation exposure on survivors. Led by James Neel, a young Army physician trained in genetics, the study actively ran for over 20 years.

Intended originally to limit itself to the effects of radiation exposure on the survivors and their offspring, the wealth of information collected allowed researchers to study genetic characteristics within a population on a scale never before attempted. Detailed clinical records were developed for survivors and over 75,000 offspring of survivors by the mid-1950s. In addition to attempting to determine the effects of radiation, other studies undertaken included the characteristics of the Japanese gene pool and the genetics of the offspring of consanguineous (having common ancestors) marriages (Neel, 1995).

The study of the genetic characteristics of discrete populations of individuals is called **population genetics**. These studies may include consideration of genetically transmitted diseases but often are used to learn more about patterns of inheritance and the rates and causes of mutations within a population's gene pool. Genetic epidemiology is more commonly thought of as the subdiscipline that studies the role of genetics in the distribution and determinants of health and disease in human populations. A closely related but distinct discipline called molecular epidemiology studies the distribution of genetic characteristics by focusing on the identification and measurement of the molecular or chemical basis of heredity and disease. The advances in scientific knowledge made possible by the HGP are blurring the distinction between these two fields because genetic epidemiology increasingly focuses on the molecular basis of genetic characteristics of disease in addition to phenotypic characteristics. In the discussion that follows, many of the techniques described were originally developed by molecular geneticists but are now an integral part of most genetic epidemiological studies of disease. For health systems planners and public health officials, this merging of genetic and molecular epidemiology can provide valuable information to help determine the need for services to treat various conditions, as well as the most effective methods of targeting services to those most likely to be affected by genetic disorders.

Genetic Techniques and Epidemiology

The primary tools used by geneticists to identify the presence and frequency of genetic characteristics within a population are: (1) phenotype identification, (2) segregation analysis, (3) linkage analysis, and (4) association analysis. Genetic epidemiologists use these tools in conjunction with traditional observational research designs methods, such as cross-sectional, case–control, and longitudinal studies. Clinicians relate information on the transmission of genes through a diagram called a **pedigree**.

Phenotype identification is one of the most basic techniques used by geneticists. This type of analysis attempts to determine the presence and magnitude of phenotypes within a family or population by identifying and classifying various observable characteristics of individuals. Phenotypes, the identifiable manifestations of a genotype, have been described in various cataloging systems. Most often, phenotype identification and analysis has been used to determine patterns of Mendelian inheritance. The most comprehensive, useful, and up-to-date catalog of phenotypes is the Online Mendelian Inheritance in Man website at http://www.ncbi.nlm.nih.gov/omim. Over 7000 distinct conditions have been cataloged with hyperlink references, allowing clinicians and researchers to easily identify phenotypic characteristics in individuals or families. Both Mendelian and non-Mendelian transmitted genetic disorders are maintained in this database. There are several problems and limitations inherent with phenotype analysis. First, the identification of a particular characteristic as a distinct phenotype is not always clear. In other words, any given characteristic, such as the shape of an eyelid, has a wide range of variations and the classification of a particular individual's eyelid as a particular phenotype is somewhat subjective. Second, phenotype analysis does not account for the various potential causes of a particular characteristic. For example, many genetic disorders can affect the expression of various facial features. Assigning a phenotype label to particular facial features may encompass a variety of unrelated genetic conditions. Thus, phenotype identification provides us with only a limited understanding of the genetic basis of the presence of a condition within a population (Ostrer, 1998).

Segregation analysis provides a deeper level of understanding about the transmission of disease, and is potentially far more useful. The approach involves estimating the ratios of inheritance of a particular genetic trait under study, thereby attempting to identify a specific genetic cause or causes from other possible explanations of a condition. There are three patterns of Mendelian genetic transmission in humans, with predictable ratios of transmission within families: autosomal dominant, autosomal recessive, and X-linked. By collecting information on disease phenotypes from family members, the mode of transmission can be inferred by comparing the observed data with goodness-of-fit statistical models based on possible modes of transmission. For example, dominant characteristics are usually transmitted at a rate of 50%, recessive traits at a rate of 25%, and X-linked traits occur at a significantly higher rate in males. Segregation analysis models can also help identify heterozygous carriers (usually unaffected individuals who only inherit one altered gene) and homozygous carriers (carriers in which both genes have the mutation). An example of the use of segregation analysis was the Cancer and Steroid Hormone (CASH) Study, which eventually led to the discovery of genetic mutations that predispose individuals to breast and ovarian cancer. Using approximately 4700 individuals with breast cancer, it was determined that there was evidence for familial clustering. The patterns of breast cancer within the families fit a model of dominant transmission, with stronger evidence of among those who had younger age of diagnosis (Claus *et al.*, 1991). The principal difficulty with segregation analysis is that not all diseases that cluster within a family are genetic in origin. Environmental risk factors, such as diet, likewise cluster within families and segregation analysis may mistakenly attribute the familial clustering of disease to genetic causes. Unless the sample of families is large enough and are from diverse origins, bias caused by nongenetic factors also can be significant. Segregation analysis is most useful if patterns of inheritance are Mendelian.

Linkage analysis is one of the more complex and powerful tools available to genetic epidemiologists. The basic principles are easily understood. Complexity occurs with the statistical calculations necessary to determine if there are linkages among two or more genes. Genes are normally inherited through a recombination of alleles from each parent for each gene. However, geneticists determined early on that there was strong evidence that different genetic characteristics were inherited together in proportions that were greater than would be expected by chance. This led to the realization that genes that are located close together on a chromosome have a greater likelihood of being inherited together rather than simply being the result of chance recombination of alleles. As the human genome has been sequenced and mapped, it has been confirmed that the closer together genes are to each other, the more likely they are to be inherited together. This is easy to understand when one remembers that recombination occurs when alleles cross over each other at one or more points, and recombine when crossover pieces break off and form new alleles. Genes that are closer together on strands are more likely to remain intact when recombination occurs. Linkage analysis is based on determining the likelihood that two or more genes (a known marker and the suspected susceptibility gene) in an individual are linked because of their close proximity on a chromosome rather than as a result of free recombination of genetic material during the process of chromosome replication. In its simplest form linkage analysis is based on testing two competing hypotheses:

H_0 = the association of two or more genes is the result of free recombination
H_1 = the association of two or more genes is the result of linkage

The null hypothesis assumes no linkage and the alternative hypothesis is that there is evidence of linkage. The ratio of the likelihood of the alternative and null hypotheses provides an indication if there is the presence of linkage. More formally, the likelihood ratio (LR) is given by:

$$LR = \text{Probability (DATA}|H_1)/\text{Probability (DATA}|H_0)$$

Typically linkage analysis results are presented in terms of the logarithm of the odds (LOD) score, which is the logarithm of the likelihood ratio. A LOD score of 3 (equivalent to a likelihood ratio of 1/1000) or more is considered to be strong evidence of linkage, meaning that the susceptibility gene is located near the marker; alternatively, a LOD score of less than -2.0 is considered evidence that the marker is associated with the condition as a result of recombination rather than being linked to the susceptibility gene. LOD scores between -2.0 and 3 are cause for analysis of additional families to confirm possible linkage (Ott, 1999). Segregation analysis detected the association between a genetic mutation and breast and ovarian cancer using data from the CASH study, which was confirmed shortly thereafter by linkage analysis. In the linkage study, 23 families with breast cancer were involved and evidence of was found between a marker on chromosome 17 and breast cancer. As in the CASH study using segregation analysis, the linkage was most pronounced in those diagnosed with breast cancer at an early age (Hall *et al.*, 1990). The results of this linkage analysis was confirmed 4 years later when the first gene for breast cancer, *BRCA1*, was found at the location hypothesized by those researchers.

Other methodologies used by genetic epidemiologists include twin studies, association analysis, and pedigree diagrams. **Twin studies** often are used as an initial method to determine whether there is a genetic basis for conditions that tend to cluster in families. Monozygotic (identical) twins are derived from the same zygote, and therefore share 100% of their genetic material, while dizygotic (fraternal) twins share on average only 50% of their genes. Because twins share a common gestational environment and typically a common rearing environment, a higher rate of disease concordance in monozygotic compared with dizygotic pairs is evidence for genetic influence. However, estimating genetic effects from twin studies is problematic if the rearing environment for monozygotic twins is more similar than that for dizygotic twins.

Association analysis is a method for examining the relationship of a known genetic marker with a disease condition in individuals. This approach commonly is implemented using a case–control research design. If the marker appears in affected individuals ("cases") at a rate greater than found in unaffected individuals ("controls"), then an association with the marker is hypothesized. The strength of associations will be greater the closer the marker is to the unidentified susceptibility gene.

A **pedigree** is a diagram of a family's genealogy that shows family members' relationships to each other and how a particular trait or disease has been inherited (see Fig. 9.2). This is a useful way of communicating the risk of any genetic disorder. Commercial software is available to facilitate construction of pedigrees.

Genetic Epidemiology Studies

Genetic epidemiology will become a major tool for assessing health risks, both in public health and to individuals, in the coming decades. The complexity of genetic factors in health can be best illustrated by surveying the types of studies in which genetic epidemiology has

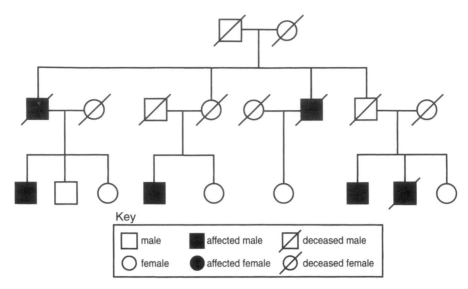

Figure 9.2. Pedigree. From National Human Genome Research Institute www.nhgri.nih.gov/dir/vip/glossary (2000).

been used. These examples also illustrate the merging of molecular and genetic epidemiology into the developing field of human genome epidemiology.

At the most basic level, genetic epidemiology has important uses for assessing the prevalence of genetic variation in the target populations. When gene variants or mutations are discovered to have an impact on health, it is important to determine the segments of the population that are most at risk. For example, various studies have attempted to determine the prevalence of the *BRCA1* and *BRCA2* mutations among different ethnic groups and subpopulations. These types of studies can help health systems planners in targeting educational and counseling programs to the populations most likely to be affected by the mutations.

Even after a genetic mutation is found to have a role in disease, the question of the magnitude of the disease risk associated with the variants must be assessed. Again, using the *BRCA1* and *BRCA2* mutations as an example, epidemiological studies can help to determine the likelihood that individuals carrying one of the mutations will actually develop breast or ovarian cancer.

Many diseases will be found to have genetic causes as well as other causes. Genetic epidemiology can be used to help determine the contribution of genetic causes to the overall disease prevalence within populations. Again, epidemiological studies have shown the contribution of *BRCA1* and *BRCA2* mutations to the overall rate of breast and ovarian cancer in populations to be less than 10% (Kahn, 1996).

Often genetic predisposition requires interaction with other genes or environmental factors before a disease manifests itself. Genetic epidemiological studies often are used to determine the risk of disease associated with these complex interactions. The use of case–control designs, where cases and controls are stratified according to an environmental risk factor, is a common approach to study gene–environment interaction. One such study attempted to determine whether there was a link between maternal cigarette smoking and cleft palate associated with a transforming growth factor-alpha (TGF-α) polymorphism mutation.

Hwang *et al.* (1995) found a significant gene by environment interaction such that among smokers the presence of a genetic mutation greatly increased risk. Similarly, a study of genetic factors associated with cholesterol levels found that beneficial effects of a certain genetic mutation on cholesterol production was only present in nonsmokers with the mutation (Pederson and Berg, 1989). As discussed above, genetic testing is the most useful method of determining whether an individual carries a particular mutation. However, before such testing can be considered for widespread use, studies must be conducted to determine the validity of such tests and how they can be most usefully implemented in health care systems. One issue of importance for health system planners is to target genetic testing to those most likely to benefit from testing. Several inherited genetic mutations have been found to be associated with an increased risk of colorectal cancer. This genetically related cancer is called hereditary nonpolyposis colorectal cancer (HNPCC). A genetic test is commercially available; but because only a small percentage of colorectal cancers are of the HNPCC type, it is important to develop criteria to screen for those who would be most likely to carry the mutation. There is a need to minimize both the number of mutation-positive cases that would be excluded from testing and the number of mutation-negative cases that would be considered for testing. Viel *et al.* (1998) identified 90 unrelated colorectal cancer patients and found a relationship between the presence of a genetic mutation and certain characteristics of the DNA in the cancerous tumors, independent of family history. This suggests that laboratory analysis of tumor material is the best available screening tool for determining whether genetic testing should be pursued. In contrast, with respect to selection of candidates for genetic testing for the *BRCA1* and *BRCA2* breast and ovarian cancer predisposition genes, several studies, including Parmigiani *et al.* (1998), have found that family history and age of onset alone can be reliable indicators of carrier status.

Health Services Management and Genetic Epidemiology

Screening

Genetics has been an important consideration in public health for many decades. The early experiences with using genetic information to improve public health illustrate many of the issues that will confront health systems planners in the coming decades. Reflecting the state of technology, for most situations the primary focus has been on identifying individuals with diseases caused by single genes, rather than more complex genetic disorders. This section will discuss how knowledge of genetic conditions has been used to identify and prevent public health problems, through screening and treatment programs. Genetic screening can be classified at three levels:

1. Population screening, which usually is directed at identifying those in a population at the highest risk of a particular genetic disorder.
2. Prenatal screening, which is intended to provide information to prospective parents who may have a family history of particular genetic disorders.
3. Family screening, which usually involves counseling and increasingly presymptomatic testing of adults who have a family history of various identifiable genetic disorders.

Prenatal screening most often is used for identifiable genetic conditions; estimates of the population prevalence have been determined for these disorders from descriptive epidemiological studies. Family screening is used to determine the presence of genetic conditions within discrete familial groups. Family screening programs are often based on a finding from population studies that the prevalence of disease causing mutations are higher among particular ethnic groups or people within particular geographic regions.

Population-Based Genetic Health Screening Service: Screening for Phenylketonuria, a Model

One of the first and most successful population genetic screening programs was designed to identify newborns susceptible to phenylketonuria (PKU). PKU is an autosomal recessive disorder with a prevalence of 1:20,000 births in the United States. Over 95% of untreated patients with PKU will become moderately to severely mentally retarded. However, the condition cannot be identified clinically until late in the first year of life, at which time irreversible developmental delays may have occurred. Dietary restriction of phenylalanine, when begun in the first weeks of life, can prevent any serious manifestations of the disease.

PKU can be detected in newborns with a relatively simple blood test, called a Guthrie test, the cost of which is less than $1.25 per newborn. Because the cost of the screening test is nominal and the disease can so easily be detected and treated, public health officials began to advocate population screening in the 1950s. By the 1960s, PKU testing was performed routinely on all newborns in the United States and many other industrialized countries.

The success of PKU population screening has led to other newborn population screening programs in the United States for single-gene genetic disorders such as galactosemia and congenital hypothyroidism, both of which can be easily detected with an inexpensive test. They also meet the criteria of being treatable, by dietary restrictions in the case of galactosemia and by hormone replacement therapy in the case of congenital hypothyroidism.

Often screening programs are directed at particular subpopulations that have a higher prevalence of a genetic disorder, such as the voluntary but routine programs to screen for Tay-Sachs disease among the Ashkenazi Jewish population or the more controversial programs to screen for sickle-cell disorder among high-risk populations such as African Americans. These programs are discussed in more detail below.

Population screening is considered appropriate when:

1. The target condition can have serious health consequences and the condition is relatively common.
2. A screening test is available that is relatively inexpensive and is reliable.
3. Treatment for the diagnosed disorder is available and accessible.

As genetic links are established for other disorders, it is likely that population screening will become used increasingly as a public health tool. Caution must be exercised in the implementation of these programs, as shown by the contrasting results of programs to screen for Tay-Sachs disease and sickle-cell disorder. Tay-Sachs disease is an autosomal recessive disorder in which a particular enzyme is deficient in those with the disease. The disease is fatal within the first few years of life. Options for carriers are to terminate pregnancies or to use artificial insemination from noncarriers. The disease is notably prevalent among Ashkenazi Jews, with a population prevalence of the recessive allele being about 1 in 30. Genetic testing is used to identify carriers of the recessive gene. If both parents are carriers, the risk of having an affected child (homozygous) is 25%. Well-planned educational and counseling programs among the susceptible population have resulted in carrier testing becoming routine and the number of Tay-Sachs births in the United States declined by more than 90% during the past 20 years

(Kaplan, 1998). Similar programs have been developed to test for more common disorders such as cystic fibrosis (Decruyenaere *et al.*, 1998).

Heterozygote testing also is available for sickle-cell disorder, which primarily affects individuals of African ancestry, although it has been found in other populations, such as among French Canadians. The disease causes red blood cells to take on a characteristic "sickling" shape, which results in low oxygen tension in the blood system. The disease is autosomal recessive and affects at least 1 out of every 600 births among African Americans. Homozygotes afflicted with the disease suffer painful episodes, damage to various body tissues, and anemia. Beginning in the early 1970s, there have been attempts to develop screening programs to test for carrier status among African Americans, without notable success in lowering the incidence of the disease. The lack of success has been attributed to a number of causes, including lack of careful planning for educational and counseling programs and lack of confidence in governmental screening programs among individuals in the target communities (Bowman, 1998).

Future of Genetic Screening Programs

Many serious health conditions have been suspected of having genetic origins. With the advent of sequencing technology made possible by the HGP, many of these associations have been confirmed, and it is likely that hundreds if not thousands of serious diseases will be shown to have a primary genetic cause. In recent years, genes causing certain forms of muscular dystrophy, some cardiac disorders, Huntington's disease, and various cancers (including some breast, ovarian, and colon cancers) have been identified. In addition, many other diseases are likely to have a genetic component, even if the precipitating cause is found to be environmental. There are numerous complex diseases, such as Alzheimer's disease, many cardiac conditions, and certain forms of cancer (Casselbrant *et al.*, 1999) that are at least partially genetically mediated.

The determination of which disorders to screen for requires the use of classic epidemiological methods combined with the tools of modern genetics. The decision about whether to offer screening and the types of screening programs involve issues of public policy and personal choice beyond the scope of epidemiology. An important factor deterring screening for many disorders will be the lack of effective treatments or interventions. In the case of prenatal screening, reproductive decisions can be made by the individuals tested. With regard to genetic testing for late-onset disorders, such as some forms of cancer, widespread screening cannot be justified unless there are viable forms of treatment or risk reduction available. In the case of heritable breast or ovarian cancer, screening for the *BRCA1* or *BRCA2* genes in the proband may help to alert female relatives about their risk for cancer. Prophylactic mastectomy is an option for genetic predisposition to breast cancer (Eeles *et al.*, 1996). In the absence of effective treatments or ethical interventions, population screening would not yield important public health benefits. In fact, there is a great risk that widespread screening for disorders for which there is no treatment would have the unintended consequence of stigmatizing individuals and promoting discriminatory practices in employment and insurance coverage.

However, for health systems planners, the availability of genetic testing, even without treatment, may be important because of public demands for such information as well as the availability of information about risk reduction strategies for individuals. The issues for health systems planners include determining the prevalence of the genetic condition within the population, the percentage of that population that is likely to desire the testing services, and the nature and extent of the services that can and should be provided.

Economic and Health Impact of Genetic Testing

What are the health and economic outcomes from the use of genetic testing? Epidemiological studies have been used to evaluate the impact of testing on morbidity, disability, mortality, and the costs of services in different populations. These types of studies are useful for health systems planners to determine how to provide services to achieve the best outcomes. For example, while PKU testing has been a notable success in decreasing the incidence of mental retardation as a public health problem, other screening programs have been less successful in affecting health because of deficiencies in follow up or other shortcomings. Screening for the sickle-cell trait discussed above is an example. By contrast, a similar screening program for Tay-Sachs carrier status among Ashkenazi Jews has been remarkably effective in reducing the incidence of that disease. However, the same fears of potential ethnic discrimination among African Americans that prevented sickle-cell screening from becoming successful are being raised in the Jewish community as new reports of discoveries of mutations for various cancers have focused on higher prevalence rates among Ashkenazi Jews (Rothenberg and Rutkin, 1998). Cost-benefit and cost-effectiveness analyses will have to be utilized (see Chapter 13) in decision making before undertaking any population-based screening or before adopted by a health plan.

Information Systems Support for Genetic Health Services

The collection and storage of genetic information will be a major challenge to health care managers. How the genetic information will be linked among data sources to support patient care management (e.g., pathology, billing information, medical records, etc.) while maintaining privacy needs to be resolved. Access to this information by patients and high-risk relatives also must be addressed. Assisting the information systems challenges is a coding scheme that allows clinicians and scientists to classify both the genetic material and mode of inheritance. Table 9.2 illustrates the coding system scheme and selected genetic diseases.

The Ethical Challenges of Genetics

Genetic information can be an invaluable resource for helping to improve the health of individuals within a population. It also carries the risk of providing the basis for stigmatization

Table 9.2. Online Mendelian Classification System

Code	Mode of inheritance	Disease example
100000	Autosomal dominant[a]	Huntington's disease
200000	Autosomal recessive[a]	Sickle cell; cystic fibrosis
300000	X-linked loci or phenotype	Muscular dystrophy, Duchenne type
400000	Y-linked loci or phenotype	Hypofertility or infertility
500000	Mitchondrial loci or phenotype	Leber hereditary optic neuropathy and dystonia
600000	Autosomal loci or phenotype[b]	Phenylketonuria

[a]Entries created before May 15, 1994.
[b]Autosomal dominant and recessive types entered after May 15, 1994.

and discrimination. Further, knowledge of the genetic predisposition to disease can prompt tremendous anxiety, particularly if such knowledge is not accompanied by satisfactory means to minimize or eliminate the risk.

The current genetic revolution is burdened with a historical background that confirms that genetic information or at least beliefs about genetic influences on health and behavior can be misused. The first genetic revolution began 100 years ago with the rediscovery of Mendel's findings from his experiments with garden peas. By the turn of the century, a movement to improve the human gene pool, called eugenics, gained support among the public and within scientific and medical circles. At its peak in the 1920s, the eugenics movement had succeeded in getting many states to adopt forced sterilization laws for mentally retarded individuals and there was strong support for euthanasia in those born with genetic abnormalities (Pernick, 1996).

The potential for abuse of the discoveries of the HGP was recognized from the beginning of the effort to decode the human genome. A significant portion of the funding for the HGP was earmarked for studies of the ethical, legal, and social implications of the project. These and other efforts have helped develop a framework for considering the ethical issues involved in utilizing genetic information in making public health decisions (see also Chapter 14).

The most sensitive and potentially most serious issues revolve around the use of genetic tests. Testing for genetic characteristics is vitally important for identifying genes responsible for life-threatening diseases. However, such testing has consequences for those tested, as well as their families and others. This is a particularly acute problem when genetic predisposition to a disease is found to have a higher incidence within particular ethnic or racial minorities. Genetic differentiation can provide an all too easy excuse for discrimination. Certain principles regarding genetic testing and services have achieved widespread acceptance within the scientific community. Some of these principles, as interpreted by the World Health Organization, are shown in Table 9.3. The guiding principles are that genetic testing always must be voluntary and that the results of such tests never should be used to stigmatize or discriminate against individuals or groups. These principles are useful for medical personnel, as well as epidemiological researchers and health systems managers, in organizing and providing genetic services.

Even with high-minded principles, advances in genetics already have created controversies that are certain to multiply as more genetic tests become commercially available. Sensitivity to privacy and issues such as the potential for individual discrimination because of genetic status and group discrimination based on the perception that a particular subpopulation has a high prevalence of a genetic disorder must be considered in implementing health care policy and services.

Conclusion

There are myriad issues in addition to the ethical issues that health care managers need to be prepared to address: issues of privacy, ownership and storage of genetic material, and insurability. Health care managers also must plan now for the challenges of providing manpower and facilities for genetic health services. This chapter has attempted to provide a brief overview of the exciting potential of the emerging field of genetic epidemiology as it impacts health care management. Epidemiology will play a major role in assessing the effects of genetics on health and in providing data for health systems planners to determine the need and character of genetic services offered to populations.

Table 9.3. General Ethical Guidelines in Medical Genetics[a]

1. Existing genetics services in a nation should be available equally to everyone regardless of ability to pay and should be provided first to those whose need is greatest.
2. Genetic counseling should be as nondirective as possible.
3. All genetics services, including screening, counseling, and testing, should be voluntary, with the exception of screening newborns for conditions for which early and available treatment would benefit the newborn.
4. All clinically relevant information that may affect the health of an individual or fetus should be disclosed.
5. Confidentiality of genetic information should be maintained except when there is a high risk of serious harm to family members at genetic risk and the information could be used to avert this harm.
6. Individual privacy should be protected from institutional third parties, such as employers, insurers, schools, commercial entities, and government agencies.
7. Prenatal diagnosis should be performed only for reasons relevant to the health of the fetus and only to detect genetic conditions or fetal malformations.
8. Choices relevant to genetics services, including choices about counseling, screening, testing, contraception, assisted procreation, and abortion following prenatal diagnosis, should be available on a voluntary basis and should be respected.
9. Adoptive children or children conceived from donor gametes should be treated equally with biological children under the guidelines.
10. Research protocols should follow established procedures for review and informed consent. Research on pre-implantation genetic diagnosis should be permitted.
11. Protocols for experimental human gene therapy should receive national review, with attention to the potential benefits or risks arising from various approaches to therapy.

[a]Adapted from *Guidelines on Ethical Issues in Medical Genetics and the Provision of Genetics Services*, World Health Organization, 1995.

Case Studies

Case Study No. 1
Screening of Genetic Disorders

The highly successful general population screening program to identify newborns with PKU was instituted because PKU is an easily detectable and treatable disorder. Untreated, the condition is likely to cause mental retardation. Tay-Sachs disease (TSD) is a fatal and devastating neurological disorder, with an average life expectancy of less than 5 years. Carrier testing for TSD also has proved to be successful among prospective Ashkenazi Jewish parents, who have a higher likelihood of being carriers of the genetic disorder than in the general population. In communities where carrier screening and testing have become the norm of practice, the incidence of TSD has declined over 90% (Kaplan, 1998). Using these programs as models, screening programs were instituted for sickle-cell disease with less success in the African-American community.

Q.1. What are some of the reasons why sickle-cell screening has been less successful than other population screening programs for genetic disorders?

Q.2. Discuss the relationship among genetic transmission patterns, social discrimination, and ethical considerations.

Q.3. Why is knowledge of and sensitivity to social and ethnic considerations important in planning genetic health care services?

Case Study No. 2
Planning Health Services for Genetic Disorders in a Developing Nation

In Oman, a tribal database has proved to be very successful in helping health care system planners and in providing a foundation for a registry for genetic specific diseases. Because the population has remained constrained by tribal boundaries in Oman, it is likely that genetic diseases will follow a similar pattern and cluster within tribes (Rajab and Patton, 1999). This is an example of genetic isolates. To maximize the use of the collected information, the tribal origin and tribal name of patients is included in all medical records.

The rare autosomal recessive Schwartz-Jampel syndrome is relatively common in Oman compared to the general population. In the past 5 years, seven cases occurred in a population of 1.5 million (0.03/1000 births). Of these seven cases, five occurred in a single tribe of 3000 individuals (10/1000 births).

Q.1. How could one use segregation analysis in this population if a genetic disorder is suspected?

Q.2. What simplifies genetic studies in this country compared to other countries?

Q.3. How could the information presented in the case be used in planning for genetic services in Oman?

Case Study No. 3
Cost-Effectiveness of Screening for Hereditary Hemochromatosis

Hereditary hemochromatosis is an inherited condition in which there is progressive abnormal deposition of iron in the heart, liver, pancreas, and other vital organs. With a prevalence as high as 1:250, it is the most common genetic disease among persons of northern European descent. The condition is an autosomal recessive, and therefore children and siblings are at increased risk for the disease. Screening is performed by measuring the serum transferrin iron saturation and ferritin levels. With early diagnosis and treatment before cirrhosis develops, an individual can have a normal life expectancy. El-Serag et al. (2000) compared the results of no screening for hereditary hemochromatosis with four screening strategies among siblings and children of a proband that incorporate testing for a hemochromatosis-associated gene (HFE).

Q.1. Draw a pedigree to illustrate an autosomal recessive mode of inheritance.

Q.2. What epidemiological information is required for this case prior to beginning a cost-effectiveness analysis of screening for hereditary hemochromatosis?

Case Study No. 4
Which Diseases to Screen for in an Outpatient Setting?

Over 5000 diseases have been found to have genetic risk factors. Among these are Alzheimer's disease, breast cancer, cystic fibrosis, Tay-Sachs disease, and neural tube defects. Screening for the genes that cause disease can aid in identifying persons at risk for the condition with the hope of altering the course of the disease when the intervention is introduced sufficiently early and is an effective intervention.

Q.1. Which diseases would the health care manager consider offering genetic screening services for in the outpatient health service setting and why?

References

Bell, J., and Haldane, J. B. S., 1937, The linkage between the genes for color-blindness and haemophilia in men, *Proc. R. Soc. Lond. [Biol]* **123**:119–150.

Boulyjenkow, V., 1998, WHO Human Genetics Programme: A brief overview, *Commun. Genet.* **1**:57–60.

Bowman, J. E., 1998, To screen or not to screen: When should screening be offered? *Commun. Genet.* **1**:145–147.

Casselbrandt, M. L., Mandel, E. M., Fall, P. A., Rockette, H. E., Kurs-Lasky, M., Bluestone, C. D., and Ferrel, R. E., 1999, The heritability of otitis media: A twin and triplet study, *JAMA* **282**:2125–2130.

Claus, E. B., Risch, N., and Thompson, W. D., 1991, Genetic analysis of breast cancer in the cancer and steroid hormone study, *Am. J. Hum. Genet.* **48**:232–242.

Decruyenaere, M., Evers-Kiebooms, G., Denayer, L., and Welkenhuysen, M., 1998, Uptake and impact of carrier testing for cystic fibrosis, *Commun. Genet.* **1**:23–35.

Eeles, R., Taylor, R., Lunt, P., and Baum, M., 1996, Prophylactic mastectomy for genetic predisposition to breast cancer: The proband's story, *Clin. Oncol.* **8**:222–225.

El-Serag, H. B., Inadomi, J. M., and Kowdley, K. V., 2000, Screening for hereditary hemochromatosis in siblings and children of affected patients: A cost-effectiveness analysis, *Ann. Intern. Med.* **15**:261–269.

Hall, J. M., Lee, J. K., Morrow, J. E., Anderson, L. A., Huey, B., and King, M. C., 1990, Linkage of early-onset familial breast cancer to chromosome 17q21, *Science* **250**:1684–1689.

Hwang, S. J., Beaty, T. H., Panny, S. R., Street, N. A., Joseph, J. M., Gordon, S., McIntosh, I., and Francomano, C. A., 1995, Association study of transforming growth factor alpha TaqI polymorphisms and oral clefts: Indication of gene–environment interaction in a population-based sample of infants with birth defects, *Am. J. Epidemiol.* **141**:629–636.

Kahn, P., 1996, Coming to grips with genes and risk, *Science* **274**:496–498.

Kaplan, F., 1998, Tay-Sachs disease carrier screening: A model for prevention of genetic disease, *Commun. Genet.* **2**:271–292.

Khoury, M. J., and Dorman, J. S., 1998, The Human Genome Epidemiology Network (HuGE Net), *Am. J. Epidemiol.* **148**:1–3.

Neel, J. V., 1995, *Physician to the Gene Pool*, John Wiley & Sons, New York.

Ostrer, H., 1998, *Non-Mendelian Genetics in Humans*, Oxford University Press, New York.

Ott, J., 1999, *Analysis of Human Genetic Linkage*, 3rd ed., Johns Hopkins University Press, Baltimore, MD.

Parmigiani, G., Berry, D. A., and Aguilar, O., 1998, Determining carrier probabilities for breast cancer-susceptibility genes BRCA1 and BRCA2, *Am. J. Hum. Genet.* **62**:145–158.

Pedersen, J., and Berg, K., 1989, Interaction between low density lipoprotein receptor (LDLR) and apolipoprotein E (apoE) alleles contributes to normal variation in lipid levels, *Clin. Genet.* **35**:331–337.

Pernick, M. S., 1996, *The Black Stork*, Oxford University Press, New York.

Rajab, A., and Patton, M. A., 1999, Analysis of the population structure in Oman, *Commun. Genet.* **2**:23–25.

Rothenberg, K. H., and Rutkin, A. B., 1998, Toward a framework of mutualism: The Jewish community in genetics research, *Commun. Genet.* **1**:148–153.

Viel, A., Genuardi, M., Lucci-Cordisco, E., Capozzi, E., Rovella, V., Fornasarig, M., Ponz de Leon, M., Anti, M., Pedroni, M., Bellacosa, A., Percesepe, A., Covino, M., Benatti, P., Del Tin, L., Roncucci, L., Valentini, M., Boiocchi, M., and Neri, G., 1998, Hereditary nonpolyposis colorectal cancer: An approach to the selection of candidates to genetic testing based on clinical and molecular characteristics, *Community Genet.* **1**:229–235.

Wilson, E. B., 1911, The sex chromosomes, *Arch. Mikrosk. Anat. Enwicklungmec* **77**:249–271.

10

Technology Assessment

Karl A. Matuszewski

With the continuous emergence of complex and expensive technologies for use in health care, how do health care managers decide which to support and which to reject? Technology assessment aids in that decision making. The assessment process considers technical characteristics of a new technology, as well as the clinical, economic, and social end points (Fuchs and Garber, 1990). Epidemiological concepts and methods are utilized in technology assessment in determining the safety, clinical efficacy, and cost-effectiveness. Technology assessment can be adequately performed only with a thorough understanding of epidemiological concepts. Specifically, familiarity with study design, measures of effect, and statistical analyses for determining the significance of effect are required to evaluate a technology for the purpose of decision making. This chapter describes the major components of technology assessment and the use of epidemiological tools in that process. Case studies at the end of the chapter allow practice in the application of epidemiological concepts and methods used in performing technology assessment.

Defining Technology Assessment and Its Function

Technology assessment is the process that examines the available evidence to form a conclusion as to the merits or role of a particular technology in relation to its possible use, purchase, or reimbursement in current medical practice. Results of clinical studies, expert opinion, hypothetical performance, economic analyses, ethical considerations, and personal value judgments all enter into the final decision regarding whether or not the technology should be viewed as investigational or an accepted standard (or state-of-the-art) of practice. This decision will have a major impact on any institution involved in or planning to acquire the evaluated technology.

Technology assessment often is undertaken to maximize the quality of patient care and

Karl A. Matuszewski   Clinical Knowledge Service, University HealthSystem Consortium, Clinical Practice Advancement Center, Oak Brook, Illinois 60523, and Department of Health Systems Management, Rush University, Chicago, Illinois 60612.

Epidemiology and the Delivery of Health Care Services: Methods and Applications, Second Edition, edited by Denise M. Oleske. Kluwer Academic / Plenum Publishers, New York, 2001.

to control health care costs. To maximize quality is to ensure that the patient receives the most effective health care services that medical science can provide at a given point in time. Technology assessment also may control costs by assisting the identification of those medical technologies that do not provide any benefit to the patient and by promoting technologies that can increase the efficiency of patient diagnosis or treatment. For instance, the introduction of a new diagnostic test with a high sensitivity and a high specificity may obviate the need for other tests that yield the same results only if performed in parallel. As an example, positron emission tomography (PET) is useful in determining the extent of myocardial infarction damage. This technology has the ability to qualitatively and quantitatively characterize myocardial ischemic tissue damage as compared to other diagnostic technologies, such as magnetic resonance spectroscopy, thallium/technetium scanning, electrocardiography, echocardiography, and blood enzyme analyses, which allow only for either qualitative or quantitative analysis (American Medical Association, 1988).

Reduced expenditures may be achieved in some cases if a technology replaces an older, more expensive one or if significant decreases in the morbidity and/or mortality of the general population are achieved. Examples include the use of a class of antibiotics called fluoroquinolones, which may be dosed less frequently but often with greater therapeutic effectiveness compared to other classes of antibiotics (Hooper and Wolfson, 1991) and the use of abciximab to reduce the rate of thrombotic complications related to angioplasty (CAPTURE Investigators, 1997).

Caution, however, should be used when claims of superiority are made for a new technology. The clinical effects found to be statistically significant should be considered with the confidence intervals for those effects (Braitman, 1991). In addition, the measurement of immediate outcomes in some studies may not always be the best indicator of ultimate clinical superiority. Likewise, statements of efficacy in the controlled study environment do not always translate into proven effectiveness in the "real world" (Diamond and Denton, 1993). The reader should be cautioned regarding interpreting the results of efficacy studies as different measures of effect may be used. For example, effect, depending on the study design used, may be represented either as a percentage relative risk reduction, absolute risk reduction, or percentage odds reduction. Effect measures calculated from a longitudinal (observational or experimental) are as follows:

> **Percentage relative risk reduction** over time $t = (I_o - I_t)/I_o \times 100\%$
> **Absolute risk reduction** = AR = $I_o - I_t$
>> Where:
>> I_o is the baseline rate
>> I_t is the rate at follow-up time t

Thus, a baseline rate of 15 readmissions per 1000 discharges and a postintervention rate 10 readmissions per 1000 discharges would be expressed as a 33% relative risk reduction, but a 5% absolute rate of reduction. Table 10.1 compares various measures of the effectiveness of antiplatelet therapy using data from Table 10.3. Note that since the incidence of the outcome is small relative to the denominator, the odds ratio is approximately equal to the relative risk. Both the relative risk and the odds ratio are expressed as ratio values less than 1 indicating that intervention reduces the risk (and the odds) of the outcome. Of the measures listed, the percentage odds reduction presents the most convincing statistical representation of the protective effect of the antiplatelet therapy.

The two factors of maximal quality and reasonable cost, which promote the appropriate and efficient use of health care resources, provide the foundation from which technology assessment is based. Payers of medical costs, either a national government (i.e., Medicare and

Table 10.1. Common Measures of Treatment Efficacy[a]

Outcome	Event rate treatment group (I_t) (%)	Event rate control group (I_0) (%)	Relative risk	Odds ratio	Relative risk reduction (%)	Odds reduction[b] (%)	Absolute risk reduction (%)
MI, stroke, or vascular death	11.45	15.02	0.76	0.73	23.77	23	−3.57

[a]From Paris-2 study, Antiplatelet Trialists' Collaboration (1994). See Table 10.3 (this volume).
[b]Percentage odds reduction = $(1 - OR)/1 \times 100\%$.

Medicaid in the United States) or private insurers, have a strong incentive to pay only for the use of cost-efficient medical services and to limit increases in taxes or higher employer/subscriber insurance premiums, respectively. At an organizational level (e.g., hospital or third-party payer), dedicated and thorough technology assessment can offer an advantage in extremely competitive markets. It enables the provider or payer to limit the selection of available technologies to those that are the most effective options and further assists in controlling the costs of providing health care (Veluchamy and Saver, 1990; Laupacis *et al.*, 1992).

Categories of Technology

The now-defunct Office of Technology Assessment (OTA) defines medical technology as "the set of techniques, drugs, equipment and procedures used by health care professionals in delivering medical care to individuals, and the systems within which such care is delivered" (Office of Technology Assessment, 1976). Systems are often not addressed by the majority of assessors of technology because of the complexity of such projects. Examples of medical technology systems include methods of healthcare delivery [e.g., health maintenance organizations (HMOs) and preferred provider organizations (PPOs)], clinical information networks, and ambulatory care. Therefore, in most cases, technology assessment includes the evaluation of the safety, effectiveness, efficiency, and appropriateness of devices, medical and surgical procedures, and pharmaceuticals promoted as improving a patient's condition or quality of life.

The targets of technology assessment are defined as follows.

Devices

Medical devices remain the major focus of technology assessment efforts (Radensky, 1991). Developments in the diagnostic imaging field bring forth a multitude of machines so complicated that they are almost instantaneously given acronyms for use as descriptors in general conversation. Computed axial tomography (CAT), magnetic resonance imaging (MRI), and single-photon emission computed tomography (SPECT) are examples of widely accepted diagnostic modalities. Positron emission tomography (PET), intravascular ultra-sound (IVU), and magnetic resonance angiography (MRA) are three examples of emerging diagnostic technologies.

Advances in therapeutic devices also are occurring at a rapid pace. For example, lasers are being used to reopen clogged coronary arteries and offer an alterative to the traditional options of open-heart surgery and coronary bypass or balloon angioplasty. Stereotactic radio-surgery using a "gamma knife" allows highly focused energy to be used in treating intra-cranial tumors, with an expected reduction in the morbidity associated with the standard surgery. Device miniaturization has also made it possible to perform many complex medical interventions outside of the hospital setting. Examples of this trend include the increasing use of portable cardiac monitoring devices and implantable drug infusion units.

Procedures

Medical and surgical procedures may be the subject of technology assessment. Examples of these include pallidotomy for Parkinson's disease, lung reduction surgery for emphysema, and gene therapy for a variety of disorders. Many other therapeutic and diagnostic procedures would benefit from early critical evaluation before becoming widely accepted as standards of medical practice.

Pharmaceuticals

An important emerging role of technology assessment is to determine the efficient and appropriate clinical uses for drugs that are approved (labeled) by the United States Food and Drug Administration (FDA) and non-FDA approved (off-label) indications, as well as those of promising new investigational agents not yet approved for marketing. The term *labeling* refers to the exact language used to delineate the clinical use of a drug (indications, dosage, adverse effects, etc.) as determined by the FDA on all promotional materials related to a drug once it has received final market approval. The need for technology assessment in the pharmaceutical area is being spurred by manufacturers who are producing increasingly sophisticated and expensive pharmaceuticals, by such means as recombinant DNA techniques, for ever-broader clinical applications.

The future clinical uses of these drugs, however, will not be completely controlled by the FDA, which has stated that it is only responsible for and interested in initial drug marketing and not in the control of the practice of medicine (Young, 1988). The use of expensive approved drugs for unsubstantiated and unapproved indications and pressure by various groups to allow more widespread use of drugs still undergoing clinical trials are two reasons why the proactive assessment of drug efficacy and cost-effectiveness offer potentially great benefits to managed care systems (Detsky, 1989). Existing authoritative sources of evaluative drug information include three major U.S. drug compendia:

- *Drug Information for the Health Care Professional* (United States Pharmacopeial Convention, 1998)
- *American Hospital Formulary Service—Drug Information* (American Society of Health-System Pharmacists, 1999)
- *Physicians GenRx* (Mosby-Year Book, 1996)

Technology Life Cycle

Regardless of the technology category, all medical technologies are subject to a predictable life cycle characterized by five distinct phases (Fig. 10.1). In the first phase of **investi-**

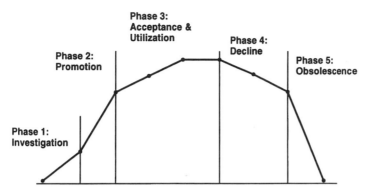

Figure 10.1. Technology life cycle. Reprinted from Matuszewski and Vermeulen (1994), with permission of the University Hospital Consortium, Oak Brook, IL, copyright, 1994.

gation, laboratory and clinical studies attempt to discover or create, refine, and package a new diagnostic or therapeutic modality. Usually at the time of pending regulatory approvals, the second phase of **promotion** is entered, and the technology is introduced to the buying community (i.e., patients, physicians, hospitals, and third-party payers). It is promoted by the sponsoring company's marketing efforts to achieve a profitable return on the investment of the first phase. A third phase, **acceptance and utilization**, is entered if the technology becomes incorporated into general medical practice. The fourth phase, **decline**, is achieved as a technology is supplanted by a superior new technology and falls out of general use or becomes a second- or third-line treatment choice. Finally, in the fifth phase of **obsolescence**, the technology is considered obsolete and is no longer appropriate, because newer technologies offer greater benefits and/or less harm. Banta and Thacker (1990) have remarked that the "diffusion of technology over time generally has been found to follow a sigmoid, or "S"-shaped, curve in which initial diffusion is slow, followed by a rapid phase, and finally ended by a flattening as saturation occurs." This corresponds to phases one through three. Murphy (1991) describes the evolution of medical technology in nine stages: invention, evaluation of safety and efficacy, implementation, marketing, general evaluation, comparison to existing alternatives, evaluation of long-term effects, modification, and replacement.

The timing and length of the phases vary. Some technologies never develop sufficient inertia to leave the investigational phase (e.g., orthomolecular therapy, which advocates high doses of vitamins), whereas other technologies may enjoy a perpetual position in the acceptance and utilization phase (e.g., X rays). Rarely, some technologies are considered obsolete and are no longer considered to be an acceptable standard of care (e.g., Garren gastric bubble for the treatment of severe obesity). Blue Cross and Blue Shield Association's Medical Necessity Program, started in 1976, was one of the earliest formal efforts to identify obsolete practices with the intent to eliminate reimbursement and change practice patterns (Banta and Thacker, 1990). Often new technologies are found to be additive and they cannot eliminate the need to perform the previous standard (Schwartz, 1987). For example, when MRI was developed, it was promoted as the ultimate imaging technology that would replace CT scans (Larson and Kent, 1989). Yet, in actual clinical practice, multiple imaging technologies (e.g., MRI, CT, X ray, ultrasound) are often performed to take advantage of incremental improvements in the available diagnostic information.

Technology assessment probably is most effective when applied in the late first phase (investigation), early second phase (promotion), or the fourth phase (decline). It is at these critical points that practices can be evaluated for possible changes to existing clinical practices and reimbursement policies (i.e., full, partial, or no payment) to achieve the greatest positive impact on patient care.

Targeting Technologies for Assessment

One difficulty in initiating a technology assessment process lies in selecting which of the many medical innovations merit an in-depth, resource-consuming evaluation. Criteria have been developed by the Council on Health Care Technology of the Institute of Medicine (IOM) for the prioritization of technology assessment topics. Primary IOM selection criteria include those technologies that have the potential to: (1) improve individual patient outcome, (2) positively affect a large population, (3) reduce treatment costs, and (4) reduce unexplained treatment variation. Secondary IOM criteria are that the assessments should address ethical/ social issues, advance medical knowledge, affect policy decision making, enhance the national assessment capacity, and be easily conducted (Institute of Medicine, 1990). Additionally, organizational criteria for selecting technologies for assessment by the Health Care Financing Administration, Georgetown's Institute for Health Policy Analysis, the National Institutes of Health Office of Medical Applications of Research, the American College of Physicians, and the American Medical Association have been published (Eddy, 1989).

Based on the review of selection criteria used by many of the major technology assessment organizations, three core criteria are proposed for targeting new medical technologies for evaluation:

1. High utilization
2. High potential for harm
3. High cost

High Utilization

Rapidly increasing, high utilization, or highly variable rates of utilization of a technology across geographic areas may signal inappropriate or excessive utilization (Leape, 1989). For example, highly variable rates across hospital service areas are noted for Medicare enrollees for coronary artery bypass graft surgery percutaneous transluminal coronary angioplasty, lumpectomy, and back surgery (Wennberg, 1996). Patient characteristics, including disease incidence, was not likely to explain this variation, but rather the availability and application of technology were felt to be closely linked areas where there was high utilization. High utilization of a technology also may be inappropriate when the cost–benefit or cost-effectiveness of the technology cannot be justified. The use of mammography in screening young women at low risk of developing breast cancer is an example where high utilization may not be desirable. For women of all races less than 50 years of age, the incidence of breast cancer is 31.7 per 100,000 and has declined 0.4% between 1987–1997, whereas among those 50 years of age and over, the incidence rate is 359.1 per 100,000 and has increased 0.5% during that same time period (Ries *et al.*, 2000). The low incidence rate in young women translates into a benefit of about 1 death prevented in 1000 women after 10 years and results in a high false-positive rate (25% over 10 years). Under this scenario, Eddy (1997) estimates that it costs approximately $150,000 for a life year saved that could otherwise be invested in some other prevention effort.

Data from the National Health Interview Survey provide information on the variation in utilization for a wide variety of medical devices, including implants (joints, dental, intraocular lenses, breasts, etc.), shunts (brain, spinal column), heart valves, and artificial arteries, veins, and ligaments by gender and age group. Provider purchasing data and third-party payer claims data are also useful for this purpose.

High Potential for Harm

Common sense dictates that different standards and assessment priorities should exist for the evaluation of technologies that have widely differing rates of risk of harm (e.g., tongue depressors versus implantable heart valves). Similarly, the assessment of the proposed use of aspirin for myocardial infarction prophylaxis may be examined with less stringent criteria than the investigational use of angiogenesis inhibitors for the treatment of a cancer that has not yet been fully evaluated by rigorous clinical drug efficacy trials. Although some advocate the necessity of assuming unknown or greater risks for severe, life-threatening conditions (e.g., AIDS), the existence of effective treatment alternatives may not justify the use of unproven or equivocal technologies.

High Cost

The time of unlimited health care spending is over. The amount of money society is willing to spend on health care services, as measured by the increasing percentage of gross national product (GNP) spent for health care, is now the subject of much debate. Payers of health care services are demanding accountability and value for their expenditures on behalf of consumers and subscribers. Although no specific price has yet been proposed by any group as being too much to pay, every new technological innovation that increases overall health care spending has a direct effect on future taxes and insurance premiums. For assessment purposes, technology costs may be examined at either the unit-of-service level or as an aggregate expense for treating an entire patient population. The results of special surveys, such as those conducted by state agencies that collect and disseminate information from the hospital discharge abstract (UB-92 form), are useful in determining high-cost procedures.

Since numerous technologies enter the marketplace each year, health care managers are constantly confronted with difficult decisions regarding which to adopt for their organization. A dynamic process of technology assessment would be helpful. Technologies that were previously assessed may be considered for possible reevaluation because the role of a technology may change over time. A method for how health care systems could prioritize technologies to assess is displayed in Fig. 10.2.

How Is Technology Assessment Performed?

There is a wide range of methods for technology assessment with varying complexity. The most common approaches include literature review and synthesis, consensus panels, decision criteria, meta-analyses, outcomes assessment, and clinical trials. Although these methods are described below as individual processes, in actual practice combinations may be used in evaluating a technology.

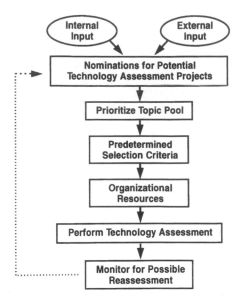

Figure 10.2. Framework for prioritizing technologies to assess. Reprinted from Matuszewski and Vermeulen (1994), with permission of the University Hospital Consortium, Oak Brook, IL, copyright, 1994.

Literature Review and Synthesis

A thorough review of the pertinent primary medical literature is a requirement for every evaluation effort. Although secondary sources (review articles and textbooks) may provide some useful interpretations of existing knowledge, articles presenting original research are the most important sources of information. Quantitative measures, particularly the results of statistical analyses, are among the most important in evaluating the effectiveness of a technology. Traditionally, a statistically significant finding is declared if the P value is less than 0.05. In accepting this value in technology assessment, this would mean that the chances are 5 out of 100 that the technology would be declared efficacious when in fact it is not. In evaluating research reports, P values as well as confidence intervals should be considered. The confidence interval conveys the range of the magnitude of the effect that can be expected if the chance occurrence of the effect has been statistically excluded. Neither the P value nor the confidence interval should be considered the sole indicators of clinical importance (Brown and Newman, 1987). Data that are pooled or cut points made without consideration of the distribution of clinical effect may occlude any true clinical significance (Greenland, 1989). Additional detail on the use of statistical criteria in evaluating data can be found in Thompson (1987) and Bailar and Mosteller (1988).

In reviewing the literature, one must be aware of the type of study from which the information was derived. Table 10.2 summarizes the level of evidence provided by common epidemiological study designs. The optimal design for evaluating a health event is a randomized clinical trial. Yet, even this design can be flawed if the study is not performed in a double-blind manner, the sample is too small, or the dropout rate or follow-up rate among the study groups is different. Guidelines for evaluating the quality of scientific studies are found in Chapter 4 (this volume).

Table 10.2. Level of Evidence about the Efficacy
of a Technology Provided by Various Study Types

Strength of evidence	Level	Study type
Strong	1	Randomized clinical trial
	2	Quasi-experimental study
	3	Longitudinal (or cohort study)
	4	Case–control study
	5	Cross-sectional study
	6	Descriptive study
Weak	7	Case series

Consensus Panels

In the **consensus approach**, topic experts review information from the scientific literature and may seek input from consumers and other medical professionals. These experts then convene to reach an agreement on responses to key questions posed in advance of the consensus conference. The expert panel may comprise members of subspecialty groups or may be multidisciplinary. Ultimately, the panel issues a consensus statement that contains recommendations for a particular health care practice. Consensus groups have made recommendations concerning albumin (Vermeulen et al., 1995), intravenous immunoglobulins (National Institutes of Health, 1990), and even procedures such as for indications for the a vaginal delivery after a cesarean section (American College of Obstetricians and Gynecologists, 1988). The National Institutes of Health (NIH) Office of Medical Application of Research is charged with managing the NIH Consensus Development Program as it applied to technology assessment (http://odp.od.nih.gov/consensus) and the dissemination of that information. Since the program's inception in 1977, more than 120 NIH consensus statements and technology assessment statements have been issued.

Decision Criteria

Decision criteria may be either quantitative or qualitative. **Qualitative criteria** may be standards or guidelines, either published or unpublished, against which a technology is tested (e.g., Blue Cross and Blue Shield Association Technology Evaluation Center criteria). This method relies heavily on the examination of the peer-reviewed literature, with the final recommendation of a technology evaluation directly related to the fulfillment of the criteria.

Quantitative criteria, such as measures of specificity, sensitivity, and positive predictive value, are important in assessing the value of a new diagnostic technology. Although sensitivity (true positive) and specificity (true negative) of the test are independent of the characteristics of the population examined, the prevalence rate of the disease affects the positive predictive value of the test. The lower the disease rate, the lower the positive predictive value and the lower the yield in finding cases with the condition. Thus, if a population has a low disease rate, the diagnostic technology may not be suitable for it despite the fact that the technology used to assess the disease has a high sensitivity and specificity. The use of decision criteria in technology assessment is illustrated by the work by Turner et al. (1988) in which MRI is compared to xeromammography for detecting breast cancer. The assessment utilizes receiver operating characteristic (ROC) curves that are constructed from plots of 1-specificity

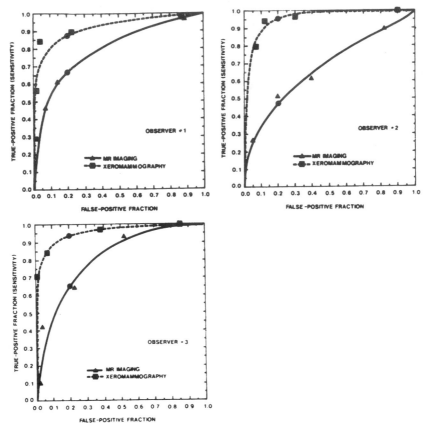

Figure 10.3. Comparison of receiver operating characteristics (ROC) curves, mammography, and magnetic resonance imaging. Reprinted from Turner *et al.* (1988), with permission of the Radiologic Society of North America, copyright, 1988.

(on the *x* axis) versus sensitivity (on the *y* axis) to assess diagnostic accuracy (Fig. 10.3) (see Chapter 2 for additional details on constructing ROC curves). The values for a curve associated with the technology that yields the highest peak in the upper-left-hand corner of the graph (the highest ratio of true positives to false negatives) represents the greatest diagnostic accuracy. In this figure, xeromammography would be preferable to MRI as the ROC curve reveals that the former has greater diagnostic accuracy.

Quantitative and qualitative criteria can be combined to facilitate achieving consensus about a technology. LeGales and Moatt (1990) describe a multicriteria decision analysis model to assess the value of screening for hemoglobinopathies. Quantitative criteria included measures of effectiveness (specificity and sensitivity of various screening measures) and cost. Qualitative measures included the rating of technical and practical feasibilities, ethical acceptability, information about follow-up time, and impact on the provision of health education.

Meta-analyses

As described in Chapters 4 and 6, a meta-analysis summarizes the intervention effect obtained from a comprehensive determination of the pool of available studies that meet

Table 10.3. Computing Statistics for a Meta-analysis[a]

To compute an effect for a single study (PARIS-2):

	Intervention	Control	Total
MI	179 (a)	235 (b)	414 (D)
No MI	1384 (c)	1330 (d)	2714
Total	1563 (n)	1565	3128 (N)

Observed (O) = 179
Expected (E) = (1563 × 414)/3128 × 206.87
Total number of events (D) = 414
Number with intervention (n) = 1563
Var $(O - E) = E(1 - n/N)(N - D)/(N - 1) = 206.87(1 - 1563/3128)(3128 - 414)/(3128 - 1) = 89.8$

To compute an effect summarized over all studies:

Odds ratio (OR) = exp(GT/SV) = exp(−158.5/561.6) = 0.75
95% CI of OR = $\exp(GT/SV \pm 1.96/(SV)^{1/2} = \exp[(-158.5/561.6) \pm 1.96/(561.6)^{1/2}] = 0.67, 0.83$

To compute the variability of effect over studies:

$X^2_{heterogeneity} = \text{Sum} [(O_i - E_i)^2/Var_i] - GT^2/SV$, with df of $n_{trials} - 1 = 12.3$, df = 10; $P > 0.1$; NS

[a]From Antiplatelet Trialists' Collaboration (1994).

predetermined criteria for inclusion in the analysis. The application of meta-analysis in assessing the effectiveness of the "technology" of antiplatelet therapy is illustrated herein. Table 10.3 summarizes the computation of statistics for a meta-analysis of data in which the odds ratio is the measure of effect. The data from each study are organized to reflect the events occurring in the intervention and the control groups. Data for these studies of antiplatelet agents are then used in Table 10.4 of the meta-analysis to determine whether or not there is a treatment effect (measured as the odds ratio) and if the treatment effect is consistent across all trials or studies (test of heterogeneity). A test statistic for heterogeneity is described in Yusef *et al.* (1985). The significance of the treatment effect for any one study or over all studies in a

Table 10.4. Meta-analysis of Antiplatelet Treatment[a]

Trial	MI, stroke, or vascular death		Statistics (antiplatelet groups only)	
	Antiplatelet	Controls	Observed (O) − expected (E)	Variance
Cardiff-1	57/615	76/624	−9.0	29.7
Cardiff-2	129/847	186/878	−25.7	64.4
Paris-1	262/1620	328/1624	−13.1	45.8
Paris-2	179/1563	235/1565	−27.9	89.8
AMIS	379/2267	411/2257	−16.9	163.0
CDP-A	76/758	102/771	−12.2	39.3
GAMIS	33/317	45/309	−6.5	17.1
ART	102/813	130/816	−13.8	49.8
ARIS	40/365	55/362	−7.7	20.7
MICRISTIN	65/672	106/668	−20.8	37.3
Rome	9/40	19/40	−5.0	4.6

[a]Grand total (GT) = O − E = −158.5; Sum of variances (SV) = 561.6.

meta-analysis can be determined from the Mantel–Haenszel–Peto test or from evaluation of the confidence intervals of the point estimate of the effect measure used. A two-tailed P value is used in case the treatment increases the risk of adverse outcomes. The methods for computing the treatment effect and its significance for the data in Tables 10.3 and 10.4 are detailed in Yusef *et al.* (1985). The results of the meta-analysis reveal that the treatment effect is significant (a reduction in the relative odds of the adverse cardiovascular outcomes), with antiplatelet therapy resulting in a significant reduction of the odds of myocardial infarction (OR = 0.75, 95% CI, 0.69, 0.82). The test statistic for heterogeneity indicates that the treatment effect is consistent across all studies (i.e., the Chi-square statistic for heterogeneity is not significant, that is, there is no heterogeneity), therefore a reduction in the likelihood of the adverse cardiovascular outcomes consistently occurs in all studies in the meta-analyses.

Problems in drawing conclusions from a meta-analysis include variation in interventions (intensity or duration), different patient populations treated, exclusion of studies for arbitrary reasons, exclusion of some and insufficient detail to identify treatment response in subgroups. Another problem emerges in the testing of heterogeneity of treatment effect as the results are dominated by larger trials and the real size of the effect in the studies pooled in the meta-analysis. Because meta-analysis is a retrospective look at data, its results should be carefully reviewed before accepted as fact. Bailar (1997) compares meta-analyses to the "gold standard" randomized clinical trials and cautions that the variability of methods in a meta-analysis can result in two meta-analyses done about the same time by investigators with the same access to the literature draw different conclusions. Table 10.5 lists several questions that should be considered in critiquing the results of a meta-analysis. Meta-analyses have been utilized to evaluate a variety of technologies, including the administration of albumin (Cochrane Injuries Group, 1998), the value of cholesterol reduction (Katerndahl and Lawler, 1999), and neonatal intensive care units (Ozminkowski *et al.*, 1987). The freeware, EPIMETA, performs meta-analysis and is available from the website http://www.cdc.gov/epo/dpram/epimeta/epimeta.htm.

Outcomes Assessment

Outcomes assessment compares the performance of a technology against standards established or recommended by expert bodies. Many organizations are developing various guidelines or practice parameters in an attempt to promote the use of outcomes assessment in evaluating new clinical technologies (see for example the National Guideline Clearinghouse at http://www.guideline.gov). Cost and intensity of care are related to real-world results

---

Table 10.5. Questions in Critiquing a Meta-analysis

- How comprehensive was the search for relevant studies (e.g., languages other than English, databases used, hand searches, contact with researchers)?
- What criteria were used to select a report for inclusion in the meta-analysis?
- What are the patient selection criteria for each study (i.e., use of same diagnostic criteria and tests)?
- Are sample sizes similar for all studies evaluated?
- Are descriptive data presented for each study included?
- Are interventions comparable?
- Are the study designs comparable?
- What are the outcomes measured in each study?
- Are the outcomes measured in the same way?
- What is the process for abstraction of data from articles used for the computation of the measure of effect (e.g., Were the abstractors blinded? How were missing data handled)?

---

using such measures as recovery speed, quality of life, ability to work, and patient preferences. Stated another way, outcomes assessment attempts to answer such practical questions as "When a physician has a few spare minutes to spend with a patient, should that time be devoted to a blood pressure check, a counseling session about dietary fat, an inquiry about possible symptoms of transient cerebral ischemia, or a demonstration of how to use nicotine chewing gum" (Laupacis *et al.*, 1988). This method seeks to maximize outputs related to limited inputs, as measured and valued by the patient or health care payer. The essential elements of performing outcomes assessment as described by Laupacis *et al.* (1988) are:

1. Comparing the consequences of doing nothing against the potential benefits of doing something.
2. Summarizing the harmful effects of the technology (e.g., side effects and toxicity).
3. Identifying patients who are at high risk and those most likely to respond to therapy.
4. Incorporating measures that allow clinicians and their patients to directly evaluate the benefits and risks of alternative therapies.

Specific outcomes of a technology can be assessed through an evaluation of changes in the relative risk, odds ratio, absolute risk, excess risk and time to event (relapse, cure, death, etc.). Health status assessment instruments, such as the *Short-Form Health Survey* (Ware and Sherbourne, 1992), the Sickness Impact Profile, the General Well-Being Index, and the Nottingham Health Profile, also may be used (Schwartz and Lurie, 1990).

Health care cost savings and the reduction of variations in treatment are the ultimate goals of outcomes assessment, when new technologies are directly compared to existing alternatives. One such example is the notion that high-dose chemotherapy and bone marrow transplantation is superior to conventional chemotherapy. Hard evidence to support such a contention, however, is limited or disputed by clinical study (Rodenhuis *et al.*, 1998).

Randomized Clinical Trials

Focused, randomized, controlled clinical trials are the gold standard of any assessment undertaking if certain criteria are met. A high-quality randomized clinical trials (RTCs) should include blinding of physicians and patients regarding treatment assignment (double-blind), hard end points not susceptible to other therapy, prior analysis of how many participants are required for study, and appropriate statistical analysis. Chalmers *et al.* (1981) describe other factors that add to the quality of a RCT. The resources required to conduct such studies may be considerable and may make them impractical for all cases where additional information is required. An RCT that demonstrated the finding that optic nerve decompression surgery is not effective, but potentially harmful (The Ischemic Optic Neuropathy Decompression Trial Research Group, 1995), is an example where this methodology worked well. However, a prospective cohort study of the effects of pulmonary catheterization was equally successful in demonstrating excess risk (Connors *et al.*, 1996).

Other Methods

Other types of analytical socioeconomic approaches have been proposed that support technology assessment efforts. These methods are explained in Bootman *et al.* (1996), Gold *et al.* (1996), and Detsky and Naglie (1990). They include the analysis of cost–benefit, cost-effectiveness, cost-utility, cost-minimization, quality of life, and cost of illness. As these methods increasingly gain acceptance, attention must be focused on their proper use. Udvar-helyi *et al.* (1992) cited the general lack of adherence to fundamental economic analytic principles in a retrospective review of 77 published journal articles. Gill and Feinstein (1994) determined that most quality of left measurements in the medical literature are also suspect.

Who Does Technology Assessment?

Technology assessment, either through formal programs or as an informal medical policy function, is performed by many groups. The perspective of the evaluating organization should be important to the reader and can be categorized in one of the following groups (the six "Ps"): payer, provider, patient, producer, political, or public (i.e., society). A distinction must be made, however, in that most nonprofit technology assessment programs generally publish their evaluations and often provide a forum for public comments. Private programs, such as those created by insurance companies, generally consider their evaluations proprietary information and do not publish or broadly circulate their technology assessment conclusions. An international directory of organizations of involved in medical technology assessment has been published (Perry *et al.*, 1998) that profiles 131 programs from 28 countries. An overview of US private-sector technology assessment also exists (Rettig, 1997). Several of the major technology assessment organizations and programs are:

US Food and Drug Administration

The US Food and Drug Administration (FDA) assesses through the drug review and approval process and device regulation system. New pharmaceutical products require an investigational drug exemption (IDE) by the FDA before a sponsor may proceed with human trials. Drugs are then scrutinized in three phases of clinical trials. Based on the accumulating strength of the data from these trials, a sponsor submits a new drug approval (NDA) application to the FDA, who either approve or reject that drug for general marketing. Devices are reviewed through the 510(k) approval process for substantial equivalence or by premarket approval (PMA) applications for unique, complex devices that require clinical studies to show positive effects. Device manufacturers are required to meet specified performance standards.

The drug approval process is extremely rigorous and for the most part has been accepted as the authoritative final word on the marketing and distribution of new drugs. This role is now changing as the result of tremendous societal pressures for new cures at any cost or at any risk to certain patient groups. Strategies developed by the FDA to deal with these external pressures are treatment investigational new drug (treatment IND) status and expedited drug review.

On the other hand, the FDA process for *device* approvals is considered by many to be modest. Studies of safety and effectiveness usually are not required for the majority of devices before they can be sold, except for devices needing a PMA application (McGivney and Hendee, 1990). This system is slowly changing, in part because of problems associated with FDA-approved heart valves and breast implants.

Agency for Healthcare Research and Quality

Formerly the National Center for Health Services Research (NCHSR) and the Agency for Health Care Policy and Research (AHCPR), the Agency for Healthcare Research and Quality (AHRQ) was established in 1989 through Public Law 101-239 to facilitate "the development, review, and updating of clinically relevant guidelines to assist health care practitioners in the prevention, diagnosis, treatment, and management of clinical conditions" (US Department of Health and Human Services, 1990a). The AHRQ currently funds 12 evidence-based practice centers that produce reports at the direction of AHRQ. Additional sponsored clinical effectiveness activities include the National Guidelines Clearinghouse and the US Preventive Services Task Force. Numerous clinical practice guidelines are available online (http://www.ahcpr.gov/clinic/cpgsix.htm) covering topics on acute pain management, Alzheimer's disease, benign prostate hyperplasia, cancer pain, cardiac rehabilitation, cataract, depression, and unstable angina, to name a few.

American College of Physicians

The American College of Physicians (ACP), through a program called the Clinical Efficacy Assessment Project (CEAP), performs consensus-driven assessments of various technologies. Started in 1981, CEAP efforts involve internal scientific policy staff, a steering committee, and external expert collaborators. Topics are chosen that are of interest to ACP members. Most CEAP reports eventually lead to position papers published in the *Annals of Internal Medicine*.

Blue Cross and Blue Shield Association

The Blue Cross and Blue Shield Association (BCBSA) evaluates new technologies through the Technology Evaluation Center (TEC), using defined criteria (Table 10.6) as a framework for the consistent evaluation of many types of technologies. In 1994, BCBSA collaborated with Kaiser Foundation Health Plan and Southern California Permanante Medical Group to expand the resources devoted to technology assessment for these groups. This joint venture allows for the purchase of TEC assessment documents by external organizations as well as selected peer-reviewed publication in the biomedical literature. TEC is an evidence-based practice center for AHRQ.

ECRI

ECRI (formerly the Emergency Care Research Institute) is a nonprofit organization, established in 1955 and chartered by the Commonwealth of Pennsylvania. ECRI's Health Technology Assessment Information Service provides summary reports on selected technologies published in *Executive Briefings*, a subscription service. Complete comprehensive reports are also available for a fee. Technology overviews are provided in the monthly newsletter *Health Technology Trends*. ECRI's assessments reflect the opinions and interpretations of ECRI staff and are targeted primarily at the hospital industry to facilitate device technology planning and acquisition needs. ECRI also is an evidence-based practice center for AHRQ and the coordinator of the National Guideline Clearinghouse.

Center for Practice and Technology Assessment (CPTA)

As a component of AHRQ, the Center for Practice and Technology Assessment (CPTA), formerly the Office of Health Technology Assessment (OHTA), evaluates the risks, benefits, and clinical effectiveness of new or unproven medical technologies being considered for Medicare coverage at the request of the Health Care Financing Administration (HCFA). Evaluations include a review of the medical literature. Participation in the assessment process

Table 10. 6. Blue Cross and Blue Shield Association Technology Evaluation Center Program Criteria

1. The technology must have final approval from the appropriate government regulatory bodies
   • This criterion applies to drugs, biological products, medical devices and diagnostics
   • A drug or biological product must have final approval from the FDA
   • A device must have final approval from the FDA for those specific indications and methods of use that Blue Cross and Blue Shield Association is evaluating
   • Any approval that is granted as an interim step in the FDA regulatory process is not sufficient
2. The scientific evidence must permit conclusions concerning the effect of the technology on health outcomes.
   • The evidence should consist of well-designed and well-conducted investigations published in peer-reviewed journals; the quality of the body of studies and the consistency of the results are considered in evaluating the evidence
   • The evidence should demonstrate that the technology can measure or alter the physiological changes related to a disease, injury, illness, or condition; in addition, there should be evidence or a convincing argument based on established medical facts that such measurement or alteration affects the health outcomes
   • Opinions and assessments by national medical associations, consensus panels, or other technology assessment bodies are evaluated according to the scientific quality of the supporting evidence and rationale
3. The technology must improve the net health outcome
   • The technology's beneficial effects on health outcomes should outweigh any harmful effects on health outcomes
4. The technology must be as beneficial as any established alternatives
   • The technology should improve the net health outcome as much as or more than established alternatives
5. The improvement must be attainable outside the investigational settings
   • When used under the usual conditions of medical practice, the technology should be reasonably expected to satisfy criteria 3 and 4

aFrom Blue Cross/Blue Shield Association (1997).

is open to all interested parties, and input is sought through announcements for comments in the *Federal Register*.

University Health System Consortium

An alliance of over 80 academic health centers, the University HealthSystem Consortium (UHC) has an effort within the Clinical Practice Advancement Center devoted to technology assessment. Started in 1989, the group produces guidelines, monographs, assessments, bulletins, briefs, and reports on new or existing medical technologies using an extensive network of medical and administrative experts and/or consultants from UHC member institutions. The assessment information is used by UHC institutions to assist in the adoption, acquisition, and utilization of new and expensive technologies. Because of its organizational structure, UHC has also been able to pursue multicenter technology surveillance projects that provide "snapshot" views of technology use in the "real world." Completed projects include ondansetron, (Vermeulen *et al.*, 1994), colony-stimulating factors (Yim *et al.*, 1995a), albumin (Yim *et al.*, 1995b), and intravenous immunoglobulins (Chen *et al.*, 2000), which compared actual drug use against "model" UHC guidelines developed by national expert panel consensus. UHC model guidelines often are submitted for peer review publication (Vermeulen *et al.*, 1995;

Ratko *et al.*, 1995; Shulkin *et al.*, 1996). Assessment documents have been available to non-UHC members for a modest fee since April 1994.

Other Assessment Centers

The Rand Corporation, a private company, is noted for its extensive experience in evaluating the appropriateness of medical procedures (Park *et al.*, 1986). Examples of private not-for-profit academic health centers that have medical assessment programs include Duke University Center for Health Policy Research and Education and Johns Hopkins Program for Medical Technology and Practice Assessment. For-profit consulting groups, often specialize in new product reimbursement and marketing assessments. Finally, most health insurance companies and health plans, to some degree, conduct technology assessment to control the premium expenditures for health care services.

International Efforts

Technology assessment is not unique to the United States. Numerous technology assessment projects are underway in many foreign countries. The Netherlands has created an advisory body known as the Health Council to begin a systematic approach toward technology assessment (Gelijns and Rigter, 1990). In Australia, the National Health Technology Advisory Panel was created in 1982 to examine technology issues (Gross, 1989). The Swedish Council on Technology Assessment in Health Care was established in 1987. Assessment is carried out by the consensus conference approach (Calltorp and Smedby, 1989). The Swiss health care system has a Medical Advisory Service to consider the safety, efficacy, advantages, costs, and other aspects of medical technology (Koch, 1987). Norway and Australia have also convened expert panels to develop consensus statements on mammography and extracorporeal membrane oxygenation, respectively (Perry *et al.*, 1991). Canada, in mid-1989, created the Canadian Coordinating Office for Health Technology Assessment (CCOHTA) to "encourage the appropriate use of health technology by influencing decision makers through the collection, analysis, creation and dissemination of information concerning the effectiveness and cost of technology and its impact on health" (http://www.ccohta.ca). Among recent assessments by CCOHTA have been comparative analyses of drug treatments for Alzheimer's disease and nonulcer dyspepsia. In 1998, the National Institute of Clinical Effectiveness was started in England to advise the National Health Service on issues of technological cost-effectiveness. The International Society for Technology Assessment in Health Care describes ongoing developments in its quarterly journal.

In addition to those described above, various technology assessment initiatives are found in Italy, Japan, Israel, South Korea, China, Finland and Germany (Koch, 1987; Perry *et al.*, 1988). As compared to the United States, efforts in technology assessment in other nations often are not as well funded and are more likely to be initiated in response to budgetary concerns.

Technology assessment projects in foreign countries are conducted by governmental, academic, as well as private organizations. International differences in the focus and application of the results of new technology evaluations can be related to the differences in the mechanism by which health care services are paid. Long-range planning and fixed budgeting in countries with national health programs set well-defined limits to the acquisition of any new technologies. Since one central source often holds most of the policymaking and reimbursement authority, tight utilization standards can be imposed on health care providers. The

United States' pluralistic health care system, from the standpoint of payers and providers, is less focused. No central policymaking authority exists to set payment and utilization limits. The assessment of new technologies, therefore, tends to be duplicative, since many organizations perform their own evaluations with little or no coordination or input from other assessment entities.

Problems in Performing Technology Assessment

Several factors effect the conclusions that are drawn from technology assessment efforts.

Lack of Evidence

Evidence on efficacy and cost-effectiveness for some new technologies is slow in accumulating for a variety of reasons, such as difficulty in performing randomized controlled trials, rarity of certain conditions to be treated, or lack of economic incentive. Even when published studies are available, problems can occur with the quality of these studies. The major study limitations most often encountered are: (1) small number of published clinical trials (excluding review articles, company promotional materials, and animal or cadaver studies); (2) small sample sizes (excluding case reports where $n = 1$); (3) lack of quantitative detail in the results section of published studies; (4) no control or randomization included in the study design; (5) emphasis on intermediate outcome results (e.g., tumor shrinkage) instead of the ultimate desired clinical outcome (e.g., survival, cure, measurable functional improvement); (6) no comparisons to alternative therapies; and (7) lack of long-term follow-up.

Lack of Agreement on How to Perform the Assessment

As described earlier, there are a variety of methods of performing technology assessment (i.e., literature review, consensus panels, decision criteria, meta-analysis, or outcomes assessment). Each method has strengths and weaknesses for which its proponents will stress the positive features. No single method is universally accepted for all potential topics and there is no guarantee that two organizations using the same method would arrive at similar conclusions.

Inconsistent Evidence

Differences in sample size, study populations, and treatment protocols are among the factors that contribute to inconsistent or inconclusive evidence. The inconsistent evidence on the effectiveness of electronic fetal monitoring (EFM) is an example of this problem. Although EFM may be useful in identifying infants at risk of neonatal seizures (MacDonald et al., 1985), EFM also has been identified as being associated with an increased risk of cerebral palsy (Shy et al., 1990).

Legal Interference

Increasingly, individuals with little or no medical or scientific background are making decisions on incredibly complex technology issues. In numerous cases (primarily in the area of bone marrow transplantation for various cancers), a judge or jury, after hearing extensive conflicting testimony from medical experts, have decided on the appropriateness of its use (Anderson et al., 1993; Ferguson et al., 1993).

Several states currently have regulations that mandate third-party payer coverage of cancer drug therapies cited in the three major drug compendia (cited earlier) or even mentioned in the literature as possibly effective. Medicare has a similar policy for unlabeled cancer chemotherapies. Anecdotal evidence, emotion, and contract language often supersede hard scientific evidence in these cases.

Breadth of Topics

It seems that there always will be more topics in need of evaluation than resources available to evaluate them. The introduction of new technologies to the health care marketplace shows no signs of slowing in the near future. If anything, the pace has accelerated. There is, unfortunately, tremendous duplication in the resources expended to evaluate a handful of controversial technologies by multiple organizations. No central coordinating body exists to maximize the information pool on all the possible technologies in need of assessment. Lacking such coordination, many marginal technologies are never evaluated.

New Information

New knowledge is constantly being presented and published. Since a technology assessment document is really a review of what is known about a technology up to its publication date, the assessment process must be ongoing to capture changes in evidence, either positive or negative (Banta and Thacker, 1990). Approval by the FDA alone for a technology is not the ultimate level of proof of appropriateness, particularly for many devices, and additional evaluation through independent studies often is necessary to form a rational, informed conclusion.

Imperfect Use of Technology

An IOM committee released a report in 1999 that estimated that up to 98,000 patients die in US hospitals every year due to preventable medical errors (Kohn *et al.*, 1999). Mistakes in medication prescribing and dispensing, as well as surgical misadventures, contributed to unsafe systems in many health care organizations that will require substantial redesign of existing checks and balances for new medical technology assimilation. If technology expectations for clinical trials cannot be safely transferred to general practice, all positive assessments will inherently overestimate expected benefits as compared to potential risks.

Future of Technology Assessment

The arrival of managed care has created a debate as to the value and role of technology assessment activities in the health care system. Important issues to be addressed regarding future technology assessment include:

- How will it be performed?
- Who will perform it? A single centralized national body or many local alliances?
- What will be the effects on medical innovation and future research?
- When and how often will new information be incorporated in technology evaluations?
- How will rare conditions be treated by the system?
- What is an acceptable cost per life year saved?

The current direction of the debate seems to bode well for formal technology assessment in the future US health care system. Capitated care, spending caps, global budgeting, practice guidelines, and the lack of opportunities to shift costs to other payers all enhance the need to know the most appropriate and efficient forms of care to minimize resource consumption. Patient satisfaction also may be improved by providing the level of care necessary or desired, thus, preventing iatrogenic complications from current system incentives to try and do anything and everything.

State-of-the-art technology will most likely be limited to a smaller number of medical centers in the future. Networks, alliances, carveout managed care contracts, joint ventures, and low reimbursement rates for primary care will result in a decline in full service providers or physician generalists and an increase in specialty services. Projected improvements in health care information systems will make every case part of a larger ongoing clinical trial of outcome effectiveness and efficiency. The dissemination of this technology information will be rapid and complete. Manufacturing principles of maximizing output will need to coexist with concerns of the US population for access to timely and comprehensive medical services. The fields of pharmacoeconomics and health system economics will spur health care providers, producers, and payers to act in concert to achieve input-to-output patient care results that use resources in a "prudent buyer" fashion.

Technology assessment should become a common part of management practice in the same manner as strategic planning and marketing. Changes in clinical services and reimbursement practices will increase the need for timely technology assessment information (Sussman, 1991). Although future clinical services will include many biotechnology products, advances in imaging, and the use of genetics to identify, monitor, and alter disease processes, a health plan, hospital, or health system may not be able to offer all the new technologies. Changes in the methods of reimbursement, such as capitation, outpatient diagnosis-related groupings (DRGs), and structured physician payment (e.g., Medicare's resource-based relative value scale physician fee schedule) are designed to limit unnecessary use of advanced technology. Cost-effectiveness evaluations and restricted use criteria for specific patient populations will become more common in medical practice as technology assessment matures as a discipline and computerized decision support software become more user-friendly.

Monetary support for technology assessment efforts will most likely come from government, private foundations, and third-party payers. Funding sources might include a percentage of future premiums paid by individuals covered by health insurance (Fuchs and Garber, 1990) or special revenue taxes and fees to manufacturers and employers. Providers, both hospitals and physicians, through alliances (e.g., University HealthSystem Consortium's Clinical Practice Advancement Center) and professional organizations (e.g., American College of Physician's CEAP) are themselves undertaking the assessment of medical technologies to protect their interests and to advance medical practice. Collaborative (e.g., BCBSA and Kaiser) efforts and broader distribution of assessment documents will strengthen technology decision implementation. Perry and Thamer (1999) advocate for a US national agency to coordinate medical assessments.

There will be an increasing use of unpublished studies and/or a greater reliance on organized treatment registry data in the evaluation of future technologies (Steinbrook and Lo, 1990; Rimm et al., 1991; Davis, 1990). Because analysis often will be undertaken in the early developmental stages of a technology, this information should be used cautiously, since it will not have the benefit of extensive peer review and will be biased by self-selection and nonrandomization of patients into treatment groups. Postmarketing trials and third-party payer claims databases will also be used to assess patient outcomes and to determine the cost-effectiveness of alternative medical technology interventions (Schwartz and Lurie, 1990), but legal issues related to electronic medical information have yet to be resolved (Hodge *et al.*, 1999). Multicenter technology surveillance using practice guidelines may become a critical method for monitoring a technology to evaluate actual practice against predefined standards.

Despite numerous established organizational processes for performing technology assessment (Perry *et al.*, 1998), individuals with no clinical or scientific background are increasingly making decisions on incredibly complex medical technology issues (Sugarman, 1990). An example to illustrate this point is a case from Washington, DC, where a US District judge ruled that HCFA could not implement a policy to deny coverage of non-FDA-approved artificial lenses to Medicare cataract patients. The judicial override of FDA approval as a minimal coverage standard suggests a lack of understanding by the courts of the ultimate purpose of drug and device regulation, which exists solely to protect the public from technologies that are not yet conclusively proven to be safe and efficacious (Appleby, 1991). Other technologies for which court-ordered reimbursement has been granted despite the lack of evidence for effectiveness include amygdalin (i.e., laetrile), immunoaugmentative therapy, and thermography (Ferguson *et al.*, 1993). This trend is disturbing.

What must be avoided in the future is antagonistic attitudes among the patient, provider, producer (i.e., the manufacturer), and third-party payer. Technology assessment offers a rational and conservative approach to the use of new medical services. However, if patients feel that they are being denied the "best" possible care, if physicians feel that their clinical actions are being unnecessarily limited, or if third-party payers use technology assessment as a shield to deny the coverage of promising medical advances, then the recommendations of technology assessment reports will be worthless, and the health care system will operate at a less than optimal level.

Summary

Who should ultimately decide what is standard therapy, state-of-the-art, or investigational: juries, judges, politicians, scientists, providers, patients, or payers? This question has no clear answer. This chapter strongly recommends that health care administrators, providers, and payers should all be familiar with the elements of technology assessment as a means of monitoring the quality and cost-effectiveness of health care delivery and should utilize epidemiological information, particularly on utilization trends and studies of risks versus benefits of new technologies. Future health care administrators, as important decision makers in new technology acquisition, must possess a comprehensive understanding of the issues involved in the process of technology assessment as well as the ability to interpret the primary medical literature knowledgeably, using epidemiological methods to assess the relative merits and limitations of new technologies. In this way, proactive technology decisions will be made, not reactive decisions based on external pressures.

Case Studies

Case Study No. 1
Solvent/Detergent-Treated Plasma

Solvent/detergent-treated plasma (SDP) is a biological product used for interventions that would otherwise require use of fresh frozen plasma (FFP). Indications include the prevention or treatment of bleeding disorders in patients with coagulation factor deficiencies, thrombotic thrombocytopenic purpura, or other clotting disorders. The solvent/detergent treatment of pooled donor plasma is a manufacturing process that effectively eliminates that potential for lipid-enveloped viruses (e.g., HIV, HBV, HCV) via transfusion transmission, at approximately twice the cost of a standard unit of FFP.

Q.1. What is the likelihood of viral transmission from FFP?

Q.2. Does SDP eliminate infectious risks of using plasma?

Q.3. Is there an alternative to using SDP or FFP?

Q.4. Has any literature been published to estimate the cost-effectiveness of SDP?

Case Study No. 2
Transmyocardial Laser Revascularization

Transmyocardial laser revascularization (TMLR) is a therapeutic procedural intervention targeted at a subset of heart disease patients. A laser is used to drill 20–40 small channels through the left ventricle, thereby creating new channels for the reperfusion of an ischemic heart area with oxygen-rich blood. The TMLR device costs approximately $200,000–500,000 and is not routinely reimbursed by third-party payers.

Q.1. Define the target population for TMLR.

Q.2. What are some alternatives for treating intractable angina patients besides TMLR?

Q.3. What two factors are important in assessing the value of TMLR, and how could they be measured in a clinical trial?

Case Study No. 3
Intensity-Modulated Radiation Therapy

Intensity-modulated radiation therapy (IMRT) is a procedural option for the treatment of a variety of solid tumors. IMRT is capable of delivering a high dose of radiation to a precisely defined target area, thus limiting adverse effects associated with less precise radiotherapy. Four systems are commercially available in the United States, and IMRT components include treatment-planning software, linear accelerator, collimator, and positioning device. System costs will vary with the availability of using existing radiotherapy equipment, but will range from a minimum of $450,000 to over $2 million.

Q.1. Name several reasons, other than to improve clinical care, why a hospital might consider acquiring an IMRT system.

Q.2. Are the effects of IMRT on local tumor control, secondary metastasis, and survival well established?

Q.3. What hospital-based committee would most likely be involved in approving IMRT?

Case Study No. 4
Intravenous Immunoglobulins

Intravenous immunoglobulin (IVIG) therapy uses a biologically derived pharmaceutical product to treat a wide range of immunological deficiency disease states. Labeled IVIG use (approved by the FDA) accounts for approximately 30% of all use, with 70% of use distributed over 70 off-label indications. The average annual treatment costs for using IVIG range from $7,000 to $15,000, depending on dosing and indication, and IVIG is usually in short supply in the United States.

Q.1. Describe several problems associated with uncontrolled use of IVIG from a health system perspective.

Q.2. Describe a strategy for evaluating an approach to controlling IVIG use from a health system perspective.

Case Study No. 5
Treatment of Benign Prostatic Hyperplasia

Benign prostatic hyperplasia (BPH) is a nonmalignant disease, primarily affecting elderly males. The gradual overgrowth of the prostate gland, blocking the urethra, leads to increasingly painful and difficult voiding. The gold standard of treatment for this condition has been transurethral resection of the prostate (TURP), a surgical procedure that has a fairly high rate of complications. New approaches to treating BPH include surgical procedure modifications, stents, drug therapies, ultrasonic aspiration, and thermotherapy.

Q.1. Describe a study design to determine which treatment strategy should be adopted in a managed care environment?

Q.2. What would be the "ideal" characteristics for a BPH treatment technology to possess in order to be performed safely on an ambulatory basis?

References

American College of Obstetricians and Gynecologists, 1988, *New Guidelines for VBAC: Statement of the Committee on Obstetrics: Maternal and Fetal Medicine*, ACOG, Washington, DC.

American Medical Association, Council on Scientific Affairs, 1988, Application of positron emission tomography in the heart, *JAMA* **16**:2438–2445.

American Society of Health-System Pharmacists, 1999, *American Hospital Formulary Service—Drug Information*, Author, Bethesda, MD.

Anderson, G. F., Hall, M. A., and Steinberg, E. P., 1993, Medical technology assessment and practice guidelines: Their day in court, *Am. J. Pub. Health* **83**:1635–1639.

Antiplatelet Trialists' Collaboration, 1994, Collaborative overview of randomized trials of antiplatelet therapy—I: Prevention of death, myocardial infarction, and stroke by prolonged antiplatelet therapy in various categories of patient, *Br. Med. J.* **308**:81–106.

Appleby, C. R., 1991, HCFA told to cover lenses still in clinical trial, *HealthWeek* **5**:4.

Aubuchon, J. P., and Birkmeyer, J. D., 1994, Safety and cost-effectiveness of solvent-detergent- treated plasma: In search of a zero-risk blood supply, *JAMA* **272**:1210–1214.

Bailar, J. C., III, 1997, The promise and problems of meta-analysis, *N. Engl. J. Med.* **337**:559–561.

Bailar, J. C., III, and Mosteller, F., 1988, Guidelines for statistical reporting in articles for medical journals, *Ann. Intern. Med.* **108**:266–273.

Banta, H. D., and Thacker, S. B., 1990, The case for reassessment of health care technology: Once is not enough, *JAMA* **264:**235–240.

Blue Cross and Blue Shield Association, Technology Evaluation Center, 1997, *TEC Criteria*, The Association, Chicago, IL.

Bootman, J. L., Townsend, R. J., and McGhan, W. F. (eds.), 1996, *Principles of Pharmacoeconomics*, 2nd ed., Harvey Whitney Books, Cincinnati, OH.

Braitman, L. E., 1991, Confidence intervals assess both clinical significance and statistical significance, *Ann. Intern. Med.* **114:**515–517.

Brown, W. S., and Newman, T. B., 1987, Are all significant *p* values created equal? The analogy between diagnostic tests and clinical research, *JAMA* **257:**2459–2463.

Calltorp, J., and Smedby, B., 1989, Technology assessment activities in Sweden, *Int. J. Technol. Assess. Health Care* **5:**263–297.

[The] CAPTURE Investigators, 1997, Randomised placebo-controlled trial of abciximab before and during coronary intervention in refractory unstable angina: The CAPTURE study, *Lancet* **349:**1429–1435.

Chalmers, T. C., Smith, H., Jr., Blackburn, B., Silverman, B., Schroeder, B., Reitman, D., and Abroz, A., 1981, A method for assessing the quality of a randomized control trial, *Control. Clin. Trials* **2:**31–49.

Chen, C., Danekas, L. H., Ratko, T. A., Vlasses, P. H., and Matuszewski, K. A., 2000, A multicenter drug use surveillance of intravenous immunoglobulin utilization in US academic health centers, *Ann. Pharmacother.* **34:** 295–299.

Cochrane Injuries Group Albumin Reviewers, 1998, Human albumin administration in critically ill patients: Systematic review of randomised controlled trials—Why albumin may not work, *Br. Med. J.* **317:**235–240.

Connors, A. F., Speroff, T., Dawson, N. V., Thomas, C., Harrell, F. E., Wagner, D., Desbiens, N., Goldman, L., Wu, A. W., Califf, R. M., Fulkerson, W. J., Vidaillet, H., Broste, S., Bellamy, P., Lynn, J., and Knaus, W., for the SUPPORT Investigators, 1996, The effectiveness of right heart catheterization in the initial care of critically ill patients, *JAMA* **276:**889–897.

Davis, K., 1990, Use of data registries to evaluate medical procedures, *Int. J. Technol. Assess. Health Care* **6:**203–210.

Detsky, A. S., 1989, Are clinical trials a cost-effective investment? *JAMA* **262:**1795–1800.

Detsky, A. S., and Naglie, I. G., 1990, A clinician's guide to cost-effectiveness analysis, *Ann. Intern. Med.* **113:** 147–154.

Diamond, G. A., and Denton, T. A., 1993, Alternative perspectives on the biased foundations of medical technology assessment, *Ann. Intern. Med.* **118:**455–464.

Eddy, D. M., 1989, Selecting technologies for assessment, *Int. J. Technol. Assess. Health Care* **5:**485–501.

Eddy, D. M., 1997, Breast cancer screening in women younger than 50 years of age: What's next? *Ann. Intern. Med.* **127:**1035–1036.

Ferguson, J. H., Dubinsky, M., and Kirsch, P. J., 1993, Court-ordered reimbursement for unproven medical technology: Circumventing technology assessment, *JAMA* **269:**2116–2121.

Fuchs, V. R., and Garber, A. M., 1990, The new technology assessment, *N. Engl. J. Med.* **323:**673–677.

Gelijns, A. C., and Rigter, H., 1990, Health care technology assessment in the Netherlands, *Int. J. Technol. Assess. Health Care* **6:**157–174.

Gill, T. M., and Feinstein, A. R., 1994, A critical appraisal of the quality of quality-of-life measurements, *JAMA* **272:**619–626.

Gold, M. R., Siegel, J. E., Russell, L. B., and Weinstein, M. C. (eds.), 1996, *Cost-Effectiveness in Health and Medicine*, Oxford University Press, Oxford, England.

Greenland, S., 1989, Modeling and variable selection in epidemiologic analysis, *Am. J. Publ. Health* **79:**340–349.

Gross, P. F., 1989, Technology assessment in health care in Australia, *Int. J. Technol. Assess. Health Care* **5:**137–153.

Hodge, J. G., Gostin, L. O., and Jacobson, P. D., 1999, Legal issues concerning electronic health information: Privacy, quality, and liability, *JAMA* **282:**1466–1471.

Hooper, D. C., and Wolfson, J. S., 1991, Fluoroquinolone antimicrobial agents, *N. Engl. J. Med.* **324:**384–394.

Institute of Medicine, Council on Health Care Technology, 1990, *National Priorities for the Clinical Conditions and Medical Technologies, Report of a Pilot Study*, National Academy Press, Washington, DC.

[The] Ischemic Optic Neuropathy Decompression Trial Research Group, 1995, Optic nerve decompression surgery for nonarteritic anterior ischemic optic neuropathy (NAION) is not effective and may be harmful, *JAMA* **273:**625–632.

Katerndahl, D. A., and Lawler, W. R., 1999, Variability in meta-analytic results concerning the value of cholesterol reduction in coronary heart disease: A meta-meta-analysis, *Am. J. Epidemiol.* **149:**429–441.

Koch, P. W., 1987, Government reimbursement policy and medical technology assessment: The case of Switzerland, *Int. J. Technol. Assess. Health Care* **3:**607–612.

Kohn, L., Corrigan, J., and Donaldson, M. (eds.), 1999, *To Err Is Human: Building a Safer Health System*, National Academy Press, Washington, DC.

Larson, E. B., and Kent, D. L., 1989, The relevance of socioeconomic and health policy issues to clinical research, *Int. J. Technol. Assess. Health Care* **5**:195–206.

Laupacis, A. L., Sackett, D. L., and Roberts, R. S., 1988, An assessment of clinically useful measures of the consequence of treatment, *N. Engl. J. Med.* **318**:1728–1733.

Laupacis, A., Feeny, D., Detsky, A. S., and Tugwell, P. X., 1992, How attractive does a new technology have to be to warrant adoption and utilization? Tentative guidelines for using clinical and economic evaluations, *Can. Med. Assoc. J.* **146**:473–481.

Leape, L., 1989, Unnecessary surgery, *Health Serv. Res.* **23**:351–407.

LeGales, C., and Moatt, J. P., 1990, Searching for consensus through multicriteria decision analysis: Assessment of screening strategies for hemoglobinopathies in southeastern France, *Int. J. Technol. Assess. Health Care* **6**:430–449.

MacDonald, D., Grant, A., Sheridan-Pereira, M., Boylan, P., and Chalmers, I., 1985, The Dublin randomized controlled trial of intrapartum fetal heart rate monitoring, *Am. J. Obstet. Gynecol.* **152**:524–539.

Matuszewski, K., and Vermeulen, L., 1994, Medical technology assessment, in *Critical Issues Shaping Medical Practice*, University Hospital Consortium, Oakbrook, IL.

McGivney, W. T., and Hendee, W. R., 1990, Regulation, coverage, and reimbursement of medical technologies, *Int. J. Radiat. Oncol. Biol. Phys.* **18**:697–700.

Mosby-Year Book, Inc., 1996, *Physicians GenRx*, St. Louis, MO.

Murphy, J. R., 1991, The assessment process: A microscopic view, *Med. Prog. Technol.* **17**:77–83.

National Institutes of Health, 1990, *Intravenous Immunoglobulin: Consensus Statement 8*, No. 5, NIH, Bethesda, MD.

Office of Technology Assessment, 1976, *Development of Medical Technology: Opportunities for Assessment*, US Government Printing Office, Washington, DC.

Ozminkowski, R. J., Wortman, P., and Roloff, D., 1987, Evaluating the effectiveness of neonatal intensive care: What can the literature tell us? *Am. J. Perinatol.* **4**:339–347.

Park, R. E., Fink, A., Brook, R. H., Chassin, M. R., Kahn, K. L., Merrick, N. J., Kosecoff, J., and Solomon, D. H., 1986, Physician ratings of appropriate indications for six medical and surgical procedures, *Am. J. Public Health* **76**:766–772.

Perry, S., and Thamer, M., 1999, Medical innovation and the critical role of health technology assessment, *JAMA* **282**:1869–1872.

Perry, S., Hanft, R., and Chrzanowski, R., 1991, Technology assessment reports, *Int. J. Technol. Assess. Health Care* **7**:68–105.

Perry, S., Garder, E. M., and Hong, R., 1998, *Directory of Health Technology Assessment Organizations Worldwide*, Medical Terminology and Practice Patterns Institute Press, Washington, D.C.

Radensky, P., 1991, Federal activities related to health and economic outcomes, *Administrative Radiology* **54**:53–55.

Ratko, T. A., Burnett, D. A., Foulke, G. E., Matuszewski, K. A., and Sacher, R. A., 1995, Recommendations for off-label use of intravenously administered immunoglobulin preparations, *JAMA* **273**:1865–1870.

Ries, L. A. G., Eisner, M. P., Kosary, C. L., Hankey, B. F., Miller, B. A., Clegg, L., and Edwards, B. K. eds., 2000, *SEER Cancer Statistics Review, 1973–1997*, National Cancer Institute, Bethesda, MD.

Rettig, R. A., 1997, *Health Care in Transition: Technology Assessment in the Private Sector*, Rand, Santa Monica, CA.

Rimm, A. A., Barr, J. T., Horowitz, M. M., and Bortin, M. M., 1991, Use of a clinical data registry to evaluate medical technologies, *Int. J. Technol. Assess. Health Care* **7**:182–193.

Rodenhuis, S., Richel, D. J., van der Wall, E., Schornagel, J. H., Baars, J. W., Koning, C. C., Peterse, J. L., Barger, J. H., Nooijen, W. J., Bakx, R., Dalesio, O., and Rutgers, E., 1998, Randomised trial of high- dose chemotherapy and haemopoietic progenitor-cell support in operable breast cancer with extensive axillary lymph-node involvement, *Lancet* **352**:515–521.

Schwartz, J. S., and Lurie, N., 1990, Assessment of medical outcomes: New opportunities for achieving a long sought-after objective, *Int. J. Technol. Assess. Health Care* **6**:333–339.

Schwartz, W. B., 1987, The inevitable failure of current cost-containment strategies, *JAMA* **257**:220–224.

Shulkin, D. J., Ratko, T. A., and Matuszewski, K. A., 1996, Model guidelines for the preoperative evaluation of patients undergoing elective surgery, *J. Clin. Outcomes Manage.* **3**:39–48.

Shy, K. K., Luthy, D. A., Bennett, F. C., Whitfield, M., Larson, E. B., van Belle, G., Hughes, J. P., Wilson, J. A., and Stenchever, M. A., 1990, Effects of electronic fetal heart rate monitoring, as compared with periodic auscultation, on the neurologic development of premature infants, *N. Engl. J. Med.* **322**:588–593.

Steinbrook, R., and Lo, B., 1990, Informing physicians about promising new treatments for severe illnesses, *JAMA* **263**:2078–2082.

Sugarman, S. D., 1990, The need to reform personal injury law leaving scientific disputes to scientists, *Science* **248**:823–827.

Sussman, J. H., 1991, Financial considerations in technology assessment, *Top. Health Care Financ.* **17**:30–41.

Thompson, W. D., 1987, Statistical criteria in the interpretation of epidemiologic data, *Am. J. Publ. Health* **77**:191–194.

Turner, D. A., Alcorn, F., Shorey, W. D., Stelling, C. B., Mategrano, V., Merten, C. W., Silver, B., Economou, S. G., Straus, A. K., Witt, T. R., and Norusis, M., 1988, Carcinoma of the breast: Detection with MR Imaging versus xeromammography, *Radiology* **168**:49–59.

Udvarhelyi, I. S., Colditz, G. A., Rai, A., and Epstein, A. M., 1992, Cost-effectiveness and cost-benefit analyses in the medical literature: Are the methods being used correctly? *Ann. Intern. Med.* **116**:238–244.

United States Pharmacopeial Convention, 1998, *Drug Information for the Health Care Professional*, Author, Rockville, MD.

US Department of Health and Human Services, PHS, Agency for Health Care Policy Research, 1990, *AHCPR Program Note*, US Department of Health and Human Services, Rockville, MD.

Veluchamy, S., and Saver, C. L., 1990, Clinical technology assessment, cost-effectiveness adoption, and quality management by hospitals in the 1990s, *Qual. Rev. Bull.* **16**:223–228.

Vermeulen, L. C., Matuszewski, K. A., Ratko, T. A., Burnett, D. A., and Vlasses, P. H., 1994, Evaluation of ondansetron prescribing in US academic medical centers, *Arch. Intern. Med.* **154**:1733–1740.

Vermeulen, L. C., Ratko, T. A., Erstad, B. L., Brecher, M. E., and Matuszewski, K. A., 1995, A paradigm for consensus: The University Hospital Consortium guidelines for the use of albumin, nonprotein colloid, and crystalloid solutions, *Arch. Intern. Med.* **155**:373–379.

Ware, J. E., and Sherbourne, C. D., 1992, The MOS 36-item short-form health survey (SF-36), *Med. Care* **30**:473–483.

Wennberg, J. E., 1996, *Dartmouth Atlas of Health Care*, American Hospital Publishing, Chicago, IL.

Yim, J. M., Matuszewski, K. A., Vermeulen, L. C., Ratko, T. A., Burnett, D. A., and Vlasses, P. H., 1995a, Surveillance of colony-stimulating factor use in U.S. academic health centers, *Ann. Pharmacotherapy* **29**:475–481.

Yim, J. M., Vermeulen, L. C., Erstad, B. L., Matuszewski, K. A., Burnett, D. A., and Vlasses, P. H., 1995b, Albumin and non-protein colloid solution use in U.S. academic health centers, *Arch. Intern. Med.* **155**:2450–2455.

Young, F. E., 1988, *Paying for Progress: Reimbursement and Regulated Medical Products*, presented to the Blue Cross and Blue Shield Technology Management Conference, Chicago, November.

Yusef, S., Peto, R., Lewis, J., Collins, R., and Sleight, P., 1985, Beta blockage during and after myocardial infarction: An overview of the randomized trials, *Prog. Cardiovasc. Dis.* **27**:335–371.

11

Health Risks from the Environment
Challenges to Health Service Delivery

Bailus Walker, Jr.

Introduction

More than 2000 years ago, a strong interrelationship between human populations and their environment was accurately assessed by Hippocrates (in the fifth century BC). In his treatise on *Air, Water and Places,* he admonished his students to observe the environment to understand the origins of disease in their patients (Francis, 1961). In this ancient context, environment refers to air, water, and soil. With increasing epidemiological data, this narrow definition is replaced by a definition that recognizes the importance of the environment that is manmade or created by society. Thus, lifestyle, homes, communities, work, and global environment enter into the definition of environment. Today, the interactions between humans and their environments, physical, chemical, biological, and social increasingly influence thinking and planning in health services. A classic model of health that embodies this orientation is the epidemiological triangle (Fig. 11.1). This model conceptualizes that health is achieved through an optimal balance among the host, agent, and the environment. The components of the model can be used to assess environmental risk according to biological, chemical, physical, psychological, and, sociological factors. Sociological and psychological factors of environmental origins are not as well delineated as biological, chemical and physical. Evidence abounds that the major disease problems facing all nations today to one degree or another are caused, mediated, or exacerbated by environmental factors (US Public Health Services, 1999; National Institute of Environmental Health Sciences, 1995). For example, without the proper disposal of waste and effective management of water resources, populations could be decimated by water or food-transmitted diseases. According to the report of the US Global Change Research Program (Patz *et al.*, 2000), there are five categories of health outcomes affected by environmental conditions: (1) temperature-related morbidity and mortality; (2) extreme weather events (storms, tornadoes, hurricanes, precipitation extremes); (3) air-pollution-related health effects;

Bailus Walker, Jr.   Environmental and Occupational Medicine Program, College of Medicine, Howard University, Washington, DC 20059.

Epidemiology and the Delivery of Health Care Services: Methods and Applications, Second Edition, edited by Denise M. Oleske. Kluwer Academic/Plenum Publishers, New York, 2001.

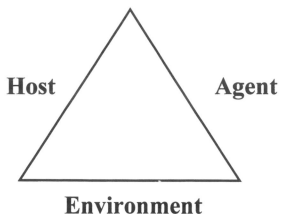

Figure 11.1. The epidemiological triangle.

(4) water- and food-borne diseases; and (5) vector- and rodent-borne diseases. Historically, the health of the environment pertaining to each of these categories has been the purview of governmental agencies. But, because of trends in public–private partnerships, this responsibility will continue to be shared. The increased availability of information (labeling of consumer products, right-to-know workplace laws, package inserts for drugs, etc.) makes it more likely that members of the public will seek advice from health care practitioners about the relationship of environmental agents to current health issues in their families and in their neighborhoods. As we learn more about the health implications of exposure to environmental agents, social and economic forces will compel the health service system to transcend the traditional diagnosis-treatment models. Thus, the purpose of this chapter is twofold: (1) to evaluate how the environment effects health status, and (2) to illustrate the use of epidemiological methods in planning and devising health care services in response to the new challenges in the environment.

Problems in Environmental Health

Most diseases today, even many transmissible ones (such as Legionnaire's disease), have environmental components. Environmental conditions that represent potential sources of health risks are numerous and can come from the home setting, workplace, or community (Table 11.1).

Gene–Environment Interaction

As mentioned in Chapter 9, environmental factors act in conjunction with normal genetic profiles as with acquired susceptibility states. As our knowledge of DNA has advanced, it

Table 11.1. Examples of Potential Sources of Environmental Health Hazards and Associated Potential Health Problems

Source	Substance(s)	Health Problem(s)
Agricultural runoff	Pesticides and herbicides	Lymphomas
Incinerators	Heavy metals (e.g., lead), particulate matter	Lead poisoning
Industrial facilities	Solvents	Cancer, reproductive impairments
Nuclear facilities	Radioactive wastes	Cancer
Landfills	Bacteria (*E. coli*), methane gas	Diarrheal diseases, death
Sunlight	Ultraviolet radiation	Skin cancer, including melanomas
Home heating units	Carbon monoxide	Death

has become clear that the impact of environmental agents on DNA, if not repaired, can affect exposed persons directly, through modification of DNA essential to the function of normal tissue. For example, the evidence mounts that most cancers result from the interactions of both genes and the environment and that genetic factors alone are thought to explain only about 5% of all cancers (Perera, 1997). Knowledge of other disease risk from gene–environment interaction will be increased as we learn more about the function of genes discovered in the Human Genome Project. In most cases, the functions of these genes and their proteins that form the body and carry out its function remain unknown.

Impact of the Environment on the Reproductive System

The extent of environmental factors in promoting reproductive dysfunction (impotence, reduced sperm concentration) and adverse pregnancy outcomes (spontaneous abortion, still-birth, congenital defects, prematurity, and low birth weight) is significant (Table 11.2). It is estimated that about 250,000 babies are born in the United States each year with birth defects, a significant number of which may be attributed to environmental factors, including deficiencies in nutrients, such as folate, or environmental contaminants. Statistics on the incidence of birth defects in various populations exist, but owing to differences in definitions and ascertainment the results are difficult to compare. More reliable data are available from Hungary (614.9 per 10,000 births) that has had a system of direct ascertainment, registration, and extensive study of birth defects since about 1970 (Czeizel *et al.*, 1993).

Environmental contaminants in the form of chemicals such as cadmium, lead, organic mercury, and some pesticides have been associated with birth defects (National Institute of Environmental Health Sciences, 1992). The medication diethylstilbestrol caused adenocarcinoma of the vagina in young women whose mothers had taken the drug during pregnancy (Paul, 1995; Mattison, 1985). Men exposed to the pesticide dibromochloropropane (DBCP), experience varying degrees of testicular toxicity including infertility. The precise scope of environmental exposures that contribute to the burden of reproductive and developmental dysfunction of men and women is unknown. Only a small fraction of the more than 75,000 chemicals in commerce today have been tested for reproductive or developmental toxicity (National Institute of Environmental Health Sciences, 1992). Cigarette smoke is well documented to be associated with low birth weight (English and Eskenazi, 1994), as well as the influence of the environment associated with low-income neighborhoods (Pallotto *et al.*, 2000).

Ionizing radiation has a potentially profound effect on reproductive function because the gametes—sperm and ovum—are radiosensitive tissues. The testis is one of the most radio-

Table 11.2. Examples of Agents Known to Affect
Human Reproductive Outcomes or Capacity

Alcohol	Ionizing radiation
Anesthetic gases	Lead
Antineoplastic drugs	Lithium
Antithyroid drugs	Methyl mercury
Arsenic	Nickel
Bovine growth hormone	Nicotine
Cadmium	Organic mercury
Chlorinated hydrocarbons	Physical stress
Dibromochloropropane (DBCP)	Plasticizers
Ethanol	Polychlorinated biphenyls (PCBs)
Formaldehyde	Tetracycline

[a]From Thomas (1993).

sensitive tissues, with low doses causing significant depression in the sperm count or temporary absence of sperm in the semen. Exposure to ionizing radiation can come from the home, workplace (e.g., mining), diagnostic X rays, disease treatment (e.g., radiation therapy for cancer), and warfare.

Impact of the Environment on the Immune System

The immune system consists of those white blood cells (lymphocytes, monocytes), humoral responses (antibodies), and tissue that influence their growth (e.g., spleen, bone marrow) that are the body's main defense against foreign materials and biologic agents. In the general population, an increasing number of people suffer from disorders of the immune system such as allergies, asthma, and AIDS. Asthma, a chronic lung disease characterized by inflammation of the airways resulting in intermittent, recurring episodes of wheezing, breathlessness, tightness of the chest, and coughing, is a growing health problem. The prevalence of asthma has increased 46% between 1982 and 1993. Increases have been documented in all age, race, and gender groups, but have been most significant among those under the age of 18 where the prevalence has increased by 80% since 1982. More than 12 million persons in the United States have been diagnosed with asthma. Environmental triggers of asthma are exposure to allergens (dust mites, pollen, mold, pet dander, and cockroach waste), strong fumes, respiratory infections, exercise, and dry or cold air. In particular, it is well known that air pollution (particulate matter and ozone) interact with allergens to increase the frequency of asthma, which in turn triggers high emergency room use when the asthma becomes uncontrollable (Tolbert et al., 2000). The current major issue is how long a time window does the effect of air pollution in any given community on health persist. Schwartz (2000) suggests that cumulative exposures of 1–2 months are significant in increasing hospitalization of older individuals whose health is already compromised and for mortality from ischemic heart disease as well as all-cause mortality. The anticipation of such air pollution information can aid in planning staffing needs of hospital emergency rooms and ambulatory urgent care centers. The US Environmental Protection Agency Air Quality web pages provide current information on levels of the major air pollutants listed in Table 11.3.

Some environmental agents such as cadmium, mercury, organic solvents, and silica dust, have been linked to autoimmune diseases in which the body's immune system destroys its

Table 11.3. Major Air Pollutants

Indoor air pollutants	Outdoor air pollutants
Tobacco smoke	Carbon monoxide (CO)
Radon	Lead (Pb)
	Nitrogen dioxide (NO_2)
	Ground-level ozone (O_3)
	Particulate matter (PM)
	Sulfur dioxide (SO_2)

other tissues (Burns *et al.*, 1996). People living near chemical waste sites have reported symptoms related to dysfunction of the immune system that suggest that mixtures of chemical pollutants may produce suppression of the immune system (National Research Council, 1992). Additionally, numerous environmental pollutants have been found to produce adverse immune system alterations (including hypersensitivity and asthmalike reactions) including lead (from gasoline, paints, ceramics, firearms), pesticides (carbamates, organophosphates), intermediates of pesticide production (dioxin, methyl isocyanates), and environments contaminated with the flame retardant polybrominated biphenyls (Thomas *et al.*, 1990). Sometimes the effect on the immune system is not so subtle. Latex, a substance contained in some inexpensive types of gloves used as protective equipment in patient care settings, can produce severe even deadly allergic reactions.

Some population subgroups are at increased risk of developing immunologic responses as a result of exposure to environmental contaminants due to their age, drug therapy, stage of physical development, or preexisting disease (e.g., asthma). For example, *in utero* exposure, infancy, and early childhood can mean increased susceptibility to environmental disease since the immune system is not fully functional until about 11 years of age. As a person ages, the immune system begins to decline. Also with age, environmental exposures may be more pronounced and/or chronic (e.g., due to workplace exposures) and modulated by personal health habits (smoking and diet), coexisting disease, or stress.

Impact of the Environment on the Nervous System

The nervous system consists of the brain, spinal cord, enervation to voluntary and involuntary organs, and the chemical substances known as neurotransmitters that convey electrical messages to the body. Similar to the immune system, exposures during early development often provoke toxic consequences rather different from the consequences inflicted on the mature nervous system. In addition to the mode of damage, differences arise in how the damage is expressed. For example, mixed behavioral syndromes of irritability, apathy, and even psychosis are early expressions in individuals with diffuse central nervous system dysfunction caused by exposure to toxic chemicals (toluene, manganese, carbon disulfide). The health and economic costs of neurobehavioral toxicity may well exceed those of cancer or other chronic diseases (Weiss and Elsner, 1996; Walker, 2000).

Environmental factors have been associated with the increased risk of brain tumors (ionizing radiation, polyvinyl chloride, formaldehyde, pesticides, and petroleum and petroleum products) (Bondy and Wrensch, 1993), and more recently to mental illness (US Department of Health and Human Services, 1999a). Chronic exposure of children to lead, either through leaded paint in the household or from the environment, is associated with the inability to concentrate, hyperactivity, decreased motor nerve conduction velocity, and depression (Weeks *et al.*, 1991; Ryan *et al.*, 1999). Again, as with the immune system, environmental challenges to the neurological system may not be able to be compensated for when the host is compromised. So the consequences of chronic lead exposure in children with sickle-cell disease may be devastating and persist well into adulthood.

Impact of the Environment on the Respiratory System

The respiratory system consists of the specialized structures of the nose, pharynx, trachea, bronchi, and lungs. The adverse effects of environmental exposure on mortality and morbidity from respiratory disorders are well known. The Clean Air Act, last amended in 1990, resulted in improvements in air quality in the United States. Yet excessive levels of the most common air pollutants (carbon monoxide, lead, nitrogen dioxide, ozone, sulfur dioxide, and particulate matter) still are observed. Ozone is the most commonly violated National Air Quality Standard. Even exposures to relatively low concentrations of ozone, a very toxic gas, have been found to affect lung function and cause respiratory inflammation in normal, healthy people, especially during exercise. Particulate matter poses major concerns for human health by affecting breathing and respiratory function, aggravating existing respiratory and cardio-vascular conditions, and damaging lung tissues (Avol *et al.*, 1984).

Since the 1970s, the importance of indoor air pollution on respiratory function has been recognized. Exposures from environmental tobacco smoke and indoor emissions from heating and cooking appliances have been consistently identified (Environmental Protection Agency, 1994; Samet and Spengler, 1998).

In addition to chemical threats to the respiratory system, ionizing radiation exposure from mining and from residential ^{222}radon decay products have been estimated to have caused up to 38,600 lung cancer deaths in the US population (Field *et al.*, 2000).

Environmental Terrorism

The increasing vulnerability of civilian populations to chemical, biological, and radiolog-ical terrorism has added a new dimension to national and international environmental health concern for those in the delivery of health care services. There is every indication that specifically biological terrorism is on the increase and that nuclear weapons are no longer the weapons of choice (Johnson, 1999). These challenges motivated the US Department of Health and Human Services and 12 public health professional societies to convene the first National Symposium on Medical and Public Health Responses to Bioterrorism in 1999 (US Department of Health and Human Services, 1999b). The first task was to determine a list of agents that could pose the greatest risk to public health and to the human-dominated ecosystem. Anthrax and smallpox are the two agents with the greatest potential for mass casualties. Both are highly lethal and are stable for transmission in aerosol and capable of large-scale production. The case fatality rate for anthrax if left untreated even before the onset of serious symptoms exceeds 80% (Chin, 2000). Spores of anthrax have been known to survive for decades under the right conditions. The US Army's Medical Research Institute reports that the former Soviet Union produced smallpox virus by the tons (Kortepeter and Parker, 1999). Plague, tularemia, ricin, and botulism also can be used (Johnson, 1999).

The next question was how our current health services system would be able to limit the number of casualties and control damage to the ecosystem. It has been recommended that even a small outbreak of smallpox could be an early warning of a more serious attack, and that prompt implementation of preventive measures could well reduce the mortality rate. Unlike chemical terrorism, biological terrorism is not immediately obvious but may appear insidiously, with primary care providers witnessing the first cases. However, the first to truly identify the problem could be hospital laboratory personnel seeing unusual strains of organisms or an epidemiologist from a hospital or from a health department tracking patterns of infectious disease hospital admissions (Pavlin, 1999).

Environmental terrorism also may be aimed at attacking plants or animals or contaminating a community's water supply. Thus, it is important to differentiate a natural outbreak from an intentional exposure of populations to biological warfare agents. In most naturally occurring outbreaks, numbers of cases gradually increase as a progressively large number of people come in contact with the reservoir of infection or other sources of the transmissible agent (e.g., contamination of a food processing facility with *Listeria*). Conversely, exposures due to environmental terrorism are most likely to be a point source, with everyone coming in contact with the agent at approximately the same time. Thus, the epidemic curve would be compressed even with physiological and exposure differences.

Environmental terrorism is not only due to chemical or biological weapons. Bombing is a significant concern and epidemiological information on injury patterns aids in planning for hospital preparedness. In the Oklahoma City terrorist bombing, spinal immobilization, field dressings, and intravenous fluids were the most common prehospital interventions. Lacerations, contusions, fractures, strains, head injuries, abrasions, foreign body removal, and eye injuries accounted for 75% of all emergency department discharge diagnoses. Use of tetanus toxoids, antibiotics, and analgesics were the most common pharmaceutical agents (Hogan *et al.*, 1999).

The two basic approaches for reducing the impact of environmental terrorism are mitigation and response. Mitigation includes all those actions that are taken before, during, and after the occurrence of a terrorist activity. Response includes health services actions taken to meet the needs of the affected community. In an environmental terrorist weapon event, there may be thousands to tens of thousands of victims. Making progress in these endeavors requires health service providers to have basic epidemiological skills and knowledge of what to expect during an environmental terrorist attack. Also essential is a robust surveillance system for detecting any emerging or reemerging disease patterns that will facilitate determining sources and preventing future exposure to biological agents. Increasingly in major metropolitan areas, hospital staffs are trained in identifying symptoms and illnesses of a biological attack and in the procedures for dealing with decontamination. Biohazard suits should be available in hospital emergency rooms and central supply departments. Decontamination showers outside hospital emergency rooms are also recommended. Biohazardous spill cleanup kits are becoming increasingly widespread, even appearing in public transportation vehicles. Last, health care managers should know their city's plan for communication and for mobilizing resources in order to cope with such an event. Table 11.4 summarizes the potential biological and chemical threats and control measures.

Climate Changes, Cataclysmic Events, and Other Disasters

Planning for the type and extent of needed health care services required to respond to cataclysmic events can also be addressed through an epidemiological framework. In addition to environmental terrorism, these events can be related to the weather (tsunamis, hurricanes, blizzards), geologic change (earthquakes, volcanic eruptions), famine, industrial accidents

Table 11.4. Examples of Chemical and Biological Agents That Could Be Used in a Terrorist Attack and Control Measures[a]

Category	Agents	Control measures
Military chemical agents (nerve agents, blister agents, choking agents, incapacitating agents, blood agents)	Sarin, mustard compounds, phosgene, chlorine, hydrogen cyanide	Reserves of antidotes, postexposure treatments, and supportive therapy (e.g., atropine, pralidoxime, diazepam, amyl nitrite, cyanide antidote kit, physostigmine, dimercaprol) Development, education and training of emergency response personnel including mental health personnel Development and review of hospital and community disaster plans Identification of governmental (e.g., local hazardous materials response teams) and nongovernmental (e.g. poison control centers) resources Dissemination of information on recognition of signs and symptoms of agents Protective equipment for emergency response personnel (full-face respiratory masks, self-contained breathing apparatuses, gloves, and liquid-proof and vapor-impermeable suits) Decontamination areas: shower areas with safe runoff disposal and eye showers Detection and identification devices for vapor and liquids (e.g., M256 detection kit)
Industrial compounds (pesticides, toxic gases, organic compounds)	Dioxin, ammonia, chlorine	Same physical supportive measures as above
Biological agents	*Bacteria*: Anthrax, plague, tularcmia	Amoxicillin, ciprofloxacin, doxycycline, penicillin G, streptomycin sulfate; chloramphenicol
	Viruses: smallpox, viral encephalitides, viral hemorrhagic fevers *Toxins*: botulinum toxin, ricin, staphylococcal enterotoxin B	Rapid assay kits or culture for anthrax spores and for botulinum toxin; botulinum antitoxin Hypochlorite solutions for decontaminating skin and surfaces Same physical supportive measures as for military chemical agents

[a]From Brennan *et al.* (1999); Inglesby *et al.* (1999); Leggiadro (2000); Sharp *et al.* (1998).

(Chernobyl nuclear accident, Bhopal gas release), loss or disruption of services (bridge collapse, contaminated water supply), and significant population displacements (civil conflicts, wars) (Combs *et al.*, 1999). The Center for Research on the Epidemiology of Disasters (1998) reports that the continents of Africa and Asia are the hardest hit, largely because of large populations and lower level of disaster preparedness. Fundamentally, unique patterns of health care needs emerge with each major event type. One of the best-documented cataclysmic events from a managerial epidemiological perspective is an earthquake. Epidemiological data indicate that the epicenter may not necessarily have the highest overall incidence of mortality and morbidity (Peek-Asa *et al.*, 2000). Epidemiological data also suggest anticipating an area larger than predicted by actual seismic activity and not to expect that injuries will emanate concentrically from the epicenter (Peek-Asa *et al.*, 2000). Instead, the geography of the affected area should be determined and then cardinal points should be identified, that is, the areas where the majority of the victims are likely to be (e.g., large buildings, apartment complexes, heavily trafficked roadways) (Alexander, 2000). Another consideration in preparing health care services for earthquakes is to understand the frequency, severity, and the types of health problems likely to be encountered. Heart attacks, multiple traumas, orthopedic injuries, head injuries, and crush injuries are common (Fig. 11.2) (Alexander, 2000). Rapid response is essential as survival is likely to be only a few hours.

War and civil conflicts are not necessarily associated with high trauma rates, but physical displacement of affected populations precipitate problems of malnutrition, diarrheal diseases, and acute respiratory infections (Brennan *et al.*, 1998). Thus, important health services concerns for these situations need to focus on nutrition, water, sanitation, shelter, the medical management of disease, and the reconstruction of public health infrastructure.

Environmental Equity

The structure of human social groups influences the acquisition and distribution of wealth, health, and resources among its members. Because of the association between income

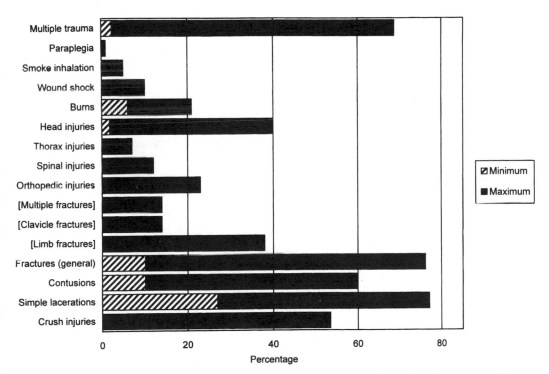

Figure 11.2. Reported proportions of various types of physical trauma in earthquake disasters. From Alexander (2000).

Table 11.5. Percentage of African American, Hispanic, and Lower Socioeconomic Populations in Census Tracts Surrounding Waste Treatment, Storage, and Disposal Facilities (WTSDF) Compared to the Proportion of These Groups in Other Census Tracts, 1994[a]

Area	African Americans	Hispanics	Persons living below the poverty line
Census tracts with WTSDF storage, disposal in area or at least 50% of their area within 2.5 miles of tract with WTSDF	24.7	10.7	19.0
Census tracts without WTSDF	13.6	7.3	13.1

[a]From Institute of Medicine (1999).

and housing, members of the lowest socioeconomic groups tend to live in substandard housing in the least desirable areas of the community or adjacent to major sources of environmental pollution (waste disposal facilities, industrial areas, abandoned toxic waste dumps) (Table 11.5). Additionally, African Americans and persons of Hispanic origin are more likely than whites to live in areas with reduced air quality. Table 11.6 displays the proportion of individuals by race living in areas affected by major air pollutants. Low-income residents living in older, poorly maintained buildings are more likely to be exposed to dangerous cockroach allergens that may increase the risk of asthma developing or precipitate an asthmatic crisis or are more likely to be near waste treatment, storage, or disposal facilities. Migrant farm workers are more likely to be exposed to hazardous levels of pesticides from agricultural exposures and lack of knowledge in safe handling and application of these. Minority groups who rely on subsistence fishing may be more exposed than the general population to accumulated pollutants such as mercury. In addition to social class, differences in environmental exposures are complex and deeply rooted in many aspects of society, such as historical preference, commerce, geography, state and local land use decisions, and other factors that affect where people live and work (National Research Council, 1999). These issues have come to be known today as issues of environmental equity. Differences in environmental exposures may explain why elevated blood lead levels and hospitalization and death rates from asthma among African American, Hispanic, and low-income persons are higher than other population groups (US Department of Health and Human Services, 2000).

Conventional epidemiology will encounter difficulties in assisting planning efforts for services that address environmental health issues in disadvantaged communities because of

Table 11.6. Percentage of African American, Hispanic, and White Populations Living in Areas Where Air-Quality Standards Are Not Attained, 1992[a]

Air pollutant	African American (%)	Hispanic (%)	White (%)
Particulates	16.5	34.0	14.7
Carbon monoxide	46.0	57.1	33.6
Ozone	62.2	71.2	52.5
Sulfur dioxide	12.1	5.7	7.0
Lead	9.2	18.5	6.0

[a]From Institute of Medicine (1999).

shortcomings in existing databases and the small populations typically involved. The Institute of Medicine, after reviewing the multiple dimensions of environmental equity, concluded that it should become a higher priority in the fields of health care services, research, education, and health policy (National Research Council, 1999).

Global Environmental Health

Global trade, travel, and communication extend the interests of all countries worldwide. This also creates global vulnerability. There are at least four routes for international transfer or acquisition of health risks: (1) the movement of people; (2) international exchange of both legal and illegal potentially toxic materials and contaminated foodstuffs; (3) the variance in environmental health and safety standards; and (4) the indiscriminate spread of medical technologies, both those with known and those with unknown safety. Of particular concern is the variance between the developed and developing economies in environmental health and safety standards. The disparity encourages multinational corporations to locate their hazardous production facilities (ergonomic or chemical) in countries that lack or do not enforce strict environmental regulations. This practice places developing nations at risk of becoming the dumping grounds for hazardous manufacturing plants and puts manufacturers who do comply with environmental health standards at a competitive disadvantage. In the United States, asbestos has been phased out because of health concerns, but the asbestos industry continues to flourish in nations such as China, Brazil, and Zimbabwe (Institute of Medicine, 1997). Nonuniform standards and weak enforcement ultimately increase the risk of environmental hazards to human health in all countries.

It has become increasingly clear that environmental deterioration, wherever it occurs in the world, has a global impact. For example, emissions and runoffs from Canada have polluted the Great Lakes shared between the United States and Canada (US Environmental Protection Agency, 1996). Largely due to combustion of fossil fuels, elimination of forest and other human activities on a global scale, compounds known as "greenhouse gases" have been accumulating in the atmosphere. Greenhouse gases include carbon dioxide (CO_2), methane, and chlorofluorocarbons (CFCs). These gases trap heat radiating from the earth's surface, raising concerns that the planet may be warming. The global impacts of climate change could add significant new stress to ecological systems that are already affected by pollution. Rising global temperatures are expected to raise sea level and change precipitation and local climate conditions. A changing global climate could also alter crop yields, water supply, and threaten human health. The most direct effect of changing climate on human health is heat stress.

Unilateral actions may address some problems in the short term, but such actions are fundamentally incapable of providing long-term solutions to global environmental health problems. Effective resolution of transnational environmental health problems requires a comprehensive approach addressing health risks and all aspects of pollution at the same time, whether they are air-, water-, or ground-based.

Recognition and Assessment of Environmentally Related Disease

Recognition of environmentally provoked diseases provides an enormous challenge to the health service systems because many different causes of disease can produce similar signs and symptoms. To determine whether the health problem seen is environmentally provoked,

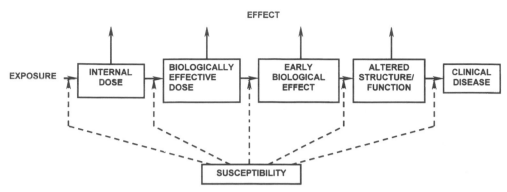

Figure 11.3. Simplified flow chart of classes of biological markers (indicated by boxes). Solid arrows indicate progression, if it occurs, to the next class of markers. Dashed arrows indicate that individual susceptibility influences the rate of progression, as do other variables. Biological markers represent a continuum of changes, and the classification of change may not always be distinct. From National Research Council, Committee on Biologic Markers (1987).

the assessment strategy includes: (1) inquiry into environmental temporal circumstances, (2) determination of whether the biological effect in a target organ is consistent with the known site of action for an agent, (3) determination of whether the agent is present in the target tissue, (4) assessment of the amount absorbed by the body in relation to that which the agent is present in the environmental media, and (5) determination of potential for coexposure (e.g., risk of radon-induced lung cancer is geometrically increased by cigarette smoking). A schematic of this relationship is displayed in Fig. 11.3.

Biological markers (or biomarkers) are measurements on biological samples (e.g., blood, urine, hair) used to aid in the determination of an environmentally provoked health problem. A detailed discussion of biomarkers, including issues of characterization, validation, and measurement techniques, is beyond the scope of this chapter. Several reviews and multi-authored books on biomarkers are available (International Agency for Research and Cancer, 1997; Lemaster and Schulte, 1995). Biomarkers are generally classified into three groups. **Biomarkers of exposure** include measurements of toxin or its metabolic product (e.g., lead in blood) in biological materials (Table 11.7). For example, the measurement of pesticides in breast milk was an approach taken in response to concerns about high levels of contamination in humans with DDT, DDE, dieldrin, and polychlorinated biphenyls (Gladen *et al.*, 1999). **Biomarkers of effect** are measurable biochemicals or other alterations within an organism that, depending on magnitude, can indicate potential or established disease. To put it another way, a biomarker of effect is the biological response that is mechanistically involved in the pathway leading to disease. For instance, chromosomal aberrations are commonly found in

Table 11.7. Examples of Biologic Specimens Used to Measure Biomarkers of Exposure to Hazardous Substances

Breast milk	Urine	Blood
Semen	Sputum	Liver tissue

tumor cells, and in some cases there is very good evidence that they play a role in carcinogenesis. Translocations (fused elements from different chromosomes) are particularly useful for quantifying certain types of acute and chronic exposures to environmental toxicants.

A **biological marker of susceptibility** is an indicator of an inherent or acquired variation in an organism's ability to respond to the challenge of exposure to a specific substance. Such markers include inborn differences in absorption, metabolism, and excretion of toxic chemicals, variations in immune systems, or other genetically determined variations in response to environmental agents. For example, the genetically determined organ reserve capacity determines the ability of the body to recover from environmental exposure. This capacity may play a role in determining the extent of an impairment.

Risk Assessment

The large number of environmental agents, their ubiquity in the environment, and their varying potential for causing health effects, requires that a system for establishing priorities and allocation of resources must be in place in order to manage population-based exposure to environmental agents. This process is known as "risk assessment." Risk assessment involves quantitatively determining the risk of disease or death in a population exposed to an environmental toxicant and relates that to the intensity and duration of exposure to that agent. The standard for risk assessment involves four steps (National Research Council, 1983):

1. Hazard identification, which concerns the capacity of the agent to cause adverse health effects (e.g., cancer, reproductive disorders), and to determine all situations or substances which the hazard in any amount can produce health effects.
2. Dose–response evaluation, which concerns the relationship between the amount of the hazardous substance absorbed and the incidence and severity of the adverse effect, duration and timing of exposure at the target organ, and the physiologic state of the individual exposed.
3. Exposure evaluation, which concerns the extent of human exposure, its source, movement of the substance through the environment, and the uptake by people (e.g., inhalation, ingestion).
4. Risk characterization, which calculates an estimated health risk expected based on cumulative exposure over an entire average lifetime in a defined population. This is obtained from information acquired in steps 1 through 3.

The cornerstones of risk assessment are studies of animals exposed to high concentrations of suspect chemicals. While it is true that "man is not a giant rat" and might not develop exactly the effect exhibited in test animals, it has been demonstrated over time that toxic effects that are shown in laboratory animals often occur in humans exposed to the same agent. Scientists do recognize, however, that animal tests may not be conclusive for humans. Virtually all elements of risk assessment are clouded with uncertainty. For instance, it is not known how many people are or will be exposed to a hazard and how much of any environmental agent will be present in a specific part of the environment. The genetic diversity and the variability of human populations in the context of any given exposure may lead to hyperresistance or hypersensitivity rendering conclusions from any single strain of controlled animal study as potential under- or overestimates of human risks. The presence of human epidemiological studies aid in confirming whether or not a positive association exists and confirms dose response animal studies (Hertz-Picciotto, 1995).

Health risk assessments have been performed for a variety of chemicals, including drinking water and disinfection by-products, lead, mercury, ozone, environmental tobacco smoke, dioxin, and ozone. The reader is advised to consult the webpages of the US Environmental Protection Agency (http://www.epa.gov) for the results of these and other risk assessments.

Although risk assessment has developed almost entirely in the context of its regulatory application, the health service practitioner is often confronted with questions from members of the public about the risk the individual faces. Indeed, the public is increasingly concerned about potential environmental risks to human health. A national survey in early 2000 showed that three in four Americans say that they or a close family member has lived in a community where one or more environmentally related problems with air, water, and food were a cause of health problem (Princeton Survey Research, 2000) (http://www.healthtrack.org.). As a result the public often wants answers to such questions as: Is the water safe to drink? Could my miscarriage be due to something in the air or water or at my place of work? What is the likelihood of cancer from fuel additives that I breathe when filling up may gas tank? As the practitioner addresses risk issues, it is important that he or she be familiar with the risk assessment process and the types of uncertainties mentioned earlier. Thus, risk communication and risk management are functions of health care managers. For example, risk assessment of the hazards of environmental tobacco smoke that resulted in a proposed Occupational Safety and Health Administration (OSHA) (1994) rule prompted many hospitals to eliminate smoking within the workplace (US Environmental Protection Agency, 1992). However, the need for regulation of ergonomic hazards faced by hospital employees who are at highest risk for occupational musculoskeletal disorders through Occupational Health and Safety Laws is still the subject of much debate.

Health Services for Environmentally Provoked Diseases

The health care services continuum considered for any health problem also is relevant to environmentally provoked diseases, namely primary prevention, secondary prevention, and tertiary prevention.

Primary Prevention

The most effective strategies for the prevention and control of environmental exposures that may provoke adverse health effects are those that prevent any contact between environmental agents and the human population. Such primary prevention strategies seek to change the social and physical environment in order to erect protective barriers between environmental agent and host. Examples of primary prevention are premarket evaluation of the toxicity of new chemical compounds (e.g., food additives), emission standards, dissemination of information (public education materials and reducing exposure to sunlight), accurate labeling of products (e.g., ragweed in some herbal teas), and encouraging consumers to read the label first before using any home cleaning or pesticide products. Communication of environmental quality goals to the public is an important prevention strategy that should be given greater priority by health care managers (US Department of Health and Human Services, 2000).

Secondary Prevention

Secondary prevention includes the early detection of the environmentally related disease through screening in order to interrupt progression. A screening test may indicate the presence of an environmentally related disease or merely a higher probability of a disease and the need for confirmatory testing. If it is performed correctly, the planning and implementation of an environmental health screening program is among the most complex procedures in health services. In developing the program, the health service professional must be familiar with clinical medicine and toxicology. In analyzing and interpreting the screening results the health practitioner must be familiar with epidemiology and understand the applicability of environmental exposure measurements. Another useful tool for secondary prevention is the reporting of excessive levels of selected environmental toxicants in body fluids by clinical laboratories to state health departments. Such reporting allows identification of the likely source of exposure, categorization of cases by location (e.g. street, census tract neighborhood), estimation of number of persons exposed, and increase of the probability of appropriate medical follow-up. Some states have developed a registry for a number of environmental toxicants, the most prominent of which is the New York State Heavy Metal Registry. However, testing and reporting for other toxicants is much less common than for lead. In addition, there is only a small number of environmental agents that can be routinely measured through monitoring of body fluids. Thus, there is an inherent limitation to this approach to environmental hazards and disease screening. It is important to emphasize that medical screening programs, however elegantly conceived or presented, are inherently less effective for disease prevention than are strategies of primary prevention. However, they may be the only practical intervention given current medical technology.

Screening for environmentally provoked diseases for which there are suitable tests is an activity that health plans should increasingly give attention to, particularly where there may be a large proportion of the membership who are exposed to some environmental agents. For example, health plans that have a large percentage of low-income members from urban areas should consider screening for lead levels among women of childbearing age (to help in preventing low birth weight) as well as in preschool children (to prevent behavioral disorders). Table 11.8 lists the recommended strategy for screening for elevated blood lead levels in children recommended by the Centers for Disease Control. In screening for environmentally provoked disease, the manager should always keep in mind national or regional goals. In the case of elevated lead levels, 4.4% of children aged 1 to 5 years had blood lead levels exceeding 10 µg/dl during 1991 to 1994. However, research results reported in 2000 showed that

Table 11.8. Centers for Disease Control and Prevention Screening Recommendations for Elevated Blood Lead Levels

Type of screening activity	Strategy
Universal screening, where risk for lead exposure is widespread	Using a blood lead test, screen all children 1–2 years and all children 36–72 months of age who have not been previously screened
Targeted screening	Using a blood lead test, screen all children 1–2 years and all children 36–72 months of age who have not been previously screened, if they meet the following criteria: Residence in a specific high-risk geographic area Membership in a high-risk group (e.g., Medicaid recipients) Positive response to any item on personal-risk questionnaire (Does your child live in or regularly visit a facility that was built before 1950? Does your child live in or regularly visit a house built before 1978 with recent or ongoing renovations? Does your child have a sibling or playmate who has or did ever have lead poisoning?)

cognitive defects can be caused by blood lead levels lower than the currently acceptable level of 10 μg/dl. This analysis drew on data from the National Health and Nutrition Examination Survey (NHANES) (Broady et al., 1999; US Department of Health and Human Services, 2000). The goal of Healthy People 2010 is total elimination of elevated lead levels in children.

Tertiary Prevention

Tertiary prevention, which includes medical intervention, is the least effective strategy for environmentally provoked disease prevention. The objective of tertiary intervention is to limit harm after harm has been done, as it is exemplified with the health problem of lead poisoning. While effective treatment for lead poisoning exists, caregivers may not recognize the problem until neurological damage is profound. Unfortunately, too, the effectiveness of tertiary intervention for environmentally provoked diseases by traditional health care services may be severely limited by the resources available and the patient returning to the same hazardous environment. Fortunately, in the case of the child with lead poisoning, state resources are likely to be available to help the family reduce the lead levels in the home. Poison control centers services are another example of tertiary prevention. For hospitals serving communities in industrial areas, access to a poison control center and a board certified toxicologist are essential. Poison control centers coordinate care for poison victims from point of exposure to information sources and therapies, as well as serving as a locus for prevention, training, and research on exposure to toxic agents.

Summary and Conclusion

There is growing evidence that the delivery of environmental health services will be considered within the broader context of the health services delivery system for several reasons:

1. A substantial portion of the national and international disease burden is environmentally related.
2. Of the three determinants of health—environment, genes, and time—only the environment is currently within the health system's control.
3. The identification, evaluation, and subsequent modification of the role of environmental factors in causing disease and premature death promise an early and major payoff in the prevention and control of disease.

With the increasing knowledge of the body's response to environmental agents, demand for services for environmental risk assessment and exposure management (including environmental engineering) will likewise increase. Synergy and support between the health service specialist and environmental control and monitoring personnel is vital because of the interactions of individuals, their work environment, the residential or home environment, and the ambient environment.

Case Studies

Case Study No. 1
The Health Consequences of a Record Heat Wave

Sustained hot weather, particularly in urban areas where there has not been a heat wave for several years, is associated with excess mortality particularly in high-risk populations. During the period July 12

Table 11.9. Selected Factors of Case Subjects and Matched Controls

Factor	Case subjects No. (%)	Controls No. (%)	Odds ratio (95% CI)
Did not leave home at least once a week	75 (27)	19 (7)	6.7 (3.0–15.0)
Lived on a top floor	83 (52)	51 (32)	4.7 (1.7–12.8)
Lived alone	156 (46)	112 (33)	2.3 (1.4–3.5)
Mental problem	52 (20)	23 (9)	3.5 (1.7–7.3)

[a]From Semenza et al. (1996).

through July 16, 1995, the daily maximum and minimum temperatures reached record highs and were accompanied by extreme relative humidity. Semenza et al. (1996) studied risk factors of heat-related death and death from cardiovascular disease during that period. The purpose of the study was to determine who was at greatest risk for heat-related death. The study sample consisted of persons who were older than 24 years of age who died in Chicago from July 14 through July 17, 1995, for whom the cause of death listed on the death certificate met one of three criteria: heat was listed as the immediate or underlying cause of death, with no reference to cardiovascular disease; cardiovascular disease was listed as the primary cause of death, with no reference to heat; or cardiovascular disease was listed as the primary cause and heat as a contributing cause of death. From this pool, 680 persons were identified and a random sample from each cause-of-death category was selected with stratification according to age, race, and date of death. Living controls were selected from the neighborhood of each decedent matched to age within 5 years. Interviews were conducted of the controls and surrogate respondents for the cases. The interview participation rate was 59.4% in the controls. Selected data from this study are displayed in Table 11.9.

Q.1. What type of study design is this?

Q.2. What are some of the factors that contributed to the risk of heat-related death? Describe the evidence in support of your conclusion.

Q.3. What other risk factors could have been studied?

Q.4. What types of biases influence the conclusions of this study?

Q.5. What services should this city provide to prevent future heat-related deaths during periods of excessively high temperatures and humidity?

Case Study No. 2
Neighbors versus Their Neighborhood

A neighborhood community association in northwest Washington, DC is concerned with what is perceived as an increased use of nonagricultural pesticides in its neighborhood—those not intended for use in producing or preserving food or crops. The chemicals are used in places where people live, work, and play, such as home, gardens, lawns, parks, and golf courses. There is no information as yet on any unusual level of symptoms or illnesses at present.

Q.1. What types of information should the community association collect?

Q.2. Propose an epidemiological study design that would determine potential health risk to consumers with exposure to pesticides through accidents, misuse, or lack of awareness of their hazards.

Q.3. How would/should the community be educated about the problem?

Case Study No. 3
Community Health Risk from an Industrial Plant

In 1984, a Union Carbide of India chemical plant released over 30 tons of methyl isocyanate into the air over the city. The plant manufactured a number of pesticides. As part of the synthesizing process the plant produced methyl isocyanate, a chemical intermediary. The methyl isocyanate was stored in a stainless steel tank and later reacted with other chemicals to produce pesticides. The most likely cause of the explosion was that a quantity of water entered the storage tank. The location of the plant in a populated area increased the number of persons exposed beyond the workers at the plant. Weather conditions exacerbated the exposures. The air was dry over the Bhopal neighborhoods. There also were other atmospheric conditions: methyl isocyanate close to the ground, near individuals' breathing zones.

Some 100,000 people living near the plant sought medical care for health problems caused by the exposure to methyl isocyanate. Entire families died, leaving no survivors, and many deaths were not recorded.

Q.1. What steps could have been taken to prevent the explosion?

Q.2. How would you determine what health care services would be needed as a result of the Bhopal explosion?

Q.3. What programs or services could have prevented significant morbidity and mortality in this community?

Case Study No. 4
Environmental Equity

During the last decade, the Pennsylvania Department of Environmental Protection has issued permits for the construction of five solid waste facilities in Chester County. The city of Chester had a long history of exposure to pollution from steel production and from manufacturing. Recently, the state issued a permit for yet another solid waste facility. Chester's residents are predominantly African American. The rest of the county is overwhelmingly white. According to a 1995 report, the city of Chester had the highest infant mortality rate and the highest death rate due to certain malignancies compared to the rest of the United States. In addition, 60% of blood samples from children living in the city of Chester exceeded the maximum 10 μg/dl of lead recommended by the Centers for Disease Control. Doctors in the community are continuously asked by their patients what they can do.

Q.1. What role should local health service providers play in addressing the concerns of Chester residents?

Q.2. What factors appear to lead to a higher prevalence of environmental hazards in low-income, minority, or inner-city communities?

Q.3. What data should be obtained by the Pennsylvania environmental authorities before approving an additional waste disposal facility?

Case Study No. 5
Global Environmental Health

In 1986 the Chernobyl nuclear power plant in the Soviet Union experienced an explosion. It resulted from the improper withdrawal of control rods and inactivation of important safety systems in violation of operating rules. The result of this failure to comply with operating procedures that caused the reactor to overheat, explode, and catch fire. The explosion caused intense radioactive pollution over all of Europe, far beyond the Soviet borders. This incident illustrates the dimensions of a nuclear disaster. While the long-term health effects of the release of radioactivity cannot be predicted with certainty, various calculations suggest that 30,000 additional cancer deaths may occur in the population over the next 70 years as a result of the accident.

Q.1. What information on ionizing radiation should health service providers have readily available?

Q.2. How can adverse health effects from ionizing radiation be prevented?

Q.3. What mechanisms could ensure the timely exchange of information on the incidents of cancer resulting from the Chernobyl explosion?

References

Alexander, D., 2000, On the spatial pattern of casualties in earthquakes, *Ann. Epidemiol.* **10**:1–4.

Bondy, M. L., and Wrensch, M., 1993, Update on brain cancer epidemiology, *Cancer Bull.* **4**:365–368.

Brennan, R. J., Waeckerle, J. F., Sharp, T. W., and Lillibridge, S. R., 1999, Chemical warfare agents: Emergency medical and emergency public health issues, *Ann. Emerg. Med.* **34**:191–204.

Broady, D. J., Pirkle, J. L., Kramer, R. A., Flegal, K. M., Matte, T. D., and Gunter, E. W., 1999, Blood lead levels in the US population, *JAMA* **272**:277–283.

Burns, L. A., Meade, B. J., and Munson, A. E., 1996, Toxic responses of the immune system, in *Casarett and Doull's Toxicology* (C. D. Klassen, ed.), pp. 355–402, McGraw-Hill, New York.

Center for Research on the Epidemiology of Disasters, 1998, *World Disaster Report*, Oxford University Press, New York.

Chin, J., 2000, *Control of Communicable Diseases in Man*, 17th ed., American Public Health Association, Washington, DC.

Combs, D. L., Quenemoen, L. E., Parrish, R. G., and Davis, J. H., 1999, Assessing disaster-attributed mortality: Development and application of a definition and classification matrix, *Int. Epidemiol. Assoc.* **28**:1124–1129.

Czeizel, A. E., Intody, Z., and Modell, B., 1993, What proportion of congenital abnormalities can be prevented? *Br. J. Med.* **306**:499–503.

English, P. B., and Eshkenazi, B., 1994, Black–white differences in serum cotinine levels among pregnant women and subsequent effects on infant birthweight, *Am. J. Pub. Health* **84**:1439–1443.

Environmental Protection Agency, 1994, *Indoor Air Pollution: An Introduction for Health Professionals*, USEPA, Washington, DC.

Field, R. W., Steck, D. J., Smith, B. J., and Kile, A. J., 2000, Residential radon gas exposure and lung cancer, *Am. J. Epidemiol.* **151**:1091–1102.

Francis, T., 1961, Biological aspects of environment, in *Proceeding of the Second National Congress on Environmental Health*, pp. 1–10, School of Public Health, University of Michigan, University of Michigan Press, Ann Arbor, MI.

Hertz-Picciotto, I., 1995, Epidemiology and quantitative risk assessment: A bridge from science to policy, *Am. J. Pub. Health* **85**:484–491.

Gladen, B. C., Monaghan, S. C., Lukyanova, E. M., Hulchiy, O. P., and Shkyryak-Nyzhnyk, Z. A., 1999, Organochlorines in breast milk from two cities in Ukraine, *Environ. Health Perspect.* **107**:459–462.

Hogan, D. E., Waeckerle, J. F., Dire, D. J., and Lillibridge, S. R., 1999, Emergency department impact of the Oklahoma City terrorist bombing, *Ann. Emerg. Med.* **34**:160–167.

Inglesby, T. V., Henderson, D. A., and Ascher, M. S., 1999, Anthrax as a biological weapon: Medical and public health management, *JAMA* **281**:1735–1745.

Institute of Medicine, 1997, *America's Vital Interest in Global Health: Protecting Our People, Enhancing Our Economy, and Advancing Our National Interest*, National Academy Press, Washington, DC.

Institute of Medicine, 1999, *Toward Environmental Justice—Research, Education, and Health Policy Needs*, National Academy Press, Washington, DC.

International Agency for Research on Cancer, 1997, *Application of Biomarkers in Cancer Epidemiology*, IARC Publ. No. 42, IARC, Lyon, France.

Johnson, J. A., 1999, Interview with Brigadier General Donna F. Barbisch, D.H.A., Senior Advisor to the Biological Warfare Improved Response Program, *J. Healthcare Manage.* **44:**329–334.

Kortepeter, M. G., and Parker, G. W., 1999, Potential biological weapons threat, *Emerg. Infect. Dis.* **5:**523–527.

Leggiadro, R. J., 2000, The threat of biological terrorism: A public health and infection control reality, *Infect. Control Hosp. Epidemiol.* **21:**53–56.

Lemaster, G. K., and Schulte, P. A., 1995, Biologic markers in epidemiology in *Molecular Epidemiology: Principles and Practice* (P. A. Schulte and F. P. Perera, eds.), pp. 81–109, Academic Press, San Diego, CA.

Mattison, D. R., 1985, Clinical manifestations of ovarian toxicity, in *Reproductive Toxicology* (R. I. Dixon, ed.), pp. 18–23, Raven Press, New York.

National Institute of Environmental Health Sciences, 1992, *Reproductive and Development Abnormalities. Human Health and Environment*, National Institutes of Health, Publications No. 92-3344, Washington, DC.

National Institute of Environmental Health Sciences, 1995, *Human Health and the Environment*, US Department of Health and Human Services, Washington, DC.

National Research Council, National Academy of Sciences, 1983, *Risk Assessment in the Federal Government: Managing the Process*, National Academy Press, Washington, DC.

National Research Council, Committee on Biologic Markers, 1987, *Biological Markers in Environmental Health Research*, National Academy Press, Washington, DC.

National Research Council, Subcommittee on Immunotoxicology, 1992, *Report of the Committee on Biological Markers*, National Academy Press, Washington, DC.

National Research Council, 1999, *Toward of Environmental Justice*, National Academy Press, Washington, DC.

Occupational Health and Safety Administration, 1994, 29 CFR Parts 1910, 1915, 1926, and 1928 Indoor Air Quality: Proposed Rule, OSHA, Cincinnati, OH.

Pallotto, E. K., Collins, J. W., Jr., and David, R. J., 2000, Enigma of maternal race and infant birth weight: A population-based study of US-born black and Caribbean-born black women, *Am. J. Epidemiol.* **151:**1080–1085.

Patz, J. A., McGeehin, M. A., and Bernard, S. M., 2000, The potential health impacts of climate variability and change for the United States: Executive summary of the report of the health sector of the U.S, National Assessment, *Environ. Health Perspect.* **108:**367–376.

Paul, M., 1995, Reproductive disorder, in *Occupational Health* (B. Levy and D. H. Wegman, eds.), pp. 543–546, Little, Brown, and Company, Boston, MA.

Pavlin, J. A., 1999, Epidemiology of bioterrorism, *Emerg. Infect. Dis.* **4:**528 530.

Peek-Asa, C., Ramirez, M. R., Shoaf, K., Seligson, H., and Kraus, J. F., 2000, GIS mapping of earthquake-related deaths and hospital admissions from the 1994 Northridge, California, earthquake, *Ann. Epidemiol.* **20:**5–13.

Perera, F., 1997, Environment and cancer: Who are susceptible? *Science* **278:**981–1192.

Princeton Survey Research Associates. National Survey of Public Perception of Environmental Health Risk (conducted April 20–30, 2000), Pew Charitable Trust and Georgetown University, Washington, DC.

Ryan, D., Levy, F., Pollack, S., and Walker, B., Jr., 1999, Protecting children from lead poisoning and building healthy communities, *Am. J. Pub. Health* **89:**823–824.

Samet, J., and Spengler, J., 1998, Indoor air pollution, *Environmental and Occupational Medicine* (W. Rom, ed.), pp. 1539–1543, Lippincott–Raven, Philadelphia, PA.

Semenza, J. C., Rubin, C. H., Falter, K. H., Selanikio, J. D., Flanders, W. D., Howe, H. L., and Wilhelm, J. L., 1996, Heat-related deaths during the July 1995 heat wave in Chicago, *N. Engl. J. Med.* **335:**84–90.

Sharp, T. W., Brennen, R. J., Keim, M., and Ryan, T., 1998, Medical preparedness for a terrorist incident involving chemical or biological agents during the 1996 Atlanta Olympic Games, *Ann. Emerg. Med.* **32:**214–223.

Schwartz, J., 2000, Harvesting and long term exposure effects in the relation between air pollution and mortality, *Am. J. Epidemiol.* **151:**440–448.

Thomas, J. A., 1993, Toxic response of the reproductive system, in *Casarett and Doull's Toxicology* (C. D. Klassen, ed.), pp. 547–580, McGraw Hill, New York.

Thomas, P. T., Busse, W. W., and Kerkvliet, N. I., 1990, Immunologic effects of pesticides, in *The Effects of Pesticides on Humans*, Vol. 18 (S. R. Baker and C. F. Wilkinson, eds.), pp. 261–295, Princeton Scientific Publishers, New York.

Tolbert, P. E., Mulholland, J. A., MacIntosh, D. L., and Ross, E., 2000, Air quality and pediatric emergency room visits for asthma in Atlanta, Georgia, *Am. J. Epidemiol.* **151:**798–810.

US Department of Health and Human Services, 1999a, *Mental Health: A Report of the Surgeon General*, US Department of Health and Human Services, Washington, DC.

US Department of Health and Human Services, 1999b, *Emerg. Infect. Dis.* **4:**491–534.

US Department of Health and Human Services, 2000, *Healthy People 2010, Conference Edition*, USGPO, Washington, DC.

US Environmental Protection Agency, 1992, *Respiratory Health Effects of Passive Smoking: Lung Cancer and Other Disorders*, Report No. EPA/600/006F, USEPA, Washington, DC.

US Environmental Protection Agency, 1996, *The Ecosystems Approach: Healthy Ecosystems and Sustainable Economies*, Interagency Ecosystems Task Force, Washington, DC.

Walker, B., Jr., 2000, Neurobehavioral toxicity, *J. Nat. Med. Assoc.* **92:**116–124.

Weeks, J. L., Levy, B. S., and Wagner, G. R., 1991, *Preventing Occupational Disease and Injury*, American Public Health Association, Washington, DC.

Weiss, B., and Elsner, J., 1996. The intersection of risk assessment and neurobehavioral toxicity, *Environ. Health Perspect. (Suppl.)* **104:**173–418.

Spanning Topics

12

Epidemiology and the Public Policy Process

Iris R. Shannon

Based on long established societal trends, the globalization of systems, including health, will accelerate into the 21st century driven by the increasing interdependence of world economic, environmental, political, health, and other interests. In Zwingle's (1999) view, globalization and its consequences are realities and not choices. The world is engulfed by an escalating technical revolution fueled by computers, the internet, telephones, cellular phones, cable television, and affordable jet travel. Dynamic and often factious debates frame multiple issues at international and national levels. A recent example was reported by Kluger (1999) regarding a "food fight" between the United States and reluctant European countries fearful of consuming genetically engineered crops. This issue has support within the United States among some concerned consumer groups and members of Congress. American television and other media sources provide opportunity for the public to be informed about and responsive to a diversity of policy issues in a timely fashion. Indeed, cyberspace is serving as a facilitating force providing the public access to scientific and lay opinions about policy issues.

Within this challenging context of domestic and international policy concerns, American governmental public health at the national, state, and local levels has responsibility for assessing population needs, providing assurance for the protection and promotion of health and for developing health policies. The core functions are population based, grounded in science as evidenced by epidemiological and other data, and based in social justice. To serve the public good, public health policymakers are expected to formulate their decisions using current knowledge and evidence. For these reasons, public health was chosen as the contextual framework for illustrating the interrelationship between epidemiology and the public policy process.

This chapter includes definitions and descriptions of terms and concepts associated with the policy process. Examples are included that explore and demonstrate the influence of epidemiology on public health policy. Opportunities to apply epidemiologic concepts to the policy process are provided in selected case studies at the end of the chapter.

Iris R. Shannon   Department of Health Systems Management, Rush University, Chicago, Illinois 60612.

Epidemiology and the Delivery of Health Care Services: Methods and Applications, Second Edition, edited by Denise M. Oleske. Kluwer Academic / Plenum Publishers, New York, 2001.

A Contextual Framework for the Relationship between Public Policy and Epidemiology: Public Health

Public Health

Definitions and parameters of public health used in this chapter are based on the Institute of Medicine/National Academy of Sciences' benchmark report, *The Future of Public Health* (1988). The Institute of Medicine (IOM) report defines the "mission" of public health as fulfilling society's interest in assuring conditions in which people can be healthy with contributions toward this end made by governmental and nongovernmental agencies. Three core functions of governmental public health were identified: (1) assessment of the health needs of populations including the systematic collection, analysis, and distribution of morbidity, mortality, and disability information; (2) assurance that services to promote and protect the health of the public are provided directly or through others; and (3) development of policy for the protection of health grounded in scientific knowledge and that serves the public interest. In its mission, public health focuses on organized community effort aimed at the prevention of disease and promotion of health through the cooperative efforts of governmental, private and voluntary agencies. Afifi and Breslow (1994) described the diagnostic tools of public health as epidemiology and biostatistics and the treatment tools of public health as health behaviors and environmental and personal health services. Wallack (1997) posited that public health is about economics, politics, communities, science and social change and how these elements "collide."

Since the publication of the core functions by the IOM in 1988, the functions have been examined, discussed, and analyzed by multiple governmental, nongovernmental, academicians, and other interested persons. A government-sponsored exploration was completed by a workgroup of the US Public Health Service's Core Public Health Functions Steering Committee (1999). In 1994, the steering committee published a list of ten essential public health services (Table 12.1) developed to increase the clarity and importance of governmental public health to the public and to policymakers. Another response to the IOM report is an ongoing 3-year public health initiative funded in 1997 by the Robert Wood Johnson and Kellogg Foundations titled "Turning Point: Collaborating for a New Century in Public Health." The Turning Point initiative was described by Berkowitz and Lafronza (1998) as a highly interactive and inclusive process with the aim of strengthening state and local public health efforts. The American Public Health Association (1998) reported that 14 states and 41 communities were funded for Turning Point projects.

Table 12.1. The Ten Essential Public Health Services[a]

1. Monitor health status to identify community problems
2. Diagnose and investigate health problems and health hazards in the community
3. Inform, educate, and empower people about health issues
4. Mobilize community partnerships and action to identify and solve health problems
5. Develop policies and plans that support individual and community health efforts
6. Enforce laws and regulations that protect health and ensure safety
7. Link people to needed personal health services and assure the provision of health care when otherwise unavailable
8. Assure a competent public health and personal health care workforce
9. Evaluate effectiveness, accessibility, and quality of personal and population-based health services
10. Research for new insights and innovative solutions to health problems

[a]From Core Public Health Functions Steering Committee (1999).

One of the core functions of public health is policy development. This population-based activity involves the assessment of needs as expressed by epidemiological and other data. Epidemiology identifies populations at health risk, the causes of health problems, and the development and measurement of interventions for the reduction or elimination of health risks. Therefore, policy development in public health represents an environment in which epidemiological and other data are used for decision making and in which public participation is inherent in the process.

National Health Objectives

For each decade since 1980, public health and public health policy have been guided by national health objectives. Each set of national health objectives has focused on prevention, considered the successes or failures of the previous decade, incorporated new knowledge and technologies, and considered changes in the organization and delivery of public health. Goals and objectives represent broad-based input from governmental and nongovernmental sources including data from national public hearings and electronic responses stimulated by a federal *Healthy People 2010* website (http://www.health.gov/healthypeople). The coming decade will challenge public health and the health care system to respond to the continuing demographic changes reflecting the needs of an older and more racially diverse population and global challenges such as including emerging infectious diseases, food supply issues, and environmental threats. The US Department of Health and Human Services (USDHHS) (1998) suggest that a number of international conditions contribute to the threat of emerging infections: "increases in international travel, importation of food, improper human and veterinary use of antibiotics, and global environmental changes increase the potential for global epidemics of infectious diseases, including emerging and reemerging diseases as well as drug-resistant strains" (pp. 22–24). International cooperation and collaboration are essential because action taken in one of country can affect the health of the world.

To respond to these and other concerns, hundreds of operational objectives are organized around two national overarching goals for the year 2010: (1) increasing the quality and years of healthy life, and (2) *eliminating* health disparities. Figure 12.1 conceptualizes the interactive and interdependent relationships implicit in efforts to achieve the year 2010 goals. An example of how objectives are organized is displayed in Table 12.2. Most objectives are formulated using epidemiological data and other studies, expert opinion, and past experience. Based on the objections of advocacy groups, differential targets for racial and ethnic minorities, people with low income, people with disabilities, women, and people in different age groups were discontinued. The presence of such differential targets was considered unacceptable and incongruent with a national goal of eliminating health disparities in the population by 2010.

Although national health objectives are not law or formal public policy, they are accepted by wide and broad consensus and considered guidelines for public policy at all governmental levels. The objectives provide direction for resource allocation, outcome measurement, and the organization and delivery of public health activity. Understanding the epidemiological underpinnings supporting national health objectives is important in efforts to inform and involve providers and the public.

Public Policy: An Interactive Process

Public policy has many definitions. Anderson's (1994) description includes the following conceptualization of public policy: "A purposive course of action followed by an actor or set

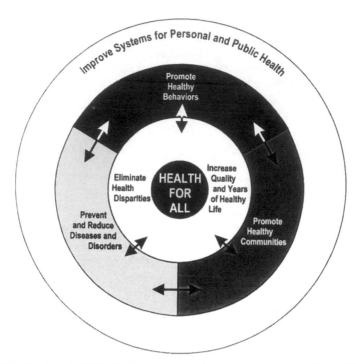

Figure 12.1. Healthy People 2010–Healthy people in healthy communities. From US Department of Health and Human Services (1998).

of actors in dealing with a problem or matter of concern" (p. 5). In Longest's (1994) view, "Public policies are authoritative decisions made in the legislative, executive, or judicial branches of government intended to direct or influence the actions, behaviors, or decisions of others" (p. 3). A commonality among public policy definitions is that public policy represents a response to demands made by an assortment of organizations and individuals. An important characteristic of public policy is that it includes outputs or what must be actually implemented and evaluated.

The **public policy process** venue is highly interactive and includes the elements of: (1) **problem identification** (defining the nature of the health care issue and who is affected); (2) **formulation** (utilizing epidemiological data and studies, expert discussions, anecdotes, public opinions, and published viewpoints); (3) **implementation** (the change directed or prescribed by rules and regulations, or allocation of resources that follows a policy mandate); and (4) **evaluation** assessing the outcomes, including both costs and progress in anticipated goals).

The policy process is congruent with the nation's political belief system, and therefore provides opportunity for public participation in the process. When the policy process is interactive and open, input from the public and epidemiological data may be used in any of the elements. However, when the policy process is closed or perceived closed, policy outcomes are more likely to reflect the values and preferences of an official elite. In the policy process, limiting public input also may limit public support and funding. Increased knowledge, trust of government, coalitional actions, belief systems, and economic and other factors influence the public's willingness to support policy actions. The political process surrounding policymaking

Table 12.2. US National Objectives Pertaining
to Diseases Preventable through Universal Vaccination[a]

Objective #14-1: Reduce or eliminate indigenous cases of vaccine-
preventable disease (VPD).

Disease	1998 baseline	2010 target
	Number of cases	
Congenital rubella syndrome	7	0
Diphtheria (people < 35 years)	1	0
Haemophilus influenzae type b[b]	253	0
Hepatitis B (people < 25 years)	945[c]	9
Measles	74	0
Mumps	666	0
Pertussis (children < 7)	3417	2000
Polio (wild-type virus)	0	0
Rubella	364	0
Tetanus (among people < 35)	14	0
Varicella (chicken pox)	4 million[d]	400,000

[a]From US Department of Health and Human Services (2000). Data
sources: National Notifiable Disease Surveillance System (NNDSS),
CDC, EPO; National Congenital Syndrome Registry (NCRSR), CDC,
NIP—congenital rubella syndrome; National Health Interview Survey
(NHIS), CDC, NCHS   varicella. Source: U.S. Department of Health and
Human Services (2000).
[b]Includes cases with type b and unknown serotype.
[c]Estimated hepatitis B cases for 1997.
[d]Based on average from 1990–1994.

is described by Anderson (1994) as "involving conflict and struggle among people (public
officials and private citizens) with conflicting interests, values, and desires on policy issues"
(p. 23).

Changes in the health system are dependent on the interaction of politics and policies, and
currently such changes lack clarity, consistency and direction. Commenting on the complexities of the policy process, Etzioni (1991) indicated the necessity for balancing economic
power, usually representing a few, with the political power, usually representing many. He also
warned that when policy analysis fails to consider the moral implications and only considers
efficiency, the outcome suffers. This admonition holds even with the increasing shift of health
policymaking to the states (Hackey, 1998). Outcomes among states may differ and depend on
factors such as regional ideology, party control, interest groups, administrative capacity, and
court decisions. However, the expectation is constant that at all levels of government health
policies should be based on science and demonstrate positive differences in the population's
health.

The Interrelationship between Epidemiology and Public Policy

Considering the numerous determinants of health, including **social, biological, environmental, behavioral** and **psychological**, the use of narrowly constructed health status measures may be problematic in policy development, planning and evaluation.

In Terris' (1985) discussion of the value of epidemiology in the policy process severe observations were made:

> Epidemiology, the study of the health of human populations, is by definition a social science. Its theory and practice have been profoundly influenced by society—by economic, social and political developments. Conversely, epidemiology has become a powerful force in the evolution and transformation of human populations and their social organization. (p. 5)

Terris posited that the powerful impact epidemiology has had on the improvement of health status in population groups resulted from applying epidemiological tools to understanding effects of social, environmental, and occupational conditions. Epidemiology has provided data to prevent many causes of illness, disability, and death. Epidemiological data and methods are used in the policy process to:

1. Identification of the nature of the health care issue, who is affected, and its relative priority.
2. Assist in planning and improving health services.
3. Monitor policy effectiveness in terms of changes in the rates of occurrence of new problems and in the rates of mortality.
4. Identify risk factors that affect the health and well-being of populations, particularly of vulnerable populations.
5. Aid in choosing among alternative policies and the allocation of resources.

The relationship between epidemiology and public policy is interactive and difficult to demonstrate schematically because of the extensive and complex nature of the policy process.

Supporting Terris' view of epidemiology's profound impact on society, the Centers for Disease Control and Prevention (CDC) announced in April 1999 that during the 20th century, life expectancy of Americans had lengthened by greater than 30 years and credited 25 years of this gain to advances in public health (Centers for Disease Control and Prevention, 1999). Accomplishments were selected on the basis of opportunity for prevention and their impact on death, illness, and disability. The list was not ranked in the order of importance and included vaccination, motor vehicle safety, safer workplaces, control of infectious diseases, decline in deaths from coronary heart disease and stroke, safer and healthier foods, healthier mothers and babies, family planning, and fluoridation of drinking water. Epidemiological data identified and supported the many public policies associated with the accomplishments made during the 20th century.

Application of Epidemiology in the Policy Process

Below are specific examples of how epidemiology and the public policy process interrelate for the promotion of health.

US Department of Health and Human Services Initiative to Eliminate Disparities in Health

Based on epidemiological evidence that race and ethnicity correlate with persistent health disparities, President Clinton announced on February 21, 1998, an Initiative to Eliminate

Racial and Ethnic Disparities in Health. The USDHHS is the lead agency for assessing, planning, implementing, and evaluating the initiative's activities and outcomes.

Problem Identification

The USDHHS (1999) selected six focus areas   representing serious health disparities among racial and ethnic minorities existing at all life stages: (1) infant morality, (2) cancer screening and management, (3) cardiovascular disease, (4) diabetes, (5) HIV/AIDS, and (6) childhood and adult immunization. Table 12.3 provides examples of disparities in these areas.

Assist in Planning and Evaluation

Although the initiative (US Department of Health and Human Services, 1999) is separate from the national health goal to eliminate health disparities by 2010, the initiative will parallel the focus of the 2010 objectives associated with this goal for the measurement of outcomes. During the progress reviews of *Healthy People 2000* held in 1997, 93 objectives were identified that represented a wide range of health problems where disparity between the general population and at least one other population group was 25% or greater (US Department of Health and Human Services, 1998) (Table 12.3). The following are the six groups used to categorize the 93 *Healthy People 2000* objectives and the number of those objectives placed in each group: (1) race and ethnicity, 54; (2) socioeconomic status, 12; (3) disability, 2; (4) gender, 5; (5) age, 14; and (6) geographic location, 2. Epidemiological evidence supports the attainment of significant national health gains as well as the uneven distribution of these gains among all population groups.

Identify Risk Factors

To eliminate health disparities by the year 2010, epidemiologists and other scientists are challenged to develop new knowledge about the determinants of disease in order to develop effective prevention and treatment interventions. The national health objectives for 2010 require new knowledge to establish a "better understanding of the relationships between health status and income, education, race and ethnicity, cultural influences, environment, and access to quality medical services" (US Department of Health and Human Services, 1998, Goal 19).

Monitor Policy Effectiveness

Measurement of program effectiveness and progress toward elimination of disparities in the six selected areas will involve epidemiological and other studies. If consistent with past national health objectives procedures, a midcourse review will be completed to determine need for adjustments or modifications of the objectives.

Aid in Allocating Resources

Where disparities are observed, health care managers and providers are challenged to find ways of translating and providing innovative and effective care to these populations. Allocation strategies, establishing need and programs, should be driven by epidemiological data.

Table 12.3. Healthy People 2000 Objectives Representing Disparities of ⩾25% between the General Population and Other Populations by Race/Ethnicity, Socioeconomic Status, Disability, Gender, and/or Geographic Location[a,b]

Race/ethnicity
  Coronary heart disease deaths (1.1)
  Sedentary lifestyle (1.5)
  Cancer deaths (2.2)
  Overweight (2.3)
  Growth retardation among low-income children (2.4)
  Colorectal cancer deaths (2.23)
  Prevalence of diabetes (2.25)
  Cigarette smoking (3.4)
  Smokeless tobacco use (3.9)
  Stroke deaths (3.18)
  Alcohol-related motor vehicle deaths (4.1)
  Cirrhosis deaths (4.2)
  Drug-related deaths (4.3)
  Teen pregnancies (5.1)
  Planned pregnancies (5.2)
  Infertility (5.3)
  Suicides (6.1)
  Homicide (7.1)
  Firearm-related deaths (7.3)
  High school completion rates (8.2)
  Unintentional injury deaths (9.1)
  Motor-vehicle crash deaths (9.3)
  Drowning deaths (9.5)
  Residential fire deaths (9.6)
  Asthma hospitalizations (11.1)
  Dental caries (13.1)
  Diagnosis/treatment of dental caries (13.2)
  Gingivitis (13.5)
  Oral cancer deaths (13.7)
  Regular dental visits (13.14)
  Infant deaths (14.1)
  Fetal deaths (14.2)
  Maternal mortality (14.3)
  Fetal alcohol syndrome (14.4)
  Severe complications of pregnancy (14.7)
  Low birth weigth incidence (14.5)
  Breast-feeding in the first 6 months (14.9)
  Prenatal care in the first trimester (14.11)
  End-stage renal disease (14.11)
  Female breast cancer deaths (16.3)
  Cervical cancer deaths (16.4)
  Diabetes deathss (17.9)
  HIV infection incidence (18.1)
  Adolescent sexual intercourse (18.3)
  Gonorrhea infection incidence (19.1)
  Primary and secondary syphilis (19.3)
  Congenital syphilis (19.4)

Race/ethnicity (*cont.*)
  Hospitalizations for pelvic inflammatory disease (19.6)
  Viral hepatitis cases (20.3)
  Tuberculosis cases (20.4)
  Influenza vaccine in last 12 months >65 (21.2)
  Pneumococcal vaccine in lifetime >65 (21.2)
  Tetanus booster in last 10 yrs (21.2)
  Preventive services receipt (21.4)

Socioeconomic status (income, education, and employment related)
  Vigorous physical activity (1.4)
  Sedentary lifestyle (1.5)
  Cigarette smoking (3.4)
  Smoking initiation by children and adolescents (3.5)
  Smoking cessation during pregnancy (3.7)
  Work-related injury deaths (10.1)
  Nonfatal work-related injuries (10.2)
  Cumulative trauma disorders (10.4)
  Diagnosis/treatment of dental caries (13.2)
  Complete tooth loss for 65 yrs or older (13.4)
  Breast cancer screening (16.11)
  Limitation of major activity (17.2)

Disability
  Sedentary lifestyle (1.5)
  Overweight (2.3)

Gender
  Smokeless tobacco use (3.9)
  Suicides (6.1)
  Diagnosis/treatment of depression (6.15)
  Homicide (7.1)
  Unintentional injury deaths (9.1)
  Drowning deaths (9.5)
  Hip fractures among adults 65 yrs and older (9.7)
  Nonfatal poisoning (9.8)
  Asthma hospitalizations (11.1)
  Cervical cancer screening (16.12)
  Gonorrhea infection incidence (19.1)
  Hospitalization for pelvic inflammatory disease (19.6)
  Tetanus booster in last 10 yrs (21.2)

Geographic location
  Regular dental visits (13.4)
  Preventive services receipt (21.4)

---

[a]From US Department of Health and Human Services (1998).
[b]Numbers in parentheses indicate the number for this objective in *Healthy People 2000: National Health Promotion and Disease Prevention Objectives.*

Infant Mortality

Although infant mortality has been consistently declining since it was first recorded in 1915 (99.9 per 1000 live births), the rate among African-American infants in 1995 was 2.4 times that of white infants and over the years and this disparity has remained largely unchanged.

Assist in Planning

Past national health objectives have set lower target levels for "special populations" experiencing excess morbidity and mortality as an incremental approach to reaching targets set for the general population. For the year 2000, the target set for the reduction of infant mortality was 7 per 1000 live births. Different targets were set for special populations as shown in Table 12.4. Targets for the 2010 objectives were set differently. For these objectives, targets were set at better than best, allowing for improvement in all groups. Hence, single targets for 2010 are given that apply to all populations consistent with the overarching goal of eliminating health disparities. For example, using the 1995 baseline of 7.6 per 1000 live births, the 2010 single target for infant mortality reduction is 5 per 1000 live births. The 1998 infant mortality rates reported by the CDC (2001) indicate significant differences continue between black and all other infants. Black infants had the highest infant mortality rate (13.8 per 1000 live births) and Japanese infants had the lowest (3.5 per 1000 live births). Successful planning and interventions to eliminate disparities in infant mortality by 2010 are contingent on the continued monitoring of infant mortality and its correlates by the CDC and other interested groups. Multidimensional interventions are needed to achieve positive modification of behavior and lifestyles that affect birth outcomes (smoking, substance abuse, poor nutrition, and stress) and access to adequate prenatal care, appropriate management of medical and social problems, and adequate parenting and child-care support.

Monitor Policy Effectiveness

Nationally, infant morality has declined steadily over the past several decades and based on 1997 data was at a record low of 7.2 per 1000 live births. According to the CDC/NCHS (1997), the infant mortality rate was 13.7 per 1000 live births for black infants and 6.0 per 1000 live births for white infants. This disparity indicates that infant mortality for black infants is

Table 12.4. Health Status Objectives from Healthy People 2000 for Infant Mortality Reduction[a]

Objective No. 14.1. Reduce the infant mortality rate to no more than 7 per 1,000 live births (baseline 10.1 per 1,000 live births in 1987)

	Infant mortality per 1,000 live births	1987 baseline	2000 target
14.1a.	Blacks	17.9	11
14.1b.	American Indians/Alaska Natives	12.5[b]	8.5
14.1c.	Puerto Ricans	12.9[b]	8

[a]From US Department of Health and Human Services (1990).
[b]1984 baseline.
NOTE: "Infant mortality rates are usually calculated by dividing the number of infant deaths in a given year (obtained from death certificates) by the number of live births in the same year (obtained from birth certificates). Race-specific infant mortality rates calculated in this way are valid only when the coding of race on both birth and death certificates is comparable" (p. 367).

more than twice that for white infants (Centers for Disease Control and Prevention/National Center for Health Statistics, 1997).

Identify Risk Factors

Schwartz and Carpenter (1999) specifically challenged researchers exploring the black and white differences in infant mortality to consider the question "What are the causes of the rate difference between blacks and whites" rather than a question that limits research to risk factors for pregnant black women. The authors concluded the following:

> When the question … is about risk differences between groups or time periods, the answer requires examination of multiple groups or multiple time periods; otherwise, a type III error can results … risk differences between individuals within a particular population may not have the same causes as differences in the average risk between 2 different populations. (p. 1179)

The authors proposed that interventions based on individual level risk factors may not change the size of the disparity between black and white infant mortality differences.

Vaccine-Preventable Diseases

As McKenzie *et al.* (1999) posit, each country has a national health agency. The primary governmental health agency in the United States is the USDHHS, which has cabinet status in the executive branch of the government. Within the USDHHS, the CDC is one of eight agencies constituting the Public Health Service. One of the offices within the CDC is the Epidemiology Program Office. The CDC's responsibility is the protection of public health through leadership and direction in preventing and controlling disease and other preventable conditions and responding to public health emergencies. Included in the CDC's functions are the analysis of disease trends and the publication of epidemiological reports on conditions of all types and causes. Other responsibilities of the CDC are the support of state and local health departments and working with the international public health agencies of other member nations of the World Health Organization (WHO).

Problem Identification

President Clinton signed the Vaccines for Children Act in 1993 targeting barriers to childhood immunizations particularly among black and Hispanic populations. The act was based on epidemiological data indicating a need to increase immunization levels among preschool children, because only 55.3% of the 2-year-old children were fully immunized. To facilitate immunizations, funding was included for extended clinic hours, increased provider and public education, community outreach, and a national tracking system for immunizations. Also, the act provided funding for purchase of vaccines to be administered in private and public settings. A study of immunization coverage by Shaheen *et al.* (2000) among predominantly Hispanic children aged 2–3 years in Central Los Angeles indicated the problem was completion of the recommended vaccinations series in a timely manner by age 2 years. Only 64.4% of the children in the study had completed the recommended series [4:3:1:3:3—four DTP/DTaP/DT, three polio, one MMR, three *Haemophilus influenzae type b* (Hib) and three Hep B].

Vaccination recommendations are determined by an Immunization Practices Advisory

Committee (ACIP) to the US Public Health Service/CDC. Voting representatives on the committee are from the American Academy of Pediatrics, American Academy of Family Physicians, American Medical Association, and American College of Physicians in addition to representatives from state health departments. Attending Committee meetings without vote, are representatives from the federal governmental agencies. Quarterly meetings of the Advisory Committee are held at the CDC offices in Atlanta, Georgia, and are open to the public. These groups can make only recommendations about immunization but cannot create public policy.

Assist in Planning

Chen and Orenstein (1996), who posit that epidemiological studies and principles, experimental and observational, play critical roles in successful immunization programs, state:

> Prior to licensure, a vaccine must demonstrate its safety and efficacy in phased clinical trials. Post-licensure, continued close monitoring of the vaccine's safety and effectiveness is needed, especially early on. But equally important to the vaccine's ultimate success is the close monitoring of the immunization program itself. (p. 99)

The authors also claim that since the introduction of routine immunizations, the incidence of several vaccine-preventable diseases has markedly decreased in the United States as well as in other areas of the world. An extensive list of vaccine-preventable diseases is found in Table 12.5. The ultimate goal of immunization is disease eradication. In his discussion of disease eradication, Hinman (1999) considered the eradication of a disease as a global term and the ultimate level of sustainability and social justice. When a disease has been eradicated, its elimination must be supported by documentation that the disease has a "zero" worldwide incidence and that immunization efforts for prevention are no longer necessary. To date, smallpox is the only disease to be so distinguished. The concept of eradication raises significant issues related to the global distribution of resources and programs needed to achieve this

**Table 12.5. World Health Organization List
of Vaccine-Preventable Diseases**

Acute respiratory virus	Pertussis
Cholera	Poliomyelitis
Diphtheria	Rotavirus
Dengue	Pneumococcal disease
Haemophilus influenzae type B	Shigella
Hepatitis B	Tetanus
Japanese encephalitis	Tuberculosis
Measles	Typhoid fever
Meningococcal Disease	Varicella (chickenpox)
Mumps	Vitamin A deficiency[a]
Neonatal tetanus	Yellow fever

[a]Vitamin A can be given during routine vaccination as a means of preventing corneal blindness in the over 75 countries where vitamin A deficiency is a public health problem.
SOURCE: World Health Organization (2001).

state. Poliomyelitis and measles are diseases with epidemiological evidence supporting that they have the potential for eradication.

Identify Risk Factors

The National Immunization Survey began in 1994 and consists of two parts: (1) a household telephone survey of immunization status age 19 to 35 months of age and requests parental permission for contacting the children's providers; and (2) a survey of vaccination providers. Because the survey asked about parents' experiences with health care providers, information about barriers to vaccinations can be obtained and used in programs aimed at decreasing vaccine-preventable diseases.

Choosing among Alternative Policies and the Allocation of Resources

The concept of eradication raises significant issues related to the global distribution of resources and programs needed to achieve this state. Poliomyelitis and measles are diseases with epidemiologic evidence supporting that they have the potential for eradication. The WHO (2000a) describes the global imitative to eradicate poliomyelitis by the end of the year 2000 the largest international disease control effort ever undertaken. The initiative began in 1988 as the result of a resolution adopted by the World Health Assembly, a delegate assembly of member nations responsible for the WHO policy. Since its adoption, polio cases have decreased from more than 350,000 to just over 5000 cases in 1999. However, the WHO also acknowledges that the "disappearing disease" polio creates another challenge: sustaining the necessary national and international commitment for polio vaccination until 2005, the date for certifying the eradication of polio. Olivé and Aylward (1999) report since 1990 when the target of 80% global coverage for polio was achieved, donor support for immunization services in developing countries has declined. The failure to eradicate polio is due mainly to insufficient resources.

Childhood Hepatitis B Infections and Hepatitis B Vaccine Use

Hepatitis B virus (HBV) disease is another candidate for eradication. More detail is provided in this example in order to understand some of the factors influencing national and international policies associated with hepatitis B vaccine (Hep B) requirements. Special emphasis in this example has been given to children.

Problem Identification

Hepatitis B is a global problem with high prevalence rates of carriers in many countries, as shown in Fig. 12.2. Hinman (1999) estimated that more than 2 billion persons are infected worldwide and 350 million persons are chronic carriers of the disease. According to the WHO (1998), most people in the developing world become infected with HBV during childhood and 8–15% of the general population become carriers.

The World Health Advisory Group on Immunization recommended that by 1997 all countries should include Hep B in their routine immunization programs; in 1998, the WHO reported that 100 countries have included the vaccine in their routine immunization programs. The increasing ease of worldwide travel and the numbers of children involved in international adoptions add to the problems associated with the spread of HBV disease.

According to the Third National Health and Nutrition Examination Survey in 1996, from

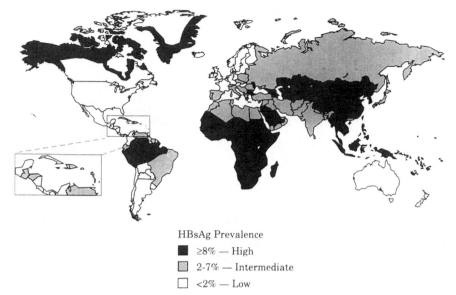

HBsAg Prevalence

■ ≥8% — High

▨ 2-7% — Intermediate

☐ <2% — Low

Figure 12.2.   Geographic distribution of hepatitis B prevalence: (■) ≥ 8%: all of Africa, Southeast Asia including China, Korea, Indonesia, and the Middle East except Israel; South and Western Pacific Islands, interior Amazon Basin, and certain parts of the Caribbean, i.e., Haiti and the Dominican Republic; (▨) 2–7%: South Central and Southwest Asia, Israel, Japan, Eastern and Southern Europe and Russia, and most of Middle and South America; (☐) < 2%: Northern and Western Europe, North America, Australia, and New Zealand. From Centers for Disease Control (1997).

data reported by state health departments, about 250,000 to 300,000 infections of HBV occurred annually in the United States over the past 20 years (US Department of Health and Human Services, 1998, pp. 22–13). It is estimated that at sometime in their lives, 1 in 20 Americans (12.5 million) has been infected with HBV and 1 in every 200 persons (1.25 million) has a chronic infection and is at risk for complications.

Assist in Planning

The US national health objectives related to HBV disease for 2010 in the proposed in *Healthy People 2010* (US Department of Health and Human Services, 1998), include the following:

- Reduce to no more than 400 chronic HBV infections in infants and young children (perinatal infections). (Baseline: 1682 chronic infections in 1995).
- Reduce to zero cases per 100,000 HBV rates in persons less than 25 years of age (except perinatal infections).
- Reduce by 75% HBV cases per 100,000 among adults more than 25 years of age.
- Reduce by 75% HBV cases in high-risk groups.

Monitor Outcomes in Terms of Rates of Occurrence and Rates of Mortality

The value of any vaccine in reducing the target disease must also be judged in terms of any adverse morbidity or mortality. The WHO (1998) reported that since 1982 when the vaccine became available, hundred of millions of persons have received the Hep B and the safety and effectiveness record of the vaccine has been outstanding. They further observed that studies have shown that the vaccine is 95% effective in preventing children or adults from developing the chronic carrier state. When Hep B vaccinations were given in countries where 8–15% of the children become chronic carriers, the carrier rate dramatically reduced to less than 1%.

Mast (1997) reported that in hepatitis B clinical trials involving 200,000 persons, about 30% of the adults and less than 10% of the children had sore arms or local swelling following the injection, and 10–15% had muscle aches, headaches, and a low-grade fever of less than 24 hours. No serious adverse events were reported.

Mast further explored evidence from the CDC that the proportion of children aged 19 to 35 months who received the recommended three doses of Hep B increased from less than 10% in 1991 when infant vaccination was first recommended to 82% in 1996. In the same time period, rates of acute HBV in children 7–10 years of age declined by 27% and in children 3–6 years of age by 62%. As of December 1997, 26% of the states had laws requiring adolescents to be vaccinated for school attendance, 29 states had laws requiring Hep B vaccination before entry into kindergarten, and 13 states required the vaccination before entry into ninth grade.

Yusuf *et al.* (1999) completed a study assessing the progress of childhood Hep B vaccinations from 1994 to 1997 using data from the National Immunization Survey (NIS) involving 32,433 households. The researchers found that 96% of the children aged 19–35 months had received one dose of Hep B vaccine and 84% had completed the three-dose schedule. The coverage with three doses increased from 41% in 1994 to 83.8% in 1996 among children 19–35 months. However, the same coverage in 1996 (83.8%) only increased to 84.6%. The slow rate of target population coverage with three doses of Hep B vaccine was described by the authors as a residual resistance to universal Hep B vaccination by some providers. Reasons given for the resistance to infant Hep B vaccine included beliefs that their patients were at low risk for HBV infection, understanding that the vaccine does not give long-term protection, parental resistance, the need for multiple injections in one visit, and limited funding at state and local levels for the Hep B vaccination program. The authors identified the need for continuing provider and parental education about the vaccination of all infants.

Identify Risk Factors

Mast (1997) posited that risks associated with HBV disease are age related. From 80 to 100% of the infants infected at birth with HBV develop chronic infections. By the age 5 years, the risk of children developing a chronic infection is similar to adults: 2–10%. Although 85% of the HBV infections occur in adults, 40% of all chronic infections were acquired during infancy, early childhood, or adolescence. HBV infections cause about the same number of long-term sequela and deaths as all other vaccine-preventable diseases combined and fewer acute clinical cases of disease than other preventable diseases. However, serious adverse events were not detected by these trials when events occurred at a frequency of less than 1 out of 200,000. A variety of rare adverse events associated with HBV have been investigated. The Vaccine Safety Committee of the Institute of Medicine, National Academy of Science (Institute of Medicine, 1994) conducted a scientific review of possible adverse consequences including those associated with the Hep B vaccine. With an examination of the epidemiological evidence consisting of observational studies, controlled clinical trials, and case studies, the committee found insufficient evidence to accept or reject a causal relationship between Hep B

Table 12.6. Institute of Medicine's Summary of the Evidence
for or against Determination of a Causal Relation—Hepatitis B Vaccine[a]

Vaccine and adverse event	Biological plausibility	Results of case reports, case studies, and uncontrolled observational studies	Results of controlled observational studies and controlled clinical trials
Hepatitis B vaccine			
Guillain–Barré syndrome	Demonstrated[b]	Indeterminate[c]	No data
Demyelinating diseases of the central nervous system	Demonstrated[b]	Indeterminate[c]	No data
Arthritis	Demonstrated[b]	Indeterminate[c]	No data
Anaphylaxis	Theoretical only	In support of causal relation	No data
Death from SIDS	Theoretical only	Indeterminate[c]	No data

[a]From Institute of Medicine (1994).
[b]Known effects of natural disease results, animal experiments, and *in vitro* studies.
[c]Data available were not for or against a causal relation.

vaccine and adverse rare diseases such as Guillain–Barré, demyelinating diseases of the central nervous system, arthritis, and sudden infant death syndrome (see Table 12.6).

Questions about vaccination safety have continuously emerged from concerned citizens. In response to these concerns, Congress passed the National Childhood Vaccine Injury Act in 1986 and the Vaccine Compensation Amendments in 1987. Litigation and the fear of litigation generated by safety concerns created economic pressures on manufacturers resulting in companies terminating vaccine production and restriction of new vaccine research and pro gram development activities. The National Vaccine Injury Compensation program created a no-fault condition that alleviated manufacturer's liability and insured the continuation of vaccine production.

Mandatory reporting of specific adverse events [Vaccine Adverse Event Report System (VAERS)] following childhood immunizations was stipulated in the legislation. Additionally, the CDC was designated to develop better information approaches in the communication of potential risks associated with vaccinations, and the US Food and Drug Administration (FDA) was designated to make changes in the vaccine package inserts to enhance their utility. Under the act, the database for VAERS is managed by the CDC and FDA. Adverse event forms are widely available and anyone can file a report, but health care providers are obligated to report specific adverse events for the vaccinations covered in the act. The Institute of Medicine, National Academy of Sciences was designated to study adverse effects of vaccines for pertussis and rubella and other vaccines commonly administered during childhood. Referring to VAERS, the Institute of Medicine (1994) indicated that this open system could result in inaccurate or poorly documented data or duplicate reports. They also observed that the data generated was more useful in monitoring adverse events and less useful for scientific analysis and determining causality. Underreporting was cited as another problem in the VAERS system.

Aid in the Choosing among Alternative Policies and Allocation of Resources

The primary policy issues in Hep B administration involve the strategies for distribution of the vaccine and recommendations regarding its use, both of which are guided by epidemiological data, but still must consider input from the public. The Hep B vaccine is administered by both public or private providers and has several advantages: it prevents the transmission of the disease between individuals, it prevents the transmission from mother to infant, and it decreases the incidence of liver cancer. Whereas childhood immunizations are affordable and accessible in the United States, in the developing world, accessibility and affordability are problematic and are assisted by the supplemental efforts of UNICEF, the WHO, the World Bank, and others. In 1998, The Bill and Melinda Gates Children's Vaccine Program reported that it contributed $100 million to increase access to immunizations in poor and developing countries (Children's Vaccine Program, 1998).

Current Hep B vaccine recommendations in the United States represent a strategy to *eliminate* hepatitis B virus transmission. Attaining national health objectives for Hep B involves: (1) the prevention of prenatal HBV by screening all pregnant women for hepatitis B surface antigen (HBAg), and (2) ensuring that all infants born to positive mothers receive the vaccine within 12 hours of birth in addition to hepatitis B immunoglobulin (and second and third at 1–2 months of age), (3) vaccinating all infants as a part of the routine childhood immunization schedule, (4) providing catchup vaccination programs for all unvaccinated children at age 11–12 years and children in populations with high rates of HBV infection and adolescents, and (5) vaccinating adults with risk factors for HBV.

Alternative public policy is being promoted by some parents who have objections to mandatory childhood immunizations. Their objections to Hep B vaccination have been more vocal, organized, and disseminated nationally through use of the Internet and other media. Siegel and Doner's (1998) cited several reasons for parental opposition to mandatory vaccinations: increased distrust of government; antiregulatory sentiment driving legislative activity at national, state, and local levels; lack of commitment to the welfare of others; loss of community principles; and loss of the concept of social justice. Many parental objections are related to concerns about vaccines safety and issues of risk or perceived risk.

The Institute of Medicine (1997), in their summary regarding a workshop on risk communication, suggested that communication must be an interactive process involving exchange of information and opinion among individuals, groups, and institutions to address experiences, beliefs, values, and attitudes of opponents and proponents. Further, the success of vaccine-preventable vaccines to decrease incidence of disease actually increases the difficulty in communicating vaccine-related risk because the reduction of disease is interpreted by some to decrease the need for vaccination protection. Decisions regarding individual immunizations are reportedly influenced by the desire to be like the majority (bandwagoning), by deciding to take advantage of high immunization rates among the majority (herd immunity) and not be vaccinated (free-riding), or by deciding to be vaccinated knowing it will protect others (altruism). Some vaccine opponents do not believe expert probability estimates because they believe themselves capable of controlling their situations in ways the experts may not have anticipated such as self-healing and the use of folk remedies. A predominant philosophical issue among opponents of vaccination focuses on beliefs of individual rights to pervade over societal good.

Proponents argue that in the presence of a compelling public health interest, government does have the right to override individual autonomy. If too many people are not vaccinated for whatever reasons, herd immunity may be threatened and the susceptibility of the community to disease increased. The uncertainty and disagreement about vaccine risks and failure to disclose what is known further erodes trust in government, providers, and manufacturers. There is incompleteness of risk communicated to parents as well as incomplete information given in manufacturers inserts. Concerns about the safety of Hep B vaccine included the use of mercury in its manufacture. The Centers for Disease Control and Prevention (2000a) reported that a Hep B vaccine without thimerosal as a preservative was produced by Merck and released in August 1999. Since March 2000, a Hep B vaccine free of thimerosal has been available to all US children.

States have mandatory vaccination laws that require children to receive certain vaccines as a condition of school attendance. Although all states provide medical exemptions, in 1997, 47 states allowed religious exemptions and 16 states allowed exemptions on philosophical grounds.

For the poorest countries in the world who cannot afford Hep B vaccine, especially Africa, the WHO indicates the challenge is to raise awareness of donor agencies so that the vaccine can be purchased.

Summary

Public policy and epidemiology function in a dynamic environment influenced by political, economic, social, and other factors. As demonstrated by the national health goal to eliminate health disparities among population groups by 2010, it will be important to have policies that demonstrate an understanding of societal determinants of health. Public policies related to vaccine preventable diseases have a long history of dependency on epidemiological data as demonstrated by the public health achievements over the last century. However, as the public becomes more educated, policy aware, and possessive of their investment in policy decisions, consideration must be given to the power and clarity of epidemiological data, their interpretation, and their usability. Mandatory Hep B vaccination for infants and preschool children is an example of a complex array of issues and opinions, strong advocacy from health providers and public health departments for continuing mandatory vaccines, and opposition from some parents who are equally as dedicated to eliminating mandatory Hep B vaccines for all infants and preschool children for a variety of reasons. In addition to antigovernment sentiments associated with health department control (mandatory immunizations), opponents to mandatory vaccination devalue the importance of herd immunity and systematically challenge the science and outcomes of related Hep B vaccine studies, particularly adverse events. As more vaccines are developed and mandated, opportunities for debate and challenges can be expected, particularly by the public. Successful public health policy based on epidemiological data depends on the quality and strength of the evidence, interactions with multiple stakeholders, and the clarity with which this information is communicated to the public.

Case Studies

Case Study No. 1
Chicago Violence Prevention Strategic Plan

Violence is a major concern for many Americans and has priority status on the public policy agenda. It is considered a public health problem requiring public health measures for its prevention and control because of its direct impact on mortality and morbidity rates. More than 200,000 acts of violence were reported to the Chicago Police Department in 1995. Because so many acts of violence are not reported, Chicago Department of Public Health (CDPH) epidemiologists used numerous databases in an attempt to establish the magnitude of the problem. The incidence of violence by demographic, socioeconomic factors, and other factors as well as time trends were identified as necessary first steps in the process of developing, implementing and evaluating strategies for prevention (Chicago Department of Public Health, 1998).

Data sets from national and local sources only reflected crimes reported to the police. Therefore, the data represented underestimates of the crimes in Chicago. For example, a 1994 Bureau of Justice Statistics National Crime Victimization Survey estimated that only 42% of the crimes had been reported to the police. Crimes against children, the elderly, intimate partners, and disabled people may not be reported. Child abuse information is collected by the Illinois Department of Children and Family Service; however, it also underestimates the problem and overrepresents welfare recipients. Based on data collected, the following information briefly describes the issues related to violence in Chicago (see also Table 12.7):

- Incidence of violence: In 1996, 211,517 victims of 83 violent crimes were reported in Chicago representing a rate of 7,598 per 100,000 residents.
- Impact on health: Between 1993 and 1995, the average annual number of deaths due to homicide was 884, representing 3% of all deaths in Chicago.
- Homicide was the leading cause of premature mortality responsible for 32,131 years of life lost representing 14% of the total years of life lost by all deaths.
- Between 1992 and 1995, it was estimated that 42 per 100,000 children aged 18 or younger required hospitalization as the result of firearm injuries.
- An emergency room study indicated that 12% of the women requesting service had been involved with domestic violence.
- The estimated annual cost of violence nationally in 1991 was $325 billion and $1.3 billion in Chicago.

Violence has long-term physical, social, and emotional consequences. At the community level, analyses suggested strong correlation between levels of violence and multiple measures of poverty.

Q.1. Sketch other tables or graphs that could be used to assess violence in this city and aid the Department of Public Health in planning prevention strategies.

Q.2. What are some risk factors for violence identified through epidemiological studies?

Q.3. What are some new policy initiatives would you undertake based on the data given and current epidemiological research on risk factors for violence?

Q.4. How can violence prevention policy initiatives proposed by the CDPH be incorporated into managed care plans?

Table 12.7 Total Crimes in Selected Chicago Populations, 1996[a]

Population subgroup	Total crimes	Rate per 100,000
Children <age 13 years	8,367	1,547
Youth age 13–19 years	33,784	12,241
Intimate partners > age 18 years (females)	38,453	3,525
Elderly age 60 years and over	7,011	1,593

[a]From Chicago Department of Public Health (1998).

Case Study No. 2
Increase Quality and Years of Healthy Life

One of the two national health goals for the year 2010 is to increase the quality as well as the years of healthy life. Babies born in 1995 are expected to live to 75.8 years. Healthy life "means a full range of functional capacity at each life stage from infancy through old age, allowing one the ability to enter into satisfying relationships with others, to work, and to play" (US Department of Health and Human Services, 2000, Goals 3). Rowe and Kahn (1998, p. 38) proposed that successful aging can be achieved by simultaneously maintaining:

- Low risk of disease and disease-related disability.
- High mental and physical function.
- Active engagement with life.

The USDHHS reports that in 1987, 90.5% of the population assessed their health status as good, very good, or excellent, and in 1994, the percentage was 90.4%. In 1988, the percentage of the population reporting they were limited in major activity due to chronic conditions was 18.9% and increased to 21.4% in 1995.

According to *Healthy People 2010*, measures of mortality and life expectancy are important for health surveillance at the state and local levels. Common measures of mortality are death rates, life expectancy, and years of potential life lost before age 75. The specific objectives using these epidemiological measures proposed in Healthy People 2010 include the following:

1. Decrease the total death rate to no more than 454 per 100,000 by 2010 (baseline: 503.9 age-adjusted death rate per 100,000 in 1995).
2. Reduce the death rate for adolescents and young adults (15–24 years) to no more than 81 per 100,000 by 2010 (baseline: 95.3 per 100,000 in 1995).
3. Reduce the death rate for adults (25–64 years) to no more than 358 per 100,000 by 2010 (baseline: 397.3 per 100,000 in 1995).
4. Increase life expectancy to 77.3 years by 2010 (baseline: 75.8 years in 1995).
5. Decrease years of potential life lost before age 75 to no more than 7,315 per 100,000 by 2010 (baseline: 8,128.2 age-adjusted years of potential life lost before age 75 per 100,000 in 1995).

For objectives 1–3 and 5, targets were set for a 10% improvement over 1995 rates. Objective 4 assumes a 10-year increase of 1.5 years.

Q.1. What are risk factors for disability in older adults?

Q.2. What factors influence life expectancy?

Q.3. What public policies should be in place to support the increasing years of life?

Case Study No. 3
Progress in Coverage with Hepatitis B Vaccine among U.S. Children

Data from the National Immunization Survey (NIS) were examined to evaluate progress in immunization coverage for HBV among children aged 19–35 months by Yusuf *et al.* (1999).

Survey data were collected via a random-digit telephone survey. Respondents were asked to provide demographic and vaccination information using written records with vaccination dates for all age-eligible children. Reports from recall were accepted in the absence of written records. Consent to obtain

Table 12.8. Coverage with Three or More Doses of Hepatitis B Vaccine among Children Aged 19–35 Months: National Immunization Survey, 1997

Racial/ethnic group	% completed (95% CI)	P-value
All children	83.7 (83.2, 84.2)	
Non-Hispanic white	84.7 (84.1, 85.3)	Reference group
Non-Hispanic black	82.7 (81.4, 84.0)	<.01
Hispanic	81.2 (79.8, 82.6)	<.01
American Indian/Alaska Native	82.9 (78.6, 87.2)	.90
Asian/Pacific Islander	87.6 (85.2, 90.0)	<.05

[a]From Yusuf et al. (1999).

information from their health care providers' records was also obtained. Surveys from all the four quarters in 1997 were examined. Displayed in Table 12.8 are the coverage estimates by racial group.

Q.1. What groups(s) have a statistically significantly lower immunization coverage despite national recommendations for 100% immunization of children with Hep B vaccine? Propose reasons that could explain the lower likelihood of vaccination.

Q.2. What potential biases could have entered into the computation of the coverage estimates?

Q.3. Search for one website that is a proponent of Hep B vaccination and one website that is an opponent. Compare and contrast the data that are used in support of the arguments for their respective positions.

Case Study No. 4
Measles—United States, 1999

An analysis of 100 confirmed cases of measles reported by state and local health departments in 1999 was reported by the CDC in the June 30, 2000, issue of *Morbidity and Mortality Weekly Report*. This epidemiologic review of measles during 1999 led to the conclusion that the rate of measles remained at less than 0.5 cases per 1,000,000 population (Centers for Disease Control and Prevention, 2000b). Of the 100 cases, 33 were imported and 67 were indigenous. Of the 67 indigenous cases, 33 were import-linked and 34 were unknown-source cases. There has been an increased percentage of imported cases in the United States since 1992 (Fig. 12.3). In 1999, imported measles occurred among 14 international visitors and 19 US residents exposed to the disease while traveling abroad.

Internationally, by WHO regions, ten cases were from Western Pacific region, six each from Eastern Mediterranean, European, and Southeast Asia regions, two from the American region, one from the African region, and the source region of two cases was unknown. Nationally, 31 states and the District of Columbia reported no confirmed cases of measles and 10 states accounted for 86% of the known cases. Thirty-two percent of the cases were over age 20 years, 26% were aged 5 to 19 years, 24% were aged 1–4 years, and 18% were less than 1 year of age.

Based on the evaluation of data indicating that 99% of the counties in the United States reported no measles cases, over 90% of the children aged 19–35 months had a first dose of measles vaccine, 98% measles vaccine coverage among children entering school, and a national serosurvey indicated that 93% of persons over age 6 years have antibody to measles, the CDC has concluded that measles is no longer endemic in the United States.

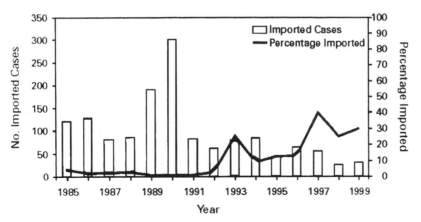

Figure 12.3. Number of imported measles cases and percentage of all measles cases that were imported by year, United States, 1999. From Centers for Disease Control and Prevention (2000b).

Q.1. What circumstances could result in measles becoming endemic again in the United States?

Q.2. Given the global implications of measles as a vaccine-preventable disease, what are the implications for national and international policy?

Case Study No. 5
International Aspects of Gender, Health, and Poverty

Globally, there have been economic gains over the last century. However, the World Health Organization (2000b) concludes that the gap between rich and poor is widening. Also, it has become clearer that poverty affects men and women differently and that a disproportionate share of the burden rests on women affecting their health. A WHO (1997) assessment of the reducing rich–poor health disparities reported that infectious diseases, maternal and perinatal conditions are killing seven times as many people among the world's poorest billion than the among the richest billion. Chronic diseases are responsible for 40% fewer deaths among the poorest billion but cancer kills twice as many and cardiovascular diseases two-thirds as many among the richest billion Dr. Gro Harlem Braundtland, Director-General, the WHO (Braundtland, 2000a), reported that the struggle for progress in the fields of "women's human rights, health and opportunities, now has a century-long history." She asked the question: "Why is the world moving so slowly?"

Poverty is defined differently in time and place. Countries define poverty as a function of their level of development, societal norms, and values. The World Bank Group (2000) measures poverty at the global level. They explain that for the purpose of global "aggregation and comparison," they use the reference lines set at $1 and $2 per day indicating levels of purchasing power parity. The estimate for 1998 (updated every 3 years) was that 1.2 billion people worldwide had consumption levels below $1 a day and 2.8 billion lived on less than $2 a day.

Examples given by the WHO (2000b) of poverty's impact on women's health include the following:

- 70% of the 1.2 billion people living in poverty are female.
- Over a 20-year period, the increase in numbers of rural poor women in 41 developing countries was 17% higher than the increase in rural poor men.

- Among the world's 900 million illiterates, there are twice as many women than men.
- Women are affected twice as much by iron deficiency anemia as men.
- Each year, 500,000 women die from pregnancy-related complications exacerbated by issues of poverty and remoteness.
- On average, women are paid 30–40% less than men for comparable work.
- In developing countries, only a small fraction of women have real economic or political power.

Women have less control over means of production such as cash, credit, and collateral and are disadvantaged in areas such as literacy, education, skills, employment opportunities, mobility, political representation, and extensive role responsibilities.

From analyses of the relationship between health and poverty reported by the WHO (2000b) a few examples are presented:

- In 20 developing countries, under age 5 mortality was found to be the greatest among women with no education and in rural communities.
- Imposition of user fees for basic services such as health care or water supply may particularly disadvantage poor women with limited decision-making power and control of income.
- In some parts of the world, social roles and cultural norms for poor women may inhibit their willingness or ability to seek health care, and in other, perceptions of masculinity keep men away from health services.
- Poverty is a significant factor behind stress and depression in women, with domestic violence a frequent contributing factor.

At the Beijing+5 Conference in June 2000, Dr. Braundtland suggested the following ways to improve women's health:

- Reducing the risk of dying at delivery (over 500, 000 die and 20 million suffer disability). Risks can be reduced with the presence of a skilled health worker during delivery.
- Women should be ensured the right to protect themselves against HIV/AIDS. In 1980, 20% of the adults infected with HIV were women and by the end of the century, 46% of HIV positive adults are women. In some parts of Africa, infection rates of adolescent girls are three to five times higher than in boys the same age.
- Rejecting all forms of violence against women: female genital mutilation, domestic violence, rape, and sexual abuse.
- Women must get the health care and attention they need in accordance with international goals set previously. The WHO analyzed 121 reports on activities on the Beijing Platform for Action. Less than half the reports identified women's health as a national priority.

The WHO (2000b) approach to the addressing the linkages between gender, health, and poverty by the Department of Health in Sustainable Development demonstrates the need for multidimensional integration in planning of gender and poverty issues. The "main principles" of the approach will examine and promote:

- Broad determinants of health affecting the poor rather than restricting the examination to a health services/health systems approach.
- The need for a strong gender and poverty perspective in the health sector reform process, with emphasis on preventive public health.
- The capacity of the roles of men and women to protect or prevent good health for themselves and others.
- A view of health as a capital asset for the poor.
- The contribution to health and sustainable livelihood for the poor of both sexes made by choice, effective participation, and control.
- Using a case study approach to assess existing policies, processes, and institutional mechanisms, contributing to integrated planning in the area of gender, health and poverty, and identifying problem areas.

Data for all efforts to improve the quality of life of poor women will be required. The Director General of the WHO (Braundtland, 2000b) spoke to the issue of criticism regarding the WHO data sources:

> In response to these questions, our position is crystal clear. We know the data are not perfect. But we also know that decision makers cannot wait for the perfect data set—they have to act on the best information they can obtain …

Q.1. Given that 1.2 billion of the 6 billion inhabiting the globe are poor, sick, and disproportionately women, what are the implications for world health?

Q.2. For a variety of reasons including resources and infrastructure, the collection of accurate health data in developing countries may be problematic particularly regarding the rural poor. What proxies or approaches would you use to determine health in women?

References

Afifi, A., and Breslow, L., 1994, The maturing paradigm of public health, *Annu. Rev. Pub. Health* **15**:223–235.

American Public Health Association, 1998, Turning point grants help strengthen public health infrastructure, *The Nation's Health* **28**:13.

Anderson, J. E., 1994, *Public Policymaking—An Introduction*, Houghton Mifflin Company, Boston.

Berkowitz, B., and Lafronza, V., 1998, Transforming our public health system, *Transform. Pub. Health* **1**:1–8.

Braundtland, G. H. (June 9, 2000a). Beijing+5 Conference. World Health Organization (July 16, 2000), http://www.who.int/director-general/speeches/2000/20000609_newyork.html.

Braundtland, G. H. (June 21, 2000b). Presentation of the world health report 2000, World Health Organization (July 16, 2000), http://www.who.int/director-general/speeches/2000/20000621_london.html.

Centers for Disease Control and Prevention, 1996, Travelers' health information on measles (September 29, 2000), http://www.cdc.gov/travel/diseases/measles.htm.

Centers for Disease Control and Prevention, 1997, *Health Information for International Travel 1996–1997*, USDHHS, Atlanta, GA.

Centers for Disease Control and Prevention/National Center for Health Statistics, 1997, Infant mortality rates by race and Hispanic origin of mother (February 17, 2001), http://www.cdc.gov/nchs/images/ibid_c.gif.

Centers for Disease Control and Prevention, 1999, Ten great public health achievements—United States, 1900–1999, *Morbid. Mortal. Week. Rep.* **48**:241–243.

Centers for Disease Control and Prevention, National Immunization Program, 2000a, Joint statement concerning removal of thimerosal from vaccines from the American Academy of Family Physicians, American Academy of Pediatrics, Advisory Committee on Immunization Practices and United States Public Health Service (June 22, 2000), http://www.cdc.gov/nip/vacsafe/concerns/thimerosal/joint_statement_00.htm.

Centers for Disease Control and Prevention, 2000b, Measles—United States 1999, *Morbid. Mortal. Week. Rep.* **49**:557–560.

Centers for Disease Control and Prevention, 2001, Infant mortality statistics show variation by race, ethnicity and state (February 17, 2001), http://www.cdc.gov/nchs/releases/00facts/infantmo.htm.

Chen, R. T., and Orenstein, W. A., 1996, Epidemiologic methods in immunization programs, *Epidemiol. Rev.* **18**:99–117.

Chicago Department of Public Health, 1998, *Chicago Violence Prevention Strategic Plan*. Chicago Department of Public Health, Chicago.

Children's Vaccine Program, 1998, Bill and Melinda Gates Children's Vaccine Program (July 12, 2000), http://www.path.org.programs/p-dis/gates_cvp.htm.

Core Public Health Functions Steering Committee, 1999, Public health in America (February 18, 2001), http://www.health.gov/phfunctions/public.htm.

Etzioni, A., 1991, in *A Responsive Society: Collected Essays on Guiding Deliberate Social Change*, Jossey-Bass, San Francisco.

Hackey, R. B., 1998, *Rethinking Health Care Policy: The New Politics of State Regulation*, Georgetown University Press, Washington, DC.

Hinman, A., 1999, Eradication of vaccine-preventable diseases, *Annu. Rev. Pub. Health* **20**:211–229.

Institute of Medicine/National Academy of Sciences, 1988, *The Future of Public Health*, National Academy Press, Washington DC.

Institute of Medicine, 1994, *Adverse Events Associated with Childhood Vaccines—Evidence Bearing on Causality*, National Academy Press, Washington, DC.

Institute of Medicine, 1997, *Risk Communication and Vaccination—Workshop Summary*, National Academy Press, Washington, DC.

Kluger, J., 1999, Food fight: The battle heats up between the US and Europe over genetically engineered crops, *Time* **154:**43–44.

Longest, B. B., 1994, *Health Policymaking in the United States*, AUPHA Press/Health Administration Press, Ann Arbor, MI.

Mast, E., 1997, *Hepatitis B Disease and Vaccine*, Paper presented at the State of Illinois Board of Health's Immunization Public Hearing on Hepatitis B and Hepatitis B Vaccine, December, Chicago, IL.

McKenzie, J. F., Pinger, R. R., and Kotecki, J. E., 1999, *An Introduction to Community Health*, Jones and Bartlett Publishers, Boston, MA.

Olivé, J. M., and Aylward, B., 1999, Poliovirus vaccine: Commentary, *Bull. World Health Org.* **77:**194–195.

Rowe, J. W., and Kahn, R. L., 1998, *Successful aging*. New York: Pantheon Books.

Schwartz, S., and Carpenter, K. M., 1999, The right answer for the wrong question: Consequences of type III error for public health research, *Am. J. Pub. Health* **89:**1175–1180.

Shaheen, M. A., Frerichs, R. R., Alexopolulos, N., and Rainey, J., 2000, Immunization coverage among predominantly Hispanic children, aged 2–3 years, in Central Los Angles, *Ann. Epidemiol.* **10:**160–168.

Siegel, M., and Doner, L., 1998, *Marketing Public Health: Strategies to Promote Social Change*, Aspen Publishers, Gaithersburg, MD.

Terris, M., 1985, The changing relationships of epidemiology and society: The Robert Cruikshank Lecture, *J. Pub. Health Policy* **6:**15–36.

US Department of Health and Human Services, 1990, *Healthy People 2000*, USGPO, Washington, DC.

US Department of Health and Human Services, 1998, *Healthy People 2010 Objectives: Draft for Public Comment*, USGPO, Washington, DC.

US Department of Health and Human Services, 1999, Eliminating racial and ethnic disparities in health (July 14, 2000), http://raceandhealth.hhs.gov/sidebars/sbinitOver.htm.

US Department of Health and Human Services, 2000, *Healthy People 2010 Objectives: Conference Edition*, USDHHS, Washington, DC.

Wallack, L., 1997, What is public health? *Propaganda Rev.* **9:**4–6.

World Bank Group, March 13, 2000, Measuring poverty (July 16, 2000), http://www.worldbank.org/poverty/mission/up2.htm.

World Health Organization (WHO) Fact Sheet/204 November 1998, Hepatitis B (July 5, 2000), http://www.who.int/inf-fs/en/fact204.html.

World Health Organization (WHO), 1997, *The World Health Report 1997*, WHO, Geneva.

World Health Organization (WHO), 1999, Ageing and health (March 6, 2001), http://www.who.int/ageing.

World Health Organization (WHO), 2000a, Global polio eradication initiative (May 22, 2000), http://www.who.int/vaccines-polio.

World Health Organization (WHO), June 2000b, Gender, health and poverty (July 14, 2000), http://www.who.int/inf-fs/en/fact251.html.

World Health Organization (WHO), 2001, Diseases and vaccines: List of diseases (February 21, 2001), http://www.who.int/vaccines-diseases/dislist.htm.

Yusuf, H. R., Coronado, V. G., Averhoff, F. A., Maes, E. F., Rodewald, L. E., Bsattaglia, M. P., and Mahoney, F., 1999, Progress in coverage with hepatitis B vaccine among US children, 1994–1997, *Am. J. Pub. Health* **89:**1684–1689.

Zwingle, E., 1999, Goods move, people move, ideas move, and cultures move, *Nat. Geographic* **196:**6–33.

13

The Contribution of Epidemiological Information in Economic Decision Making

Gerald L. Glandon

Introduction

Epidemiology aids planners in identifying areas with high rates of health care problems and characterizes population subgroups who are affected. Left to market forces, the allocation of health care resources are likely to result in inequities and areas of under- or overutilization as described in Chapter 1 (this volume) and areas of real need overlooked. Cost benefit analyses (CBA) and Cost effectiveness analyses (CEA) are closely related economic techniques that use epidemiological information to assist decision makers to allocate resources to their most highly valued use. At the macrolevel, government organizations (federal, state, or local) use the results of these analyses to formulate national health care policy and answer questions such as, "Should we vaccinate all infants against hepatitis B?" (Krahn and Detsky, 1993). Application of these techniques to decisions at the microlevel (industry, firms, health plan, or hospital) also has become common (Glandon and Buck, 1994). Managerial decisions regarding technology acquisition, strategic affiliation, or strategic program development (transplant program) may benefit from application of CEA or CBA.

When considering the adoption of a new health policy initiative, technology, or other significant business venture, the critical decision criteria is, "Does the proposed activity increase or decrease benefits or health outcomes and does it increase or decrease costs?" As described most recently by O'Brien *et al.* (1997), a proposal that appears to raise cost and lower benefits or outcome and can be easily rejected. Similarly, if costs fall and benefits increase, adoption is not a real question. The more difficult cases are those in which costs and benefits decrease or more commonly both costs and benefits increase. In these instances, formal cost-benefit or cost-effectiveness analysis is required. Under these conditions, the decision to invest, adopt, or utilize depends on the relative changes in costs and benefits or

Gerald L. Glandon   Department of Health Services Administration, University of Alabama at Birmingham, Birmingham, Alabama 35294.

Epidemiology and the Delivery of Health Care Services: Methods and Applications, Second Edition, edited by Denise M. Oleske. Kluwer Academic / Plenum Publishers, New York, 2001.

outcomes, and thus the precise definition, measurement, and valuation of each becomes important (Eisenberg, 1989).

For many decisions, prices provide reliable signals that guide business decisions. However, prices may be poor guides in select instances (Dranove *et al.*, 1991). Public goods represent a class for which market prices do not signal true or total costs or benefits. In this case, firms or government agencies may over- or underinvest in some program. Further, even if a firm operates in a conventional market with appropriate prices for its products, it rarely uses prices for internal transactions of goods and services. Detailed cost assessment and subsequent CEA or CBA are techniques that can assist in making those decisions (Gold *et al.*, 1996; Glandon and Shapiro, 1988, for discussions). Therefore, just as the government needs a decision-making tool, health care management needs analytic methods to help decide which investment decisions are beneficial to the processes of health care delivery and which are not.

This chapter will review the basis for application of CBA and CEA, which is the public health nature of many goods and services for which these techniques are used in decision making. Next, the methodology for these techniques will be reviewed. Third, application of these techniques will be presented. Finally, future prospect and impediments to widespread use of epidemiological data by CBA and CEA will be discussed.

Background: Public Goods

Use of CBA and CEA are now widespread. Applications of CBA or CEA abound from a wide range of specific health-related issues, including prenatal and infant nursing home visitation (Olds *et al.*, 1993), home rehabilitation of the elderly (Melin *et al.*, 1993), early prostate cancer detection or screening for cervical cancer (Littrup *et al.*, 1993; Goldi *et al.*, 1999), lithotripsy versus surgery for gallstones (Bass *et al.*, 1991), elective surgery for intracranial aneurysms (King *et al.*, 1995), and occupational therapy services (Trahey, 1991). The question of why these techniques arose and in particular why they arose in health care applications reveals much about the technique. While these techniques have had many direct clinical applications even in the early years (Pauker and Kassirer, 1975; McNeil and Adelstein, 1976; Weinstein and Stason, 1977), most of the applications of CBA and CEA arose initially from the need to deal with the public goods nature of many health care services.

Government Provision of Public Goods

Government first used CBA for such projects as river and harbor development, flood control/irrigation, and later, national defense programs where markets did not exist to ensure provision of an optimal quantity of these goods or services by the private sector (Gold *et al.*, 1996; Warner and Luce, 1982). National defense is the classic example of a public good. Private firms cannot effectively produce and sell the appropriate quantity of national defense despite its value because of its public good characteristics. National defense, once produced, confers benefits to all individuals in society, even to those external to the transaction. When these benefits, called externalities, exist widely, the result is suboptimal payment for and provision of the service. Because they receive the benefit even if they do not pay, some people will not willingly pay for the service to be provided. In these cases, the government is often called on to rectify the failure of the market to provide the appropriate level of the good by creating or regulating the market or by providing services directly. Examples in addition to national defense include control of infectious diseases, basic research for new pharmaceuticals, and industrial pollution.

To see how this applies to health care, consider an infectious disease such as pneumonia. Individuals have a self-interest in reducing exposure to this infectious disease. This reduction occurs through vaccination, rapid isolation of those infected, and application of treatment for those infected. Interventions appear to be effective and cost little per year of life gained (Tengs *et al.*, 1995). Each individual has a risk of adverse health consequences from contacting pneumonia and will make a decision to vaccinate and isolate and treat based on personal expected costs and benefits. However, individual decisions do not consider the external costs imposed on society at large of having pneumonia and potentially infecting others. Because each individual only considers the private costs and benefits, they may reason that if all their neighbors effectively pay for protection from this disease, they will receive the benefits and there is no need to pay. If everyone else is protected, it is unlikely that the disease could infect any single individual.

Private firms trying to provide protection to a community from pneumonia consequently provide less than the optimal levels of protection because no individual will voluntarily pay for the benefits that accrue external to the decision maker. However, under this scenario, some individuals may not purchase and take the vaccine. A private market for this service will not capture all people because some would not pay. Only by having the government mandate the use of vaccines and the rapid isolation and treatment of those infected and force all citizens to pay can the optimal level of protection be provided. The political process, not an economic market, will determine optimal levels of vaccination and treatment of pneumonia and similar goods and services (Weisbrod, 1983).

Further, because there is no market for these public goods, there are no prices to act as signals of social value. Prices serve as a mechanism or signal for allocating goods and services to the most highly valued (optimal) use. External resource allocation rules may be required if prices do not exist. In the absence of market prices, CBA and CEA provided a set of rules to help the government decide what, how, and for whom to produce (Warner and Luce, 1982; Weisbrod, 1983).

Health Care and Public Goods

While the extreme case of total failure of the market to function is the rationale for a number of government public health activities, often the market exists but does not provide the appropriate level of a good or service. If prices do not act as appropriate signals, there may be a misallocation of production. Posted prices for health care services are highly unreliable indicators of resource costs (Dranove *et al.*, 1991; Warner and Luce, 1982; Weinstein *et al.*, 1996) for the following four reasons:

- Health care prices are unreliable because insurance shields consumers from most of the effects of health care prices. In total, private or government payers cover about 80% of all health expenditures. Out-of-pocket expenditures for direct elements of cost are relatively minor except for select services (nursing home care and dental services). As a result, the market for most health care services is unable to effectively enforce a true market price.
- Even without the insurance issue, the problem of using prices is still complex. Because of the way health care providers have been paid by government payers, charges,

reimbursement, and costs may not be related. Stated prices for health care services often do not reflect either the ultimate exchange price or any concept of costs (Dranove *et al.*, 1991). For example, a hospital may charge $12,000 for a patient's hospital stay, be paid (reimbursed) $7,700, and have estimated costs of $6,850. What is the "price" of care in this case and how does anyone respond to those confused price signals?

- A related problem is that many services and programs that are being evaluated already exist within the firm. However, prices often are not used to transact goods and services within an individual firm. Therefore, management needs an analysis method to help it decide which investment decisions are beneficial to the firm and which programs should be expanded and which eliminated. Detailed costing and subsequent CEA and CBA are techniques that can assist in making those decisions.

- Finally, there are often substantial indirect costs associated with receiving medical services that are not reflected in prices. For example, the costs of surgery clearly includes the hospitalization expenses, physician fees, nurse time, and so forth, but it should also include the opportunity cost time spent by the patient in surgery (preop, admission and postop time) and the time lost from work during recovery and spent in follow-up care.

Overview of the Definition and Core Elements of Cost–Benefit Analysis and Cost-Effectiveness Analysis

CBA is a process that systematically measures the net incremental costs and the net incremental benefits associated with alternative methods of addressing a problem. Formally it is the ratio of net incremental costs to net incremental benefits with greater ratios, implying that costs are high relative to benefits. The purpose of using this ratio is to assist decision makers in selecting among a range of solutions. CBA assigns dollar values to all the costs and to all the benefits of a proposed investment, program, or technology. By performing this analysis on a number of alternative uses of scarce resources, the alternatives can be compared on a relatively even footing. Decisions can be made where to invest by selection the alternative with the lowest ratio first and then selection options with successively higher ratios until you have no more to spend. This method assures that the alternatives with the greatest benefits relative to costs are selected first.

CEA differs from CBA only in that certain beneficial consequences or outcomes of a program or technology are evaluated in nonmonetary terms, e.g., "life years" saved. The numerator contains the net incremental costs and the denominator contains the net increment in health outcome (Weinstein *et al.*, 1996). The origin of this technique was the realization that outcomes or benefits for CBA such as mortality or morbidity are difficult to quantify in monetary terms from a social, organizational, or individual perspective. The similarity between the two has been noted, however (Phelps and Mushlin, 1991).

A challenging component to measurement of the lives saved as measured by CEA is that not all those saved lives are equivalent. As a result, analysts often modify the life year or other outcome by applying a higher weight to those years that consumers value highly and a lower weight to those years that are less valuable to patients. The current consensus is that the modification should be the health-related quality of life (QOL) associated with that year; however, there is a great deal of debate on the appropriate QOL measure (Guyatt *et al.*, 1997; Kaplan, 1993; MacKeigan and Pathak, 1992; Revicki and Ehreth, 1997; Weinstein *et al.*, 1996). For example, some patients have a choice between bypass surgery and medical management of coronary artery blockage. Life expectancy might be no different between the two options, and in fact the mortality risk from surgery might yield more years of expected life for medical management. However, the patient's evaluation of those additional years may differ between the two options. If physical function is not as great with a medical as opposed to a surgical intervention, the added years of life might be worth less to the patient. Only by weighting those additional years by their value to the patient can the alternatives be evaluated correctly.

The performance of a CBA or CEA requires the analyst to follow standard research evaluation protocols that have been widely described with respect to health care (Glandon and Shapiro, 1988; Gold *et al.*, 1996; Siegel *et al.*, 1996; Torrance *et al.*, 1996; Warner and Luce, 1982). The steps in the performance of CBA and CEA are summarized in Table 13.1. While they may differ in small detail, the nature of the steps in the processes is generally as follows:

1. *Identify objectives of the CBA or CEA analysis.* What are the expected outcomes of the analysis? Identifying the key objectives represents the crucial means of both limiting and defining the study. The objectives may be the direct outcome of interest or may be intermediate or distal from the ultimate goals. For example, pharmacological interventions might be able to reduce mortality and morbidity from heart disease, but these outcomes might take years to observe. Lowering blood cholesterol, an intermediate outcome, is closer to the pharmacological intervention, and thus is often selected as the outcome of interest (Schulman *et al.*, 1990). Similarly, outcomes of a clinical information system may be designed to improve the quality of care by providing rate numbers to be used to monitor, review, and improve processes (e.g., immunization rates for an HMO membership). The link between alternative clinical information systems and quality may not be strong, however, because a number of factors may influence overall quality. Consequently, the evaluation of the system may be conducted in terms of its ability to deliver standardized reports in a timely and accurate manner. Finally, childhood vaccinations may improve life expectancy and quality of life 50 to 70 years after application. However, vaccination programs may adopt current vaccination rates as their objective because of the time it takes to evaluate the primary outcome of interest.

2. *Specify alternatives.* The comparison group(s) to the core technology or program. A comprehensive list of alternatives must be identified so that the technology or program in question is properly challenged. An option judged better than the best alternatives gives greater confidence in its merits. Alternatives selected for convenience may not provide a true test of the technology being considered. Less than competitive alternatives may be selected through ignorance. However, the political situation within a firm or at the governmental level may induce analysts to select inappropriate alternatives. For example, the relevant alternative to a proposed information system application is almost never "no system." Analysts must consider the next most sophisticated option to make a valid comparison. Epidemiological studies can provide data from which to models of alternatives based on the natural history of

---

**Table 13.1. Steps in the Performance of a Cost-Benefit Analysis (CBA)
and Cost-Effectiveness Analysis (CEA)**

1. Identify objectives of the CBA or CEA analysis
2. Specify alternatives
3. Develop a framework for analysis
4. Measure costs
5. Measure benefits (in dollars for CBA and in outcomes for CEA)
6. Apply appropriate discounting
7. Perform sensitivity analysis
8. Consider equity of distribution of costs and benefits

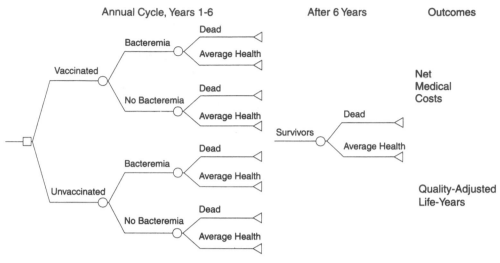

Annual Cycle, Years 1-6   After 6 Years   Outcomes

Bacteremia — Dead / Average Health

Vaccinated   Net
                                                             Medical
No Bacteremia — Dead / Average Health   Costs

                                        Survivors
                                        Dead / Average Health

Bacteremia — Dead / Average Health

Unvaccinated   Quality-Adjusted
                                                             Life-Years
No Bacteremia — Dead / Average Health

Figure 13.1.   Decision model. From Sisk *et al.* (1997).

the health outcomes. The specification of alternatives is aided through use of a decision model (Fig. 13.1). For example, cost accounting systems based on standard costs may provide more accurate information regarding the financial consequences of treating different types of patients. Compared to the alternative of the complete absence of patient-specific cost information, implementing a cost-accounting system based on standard costs always should be beneficial. However, standard costs may not be as good when compared to a more appropriate alternative of cost estimates based on cost to charge ratios, which, while less accurate, provide useful information concerning patient costs.

3. *Develop a framework for analysis.* The framework for analysis is defining how care is organized and delivered. How the process works and what does the technology do? This understanding is crucial when trying to determine what resources are required and what are the likely and unexpected outcomes of a process. For this purpose, the health care delivery system can be viewed as a production process. This framework for analysis treats labor, machines, and supplies as specific inputs that when combined in a precise manner may produce measurable output. For clinical technologies such as the directly observed treatment system (DOTS) for pneumonia, one must understand all aspects of the clinical management of pneumonia so that all resources can be identified and threats to treatment outcome can be considered (US Agency for International Development, 1997). The same applies to nonclinical technologies. For example, information system alternatives under consideration constantly in clinical setting represent different production technologies from the perspective of the hospital or clinic. Evaluation of these technologies implies that the analyst must understand what function the information system is intended to accomplish, what resources are required to implement the technology, and to fully grasp how the technology performs.

4. *Measure costs.* The measurement of costs involves the identification, selection of a measurement tool, and valuation of the relevant incremental resources used in the process relative to the outcome(s) under study. Table 13.2 presents a representative set of cost categories, common measurement unit, and valuation methods. This presentation is by no

Table 13.2. Components of Direct and Indirect Cost Categories

Cost categories	Elements	Quantity	Value measure
Direct Costs			
Institution macro	Hospital encounter	Admission	Charge or payment
		Day of stay	Charge or payment
		ER visit	Charge or payment
	Clinic encounter	Visits	Charge or payment
		Procedure	Charge or payment
	Ancillary encounter	Procedure	Charge or payment
Institution micro	Labor		
	Nursing	Hours	Market wage
	Physician	Visits	Market wage
	Technician	Procedures	Market wage
	Managerial	Hours	Market wage
	Office/support	Hours	Market wage
	Supplies		
	Medical supplies	Count	Market price
	Office supplies	Count	Market price
	Equipment		
	Medical equipment	Count	Market price
	Office equipment	Count	Market price
	Capital		
	Space	Square foot	Market rental
Provider	Physician	Visits	Charge or payment
	Nurse	Visits	Charge or payment
	Pharmacy	Consultation	Charge or payment
	Allied health	Consultation	Charge or payment
Equipment and supplies	Assistive devices	Count	Market price
	Home alterations	Count	Market price
	OTC drugs	Count	Market price
Indirect costs			
Patient	Travel	Hours	Market wage
	Wait for treatment	Hours	Market wage
	Receive treatment	Hours	Market wage
	Lost work time	Hours	Market wage
	Lost work productivity	Hours	Market wage
FamilyMember(s)	Travel	Hours	Market wage
	Wait for treatment	Hours	Market wage
	Receive treatment	Hours	Market wage
	Lost work time	Hours	Market wage

means exhaustive but provides a guide to begin the costing process. There are numerous approaches to costing as outlined in many recent studies (Schulman *et al.*, 1996):

- *Cost identification* is the delineation of all the processes required to produce or provide the resources. There are two primary components of costs that need to be identified, direct and indirect. In a health care application, direct costs are "the value of resources used in the treatment, care, and rehabilitation of persons with the condition under study" (Kirschstein, 2000). Indirect costs "represent the value of economic resources lost because of disease related work disability or premature mortality" (Kirschstein, 2000; Jacobs and Fassbender, 1998). For example, mandating the inactivated polio vaccine into the immunization schedule requires full understanding of not only the cost of the vaccine but the process for storage, distribution, administration and the consequences of administering the alternative active vaccine (Miller *et al.*, 1996).

In addition, costs can be classified as variable or fixed. Variable costs are those that grow or shrink with the level of activity. For example, in a well-run hospital, as the number of inpatient days increase or decrease, the number of nurses employed also will increase or decrease. The resulting nursing labor costs are variable. On the other hand, costs of physical structure of the hospital, certain labor classes and some medical equipment does not vary for even relatively large changes in volume. These are examples of fixed costs. The current consensus is to include an estimate of fixed costs in the cost side of CEA or CBA (O'Brien *et al.*, 1997).

- *Measurement* consists of the counting or quantification of resources used in the process for each of these cost elements. Depending on the type of study, measurement might be simple. For clinical trials it usually involves monitoring the defined utilization of health resources by the subjects. Only if subjects are receiving significant care outside of the defined protocol will this pose a problem. Often, however, the measurement step utilizes data from external studies. Miller *et al.*, (1996), for example, rely on historical data on vaccine activated polio from the CDC to derive the annual activated vaccine polio incidence. Other examples might include disease incidence rates, cure rates, rates, and side effects of treatment.

- *Valuation* is the assignment of a monetary value for the resources that have been identified and measured. The general principle is that opportunity cost represents the appropriate value of the resource consumed, but in health care there if often a divergence between posted price and opportunity cost. As a result in performing CBA or CEA the contingent value must be determined. The Panel on Cost-Effectiveness in Health Care and Medicine recognized this in developing core methodology and stated, "when prices do not adequately reflect opportunity costs because of market distortions, they should be adjusted appropriately" (Weinstein *et al.*, 1996, p. 1255). For markets for most goods and services, prices serve as an effective mechanism for determining the relevant cost per unit of service used. Individual consumers and providers use prices as the signals to purchase more or less (consumers) or produce more or less (providers). Where these market-determined prices do not exist or are not reliable, however, costing studies are needed to help make decisions. For example, Miller *et al.*, (1996) employed the average court settlement for those children who contacted polio from the immunization as an approximation of the "cost" of expected side effects.

5. *Measure benefits (in dollars for CBA; in outcomes for CEA).* The identification of the outcomes of the process under study represents a complex component of the process. Benefits determination goes through the same components of cost, identification, measurement, and valuation as we observed in item #4 above. For CBA, benefits require the analyst to place a monetary value on the outcome. The scope of benefits to be included must be defined carefully. Particularly in the health care field, in addition to firm-specific benefits (e.g., more patients per day), societal gains such as live-years saved, morbidity reduced, or function restored may need to be considered (Gold *et al.*, 1996; Weinstein *et al.*, 1996). Since many of these benefits are rarely priced and transacted in a market, they do not lend themselves to valuation by

accounting systems. For example, assigning a value to life or to improved function represents a major economic challenge and the primary reason that "social" CBA and CEA is performed.

      6. *Discount monetary values.* Knowledge of technology's life cycle determines timing of benefits and costs. For a valid comparison, all costs and benefits must be measured at the same time. Unless all benefits and costs occur at the same time, they must be discounted to a common period (Gold *et al.*, 1996). Discounting is the method of translating future health outcomes and costs to their value today. Typically, projects have startup costs that occur primarily in an early period and operating costs that continue over time. Depending on the application, projects may have periodic maintenance or enhancement costs. To compare costs with benefits that are realized at different points in time, both must be discounted to a common period. To discount you must consider the appropriate project life cycle and the appropriate discount rate. The discount rate is the rate at which future values of outcomes and costs are translated into today's value. It answers the question, "What is a dollar worth that you receive a year from now worth today? Once a discount rate and project life cycle ("*n*" years) are selected, the stream of benefits or outcomes and costs which result can be reduced to a discounted present value (PV) using the following equations:

$$\text{PV benefits} = B_0 + B_1/(1 + r_1)^1 + B_2/(1 + r_2)^2 + \ldots + B_n/(1 + r_n)^n$$
$$\text{PV costs} = C_0 + C_1/(1 + r_1)^1 + C_2/(1 + r_2)^2 + \ldots + C_n/(1 + r_n)^n$$

where B_n and C_n represent the net benefits and net costs accrued in the *n*th year. Benefits and costs are discounted to the base year "0." The term, r_n is the discount rate in the *n*th year. For simplicity, the discount rate is usually assumed equal for all years. Because the discount rate is positive, benefits or outcomes realized and costs incurred in the future are worth less than benefits or outcomes realized today in present value terms. Because the denominator in the above equations gets larger the further you have moved from the base year, benefits and costs in the distant future are worth much less than benefits or costs from the near future.

      The rate of discount commonly used for social CBA or CEA analyses is 3%. This discount rate is used to represent the pure effects of time on present value and represents the value society places on getting resources today as opposed to next year. Many consider this rate low because they observe interest rates being substantially above 3% in the real world. However, this pure discount rate ignores the effects of inflation. It is the custom for most analysts to ignore inflation in these calculations for two reasons. First, if inflation were added, the discount rate would be the pure 3% plus expected inflation (currently another 3–4%). However, if you raise the discount rate to include inflation, the monetary value of benefits and costs also would have an inflation factor included (Gold *et al.*, 1996; Warner and Luce, 1982). The net effect of including inflation in the discount and in the monetary measures of benefits and costs is zero. If future benefits B_n and costs C_n and the discount rate increase by the same expected inflation, there is no effect on the present value. Second, including expected inflation requires that you derive an estimate of expected inflation, which is a difficult task at best. Consequently, most analysts do not directly account for inflation in CBA or CEA.

      7. *Perform sensitivity analysis.* By their nature, performing CBA and CEA require addressing substantial uncertainty. Sensitivity is the process of testing the effects of changes in key model parameters on the computed CBA or CEA. Assumptions are usually made about likelihood of mortality or morbidity, severity of event side effects, costs of treatment, and other events. The sensitivity of CBA or CEA analyses must be examined because of the potential inaccuracy of the estimates of certain parameters. If small changes in the value of a single parameter had unusually large impacts on aggregate costs or benefits, conclusions should be drawn with caution. The usual approach to this issue is to recompute CBA or CBA

with variations in key parameters from "best" to "worse" case. This gives direct evidence of how much aggregate findings vary or are sensitive to changes in the parameters. For example, Miller *et al.*, (1996) analyzed the cost effectiveness of incorporating inactivated poliovirus vaccine (IPV) in childhood immunizations. This strategy eliminates vaccine-associated paralytic poliomyelitis (VAPP) cases when compared to live attenuated oral poliovirus vaccine (OPV) but costs more to administer. Their base case was the "worst" case for adopting VAPP in that it saved only 9.5 cases per year. In this case, IPV cost $3.0 million per life saved compared to OPV. However, under the best outcome for VAPP it might avoid 12.17 cases per year. This sensitivity in the effect parameter lowered by cost per life saved by 33% to $2.0 million.

8. *Consider the equity of the distribution of the costs and benefits.* Applications should consider the equity of the distribution of costs and benefits. Because these analyses usually apply to social programs, who bears the costs and who receives the benefits can be as important to decision makers as the total level of costs and benefits. A social program that generates benefits to an affluent subclass of the population but has costs borne by all would not be as positively evaluated because it distributes benefits to those least in need (Warner and Luce, 1982). In recent years, the evaluation of programs aimed at improving the health status of the poor has become a high priority. Recently, the United Nations (2000), the World Bank (Deininger and Squire, 2000), and the US Census (Dalaker, 1999) among others have published studies on the nature and extent of poverty and the growing income inequality of the world's population. Efforts to address these problems are underway and will require significant efforts on a number of fronts; however, consideration of the distribution of benefits and costs as opposed to just the level likely will increase in the future. Interestingly, defining low-income people increases the difficulty in designing programs to help those in poverty. For example, in the United States, income has a complex definition. Income is the amount of money income received in the preceding calendar year by persons over age 15 from each of the following sources: earnings, unemployment compensation, workers' compensation, social security, supplemental security income, public assistance, veterans' payments, survivor benefits, disability benefits, pension or retirement income, interest, dividends, rents, royalties, and estates and trusts, educational assistance, alimony, child support, financial assistance from outside of the household, and other income. Each term has a definition as well. Poverty on the other hand includes only money income before taxes and excludes any capital gain or noncash payments (Dalaker, 1999). In the United States in 1998, the poverty threshhold is $16,660 for a family of four and $10,634 for a family of two.

Cost-Effectiveness Analysis, Epidemiological Data, and Application to Managerial Decision Making

This section will combine the application of a CEA with experiences the author has had in developing countries in which epidemiological data were critical in the decision making of officials in ministries of health. Burman *et al.* (1997) summarized the problem worldwide by reporting increases in tuberculosis (TB) rates and provided a cost-effectiveness analysis of alternative treatment programs. The increase in rates of active TB internationally has been an ongoing cause of concern to public health and other officials. Recent evidence is that the rate may have doubled in recent years (Raviglione *et al.*, 1995). A number of factors are related to that increase, but even more important, Burman *et al.* (1997) suggest that the increase in cases resistant to conventional therapy has more than doubled since the early 1980s.

Treatment regimens for TB have been well established and appear generally effective. Clinical trials suggest that cure rates approach 95% (Combs *et al.*, 1990). While examples of success of clinical trial protocol are less impressive, the directly observed treatment (DOT) administration of drugs appears to be the solution. The CDC (1993) recommends that the use of DOT generally be adopted.

The perception that DOT is more costly may be the reason for failure to adopt this procedure for administering it uniformly. Burman *et al.* (1997) provide the first US-based cost-effectiveness analyses of DOT versus self-administered therapy (SAT). An application of the above methodology is applied in the following eight steps using data from Burman *et al.* (1997):

1. *Identify study objectives.* Given the increase in incidence of TB worldwide, many analysts have begun a search for a solution. Despite strong clinical evidence that drug therapy can be effective against most strains of TB, it is not uniformly accepted because it is viewed as an expensive form of treatment. Consequently, the objective of their study was to test the cost-effectiveness of DOT versus SAT. Costs included resources used in treatment and outcomes were treatment.

2. *Specify alternatives.* The alternatives for this analysis were DOT and SAT. DOT used a 62-dose regimen of isoniazid, rifampin, pyrazinamide, and streptomycin for 4 months. A nurse is responsible for administering the dose, and thus validates the directly observed portion of the name. Cure was defined as being TB free during the 6-month period of therapy and for 6 months following therapy. All failure is treated by hospitalization irrespective of cause of failure. SAT is daily isoniazid, rifampin, pyrazinamide, and ethambutol for 2 months. This is followed by isoniazid and rifampin for 4 months. All drugs are administered by the patient or the caregiver.

3. *Specify the framework for analysis.* The primary issue of concern in this case is to understand why there might be differences in cure rates and costs in the two arms. Because the drugs have been shown to be effective in clinical trials, the difference in outcomes appears to be a result of failure of the patient to comply with the SAT portion of the study. The use of nursing time to administer the drugs and the patient's time to travel to the nurse for this administration clearly raised the observable costs of DOT relative to SAT. However, costs of treating the higher failure rate for SAT may offset this high initial cost. The perspective is total system costs; thus, all costs are relevant to the analysis.

4. *Measure costs.* Costs related to these alternative treatment methods (SAT and DOT) can be presented for initial treatment and for drug-susceptible or multidrug-resistant treatment failure. The authors have identified, measured, and valued all of the elements of the initial treatment for the two methods and those costs are summarized in Table 13.3.

The second category covers the costs associated with managing the care for those patients who failed initial therapy and consists of patients who still can be treated (drug-susceptible) and those with multidrug resistant strains. The categories of cost include the diagnosis of the continued TB problem, hospitalization, outpatient treatment posthospitalization, and patient time costs. Specific estimates of these costs are presented in Burman *et al.* (1997) are presented in Table 13.4.

These are the results from a specific study and the cost estimates and number of units presented might differ in other settings (Burman *et al.*, 1997). Examination of the detailed assumptions employed in the original data collection should be easily updated to a particular location and time. Analysts could easily substitute alternative protocols and area-specific unit costs to apply this methodology to other settings.

**Table 13.3. Determination of Direct and Indirect Costs
for Cost Effectiveness Analysis of DOT and SAT Tuberculosis Therapy**

	DOT		SAT	
Cost category	No. of Units	Cost	No. of Units	Cost
Drugs and diagnostic tests	—	$587[b]	—	$1154[c]
Patient time cost[d]	62 visits	$911	8 visits	$118
Nursing cost ($25.28hr)	0.25 hr/dose × 62 visits	$392	0.33 hr/visit × 8 visits	$67
Delivery of DOT dose	0.2 × 62	$227	NA	—
Total treatment costs		$1206		$1227
(1.25 hours/visit × $11.75/hr)				
Total cost		$2117		$1339

[a]DOT, directly observed therapy; SAT, self-administered therapy.

[b]Antituberculous drugs, sputum culture (4 @ $58.50 ea.), chest radiograph (2 @ $40 ea.), and serum bilirubin (5 @ $16 ea.).

[c]Anti-tuberculosis drugs ($584), sputum culture (7 @ $58.50 ea.), chest radiograph (2 @ $40ea.), and serum bilirubin (5 @ $16 ea.).

[d]1.25 hours per visit at $11.75 per hour.

5. *Measure benefits*. In this analysis, benefits are a cured case of TB. The cure rate for DOT is assumed to be 94.5%, while the cure rate for SAT is 79%. In addition, for those cases where the primary therapy fails, there is a higher rate of multidrug-resistant TB for SAT treatment (29% vs. 16%) as a result of the observed, interrupted SAT treatment. Consequently, DOT patients have fewer failures overall and fewer high-cost failures. DOT avoids costly hospital treatments due to failure and also highly costly treatment for multidrug-resistant cases. Again, these are the results from a specific study and the benefits of therapy might differ in other settings (Burman *et al.*, 1997).

Putting these benefits and cost data together yields the odd finding that DOT has better outcomes from initial treatment (94.5% vs. 79%) and lower costs. The cost-effectiveness ration defined in this case as the cost per additional treatment success is actually negative (−$52,700), as presented in Table 13.5.

6. *Apply discounting*. The discounting is the process of transforming future values of outcomes and costs into today's value. In this example, most of the costs and benefits of treatment alternatives occur in a single year, thus only a limited amount of discounting is required in these analyses. However, the treatment of multidrug-resistant tuberculosis extends over a 3-year period and those costs should be discounted (data in Table 13.4 are not

Table 13.4. Direct and Indirect Costs of Tuberculosis Treatment Failure

Cost category	Drug-susceptible failure	Multidrug-resistant failure
Diagnosis	$ 354	$ 687
Hospitalization	$7,820	$15,740
Outpatient DOT	$1,317	$13,926
Patient time	$3,384	$16,920
Total treatment failure costs	$2,875	$47,273

Table 13.5. Computation of Cost-effectiveness and Cost-effectiveness
Ratio of DOT Tuberculosis Treatment

Treatment option	Cure costs	Failure Drug susceptible	Failure Multidrug resistant	Total treatment cost	Outcome (cure rate)
DOT	$2117	$12,875	$146,271	$3999	94.5%
SAT	$1339	$12,875	$146,271	$12,167	79.0%
Difference	$776	$0	$0	−$8168	15.5%

Cost effectiveness (CE) ratio	=	Incremental costs/Incremental outcome
	=	[−$8168/15.5%]
	=	−$52,700

discounted). Treatment costs are primarily concentrated in year 1, but $10,644 occur in year 2, and another $5,322 occurs in year 3. In this case, the authors used a discount rate of 5%. The discounted costs in years 2 and 3, respectively, $10,137 and $4,827. At 5% the total discounted costs of treating multidrug-resistant TB is $146,271.

7. *Perform sensitivity analysis.* Sensitivity is the process of testing the effects of changes in key model parameters on the computed CBA or CEA. Sensitivity could be applied in a number of ways to this analysis. Variation in individual cost parameters, discount rates, or treatment protocols might vary. However, the most instructive and realistic application of sensitivity analysis is evaluating the assumptions about the epidemiological rate measures of effect or benefit used. In the example used about TB treatment, sensitivity analysis is used to evaluate the ranges of treatment failure rates and rates of alternative types of drug resistance found. One might imagine that the success rates of SAT and the proportion of multidrug resistance for failure might vary as the population's understanding of the importance of treatment continuation increases. This could have a large impact on the final evaluation of SAT relative to DOT because of the extremely high cost of treatment failures. As the numbers in Table 13.6 indicated, DOT loses much of its relative value to SAT if steps can be taken to lower the rate of multidrug-resistant cases. This suggests that education might be a worthwhile intervention to explore.

Application of the DOTs methodology in international settings can also be of value. As indicated above, TB is an ongoing problem in a number of countries. Experience in Kazakhstan indicates that there may be as many as 52,000 active cases of TB in that country with 14,000 new cases per year. Current treatment protocol is hospitalization for an extended duration with minimal drug therapy. This is an issue of social policy with regard to continuing to fund the hospitals that provide treatment as opposed to devoting scarce resources to DOT.

While much of the data are uncertain, with some assumptions we can apply the cost-effectiveness analysis to this international problem. In this case, it appears that conventional treatment is a 60-day hospital stay and that is being compared to DOT. Success rates are not certain, but for analysis sake we can assume that hospitalization success would be no greater than success for SAT described above and probably significantly lower; thus, we used 75% versus 79%. We assume that even DOT will be less successful in this setting (80% vs. 84.5%). On the cost side, assume that ambulatory therapy is about 25% as costly in Kazakhstan as in the United States example; thus, we used $529.25 (25% of $2117). Hospitalization is 5% as costly and we used $643.75 (5% of $12,875) for drug-susceptible failure and $7313.55 (5% of

**Table 13.6. Sensitivity of Cost-effectiveness Ratios of Tuberculosis
Treatment Options to Changes in SAT Treatment Effects**

Treatment option		Standard rate	Higher SAT success rate	Lower SAT multidrug-resistant rate
DOT cost		$3999	$3999	$3999
Cure	$2117	.945	.945	.945
Failure prob.:		.055	.055	.055
Drug susp.	$12,875	.84	.84	.84
Multidrug	$146,271	.16	.16	.16
SAT cost		$12,167	$9073	$8225
Cure	$1339	.79	.85	.79
Failure prob.:		.21	.15	.21
Drug susp.	$12,875	.71	.71	.85
Multidrug	$146,271	.29	.29	.15
Cost difference (DOT − SAT)		−$8168	−$5074	−$4226
Treatment difference (DOT − SAT)		.155	.095	.155
Cost effectiveness ratios[a] (cost/cure)		−$52,700	−$53,400	−$27,300

[a]Cost effectiveness ratio = incremental cost/incremental outcome. In this case negative values of the cost effectiveness ratio indicate that you spend fewer resources and get better outcomes from DOT treatment. Therefore, even with substantial variation in estimates of effectiveness, DOT treatment saves substantial resources per successful case treated.

$146,271) for multidrug-resistant failure. All other treatment parameters are the same. Table 13.7 presents the results of applying these assumptions to a CEA in millions of US dollars for the assumed 14,000 new cases. This analysis, though filled with uncertainty, indicates that adopting DOT in Kazakhstan would generate substantial savings and generate a large increase in cure rates. The policy decision should not be difficult make when placed in these terms. Resistance to adopting accepted methodology for TB treatment yields poor outcomes and increases health care spending.

Table 13.7. Computation of Cost-Effectiveness Ratio of Tuberculosis Treatment Options[a]

Treatment cost	Cure costs[b]	Drug susceptible	Multidrug resistant	Total treatment cost	Outcome (cure rate)
DOT	$7.41	$1.44	$4.12	$12.97	80%
Hospitalization	$40.50	$0.00	$25.77	$66.27	75%
Difference	−$33.09	$1.44	−$21.65	−$53.31	5%
Cost effectiveness (CE) ratio	=		Incremental cost/incremental outcome		
	=		[−$53.31 million/700 (5%*14,000)]		
	=		−$76,143		

[a]Therefore, the adoption of DOT is a highly beneficial alternative to their current standard practice generating about $76,000 in savings per additional patient cured.
[b]All cost estimates are in millions of US dollars.

Conclusion

This chapter reviewed the epidemiological basis for the application of CBA and CEA in health care management situations. The public health nature of many health care goods and services promoted the development and application of these techniques to decision making and increasingly compel their use in the private sector.

In the simplest way all costs and benefits that economists use in their analysis have their origin in the underlying epidemiology of the patients under study. One can think of CEA as placing monetary value on basic incidence and prevalence measures when related to a disease process. This is not to say that there is not added value of formalized CBA and CEA when applied to health questions. As the case for TB management using commonly accepted DOT illustrated, the social, political, and economic decisions regarding treatment alternatives are made clearer through economic analysis. The epidemiological argument that DOT had superior outcomes is fine, but also showing that those outcomes could be achieved while lowering costs makes the argument compelling.

It is not often, however, that this clear an outcome exists. Careful identification, measurement, valuation, and analysis of costs and outcomes are necessary in most cases. The improved availability and quality of epidemiological data will result in the increasing use of CBA and CBE in making population-based assessments of the resource demands of adding or subtracting health care benefits.

Case Studies

Case Study No. 1
What Is the Most Cost-Effective Treatment for Tuberculosis?

Tuberculosis (TB) has increased dramatically in the United States and throughout the world since the mid-1980s. The incidence of TB is still low in the United States, but rates of reported active TB have increased worldwide and doubled in developing countries. Along with the overall increase in TB is an even more rapid increase in drug-resistant strains. While clinical trial evidence has demonstrated a highly efficacious treatment regimen for active TB, it has been less effective in practice. As a result, directly observed treatment (DOT) has been proposed as an alternative to self-administered therapy (SAT). Using

Table 13.8. Costs Associated With DOT and SAT Treatments for Multidrug-resistant Tuberculosis

Cost category	DOT	SAT
Initial treatment	$2,117	$1,339
Treatment	$1,206	$1,221
Patient time	$911	$118
Drug-susceptible failure	$12,875	$12,875
Diagnosis and treatment	$9,491	$9,491
Patient time	$3,384	$3,384
Multidrug-resistant failure[a]	$146,271	$146,271
Diagnosis and treatment	$125,995	$125,995
Patient time	$20,276	$20,276

[a]Treatment extends over 3 years. Costs are discounted at 5%.

data from a number of sources, we find that the "cure" rate for DOT is greater than that of SAT, 94.5% to 79.0%, respectively, and conditional on failure of initial cure, the SAT cases have a greater probability of multidrug-resistant cases, 29% to 16% (Burman *et al.*, 1997). Many resist adopting the DOT protocol because of its assumed greater cost. Table 13.8 summarizes the costs associated with various aspects of these two treatment alternatives.

Q.1. Which treatment protocol (DOT or SAT) cures more patients?

Q.2. What is the cost-effectiveness ratio of the DOT protocol for both direct and total costs?

Q.3. What are potential biases in the data for this analysis?

Q.4. Why is the effectiveness of SAT lower than DOT?

Q.5. What treatment strategy would you employ if you were the Minister of Health of a central Asian country and why?

Case Study No. 2
Health and Economic Benefits of Weight Loss

Obesity in the United States has increased from estimates of 25% of the population in the late 1970s to about 35% in the 1990s. There is evidence that obesity has a role in a variety of diseases including hypertension, type 2 diabetes, coronary heart disease, and stroke. The increased risk that obesity plays can be reversed if weight is reduced. Recent research has estimated the medical treatment cost savings for five diseases (heart disease, stroke, hypertension, hypercholesterolemia, and type 2 diabetes) associated with a sustained 10% weight loss by age, gender, and an index of obesity (Oster *et al.*, 1999). The cost of "reducing" weight for obese persons is assumed to vary by age and gender and is incurred in the base year and every 10 years until death. Health costs avoided and costs are assumed to extend to age 99. Table 13.9 summarizes the health costs avoided (benefits) and costs of reducing weight by age, gender, and starting weight.

Q.1. Which gender and age-group has the highest benefit-to-cost ratio for weight loss program?

Q.2. How does initial weight relate to the benefit to cost ratio?

Q.3. What are the potential biases in the data for this analysis?

Table 13.9. Health Costs Avoided and Costs of Weight Loss[a]

Gender and age group	Weight categories		
	27.5 kg/m^2	32.5 kg/m^2	37.5 kg/m^2
Men age 35–44			
Health costs avoided	$2300	$3500	$4900
Costs of weight loss[a]	$700	$800	$900
Women age 35–44			
Health costs avoided	$2200	$3300	$4600
Costs of weight loss[a]	$750	$850	$950

[a]This is cost of weight loss episode. Total cost consists of treatment during the initial year and every 10 years until death. These costs should be discounted at 3%.

Q.4. Why do the health costs avoided by weight loss increase with initial weight?

Q.5. What is your conclusion concerning the appropriateness of weight loss programs?

Case Study No. 3
Inactivated Poliovirus Vaccine and Routine Childhood Immunizations

Poliomyelitis incidence essentially has been eradicated since the late 1970s. Since 1980, the only cases in the United States have been "imported" or vaccine associated. The question of using inactivated poliovirus vaccine (IPV) as opposed to live attenuated oral poliovirus vaccine (OPV) has been raised repeatedly during this period. The question of the efficacy of IPV has not been questioned, but cost effectiveness is less clear. Currently, there are essentially three dosing options being seriously considered: four doses of OPV; two doses of IPV followed by two doses of OPV; or four doses IPV. IPV is more costly to administer but totally avoids the potential of vaccine-activated polio (Table 13.10).

Q.1. What is the total of incremental costs for the three immunization options?

Q.2. What are the cost differences of the competing alternatives?

Q.3. What are the cost-effectiveness ratios for the alternative immunization schedules?

Q.4. What immunization policy would you favor and what additional information would you want to consider before making this decision?

Case Study No. 4
Cost-Effectiveness of Magnetic Resonance Imaging for Internal Derangement of the Knee

Patients with internal derangement of the knee (IDK) often have arthroscopic surgery of the knee as either a diagnostic or therapeutic procedure. This costly, invasive procedure adds to national health care

Table 13.10. Costs and Health Costs Avoided through Childhood Vaccination[a]

Category	OPV	IPV	2IPV/2OPV
Annual VAP cases per year	9.5	0	4.75
Compensation per VAP case	$1.2M		
Efficacy of avoiding VAP	0%	100%	50% (32%–68%)
Vaccine prices per dose			
Public	$2.27	$5.28	$3.78
Private	$10.18	$11.55	$10.87
Weighted average	$6.22	$8.42	$7.32
Doses			
First	4.0 million		
Subsequent	11.4 million		
Administration cost (per visit)	$9.40	$9.40	$9.40
Clinic travel cost (per visit)	$3.00	$3.00	$3.00

[a]OPV, oral polio vaccine; IPV, inactivated polio vaccine; VAP, vaccine-activated polio.

Table 13.11. Direct, Indirect, and Total Costs
per Patient for Internal Knee Derangement

Category	Direct	Indirect	Total
Arthroscopy, diagnostic	$539	$298	$837
Arthroscopy, therapeutic	$673	$297	$970
MRI	$216	$19	$235

*a*From Suarez-Almazor *et al.* (1999).

expenditures and carries some surgical and anesthetic complication risk. Studies have demonstrated that magnetic resonance imaging (MRI) can reliably detect lesions of the cruciate ligaments and menisci (Suarez-Almazor *et al.*, 1999). Consequently, there is the potential to use MRI as a means of identifying patients without treatable lesions, thus avoiding costly arthroscopy surgery. Extensive analyses have been performed on patients presenting with IDK and the following general information has been found: The percentage of arthroscopies avoided is assumed to be 10% with a range from 5 to 16%. Costs include direct and indirect costs. Direct costs consist of orthopedic surgeon fee, anesthesia, operation room costs (including overhead), drug costs, four physical therapy visits, and one follow-up visit with surgeon. Indirect costs were time off work assuming that 67% of patients were in the workforce. Five days of lost work were assumed for the surgery and 2.5 hours of lost work for an MRI. The costs are summarized in Table 13.11.

Q.1. What is the cost per arthroscopic surgery avoided assuming social (total) costs are considered?

Q.2. What is the cost per arthroscopic surgery avoided considering only direct costs?

Q.3. Perform sensitivity analyses on the social cost estimates to determine best and worst case estimates?

Q.4. What screening policy would you propose given the data presented? What additional information might you want to obtain?

References

Bass, E., Steinberg, E., Pitt, H., Saba, G., Lillemoe, K., Kafonek, D., Gadacz, T., Gordon, T., and Anderson, G., 1991, Cost-effectiveness of extracorporeal shock-wave lithotripsy versus cholecystectomy for symptomatic gallstones, *Gastroenterology* **101**:189–199.

Burman, W. J., Dalton, C. B., Cohn, D. L., Butler, J. R., and Reves, R. R., 1997, A cost-effectiveness analysis of directly observed therapy vs. self-administered therapy for treatment of Tuberculosis, *Chest* **112**:63–70.

Centers for Disease Control and Prevention, 1993, Tuberculosis control laws—United States, 1993: Recommendations of the Advisory Council for the Elimination of Tuberculosis (ACET), *Morbid. Mortal. Week. Rep.* **42** (RR-15):1–28.

Combs, D., O'Brien, R., and Geiter, L., 1990, USPHS Tuberculosis Short-Course Chemotherapy Trial 21: Effectiveness, toxicity, and acceptability. The report of final results, *Ann. Intern. Med.* **112**:397–406.

Dalaker, J, 1999, US Census Bureau, Current Population Reports, Series P60-207, *Poverty in the United States: 1998*, US Government Printing Office, Washington, DC.

Deininger, K., and Squire, L., 2000, Economic growth and income inequality: Reexamining the links, Worldbank, http://www.worldbank.org/fandd/english/0397/articles/0140397.htm.

Dranove, D., Shanley, M., and White, W., 1991, How fast are hospital prices really rising? *Med. Care* **29**:690–696.

Eisenberg, J. M., 1989, Clinical economics: A guide to the economic analysis of clinical practices. *JAMA* **262**:2879–2886.

Glandon, G., and Buck, T., 1994, Cost-benefit analysis of medical information systems: A critique. in *Evaluating*

Health Care Information Systems: Methods and Applications (J. Anderson, Aydin, C., and Jay, S. eds. pp. 164–189, Sage Publications, Thousand Oaks, CA.

Glandon, G., and Shapiro, R., 1988, Benefit-cost analysis of hospital information systems: The state of the (non) art, *J. Health Human Res. Admin.* **11:**30–92.

Gold, M., Siegel, J., Russell, L., and Weinstein, M., 1996, *Cost-Effectiveness in Health and Medicine*, Oxford University Press, New York.

Goldie, S. J., Weinstein, M. C., Kuntz, K. M., and Freedberg, K. A., 1999, The costs, clinical benefits, and cost-effectiveness of screening for cervical cancer in HIV-infected women, *Ann. Intern. Med.* **130:**97–107.

Guyatt, G., Naylor, D., Juniper, E., Heyland, D., Jaeschke, R., and Cook, D., 1997, Users' guide to the medical literature, XII how to use articles about health related quality of life, *JAMA* **277:**1232–1237.

Jacobs, P., and Fassbender, K., 1998, The measurement of indirect costs in the health economics evaluation literature. A review, *Int. J. Technol. Assess. Health Care* **14:**799–808.

Kaplan, R., 1993, Quality of life assessment for cost/utility studies in cancer, *Cancer Treat. Rev.* **19**(Suppl. A):85–96.

King, H., Glick, H., Mason, E., and Flamm, E., 1995, Elective surgery for asymptomatic, unruptured, intracranial aneurysms: A cost-effectiveness analysis, *J. Neurosurg.* **83:**403–412.

Kirschstein, R., 2000, Disease-specific estimates of direct and indirect costs of illness and NIH support: Fiscal year 2000 update. Department of Health and Human Services, National Institutes of Health (June 2, 2000) http://www1.od.nih.gov/osp/ospp/ecostudies/COIreportweb.htm.

Krahn, M., and Detsky, A., 1993, Should Canada and the United States universally vaccinate infants against hepatitis B? A cost-effectiveness analysis, *Med Decision Making* **13:**4–20.

Littrup, P. J., Goodman, A. C., and Mettlin, C. J., 1993, The benefit and cost of prostate cancer early detection, *CA-A Cancer J. Clinicians* **43:**134–149.

MacKeigan, L. and Pathak, D., 1992, Overview of health-related quality-of-life measures, *Am. J. Hosp. Pharm.* **49:**2236–2245.

McNeil, B., and Adelstein, J., 1976, Determining the value of diagnostic and screening tests, *J. Nuclear Med.* **17:**439–448.

Melin, A., Hakansson, S., and Bygren, L., 1993, The cost-effectiveness of rehabilitation in the home: a study of Swedish elderly, *Am. J. Public Health* **83:**356–362.

Miller, M., Sutter, R., Strebel, P., and Hadler, S., 1996, Cost-effectiveness of incorporating inactivated poliovirus vaccine into the routine childhood immunization schedule, *JAMA* **276:**967–971.

O'Brien, B., Heyland, D. Richardson, S., Levine, M., and, Drummond, M., 1997, Users' guide to the medical literature, XIII, how to use an article on economic analysis of clinical practice, B. What are the results and will they help me in caring for my patients? *JAMA* **277:**1802–1806.

Olds, D., Henderson, C., Phelps, C. Kitzman, H., and Hanks, C., 1993, Effect of prenatal and infancy nurse home visitation on government spending, *Med. Care* **31:**155–174.

Oster, G., Thompson, D., Edelsberg, J., Bird, A. P., and Colditz, G. A., 1999, Lifetime health and economic benefits of weight loss among obese persons, *Am. J. Pubic Health* **89:**1536–1542.

Pauker, S., and Kassirer, J., 1975, Therapeutic decision making: A cost-benefit analysis, *N. Engl. J. Med.* **293:**229–234.

Phelps, C., and Mushlin, A., 1991, On the (near) equivalence of cost-effectiveness and cost-benefit analyses, *Int. J. Technol. Assess. Health Care* **7:**12–21.

Raviglione, M., Snider, D., and Kochi, A., 1995, Global epidemiology of tuberculosis. Morbidity and mortality of a worldwide epidemic. *JAMA* **273:**220–226.

Revicki, D., and Ehreth, J., 1997, Health-related quality-of-life assessment and planning for the pharmaceutical industry, *Clin. Ther.* **19:**1101–1115.

Schulman, K., Kinosian, B., Jacobson, T., Glick, H., Willian, M., Koffer, H., and Eisenberg, J., 1990, Reducing high blood cholesterol level with drugs: Cost-effectiveness of pharmacologic management, *JAMA* **264:**3025–3033.

Schulman, K., Burke, J., Drummond, M., Davies, L., Carlsson, P., Gruger, J., Harris, A., Lucioni, C., Gisbert, R., Llana, T., Tom, E., Bloom, B., Willke, R., and Glick, H., 1998, Resource costing for multinational neurologic clinical trials: Methods and results, *Health Econ.* **7:**629–638.

Siegel, J., Weinstein, M., Russell, L., and Gold, M., 1996, Recommendations for reporting cost-effectiveness analyses, *JAMA* **276:**1339–1341.

Sisk, J. E., Moskowitz, A. J., Whang, W., Lin, J. D., Fedson, D. S., McBean, A. M., Plouffe, J., Cetron, M., and Butler, J., 1997, Cost-effectiveness of vaccination against pneumococcal bacteremia among elderly people, *JAMA* **278:**1333–1339.

Suarez-Almazor, M., Kaul, P., Kendall, C., Saunders, L., and Johnston, D., 1999, The cost-effectiveness of magnetic resonance imaging for patients with internal derangement of the knee. *Int. J. Technol. Assess. Health Care* **15:**392–405.

Tengs, T., Adams, M., Pliskin, J., Safran, D., Siegel, J., Weinstein, M., and Graham, J., 1995, Five hundred life-saving interventions and their cost-effectiveness, *Risk Anal.* **15:**369–390.

Torrance, G. W., Siegel, J. E., and Luce, B. E., 1996, Framing and designing the cost-effectiveness analysis, in *Cost-Effectiveness in Health and Medicine* (M. Gold, J. Siegel, L. Russell, and M. Weinstein, eds. pp. 54–81, Oxford University Press, New York.

Trahey, P., 1991, A comparison of the cost-effectiveness of two types of occupational therapy services, *Am. J. Occup. Ther.* **45:**397–400.

United Nations, 2000, Overcoming human poverty: UNDP Poverty Report, 2000 http://www.undp.org/povertyreport/exec/english.html.

US Agency for International Development, 1997, *Tuberculosis Initiative in Central Asia*, US Agency for International Development, Department of State, http://www.usaid.gov.

Warner, K., and Luce, B., 1982, *Cost-Benefit and Cost-Effectiveness Analysis in Health Care: Principles, Practice and Potential*, Health Administration Press, Ann Arbor, MI.

Weinstein, M., and Stason, W., 1977, Foundations of cost-effectiveness analysis for health and medical practices. *N. Engl. J. Med.* **296:**716–721.

Weinstein, M. C., Siegel, J. E., Gold, M. R., Kamiel, M. S., and Russell, L. B., 1996, Recommendations of the panel on cost-effectiveness in health and medicine, *JAMA* **276:**1253–1258.

Weisbrod, B. A. 1983, *Economics and Medical Research*, American Enterprise Institute, Washington, DC.

World Bank, 1999, Living standards measurement study of the World Bank (December 20, 2000), http://www.worldbank.org/lsms/index.htm.

14

Ethics, Epidemiology, and Health Service Delivery

Sana Loue

Introduction

Important advances have occurred in epidemiology and health services in the last century. Many of these developments have been coextensive with or have resulted from significant historical events, such as the experiments conducted by Nazi physicians (Lifton, 1986), the Tuskegee syphilis study in the United States (Brandt, 1985), and the Cold War radiation experiments (Welsome, 1999) and the consequent increase in concern for individuals' ability to consent to participation in health experiments and the confidentiality of information relating to individuals. Scientific advances, such as the identification of specific genes and their association with particular diseases, and the development of new systems of health care delivery, such as health maintenance organizations, also have given rise to increased concerns for the development of safeguards for the individual and for society.

Accordingly, these events and advances require that ethics be considered in management decision making, especially as the consequences of this decision making involve impacts on large populations. Very generally, ethics can be defined, as involving questions relating to morality, moral disagreements, and conflicting judgments about particular issues. Examples of ethical dilemmas include the debates within a hospital regarding the provision of abortion services or the passage of legislation that would permit physician-assisted suicide. The inclusion of provisions for end-of-year bonuses in physician employment contracts that are tied to nonutilization of health services, particularly of hospitalization, similarly raise ethical concerns.

The first portion of this chapter sets forth various but not all approaches or strategies that can be utilized in resolving ethical dilemmas. At a less general level, there are ethical principles that flow from these approaches and that provide the basis for rules or norms. A rule is a general statement that states that something should or should not be done because it is right

Sana Loue   Department of Epidemiology and Biostatistics, School of Medicine, Case Western Reserve University, Cleveland, Ohio 44106.

Epidemiology and the Delivery of Health Care Services: Methods and Applications, Second Edition, edited by Denise M. Oleske. Kluwer Academic / Plenum Publishers, New York, 2001.

or wrong. The second portion of this chapter focuses on principles and rules that have evolved to guide the design and conduct of research studies. Because the health care manager often will have within his or her institution research studies, support for the ethical conduct of such studies is now an essential component of management practice. The case studies at the close of this chapter ask you to make judgments regarding specific situations and to delineate the principles on which you relied and the strategies that you utilized to arrive at those judgments.

Approaches to Resolving Ethical Dilemmas

When confronted with an ethical dilemma, a convenient approach is to select a framework or strategy for attempting a resolution. Table 14.1 summarizes various approaches and the criteria used to judge "rightness" and "wrongness" using that framework. These strategies are also detailed below.

Principlism

Central to principle-based theory is the existence of governing principles that enunciate obligations (Beauchamp and Childress, 1994). The term *principlism* often is used to refer to four standard principles derived from the Nuremberg Code (1949), and further elucidated by the Helsinki Declarations. Principlism, in essence, is the overriding approach utilized in the United States and in the research context is reflected in regulations promulgated by various agencies of the federal government. These principles are respect for persons, nonmaleficence, beneficence, and justice (Beauchamp and Childress, 1994).

Respect for persons encompasses the concept of informed consent. In turn, informed consent requires capacity, voluntariness, disclosure of information, and understanding. Capacity or the lack of it, is often determined by reference to one of three standards: (1) the ability to state a preference, without more; (2) the ability to understand information and one's own situation; and (3) the ability to utilize information to make a life decision (Appelbaum and Grisso, 1988). Voluntariness refers to the individual's ability to consent or refuse a treatment or procedure or participation without coercion, duress, or manipulation (Beauchamp and Childress, 1994).

The concept of disclosure focuses on the provision of information to the patient or research participant. Ethically, the health care provider or researcher must disclose the facts

Table 14.1. Strategies and Criteria for Ethical Evaluation of Alternative Courses of Action

Strategy	Criteria for judging "rightness" or "wrongness"
Principlism	Respect for persons, beneficence, nonmaleficence, justice
Casuistry	"Discover" ethical principles from case through examination of that case, past analogous cases, and principles derived from past cases
Communitarianism	Balance between social forces and the individual, community and autonomy, common good and liberty, individual rights and social responsibility
Feminist ethics	Emphasis on relations and caring; content of issue
Utilitarianism	Weigh "good" and "bad" consequences to welfare resulting from each alternative course of action; select course of action that maximizes "good" consequences to welfare

that the patient or research participant would consider important in deciding whether to consent or to withhold consent, information that the health care provider or researcher believes is material, the purpose of the consent, and the scope of the consent, if given (Beauchamp and Childress, 1994). In the health care context, the provider also must give his or her recommendation. Legally, additional information may be required. For instance, legally a physician may be required to disclose personal interest that may affect his or her judgment, whether or not those interest are related to the patient's health (*Moore v. Regents of the University of California*, 1990).

Understanding is related to the disclosure of information in a way that can be understood. Studies have shown, for instance, that information provided to prospective participants in research studies often is written at a level above the participants' educational level (Hammerschmidt and Keane, 1992; Meade and Howser, 1992) and often includes unfamiliar words, long words, and long sentences (Rivera *et al.*, 1992). Understanding also may be impeded in situations where the patient or research participant comprehends the information but refuses to accept the information. For instance, a patient may refuse to consent to an HIV test where she intellectually understands what behaviors may subject an individual to an increased risk of transmission, but believes that such a test is unnecessary for her because she is not ill and she believes that HIV-infected persons must look and feel sick.

Nonmaleficence refers to the obligation to refrain from harming others. Conversely, the principle of beneficence "refers to a moral obligation to act for the benefit of others" (Beauchamp and Childress, 1994, p. 260). This must be distinguished from benevolence, which refers to the character trait of one who acts for the benefit of others. Although some beneficent acts may be admirable, they are not necessarily obligatory, such as the donation of blood or an organ to another. The principle of justice refers to the distribution of the benefits and burdens, e.g., of health care and of research. How those benefits and burdens should be distributed is the subject of intense and ongoing debate.

The principlistic approach has been criticized on a number of grounds. First, the principles themselves can be in conflict in specific situations and they provide little or no guidance in resolving such conflicts. For instance, the principle of respect for persons would suggest that a woman has the right to decide whether or not to participate in a clinical trial for a new drug designed to reduce transmission of a sexually transmitted disease, based on receipt of all information material to that decision-making process. Beneficence, however, would argue that she should not be permitted to participate because of the unknown and unknowable risks to any future unborn children. Second, principlism does not have a systematic theory as its foundation (Green, 1990).

Casuistry

Casuistry refers to a case-based system of ethical analysis (Jonsen, 1995). Artnak (1995) has summarized the techniques utilized in casuistical analysis as consisting of three features: typification, relationships to maxims, and certitude (Artnak, 1995). Typification refers to a comparison of the case at hand with the caregiver's past experiences and identification of the similarities and differences between the instant case and those that preceded it. Relationship to maxims refers to reliance on "rules of thumb," which consider the characteristics of the situation at hand. Certitude refers to the certainty of the outcome in relationship to all the alternative courses of action that are available. In essence, casuistry represents a "bottom-up" approach to the development of knowledge, rather than a "top-down" approach, as is perceived to be the case with principlism (Arras, 1991).

Unlike principlism, which sets forth principles to be applied in specific cases, casuistry discovers ethical principles in the cases to be analyzed (Jonsen, 1986). Jonsen (1995; p. 241) has defined what makes a "case":

> A case is a confluence of persons and actions in a time and a place, all of which can be given names and dates. A case, we say, is concrete as distinguished from abstract because it represents the congealing the coalescence, or the growing together (in Latin, *concrescere*) of many circumstances. Each case is unique in its circumstances, yet each case is similar in type of other cases and can, therefore, be compared and contrasted. Cases can be posed at various levels of concreteness. Some will be composed of quite specific persons, times, and places; others will describe an event or practice in more diffuse terms, such as the "case of the Bosnian war" or the "case of medical experimentation." I refer to cases of the latter sort as "great cases."

The principles thus derived are subject to revision because they are intimately linked to their factual surroundings, which vary between cases and over time. Casuistical analysis, then, "might be summarized as a form of reasoning by means of examples that always point beyond themselves" (Arras, 1991, p. 35). This is similar to the development of common law, which derives from the analysis of judicial opinions. Each subsequent case is examined based on similarities and differences with similar cases that preceded it: "The ultimate view of the case and its appropriate resolution comes, not from a single principle, nor from a dominant theory, but from the converging impression made by all of the relevant facts and arguments that appear (Jonsen, 1995, p. 245). This can be contrasted with the principlistic approach, which is more analogous to a code-based system of law, in which a situation may be resolved by reference to a prior codification of rules pertaining to such situations. Arras (1991) has argued that the emphasis on the development of principles from cases, rather than the reverse, requires the utilization of real cases, rather than hypothetical ones. Hypothetical ones, he argues, tend to be more theory-driven, rather than practice-driven.

There is a specific method to effectuate case comparison. First, the midlevel principles relevant to a case and role-specific responsibilities are identified. Potential courses of action must be determined. Third, the case is compared to others that are similar. Fourth, for each identified course of action, a case must be identified in which the option under consideration is justified. These justified cases are termed "paradigms" (Kuczewski, 1994). A paradigm case is

> [a] case in which the circumstances were clear, the relevant maxim unambiguous and the rebuttals weak, in the minds of almost any observer. The claim that this action is wrong (or right) is widely persuasive. There is little need to present arguments for the rightness (or wrongness) of the case and it is very hard to argue against its rightness (or wrongness). (Jonsen, 1991, p. 301).

New cases are then compared to a set of paradigm cases and a paradigm that is similar to the new case is identified. This identified similar paradigm then serves as a guide for action in the new case (Kuczewski, 1994). A paradigm is "the ultimate justification of moral action (Kuczewski, 1994, p. 105), although it must be recognized that some paradigms may be more stable than others.

Jonsen and Toulmin (1988) have characterized the work of the National Commission for the Protection of Human subjects of Biomedical and Behavioral Research as casuistic in nature. The commissioners hail from a variety of academic and nonacademic disciplines. They analyzed paradigmatic cases involving harm and fairness and then extended their analysis to more complex situations raised by biomedical research, essentially utilizing an incremental approach to the examination of difficulties encountered in research.

Arras (1991) has identified numerous strengths of casuistry. First, this method encourages the development of detailed case studies, because their facts are critical not only in resolving the issue(s) at hand, but also in the resolution of case situations that do not yet exist. Second, the case-based approach encourages reliance not merely on a single case, but rather on a sequence of cases that relate to a central theme. Third, this strategy will require in-depth examination of exactly what issues are being raised in a particular situation.

These same characteristics, however, are weaknesses as well as strengths. For instance, it is unclear what situations and how a situation is to constitute a "case" meriting in-depth examination. Second, casuistry does not provide guidance on how detailed a case must be to be adequate, since a case necessarily involves multiple perspectives, numerous facts, and various issues. Third, the resolution of new situations requires reference to previous situations that embody similar issues and/or facts, but no guidance is available as to how to group cases thematically (Arras, 1991). The reader is advised to consult Artnak and Dimmitt (1996) for an example of how casuistry is used to evaluate ethical issues concerning patient privacy and confidentiality in matters that deal with violence and abuse.

Communitarianism

Communitarianism is premised on several themes: the need for a shared philosophical understanding with respect to communal goals and the communal good, the need to integrate what is now fragmented ethical thought, and the need to develop "intersubjective bonds that are mutually constitutive of [individuals'] identities" (Kuczewski, 1997, p. 3).

Etzioni (1998) has distinguished between the "old communitarians" and the "new communitarians." The former are characterized by their emphasis on the significance of social forces and bonds (Etzioni, 1998); the latter focus on the balance between social forces and the individual, between community and autonomy, between the common good and liberty, and between individual rights and social responsibility (The Responsive Communitarian Platform: Rights and Responsibilities, 1998, p. xxv). The new communitarians, then, are concerned with a dual danger: the society whose communal foundations are deteriorating and the society in which individual freedoms are negated. New communitarians advocate the promotion of prosocial behavior through persuasion, rather than through coercion (Etzioni, 1998).

Unlike principlism, which focuses on the rights of the individual, communitarianism examines communal values and relationships and attempts to ascertain which are present and which are absent. Where communitarianism emphasizes the need for a common vocabulary and shared understanding casuistry rejects such a foundation, arguing that it is the "breakdown of tradition [that] forces reexamination of particular instances of action and a return to concrete practical reasoning" (Kuczewski, 1982, p. 61).

One difficulty of communitarianism lies in the ability to define what constitutes the relevant community. Etzioni (1998, pp. xiii–xiv) has offered the following:

> Communities need not be geographically concentrated....
> Communities are not automatically or necessarily places of virtue. Many traditional communities that were homogenous, if not monolithic, were authoritarian and oppressive. And a community may lock into a set of values that one may find abhorrent....
>
> However, contemporary communities tend to be new communities that are part of a pluralistic web of communities. People are, at one and the same time, members of several

communities, such as professional, residential and others. They can, and do, use these multi-memberships ... to protect themselves from excessive pressure by any one community.

What is the scope of communities? It is best to think about communities as nested, each within a more encompassing one ... Ultimately, some aspire to a world community that would encapsulate all people. Other communitarians object to such globalism and suggest that strong bonds and the moral voice, the essence of communities, mainly are found in relatively small communities in which people know one another, at least to some extent, as in many stable neighborhoods.

Feminist Ethics

Purdy (1992) has delineated four tasks that can be accomplished by feminist ethics: (1) the provision of an emphasis on the importance of women ad their interests; (2) the provision of a focus on issues especially affecting women; (3) the reexamination of fundamental assumptions; and (4) the incorporation of feminist insights from other fields into the field of ethics. Sherwin (1992) assigns to feminist medical ethics the responsibility of developing conceptual models that will restructure the power associated with healing, to allow individuals to have the maximum degree of control possible over their own health. Accordingly, feminist ethics is often concerned with the content of the discussion (Warren, 1992), such as reproductive technologies, the rationing of medical care, the participation of women in research, and physician–patient communication. Feminist ethics as an approach subsumes several alternative approaches, including the ethic of care and relational ethics, discussed below.

The Ethic of Care

The ethic of care derives from Gilligan's (1982) empirical observations that found that men tend to resolve situations utilizing an ethic of rights, with an emphasis on fairness, while women tend to rely on an ethic of caring that focuses on needs, care, and the prevention of harm. Gilligan, then, did not dispute that differences exist between men and women. Rather, Gilligan maintained that society had placed a greater value on individual achievement, thereby devaluing the caretaking roles fulfilled by women. The ethic of care, then, rejects the cognitive emphasis of other approaches to ethical analysis and emphasizes the moral role of the emotions. The detachment inherent in the cognitive approaches is criticized precisely because it fails to recognize the attachment inherent in relationships.

The ethic of care has been criticized on a number of bases. First, Nicholson (1993) has argued that our understanding of reality need not be limited to two different modes. Tronto (1993) has asserted that the advocates of an ethic of care have not adequately explored and explained the assumptions on which this moral position is premised.

Relational Ethics

Noddings (1984), like Gilligan, has criticized traditional ethical theories for their undervaluing of caring and their counterintuitive approach to issues arising in the context of relationships. Noddings goes further than does Gilligan, however, and argues that an ethics of care is better than, not only different from, an ethic of justice. Noddings' objections to universalism are moderated by her observation that the caring attitude that underlies her ethical view is, in itself, universal.

> Noddings (1984, p. 5) maintains there exists a natural caring: The relation of natural caring will be identified as the human condition that we, consciously or unconsciously, perceive as "good." It is that condition toward which we long and strive, and it is our longing for care—to be in that special relation—that provides the motivation for us to be moral. We want to be moral in order to remain in the caring relation and to enhance the ideal of ourselves as one-caring.

She argues that an ethic of caring can be taught as easily as an ethic of rules and principles. Moral development does not require the replacement of natural caring with ethical caring.

Noddings asserts that relational ethics encompasses two types of virtues. The first is that set of virtues that belong to the relationship of the people involved. The second set consists of those virtues that belong to the individuals involved in the relationship, such as honesty. Noddings frames most situations in terms of relational dramas, arguing, for instance, that even a decision relating to euthanasia should be made in consultation with those who will be affected by the patient's suffering and dying. There is an underlying assumption that such consultations and discussions will result in a decision by consensus.

Tong (1993) and others (Card, 1990; Hoagland, 1991) have criticized Noddings relational ethics on a number of grounds. Tong disputes the notion that consensus will be reached through discussions involving members of a relational network. Tong notes that most individuals are members of networks that are not altogether healthy ones. Hoagland has criticized Noddings' (1) reliance on unequal relationships as the basis for her assertions; (2) assumption that the individual providing the care is in the best position to know what is good for the person receiving the care; (3) assumption that inequalities in abilities, rather than power, necessarily render a relationship unequal; and (4) advisory that the cared-for blindly trust their caregivers, pointing out that this would result in the vulnerability of those receiving the care and potentially subject them to abuse. Hoagland further advises that Noddings has failed to distinguish between receptivity to caring and reciprocity of caring, and by emphasizing receptivity has failed to incorporate into her model the kind of respect that is truly necessary for a moral relationship.

Feminist theory has been criticized as being underdeveloped, too contextual and hostile to principles, and overly confined to the private sphere of relationships (Beauchamp and Childress, 1994). The ethic of care also has been recognized as providing an important corrective to rights-based theory and a focus on impartiality, to the neglect of sensitivity and practical judgment (Beauchamp and Childress, 1994).

Utilitarianism

The theory of utilitarianism is premised on the idea of utility: That the "aggregate welfare is the ultimate standard of right and wrong" (Reiman, 1988, p. 41). The "right" course of action is determined by summing the "good" consequences and the "bad" consequences to welfare that may result from each alternative course of action and selecting that course of action that appears to maximize the "good" consequences to welfare. Utilitarianism, then, values an action based on its utility-maximizing consequences and as a result has been known as consequentialism (Williams and Smart, 1973).

How to measure gains and losses to welfare, however, is far from simple and to a great degree depends on which values are most important and how they are to be weighed. For instance, the maximization of good can be premised on the value of happiness, i.e., whichever course of action produces the greatest degree of happiness, or it can refer to the maximization of goods valued by rational persons. Mill (1863/1998, p. 124) explained what the maximization of happiness means:

> [T]he ultimate end, with reference to and for the sake of which all other things are desirable—whether we are considering our own good or that of other people—is an existence exempt as far as possible from pain, and as rich as possible in enjoyments, both in point of quantity and quality; the test of the quality and the rule for measuring it against quantity being the preference felt by those who, in their opportunities of experience, to which must be added their habits of self-consciousness and self-observation are best furnished with the means of comparison.

Quality was to be assessed as follows:

> If I am asked what I mean by difference in quality of pleasures, or what makes one pleasure more valuable than another, merely as a pleasure, except its being in greater amount, there is but one possible answer. Of two pleasures, if there be one to which all or almost all who have experience of both give a decided preference, irrespective of any feeling of moral obligation to prefer it, that is the more desirable pleasure. If one of the two is, by those who are competently acquainted with both, placed so far above the other that they prefer it, even though knowing it to be attended with a greater amount of discontent, and would not resign it for any quantity of the other pleasure which their nature is capable of, we are justified in ascribing to the preferred enjoyment a superiority in quality so far outweighing quantity as to render it, in comparison, of small account. (Mill, 1863/1998, p. 123).

Mill's explanation fails to explain, however, how much experience is required or sufficient to assess the quality of a particular end and how one person's competence is to be judged. Mill did address, however, the difficulty in assessing even what is to be accepted as "good":

> Questions of ultimate ends are not amenable to direct proof. Whatever can be proved to be good must be so by being shown to be a means to something admitted to be good without proof. The medical art is proved to be good by its conducing to health; but how is it possible to prove that health is good? (1863/1998, p. 119)

Unlike Mill, Bentham (1962) proposed that individuals consider intensity, duration, certainty, propinquity, fecundity, purity, and extent in assessing the utility of specified actions for specified individuals.

The role of rules in utilitarianism is somewhat controversial. Some utilitarians ("act utilitarians") would argue that rules provide a rough guide but do not require adherence where the greatest good in a particular circumstance may result from breach of the rule. Others emphasize the importance of the rule in maximizing the "good" consequences, as demonstrated by one utilitarian in discussing the importance of truth telling in the context of the physician–patient relationship:

> The good, which may be done by deception in a few cases, is almost as nothing, compared with the evil which it does in many, when the prospect of its doing good was just as promising as it was in those in which it succeeded. And when we add to this the evil which would result from a general adoption of a system of deception, the importance of a strict

adherence to the truth in our intercourse with the sick, even on the ground of expediency, becomes incalculably great. (Hooker, 1849, p. 357)

Smart (1961) has advocated a third possibility, that of sometimes relying on rules.

Utilitarianism has been criticized on numerous grounds. Beauchamp and Childress (1994) have argued that utilitarianism appears to permit blatantly immoral acts where such acts would maximize utility. As a result, the appropriateness of including utilitarians on institutional review boards has been called into question (Reiman, 1988). Tong (1993) has detailed the difficulty inherent in the utilitarian perspective. Utilitarians do not, for instance, want to defend preferences that are discriminatory. Consequently, they may attempt to distinguish between acceptable and unacceptable preferences or rational and irrational preferences, classifying those that are discriminatory as unacceptable and/or irrational. However, distinguishing between rational/irrational and acceptable/unacceptable may be equally difficult. Additionally, a utilitarian perspective requires that an individual subvert his or her preference to the larger good, something that many may be unwilling to do. Williams and Smart (1973) have noted the difficulty in even establishing causality to determine utility, e.g., whether a particular action is related to a particular consequence or whether a situation is so attenuated from an action that it cannot be said to be a consequence of it.

Donagan (1968) has asserted that utilitarianism fails to distinguish between those actions that are morally obligatory and those that are performed based on personal ideals and are above and beyond the call of moral obligation. In a similar vein, Williams and Smart (1973, p. 97) have noted that utilitarianism essentially creates negative responsibility:

It is because consequentialism attached value ultimately to states of affairs, and its concern is with what states of affairs the world contains, that it essentially involves the notion of *negative responsibility*: that if I am ever responsible for anything, then I must be just as much responsible for things that I allow or fail to prevent as I am for things that I myself, in the everyday restricted sense, bring about. Those things must also enter my deliberations, as a responsible moral agent, on the same footing. What matters is what states of affairs the world contains, and so what matters with respect to a given action is what comes about if it is done, and what comes about if it is not done, and those are questions not intrinsically affected by the nature of the causal linkage, in particular by whether the outcome is partly produced by other agents.

Despite its obvious shortcomings, the utilitarian perspective has various strengths. First, the emphasis placed on consideration of the consequences potentially serves to maximize beneficence, when it is the good of all that is the ultimate goal. As Sen (1987, p. 75) has observed, "Consequentialist reasoning may be fruitfully used even when consequentialism as such is not accepted. To ignore consequences is to leave an ethical story half told." Second, because utilitarianism appears to demand from individuals extraordinary service, the perspective challenges individuals to rise above an ordinary level of function. Application of the utilitarian approach in ethical decision making is considered in the formulation of quality-adjusted life years (QALYs) (Burrows and Brown, 1993). Here the ethical decision is how to promote economic efficiency in the use of rationed funds for health care and yet maximize health outcomes. The development of QALYs and disability adjusted life-years (DALYs) becomes problematic to some when ethically viewed from the utilitarian approach as social choice then emphasizes the net sum of benefits without regard to the distribution of benefits to the population. The development of clinical practice guidelines is another example of this conflict and the utilitarian approach to addressing a health care utilization problem (Panek, 1999).

Principles, Rules, and Guidelines

Numerous documents exist that provide guidance in the implementation of epidemiological or clinical research. These documents, however, represent a "gold standard" of conduct; there is no legal requirement that a researcher comply with their provisions, except to the degree that they are incorporated into federal regulations or state laws governing the conduct of research or into contracts with private sources of research monies. Hence, if clinical research does not comply with the provisions set forth by those regulations, withholding of revenue and liability matters may arise until compliance is assured. The documents that influence health care practices are described below.

The Nuremberg Code and Declaration of Helsinki

The Nuremberg Code (1949) was promulgated in response to the experiments conducted during World War II in the Nazi concentration camps. The code enumerates ten basic principles that are deemed to be universally applicable to research involving human subjects:

1. The prospective participant's voluntary consent is essential.
2. The results to be obtained from the experiment must be beneficial to society and those results cannot be obtained through any other means.
3. The study must have as its foundation the results of animal experiments and a knowledge of the natural history of the disease so that the anticipated results justify the conduct of the experiment.
4. All unnecessary physical and mental injury or suffering must be avoided during the course of the experiment.
5. No experiment should be conducted if it is believed that death or disabling injury will occur, except where the research physicians also serve as research participants.
6. The degree of risk should not exceed the humanitarian importance of the problem being addressed.
7. Adequate facilities and preparations should be used to protect the participant against death or injury.
8. Only scientifically qualified persons should conduct the experiment.
9. The participant has a right to end his or her participation at any time if he or she reaches a point where continuation seems impossible.
10. The scientist in charge must be prepared to end the experiment if there is probable cause to believe that continuing the experiment will likely result in the injury, disability, or death of the research participant (World Medical Association, 1991b).

The Nuremberg Code has been subject to a great deal of criticism, particularly for its failure to distinguish between therapeutic clinical research and clinical research on healthy participants and to provide a review mechanism for researchers' actions (Perley *et al.*, 1992). These deficiencies and the resulting discussions ultimately led to the formulation and adoption of the Declaration of Helsinki.

The Declaration of Helsinki was initially adopted by the World Medical Association in

1964. Unlike the Nuremberg Code, the Declaration: (1) allows participation in research through the permission of a surrogate, where the actual participant is legally or physically unable to consent to his or her participation; and (2) distinguished between clinical research combined with professional care and nontherapeutic clinical research. Later revisions in 1975, 1983, and 1989 further emphasized the need for an individual's voluntary informed consent to participate in research (World Medical Association, 1991a). Unlike later documents, the Helsinki Declaration emphasizes the role of physicians in conducting research and does not impose a requirement of review of research protocols by an independent body prior to the initiation of the research.

Although the Nuremberg Code has often been called "universal," it is clear that this is not the case. For instance, the expert witnesses who appeared at the Nuremberg trial indicated that the standards that they were reciting for the conduct of experimentation involving human subjects were already in place in the United States. However, as we saw from the discussion above, this was far from accurate. Additionally, these experts utilized the writings of Western civilization as the basis for their assertions, without regard to other traditions (Grodin, 1992). Universalists contend that the universal recognition and/or adoption of specified standards is critical in order to prevent the exploitation of more vulnerable and less sophisticated populations and societies. Pluralists and relativists argue in response that the imposition of Western standards on a society constitutes yet another form of exploitation. The concept of informed consent, for instance, reflects the concept of an individual as a freestanding being, whose decisions are independent of the expectations or considerations of others. This is a uniquely Western concept of the individual and as such fails to provide essential guidance to the conduct of research in societies and cultures where concepts of personhood may differ greatly (see Loue *et al.*, 1996).

The International Covenant on Civil and Political Rights

The International Covenant on Civil and Political Rights (ICCPR) was drafted by an international committee following World War II. Although it was entered into force in 1976, the United States did not ratify it until 1992. As of 1997, it had been ratified by more than 115 countries, representing more than two thirds of the world's population (Rosenthal, 1997). Article 7 of ICCPR provides that: "No one shall be subjected to torture or to cruel, inhuman or degrading treatment or punishment. In particular, no one shall be subjected without his free consent to medical or scientific experimentation." In essence, the clause links nonconsensual experimentation to torture and inhuman or degrading treatment, one of the most fundamental prohibitions of international law.

The article itself, however, fails to provide any guidance with respect to experimentation. That inadequacy is addressed in part by General Comment 20, adopted by the Human Rights Committee in 1992:

> Article 7 expressly prohibits medical or scientific experimentation without the free consent
> of the person concerned ... The Committee also observes that special protection in regard to
> such experiments is necessary in the case of persons not capable of giving valid consent,
> and in particular those under any form of detention or imprisonment.

Unlike the Nuremberg Code and the Helsinki Declaration, discussed above, and the CIOMS documents, discussed below, the ICCPR is binding on those countries that have ratified it; the countries agree to enforce the ICCPR through their own legal systems (Vennell, 1995). Although ratifying countries must report to the United Nations Human Rights Committee the mechanisms that they have adopted to effectuate the provisions of ICCPR, there is no international mechanism for the enforcement of the ICCPR provisions (Rosenthal, 1997). In the United States, the treaty is non-self-executing, so that a private right of action does not exist (Stewart, 1993).

CIOMS and WHO International Guidelines

International documents were later developed to provide further guidance in the conduct of research involving humans and to address some of the deficiencies of the Nuremberg Code and the Helsinki Declaration. The *International Guidelines for Ethical Review of Epidemiological Studies* were compiled by the Council for International Organizations of Medical Sciences (CIOMS, 1991) specifically to aid researchers in the field of epidemiology to resolve moral ambiguities that may arise during the course of their research. The *International Ethical Guidelines for Biomedical Research Involving Human Subjects* (CIOMS, 1993), prepared by CIOMS and the World Health Organization (WHO), set forth a statement of general ethical principles, 15 guidelines, and relevant commentary reflecting both the majority and minority points of view. These two documents, in particular, reflect the potential for heterogeneity across cultures in which the research is to be conducted, and diversity of discipline among the investigators carrying out the research studies. As such, they reflect broadly stated principles and offer various mechanisms for the application of those principles, which may differ greatly among cultures. The WHO's (1995) *Guidelines for Good Clinical Practice for Trials on Pharmaceutical Products* provides additional guidelines for the conduct of clinical trials.

United States Guidelines and Regulations

Many of the ethical principles enunciated by the international documents have been incorporated into and operationalized by federal regulations governing research involving human participants, essentially transforming certain ethical standards into legal requirements. These include, for instance, the requirement that prospective research participants be made aware that they will be participating in research rather than receiving clinical care; the requirement of informed consent as a prerequisite to an individual's participation in research, or assent and consent of an authorized individual or entity where informed consent is not possible; the requirement that participants be allowed to withdraw from participation in a study at any time; and the requirement that there be a balancing of risks and benefits to the participants. Unlike the Nuremberg Code and the Helsinki Declarations, however, the regulations also set forth a standard for research conduct, including the avoidance of conflicts of interest and sanctions for scientific misconduct and misuse of human participants.

The American College of Epidemiology has proposed guidelines to assist researchers in fulfilling their professional responsibilities. These guidelines reflect core values of the profession and provide a foundation for the discussion of ethical issues that may arise during the course of professional practice (Weed and Coughlin, 1999). These guidelines focus on many of the same issues as the federal regulations, such as the protection of human participants and the avoidance of conflicts of interest. Unlike both the international documents and the federal regulations, however, these guidelines also focus on standards of practice among those engaged in epidemiology-related endeavors.

Operationalizing Codes, Guidelines, and Regulations in the Context of Research and Patient Care

Regardless of the theoretical approach that is ultimately pursued in resolving an ethical conflict, managers, researchers, and clinicians will at some time be faced with issues relating to quality of care, informed consent, confidentiality, and situations that may present conflicts of interest, e.g., employment or contracts or patent rights. It is beyond the scope of this chapter to address all such issues. Accordingly, this discussion focuses on the operationalization of the codes, guidelines, and regulations discussed above in relation to informed consent and confidentiality in the context of research. Additional resources should be consulted for a discussion of these concepts in the context of patient care.

In reviewing these concepts and their application to the research context, it is important to note that a situation may not clearly constitute research. For instance, patients are admitted on a daily basis to a hospital for medical care, without being asked to participate in a study. Later, a physician– researcher decides that it would be interesting and valuable to examine the outcomes of two different procedures commonly used to address a particular heart condition. Consequently, he or she undertakes a study, relying on chart reviews and laboratory reports of eligible patients for his or her data. It is not necessary in this study to know a particular patient's identity. The patients whose records are under review for the research never consented to participate in research. The study may be undertaken for any of a number of purposes including the acquisition of knowledge that may help others in the future, the desire to identify "best practices," and/or a desire to maximize profit by encouraging the use of the least costly of the two procedures. Should patients in such a situation be approached for their consent to examine their medical records? Is the purpose for which the study is undertaken relevant?

Informed Consent

As we have seen, the Nuremberg Code (World Medicine Association, 1991b) specifies that participation of an individual in research requires voluntary consent:

> The voluntary consent of the human subject is absolutely essential.
> This means that the person involved should have legal capacity to give consent; should be so situated as to be able to exercise free power of choice, without the intervention of any element of force, fraud, deceit, duress, over-reaching, or other ulterior form of constraint or coercion; and should have sufficient knowledge and comprehension of the elements of the subject matter involved as to enable him to make an understanding and enlightened decision. The latter element requires that before the acceptance of an affirmative decision by the experimental subject there should be made known to him the nature, duration, and purpose of the experiment; the method and means by which it is to be conducted; all inconveniences and hazards reasonably to be expected; and the effects upon his health or person which may possibly come from his participation in the experiment. (p. 266)

The first guideline of the *International Guidelines for Biomedical Research Involving Human Subjects* (CIOMS and WHO, 1993, p. 13) provides that:

> For all biomedical research involving human subjects, the investigator must obtain the informed consent of the prospective subject or, in the case of an individual who is not capable of giving informed consent, the proxy consent of a properly authorized representative.

As we have seen, the International Covenant on Civil and Political Rights, which is legally binding on signatory nations, has been interpreted as requiring informed consent.

The requirement of informed consent, however, is not limited to biomedical research. For instance, it also applies to research relating to peoples' attitudes toward disease and peoples' sexual behavior, both of which can be classified as health research and neither of which would be thought of as biomedical research. Similarly, the *International Guidelines for the Ethical Review of Epidemiological Studies* (CIOMS, 1991, p. 11) provides in its first Guideline:

> When individuals are to be subjects of epidemiological studies, their informed consent will usually be sought. For epidemiological studies that use personally identifiable private data, the rules for informed consent vary ... Consent is informed when it is given by a person who understands the purpose and nature of the study, what participation in the study requires the person to do and to risk, and what benefits are intended to result from the study.

Why is informed consent so integral to each of these documents? We can look to each of the ethical theories for guidance. Utilitarianism seeks to maximize good. Involvement of individuals in research without their understanding or their permission or against their will may lead to a distrust of science and scientists, harm to the individuals, and the questionable validity of the research findings, a result that could hardly be thought of as the maximization of good by any definition. A casuistic analysis of past instances of experimentation involving human beings reveals considerable long-term and short-term harm to both individuals and the larger society in those instances in which research was conducted on unknowing and/or involuntary subjects. Consider, for instance, the Nazi experiments, the Tuskegee experiment, Willowbrook, and the Cold War radiation experiments, to name but a few. Communitarianism emphasizes communal values and relationships. Accordingly, it can be argued that the integrity of a community cannot be established and preserved and its values enhanced without recognition of the integrity of its component parts.

Integral to the concept of informed consent, as it traditionally has been applied by Western nations, is the concept of the individual as an autonomous being. This conceptualization of the individual, however, may be discordant "with more relational definitions of the person found in other societies ... which stress the embeddedness of the individual within society and define a person by his or her relations to others" (Christakis, 1988, p. 34). In some cultures, including some communities in the United States, decisions may be made in consultation with community and/or family leaders. Individuals may not even consider refusing a request to participate once permission has been given by a community leader or a family representative (Hall, 1989). Indeed, insistence on informed consent in a "Westernized manner" without consideration of the cultural context may produce harm:

> [S]eeking informed consent to research from individuals [in certain developing world settings] may tend to weaken the social fabric of a nonindividualistic society, forcing it to deal with values it does not hold and possibly sowing disorder that the community will have to reap long after the investigators have gone home.... It is questionable that [our Western individualism] had been an unmitigated good for our own civilization and very questionable that it is up to standard for export. We ought, in truth, to be suitably humble about the worth of procedures [individual consent] developed only to cater to a very Western weakness.... How can it be a sign of respect for people, or of our concern for their welfare, that we are willing to suppress research that is conducted according to the laws and cultures of the countries in which it is being carried out? (Newton, 1990, p. 11)

Similarly, though, the position of ethical relativists—that actions are defined as right or wrong in the context of a specific culture and, consequently, are not subject to judgment—may result in harm. After all, the Nazi experiments were conducted in accordance with laws that permitted such activity.

It is critical that consent procedures be adapted, as appropriate, to accommodate such differences, without abandoning the need for informed consent (WHO, 1989). Individual informed consent serves various purposes, including (1) serving as a reminder against using human beings merely as means; (2) requiring additional thoughtfulness on the part of the investigators by requiring them to explain the study; (3) regularizing relations between research participants and investigators; and (4) safeguarding individuals from invasions of their privacy (Capron, 1991).

As an example, Hall (1989) has reported on a model of informed consent used in Gambia, which appears to accommodate local concerns while still fulfilling the purposes of informed consent. Consent from the individual follows a series of permissions and negotiations of consensus, beginning with the government and then proceeding to the chief of the district, the head of the village, village meetings, and ultimately to each individual to ask consent for participation. This resolution exemplifies the concept of ethical pluralism, which differs from both ethical universalism and relativism in four important respects: (1) it requires on ongoing dialogue between ethical systems; (2) it requires the negotiation between ethical systems with regard to a specific situation; (3) it requires an assessment by each ethical system of itself and the "dissonant" system; and (4) it demands the acknowledgment that some ethical conflicts are irresolvable but must be addressed and dealt with nevertheless (Christakis, 1996). The *International Guidelines for Ethical Review of Epidemiological Studies* (CIOMS, 1991, Guideline 5, at pp. 12–13) recognizes the need for such accommodations:

> When it is not possible to request informed consent from every individual to be studied, the agreement of a representative of a community or group may be sought, but the representative should be chosen according to the nature, traditions, and political philosophy of the community or group. Approval given by a community representative should be consistent with general ethical principles. When investigators working with communities, they will consider communal rights and protection. For communities in which collective decision-making is customary, communal leaders can express the collective will. However, the refusal of individuals to participate in a study has to be respected: a leader may express agreement on behalf of a community, but an individual's refusal of personal participation is binding.

Loue and colleagues (1996) have reported an alternative form of accommodation in Uganda, through the incorporation of a waiting period between the time an individual is initially approached regarding participation in a study and actual signing of the informed consent and entry into a study, in an attempt to reconcile concepts of individual autonomy with Ugandan traditional law.

The various international documents enumerate the components of informed consent: voluntariness, information, understanding, and the capacity to consent, and United States regulations demand that practices be established to effectuate these elements. It is important to recognize that the elements of informed consent are interwoven. For instance, although recruitment relates to voluntariness, it is clearly related to the information provided. It is related to the principle of justice, as well as the principle of respect for persons. Similarly, the manner in which information is provided is relevant to the ability of the participants to understand. A well-designed informed consent process considers and incorporates the complexities and subtleties of such relationships in the context of the particular study's goals and procedures, while recognizing the concerns and characteristics of the participant and target populations. Suggestions for the development of an informed consent process are enumerated in Table 14.2. Additionally, the reader is advised to consult the federal Office of Human Research Protections website (http://ohrp.osophs.dhhs.gov) for regulations, ethical principles Institutional Review Board Guidebook, and other materials relevant to the protection of human research subjects.

Confidentiality and Privacy Concerns

Concern for a participant's privacy and for the confidentiality of the information that he or she provides in the context of research. These same principles should be applied as a manner of routine patient care arises regardless of one's ethical framework. A respect for persons would dictate that participants be afforded sufficient privacy and confidentiality to safeguard their interest and to ensure that they are not simply viewed as a means. Nonmaleficence suggests that access to information about participants should be restricted so as to minimize the harm that could ensue if it were disclosed.

The concern for confidentiality and privacy is reflected across the relevant international documents. The Helsinki Declaration (World Medical Association, 1991a) provides,

> The right of the research subject to safeguard his or her integrity must always be respected. Every precaution should be take to respect the privacy of the subject and to minimize the impact of the study on the subject's physical and mental integrity and on the personality of the subject.

However, there are limits to an investigator's ability to assure confidentiality. The existence of these limitations is recognized by the CIOMS documents, which caution the investigator to provide the research participants with information relating to these restrictions.

> The investigator must establish secure safeguards of the confidentiality of research data. Subjects should be told of the limits to the investigators' ability to safeguard confidentiality and of the anticipated consequences of breaches of confidentiality. (CIOMS and WHO, 1993, Guideline 12, p. 35).
> Research may involve collecting and storing data relating to individuals and groups, and such data, if disclosed to third parties, may cause harm or distress. Consequently, investigators should make arrangements for protecting the confidentiality of such data by, for example, omitting information that might lead to the identification of individual subjects, or limiting access to the data, or by other means. It is customary in epidemiology to aggregate numbers so that individual identities are obscured. Where group confidentiality cannot be maintained or is violated, the investigators should take steps to maintain or restore a group's good name and status.... Epidemiologists discard personal identifying information when consolidating data for purposes of statistical analysis. Identifiable personal data will not be used when a study can be done without personal identification (CIOMS, 1991, Guideline 26, pp. 17–18).

These limitations may include, for instance, laws mandating the reporting of partner, child, or elder abuse; a duty to warn individuals of imminent threat to their lives by another individual; the mandated reporting to the state or local health department of specified disease states, such

Table 14.2. Essential Categories of an Informed Consent and Representative Elements

Category	Elements included
Information	The study involves research
	The purpose of the study
	The expected duration of the individual's participation
	A description of the procedures
	The identification of procedures that are experimental
	A description of any foreseeable risks or discomforts to the participant
	A description of any benefits to the participant that can be reasonably be expected from the research
	A statement disclosing appropriate alternative treatments or procedures that may be beneficial to the participant
	A description of the extent to which confidentiality will be maintained
	An explanation as to whether any compensation or medical treatment is available where the experiment involves more than minimal risk and where additional information may be obtained regarding the compensation or if injury occurs
	A statement that participation is voluntary
	A statement that the participant may withdraw at any time without penalty or loss of benefits to which he or she is otherwise entitled
	A statement that refusal to participate will not result in a loss of benefits to which the individual is otherwise entitled
	A statement of the circumstances under which participation may be terminated involuntarily (optional under federal regulations)
	The consequences of the participant's withdrawal and the procedures for such (optional under federal regulations)
	A statement that the procedure or treatment may involve risks to the participant, embryo, or fetus that are unforeseeable (as appropriate to study)
	Costs to the participant of withdrawal (as appropriate)
	A statement that significant new findings that develop during the course of the research and that may affect the participants' willingness to continue will be provided (optional under federal regulations)
Understanding	The written consent form or information sheet to be provided to the participant if consent is given orally or is written in the language best understood by the participant
	The written consent form or information sheet is written at a reading level that can be understood by the participants
	Alternative mechanisms are employed to convey the necessary information, as appropriate, e.g., video, an incremental information process
Capacity	The participant has legal capacity to consent
	If the participant does not have legal capacity to consent, procedures have been implemented to obtain permission from the appropriate, authorized individual or entity and the participant has provided assent to the extent possible (see text for discussion of when assent is required)
	If the participant is cognitively impaired, he or she has been assessed for the extent of that impairment to determine if consent is possible
	If the participant is cognitively impaired so that consent is not possible, permission to proceed has been obtained from an authorized individual or entity and additional protections have been implemented to protect the participant from harm

as syphilis or AIDS; the reporting to the police of wounds resulting from specified weapons or events, such as gunshots; and the monitoring of patient records by state, federal, and/or accreditation authorities and entities for quality assurance.

Various practical mechanisms can be instituted that will help to reduce the possibility that confidentiality of one or more of the research participants or patients will be breached. This can include the (1) use of unique identifiers, (2) restriction of employee and volunteer access to files and to lists containing both the unique identifiers and the individuals' names, (3) use of locked file cabinets and locked offices, (4) use of passwords or codes to access data stored on computers (Torres *et al.*, 1991), (5) provision of comprehensive training for employees on the ethical and legal principles underlying the confidentiality protections and the mechanisms in place to effectuate these protections (McCarthy and Porter, 1991), and (6) development of an internal procedure for the release of data (Koska, 1992).

Conclusions

Along with the tremendous advances in science and information technology in this millennium have risen the challenges of decisions of protecting individual rights relative to common goods. Ethics provides a framework for interpreting the risk information derived in epidemiological studies allowing managers to take a course of action that is appropriate both for the institution as well as the patients served.

Case Studies

Case Study No. 1
Providing Immunization Services

Poliomyelitis is a viral infection affecting primarily infants and children that is transmitted through person-to-person contact. The most serious effects of the infection include paralysis of the limbs, resulting in disability, and paralysis of the muscles of respiration, which may result in death (Chin, 2000). The disease was officially certified as eradicated in the Western hemisphere in 1991 (Centers for Disease Control, 1997) primarily due to the widespread use of vaccines and the establishment of herd immunity (Griffiths, 1999). Children in the United States remain at risk for the disease due to exposure of the virus imported from other countries, such as through immigration of infected persons and exposure to the risks of live oral polio vaccine (OPV) (Wadsworth, 1999). The risk of vaccine-associated paralytic poliomyelitis (VAPP) has been estimated to be 1 case per 2.4 million doses; the greatest risk is associated with the administration of the first of the two doses, with 1 case per 750,000 doses (Strebel *et al.*, 1992).

With growing frequency, well-educated parents who present their infants for emergency services at health facilities have not had their young children immunized against polio. The parents in such cases have cited numerous reasons for their refusal of vaccine from their primary care physician, including religious grounds, fear of provoking a delayed autoimmune response, the lack of necessity for the vaccine in view of the existing herd immunity and the official eradication of the disease, and the desire to be free from "government control."

Q.1. Should immunization services be provided in the context of emergency department visits? What are the ethical, financial, and logistical arguments for and against such a practice?

Q.2. What are your ethical obligations to the community as a whole with respect to immunizations? To an individual child? How do you balance these interests?

Q.3. How would your response to question 2 above differ, if at all, if the disease in question were still highly prevalent and easily transmissible, with serious health consequences?

Case Study No. 2
Reporting Partner Violence

Your state legislature is considering the passage of a bill that would mandate the reporting of cases of intimate partner violence (IPV) by all physicians to law enforcement agencies. Supporters of this measure argue that this requirement will result in more precise population-based estimates of the incidence of IPV from the data that are garnered and will make the criminal justice system more responsive to the needs of IPV victims, who often suffer severe health consequences as a result of the violence (Campbell and Lewandowski, 1997). Proponents of the measure further claim that the resulting data can be utilized to guide the development of appropriate and effective community resources and interventions and to increase public awareness of the issue.

Q.1. What are the policy arguments for and against the adoption of a reporting requirement to law enforcement agencies versus the reporting of cases to (1) a public health department or (2) a registry developed specifically for partner abuse?

Q.2. What ethical concerns are raised by a reporting requirement in general? How do these concerns differ, if at all, between reporting to a law enforcement agency and reporting to a health department or registry?

Case Study No. 3
The Use of Biomarkers in Epidemiological Research

Biomarkers are "indicators signaling events in biological systems or samples" (Koh and Jeyaratnam, 1998, p. 28). They may be markers of exposure, or effect, or of susceptibility to disease or increased sensitivity to specified exposures (Koh and Jeyaratnam, 1998). Biomarkers are being used with increasing frequency in epidemiological research. Some such markers have not yet been quantitatively linked to the risk of disease at either a group or individual level and consequently have no clinical meaning. Others have been so linked, i.e., validated. However, epidemiological studies yield group, rather than individual results, so that the estimate of risk applies to the group as a whole and may not apply to an individual member. Individual risk may be calculated using a risk function equation if the marker has been validated for disease (Schulte, et al., 1997).

Q.1. What are the individual- and societal-level risks and benefits potentially associated with the use of biomarkers in research? As a population-based screening tool? In an employment context?

Q.2. Should study findings regarding the (non)existence of an individual's biomarkers be released to each study participant? What are the ethical arguments for and against such disclosure?

Q.3. What ethical concerns are raised in conjunction with the dissemination of study findings to the public? How can such concerns be addressed on a policy level? At the level of the health care manager and his or her institution?

Case Study No. 4
The Epidemiology of Do-Not-Resuscitate (DNR) Orders

Various cross-sectional studies indicate that the proportion of patients who have DNR orders in their charts varies from less than 1% to 14% in intensive care units and from 3% to 10% in hospital wards (Wenger *et al.*, 1995). Decisions about resuscitation may reflect a patient choice and/or prognosis, the integrity of the physician–patient relationship and communication, the community standard of practice, costs associated with end of life care and the ability and willingness of the patient and/or health care facility and insurer to underwrite those costs. And, in cultures in which the individual is defined in relation to others in the family, the decision may also reflect the input of various family members.

An observational study of a nationally representative sample of 14,008 Medicare patients hospitalized with congestive heart failure, acute myocardial infarction, pneumonia, cerebrovascular accident or hip fracture found that, even after adjustment for sickness at admission and functional impairment, DNR orders were assigned more often to individuals who were older, who were women, or who were suffering from dementia or incontinence.

Q.1. What are the various explanations that exist that would explain the increased frequency of assigning DNRs to these groups of patients?

Q.2. What ethical concerns may be prompted by the differences found in DNR assignment?

Q.3. How would your resolution of the ethical concerns identified in Q.2 above vary depending on your approach, e.g., principlism versus utilitarianism versus feminist ethics?

Case Study No. 5
Informed Consent in Evaluating Education Given through a Genetics Clinic

The Comprehensive Breast Center (CBC) of Freeway Medical Center offers a genetics screening clinic to women. The purpose of this clinic is to provide counseling and blood screening for the *BRCA1* and *BRCA2* genes known to be associated with the occurrence of both breast and ovarian cancer. Little is known about the most effective way of teaching women about their risk to these types of cancer. The CBC proposes conducting a study designed to compare two types of educational methods, one that uses computer software to construct a pedigree as an instructional aid and one in which a pamphlet describing the risk is given. Women will be recruited from the surrounding community that has a population at high risk for breast cancer. Before beginning the study, the CBC submits its research proposal to its Institutional Review Board (IRB) for approval. An IRB is the entity that assures that a research study is in compliance with the regulations of the federal Office of the Protection of Research Subjects. All research studies conducted at a health care organization or facility (including doctors' offices) must be approved by an IRB, regardless of whether or not outside funding is used for the conduct of research, before the research study begins.

Q.1. Prepare an informed consent form that could be given to women who participate in this evaluation research study.

Q.2. Should the consent form be modified if a large number of women are expected to be enrolled in the study cannot read or speak English?

References

Appelbaum, P. S., and Grisso, T., 1988, Assessing patients' capacities to consent to treatment, *N. Engl. J. Med.* **319:**1635–1638.

Arras, J. D., 1991, Getting down to cases: The revival of casuistry in bioethics, *J. Med. Phil.* **16:**29–51.

Artnak, K. E., 1995, A comparison of principle-based and case-based approaches to ethical analysis, *HEC Forum* **7:**339–352.

Artnak, K. E., and Dimmitt, J. H., 1996, Choosing a framework for ethical analysis in advanced practice settings: The case for casuistry, *Arch. Psychiatr. Nur.* **10:**16–23.

Beauchamp, T. L., and Childress, J. F., 1994, *Principles of Biomedical Ethics*, 4th ed., Oxford University Press, New York.

Bentham, J., 1962, An introduction to the principles of morals and legislations, in *Utilitarianism and Other Writings*. The New American Library, New York.

Brandt, A. M., 1985, Racism and research: The case of the Tuskegee syphilis study, in *Sickness and Health in America: Readings in the History of Medicine and Public Health*, (J. W. Leavitt and R. I. Numbers, eds.), (pp. 331–343), University of Wisconsin Press, Madison, WI.

Burrows, C., and Brown, K., 1993, QALYs for resource allocation: Probably not and certainly not now, *Aust. J. Public Health* **17:**278–286.

Campbell, J., and Lewandowski, L. A., 1997, Mental and physical health effects of intimate partner violence on women and children, *Psychiatr. Clin. N. Am.* **20:**353–374.

Capron, A. M., 1991, Protection of research subjects: Do special rules apply in epidemiology? *Law Med. Health Care* **19:**184–190.

Card, C., 1990, Caring and evil, *Hypatia* **5:**101–108.

Centers for Disease Control and Prevention, 1997, Poliomyelitis prevention in the United States: Introduction of a sequential vaccination schedule of inactivated poliovirus vaccine followed by oral poliovirus vaccine: Recommendations of the Advisory Committee on Immunization Practices (ACIP), *Morbid. Mortal. Week. Rep.* **46:** 1–25.

Chin, J., 2000, *Control of Communicable Disease Manual*, 17th ed., American Public Health Association, Washington, DC.

Christakis, N. A., 1988, The ethical design of an AIDS vaccine trial in Africa, *Hastings Center Rep.* **18:**31–37.

Christakis, N. A., 1996, The distinction between ethical pluralism and ethical relativism: Implications for the conduct of transcultural clinical research, in *The Ethics of Research Involving Human Subjects: Facing the 21st Century* (H. Y. Vanderpool, ed.), pp. 261–280, University Publishing Group, Frederick, MD.

Council for International Organizations of Medical Sciences (CIOMS), 1991, *International Guidelines for Ethical Review of Epidemiological Studies*, CIOMS, Geneva.

Council for International Organizations of Medical Sciences (CIOMS), World Health Organization (WHO), 1993, *International Ethical Guidelines for Biomedical Research Involving Human Subjects*, CIOMS and WHO, Geneva.

Donagan, A., 1968, Is there a credible form of utilitarianism? in *Contemporary Utilitarianism* (M. Bayles, ed.), pp. 187–202, Doubleday and Company, Garden City, NY.

Etzioni, A., 1998, Introduction: A matter of balance, rights, and responsibilities, in *The Essential Communitarian Reader* (A. Etzioni, ed.), pp. ix–xxiv, Rowman & Littlefield, Lanham, MD.

Gilligan, C., 1982, *In a Different Voice: Psychological Theory and Women's Development*, Harvard University Press, Cambridge, MA.

Green, R., 1990, Method in bioethics: A troubled assessment, *J. Med. Phil.* **15:**188–189.

Griffiths, P. d., 1999, Defending vaccines from the enemy within, *Re. Med. Virol.* **9:**145–146.

Grodin, M. A., 1992, Historical Origins of the Nuremberg Code, in *The Nazi Doctors and the Nuremberg Code: Human Rights in Human Experimentation* in (G. J. Annas and M. A. Grodin, eds.), pp. 121–144, Oxford University Press, New York.

Hall, A. J., 1989, Public health trials in West Africa: Logistics and ethics, *IRB* **11:**8–10.

Hammerschmidt, D. E., and Keane, M. A., 1992, Institutional review board (IRB) review lacks impact on readability of consent forms for research, *Am. J. Med. Sci.* **304:**348–351.

Hoagland, S. L., 1991, Some thoughts about "caring," in *Feminist Ethics* (C. Card, ed.), pp. 246–263, University of Kansas Press, Lawrence.

Hooker, W., 1849, *Physician and Patient*, Baker and Scribner, New York.

Jonsen, A. R., 1986, Casuistry and clinical ethics, *Theoret. Med.* **7:**65–74.

Jonsen, A. R., 1991, Casuistry as methodology in clinical ethics, *Theoret. Med.* **12:**295–307.

Jonsen, A. R., 1995, Casuistry: An alternative or complement to principles? *Kennedy Inst. Ethics J.* **5:**237–251.

Jonsen, A. R., and Toulmin, S., 1988, *The Abuse of Casuistry*, University of California Press, Berkeley.

Koh, D., and Jeyaratnam, J., 1998, Biomarkers, screening and ethics, *Occup. Med.* **1:**27–30.

Koska, M. T., 1992 (Jan. 5), Outcomes research: Hospitals face confidentiality concerns, *Hospitals* 32–34.

Kuczewski, M. G., 1994, Casuistry and its communitarian critics, *Kennedy Inst. Ethics J.* **4:**99–116.

Kuczewski, M. G., 1997, *Fragmentation and Consensus: Communitarian and Casuist Bioethics*, Georgetown University Press, Washington, DC.

Lifton, R. J., 1986, *The Nazi Doctors: Medical Killing and the Psychology of Genocide*, Basic Books, New York.

Loue, S., Okello, D., and Kawuma, M., 1996, Research bioethics in the Ugandan context: A program summary, *J. Law Med. Ethics* **24:**47–53.

McCarthy, C. R., and Porter, J. P., 1991, Confidentiality: The protection of personal data in epidemiological and clinical research trials, *Law Med. Health Care* **19:**238–241.

Meade, C. D., and Howser, D. M., 1992, Consent forms: How to determine and improve their readability, *Oncol. Nurs. Forum* **19:**1523–1528.

Mill, J. S., 1863, Utilitarianism, in *Ethics: The Big Questions* (J. P. Sterba, ed.), pp. 119–132, Blackwell Publishers, Malden, MA (1998).

Moore v. Regents of the University of California, 793 P.2d479 (Cal. 1990).

Newton, L., 1990, Ethical imperialism and informed consent, *IRB* **12:**11.

Nicholson, L. J., 1993, Women, morality, and history, in *An Ethic of Care: Feminist and Interdisciplinary Perspectives* (M. J. Larrabee, ed.), pp. 87–101, Routledge, New York.

Noddings, N., 1984, *Caring: A Feminine Approach to Ethics and Moral Education*, University of California Press, Berkeley.

Panek, W. C., 1999, Ethical considerations related to outcome studies-based clinical practice guidelines, *J. Glaucoma* **8:**267–272.

Perley, S. S., Fluss, S. S., Bankowski, Z., and Simon F., 1992, The Nuremberg Code: An international overview, in *The Nazi Doctors and the Nuremberg Code: Human Rights in Human Experimentation* (G. J. Annas and M. A. Grodin, eds.), pp. 149–173, Oxford University Press, New York.

Purdy, L. M., 1992, A call to heal ethics, in *Feminist Perspectives in Medical Ethics* (H. B. Holmes and L. M. Purdy, eds.), pp. 8–13, Indiana University Press, Bloomington, Indiana.

Reiman, J., 1988, Utilitarianism and the informed consent requirement (or: should utilitarians be allowed on medical research ethical review boards?) in *Moral Theory and Moral Judgments in Medical Ethics* (B. A. Brody, ed.), pp. 41–51, Kluwer Academic, Boston.

The Responsive Communitarian Platform: Rights and Responsibilities, 1998, in *The Essential Communitarian Reader* (A. Etzioni, ed., p. xxv–xxxix, Rowman & Littlefield, Lanham, MD.

Rivera, R., Reed, J. S., and Menius, D., 1992, Evaluating the readability of informed consent forms used in contraceptive clinical trials, *Int. J. Gynecol. Obstet* **38:**227–230.

Rosenthal, E., 1997, The International Covenant on Civil and Political Right and the Rights of Research Subjects, in *Ethics in Neurobiological Research with Human Subjects: The Baltimore Conference on Ethics* (A. E. Shamoo, ed.), pp. 265–171, Overseas Publishers Association, Amsterdam.

Schulte, P. A., Hunter, D., and Rothman, N., 1997, Ethical and social issues in the use of biomarkers in epidemiological research, in *Application of Biomarkers in Cancer Epidemiology* (P. Toniolo, P. Boffetta, P. Shuker, N. Rothman, B. Hulka, and N. Pearce, Eds.), pp. 313–318, International Agency for Research on Cancer, Lyons, France.

Sen, A. K., 1987, *On Ethics and Economics*, Basil Blackwell Publishing, Oxford, England.

Sherwin, S., 1992, Feminist and medical ethics: Two different approaches to contextual ethics, in *Feminist Perspectives in Medical Ethics* (H. B. Holmes and L. M. Purdy, eds.), pp. 17–31, University of Indiana Press, Bloomington.

Smart, J. J. C., 1961, *An Outline of a System of Utilitarian Ethics*, University Press, Melbourne.

Stewart, D. P., 1993, United States ratification of the Covenant on Civil and Political Rights: The significance of the reservations, understandings, and declarations, *DePaul Law Rev.* **42:**1183–1207.

Strebel, P. M., Sutter, R. W., Cochi, S. L., Biellik, R. J., Brink, E. W., Kew, O. M., Pallansch, M. A., Orenstein, W., and Hinman, A. R., 1992, Epidemiology of poliomyelitis in the United States on e decade after the last reported case of indigenous wild virus-associated disease, *Clin. Infect. Dis* **14:**568–579.

Tong, R., 1993, *Feminine and Feminist Ethics*, Wadsworth Publishing Company, Belmont, CA.

Torres, C. G., Turner, M. E., Harkess, J. R., and Istre, G. R., 1991, Security measures for AIDS and HIV, *Am. J. Public Health* **81:**210–211.

Tronto, J. C., 1993, Beyond gender difference to a theory of care, in *An Ethic of Care: Feminist and Interdisciplinary Perspectives* (M. J. Larrabee, Ed.), pp. 240–257, Routledge, New York.

Vennell, V. A. M., 1995, Medical research and treatment: Ethical standards in the international context, *Med. Law Int.* **2:**1–21.

Wadsworth, L., 1999, Polio immunization: Dealing with new recommendations and helping parents understand the changes, *J. Pediatr. Health Care* **13:**S21–S30.

Warren, V. L., 1992, Feminist directions in medical ethics, in *Feminist Perspectives in Medical Ethics* (H. B. Holmes and L. M. Purdy, eds.), pp. 32–45, University of Indiana Press, Bloomington.

Weed, D. L., and Coughlin, S. S., 1999, New ethics guidelines for epidemiology: Background and rationale, *Ann. Epidemiol.* **9:**277–280.

Welsome, E., 1999, *The Plutonium Files*, Dial Press, New York.

Wenger, N. S., Pearson, M. L., Desmond, K. A., Harrison, E. R., Rubenstein, L. V., Rogers, W. H., and Kahn, K. L., 1995, Epidemiology of do-not-resuscitate orders: Disparity by age, diagnosis, gender, race, and functional impairment, *Arch. Intern. Med.* **155:**2056–2062.

Williams, B., and Smart, J. J. C., 1973, *Utilitarianism, For and Against*, Cambridge University Press, Cambridge, England.

World Health Organization, 1989, February 27-March 2, Criteria for international testing of candidate HIV vaccines, WHO, Geneva.

World Health Organization, 1995, *Guidelines for Good Clinical Practice for Trials on Pharmaceutical Products*, WHO, Geneva.

World Medical Association, 1991a, Declaration of Helsinki, *Law Med. Health Care* **19:**264–265.

World Medical Association, 1991b, The Nuremberg Code, *Law Med. Health Care* **19:**266.

Suggested Answers to Selected Case Study Questions

Chapter 1

Case Study No. 1:
Racial Differences in the Incidence of Cardiac Arrest and Subsequent Survival

A.1. Differences in risk factors. Blacks have more hypertension, left ventricular hypertrophy, and end-stage renal disease that are risk factors for cardiovascular disease. There also may be differences in access to treatment for these risk factors. Social or cultural factors or lack of knowledge may prevent blacks from avoiding these risk factors. Lack of knowledge about recognizing the signs and symptoms of cardiac disease also may prevent blacks from seeking needed help for the treatment of risk factors.

A.2. Factors influencing survival, or prognostic factors, include age, initial cardiac rhythm, whether or not the cardiac arrest was witnessed, whether or not cardiopulmonary resuscitation was initiated by a bystander, response time, socioeconomic status, and location of victim.

A.3. The city department of public health could work with a local Red Cross, hospital, fire department, or American Heart Association to teach members of the community first aid and cardiopulmonary resuscitation techniques and how to use the emergency response system.

Case Study No. 3: Rural Populations and Public Health Services

A.1. From the most recent census obtain additional information on population characteristics: number of persons <5, 5–18, and 65 years of age and over; percentage of population in poverty; percentage covered by Medicaid. Obtain information on the number of primary care providers in the county, health status indicators such as birth rate, cause-specific death rates, immunization rates, and infectious disease patterns.

A.2. Arrange for community town halls meetings on the matter. Contact local development associations to determine whether any new economic initiatives are being planned.

Case Study No. 5:
Why Aren't 100% of Children Immunized Against Common Childhood Illnesses?

A.1. Inaccurate record keeping on the part of the office staff could have failed to flag the charts of children who were "due" for a vaccination. Interruptions in the access of the independent practice association to vaccine supplies. Problems with vaccination production by commercial suppliers due to increased regulation of vaccination formulation processes. Children may not necessarily see the same physician at each encounter. Lack of continuity with provider has been identified as a barrier to immunization.

A.2. Lack of knowledge about the appropriate administration of vaccinations during an episode of acute childhood illness; reluctance to allow children without insurance for immunization into their practice; lack of evening and weekend hours for working parents.

Chapter 2

Case Study No. 2: Inappropriate Emergency Department Visits
by Members of a Health Maintenance Organization (HMO)

A.1. To determine agreement beyond chance, the kappa statistic should be computed:

$$P_o = (257\text{-}1411)/1745 = .96$$
$$P_e = \{[(277 \times 314)/1745] + [(1468 \times 1431)/1745]\}/1745 = .72$$
$$k = (P_o - P_e)/(1 - P_e) = (.96 - .72)/(1 - .72) = .86$$

A.2. The kappa of .86 indicates that there was excellent agreement between the two physicians. Therefore, use of criteria to determine what is an appropriate emergency room visit promotes the achievement of reliability.

Case Study No. 3: A Breast Cancer Screening Program

A.1. First, compute the number of women with breast cancer:

$$250,000 \times 0.3\% = 750 \text{ women}$$

Next, find the number of true positives:

$$750 \times 95/100 = 742$$

A.2. Continuing with the information from Q.1, obtain the number of women without breast cancer:

$$250,000 - 750 = 249,250$$

Determine the number of false positives:

$$249,250 \times (1\text{--}99/100) = 2,492$$

The data from Q.1 and Q.2 result in the following 2×2 table:

	Breast cancer		
Mammography result	Yes	No	
Positive	742	2,492	
Negative	8	246,758	
Total	750	249,250	250,000

A.3. Yes. The specificity and sensitivity are both high. Thus, you have a high probability of accurately classifying a woman who is positive from mammography screening to truly have breast cancer. You also have a high probability of determining that if a woman tests negative, she does not have the disease; only eight women are false negatives.

Chapter 3

Case Study No. 1: In-Hospital Mortality from Hip Fractures in the Elderly

A.1. Age-specific mortality rates:

$$Rate_{65-69 \text{ years of age}} \text{ per } 100 = 68/2542 \times 100 = 2.68 \text{ per } 100$$
$$Rate_{70-74 \text{ years of age}} \text{ per } 100 = 140/3842 \times 100 = 3.64 \text{ per } 100$$
$$Rate_{75-79 \text{ years of age}} \text{ per } 100 = 216/5374 \times 100 = 4.02 \text{ per } 100$$
$$Rate_{80-84 \text{ years of age}} \text{ per } 100 = 297/6541 \times 100 = 4.54 \text{ per } 100$$
$$Rate_{>85 \text{ years of age}} \text{ per } 100 = 618/9071 \times 100 = 6.81 \text{ per } 100$$

Race-gender specific mortality rates:

$$Rate_{\text{white males}} \text{ per } 100 = 392/4970 \times 100 = 7.87 \text{ per } 100$$
$$Rate_{\text{white females}} \text{ per } 100 = 847/20,675 \times 100 = 4.10 \text{ per } 100$$
$$Rate_{\text{black males}} \text{ per } 100 = 38/506 \times 100 = 7.51 \text{ per } 100$$
$$Rate_{\text{black females}} \text{ per } 100 = 62/1209 \times 100 = 5.13 \text{ per } 100$$

The mortality rate increases with advancing age. White males are at highest risk for death followed by black males, black females, and white females.

A.2. The higher death among males may be due to a higher proportion of the injuries associated with more serious injuries incurred in motor vehicle accidents, assaults, and falls from heights.

A.3. Since there is a smaller number of deaths in the cells resulting from the cross-tabulation of age group, gender, and race, this was done in order to have stable rates in the population subgroups examined.

A.4. Death certificates.

A.5. Deaths may not have been recorded on the hospital discharge abstract as there may not be a legal requirement for doing so, since death certificates are viewed as the standard mechanism for reporting this event. This would underestimate the inpatient mortality rate. Persons with a hip fracture may be readmitted for management of the hip fracture. This also could underestimate the rate because these persons would artificially increase the denominator. If procedure codes are not used concurrently with diagnosis code, persons with hip fracture may be missed. If in-hospital death occurred in the unidentified case, the rate could also be underestimated; otherwise the rate would be overestimated.

Case Study No. 2: Medicaid Prenatal Care: Fee-for-Service Versus Managed Care

A.1.

Payer	Low birth weight	Normal weight	Total
Managed care	276	5,846	6,122
Fee-for-service	821	12,632	13,453

Odds ratio = 276/5846 ÷ 821/12,632 = 0.73.

Among Medicaid women, the likelihood of a low birth weight baby is less in the managed care group than in the fee-for-service group.

Case Study No. 3: Gender Differential Trends in Prevention, Diagnosis, Classification, and Treatment of Coronary Heart Disease (CHD)

A.1. Age-specific mortality rates by gender.

A.2. Males, 65–74 years of age, for both questions.

A.3. In general, mortality rates among men showed a steeper decline than among women.

A.4. There may be a greater public awareness of risk factors among men and a higher rate of preventive health behaviors aimed at reducing these factors. Some studies show that there may differences in seeking and obtaining care, with women experiencing more delays in the recognition and treatment of CHD.

A.5. CHD in women may be underdiagnosed due to delays in symptom recognition by patient.

A.6. Initiate an educational campaign to educate women members about the fact that heart disease is a leading cause of morbidity and mortality among women. Include in the educational campaign information about actions members can take to help reduce their risks that both prevention (e.g., reducing the amount of dietary fat intake), secondary health intervention (cholesterol screening, blood pressure screening), and tertiary intervention (encourage cardiac rehabilitation).

Case Study No. 5: Risk Factors for Coronary Artery Disease (CAD)

A.1. RR = 12.6 per 100 population/7.7 per 100 population = 1.64

A.2. A RR of 1.64 means that smokers are 1.64 times more likely to develop CAD than nonsmokers.

$$\text{A.3. PAR } \% = [P_e (RR - 1)]/1 + P_e (RR - 1)] \times 100\%$$
$$= [0.42(1.64 - 1)]/1 + 0.42(1.64 - 1) \times 100\%$$

A.4. In this case, the RR helps define causation and provide an estimate of the degree to which a risk factor plays a role for an individual. The RR indicates that smoking elevates one's chances of developing CAD and, therefore, health promotion services should include methods for assisting an individual in quitting smoking.

Chapter 4

Case Study No. 1: Applying the Scientific Method to Develop a Strategy for Assessing HMO Performance in Preventive Practice

A.1.

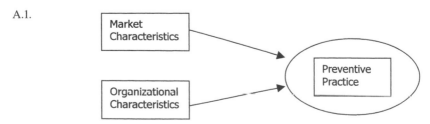

A.2. Market characteristics are not associated with preventive practice for elderly persons in HMOs in an urban area. Note that you should specify the independent variable before the dependent variable. The population in which the hypothesis is to be tested should also be specified (HMOs in an urban area in this case).

A.3. Multiple linear regression analysis or structural equation modeling (LISREL). Since most of the independent and the dependent variables are interval level of measurement, the linear regression technique is the most powerful. Also, there is only one dependent (or outcome) variable: prevention score. Before applying this statistical test to your data, you should evaluate the distribution of your independent and dependent variables to make sure they meet the normality assumption of these statistical tests.

A.4. Determine which of the factors are statistically significantly associated with prevention score. Determine that confounding has been accounted for either by design or statistical control.

Case Study No. 5: Developing a Conceptual Framework
for Community-Based Violence Prevention

A.3. The 1995 National Alcohol Survey for information at the individual level (e.g., violent behaviors, individual and household-level variables). The US Census for 1990 for information on community level education, unemployment, and income.

A.4. Multilevel analysis.

Chapter 5

Case Study No. 1: Strategic Planning for a County Health Department

A.1. Yes. Although the situation is one full of change, there is no evidence of a crisis situation. Strategic planning could help the Health Department effectively address these changes and chart its future direction.

A.2. No. The executive director is new; he lacks a sense of the organization's history, and he received mixed messages when members of the Health Department's board shared their vision of where the department should go in the future. Staff of the organization have never had the opportunity to reflect formally on the organization's mission. There is a policy and procedures manual that was compiled some time ago. It describes the mandates of health departments if they are to receive state monies as local public health agencies. The role the department has taken on as a provider of mental health services (a role not essential for health departments) was not addressed in the dated publication (which rarely had been removed from the shelf in recent years anyway). Developing consensus on a mission for the Health Department is a step appropriate for inclusion in the strategic planning process.

A.3. The types of data appropriate for review by the Health Department include the following: financial data pertinent to funding of the department's programs and service-specific income and expense data; statistical reports that present data relevant to trends in the utilization of services and to the characteristics of those served; county- and statewide morbidity data for reportable diseases and vital statistics (contained in reports prepared by the Illinois Department of Public Health); census data for the county and other data describing the demographic and socioeconomic characteristics of county residents; reports by state agencies (such as the Department of Mental Health and Developmental Disabilities) that provide an inventory of services available for treatment of acute and chronic illnesses and other dysfunctions and present data pertinent to the assessment of unmet health needs (for a range of medical treatment, habilitative, and supportive services); and data pertinent to the availability of health personnel (such as child psychologists, certified addiction counselors, and therapists of various kinds).

Because some board members expressed the opinion that the Health Department should do more to monitor and improve the environment, it also is appropriate that data be compiled to assess the status of the county's environment against standards for land, air, and water quality. Sources of data may include results from periodic testing of soil, water, and air by the Health Department, governmental reports, and studies of "watchdog" and consumer advocacy organizations. Morbidity and mortality data for the county also could be reviewed to determine whether the county has a higher incidence of diseases that appear to have a link to environmental pollutants.

A.4. The data identified above could be utilized to gain awareness of the health status of the county's population relative to a meaningful comparison group (such as the population of the state) and to assess possible causes for discrepancies from the norm. The data can facilitate an understanding of the variables (such as age, economic and occupational status, and environmental conditions) that influence health needs and demands.

A.5. Members of the county board, the executive director, and staff (all or some) certainly should be involved in the process. Representatives of local businesses, other service agencies, and the community at large also may be invited to participate in the process. There is no standard answer to this question, but it is important to have a basis for justifying selection of planning participants. A process that is open and democratic probably has a better chance of success than one that appears closed and autocratic.

A.6. The case does not suggest evidence that the Health Department has personnel knowledgeable about strategic planning. The executive director and board president should evaluate the capabilities that can be applied to a strategic planning process. If the commitment to undertake the process is sufficient, the executive director and the Board can agree to seek expert help and contract with consultants who can assist in the process. Other potential problems could be avoided if adequate attention is given to planning the planning, to selecting a process tailored to the needs of the organization, and to establishing other conditions that are associated with effective strategic thinking and action.

Case No. 2: Strategic Planning for Inpatient Rehabilitation Services

A.1. A comprehensive study could include assessment of the following factors:

- The need for comprehensive rehabilitation among the population in communities traditionally served by the hospital (with consideration given to sociodemographic variables such as age and income levels) as well as epidemiological variables (causes of morbidity and mortality, incidence of work injuries and illnesses that could increase the need for work rehabilitation programs).
- The diagnoses of patients currently utilizing the hospital (to assess whether the hospital was already providing acute care services to substantial numbers of patients who were likely candidates for rehabilitation and to determine the impact of more aggressive need identification on occupancy).
- Financial implications of operating a larger, exempt unit.
- The perceived need among the hospital's physicians for expansion of inpatient rehabilitation services and the physicians' willingness to refer patients to the hospital's rehabilitation service rather than identifying other resources in the community for meeting the needs of patients.
- Competitors in the rehabilitation business (their levels of success, the programs offered and those not available).

- The unit's current ability to achieve established clinical outcomes and to satisfy other quality standards and expectations of consumers and stakeholders.

A.2. No. It made a decision to involve consultants to expedite the process. This was probably a responsible decision, considering that the management team lacked adequate time and expertise to address the problem itself. There is no absolute formula for success in strategic planning. However, the management team worked with consultants to design a process with a high probability of success. The consultants did the research and analytical work usually associated with a situational analysis. However, the management group maintained involvement in the process and carefully reviewed the work of the consultants to ensure that there would be adequate confidence in conclusions and ownership of recommendations. The hospital's management team became more educated and informed of the issues as the process proceeded; this facilitated good judgment and decision making on their part. The management team also gave full consideration to what needed to be done to begin implementation of some of the recommendations of the consultants.

A.3. There's no right or wrong answer to this question. Certainly, other approaches might have worked as well or better. The hospital wanted to get a certificate-of-need (CON) permit, which was necessary to achieve formal recognition of the unit and to gain authorization of capital expenditures that the hospital had budgeted to improve the physical environment of the unit. It obtained the permit, but not without difficulty because it initially failed to give attention to the politics associated with the CON regulatory process. The hospital wanted the rehabilitation unit to gain exemption and to achieve a more favorable "bottom line." Both objectives also were attained. Therefore, unless the management team had other objectives that were not accomplished, the process worked.

Chapter 6

Case Study No. 1: Evaluation of an Influenza Vaccination Program

A.1. A case–control study could be designed for all those who received the vaccination (as the cases) and a control group from the community of those who did not get the vaccination.

A.2. A variety of factors would need to be assessed, including but not limited to age, gender, date of vaccination, type of vaccination, onset of flu symptoms, and coexistence of other illnesses.

A.3. Incidence rates should be compared. A logistic regression could be performed using measures to control for differences between the groups to calculate the odds of still getting the flu after vaccination.

A.4. Anticipating that incidence of flu among those who were vaccinated is lower than among those who were not, this information could be made part of a mass media campaign to educate the elderly and solicit participation in subsequent years.

Case Study No. 2: Impact of a Smoking Prevention Program

A.1. An assessment of prevalence of tobacco use in the community and in the school-based population is an initial step. Calculating prevalence rates and relative risk for cancer given population information might be possible.

A.2. A survey might be done to assess knowledge and awareness. It could establish a baseline for the evaluation of the intervention to prevent tobacco use.

A.3. A longitudinal study could be done to monitor children over time. If an intervention is implemented at a number of schools and not at others, the results across schools could be compared to assess effectiveness over time using a quasi-experimental design.

Case Study No. 3: Evaluation of Exposure to Tuberculosis (TB)

A.1. Screening of the staff of the hospital would have to be done immediately. Current patients also should be screened. In addition, other patients who had been discharged also should be notified to undergo testing. Timing of how far back discharged patients might have to be tested will depend on identification of positive cases and potential exposure of patients.

A.2. For staff who may be carriers, the units that they worked in, patient population demographic information, people who they may have come in contact with who also might be exposed.

A.3. A historical prospective comparison of staff screening for TB could be done.

Case Study No. 4: Evaluating a Community-Based Hypertension Control Program

A.1. Changes in the prevalence of hypertension, prevalence of controlled hypertension, and cardiovascular mortality rates are appropriate criteria.

A.2. This is quasi-experimental because of the inability to randomize persons in the community into an intervention or control group.

A.3. Factors other than the intervention could contribute to the outcome experienced by the population overtime.

A.4. The program was effective. The prevalence of controlled hypertension was significantly increased in only the intervention counties. In addition, the percentage of the population with hypertension declined in the intervention counties, but not significantly in the control counties.

A.5. An audit of the process could have been done and accounted for in the follow-up survey. That is, attention could have focused on delineating the types of interventions for high blood pressure control to which those surveyed were exposed. It also would be relevant to assess how long survey respondents had lived in the county (to assess the duration of exposure to the various intervention approaches).

Chapter 7

Case Study No. 1: Managing a Hospital-Specific Cesarean Section Rate

A.1. Select appropriate team members and review the current processes.

A.2. First, the number of newborn deliveries must be identified (the denominator). This may be done using International Classification of Diseases (ICD) codes for procedures, diagnoses, or other internal coding schemes for identifying the newborn (such as an admission code). Then, the numerator must be defined. Either codes from the ICD or using diagnosis-related groups can be used.

A.3. A flowchart could be used to understand the current process. Run charts (line graphs) and control charts would be constructed once data are available. Use a cause–effect diagram to help identify the source(s) of the problem(s).

A.4. The rate measures used are only crude rate measures and not risk adjusted. Typically, cesarean section data reviewed by hospitals for quality improvement initiatives are derived from billing claims (not from birth certificate data) that are derived from coded medical records. Therefore, the data are influenced by the experience and knowledge of hospital coders and the timeliness of data submission to the state agency that collects and reports the hospital utilization data.

A.5. Feedback to physicians on individual cesarean section rates, practice guideline for management of active labor, patient education for candidates for vaginal birth after cesarean section, and implemented policy for preapproval of scheduled cesarean or scheduled inductions of labor.

Case Study No. 2: Measuring and Improving Patient Satisfaction

A.1. The first two hospitals have the same percentage of patients rating their satisfaction a "1" and a "2," yet there is a big difference in the overall percentile ranking of the two hospitals. Only a small percentage of patients respond with a rating of poor or very poor. The real difference is in the percentage of patients providing a score of "5." Therefore, the opportunity may not be getting the low scores up to the top, but rather putting efforts toward bringing the scores of "4" to scores of "5."

A.2. According to the PDCA cycle, to fix a problem, a process must be studied. Once data are evaluated, team members must decide on a plan for improvement. To study patient satisfaction, further analyses should be conducted to determine which areas are in need of improvement. The data could be stratified by service line, unit, or patient population. Examine the data according to the various dimensions measured by the experience to pinpoint trouble areas, such as provider interactions, facility conditions, meals, pain management, and so forth. Correlate findings with those of other quality-related programs such as case management, utilization management, or risk management. A control chart can be constructed to examine whether the findings have been consistent (stable) over time. A comparison chart can be used to examine how closely the data match that of other organizations. Once areas for improvement are identified, a team could be formed to further analyze issues. Deming (1986) believes it is important to involve those closest to the process, thus consider for team membership a patient representative and a sample of key individuals who interact with patients.

A.3. Check sheets, histograms, and Pareto diagrams may be used to display levels of patient satisfaction according to various dimensions of care. Once the team has narrowed down the area(s) in need of improvement, a cause-and-effect diagram can be constructed to help identify causes of dissatisfaction. If the causes point to a process in need of fixing, the team can work to construct a flow diagram to identify areas where value can be added and/or inefficiencies corrected. If the satisfaction measurement will be continued over time, a trend chart and/or control chart might be useful to examine the stability of the process. In addition, a comparison chart would offer ease in identifying how the facility compares with others.

A.4. Create a cause-and-effect diagram—"Patient Units Are Noisy"—and list all the sources of noise and why these noises happen. Using a check sheet, collect data on noise levels through observation. Break data into categories of type of noise. Involve the team in a brainstorming session on how to create a warm atmosphere. If there is no budget for remodeling, challenge them to generate no-cost or low-cost options.

A.5. Implement on a small scale, such as one patient unit, and measure the effect of the change. If successful, implement on a larger scale.

Case Study No. 3: Investigation of a Medical Error

A.1. The team should include persons who interacted with the patient and/or were responsible for various aspects of surgical preparation. The risk manager, in-house attorney, and senior leaders may be involved. Refrain from any punitive action and encourage honest interaction. Set ground rules for discussion, such as those used for brainstorming.

A.2. Review all medical record documents, unit logs, and preadmission documentation. Keep these documents available for reference during team discussions. Construct a cause-and-effect diagram titled "Reasons for Wrong-Site Surgery." Ask the team members to openly offer thoughts on causes, in particular those related to the process, as opposed to blaming individuals. Construct a flow diagram to map out the patient's course, beginning with early preparation for admission and surgery. Look for pitfalls in the process.

A.3. A new flow diagram should be constructed, this time representing the improved process. The new process should be implemented in a pilot phase and evaluated by the team as to its effectiveness. To ensure that the process is being maintained, follow-up checks should be conducted to assure quality control.

Chapter 8

Case Study No. 1: Decreasing Hepatitis B Virus Infection in Health Care Workers

A.1. The policy regarding incentive encouragement is the most effective. The prevalence ratio of vaccinated to those not vaccinated is 1.6. The 95% confidence interval of 1.4–2.0 does not contain 1.0. This means that the ratio is statistically significantly elevated.

A.2. Tracking system used to monitor coverage is the least effective. The prevalence ratio is the lowest. In addition, the 95% confidence interval contains 1.0. This means that the tracking system is not statistically associated with an increased vaccination rate.

A.3. Persons who are immunized may not have responded to the survey. Persons may not accurately recall their immunization status.

A.4. Employee health personnel staffing levels may be inadequate to mount large-scale education programs, send reminder letters, or to track immunization schedules.

Case Study No. 2: Outbreak of Hepatitis B Virus (HBV) Infection among Hemodialysis Patients

A.1. The shared multiple-dose vial.

A.2. Since HBV survives well in the environment, blood-contaminated surfaces that are not routinely cleaned and disinfected are a reservoir for transmission of HBV. Staff also can transfer HBV to patients from contaminated surfaces by their hands or through use of contaminated equipment and supplies.

A.3. Strict adherence to universal precautions should be practiced. Serum specimens from all susceptible patients should be tested monthly for hepatitis B surface antigen (HBsAg). HBsAg-positive patients should be isolated by room, machine, instruments, medications, supplies, and staff. No instruments, medications, or supplies should be shared. Multidose medication vials should be avoided, but if necessary, medications must be prepared in a clean centralized area separate from areas used for patient care, laboratory work, or refuse disposal. Areas for clean and contaminated items should be clearly established. Blood specimens should be handled with gloved hands and stored in a designated area away from central supply and medication preparation areas. Hepatitis B vaccination for susceptible patients should be encouraged.

Case Study No. 3: Methicillin-resistant *Staphylococcus aureus* (MRSA): A Prevalent Nosocomial Pathogen in US Hospitals

A.3. Handwashing, gloving, masking and eye protection, gowning, appropriate device handling, and appropriate handling of laundry should be implemented. Wash hands after touching blood, body fluids, secretions, excretions, and contaminated items, whether or not gloves are worn. Wash hands after tasks and procedures on same patient and between patient contacts. Wear gloves when touching blood, body fluids, secretions, excretions, and contaminated items. Wear mask and eye protection during patient care activities and procedures that are likely to result in sprays or splashes of blood, body fluids, excretions, or secretions. Wear a gown to protect skin and prevent soiling of clothes during patient care activities and procedures likely to result in sprays or splashes of blood or body fluids. Handle, transport, and process used patient care equipment or devices soiled with blood, body fluids, excretions, or secretions in a manner that prevents skin and mucous membrane contact, contamination of clothing, and transfer of microorganisms to other environments and patients. Handle, transport, and process linens soiled with blood, body fluids, excretions, or secretions in a manner that prevents mucous membrane and skin contact, contamination of clothing, and transfer of microorganisms to other environments and patients.

Chapter 9

Case Study No. 2: Analysis of Genetic Disorders in a Tribal Setting

A.1. The patterns of a disorder's appearance in different families can be used to determine, through segregation analysis, the mechanism of inheritance of the disorder, that is, whether or not there is Mendelian transmission, and if so, whether the disorder is autosomal dominant, autosomal recessive, or X-linked. This will aid in determining which relatives should be screened using what method of screening.

A.2. The population is relatively homogeneous and genetic traits are less likely to be influenced by intermarriage with outsiders.

A.3. By identifying which tribes have the highest incidence of Schwartz–Jampel syndrome, screening and follow-up health care resources can be targeted to that tribe.

Case Study No. 3: Cost-Effectiveness of Screening for Hereditary Hemochromatosis

A.1.

Key

Proband   Unaffected   Affected   Carrier

Figure 9.3.   Pedigree illustrating an autosomal recessive method of inheritance.

A.2. Determine the (1) specificity and sensitivity of the all four testing methods, (2) prevalence of children that are homozygous, (3) prevalence of siblings that are homozygous, and (4) incidence of cirrhosis in those with hereditary hemochromatosis.

Case Study No. 4: Which Diseases to Screen for in Outpatient Settings?

A.1. Gene location and mechanism of inheritance should be established. Information on the incidence and prevalence of disease and the consequences of the diseases should be considered. Information on the variation of incidence in population subgroups served by the outpatient clinic (to target screenings and interventions) also should be known. There must be clear evidence that asymptomatic people can be identified using the screening test. There must be high specificity and sensitivity of the screening method. Effective therapy for the condition, if identified, must be available.

Chapter 10

Case Study No. 1: Solvent/Detergent-Treated Plasma (SDP)

A.1. The likelihood of viral transmission from fresh frozen plasma (FFP) is very low, with rates of transmission estimated at 1:676,000 for HIV, 1:63,000 for HBV, and 1:103,000 for HCV. Risk increases with multiple transfusions (Schreiber *et al.*, 1996).

A.2. No. Bacterial contamination is theoretically possible, and the infectious risk of nonlipid-envelope viruses (e.g., parvovirus B19 and hepatitis A) is not eliminated.

A.3. Donor-retested plasma is a third option that uses plasma from a single donor after a specified period of quarantine time.

A.4. AuBuchon and Birkmeyer (1994) estimated a cost-effectiveness ratio for SDP at slightly less than $300,000 per quality-adjusted life year, using a model that understated the actual acquisition cost of SDP by 50%.

Case Study No. 2: Transmyocardial Laser Revascularization (TMLR)

A.1. TMLR patients are those that are not candidates for CABG or PTCA procedures, because they may have diffuse atherosclerosis, distal stenosis, or small arteries, or are unresponsive to pharmacological management.

A.2. Chelation therapy, enhanced external counterpulsation, heart transplantation, neural stimulation, and urokinase injection.

A.3. Safety, as measured by morbidity and mortality of TMLR to an appropriate alternative treatment, and efficacy, which could be determined as an improvement in symptoms as measured by a validated angina scale (e.g., New York Heart Association Angina Classification System).

Case Study No. 3: Intensity-Modulated Radiation Therapy (IMRT)

A.1. Remain competitive in marketplace, enhance institutional reputation, improve oncology staff recruitment, increase patient referrals, or augment research opportunities.

A.2. No. Randomized controlled trials have definitely proven advantages on these effects for IMRT versus standard treatment.

A.3. Capital equipment committee.

Case Study No. 4: Intravenous Immunoglobulins (IVIG)

A.1. (1) Cost—annual pharmacy budget for this item is often substantial; (2) availability—short national supply of IVIG often results in limited inventory locally; and (3) reimbursement difficulties—third-party payers often will not cover off-label uses.

A.2. (1) Evaluate the biomedical literature to identify all the possible uses of IVIG; (2) characterize these uses based on the strength of published evidence as acceptable, unacceptable, or promising but unproven; (3) examine existing health system use and compare to guidelines developed in 2; (4) educate clinicians on appropriate use; and (5) develop monitoring and feedback mechanisms to control IVIG use.

Chapter 11

Case Study No. 1: The Health Consequences of a Record Heat Wave

A.1. Case–control study.

A.2. The strongest risk factor from Table 11.9 is "did not leave home at least once a week." The crude odds ratio (OR) is 6.7. The 95% confidence limits of 3.0 and 15.0 (since 1 is not contained) indicate that the OR represents a statistically significant relationship between the exposure and outcome (death from heat wave). The strength of the OR suggests that it is not likely to be a chance occurrence.

A.4. Living controls but proxy respondents for the cases were interviewed.

A.5. Form a seasonal group to prospectively monitor climactic conditions (heat and humidity). Utilize health aides from the Department on Aging to go to neighborhoods, particularly those with high density elderly and poverty and high rise buildings, to monitor conditions of elderly.

Case Study No. 2: Neighbors versus Their Neighborhood

A.1. Name of the compounds being used, their amount and frequency, and the specific areas being covered. Information on the known acute toxicity or other health hazards (e.g., effects on pregnant women) can be obtained from the Environmental Protection Agency (EPA).

A.2. Cross-sectional study design of exposure (yes vs. no) compared to presence of recent symptoms of pesticide exposure, and use of protective measures or safe-handling practices (yes vs. no) and presence of recent symptoms of pesticide exposure.

A.3. Convene a community meeting to discuss what is known about health effects of pesticides and risk of human exposure through air, water, food, or bystander exposure. Information brochures for health care providers and for the public on safe and proper handling of pesticides (including reading the label). Public service announcements by the local EPA, television, and radio.

Case Study No. 3: Community Health Risk from an Industrial Plant

A.1. Better plant design and facilities for storing chemicals. Training of workers in emergency procedures.

A.2. Surveys, epidemiological studies. Longitudinal studies comparing exposed and nonexposed persons to ascertain incidence and mortality of disease.

A.3. Emergency planning. Community awareness of plan. Land-use planning in locating industrial plants. Adequate information about industrial chemicals used in the area for health care providers. Properly trained and equipped emergency response personnel. Cooperation of industry, labor, government, and medical personnel in planning for environmental emergencies. Local department of public health could take the lead in these efforts.

Case Study No. 4: Environmental Equity

A.1. Recommend blood lead screening for children according to CDC protocol. Send chips of peeling pain or dust wipes of residence to an environmental laboratory for analysis in areas at high risk for poverty. Be familiar with state-mandated resources for residential lead identification and removal programs.

A.2. Paint deterioration in older, poorly maintained housing and lead dust from the environment from proximity near industry with lead by-products.

A.3. Population size, density, and time trends; proximity to water supply; geologic stability; the nature of existing proximate pollution sources; community attitudes about the presence of the additional waste facilities.

Case Study No. 5: Global Environmental Health

A.1. Know where the main sources of radiation are in the community and what forms of radiation they emit and the different adverse effects caused by different forms of radiation.

A.2. Appropriate design and operation of sources producing ionizing radiation. Education of members of the public as to what action they should take in response to nuclear disasters. Prevent unnecessary exposure through certifications and regulations.

A.3. Links among health officials at national and international levels. Disease surveillance networks. Multinational cooperative agreements among governments.

Chapter 12

Case Study No. 1: Chicago Violence Prevention Strategic Plan

A.1. Consider using geographic information software to identify community areas at highest risk for violence or if different violence patterns emerge in different communities (e.g., drug crimes).

A.2. Substance abuse, mental health problems, family stress, family isolation, weapons possession, and lack of access to mental health or community support services.

A.3 Examples of policies would include the creation of an Office of Violence Prevention within the Chicago Department of Public Health. Specific program initiatives would need to span housing, mental health, family planning, and social services. Increased public health nurse and clinic professionals training aimed at interventions to families with young children aimed at preventing and identifying stressful situations (family and community), providing counseling, and anticipatory guidance and referral to other agencies as needed.

A.4. The Chicago Department of Public Health suggests that through quality assurance programs and information systems, managed care plans can promote the standardized use of protocols for screening for substance abuse and to monitor the providers in their compliance with these protocols. In addition, managed care plans can determine the prevalence of certain diagnoses or conditions (risk factors) related to violence within the contracted populations they serve through the examination of encounter data and to develop prevention programs accordingly.

Case Study No. 2: Increase Quality and Years of Healthy Life

A.1 Chronic disabling diseases (such as arthritis), physical inactivity, obesity, and smoking.

A.2. High mortality rates early in life such as that resulting from high infant mortality, homicide in youth, and AIDS in young African Americans.

A.3. Policies supporting primary and secondary prevention in the elderly focused on quality of life and longevity issues. According to the World Health Organization (1999), examples include:

- Promoting the benefits of healthy lifestyles, especially promoting physical activity.
- Legislation on sales and advertising of alcohol and tobacco.
- Ensuring access to health care and rehabilitation services for older people.
- Adapting physical environments to existing disabilities.

Other policies are needed that provide additional social systems for the elderly needing resources such as caretakers, meal services, daycare facilities for the disabled, legal services, recreation, and funding for wellness home and community health services.

Case Study No. 4: Measles—United States, 1999

A.1 Endemic measles can be reestablished in the United States if vaccination coverage declines. High coverage and strong surveillance are essential to maintaining the current status of measles in the United States.

A.2. Eradication, control, or elimination of a disease in our global society is dependent on international planning and cooperation through the WHO, including the sharing of resources (goods and services) when necessary as well as technology to developing countries. International certificates of vaccinations for diseases when epidemic in a country may be required or policy as a condition of entry into that country. The United States recommends that children 12–15 months and older visiting countries where measles is an endemic disease be vaccinated before entry into that country (CDC, 1996). An example of a disease requiring a certificate of vaccination for entry into some countries is yellowfever. The political, economic, social, and cultural implications of mandating vaccinations when applied to global control of vaccine-preventable diseases are complex.

Chapter 13

Case Study No. 1: What Is the Most Cost-Effective Treatment for Tuberculosis?

A.1. Out of a cohort of 100 patients, directly observed treatment (DOT) will cure 15.5 more patients after initial therapy (94.5 per 100–79.0 per 100).

A.2. The cost per cure is negative for DOT protocol irrespective of how costs are determined. The ratio is −49,961 per cured patient considering only direct health care costs and −52,697 per cured patient when all costs are considered.

A.3. All cost estimates were taken from specific cases convenient to the researchers such as specific facility charges for treatment, facility cost-charge ratios, test charges, and so on.

A.5. The minister of health should adopt the DOT strategy both to reduce health care costs and to improve patient outcomes.

Case Study No. 2: Health and Economic Benefits of Weight Loss

A.1.

Gender and age group	27.5 kg/m^2	32.5 kg/m^2	37.5 kg/m^2
Men age 35–44			
Health costs avoided	$2300	$3500	$4900
Discounted PV of cost	$2389	$2371	$3073
Benefit/cost ratio	0.96	1.28	1.59
Women age 35–44 years			
Health costs avoided	$2200	$3300	$4600
Discounted PV of cost	$2651	$2902	$3243
Benefit/cost ratio	0.86	1.14	1.42

A.2. The benefit-to-cost ratio increases with higher weight to height for both males and females.

A.3. Because causal linkages between weight and incidence rate of a specific disease are not clear, reductions in weight may not reduce incidence in disease.

A.4. There appears to be a positive relationship (dose–response) between obesity and cost of adverse medical problems. Greater initial weight appears to increase the likelihood of all/most diseases.

A.5. Weight loss programs have a benefit to cost ratio that increases with the initial weight to height ratio. Consequently, targeting weight loss programs to those with at least a current status of 37.5 kg/m^2 would be suggested. Enrolling individuals in a weight loss program with an initial status of 27.5 kg/m^2 or less is not recommended. These programs should not differentiate by gender because benefit to cost ratios do not seem to differ by gender.

Case Study No. 3: Inactivated Poliovirus Vaccine (IPV) versus Oral Polio Vaccine (OPV) as Routine Childhood Immunizations

A.1.

Category	Cost	Cost avoided	Net cost
OPV	$286.7 M	$0 M	$286.7 M
IPV	$320.6 M	$11.4 M	$309.2 M
IPV/OPV	$303.7 M	$5.7 M	$298.0 M

A.2. OPV is base
IPV $22.5 M (309.2–286.7)
IPV/OPV $11.3 M (298.0–286.7)

A.3. OPV is base
IPV $22.5 M/9.5 cases avoided = $2.37 M per polio case avoided.
IPV/OPV $11.3/4.75 cases avoided = $2.38 M per polio case avoided.

A.4. Either IPV-related option appears costly per polio case avoided. OPV should be maintained as the desired immunization policy. However, the driving factor in this decision is the cost per dose difference between the two types of vaccine. If policy moves totally to IPV would that have an effect on the cost per dose (due to increased volume, etc.)? This is important because if the cost of IPV vaccine falls by 10 or 20%, the cost per case avoided falls dramatically. For example, a 10% vaccine cost reduction lowers IPV unit vaccine cost to $7.58 and lowers net cost of this strategy to $296.3 M (from \$309.2 M). The difference between IPV and OPV then falls to \$9.5 M or about \$1.0 M per case avoided.

Case Study No. 4: Cost-Effectiveness of Magnetic Resonance Imaging (MRI) for Internal Derangement of the Knee

A.1.

Category	Arthroscopies averted (%)	Strategy 1 no MRI \$ per person	Strategy 2 MRI \$ per person	Incremental costs of MRI \$ per person	Cost per arthroscopy averted
Base: Social costs	10%	\$975	\$1108	\$151	\$1514
Worst case	5%	\$964	\$1156	\$192	\$3850
Best case	16%	\$949	\$1050	\$101	\$632
Base: Direct costs	10%	\$660	\$822	\$162	\$1624
Worst case	5%	\$666	\$855	\$189	\$3773
Best case	16%	\$651	\$782	\$130	\$813

A.2. See above.

A.3. See above.

A.4. Probably would not adopt the MRI screening policy from either the social or private point of view. Because there are not that many arthroscopies avoided using the MRI diagnostic process, the potential savings from avoiding surgery does not compensate for the costs of the MRI test being performed on these patients. Additional information that might mitigate this conclusion include the potential for reduction in the cost of the MRI diagnostic procedure due to increased volume and more information about potential indirect costs or quality of life associated with arthroscopy. It is possible that this analysis underestimated the indirect costs of avoided surgery by only using value of lost work time. Quality of life for those not having to have surgery might increase benefits somewhat, but probably not sufficiently to justify surgery, however.

Chapter 14

Case Study No. 2: Reporting Intimate Partner Violence

A.1. An assaultive partner may be less likely to repeat the assaultive behavior if he or she knows that he or she will face legal consequences, including imprisonment. However, if the police response does not address the situation effectively, it is possible that partner violence will be encouraged because the assaultive partner will come to believe that there are no consequences for his or her actions. Public health departments may be more likely over time to approach the issue of partner violence form a prevention perspective, unlike the police, who have a law enforcement orientation. Compared to both the public health department and the police, the reporting of such events to a registry would potentially permit the development of a more comprehensive database that could be used to develop more targeted and effective prevention and intervention programs.

A.2. The mandated reporting of the violence limits the autonomy and privacy of the victim and, depending on the circumstances, may increase the risk of harm following the report. Public health departments have significant experience in maintaining confidentiality of records, such as reports of infectious disease and contact tracing procedures. Most registries also operate under strict guidelines relating to confidentiality. Many reports filed with the police are available for public inspection, thereby compromising an individual's privacy and potentially increasing his or her risk of future harm.

Case Study No. 4: The Epidemiology of Do-Not-Resuscitate (DNR) Orders

A.1. Individuals who are older are more likely to be sicker, thereby justifying a DNR. Individuals who are suffering from dementia may not have expressed their wishes to their physicians or family prior to the onset of their dementia and are unable to do so, so that the providers and/or family must try to determine what the patient would have wanted and/or what would be best for the patient under the circumstances.

A.2. Conflicts of interest may exist in the specification of DNR physician orders. For example, (1) the family does not have the resources or the energy to care for the relative so asks that a DNR order be placed in the chart, although it may not be the wish of the patient, or (2) the hospital believes that older individuals have already lived their lives and that an extension of life and consumption of the requisite resources is unwarranted, given the scarcity of resources and perhaps the patients' inability to pay for care. Women may face denial of procedures more frequently than men. Alternatively, the seriousness of their health condition is not recognized as early as it should be due to provider lack of knowledge of women's health and/or unwillingness to address seriously women's complaints, so that women are hospitalized/undergo procedures at more advanced stages of illness.

A.3. Briefly, utilitarianism seeks to achieve the maximum good. In this situation, it might be theorized that DNR orders are warranted based on the patients' medical status, that there is a limited amount that can be done, that resources are limited, and that it serves the greater good to limit access to limited resources by those who would consume a great deal of them and offer little economically in exchange, e.g., through employment. A principlistic examination would focus on respect for persons, beneficence, nonmaleficence, and justice in the context of the factual situation and would likely conclude that the entry of a DNR order is a matter to be decided by the patient. Feminist ethics would be concerned not only with the patient, but also with the effect of the DNR order on the patient's relations with caregivers, family, friends, and so forth, and the implications of any changes in those relations as a result of the order.

Appendix

Websites for Health Care Managers Thinking Epidemiologically

The editor recommends that all health care managers visit each of these websites in this section to familiarize themselves with the type and amount of information that are available for health planning and evaluation. The websites were selected because of easy access to online data for this purpose. Since these websites also are now likely to be frequented by consumers of health care, health care managers must be prepared to respond to consumer requests for information and services as may be prompted through searches from the worldwide web.

Commercial

General search engine (originated at Stanford).
http://www.yahoo.com

ask Dr. Weil
Dr. Weil's integrative medicine and self-healing-oriented site
http://www.drweil.com

drkoop.com
"The Best Prescription is Knowledge." Health news, family health, health resources, health and wellness, community, conditions, and concerns.
http://www.drkoop.com

Elements: Visionary Health Insurance and Wellness Program
Featuring personalized health improvement profiles and direct links to traditional and complementary providers.
http://www.elementswellness.com

HealthNetwork.com/WebMD
Builds on cable/video programming. Original programming live, breaking news, exercise and nutrition guides, expert medical advice and in-depth information; interactive.
http://ahn.com

Center for Studying Health System Change—HSC Data Files
1996–1997 HSC household and physician surveys.
http://www.hschange.com

Health Central
Health news, health profiles and information, tips, disease and condition library, Dr. Dean Edell.
http://www.healthcentral.com

HealthPartners Consumer Choice System
Information to select a provider, clinic, or care network; compare care networks or hospitals on quality and satisfaction.
http://www.consumer-choice.com

HealthGrades.com
Health care report cards on hospitals, physicians, health plans, nursing homes; choosing a hospital, physician, health plan, nursing home, chiropractor, dentist, acupuncturist, naturopathic physician, assisted living residence.
http://www.healthgrades.com

Health Pages: The Voice of the Health Care Consumer
Physician directory where patients grade and comment on their doctors, compare insurance plans, and explore health care options.
http://thehealthpages.com

Intelihealth
Johns Hopkins Health Information. Health issues, drug search, medical dictionary, diseases and conditions, health assessments.
http://www.intelihealth.com

iVillage.com: The Women's Network
The leading women's health network.
http://www.ivillage.com

Mylifepath
Blue Shield of California provides health information and links to providers and products.
http://www.mylifepath.com

Onhealth
Health information: draws from major medical journals. Diseases and conditions, women, family, baby, alternative, lifestyle, food and fitness, library, community, shopping, and news.
http://www.onhealth.com

Press, Ganey Services
Provider information including research and best practices, published articles and accreditation news.
http://www.pressganey.com

RealAge
A personalized age assessment and health risk reduction plan
http://www.RealAge.com

Web Medicine
Consumer health information linked to provider/payer e-commerce resources.
http://www.webmed.com

US Government

Federal Government

The Agency for Healthcare Research and Quality (AHRQ)
The Medical Expenditure Panel Survey (MEPS)

A nationally representative survey of health care use, expenditures, sources of payment, and insurance coverage for the US civilian noninstitutionalized population, as well as a national survey of nursing homes and their residents.

Healthcare Cost and Utilization Project (HCUP)

Comprises a family of administrative longitudinal databases—including state-specific hospital discharge databases and a national sample of discharges from community hospitals—and powerful, user-friendly software that can be used with both HCUP data and with other administrative databases.
http://www.ahcpr.gov/data

Administration on Aging

Provides information on health, social, and economic needs of the elderly including legislation and implementation of US government entitlement programs for the elderly.
http://www.aoa.dhhs.gov

Bureau of Labor Statistics

This is the principal data source agency for the US federal Government in the fields of economics and labor statistics.
http://stats.bls.gov

Center for the Evaluation of Risks to Human Reproduction

Provides the latest information about potentially hazardous effects of chemical on human reproduction and development.
http://cerhr.niehs.nih.gov

Center for Information Technology (CIT)

To provide, coordinate, and manage information technology and to advance computational science.
http://www.cit.nih.gov/home.asp

Centers for Disease Control and Prevention

To promote health and quality of life by preventing and controlling disease, injury, and disability. Includes 11 center, institute, and offices. Information on travelers' health, health topics A-Z, publications, software and products, data and statistics, training and employment.
http://www.cdc.gov

- **National Center for HIV, STD, and TB Prevention**
  To prevent HIV infection and reduce the incidence of HIV-related illness and death, in collaboration with community, state, national, and international partners.
  http://www.cdc.gov/nchstp/od/nchstp.html
- **National Center for Chronic Disease Prevention and Health**
  Plans and coordinates a program to prevent premature mortality from chronic illness.
  http://www.cdc.gov/nccdphp/index.htm
- **CDC WONDER**
  Easy-to-use system that provides a single point of access to a wide variety of CDC

reports, guidelines, and numeric public health data.
http://wonder.cdc.gov/

Comprehensive Epidemiologic Data Resource Program (CEDR), US Department of Energy
Epidemiologic data sets on radiation health effects available for downloading
http://cedr.lbl.gov

Department of Health and Human Services
Medical and social science research; preventing outbreak of infectious disease; assuring food and drug safety; Medicare; financial assistance for low-income families; child support enforcement; improving maternal and infant health; Head Start; preventing child abuse and domestic violence; substance abuse treatment and prevention; services for older Americans; comprehensive health services delivery for American Indians and Alaska Natives.
http://www.os.dhhs.gov

Department of Veterans Affairs
Searchable database of active VA-funded research programs; Health Services Research and Development Service.
http://www.va.gov/va.htm

Environmental Protection Agency
To protect human health and to safeguard the natural environment. Programs: reinvention activities, general interest, media, industry partnerships, state, local and tribal projects, geographic, research.
http://www.epa.gov

FedStats
Statistics from over 100 agencies in US Federal Government for the public.
http://www.fedstats.gov

Health Care Financing Administration
Information on Medicare and Medicaid; research initiatives and publications of Office of Research and Demonstrations.
http://www.hcfa.gov

Healthfinder
Information for patients regarding quality of health plans, primary care providers, long-term care facilities, hospitals, and treatments.
http://www.healthfinder.gov

Medicare
The official US government site for general Medicare information.
http://www.medicare.gov

National Center for Health Statistics (NCHS)
NVSS Births: 1998 data; births, marriages, divorces, and deaths: 1999. National Nursing Home Survey. National Health Interview Survery on Disability. NHIS Data Release. Collection systems: NHANES, NHCS, NHIS, NIS, NSFG, SLAITS, Vital Statistics. Initiatives: Aging, Classification of Diseases, Healthy People. FASTATS A to Z. FEDSTATS, AIDS/HIV information, aging, elderly care, alcohol and drug information (PREVLINE), cancer information, cardiovascular disease, CDC, child health, consumer information, diseases, electronic

records, environment, Federal Depository Library, food and nutrition, funding and grants, health information, health insurance, health promotion, heart disease and stroke, Hispanic health, immunizations, Indian health, injuries, international data, medication, prescriptions, oral health, state governments, statistics, women's health, web searching tools.
http://www.cdc.gov/nchs

- Most recent data sets and updates from the NCHS are stored at this FTP directory ftp://ftp.cdc.gov/pub/

National Guideline Clearinghouse (NGC)
Evidence-based clinical practice guidelines and related abstract, summary, and comparison materials widely available to health care professionals. Operated by US Department of Health and Human Services, AHRQ, in partnership with the AMA and the AAHP.
http://www.guideline.gov/index.asp

National Health Care Indicators and Expenditures Indicators
Contains data and analysis of recent trends in health care spending, employment and prices.
http://www.hcfa.gov/stats/stats.htm

National Institute on Alcohol Abuse and Alcoholism
NIAA publications and databases, news and events, grants information.
http://www.niaaa.nih.gov

National Institute on Drug Abuse
Events calendar, grants and contracts, publications and brochures, such as NIDA Notes.
http://www.nida.nih.gov

National Institutes of Health
Conducts and supports research and fosters communication of biomedical information. Composed of 25 separate institutes and centers.
http://www.nih.gov/about/nihnew.html

- **National Cancer Institute (NCI)**
  http://www.nci.nih.gov
  A color atlas of geographic patterns of cancer death rates is available through the NCI.
  http://www.nci.nih.gov/atlas
- **National Center for Complementary and Alternative Medicine**
  http://nccam.nih.gov
- **National Center for Research Resources (NCRR)**
  http://www.ncrr.nih.gov
- **National Eye Institute (NEI)**
  http://www.nei.nih.gov
- **National Heart, Lung, and Blood Institute (NHLBI)**
  http://www.nhlbi.nih.gov/index.htm
- **National Human Genome Research Institute (NHGRI)**
  http://www.nhgri.nih.gov
- **National Institute on Aging (NIA)**
  http://www.nih.gov/nia
- **National Institute on Alcohol abuse and Alcoholism (NIAAA)**
  http://www.niaaa.nih.gov

- **National Institute of Allergy and Infectious Diseases (NIAID)**
  http://www.niaid.nih.gov
- **National Institute of Arthritis and Musculoskeletal and Skin Diseases (NIAMS)**
  http://www.nih.gov/niams
- **National Institute of Child Health and Human Development (NICHD)**
  http://www.nichd.nih.gov
- **National Institute on Deafness and Other communication Disorders (NIDCD)**
  http://www.nih.gov/nidcd
- **National Institute of Dental and Craniofacial Research (NIDCR)**
  http://www.nidr.nih.gov
- **National Institute of Diabetes and Digestive and Kidney Diseases (NIDDK)**
  http://www.niddk.nih.gov
- **National Institute on Drug Abuse (NIDA)**
  http://www.nida.nih.gov/NIDAHome1.html
- **National Institute of Environmental Health Sciences (NIEHS)**
  http://www.niehs.nih.gov
- **National Institute of General Medical Sciences (NIGMS)**
  http://www.nigms.nih.gov
- **National Institute of Mental Health (NIMH)**
  http://www.nimh.nih.gov
- **National Institute of Neurological Disorders, and Stroke (NINDS)**
  http://www.ninds.nih.gov
- **National Institute of Nursing Research**
  http://www.nih.gov/ninr
- **National Library of Medicine (NLM)**
  http://www.nlm.nih.gov

National Library of Medicine
MEDLINE, MEDLINE*plus*, databases, publications, training, grants, research programs, computational molccular biology, medical informatics, announcements, exhibits, jobs, contracts
http://www.nlm.nih.gov

Naval Health Research Center, Health Sciences and Epidemiology
Conducts research and development to improve the clinical and medical information systems available to operational commanders, medical planners, environmental health and preventive medicine staff, and field medical providers engaged in the prevention, control, and treatment of illnesses and injuries in deployed military forces.
http://www.nhrc.navy.mil

Occupational Safety and Health Administration (OSHA)
Sets standards for workplace health and safety.
http://www.osha.gov

Surveillance, Epidemiology, and End Results (SEER) Program of the National Cancer Institute
Most authoritative source of information on cancer incidence and survival in the United States. Information on more than 2.5 million cancer cases included. SEER data, publications, and resources are available free of charge.
http://www-seer.ims.nci.nih.gov

United States Census Bureau
Preeminent collector and provider of timely, relevant, and quality data about the people and economy of the United States.
http://www.census.gov

United States Public Health Service
http://www.os.dhhs.gov/phs

- **Administration for Children and Families (ACF)**
  http://www.acf.gov
- **Administration of Aging (AOA)**
  http://www.aoa.gov
- **Agency for Healthcare Research and Quality (AHRQ)**
  http://www.ahrq.gov
- **Agency for Toxic Substances and Disease Registry (ATSDR)**
  http://www.atsdr.cdc.gov
- **Centers for Disease Control and Prevention (CDC)**
  http://www.cdc.gov
- **Food and Drug Administration (FDA)**
  http://www.fda.gov
- **Health Care Financing Administration (HCFA)**
  (Medicare and Medicaid)
  http://hcfa.hhs.gov
- **Health Resources and Services Administration (HRSA)**
  http://www.hrsa.gov
- **Indian Health Service (HIS)**
  http://www.ihs.gov
- **National Institutes of Health (NIH)**
  http://www.nih.gov
- **Program Support Center (PSC)**
  http://www.psc.gov
- **Substance Abuse and Mental Health Services Administration (SAMHSA)**
  http://www.samhsa.gov

United States Department of Commerce
Promotes job creation, economic growth, sustainable development, and improved living standards for all Americans. Makes possible daily weather reports; facilitates technology that is used in the workplace and home; supports the development, gathering, and transmission of information essential to competitive business; conducts the constitutionally mandated decennial census.
http://204.193.246.62

State Government

Council of State Governments
http://www.csg.org

NASIRE
http://www.nasire.org
The leading forum for addressing opportunities, implications, and challenges of improving the business of government through the application of information technology.

Robert Wood Johnson Foundation for State Health Policy Home Page
http://www2.umdnj.edu/shpp/homepage

University of Indiana Virtual Law Library
http://www.law.indiana.edu

Washburn Law School State Government and Legislative Info Site
http://www.washlaw.edu

All Known State Websites Pertaining to Health Care

Alaska Department of Health and Social Services
http://health.hss.state.ak.us

Arizona Department of Health Services
http://www.hs.state.az.us

California Health and Human Services
http://www.chhs.ca.gov

Connecticut Department of Social Services
http://www.dss.state.ct.us

Colorado Department of Health and Human Services
http://www.state.co.us/gov_dir/agencies.html

Florida Agency for Health Care Administration (AHCA)
http://www.fdhc.state.fl.us

Georgia Statewide Academic and Medical System
http://www2.state.ga.us/Departments/DOAS/GIST

Idaho Department of Health and Welfare
http://www2.state.id.us/dhw/hwgd_www/home.html

Illinois Department of Public Health
http://www.idph.state.il.us

Kansas Department of Human Resources
http://www.kdhe.state.ks.us

Kentucky's NASIRE State Search: Health, Human Services and Welfare
The Cabinet for Health Services
http://cfc-chs.chr.state.ky.us

Maine Bureau of Health
http://janus.state.me.us/dhs/boh/index.htm

Massachusetts Department of Public Health
http://www.state.ma.us/dph/dphhome.htm

Michigan Department of Community Health
http://www.mdch.state.mi.us

Minnesota Department of Health
http://www.health.state.mn.us

Mississippi Division of Medicaid
http://www.dom.state.ms.us

New Jersey Department of Health and Senior Services
http://www.state.nj.us/health/index.html

New York State Department of Health
http://www.health.state.ny.us

North Carolina Department of Human Resources
http://www.dhhs.state.nc.us

North Dakota Health Department
http://www.ehs.health.state.nd.us/ndhd

North Dakota Department of Human Services
http://lnotes.state.nd.us/dhs/dhsweb.nsf

Oregon Department of Human Services
http://www.hr.state.or.us

Pennsylvania Department of Health
http://www.health.state.pa.us

Rhode Island Department of Health
http://www.health.state.ri.us

South Carolina State Department of Health and Environmental Control
http://www.state.sc.us/dhec

South Dakota Department of Health
http://www.state.sd.us/doh

Tennessee Department of Health
http://www.state.tn.us/health

Texas Department of Health
http://www.tdh.texas.gov

Utah Department of Health
http://hlunix.ex.state.ut.us

Virginia Department of Health
http://www.vdh.state.va.us

Washington State Department of Health
http://www.doh.wa.gov

Wisconsin Department of Health and Family Services
http://www.dhfs.state.wi.us

Private Organizations

American Cancer Society
Information for the lay public and health care professionals on current trends in cancer prevention, diagnosis, and treatment. Statistical trends and online journal available.
http://www.cancer.org

American College of Epidemiology

The professional organization dedicated to continued education and advocacy for epidemiologists in their efforts to promote the public health.
www.acepidemiology.org

Citizens for the Right to Know

A California consumer advocacy group offers tips for choosing a health plan.
http://www.rtk.org

Cochrane Library

The Cochrane Database of Systematic Reviews (CDSR): a collection of databases containing systematic, up-to-date review of the effects of health care.
http://www.library.mcgill.ca/cdroms/colib.htm

Electronic Hallway

University of Washington. Teaching cases and exercises; role plays; teaching workshops, editorial assistance, peer-reviewed case journal.
http://www.hallway.org

Epidemiology and Public Health (Public health, biosciences, medicine)

Government agencies and international organizations; university sites; professional societies and organizations; cancer, cardiovascular, diabetes, infectious disease, and AIDS; hospital epidemiology and infection control; genetic and molecular, social behavioral, environmental, nutrition, reproductive health and population studies; biostatistics and mathematical modeling; data sources, publications, meetings/courses, computing resources, news and discussion groups, FAQ.
http://chanane.ucsf.edu/epidem/epidem.html

Federation of American Scientists, ProMED Initiative

Global monitoring of emerging diseases: AHEAD/ILIAD and PROMED mail reporting network.
http://www.fas.org/promed

Hardin Library for the Health Sciences

Information/references, education services, educational multimedia facility and electronic classroom, IHIO, National Laboratory for the Study of Rural Telemedicine, Healthnet, MD consult, journals, indexes/databases, HealthWeb, lists for health subjects, OASIS, health information resource for health providers and patients.
http://www.arcade.uiowa.edu/hardin

Joint Commission on Accreditation of Healthcare Organizations

Information for providers, consumers and employers on the safety and quality of care provided to the public through the provision of health care accreditation and related services that support performance improvement in health care organizations.
http://www.jcaho.org

Massachusetts Health Quality Partnership

Results from the 1998 project and information on the objective and methodology of the project.
http://www.mhqp.org

Mayo Clinic Health Oasis

Reliable information for a healthier life; news; centers for diseases.
http://www.mayohealth.org

Metro Chicago Information Center
An independent, nonprofit research organization committed to increasing the quality, quantity, and accessibility of information about human conditions and the quality of life in the Chicago Metropolitan area.
http://www.mcic.org

National Academy of Science
Private, nonprofit society engaged in scientific and engineering research.
http://www.nas.edu

National Committee for Quality Assurance (NCAQ)
Information for consumers and health care organizations regarding NCQA accreditation, links to other health care websites. Source of information on quality indicators for managed care plans. Maintains the Health Plan Employer Data and Information Set (HEDIS® 1999) for benchmarking health plan quality.
http://www.ncqa.org

Osteoporosis Society of Canada
A Canadian charity serving persons who have or are at risk for osteoporosis through education, empowerment, and community support. Provides an on-line assessment of calcium intake.
http://www.osteoporosis.ca

Picker Institute Homepage
Patient survey information and links to other websites with patient/consumer focus.
http://www.picker.org

Quality Measurement Advisory Service
Assists state and local healthcare coalitions, purchasing groups, and health information organization to measure health care quality.
http://www/qmas.org/default.htm

International

National Health Service (NHS)
Describes current initiatives of the medical care system for Great Britain.
http://www.nhs50.nhs.uk

Pan American Health Organization
An international agency specializing in health.
http://www.paho.org

United Nations Population Information Network (POPIN)
Electronic information on world population trends including migration and development.
http://www.undp.org/popin

University of Bergen
Compilation of resources of family physicians that link a rich variety of sites across the world.
http://www.uib.no/isf

The World Bank Group
A group of five closely associated institutions: the International Bank for Reconstruction and Development, International Development Association, International Finance Corporation, Multinational Investment Guarantee Agency, and the International Centre for Settlement of

Investment Disputes. Initiatives are aimed at reducing poverty and promoting social justice and equity. Economic and social indicators on countries are available.
http:///www.worldbank.org

World Health Organization (WHO) Report on Infectious Diseases: Removing Obstacles to Healthy Development
A review of the report's key messages; presentation and index of graphs and figures; presentation and index of WHO initiatives; a test-only version; contact points for further information.
http://www.who.int/infectious-disease-report

The World Medical Association, Inc.
Provides a forum for its member associations to communicate freely, to cooperate actively, to achieve consensus on high standards of medical ethics and professional competence, and to promote the professional freedom of physicians worldwide.
http://www.wma.net

Slide Presentations

HIV/AIDS Surveillance—General Epidemiology
Describes trends in HIV/AIDS over time, variation by geographic area, and population subgroups through downloadable .pdf or .ppt formats.
http://www.cdc.gov/graphics.htm

ICD-10-Procedure Coding System (ICD-10-PCS)
On-line slide presentation to describe differences between ICD-9-CM procedure coding and ICD-10 procedure coding.
http://www.hcfa.gov/stats/icd10/icd10pcs.pdf

Supercourse: Epidemiology, the Internet and Global Health
Compilation of lecture materials, including slide presentations on various contemporary and classical epidemiology topics. On-line viewing available. Maintained by faculty from the University of Pittsburgh.
http://www.pitt.edu/~super1/main/index.htm

Glossary

Adjusted rates   A summary rate that is produced by arithmetically weighting the specific rates in a study population by the proportion of persons in a reference population for each specific rate category. This removes the effect of population characteristics influential on an outcome to permit comparison of groups of individuals or populations with respect to incidence or mortality rates.

Alpha level   An arbitrary value that indicates the threshold probability for rejecting a true null hypothesis. Also known as the "level of significance."

Alternative hypothesis (H_A)   Makes a statement about the values of population parameters and is phrased to contradict the null hypothesis.

Attributable risk   The proportion of excess risk of disease or health problem that is associated with exposure to a risk factor.

Beta level   Probability of accepting a false null hypothesis.

Bias   Any difference between an observed value and the true parameter.

Case–control study   Individuals are selected on the basis of the presence or absence of an outcome. Evidence of a factor suspected as causative of the outcome is sought by comparing its prevalence among those who have the outcome factor (cases) to those who do not (controls).

Case-fatality rate   Number of persons dying of a condition divided by the number diagnosed with the condition within one year or less.

Carrier   An infected person or other vertebrate who harbors a transmissible agent without discernible clinical disease and who serves as a potential source of infection.

Causation   A process of identifying an outcome resulting from exposure(s) using a study design, that employs a comparison group.

Causative factor   A variable that is linked to producing an effect, either by itself or in combination with some other factor. It must precede the effect in a time interval consistent with the anticipated effect.

Censored observation   Cases in which the outcome of interest (e.g., death) has not been observed. Term used in survival or failure-time analysis.

Clinical outcomes   The health status changes or effects individual patients experience resulting from the delivery of health care; are measured in terms of the patient's perspective as morbidity, mortality, functional abilities, and satisfaction with care.

Coefficient of variation   Relates the variability of a set of scores to the average size of the set of scores (as a percent). Coefficient of variation = standard deviation ÷ mean × 100%.

Cohort   Group of individuals who share a common experience or event and who pass through time together. Cohorts could be defined by birth year, death year, or exposure to a common source (e.g., atomic bomb survivors).

Competitor analysis   An assessment of an organization's position in the marketplace relative to other entities (individuals, groups, or organizations) which may compete for the same customers or valued resources or otherwise interfere with an organization's ability to serve its selected markets.

Competitor   An individual, group, or organization, which competes for the same customers or valued resources or otherwise interferes with the ability of another entity to engage in exchange with a targeted market.

Confidence interval   Represents a range of values for a point estimate of a parameter (mean, proportion, odds ratio, difference between means) within which the true population parameter is expected to lie within a given level of probability.

Construct   An underlying, not directly observable concept of which measurement is desired. For example, "severity of illness" and "quality of life" are constructs.

Construct validity   An instrument exhibits construct validity when it is seen to correlate with other trusted measures of the phenomenon being measured and it is able to discriminate between groups that have known differences.

Consumer price index (CPI)   A measure of the average change in price over time in a fixed "market basket" of goods and services purchased either by urban wage earners and clerical workers or by all urban consumers.

Cost-benefit analysis (CBA)   An analytic tool for estimating the net social benefit of a program or intervention as the incremental benefit of the program less the *incremental cost*, with all benefits and costs measured in dollars.

Cost-effectiveness analysis (CEA)   An analytic tool in which costs and effects of a program and at least one alternative are calculated and presented in a ratio of incremental cost to incremental effect. Effects are health outcomes, such as cases of a disease prevented, years of life gained, or quality-adjusted life years, rather than monetary measures as in cost-benefit analysis.

Cost-effectiveness ratio   The incremental cost of obtaining a unit of health effect (such as dollars per year, or per quality-adjusted year, of life expectancy) from a given health intervention, when compared with an alternative.

Crude rate   All events in a population in a calendar year multiplied usually by 1000. The crude death rate represents the probability of dying from all causes and is affected by the age distribution of the population under consideration.

Customers   In a health care situation, those individuals utilizing services offered by a health care provider; a term frequently favored over the term "patients," as it is suggestive of a scenario in which the consumer has a choice among alternatives for the satisfaction of a health-related need or want.

DALYs (disability adjusted life years)   A summary measure that is the sum of years of life lost due to premature mortality and the years lived with disability adjusted for severity of the disability.

Decision analysis   An explicit, quantitative, systematic approach to decision making under conditions of uncertainty in which probabilities of each possible event, along with consequences of those events, are stated explicitly.

Decision tree   A graphic representation of a decision, incorporating alternative choices, uncertain events (and their *probabilities*), and outcomes.

Demand   In the context of health care, the amount of service actually utilized or the amount of service considered necessary to meet need as perceived subjectively or as determined "objectively" by application of a formula.

Demography   The study of human populations in reference to such variables as size, distribution, and composition and to the dynamics of fertility, mortality, and migration.

Dependent variable   The variable that is the result of some antecedent or independent variable. Sometimes called the response or outcome variable.

Diagnosis   Identifying a target disorder based on objective laboratory or clinical standards.

Direct costs   The value of all goods, services, and other resources that are consumed in the provision of an intervention or in dealing with the side effects or other current and future consequences linked to it.

Direct medical costs   The value of health care resources (e.g., tests, drugs, supplies, health care personnel, and medical facilities) consumed in the provision of an intervention or in dealing with the side effects or other current and future consequences linked to it.

Disability days   Days in which activity is restricted due to either short-term or long-term health problems or conditions.

Discounting   The process of converting future dollars and future health outcomes to their present value.

Discount rate   The interest rate used to compute present value, or the interest rate used in discounting future sums.

Double-blinded   The administration of an intervention where neither the person receiving the intervention nor the person administering the intervention know the nature of the treatment.

Economies of scale   The situation where cost of production per unit of output decreases as the total volume of output increases. This may come about because of more efficient use of labor or equipment, or ability to specialize productive processes.

Effectiveness   The extent to which medical interventions achieve health improvements in real practice settings.

Effect size   A standardized measure of change in some variable measured using a "before and after" design in a group or a difference in such changes between two groups. It is the mean change divided by the standard deviation of changes across individuals.

Efficacy   The extent to which medical interventions achieve health improvements under ideal circumstances.

Effectiveness   The impact of an intervention in practical application, such as a community setting.

Efficacy   Determines whether a medical technology or other intervention technique works under controlled conditions or a set of guidelines or conditions, ideally through a randomized clinical trial; it is the result of positive outcomes minus negative outcomes.

Endemic   The usual or constant prevalence of a disease or infection in a human population in a defined geographic area.

Environmental scanning   An organizational function designed to ensure that the organization is aware of change relative to the forces and character of its environment so that both the threats and opportunities inherent in the environment are recognized.

Epidemic   The occurrence of cases in excess of expected. Expected values are defined from historical rates in the population or the occurrence of two or more cases of a condition not normally expected in a population.

Etiology   The sum of the knowledge regarding the cause of a disease.

Excess risk   The arithmetic difference between two measures of risk.

External environment   Individuals, groups, or other organizations that exist outside the boundaries of a focal entity as well as the political, economic, social, and technologic forces which impact the entity's operations.

False-negative probability   Probability of those with an outcome whose test results are negative for the outcome of interest. Inversely related to sensitivity.

False-positive probability   Probability of those without an outcome whose test results are for outcome. Inversely related to specificity.

Functional status   An individual's effective performance of or ability to perform roles, tasks, or activities (e.g., to work, play, maintain the house). Often functional status is divided into physical, emotional, mental, and social domains, although finer distinctions are possible.

Gap analysis   An analysis that attempts to quantify a deficit by comparing an ideal situation with the current situation or the situation as it would be in the future without some form of intervention.

Goal   A broad statement indicating general direction toward a desired future state.

Hazard rate   Number of persons having an adverse outcome before time $t+1$ who were outcome free until time t divided by the number at risk between t and $t+1$ time. Synonym is failure rate.

Health   A state of complete physical, mental, and social well-being and not merely the absence of disease or infirmity.

Health outcomes   Injury and disease morbidity and mortality resulting from the intervention of health care services.

Health promotion   Activities related to individual lifestyle to prevent disease, disability, and injury, e.g., physical fitness, nutrition counseling, tobacco cessation programs, family planning.

Health protection   Environmental or regulatory interventions aimed at large groups, e.g., air quality standards, seat belt laws, water fluoridation.

Health-related quality of life   As a construct, health-related quality of life refers to the impact of the health aspects of an individual's life on that person's quality, of life, or overall well-being. Also used to refer to the value of a health state to an individual.

Health state   The health of an individual at any particular point in time. A health state may be modified by the impairments, functional states, perceptions, and social opportunities that are influenced by disease, injury, treatment, or health policy.

Health status measures   Systems used to define and describe health states (e.g., a multi-attribute health status classification system).

Herd immunity   Populations protected from infection due to the presence of immune persons. The degree of protection achieved depends on age of immunity, season of the year, timing of introduction of susceptibles, and disease reproduction rate.

Iatrogenic injury   An injury occurring as a result of medical care or health care management.

Immunity   Resistance of the host associated with the presence of antibodies or cells having a specific action on the invading microorganism or on its toxin.

Inapparent infection   Presence of infection in a host without the occurrence of recognizable clinical signs and symptoms.

Incidence   Number of new cases.

Incidence rate $\dfrac{\text{No. of new cases}_t}{\text{Population at risk}_t} \times 10^k$

where t is a time period and k is some factor of 10. A change in the incidence rate means that there is a change in the balance of etiologic factors, some naturally occurring fluctuation, or possibly the application of an effective control program.

Incremental cost   The cost of one alternative less the cost of another.

Incremental cost effectiveness (ratio)   The ratio of the difference in costs between two alternatives to the difference in effectiveness between the same two alternatives.

Indirect costs   A term used in economics to refer to productivity gains or losses related to illness or death; in accounting it is used to describe overhead or fixed costs of production.

Incubation period   Time between the entry of a microorganism into a host and the first signs and symptoms of disease.

Independent variable   The variable that is manipulated to cause or influence an outcome. In experimental studies, this is the intervention. Sometimes called the antecedent variable.

Infection   The entry and establishment of a transmissible agent in host tissue resulting in cellular injury.

Internal environment   The situation of an organization as characterized by its structure and resources or inputs; the elements associated with an organization's internal environment are generally those under direct control and within defined organizational boundaries.

Kappa statistic   A measure of agreement (reliability) for categorical variables beyond chance alone. A kappa (k) = 1 indicates perfect agreement. The significance of the k statistic is assessed with a z score.

Likelihood ratio   Ratio of the probability that persons with the outcome have an observed value of a test to the corresponding probability among people without the outcome. Likelihood ratios are expressed as odds. Likelihood ratios do not vary with prevalence. Good for examining likelihood of outcome at various levels of a test.

Longitudinal study   Individuals are selected in consideration of varying degrees of exposure to suspect factor but are not known to possess the outcome associated with the factor under study. The purpose of this study is to examine the rate of occurrence of particular outcome with various levels of some causative factor(s). The group selected for study can be a sample from the general population or a select group, e.g., individuals in certain occupations. It also is possible to conduct a prospective study by defining a past date for a specific group (e.g., HMO enrollees) investigation. Follow-up information concerning the outcome is reconstructed, if necessary, through a number of sources including death certificates, hospital records. This latter approach also may be termed historical prospective or retrospective.

Market   The set of all people who have an actual or potential interest in a product or service.

Market analysis or audit   An analytic process associated with planning, which is initiated for the purpose of defining and characterizing the market and its needs, wants, or preferences.

Market area   The place or location that is associated with the actual or potential markets (or customers), which an organization targets or selects for delivery of one or more products or services.

Marketing   A managerial function encompassing planning, analysis, implementation, and control activities, which are undertaken to bring about the voluntary exchange of valued resources between two or more parties; a set of activities that are designed to facilitate the satisfaction of the resource-dependency needs of an organization.

Market segment   A subset of a larger market (or set of al people who have an actual or potential interest in a product or service); members of such a subset are homogeneous in regard to defined demographic, geographic, psychographic, or behavioristic variables and adequately distinct from other market segments to justify delineation of specific marketing strategies.

Marginal rate of return   The percent gain per time period (e.g., per year) from diverting $1 of consumption to investment. For example, if the marginal rate of return is 6% annually, a dollar invested today will yield $1.06 one year hence.

Medicaid   A government health insurance program that is designed to provide care for those families and individuals who are unable to afford necessary medical care.

Medicare   A federally financed health insurance plans for elderly persons, individuals receiving Social Security disability payments, and most persons with end-stage renal disease. Medicare Part A provides hospital insurance. Medicare Part B can be purchased for a monthly premium to pay for medical expenses.

Medical technology   Therapeutic or diagnostic devices, medical or surgical procedures, pharmaceuticals, or combinations thereof.

Medication error   A preventable event that leads to or causes patient harm of inappropriate medication use. Types of medication errors include drug allergy, too rapid intravenous fluid flow rate, wrong route, and wrong dose.

Meta-analysis   A systematic method using statistical analyses that combines data from independent studies to obtain a quantitative estimate of the summary effect of an intervention on an outcome.

Mission statement   A statement that describes an organization's reason for being, its business, the products or services it offers, the market(s) it intends to serve, and features that distinguish the organization from others.

Morbidity   The condition of being affected by a disease, illness, or symptoms. It may be newly onset case (incidence) or an existing condition (prevalence).

Mortality rate   Number of deaths in a time period/population at risk times a factor of 10.

Negative predictive value   Probability that a person with a negative test result does not have the outcome. It is the same thing as the posttest likelihood or posterior probability of no disease.

Nosocomial infection   An infection in a patient or staff member emerging as a result of exposure to a source within a health care facility.

Null hypothesis (H_O)   Makes a statement about the value of a population parameter to be statistically evaluated, phrased to negate the possibility of a relationship between the independent and dependent variables.

Objective   A specific statement that indicates in measurable terms what an organization intends to accomplish and when in order to progress toward fulfillment of a goal objective.

Odds   Ratio of the occurrence of an attribute that exists in a sample or population relative to it not existing.

Odds ratio (OR)   The ratio of one odds to another. In a case–control study, the odds ratio compares the odds of exposure among the cases to the odds of exposure among the controls. The odds ratio in longitudinal and cross-sectional studies compares the odds of the outcome among the exposed relative to the odds of the outcome among those not exposed. The odds ratio is a descriptive measure of the strength of the relationship between an exposure factor and an outcome.

Open systems theory   A theory that recognizes the importance of the interface or optimum fit between an organization and its environment and attempts to explain organizational behavior by viewing the organization as an open system that must interact with other entities in its environment in order to acquire resources and disburse its goods or services.

P **Value**   The probability associated with a test statistic. Indicates how extreme the observed parameter is relative to a distribution. A *P* value of less than .05 generally is accepted as meaning that the results of the statistical test are unlikely to be due to chance alone. It also means that for a given test statistic the values observed are less than 5 times out of a 100 as extreme as the one observed.

Pathogenicity   The ability of a biological agent to cause disease in a susceptible host.

PESTs   An acronym for the political, economic, social (demographic), and technological forces that exist in an organization's external environment and determine the nature of the threats and opportunities confronting an organization.

Population   The universe of all possible observations given a set of rules.

Position   In the context of marketing, a comparative measurement of the standing of an organization or of each of its products and services relative to competitors and their products or services.

Positive predictive value   Probability that a person with a positive test result has the outcome. It is used to assess yield of cases for screening efforts and is the same as the posttest likelihood or disease or posterior probability of disease. It is the proportion of individuals in the population with a characteristic at a specified point or period of time. It is the same as the pretest likelihood of disease or the prior probability of disease. The lower the prevalence rate, the lower the predictive value of a positive test.

Present value   The value to the decision maker now of outcomes occurring in the future.

Prevalence   Is the number of individuals in a population with the attribute of interest. Prevalence includes both previously diagnosed as well as new cases of a disease. Prevalence is a function of both the incidence and duration of the disease.

Prevalence rate $\dfrac{\text{Total number of new and old cases}_t}{\text{Total population}_t} \times 10^k$

where t designates a time interval and k is some factor of 10. The cases must come the same population in the same time period.

Primary data   Information that is collected by the manager or researcher using any study designs, such as randomized controlled trials or observational studies.

Primary prevention   Measures designed to prevent the onset of a disease or health problem (e.g., immunizations, health education).

Prognosis   Forecasting the outcome of interest in a cohort or person initially free of the outcome of interest.

Prognostic factor   A variable that affects the course of a disease or other health problem or outcome.

Random sample   A subset of observations drawn from populations in such a way that each observation contained in population has an equal chance of being included in the sample.

Receiver operating characteristic (ROC) analysis   A graph of a pair of true positive and false positive pairs used to evaluate the accuracy of a diagnostic test. The x axis is 1-specificity or 1-"true negatives"; the y axis is sensitivity or "true positives." A way to determine the optimal cutoff point in consideration of diagnostic error. The optimal curve (test with the least diagnostic error) is one in which the x and y coordinates are maximal at the upper left of the graph.

Relative risk (RR)   A ratio of the incidence rate among exposed divided by the incidence rate among the nonexposed. If the RR is greater than 1, the exposure factor increases risk of the outcome occurring. If RR is less than 1, exposure is protective for the outcome.

Research hypothesis   Makes a statement about a presumed relationship between an independent variable(s) and a dependent variable within a population, e.g., fewer medication errors will occur when the nurse–patient ratio is at least 1:10.

Resource dependency   A facet of open systems theory that holds that the behavior of an organization is influenced by the need to relate to other organizations in the environment in order to obtain resources essential for organizational survival and for production of outputs (or the goods and services of the organization).

Risk   The probability that an event will occur within a defined population during a specified time.

Sample   A subset of observations drawn from a population.

Secondary data   Data that already exist, having been collected for another purpose; data that may contribute to the understanding of a marketing situation or problem, although it may not be entirely responsive to the information needs of a current situation since the data were previously collected for some other reason.

Secondary prevention   Measures that identify or treat persons who have a disease or risk factors, but who are not yet experiencing symptoms of the disease (e.g., Pap smears, blood pressure screening).

Sensitivity   The ability of screening test to give a positive finding when the person tested truly has the disease. % Sensitivity =

$$\frac{\text{Persons with disease detected by screening test}}{\text{Total number of persons with the disease}} \times 100\%$$

Sensitivity analysis   Mathematical calculations that isolate factors involved in a decision analysis or economic analysis to indicate the degree of influence each factor has on the outcome of the entire analysis. Specifically measures the uncertainty of the probability, distributions.

Sentinel event   Any unexpected occurrence in the course of providing health care that results in death, serious physical or psychological injury, loss of function, or other events as defined by an accrediting body (e.g., infant discharge to wrong family, rape, patient suicide).

Situational analysis   An assessment of an organization's situation in terms of its market(s), the forces in its external environment, competitors, the internal aspects of the organization associated with its resources and capabilities, and the performance of the organization relative to expectations.

Specific rate   Rate pertaining to a segment or subgroup of a population, e.g., sex-specific rate. Represented as per 100,000 population in community assessments.

Specificity   The ability of the test to give a negative finding when the person tested is free of the disease under study. % Specificity =

$$\frac{\text{Persons without the disease who are negative to the screening test}}{\text{Total number of persons without the disease}} \times 100\%$$

Stakeholder   An entity (individual, group, or organization) that has an interest in or influence on a specified organization.

Sterilization   The complete destruction of biological agents on or in an object, usually by means of heat (e.g., autoclave) or chemicals.

Strategic planning   A systematic process for setting future direction, developing effective strategies, and ensuring that an organization's structure and systems are compatible with long-term survival and success.

Strategy   A set of decision rules developed for the purpose of guiding an organization's behavior under varying circumstances; a pattern or plan for integrating an organization's mission, resources, and activities into a cohesive whole.

Surveillance   The systematic collection, tabulation, analysis, and feedback of information about all those at risk for a particular condition regarding the occurrence of the condition. Surveillance also involves the implementation of strategies to reduce risks and prevent outbreaks. Surveillance may be targeted, i.e., focused on high-risk populations (ICU patients), passive (the review of microbiological reports from a transplant unit), or active (case finding of needlestick injuries).

Survival curve   Graphic representation of the cumulative probability of death, survival, or other end-point determined from the follow-up of a defined group of persons at risk for the event.

SWOT analysis   An assessment of the strengths and weaknesses of an organization (as represented by the resources under the organization's control and the resulting organizational capabilities) and the opportunities and threats (SWOT) existing in an organization's external environment and determined by the political, economic, sociodemographic, and technological forces in that environment.

Technology assessment   The evaluation of the safety, effectiveness, efficiency, and appropriateness of devices, organization of services, medical and surgical procedures, and pharmaceuticals as promoted for improving a patient's condition or quality of life.

Tertiary prevention   Measures or services that are designed to prevent recurrence, death, or further disability in persons with clinical illness (e.g., cardiac rehabilitation, calcium plus vitamin D supplementation in elderly persons).

Time costs   The time a patient spends seeking care or participating in or undergoing an intervention.

Time horizon   The period of time for which costs and effects are measured in a cost effectiveness analysis.

Type I error   An error committed when a true null hypothesis is rejected; occurs when the sample is too large.

Type II error   An error committed when a false null hypothesis failed to be rejected; occurs when the sample is too small.

Uncensored observation   The event of interest has occurred in the case (e.g., death). Term used in survival or failure-time analysis.

Utility   A concept in economics, psychology, and decision analysis referring to the preference for or desirability of a particular outcome. In the context of health-related quality-of-life measurement, utility refers to the preference of the rater (usually a patient or a member of the general public) for a particular health outcome or health state.

Index

An italicized number signifies that the entry is in a figure.

Absolute risk reduction, 236
Acceptability, 136–137
Accessibility, 13, 135
Adjusted rates, 60; *See also* Standardization of rates
Affinity diagram, 171
Age adjustment, 60
AIDS (acquired immunodeficiency syndrome), 104, *194, 195*
   classification of, 39
   See also Human Immunodeficiency Virus
Airborne disease, 203
   control measures, 204
Airborne precautions, *205*
Air pollutants, *265*
Allele, defined, 218
American College of Epidemiology, ethics guidelines, 340
Association analysis, 225
Autoregressive integrated moving average (ARIMA) model, 149
Availability
   defined, 13
   related to health care utilization, 13

Behavioral Risk Factor Surveillance System, of the Centers for Disease Control and Prevention, *45*, 57
Benchmarking, defined, 164
Best practices, 162–163
Biologic markers
   definition, 272
   of effect, 272
   of exposure, 272
   of susceptibility, 273
Bloodborne disease
   exposure control measures and plans, 199, *200*
   hepatitis B (HBV), 197, 198
   human immunodeficiency virus (HIV), 197, 198
   prevention and control, 199
   standard precautions, *202*
Brainstorming, defined, 171

Carrier, defined, 193
Case, making for ethical analysis, 332
Case-control study, 142
   advantages and disadvantages, 143
   purpose of, 142
   selection of control group, 142
   See also Study designs
Case-fatality rate, *58*
Case management, 163
Casuistry, 331
Causal analysis
   multiple outcomes, 149
   qualitative causal criteria, 90–92
Causality
   definition, 90
   steps in evaluation of, 79
Causal inquiry, seven steps, *79*
Cause-and-effect diagram
   defined, 172
   examples and construction of, 172–173
Census, *45*
Centers for Disease Control and Prevention, 54
Classification systems
   defined, 38
   diseases, 38
   functional ability, 40
   infectious agents, 192
   injuries, 40
   Mendelian, *230*
   mental and behavioral disorders, 41
   organizations, 42
   procedures, 43
   quality of life, 41
Clinical practice guidelines
   critical success factors, 162
   key features of, 162
Clinical trials, ethical guidelines, 340
Clinical Value Compass, 164–165
Coefficient of variation, 36
Coherence, causal criteria, 91
Cohort, 143

Cohort study, 143; *see also* Longitudinal studies
Communicable disease reporting, *194*, 197
Communitarianism, 333, 342
Community, definition of relevant, 333
Comparison charts, 179, *180*
Competitive (or competitor) analysis, 111–112
Conceptualization, 80
Confidence interval, 67
Confidentiality and privacy concerns, 344
Consent, informed, elements of, *345*
Consistency, causal criteria, defined, 91
Construct validity, 34
Content validity, 34
Continuity, defined, 136
Continuous quality improvement, 158
Control chart
    definition and example, 177
    formulae for, 178
    steps in preparing, 178
Control of confounding, 90
Correlation coefficient, 36
Cost–benefit analysis, 312
    defined, 150, 312
    steps in performance of, *313*
Cost-effectiveness analysis (CEA), 312
    computation of cost-effectiveness ratio, *321*
    defined, 150, 312
    epidemiological data, 318
    steps in performance of, *313*, 318
Cost components, *315*
Cost identification, 314, 315
Costs and benefits, equity of distribution of, 318
Council for International Organizations of Medical
    Sciences, 340
Cox regression, 148–149
Criterion validity, 34
Critical paths. *See* Clinical practice guidelines
Cross-sectional study, 141
    limitations, 141
    See also Study designs
Crude rates, 58, *60*

Death certificate, as a source of information about
    deaths, 55, *56*
Decision criteria, 243
Decision model, *314*
Declaration of Helsinki, 338
Deductive inquiry, 77
Dependent variable, 82
Descriptive epidemiologic measures, 68
Diagnostic related groups (DRGs), 181
Directly observed treatment (DOT), 319
    and benefits compared to self-administration of
      treatment (SAT), 320, *321*
Direct rate adjustment, 60–61, *62*; *See also*
    Standardization of rates
Disability, defined, 40

Disability-adjusted life expectancy (DALE), 139–140
Disability-adjusted life years (DALYs), 64, 103
Disasters, environmental, 267
Discounting, defined, 317
Disparities, health, *292*

Ecological fallacy, 89
Economic decision-making, 309
Effectiveness, 136
Efficacy, 139
Efficiency, defined, 136
Environment
    impact on the immune system, 264
    impact on the nervous system, 265
    impact on the reproductive system, 263
    impact on the respiratory system, 266
Environmentally related (or environmentally
      provoked) diseases, 274
    health services for
      primary prevention, 274
      secondary prevention, 274
      tertiary prevention, 276
    recognition and assessment, 271–272
    risk assessment, 273
Environmental equity, 269
Environmental terrorism, 266
Epidemic, 196
    definition, 196
    role of health care manager, 196
Epidemiological framework
    health system characteristics and health status of
      populations, 18
    population-based focus for health care delivery, 15
    questions to answer to address health problems, *21*
Epidemiological measures
    ratio measures, 64
    specific rate measures, 58, *59*
    summary rate measures, 58
Epidemiological model for health care delivery, 4
Epidemiologic triangle, *262*
Epidemiology
    applying in health care management practice, *21*
    defined, 3
    determining distribution of needs (disease), 16–17
    formulating and evaluating public policy, 20, 290
    monitoring health system performance, 19–20
    monitoring, service population size, 15
    planning and evaluating health services, 134
    understanding genesis and consequences of health
      problems, 18
Ethical evaluations, approaches for resolving, *330*
    casuistry, 331
    communitarianism, 333
    feminist ethics, 334
    principlism, 330
    utilitarianism, 335
Ethic of care, 334

Ethics
  defined, 329
  in epidemiology, 340
  in medical genetics, *232*
Ethics of genetic disease screening, 230
Evaluation, in health care
  defined, 133
  process, 137–138
  purposes, 133
  use of epidemiological principles and methods in, 133
  See also Health system, evaluation criteria
Evaluation criteria, conceptual frameworks for
    specifying and measuring impact, 138–140
  RE-AIM (reach, efficacy, adoption, implementation, and maintenance) model, 139
  SPO (structure, process, outcome) classification, 139
  WHO systems level framework and five dimensions of, 139
Exchange theory as the foundation of marketing, 105
Exon, defined, 219
Experimental studies, 144–145
  quasi-experimental studies, 145
  time series design, 145
Exposure
  in developing infectious disease, 195

False negative, 34
False positive, 34
Feminist ethics, 334
Fertility rates, *58*, 100
Flow chart, 173, *174*
Functional ability, classifications of, 40–41

Gap analysis, 113
Gene-environment interaction, 262
Genetic epidemiology, studies, 226
  of BRCA1 and BRCA2, 226
Genetic epidemiology and health services management, 227
Genetic health services, 227, 229
  and information needs and systems, 229, 230
Genetic linkage, 219
Genetic mapping, 220
Genetic screening (testing), 227, 228, 229
  conditions for appropriateness, 228
  economic and health impact, 230
  example of phenylketonuria screening, 228
  future of, 229
  levels of
    family, 228
    individual, newborns, 228
    population, 228, 229
  prenatal, 227, 229
Genetics, ethical challenges of, 230
Genetics and epidemiology of
  genetic techniques and tools, 223

Genetic and epidemiology of (*cont.*)
  genetic techniques and tools (*cont.*)
    association analysis, 225
    linkage analysis, 224
    pedigree, 223
    phenotype identification, 223
    segregation analysis, 224
  twin studies, 225
Genotype, defined, 218
Global environmental health, 271
Goal, defined, 115

Hazard rate, 53
Health
  classification of, 38
  definition of, 14
  environment and, 261
  global, 271
  measures of, *9*, *10*, 14
  needs, 6, 8, 16
  outcomes, 15, 261–262
Health care quality management
  defined, 157
  interrelationship with epidemiology, 157
Health Plan Employer Data and Information System;
    see HEDIS
Health services
  for environmentally provoked diseases, 274
  evaluation, 134
  prospects of, 150
  public, *286*
Health status, 168
Health system
  defined, 137
  evaluation criteria, *134*
HEDIS (Health Plan Employer Data and Information System), 166–167
Helsinki Declaration, 339
Hepatitis B
  adverse events from vaccination, 299
  geographic distribution, *297*
  rates of occurrence, 296, 298
Herd immunity, 300
Histogram, 175
Historical prospective study, 143
Host susceptibility, 195
Human Genome Epidemiology Network (HuGE Net), 221
  web sites for, *222*
Human Genome Project, 219
  epidemiology and, 221, 222
  international implications of, 221
Human Immunodeficiency Virus (HIV)
  epidemiology of, 198–199
  transmission of, 197
Hypothesis
  defined, 83

Hypothesis (cont.)
  formulation of and template for, 82
  testing, 83

Immune system
  definition, 264
  impact of the environment on, 264
Immunity
  defined, 195
  herd, 300
  types, 195
Incidence
  density rate, 52
  rate, 51
  sources of information, 54
Incubation period, defined, 193
Independent segregation of genes, law of, 218
Independent variable, 82
Indirect adjustment, 61–62, 63
Inductive inquiry, 77
Infant mortality rate, 14, 58, 180, 293
Infection control, management responsibilities, 196, 197, 198
Infectious disease control
  special considerations by health care setting
    ambulatory care, 208
    behavioral health, 211
    home care, 209
    hospice, 210
    inpatient acute care, 207
    long-term care/skilled nursing facility, 209
  See also Bloodborne disease
Infectious diseases
  concepts of, 192
  drug-resistant, 203
  emergence of, 192
Informed consent, defined, 341
  essential categories of, 345
Institutional Review Board (IRB) defined, 348
Integrated requirements model (IRM) for primary care resource planning, 113
Internal organizational audit, 112–114
  defined, 112
  understanding of strengths and weaknesses, 112
International Classification of Diseases (ICD), 38, 39
International Covenant on Civil and Political Rights, 339
International Ethical Guidelines for Biomedical Research Involving Human Subjects, 341
International Guidelines for Ethical Review of Epidemiological Studies, 342
Intervention effects
  methods for analyzing, 145–149
Introns, 219

Kappa statistic, 36, 37

Law of independent assortment of alleles, 218
Level of measurement, 31
Level of significance, 83
Life expectancy defined, 14–15
Likelihood ratio, defined, 35, 36
Likelihood ratio in genetic analysis, 225
Likert-type ordinal scale, 31, 168
Linkage analysis, 219, 224
Lod score, 225
Logistic regression model, 84–85, 146
Longitudinal study (prospective or cohort study), 143–144
  advantages and disadvantages of, 144
  purposes of, 143
  types of, 143

Malcolm Baldrige National Health Care Quality Award, 181–183
Map, genetic, 221
Market, defined, 108
Market analysis, 108–110
Marketing, 105
Measurement, logistics of, 38
Measurement error
  control of, 44
  defined, 43
  sources of, 44
Measurement of benefits, 316, 320
Measurement of costs, 314, 319
Measurement of resources, 316
Mendelian Classification System, 230
Mendel's laws, 218
  exceptions to, 218
  independent segregation of genes, 218
  law of independent assortment of alleles, 218
Meta-analysis
  computing effects, 245
  critiquing, 246
  defined, 92
  summarizing effect, 149
  in technology assessment, 244
Microbiologic agents, categories of bacteria, fungi, parasites, viruses, 193
Mission statement, key elements of, 107
Multilevel analysis, 87

National Center for Health Statistics, 55
National Committee for Quality Assurance, 161, 166
National Death Index, 55
National Health Interview Survey, 45
National Health Objectives, 287
National Immunization Survey, 296
Needs, health, 16
Nervous system, impact of the environment on, 263
Nosocomial infection, 207
Nuremberg Code, ten basic principles of, 338

Observational studies, types, 140, *141*
  case-control, 142–143
  case series, 140
  cohort, 143
  cross-sectional, 141
  descriptive, 141
  longitudinal or prospective, 143
Odds, defined, 66
Odds ratio, defined, 66
Office for Human Research Protections, 344
Operational definition, 81
ORYNX initiative of Joint Commission on
     Accreditation of Healthcare Organizations,
     166
Outbreaks, disease
  managing, 195–197
  reasons for occurrence, 195
Outcome measures, *170*
Outcomes
  assessment, 139, 246
  clinical, 167
  health, 139

P value, 242
Pareto chart, 175, *176*
Pathogenicity, defined, 193
Pedigree, 225, *226*
PESTs (political, economic, social technological
     forces), 110
Phenotype, defined, 223
Plan, Do, Study, Act (PDSA) cycle, 164, *165*
Planning, 137
Population
  characteristics impact on disease patterns, 101
  defined for health services delivery, 4, 134
  factors affecting size, *16*
  sources of data, 5–6
  trends, 6, *7*, *8*, *17*, 100, *101*
Population attributable risk (PAR) percent, 67
Population genetics, defined, 223
Population pyramids, 101, *102*
Practice guidelines, clinical, 162
Present value (PV)
  discount rate, 317
  formulae for benefits and costs, 317
Prevalence
  defined, *34*
  rate, 53–54
  sources of data, 55
Prevention
  for environmentally-provoked diseases, 274
  primary prevention, 10, *11*, 274
  secondary prevention, 10, *11*, 274–276
  tertiary prevention, 10, *11*, 276
Principlism, definition, 330
Privacy: *see* Confidentiality and privacy concerns
Problem, identification and specification, 79

Process measures, 139, 167, *170*; *see also* Evaluation
    criteria
Program evaluation, 133
  conceptual dimensions, *134*
  design considerations, 140
Programmatic quality initiatives
  defined, 160
  examples of, 160
Propositions, definition of, 78
Prospective study (longitudinal), 143
Public goods, 310
  and applications of CBA and CEA, 310
  and government provision of, 310
  and health care, 310
Public health
  definition, 286
  services, *286*
Public policy process, 287, 288

Quality
  defined, 135
  dimensions of, 159
  See also Program evaluation
Quality assessment, 114–115, 135
Quality audits, *106*, 114
Quality control tools, statistical, 173–181
  check sheet, 175
  comparison charts, 170–180
  control chart, 177–179
  histogram, 175
  Pareto chart, 175–176
  run chart, 177
  scatter diagram, 176
Quality improvement tools, qualitative, 170–173
  affinity diagram, 171
  brainstorming, 171
  cause-and-effect diagram, 172
  flowchart, 173, *174*
Quality management in health care, 158
  definition, 158
  organizational approaches to, 159
  performance standards, 161
  planning, 160
  programmatic options in, 159–160
Quality measurement, 166
  clinical outcomes, 167
  data sources, 168
  health status, 168
  levels of, 169–170
  process measures, 167
  sampling, 169
  satisfaction, 167–168
Quality of life, 41
Quasi-experimental studies, 145

Randomization, random sample, defined, 144
Randomized clinical trial (RCT), 247

Random sample, 169
Rate, uses of, 68, 169, 170
Ratios, uses of, 68, 170
Receiver operating characteristic (ROC) curves, 35, 244
Relational ethics, 334
Relative risk (RR), 66
    percentage reduction, 236
Reliability, 36
Reportable (notifiable), 193, *194*
Reproductive health
    agents affecting, *264*
    impact of the environment on, 263
Reservoir, for infectious agents, 193
Respiratory system, impact of the environment on, 266
Review of literature, 80, 242
Risk adjustment, 181
Risk assessment, process for environmentally provoked diseases, 273
Risk factor, 64–65
Risk management, 163
Risk ratio, 65
Run chart, 177

Sampling, 169
Satisfaction, patient, means of measuring, 168
Scatter diagram, 176
Scientific inquiry, 75
    characteristics of, 76
    conceptualization, 80
    logic of, 77
        and deductive inquiry, 77
        and inductive inquiry, 77
        stages in (seven steps), *79*
    model selection, 80
    review of literature, 80, *81*
    theoretical framework, 80
Screening
    for environmentally provoked diseases, *275*
    genetic, 227
    for phenylketonuria, a model, 228
    programs 229
Segregation analysis 225
Selecting a statistical test, 84
Sensitivity, defined, 34
Sensitivity analysis (in CBA and CEA), 317
Small area analysis, 141
Specificity, defined, 34
Specific rate, 58, *58, 59*
Stakeholders
    defined, 114
    examples of, 115
Standard, performance, 161–162
Standardization of (adjusted) rates, 60
    direct adjustment, 60
    indirect adjustment, *63*

Standard precautions, *202*
Statistical tests, selection, 84, *85*
Strategic planning
    application of epidemiology, 105
    conceptual framework, theoretical basis, 104–106
    data resources for, 117, 118–119
    defined, 104, 106
    epidemiological basis, 99
    process steps, 108–115, 116–117
    SWOT analysis, 117–119
    theoretical basis, 104–106
    tools for, 117–119
    worksheets (sample) for use in strategic planning, 120–121
Structural equation models (SEM), 85–86, 149
Structural measures of evaluation, 139
Study design, selection of, 82, 140
Study designs, 140, *141, 243*
    descriptive studies, 141
    in evaluation, 140–150
    experimental studies, 144
    observational studies, 140
Study variables, quantification of, 80
Summary rate measures, 58
Surveys
    advantages and disadvantages, *30*
    types of, 30
Survival analysis, 147–149
    Cox regression, 148–149
    Kaplan–Meier (product limit) survival estimate, 147, *148, 149*
    log-rank test, 148
    survival curve, *149*
SWOT analysis, 117–119

Technology assessment
    criteria for, 240
    defined, 235
    framework for prioritizing technologies, *242*
    organizational efforts, 248–251
    problems in performing, 252
Technology life cycle, 238
Terrorism, environmental, 267
    control measures, 268
Theoretical framework, 80
Theory formulation approaches, 77
    deduction, 77
    induction, 77
Time series design, 145
Total Quality Management (TQM), defined, 158
Transmission of disease
    modes (route) of transmission, 193, *195*
    portal of entry, 193
    portal of exit, 195
    vehicles of, 194
Tuberculosis (TB), 203
    control measures and plans, 204–207

Tuberculosis (*cont.*)
  transmission of, 203

Utilitarianism
  role of rules, 336
  theory of, defined, 335
Utilization management, 162–163
Utilization of health care services
  changing patterns, 111
  determinants or influences of, 12
  proxy measure of need, 8
Vaccine preventable diseases, *289, 295*

Validity
  defined, 33
  evaluation of, 34
Variance tracking, defined, 162
Variation
  assessment of, 180
  common cause, 180
  special cause, 180
Virulence, 193
Viruses, 192

Years of potential life lost (YPLL), 63, *64*